Commentary On
J. William Fulbright and His Time

WILLIAM H. GRAY, III, President and CEO, United Negro College Fund, former Congressman from Pennsylvania and Majority Whip, U.S. House of Representatives:

"*J. William Fulbright and His Time* is a superbly written and informative book that provides a unique and refreshingly candid perspective on the life of William Fulbright and the evolution of his views on Vietnam and the civil rights movement."

NORMAN A. GRAEBNER, University of Virginia, Professor Emeritus of American Diplomatic History; former Harmsworth Professor of American History, Oxford University

"Only the efforts of a major scholar of J. William Fulbright's career, especially in legal and foreign affairs, aided by a leading Arkansas journalist of the past half century, could produce a biography of such erudition, detail, and enlightenment.

On its pages Fulbright emerges as a man of remarkable wit, perception, honesty, and capacity to learn. Lee Riley Powell's penetrating analyses of issues and events demonstrate Fulbright's occasional lapses as well as his many political and intellectual triumphs, especially the renowned Fulbright Program for global educational exchange and his long, effective examination of U.S. policy toward Vietnam and China. Fulbright was indeed a preeminent member of Congress through decades of challenge and change, worthy of this prodigious and scholarly endeavor."

LEE WILLIAMS, Administrative Assistant to Senator Fulbright

"Powell's superb biography is likely to stand for some time as the definitive work yet done on the amazing life of the man who changed the history of the world and shortened our longest and most tragic war."

FEDERAL JUDGE HENRY WOODS (former leader of the STOP campaign against Gov. Orval Faubus in 1957-58 during the Little Rock desegregation crisis)

"*J. William Fulbright and His Time* is an impressive work of legal scholarship on the part of Lee Powell. The book is based on monumental research over a 17-year period in the J. William Fulbright Papers, Library of Congress, the National Archives, Presidential libraries, judicial opinions, and other primary sources. Lee Powell is admirably objective. He analyzes the weaknesses in Fulbright's civil rights record—especially in the era of massive resistance to the *Brown* decision—without becoming shrill, yet he also carefully points out some of the favorable features in Fulbright's record in his later years, particularly his opposition to the nomination of the racist Harrold Carswell to the Supreme Court.

This elegantly written, superb biography will be of interest to all students of American constitutional history from the Roosevelt administration to the present."

J. WILLIAM FULBRIGHT

AND HIS TIME

J. WILLIAM FULBRIGHT

AND HIS TIME

A POLITICAL BIOGRAPHY

BY

LEE RILEY POWELL

FOREWORD BY PRESIDENT BILL CLINTON

GUILD BINDERY PRESS
MEMPHIS, TENNESSEE

Published in Memphis, Tennessee
by Guild Bindery Press, Inc.

Library of Congress Cataloging-in-Publication Data

Powell, Lee Riley
J. William Fulbright and His Time/Lee Riley Powell—1st ed. in the U.S.A.
      p.   cm.
      I. Title.
      ISBN# 1-55793-060-0
      95-81669   CIP

Editor and Publisher: Randall Bedwell
Managing Editor: Robbin Brent, RBrent&Company
Jacket and Book Design: Beverly Cruthirds, Cruthirds Design
Inside-Jacket Copy: Robert L. Kerr

published in the United States by

GUILD BINDERY PRESS
Post Office Box 38099
Memphis, Tennessee 38183

First Edition
10 9 8 7 6 5 4 3 2 1

For the memory of
James O. Powell, Jr.
Accomplished lawyer, cherished son and brother

Fulbright and the author, Lee Riley Powell, in Little Rock in the offices of the old *Arkansas Gazette* at the time of the publication in 1984 of Powell's previous book, *J. William Fulbright and America's Lost Crusade (foreword by J. William Fulbright)*, an analysis of Fulbright's opposition to President Johnson's Vietnam policy. (James Powell's files)

Author's Note

I have written this biography of J. William Fulbright over a period of 17 years. It is based primarily on extensive research in the primary sources, including the J. William Fulbright Papers at the University of Arkansas in Fayetteville, Arkansas; the National Archives; the Library of Congress; Congressional hearings and debates; decisions of the United States Supreme Court and the lower federal courts; the Orval E. Faubus Papers and Brooks Hays Papers, both at the University of Arkansas in Fayetteville; the Libraries of Presidents Harry S. Truman, John F. Kennedy and Lyndon Baines Johnson; and the books, speeches and other writings of Senator Fulbright. It is written largely from the broad perspective of a constitutional law scholar, albeit one who has also taken part as a political aide in the turbulent world of Congressional politics. Fulbright was a lawyer, constitutional law professor, and lawmaker in his career, so my attention to the law in this biography is natural. My views on constitutional history were deeply influenced by Fulbright, but also by my experience in Congressional politics on Capitol Hill; my legal work in the federal court system; and by my experience at the University of Virginia Law School, particularly by the lectures and writings of Professors A.E. Dick Howard, Michael Klarman, John C. Jeffries, Jr., Richard Merrill, and Visiting Professor John Hart Ely. I also studied recent American political history at the University of Virginia Graduate School, where Norman Graebner, the distinguished professor emeritus of American foreign policy, and Paul Gaston, who is one of the most perceptive historians of the South, also contributed greatly to my understanding of Senator Fulbright and his place in recent American history. I do not write entirely from the cloister of academe, however, for I have continued to ply my trade as a legal scholar as a lawyer on the staff of U. S. District Judge William R. Wilson, Jr., in recent years; and in the 1980s I was the communications director and legislative research assistant to Congressman Bill Alexander. My father has also attempted to bring this book down from the ethereal regions of constitutional scholars into the real world; he was Editor-in-Chief of this biography, bringing to bear his 40 years of experience in analyzing Southern politics as editorial editor of the *Arkansas Gazette*, and earlier, associate editor of the *Tampa Tribune*.

My analysis and years of research regarding Senator Fulbright included long stretches of time when I was younger when I devoted all day every day to research in the Fulbright Papers at Fayetteville or reading in the literature of the history of post-war America. I wrote research papers on the senator's career in constitutional law seminars and other research projects in law school and graduate school, and when I lived in Washington working on the Hill I was able to visit with Fulbright at regular intervals as we debated his career and discussed the tribulations and hopes of the present. My father and I have interviewed the senator more than 100 times since the late 1950s, and although the heart of this book is based upon the documentary sources listed above, we have also added insights from our extensive personal contacts with the senator over the decades.

My interpretations of Senator Fulbright's public policy positions are fundamentally favorable. No objective, thoughtful observer has ever had any serious reservations about the great achievements of the Fulbright Fellowship program, and his courageous opposition to the witch hunts of Joe McCarthy in the 1950s was one of the impressive displays of political courage in our nation's recent history. The Fulbright Program is treated in many passages of this book from 1946 to the end of Fulbright's career; the most detailed treatment of the Program is in Book Six, "Fulbright and His Legacy," which contains a long section analyzing the achievements of the Program. By his drafting and leadership in supporting the Fulbright Resolution of 1943, Fulbright played an impressive role as a young congressman in supporting American entry into what would become the United Nations. The senator was deeply disappointed by the serious weaknesses of the UN as early as 1945 and remained realistic about the body throughout his life, yet he remained a forceful advocate of strengthening the body and ultimately transforming it into a forceful collective security organization. Fulbright also displayed a thoughtful critique of Secretary of State John Foster Dulles' rigid Cold Warrior policies in the 1950s. In early 1961, he was the only adviser at the final strategy session before the Bay of Pigs invasion who warned the President not to go through with that doomed expedition. In the early years of the Cold War, Fulbright was often critical of Soviet policies; however, in the Stalinist era such a position was justifiable, and Fulbright never carried his anticommunism to the hysterical depths of the McCarthyites.

Despite my generally favorable analysis of Fulbright's basic positions and approach to public life, there are two arenas in which I have found serious flaws in his record. First, in the years roughly from 1961 to mid-1965, Fulbright embraced the typical Cold Warrior notion that the role of Congress was to support the President publicly; any dissent must be expressed privately, lest the public discord weaken the government in its effort to bring about a vigorous policy. Fulbright relished his role as the senior foreign policy adviser to Presidents Kennedy and his old friend, Lyndon Johnson, in the early 1960s, and he adopted the elitist view that foreign policy must be left to the "experts." His philosophy during that era was seriously misguided, as he would later admit. When he confined his grave reservations about President Johnson's policies in 1964 and early 1965 to private memoranda or conversations at the White House, yet publicly supported the President, he accomplished nothing except to deprive himself of any political influence he might have had upon public opinion and to strengthen the executive's ability to pursue its tragically mistaken policies in Vietnam. The classic example of his mistaken attitude in that era was his support for the Gulf of Tonkin Resolution in 1964; while it is true that the administration deceived the senator regarding that episode, Fulbright had unwisely substituted his personal trust for President Johnson for the proper, adversarial, institutional relationships between the legislative and executive branches. The Framers of the Constitution were wise to provide checks and balances in the American system, but if one branch abdicates its role to another, American policy will unavoidably fail.

After realizing the basic errors and futility of his elitist strategy in the early 1960s, Fulbright had the wisdom and flexibility to change his position. He would ultimately become one of the most eloquent critics of the elitist view that the foreign policy "experts" must control American diplomacy without interference from the amateurs in Congress or the American public. His thoughtful, courageous dissent against Johnson's policies in the

Dominican Republic and Vietnam beginning in 1965-1966 inaugurated a searching reappraisal of American foreign policy, began to weaken the domination of the rigid Cold Warrior consensus, and led a re-assertion of Congress' proper constitutional role in the American system. If he had been an elitist in the early 1960s, by the mid-1960s and for the rest of his lengthy career in Congress he advocated a full public debate and dissemination of knowledge to the American people about the government's foreign policies. He led the movement for changes in America's policy toward China that culminated in the Nixon-Kissinger breakthrough to the mainland in the early 1970s, and he was a valiant supporter of detente with the Soviet Union.

The second area in which I disagreed strongly with the senator concerned civil rights. Indeed, by far the most serious flaws in his record centered on the dilemma of race relations. Books Three and Five of this biography deal in great detail with the senator's compromises on this issue: his signing of the Southern Manifesto condemning the Supreme Court's historic decision in *Brown v. Board of Education*, his votes against the major civil rights legislation, and his silence in the 1957 Little Rock Central High crisis while Governor Orval Faubus flouted the rule of law. While I have presented his justifications for his record, I ultimately do not find them convincing. I discussed these issues at great length with him, but never could obtain any real expression of error regarding those turbulent years; there was nothing he could do, he would say, and the forces of racism were simply too powerful. When I suggested the alternatives of at least supporting *Brown* at the height of the Central crisis not as a correct decision, but simply on the traditional grounds of respect for the rule of law, he once replied, "Well, you could speculate about that but I had no desire for martyrdom." The Faubus era of the 1950s and much of the 1960s is explored in detail in this work. My father, of course, was directly involved in those events as an editorial editor, and his comments and recollections of the era have added (I hope) a fresh approach and life to the story.

In spite of my strong conviction that Fulbright's civil rights record was his greatest flaw, I have still avoided the simplistic tendency to dismiss him as a "racist" or a hypocrite. Fulbright indeed was no racist, and the criticism of him in this regard should be objective and fair enough to be tempered by recognition of some of his achievements in this area late in his career. He was one of the few Southern senators to vote for Thurgood Marshall's elevation to the Supreme Court in 1967, and in a debate that was dominated by civil rights issues, Fulbright courageously played a crucial role in blocking the nomination of the racial extremist, Harrold Carswell, to the Court. He voted for the extension of the Voting Rights Act in 1970. The description of him as a "racist", as one writer has recently done, is shrill and superficial. Had he been a racist, it would have been easy for him to have played upon segregationists' prejudices to his political benefit in the late 1950s, yet Fulbright never did. Criticisms of his civil rights record should be tempered by the knowledge of his ability to change—though never in anything approaching his flexibility and wisdom in foreign policy issues—and his positive votes late in life.

As the title indicates, this book places Fulbright's career in the broad context of his time. In particular, the chapter on Southern "massive resistance" against the Brown decision in the 1950s contains a thorough examination of the pertinent civil rights issues in Arkansas, the South, and at the national level. The signing of the Southern Manifesto and the 1957 Little Rock Central crisis were probably the most painful and poignant controversies in Fulbright's career, and these episodes will be placed in their broad historical setting.

One of Fulbright's legacies will also be his influence upon his protege and former staff member, and later President of the United States, Bill Clinton. I have attempted to provide an objective analysis of President Clinton and Fulbright, particularly in the context of the Vietnam draft controversy, but it is too early to tell what the overall verdict of history will be upon Bill Clinton, and I have avoided making any predictions in that regard. With regard to Fulbright, however, it is not too early to venture the proposition that he will be regarded at the plane of Daniel Webster and Henry Clay among the giants of the United States Congress.

Norman Graebner read and critiqued most of the material on the Cold War and Vietnam when I worked with him at the University of Virginia Graduate School. Michael Klarman read Book Three, the first draft of which I wrote at the University of Virginia Law School. I worked with Paul Gaston in a civil rights seminar regarding Fulbright's civil rights positions in the latter part of his career. Regarding my knowledge of constitutional law, I am particularly indebted to Professor A.E. Dick Howard of the University of Virginia Law School; Professor Howard is recognized as one of the most distinguished constitutional law scholars in America. Professors Franklin Wright and James Lanier of Rhodes College in Memphis critiqued earlier versions of the manuscript. I have also received comments from Professor Robin Winks of Yale and F. Ray Marshall of the University of Texas. I am responsible for any mistakes in the book, of course.

Over the years, the most important editors of this book were the scholars with whom I worked at the University of Virginia Law School and the University of Virginia Graduate School. For the final round of editing, my father was the chief editor. He suffers from a liberal bias, but on the other hand he works for free, so I shouldn't complain. The editors at the Guild Bindery Press, of course, gave a close reading to the entire manuscript. Associate Editor was Ernest Dumas, formerly of the *Arkansas Gazette*, and now a journalism professor at the University of Central Arkansas and a columnist for the *Arkansas Times*. Assistant Editors in one round of editing were Evelyn Saldana, Program Coordinator of the International Center, University of Arkansas at Little Rock (Ms. Saldana is from Guatemala and came to Little Rock through the Fulbright Exchange Program); Robert McCord, also formerly of the *Gazette*, and now a columnist and famous television commentator; Beth Deere, Esq., of the U.S. District Court for the Eastern District of Arkansas; and Josh Wheeler, Esq., of the Thomas Jefferson Center for the Protection of Free Expression in Charlottesville, Virginia. Many librarians and archivists have helped me over the years, and they have my great appreciation. In particular, Betty Austin of the J. William Fulbright Papers in Fayetteville combined the skills of an archivist with the understanding of someone who has an extensive knowledge of American history. Her help was absolutely invaluable in my research, from 1980 to 1995.

Parts of this book were published, in a different form, as *J. William Fulbright and*

America's Lost Crusade: Fulbright, the Cold War and the Vietnam War (Little Rock: Rose, 1984; Expanded edition, 1988). That book received favorable reviews, as well as complimentary comments from Professor Robin Winks of Yale, F. Ray Marshall, President Carter's Secretary of Labor and later Professor at the University of Texas, the late LeRoy Collins, former Governor of Florida, Senator Edward Kennedy, Senator George McGovern, and Dee Brown. The book was used as a text in several political science courses at the University of Arkansas at Fayetteville and the University of Arkansas at Little Rock.

Senator Dale Bumpers and Claiborne Pell of Rhode Island helped me to obtain access to some Senate Foreign Relations Committee documents. The late Congressman Claude Pepper and the late Senator John Sparkman graciously consented to interviews back in the late 1970s and early 1980s.

A special thanks to Randall Bedwell and all the staff of the Guild Bindery Press of Memphis for all their work on this book.

President Clinton is admirably suited on intellectual grounds to write the foreword, since he is a former member of Senator Fulbright's staff, a Rhodes Scholar, a Yale Law School graduate, and a former constitutional law professor. The President certainly has my great appreciation for the foreword.

J. William Fulbright generously took the time to write an Afterword on American foreign policy during the Cold War, as well as detailed commentaries on the drafts of the book's chapters as I mailed them to him over the years, and he was gracious with his time in talking to me at great length on many occasions, despite my occasional argumentativeness. He won most of the debates.

Lee Riley Powell
October, 1995

CONTENTS

FOREWORD

by President Bill Clinton

It is with great pleasure that I write this foreword to *J. William Fulbright and His Time*. Lee Riley Powell devoted 17 years to this wonderful book. I imagine it was much more than that. Any Arkansan—indeed any American who has followed the course of our nation and the world through the triumphs and turbulence of the 20th century—knows that we have spent our entire lives touched by the ideals and actions of J. William Fulbright. And though Senator Fulbright passed away in early 1995 at the age of 89, we can be certain that he will be with us as long as the dream of America is alive

Lee Powell, as he notes in his introduction, received plenty of wise editorial advice from his father, James O. Powell, who for 25 years was the editorial page editor of the Arkansas Gazette. It's worth mentioning that between the two of them they interviewed Bill Fulbright more than 100 times. This is no mean feat. Back in 1968, I had the privilege of driving the Senator around Arkansas during his campaign for reelection and I can tell you firsthand that keeping pace with his formidable intellect took about every ounce of wit I could muster.

Senator Fulbright was a remarkable man. In the work he did, in the words he spoke and in the life he lived, Bill Fulbright—teacher, university president, public servant, statesman—stood against this century's most destructive forces and fought to advance its brightest hopes. He lived a life of passion tempered by reason.

He believed in the American idea, but respected others who saw the world differently. He loved politics, but cautioned against the arrogance of power. He cherished education as the answer to our common problems and to our personal dreams, but he knew there would always be more to learn. He understood the value of reasoned conflict, but never permitted it to come at the expense of common ground.

"The Great Dissenter," as he was called, knew very well that conflict can be the engine of progress in a democracy. He also knew that the tensions created by our great diversity of experience and opinion must be balanced by civility and mediated by the recognition that we share a philosophical heritage in the Declaration of Independence and the Constitution. We should, as he did, fight hard for what we believe in. We can, as he did, challenge our leaders if that is the course of our convictions, but we must, as he did, do so with respect and without anger. It was in this spirit that Bill Fulbright warned President Kennedy not to go through with the Bay of Pigs expedition. He was one of the few advisers close to the President to take such a stand. From where I sit now, I understand better than ever before the value of such honest, principled dissent.

Time and again, for 32 years as Congressman, as a Senator, as a Chairman of the Foreign Relations Committee, Bill Fulbright worked for progress and peace, often against great odds and sometimes at great personal cost. He expanded opportunities for Americans who needed help to make the most of their lives. He was a driving force behind the United Nations, the Marshall Plan, and NATO. He took a long, lonely stand against Joseph McCarthy. He fought a long, lonely fight to change our course in Vietnam. He struggled mightily to remind us that the forces of freedom would win the Cold War if we could just avoid nuclear war—what he called his generation's power of veto over the next. And in the chill dawn that followed Hiroshima, he brought about the creation of the international exchange program that will live as his most profound legacy to world peace and understanding.

The Fulbright Scholarship Program embodies Senator Fulbright's faith—people of all backgrounds learning side by side, building what he called "a capacity for empathy, a distaste for killing other men, and an inclination for peace."

The idea behind the program was a simple one. And it informed Bill Fulbright's life. It was the eternal search for common ground—the belief that the ethnic and religious and political differences that divide us are vastly less important than our shared bonds of humanity. Bill Fulbright was one of the first Americans to try to get us to think seriously about the Islamic world. He was one of the first Americans to try to get us to understand the rich and varied cultures of Asia.

This conviction in the hopefulness of connection shaped the contours of his life. And it is in the spirit behind the wonderful program he created. Next year will be the 50th anniversary of the Fulbright Program, which includes as its alumni Nobel Prize winners, members of Congress, and leaders for peace and freedom the world over. The list also includes many not so famous people who journeyed abroad and then returned home to live out quietly the promise of Senator Fulbright's vision. More than 120,000 students from more than 130 countries have come to the United States to study; more than 90,000 Americans have gone overseas to learn and to grow. No matter what their native tongue, all of them are now known by the same name—Fulbrights.

Those of us from Arkansas, those of us who worked for him over the years, in the Congress and on his campaigns, are Fulbrights, too. It would be impossible to overstate the impact he had on generations of young people in our state. It gave us tremendous hope to know that we had a Senator in Washington who could double the I.Q. of any room he walked into. He made us believe that education could lift us up. He convinced us that our obligation was to build our minds and use them as he did, in the action and passion of our times. And he taught us that it was acceptable for us to change our minds—if the facts and our convictions led us in a new direction. In this light, it must be remembered that while many of us disagreed strongly with his early positions on civil rights, he did, in his later years, contribute to the effort to ensure equal opportunity for all Americans. He was one of the few Southern Senators to vote for Thurgood Marshall's elevation to the Supreme Court in 1967. In 1970, he voted to extend the Voting Rights Act.

Most importantly, Bill Fulbright made us believe in the power of reason over fear. During his 1968 reelection campaign, a time when this country was literally being torn apart by the war in Vietnam, the Senator and I stopped by a feed store in a small town in the southwest part of the state. When we walked in, a man in overalls came up to the Senator, looked him right in the eye, and said, "I wouldn't vote for you if you were the last person on Earth." Senator Fulbright sat down on a big sack of seed and said, "Well, why?" And the man replied, "Because you're letting the Communists in. They're everywhere. Today it's Vietnam; tomorrow it will be—they're everywhere."

So the Senator looked around the store slowly, paused, and then said, "I didn't see any when I came into town. Where are they and what do they look like? I wouldn't recognize one." Bill Fulbright was always trying to understand and he was always trying to be understood. I wish he had been alive to see our nation normalize relations with Vietnam. It would have made him proud to know that Americans who were so deeply divided over the war a generation ago came together, bound up the wounds of the past, and moved on toward common ground for the future.

In a speech she gave to the American Chamber of Commerce in Berlin recently, Harriet Fulbright, who was accepting a distinguished award for her husband, spoke of his accomplishments in the context of the times in which he lived. In the late 1940s and early 1950s, she reminded the audience, as the United States was acclimating itself to the Cold War world, talk of leadership, freedom, and education—ideas that may seem simple, self-evident, and commonplace today—was often considered radical, even dangerous. Back then, for taking such daring stands, Senator Fulbright was subjected to fierce criticism.

Then she quoted from a letter the Senator received some 30 years ago. Senator Fulbright got a lot of very emotional mail, but this letter affected him particularly. "Dear Senator Fulbright," the letter began:

"I have never voted for you. I have never missed a chance to belittle you. But deep inside me, there is a nagging suspicion that I have been wrong. If this world plunges headlong toward what well may be its destruction, it gets increasingly harder to hear lonely voices, such as yours, calling for common sense, human reason, and the respect for the brotherhood of man. But be of good cheer, my friend; keep nipping at their heels. This old world has always nailed its prophets to trees, so don't be surprised at those who come at you with hammers and spikes. Know that those multitudes yet unborn will stand on our shoulders. And one among them will stand a little higher because he is standing on yours."

After reading this letter, Senator Fulbright closed his office door, ordered his calls held, and wrote out an answer by hand. We don't know what he said. He kept it to himself. It was a rare private moment for a man who spent his entire life in service to his country, and to the world. In Fayetteville, where Bill Fulbright grew up, there is a statue of him in the town square with the following inscription: "In the beauty of these gardens, we honor the beauty of his dream—peace among nations and free exchange of knowledge and ideas across the earth." Bill Fulbright left us more than a dream. He left us the power of his example. It is a noble, timeless example, and one that is captured admirably in this book.

PROLOGUE

J ames William Fulbright was a United States senator for 30 years, and in 1974, when
he lost his Senate seat in the Arkansas primary election, it was clear that his career in
Congress had been extraordinary if not unique. Two decades later, the place earned by
Fulbright in American history was in sharper focus. No senator in this century has had
greater influence on our foreign policy; his critical dissent in the Cold War and in the
Vietnam War, his opposition to the unbridled exercise of American power, his disbelief in a
Pax Americana, and his sponsorship of the celebrated Fulbright scholarships made an
enduring imprint on both foreign policy per se and the way the Americans and other
nations regard each other.

Fulbright was not admired by presidents—with the exception of John F. Kennedy in his
short tenure—because the senator came into conflict with them almost inevitably during
and even before his record 15-year tenure as chairman of the Foreign Relations Committee.
Harry Truman called him "an overeducated Oxford S.O.B.,"[1] and Lyndon Johnson broke off
a close friendship with Fulbright after the senator began speaking out against the Vietnam
War. But he won great respect in the nation's intellectual community as well as (grudgingly) in Congress, and Walter Lippmann paid him the ultimate compliment: No one else [in
the government] is so powerful and so wise."[2] His record in domestic affairs had its aberrations, notably in his insensitivity to civil rights, but his work in foreign affairs was a powerful legacy.

When Fulbright left the Senate, his name had become known throughout the world for
two principal reasons. Early in his career in Congress, he had sponsored and President
Truman signed into law a program of international scholarships that bore his name. Today,
they have been in existence a half-century and most of the countries of the world are joined
in the exchange of Fulbright scholars. The Oxford scholar R.B. McCallum commended the
Fulbright program—founded by the Arkansan he had tutored in the Rhodes Scholarship
program many years before—as the greatest dispersal of scholars across the face of the earth
since the fall of Constantinople. As the scholarships were becoming a world institution,
Fulbright was appointed to the Foreign Relations Committee and in 1959 assumed the
chairmanship at a time when the chairmen of the major committees in Congress were at the
zenith of their power. He held the chair of Foreign Relations for 15 years, the longest chairmanship of that famed committee in American history, and he gradually became the pre-

manship of that famed committee in American history, and he gradually became the pre-eminent figure in congressional opposition to the Vietnam War and in congressional restraint upon the prosecution of the Cold War generally. In 1966 he conducted hearings that focused national attention upon the ominous course of the war and revealed its tragic folly, underscoring its terrible cost in blood and treasure.

Fulbright changed the role of the Senate Foreign Relations Committee in influencing the foreign policy of the country. His immediate predecessor, Theodore Green of Rhode Island, at 91, had become barely able to function by the time Lyndon Johnson, the majority leader, persuaded him to step down. Earlier, Senator Walter George's role as chairman had been to support the President, Eisenhower or whomever, regardless, in the tradition of maintaining a bipartisan foreign policy; it was a tradition left over from World War II.

Fulbright, in his turn, began to reassert the authority of the committee as a force for independent thought and, recurrently, dissent. In 1961, when Kennedy made the first great blunder of his administration at the Bay of Pigs, Fulbright's was one of the few voices (Chester Bowles' and Arthur Schlesinger's were the others) raised against it in Kennedy's war counsels. Kennedy might have wondered then if he should have followed his first instinct in late 1960 and chosen Fulbright as Secretary of State instead of Dean Rusk. But whatever Kennedy's conjecture after the Bay of Pigs, Fulbright's role as a dissenter had begun to emerge, and Kennedy respected him for it, for Kennedy had no illusions about the failed invasion of Cuba. At the time, he got off a famous joke: "It's like Eisenhower; the worse I do the more popular I get."

The role of the foreign relations dissenter did not develop fully in the short years of the Kennedy administration nor in the first years of Lyndon Johnson's administration. President Johnson and Fulbright had been close friends and colleagues in the Senate, and Fulbright at first mistakenly believed that Johnson would pursue a "moderate" approach in southeast Asian policy, even endorsing the strike after the Gulf of Tonkin episode, which Fulbright was later to regret bitterly. But in 1965 and 1966 Fulbright came slowly to the conclusion that he had been lied to by the President and that the war was a tragedy. Fulbright became the leading opponent of the war in Congress and, even if he was not the first to speak out against the war— Senators Ernest Gruening of Alaska and Wayne Morse of Oregon had preceded him—he was the man who exercised the power of his chairmanship. It was he more than anyone else who set in motion the forces that eventually brought the war to an end.

It was nearly a decade before President Nixon and Henry Kissinger belatedly worked out the agreement with North Vietnam that enabled the United States to withdraw from Indochina, but at last the end did come. Nixon himself had taken about five years to accomplish the withdrawal that Fulbright had called for years earlier; but Fulbright had established himself as the conscience of America in the eyes of people throughout the world. He led the way toward the national consensus that would guard against future Vietnams and at the same time joined Nixon and Kissinger in developing detente with the Soviet Union and China. It remained for the Encyclopedia Americana to make the precise judgment, describing Fulbright as "the most articulate critic of American policy in Southeast Asia and an outspoken defender of congressional prerogatives in the conduct of American foreign affairs."

History tends to create an aura around every national figure, even if revisionists may work to tear his record down, and in the case of Fulbright the passage of a few decades may establish his name early in the 21st century alongside legendary figures of the nineteenth century—Daniel Webster and Henry Clay. As the *New York Times* would write upon his death in 1995, J. William Fulbright was one of the giants of the United States Congress in the 20th century.

Book One:
J. William Fulbright of Arkansas

I. FROM THE OZARKS TO OXFORD

J. William Fulbright became a scholar and a cosmopolitan intellectual and, at the same time, in rare combination, a politician who managed to get elected and re-elected to the United States Congress for 32 years, the first two in the House of Representatives. His intellect and urbanity were acquired principally in three universities: the first one small and obscure (then) in his home state; the second celebrated, Oxford University; and the third, George Washington University, where he graduated with distinction from a highly respected law school. Nothing in his lineage made his career predictable, for his father, Jay Fulbright, was a farmer (at first) of German immigrant stock, and his mother, Roberta Waugh, of English descent, was likewise reared on a farm.[3] There was little in the family history to foretell that he would have a forceful impact upon U.S. foreign policy in the 20th century.

He was born in Sumner, Missouri, in 1905, 12 years after Jay Fulbright and Roberta Waugh were married, but the Missouri origin is largely a technicality, for his family moved to Fayetteville, Arkansas, less than a year later, the father pursuing business opportunity and a less rigorous climate. In any case it was in Arkansas that Fulbright spent his childhood and adolescent years and began the university associations that fashioned his philosophy and his career in public life. It was Arkansas, a poor and undeveloped state, confused by legacies from both the hillbilly frontier and the Southern plantation society, that gave to J. William Fulbright his constituency and "power base" for the congressional service that spanned a third of a century. A short distance away from Fayetteville was the frontier of Oklahoma, which had been opened to settlers 17 years before and was still a territory. Only a few decades before, Mark Twain had depicted the people of Arkansas in his unforgettable, colorful prose: he quoted one Arkansan as saying, "Whoo-oop! I'm the original iron-jawed, brass-mounted, copper-bellied corpse-maker from the wilds of Arkansas! Look at me!... and lay low and hold your breath, for I'm 'bout to turn myself loose." The Arkansans, in Twain's hyperbole, were "prodigious braggarts; yet, in the main, honest, trustworthy, faithful to promises and duty, and often picturesquely magnanimous."[3a] Future generations of Arkansans would be acutely sensitive to the reality that many people outside the state could see only the stereotypes of backwardness and hillbilly braggodocio, but not the qualities that Twain could see: their diligence, honesty and magnanimity. Of course, categorizing an entire state of Americans as sharing similar traits was an inherently oversimplified and inaccurate activity, since the diverse delta, mountains, and central regions of the state produced a kaleidoscope of different peoples; but if any one man could dispel the stereotype of the hillbilly, braggart Arkansan, it would be the cosmopolitan, thoughtful son of Jay Fulbright.

Jay Fulbright was far too prodigious and businesslike to fit the redneck image of an "Arkansas braggart." One of the salient qualities of the Fulbrights was their work ethic. The first of the clan to set foot on American soil was Johan Wilhelm Volprecht, who was born in Berlin and arrived in Pennsylvania in 1740. The Volprechts anglicized their last name and moved steadily westward, to Indiana and then northwest Missouri, usually tilling the rich American soil to make a living.[3b] Jay was born a year after the Civil War ended and attended the University of Missouri one year, but he was an indifferent student and never cared much for books. Roberta Waugh's family lived on a farm near Jay Fulbright, the Waughs having come to Missouri from Virginia in the 1840s. What Jay was interested in was making money. He was a shrewd businessman, always out to acquire more, after the time-honored pattern of those who regard making money as a game. He had successes in Missouri but in Fayetteville he began practicing entrepreneurship in every direction. At his death in 1923 he owned all or part of several small banks in the area, a hotel, a wholesale grocery, a Coca-Cola franchise, an icehouse, and, significantly, a newspaper.[4] It was the newspaper, the Fayetteville *Daily Democrat*, that became the vehicle for launching Roberta Fulbright and indirectly her son, Bill, into the world of public affairs and politics.

What Jay Fulbright taught his son, clearly, was to value money, even if Jay's was not the world of ideas that came to dominate the life of his son. Bill Fulbright was always concerned with financial security and had a sense of frugality that was the source of light humor among his old friends before and after he became a United States senator. Observers of the Fulbrights have noted the marked differences between the father and son in their maturity, the contrast in their horizons, but nevertheless the record indicates that Jay Fulbright and Bill Fulbright got along very well, with mutual respect and affection. Jay and the older son, Jack, were never close, and it was Bill who joined his mother in managing the family enterprises after the unexpected death of his father in 1923.[5]

It was Roberta Fulbright whose influence, more than any other, set Bill Fulbright on the course that was to take him to the locus of power, Washington, and into the arena of world affairs. In the universities several teachers had a profound effect on Fulbright and opened the horizons of his intellect, but the hand that rocked his cradle and guided him in his formative years, especially in certain critical decisions, was the strongest force moving him toward a career far removed from the little university town of Fayetteville.

Roberta, too, had studied a short while at the University of Missouri and, in her case, higher education took hold. She studied journalism and liked it so much that when her husband died she became editor of their newspaper, the *Daily Democrat*.[6] It was a time when independent, family-owned newspapers set the tone of public dialogue in many communities and states. There was no television, and chain ownership was the exception. Roberta wrote a personal column ("As I See It") and plunged into politics and Arkansas affairs. The *Daily Democrat* was lively and progressive, evocative on a small scale of another family-owned newspaper, the *Arkansas Gazette*, published at Little Rock, which influenced the public thought of Arkansas during both the 19th and 20th centuries, particularly the 20th. Roberta Fulbright's interest in politics soon put her into forceful argument on behalf of an able, dynamic candidate for governor named Carl Bailey, who got elected in 1936 and set in motion events that were to send Bill Fulbright to Congress.

Roberta Fulbright wrote with style. Her newspaper column and her letters indicate that she was a woman with a natural talent for expression and a sense of realism about life and about people. If her formal education stopped at one year in college, writers nonetheless are born, not made, and she was prepared to make the effort, to *work* at writing, as most writers must if they are to be successful in their trade. After her husband died and she took over the newspaper, she didn't have to write a column of opinion, but she wanted to. She would stay up at night, writing her pieces in longhand, before turning them in to a typographer who knew how to decipher her scrawl.

Her column revealed a wry sense of humor. The death of Jay Fulbright had left her scrambling to carry on the several Fulbright businesses. She felt overwhelmed at times, even as she recalled her family's tight circumstances when she was a child. "I was born in arrears," she wrote, adding: " I've remained in arrears through a long heavy life-time ... no matter what I do, or give, or stand for, I'm still in arrears. So I've about decided to let the matter stand 'in arrears,' and let it be graven on my tombstone."[7]

She did not indulge herself in illusions about the nature of people, at least not after the death of Jay Fulbright left her to preside over the family enterprises, with some help from her son, Bill. She was shocked to find some of her late husband's associates trying to take advantage of her inexperience and their perception of her presumed "deficiencies as a woman." Years later she wrote in a column that she had looked for help from old friends in the businesses and found, instead, that "resentment and distrust were ever present." She learned that there is a certain savagery in the capitalist system, and wrote that it was "hard to do business with friends and difficult to be too friendly in your business." She found in business, firsthand, a certain "selfish brutality," which was particularly evident in a time of rampant free enterprise, the roaring Republican 1920s.[8]

In her life and her writings, Roberta Fulbright showed traits of personality that were to be reflected later in her son, the senator. She sometimes wondered if she wasn't making all manner of mistakes of judgment and if her efforts were really worth much;[9] at the same time she could be stubborn, or resolute, whichever word applied in a given set of circumstances. The same could be said of Senator Fulbright, who could stand like a rock against an appropriation for Joseph McCarthy or against continuing the Vietnam War, but could never believe that he had really erred in his votes against civil rights legislation.

The convictions of Roberta Fulbright set the stage for her son's political orientation as a Democrat, but not as a conservative Democrat in the familiar, tiresome mode of the time. She was a staunch backer of the New Deal and of a free construction of the "general welfare" clause in the Constitution. In 1936 she wrote that the entire life of the Constitution had been marked by "violent stretchings and squeezings," and that the Republicans had found it "useful propaganda [in 1936] to squeeze in and say that 'Mr. Roosevelt would invalidate the Constitution.'" Her newspaper endorsed Roosevelt every time. In 1940, she wrote of FDR: "He is really a great Democrat and by that we mean he is the greatest living exponent of the Democratic idea that everyone is entitled to opportunity, that government is for the people and by the people and that freedom is a human right." She went on to conclude: "We hail our President as a matchless leader. May increased wisdom be his portion."[10]

Roberta Fulbright 's views on government evoked principles that are fresh and strong and yet seem old-fashioned in the 1990s, an era when right-wing cynics seem to make more noise than anyone else in the land. How often does one hear, this late in the century, an appeal to "support your government" after the fashion of a column she wrote in 1938. "The democratic mode of government," she declared, "is one that must be maintained by those governed, not the other way around." She compared the duty to government with the duty to family, in a way that echoed The Apostle Paul.

Taxes! "No one really loves to pay taxes but they are the lifeblood of government everywhere," she wrote.[11] She knew that taxes are essential in a civilized society. She would have been shocked, surely, at the current fashion for demonizing the figures who are elected to run government at every level.

Roberta Fulbright was a feminist ahead of her time, although she was not strident and belligerent in her views of the traditional, male-dominated society. She wrote that "so long as a woman does poorly and the lords of creation can say, 'O, it's nothing but a fool woman,' they are fairly content, for they must, every mother's son of them, have a woman to do much of the work ... but let a woman do well and she is all but burned at the stake."[12]

She was familiar with prejudice against women and in a column in 1939 she compared such prejudice to anti-Semitism. She proclaimed "an advance tip to the next generation: when you emerge from your chrysalis don't be either a woman or a Jew," adding: "While they are two of the best specimens of the human race, they can stir up more prejudice per square inch, than any other of the species ... To my mind, this unreasoning prejudice which kindles at the advent of a smart Jew or a smart woman almost always spells the superiority of both."[13]

It was inevitable that Roberta Fulbright in her advocacy of equal rights for women would be an enthusiastic supporter of Hattie Caraway, of Arkansas, the first woman to be elected to the United States Senate. As it turned out, Senator Caraway was the most forgettable figure in the Senate in her two terms; she never said anything or did anything except vote a straight Democratic line. Caraway eventually would become one of the candidates Bill Fulbright would defeat in the 1944 Senate race in Arkansas, although by that time she was not a strong candidate and Fulbright's most serious opposition would come from other (as will be discussed later in this book) politicians, primarily Homer Adkins.

The Fulbright column in the *Daily Democrat* (later called the *Northwest Arkansas Times*) ranged across every subject that crossed her mind, from gardening to the turn of the seasons to the deep issues of the times. She vacillated on prohibition. She was brought up on it, practiced it, supported it, but after 15 years she had a "swerve of reason" and turned against it. After repeal, she concluded it had set "the nation on a debauch." She wrote that "forbidden or not, forbidden drink seems to lure and is a demon to be wrestled with."[14]

Her view on Prohibition did not stick with her celebrated son, who would have a drink in the evening throughout much of his life. In 1991, in an interview with a Japanese journalist, he spoke lightly of the rigors of the temperance movement: "My father neither drank nor smoked but he died very young. Seeing that, I later decided I had better drink and smoke to live longer."[15] In 1993 the senator suffered a severe stroke, one that left him partially paralyzed with his speech impaired, and one of his compensations in his daily life then was the drink that he had every day at sundown.[16]

If Fulbright's career as a historic figure in the U. S. Congress was not predictable in the record of his forbears, neither could the strength of character demonstrated in the greatest crisis of his career, Vietnam, be attributed to any early testing in the crucible of adversity. He never knew hardship; he never lived in a log cabin or studied by candlelight or even worked his way through school. In fact, Fulbright's youth was an idyll of small-town happiness and success. Life was good and, in truth, easy. The Fulbrights were prominent and well-to-do and lived in a beautiful colonial home overlooking the town. His relationship with his father was good and his mother adored him. He made decent but not exceptional grades, studying enough to satisfy his parents. He had standing with his peers as a natural athlete and successful politician; he became a Big Man on Campus at the University at Fayetteville. He was president of the student body, popular with the girls, and a football hero forever remembered in the annals of the Arkansas Razorbacks for his heroics in winning a game with Southern Methodist University.[17] Interestingly, scholarship had low priority in his early years, until after he won a Rhodes Scholarship, at a time when few Arkansans even knew about Rhodes Scholarships and when athletic accomplishment was an important factor in the awards under the will of Cecil Rhodes. Certainly luck was with Bill Fulbright in his early years.

Fulbright's boyhood was as idyllic as his adolescence. In his earliest years at Fayetteville, before Jay Fulbright became one of Washington County's richest men with his several successful enterprises, the Fulbrights lived on a thousand-acre farm outside of town. There Bill Fulbright lived the life dear to boys the world over: He hunted and fished, and camped with his father on the White River, a mountain stream celebrated for its beauty. He took care of horses on the farm and enjoyed it; he loved to ride bareback, like a circus performer, and would ride into town. One of his early, cherished memories was winning the horse-harnessing contest at the Washington County Fair, under the eyes of his father, who was the fair chairman.[18]

As a lad, Fulbright showed that he was uncommonly blessed with common sense, although when he grew up and went to Oxford and George Washington University, and afterward, his detractors called him an egghead. Jay and Roberta Fulbright required of their children that they go to school in the summer or work in one of the family businesses. Bill Fulbright chose school, every time, without hesitation, for he did not care for manual toil. "I can always remember how awful it was when I worked once at my father's feed grain wholesale company, shoveling corn and wheat from a boxcar on to a conveyor belt. It was so hot and disagreeable, and the dust came down the neck. A person felt sick and horrible all over. That was why I decided it was much nicer and better to go to summer school."[19]

His distaste for common labor helped him enter college at 16 and graduate at 19, accomplishments that prepared him well for the unknown dramas that lay ahead.

Fulbright was one of six children, and the relationships among them afford interesting commentary for psychologists, although Fulbright remarked in his twilight years that it was too much for him to try to analyze. He had four sisters and one brother, who was six years older. Bill was the darling of the women in the family and sometimes felt a little stifled by them, or so he said in 1991 in an interview. He claimed that in his early years he didn't have much interest in girls because there were so many of them in his household.[20] In any case he was never far from the feminine influence from the time of his youth through two marriages, both of which were eminently successful . He adored his wife Betty and when she became ill, remarked that he didn't know how he could do without her, but after she died he married again, at 85. His second wife was another loving admirer, Harriet Mayor, who had performed significant work for the Fulbright scholarship program.

His relationship with his older brother, Jack, seems to have been one of fierce sibling rivalry. Jack didn't get along with either his father or his little brother. Bill Fulbright, look-.ing back over his life, said that his brother would rough him up when they were children. Jack left Fayetteville early, attended the University of Missouri and played on the varsity football team, then settled in Missouri; he died in 1968. The senator said in 1991 that Jack had apologized to him before he died for his behavior in the early years.

"Jack acted as if he were very superior to me and didn't bother much with me," Fulbright recalled of his much taller and physically more powerful brother, adding: "He pushed me around, giving me a hard time. I think I was a nuisance to him, always in his way with our parents showering me with affection."[21]

Fulbright's success in politics was presaged in his election to the highest student offices when he entered the university. But his experience testified to a rule of politics that is often disregarded in popular myth. Some politicians do win their offices largely on gregariousness and warmth of personality, but others gain popular favor through respect. Over decades Fulbright's friends and supporters and associates, from the time of his youth onward, knew that he was not a natural politician in the commonly accepted sense. In high school and college there was a certain reserve in his manner; then and later he had few close friends. He kept a measure of distance between himself and most of the people he knew, even though he was a great conversationalist on serious issues and gracious in meeting people even at the peak of his power. In the early years and through a 32-year-career in government, his greatest political asset was in a popular willingness to admire his intellect, his power of articulation and his stubborn resolve to fight for certain principles he regarded as of paramount interest to the country. His Arkansas constituents elected him to the Senate five times not because they loved him, as the voters in Massachusetts have loved the Kennedys, but because most Arkansans were proud of him and of the reputation that he had attained around the world. In the beginning, in the small-town setting of Fayetteville, he succeeded because of wide-ranging interests and extracurricular athletic ability, and his position in what was possibly the richest and most influential family in the town. His success in the early years, as later, was based on respect.

He never acquired the glad-handing style that is a stereotype for politicians. Friends and enemies alike noted his sense of reserve, which his enemies called snobbery. One could not say of Fulbright that his thoughts were his own, for his thoughts on the great issues of the country and the world were set forth profusely in thousands of speeches in thousands of forums and in books like *The Arrogance of Power*, hearings, and magazine articles. But he was always a private man. Here, if the biographer looks for parental influence, the example was set by Jay Fulbright, who was regarded outside his family as distant, even aloof.[22]

It was the death of his father, in 1923, when Bill Fulbright was 18, that brought the family a sense of crisis and precipitated events that were to send the son forth to a career 'in government. Roberta got into journalism and, in consequence, into politics. In her innocence she had thought that the business world of Fayetteville would help her, the bereaved widow, but instead she encountered a savage competitive spirit that was ready to make capital of her disadvantage. She survived, and preserved, with help from Bill, the family legacy.

Meantime, young Fulbright finished, at 19, his undergraduate work at the University, added a semester in the law school and came under the influence of two brilliant professors who opened new vistas of learning and ideas. One was Julian Waterman, the founder and dean of the law school, whose name the law school's administration building bears today. Waterman treated Fulbright as an equal. The other professor was Claude Pepper, a native of Alabama, who later moved to Florida and fashioned two singular careers in the U.S. Congress, the first as a senator and the second, 12 years after he was defeated in a bid for re-election, in the U.S. House of Representatives.

The influence of Claude Pepper upon Fulbright was significant. He taught Fulbright a course in law that spring of 1925, and to hear Pepper lecture was in itself an adventure. He was to become known in Florida, and in Congress, for his dazzling eloquence. Neither the professor nor the pupil could know that they were to meet again in Washington and leave, separately, their imprints upon the century.

Pepper taught Fulbright while the promising student was waiting for his Rhodes scholarship to begin. The teacher was only five years older than the pupil. At 24, Pepper was fresh out of Harvard Law School and was a dashing figure at the University of Arkansas. "He was a genius and flamboyant," Fulbright recalled in an interview in 1991. Pepper "brought something of the excitement of the big city to the small farm town. Pepper later entered Congress and was noted for his superb speeches and his thoughtful liberalism."[23]

Claude Pepper got his undergraduate degree at the University of Alabama, where he was a Phi Beta Kappa, but after Harvard and his soujourn in Arkansas, he settled in Florida, practicing law at Perry and Tallahassee. He entered politics and in 1936 was elected to the U.S. Senate, where he served 14 years. He was a wonderful orator, unforgettable in appearance; he had a big red nose and jet black hair and wore great black horn-rimmed spectacles. He was an unhyphenated Democrat who salted his partisanship with humor. On one occasion, addressing the Florida legislature in the late 1940s, he noted that there was one Republican in the entire assembly—"the two-party system in the ideal proportions."[24] In the Senate Pepper was recognized as a flaming New Dealer and internationalist; he was close to Roosevelt but, later, like Fulbright, did not get along with Truman. At times during the Truman administration Fulbright and Pepper delivered speeches questioning some of Truman's foreign policies, although Pepper was much more sharply critical at the time of what he regarded as certain excessively hard-line Cold War policies than was Fulbright. By 1950 Florida politics had taken a hard swing to the right and Pepper was beaten in the primary by a young congressman, George Smathers, who had been a Pepper disciple. It was a bitter defeat for Pepper, who seemed to be finished, but in 1962 he ran for the House of Representatives in a Miami district and won. He then served in Congress another 27 years and became known as the foremost champion of the causes of the elderly. At his death, at 89, he was chairman of the powerful House Rules Committee.

The widespread respect for Claude Pepper was shared by his former pupil at the Arkansas law school and colleague in Congress. Fulbright said of Pepper: "He was the mentor I trusted most, a good advisor to me until his death [in 1989]."[25]

Julian Waterman, in his prior turn, was not to become a national figure, like Pepper, but he was Fulbright's first mentor outside the family. His influence on Fulbright was profound. He was a member of an old Arkansas family, his father having been the first permanent settler in the little town of Dumas. At the time, Arkansas was still a territory. The father moved to Pine Bluff, where Julian was born and reared. Julian went to Tulane for an A.B. degree (Phi Beta Kappa) and to Michigan for a master's in economics before joining the faculty at the University of Arkansas. On leave from the University, he earned a law degree at the University of Chicago, graduating at the top of his class. Shortly afterward he was commissioned by John C. Futrall, president of the University of Arkansas, to organize a law school at Fayetteville. He made his survey, went to Harvard to hire Claude Pepper, and the two of them became professors of the new law school, which Fulbright attended a semester while he was waiting to go to Oxford.[26]

Fulbright, throughout his life, remembered Waterman as an exemplar and friend. Waterman encouraged him to apply for a Rhodes Scholarship and later arranged to bring him back to the law school faculty at Fayetteville, after Fulbright had taken a law degree at George Washington University. Waterman was Jewish (his family immigrated from Germany) and he reminded Fulbright "of the old Jewish rabbis who were the leading intellectuals of their community." Waterman was dignified and scholarly, Fulbright recalled, and "he taught me the rigors and the joys of learning."[27] Waterman continued a close association with Fulbright until he died in 1943; he was only 52.

As Fulbright reached maturity, two seminal events set the course of his life. One was the death of his father, which launched Roberta Fulbright into journalism and politics; the other was an invitation from the dean of the graduate school at the University of Arkansas to apply for a Rhodes Scholarship. Fulbright knew nothing about the scholarship even though it was already celebrated in the academic world. Arkansas was allotted two scholarships every three years under the system obtaining then. The competition was not nearly as formidable as it was to be four decades later when another Arkansan named Bill Clinton would win his own Rhodes. In any case, Fulbright was encouraged by his mother and Professor Waterman to make the application, and he went down to Little Rock for the interviews.

Fulbright's record as an undergraduate had been fairly ordinary, with a B average, although he had entered college and graduated precociously. Even so, he had three advantages that would carry the day. He was a superior athlete, and Cecil Rhodes had specified athletics as one of the governing criteria in his scholarships. Second, Fulbright had a presence, in presenting himself and his views, which would serve him throughout his career. Third, he had good connections, which supported the politics of his application. Fulbright recalled, humorously, a lifetime later, that it didn't hurt to have the president of the University of Arkansas—John C. Futrall—as the chairman of the Rhodes selection committee. In the summing up, luck, as well as merit, was on Fulbright's side.

In mid-December 1924 Fulbright won the award, which was to take him to Oxford for three years, beginning in the fall of 1925. Meantime, Fulbright had his classes under Claude Pepper, and thus the lapse itself served Fulbright well.

In the late summer of 1925 Fulbright and his mother took a train to New York; there he and 25 other scholars assembled at a hotel. Fulbright and his group took an eight-day voyage across the Atlantic on the Cunard White Star, docked at Southampton and then traveled north 70 miles to the college town of Oxford. It was the beginning, Fulbright recalled, of "the most wonderful time of my life."[28]

Cecil Rhodes' concept of what his scholarships would achieve turned out to be quite different from the actual experience. When he died in 1902, he thought that his bequest would encourage generations of bright students from England, the United States and Germany to become political leaders, statesmen, who would fashion the history of the world. He thought that eventually a union of these three powers would dominate the world. In practice, Germany became the enemy of the other two in two world wars and the scholarships for Germans were twice suspended. Rhodes would also have been disappointed in the general disposition of his scholars not to enter politics and government. By the time that Bill Fulbright entered Oxford, it was already clear that most of the Rhodes Scholars were going into academics, the law, medicine, business and even journalism.[29] As it turned out, J. William Fulbright was one of two Arkansans who became leading figures in government as Rhodes intended. The other was Bill Clinton, a Rhodes Scholar who worked briefly for Fulbright in the U.S. Senate in the late 1960s and was inaugurated President of the United States in 1993.

Fulbright spent three years in Pembroke College at Oxford. He spent his long vacations traveling in Europe, learning to speak French in Paris, once traveling through Europe to Warsaw with a Polish student on an old automobile that Fulbright bought for about $500.[30] In those three years the horizons of the world opened up for the young Arkansan from the little country town of Fayetteville.

Fulbright shared quarters at Pembroke College with a student from Kansas. There were about 150 students at the college, and they lived apart from the rest of the world. When they went into town, they had to wear gowns for identification and had to be back on the campus at 9 p.m. Fulbright recalled that once he violated the curfew and had to shinny over the college wall to get back to his quarters; one violation was enough, as he realized that he had risked expulsion.

The students at Pembroke had ideal circumstances for scholarship. Each apartment had a bedroom and sitting room, and a manservant (called a "scout") to build fires, clean up, serve breakfast, lunch and tea, and meet all the routine needs of the students. The "scouts" were servants in the familiar English tradition: they did not consider other occupations, as a rule, but were dedicated to the service of the college, and one generation of scouts would pass the jobs along to the next. Every detail was calculated to enhance scholarship and healthy living. Life at Oxford was recalled vividly by Gaston Williamson, later a prominent lawyer in Little Rock, who graduated at Exeter College, Oxford, in 1937: "Even more enchanting to American students than the physical aspect is the life one leads at Oxford. Mornings are spent in study, the early afternoon in games. Most students go out for some sort of sport, and the competition between the various colleges is sharp and healthy. During the winter, when night comes early and curtains have been drawn against the cold wet darkness outside, a pot of hot tea, buttered crumpets and cakes among a congenial group of friends will put most anyone in a glowing, expansive mood."[31]

In his own time at Oxford, Fulbright studied the liberal arts with emphasis on history and literature. Later he recalled that he suddenly realized how little he knew coming out of the small town life back home. He studied modern history, which he said began with ancient Greece. He read Aristotle and Plato and other Greek philosophers of the fourth and fifth centuries B.C. He discovered that he couldn't write a satisfactory sentence and thus, under the guidance of his tutor, writing was one of the things he learned to do. It would prove indispensable to him in his careers, in academics (briefly) and in government. He knew little about English literature, so he wrote one of his early theses on Sherwood Anderson, the American author who was popular at the time but not well known to the British students at Oxford, who looked down on American writers.

Fulbright was a natural athlete and he joined the rugby, lacrosse and tennis teams at Oxford, displaying the same kind of ability that he had at the University of Arkansas. He became a member of the international lacrosse team that toured America playing college teams in the summer of 1926. The team was invited to the White House, where Bill Fulbright met President Calvin Coolidge. He joined a social club called The Teasel, and he learned to drink and smoke. He also joined the Johnson Club, named after Samuel Johnson, who had been a Pembroke student. The club had 20 members and Fulbright was the only American in it.

It was at Oxford that Fulbright encountered his third exemplar. His tutor was a young Scotsman named R. B. McCallum, who was to shape Fulbright's future even more power- fully than Julian Waterman and Claude Pepper.

Ronald Buchanan McCallum's career at Pembroke began in 1925 and his maiden year there at Oxford coincided with the arrival of Fulbright as a Rhodes Scholar. McCallum was assigned as Fulbright's tutor. They met on a bright autumn afternoon and went cycling to the tomb of William Lenthall, speaker of the Long Parliament. It was the beginning of a life- long friendship treasured by both men. Decades later, McCallum wrote Fulbright, the sen- ator: "One of my greatest satisfactions is in seeing how far some of my pupils have gone in life and what they have achieved, you above all. I am most grateful for the continuing friendship."[32]

McCallum himself, like Claude Pepper, was only a few years older than Fulbright. He was a young Scottish Presbyterian, who had held a Commonwealth scholarship at Princeton University and understood American manners and customs. He was just seven years Fulbright's senior. Fulbright recalled, in looking back over his lifetime, that McCallum was "very patient with me" and unusual in his tolerance—"there weren't many people like him in all of Oxford." Fulbright credited McCallum for a stay at Oxford that was always enjoy- able, free of any sense of inferiority or frustration. Under the system, McCallum would assign to Fulbright a week's readings and the pupil would write a report by week's end. McCallum would rewrite it. Fulbright learned much about writing from McCallum and the tutor stirred in the pupil an interest in politics and government that was to fashion Fulbright's career.

McCallum was a classical British liberal and a dedicated member of the Liberal Party. His scholarship and publications over decades at Pembroke were centered upon the work and policies of the Liberal Party, its emphasis upon the individual, its concern against con- centration of excessive power in business or in labor unions. Another of McCallum's themes was the need for an international organization, first the League of Nations and later the United Nations, that would guard the peace following world war.[33] As Professor Kurt Tweraser has noted, there were suggestive parallels in the views of R. B. McCallum and those of Senator Fulbright, the father of the Fulbright scholarships and later chairman of the Senate Foreign Relations Committee. Fulbright left Oxford with a cosmopolitan view that dominated his thinking in foreign policy throughout his career. McCallum and Fulbright exchanged letters for 25 years after Fulbright was elected to the Senate in 1944. McCallum became Master of Pembroke College, where he taught until 1967. He died in May 1973.

The young Oxford don and his pupil worked on comparative government, noting the differences in the British parliamentary system and the American system of separation of powers and set terms in office. Fulbright developed a preference for the parliamentary system that he expressed recurrently throughout his life. Occasionally, it got him into trouble, as in 1946 in his celebrated remark that it would be better for Harry Truman to resign than to have to govern with the opposition party, the Republicans, in control of both houses of Congress. Truman resented the remark bitterly, even if Fulbright meant it as a throw-away line, an academic thought. This was the occasion when the celebrated characterization of Fulbright as "an overeducated Oxford S.O.B." was attributed to the peppery, profane Truman. The term became part of the Washington folklore, and, indeed, Truman was famous for such private observations. On one occasion he said that the "senior senator from Florida [Claude Pepper] is a shitass," according to the late Walker Stone, who was editor of the Scripps Howard newspapers.[34]

At Oxford, under McCallum's tutelage, Fulbright developed an affection and respect for Britain and for the British form of government that endured, in the same way that McCallum's concept of an international peacekeeping force endured in Fulbright's principles.

In June 1928, Fulbright was graduated from Oxford. There were four levels of graduation, and Fulbright took a second, which satisfied him. His had been a well-rounded time at the University, for he had won awards in athletics and been elected to offices in the social clubs. Half of each year he had spent in class at Oxford and, during the other half, he lived much of the time on the continent, as the dons at Oxford intended. His eyes were opened to the life and culture of Western Europe as well as of England. Graduation cleared the way for living on the continent for most of another year. It was an exciting experience for the young man raised in Arkansas, and offered a persuasive argument against the peculiarly American concept that every red-blooded American boy is duty-bound to finish college and go to work, gainfully, at once. The Fulbrights had money and Roberta was determined to spend it freely in giving her adored son a life rich in culture and leisure. The son was not hustled back to Fayetteville to run the family businesses. Instead, his mother joined him for graduation, and then the two of them, with friends, made the summer grand tour across France and Switzerland to Vienna. At summer's end, Roberta returned to Fayetteville and Fulbright settled in to spend the fall and winter in Vienna. His mother allowed him $200 a month for living expenses and, at the time, that was a lot of money. He went to the opera and got into the cafe society of Vienna, where European writers and artists commingled in the street cafes with expatriates, including newspaper correspondents who were to become household words in America, in the tumultuous events of the thirties. Fulbright met William L. Shirer and John Gunther and Dorothy Thompson. He became friends with a Hungarian correspondent named Mike Fodor, who wrote for the *Manchester Guardian* and the *New York Evening Post*.

Fodor was one of the leading correspondents, and he took a liking to the young Arkansan. He was one of the most informed writers in Europe and he allowed Fulbright to become sort of a protege; he invited Fulbright in the spring of 1929 to accompany him on an annual trip he made through the Balkans and Greece. Fodor designated him as correspondent for one of his lesser clients, thus giving Fulbright entree to the sources of power. It was a particularly memorable experience for Fulbright, but it was cut short in Greece when Fulbright came down with quinsy, a throat infection that left him ill and miserable. He had to return to the United States and home to Arkansas, sick throughout the journey. His carefree travels in Europe were over and he took up at Fayetteville where he left off, helping manage the family businesses and, perhaps, pondering what to do next.[35]

In the summer of 1930, fate, or happenstance, or whatever, took him to Washington for what was to have been a short stay managing the estate of an old friend whose father had just died. There he met Betty Williams, the daughter of an aristocratic Philadelphia family. This event was later described by Fulbright in his old age as one of several accidents that determined the course of his life. Fulbright and Betty Williams were immediately attracted to each other, but Betty told him that he, the Rhodes Scholar, needed further education. He agreed and entered George Washington University Law School, to be near her as much as to learn the law. While they were courting he was working toward a law degree, but the romance encountered difficulty because her parents, her mother, especially, didn't want to bring a yokel from Arkansas into the family. Fulbright thought Philadelphians were snobs, and he told Betty they had better break it off; they parted as good friends.

Two months later she contacted him and went down to Washington to see him over her mother's objection. Roberta Fulbright also had some misgivings at the time about whether a Philadelphia socialite would be able to adjust to Arkansas, although after their marriage she would later tell Betty that of all Bill's dates, she was "the best of the litter." They were married soon after, in the summer of 1932.[36]

In 1991, when he was an old man, Fulbright spoke with the candor of his age about life and women, using language that would irritate, to say the least, many members of the feminist movement. He said, of his courtship and marriage to Betty Williams: "There's no accounting for what women will do. Maybe at the ripe old age of 25 she was just getting nervous when she renewed our courtship. No one can explain women. They are very peculiar creatures."

The marriage was a blessing for both parties. They got along well, had two daughters, and worked the campaign trail together—Betty more so than Bill—when Fulbright got into politics. Betty's skills in socializing with people from all persuasions and socio-economic levels were tremendously beneficial to her husband, who often found it difficult to engage in small talk. Her long illness and death in the 1980s were presaged by serious illness in the 1970s when Fulbright, reflecting on the depth of their feeling, told an Arkansas editor that he simply did not know how he could get along without her.[37]

Fulbright finished law school second in his class of 135 students, showing what he could do when he set his mind to academics. As an undergraduate and at Oxford he had been content with good but not exceptional marks. His record as one of the top two students at a nationally known law school demonstrated his clear abilities as an exceptional legal scholar. He proceeded from law school to become a special assistant attorney general in the Justice Department's anti-trust division. Here he handled some routine business, but he became acquainted with Adlai Stevenson, then a young lawyer in the Agricultural Adjustment Administration, and he took part in the historic litigation called the "sick chicken case," involving the National Recovery Administration and the law that created it, the National Industrial Recovery Act. Twenty years later, Fulbright would be a strategist in Stevenson's second presidential campaign. In the NRA litigation, Fulbright was assigned to assist a lawyer named Walter Rice in enforcing the NRA code against a poultry firm in Brooklyn run by four brothers named Schechter. In the Schechter case, Fulbright joined Rice in a jury trial in Brooklyn against the poultry firm. The government had charged the Schechters with conspiring to violate provisions of the NRA and the fair practices code for the New York metropolitan area. The case involved the "live poultry code," which contained maximum-hour and minimum-wage provisions and prohibited various practices considered "unfair methods of competition." It was a historic case, testing the NIRA's constitutionality and dealing with the issue of the federal government's authority to act regarding local industry on the grounds that its business affected interstate commerce. Rice and Fulbright won, as the jury found the defendants guilty on 19 counts.

Fulbright and Rice were jubilant, but the Schechters appealed and the Solicitor General—Stanley Reed—took over for the government, only to ultimately lose in the Supreme Court. *Schechter Poultry Corp. v. the United States*, 295 U.S. 495 (1935). The NIRA had attempted to permit representatives of labor and management in each industry to meet and design codes of "fair competition." The goal was to help stabilize wages and prices in order to halt their decline. The President was to approve the "codes" after making several findings, including: first, that there were "no inequitable restrictions on admission to membership," and second, that the codes were not designed to promote monopoly or to oppress small enterprises.[38a] The Court invalidated the Act on the grounds that it impermissibly delegated a legislative function to the President. Fulbright at the time felt that the Supreme Court's decision reflected the arch-conservative attitude of many of the Justices at that time—a criticism of the Court certainly shared by President Roosevelt and by many other New Dealers—in striking down one of the most famous pieces of legislation of FDR's famous first "100 days."[38b] Speaking of Justice James McReynolds, Justice Willis Van Devanter, and the other "four horsemen," Fulbright would later vividly recall his belief as a young lawyer that they were ""old-fogey reactionaries.""[38c]

Fulbright was certainly correct in his concern about the reactionary tendencies of McReynolds and the most conservative bloc on the Court at that time, for in many decisions in that era the conservative justices had rigidly opposed government intervention in the economy. However, in retrospect, *Schechter* was not the benighted decision that some New Dealers condemned it as in 1935; the Court was unanimous in the result, with even the brilliant progressive Justice, Louis Brandeis, joining in the opinion. Brandeis had frequently dissented from the conservative majority when the Court blocked efforts of the federal government to intervene in the economy. Some liberal critics of the NRA felt that the codes gave too much power to the largest economic organizations within each industry. Senator Hugo Black of Alabama, for example, opposed the NRA (except for the provisions dealing with appropriations for public works), saying at the time of its passage that "it created committees of businessmen at various parts of the country to set up commissions and draw what I considered to be laws. And it also provided for the suspension of the anti-trust act... I'm interested in the consumers, and as I understand this bill, it proposes to do away with the anti-trust act and leave the control of prices to businessmen meeting in common. I remember from Adam Smith that he said if you let a group of businessmen get together even for a dinner to talk among themselves, that the public's going to suffer. And that's the way I feel about this NRA."[38d]

Although Senator Black engaged in some populist hyperbole, the concern about the strength of big business and industry in the NRA codes was legitimate. The opinion in *Schechter*, in fact, expressed concerns about overweening executive power that Fulbright would decry—in a quite different context—later in his career. Of course, Fulbright's role and perspective as a young executive branch lawyer differed entirely from his later role as a legislator. "The Congress is not permitted," Chief Justice Charles Evans Hughes wrote for the *Schechter* Court (which was unanimous in the result, although Harlan Stone and Benjamin Cardozo joined in a concurring opinion), "to abdicate or to transfer to others the essential legislative function with which it is thus vested." *Schechter*, at 529. The Court asked what was meant by "fair competition" as that term was used in the Act; was it "a convenient designation for whatever set of laws the formulators of a code for a particular trade or industry may propose and the President may approve as being wise and beneficient provisions for the government of the trade industry in order to accomplish the broad purposes of rehabilitation, correction, and expansion which are stated in the first section [of the Act]." The Court asked if Congress could delegate its legislative authority to trade or industrial associations so as to empower them to enact the laws they deem to be wise for the rehabilitation of their trade or industry. The answer was resoundingly in the negative: "Such a delegation of legislative power is unknown to our law and is utterly inconsistent with the constitutional prerogatives and duties of Congress." *Schechter*, at 537.

Based upon the venerable principle of American constitutional law that courts do not sit to grant advisory opinions, the *Schechter* Court should have stopped with its discussion of delegation, which was sufficient to invalidate the NRA. But in a much more dubious section of the opinion, Chief Justice Hughes went on to elaborate upon the old distinction between "direct" and "indirect" effects on interstate commerce: although the bulk of the Schechter poultry came from without the state, Hughes contended that it came to a "permanent rest within the state" (that is, it was eaten there) and hence sale within the state was not part of the flow of interstate commerce. It was this section of the opinion that most alarmed Fulbright and would give rise to President Roosevelt's famed response that the Court's rejection of the idea of "indirect" effects on interstate commerce had turned back the Constitution to the "horse-and-buggy days" when the economy was essentially local and many people were self-supporting in local areas.[38e] The New Dealers might have taken some solace in the much more perceptive concurring opinion of Cardozo and Stone, which expressly declined to accept the majority's distinction between direct and indirect effects upon commerce as the touchstone of universality. The concurrence thundered that the NRA was "delegation running riot," but there was a vital distinction on the commerce clause question: where Hughes would apparently deny that indirect effects on interstate commerce even of vast magnitude would qualify an industry for national regulation, Cardozo and Stone were willing to consider the particular situation in each case. The apparent determination of the Court to announce a broad constitutional principle in dictum was disturbing to astute constitutional lawyers; as Felix Frankfurter and Henry Hart aptly wrote, "Against such advisory pronouncements the constitutional theory and practice of a century and a half unite in protest."[38f]

In the desperate conditions of the Depression, Roosevelt had adopted a commendable spirit of experimentation, and many of the administration's experiments were historic successes; but the NRA, unfortunately, was an exception to that rule. The NRA was not successful in achieving its economic recovery goals, and in fact the National Labor Relations Act, Social Security Act and other New Deal legislation proved far more important. In such decisions as *Morehead v. New York ex rel. Tipaldo*, 298 U.S. 587 (1936), in which the Supreme Court invalidated a state minimum wage protection for women as violating due process, a five-person majority on the Court had invalidated reform legislation. Fulbright's aversion to such decisions as *Morehead* was justified.

In *Schechter*, Fulbright was effectively playing his role as a New Deal lawyer. The way the case turned out, Fulbright was able to argue for the rest of his life, half seriously, that he and Walter Rice would have won had they been left to conduct the appeal. He couldn't prove it nor could anyone disprove it.[39] His work in the Justice Department, in any event, was a marvelous learning experience in law and public policy, and his success at the trial level in Schecter suggests that he would have made a successful trial lawyer, had he chosen that career route. He left the Justice Department before the administration's concerns about the "four horsemen" on the Court led to the notorious "Court-packing episode," so Fulbright was spared any involvement in that regrettable controversy. Later he would reflect that Roosevelt had erred in the Court-packing episode. In any event, the make-up of the Court was changed by the later appointments Roosevelt made, as well as by the transition in Justice Roberts' position on some major cases.[39a]

In 1935, Fulbright had decided to leave the Justice Department to take a job as a law professor in the George Washington law school. He seemed to prefer teaching to lawyering. After a year he and Betty decided to return to Fayetteville, where DeanWaterman and Professor Robert Leflar were entreating him to come join the faculty and Roberta Fulbright was always saying she needed him to help run the family's affairs. The opportunity for Fulbright to return to Arkansas was created by Professor Leflar's acceptance of a visiting professorship at the University of Missouri in 1936-37; Fulbright taught Leflar's courses during the Missouri professorship. Leflar, who remained vigorous and brilliant well into his eighties, would recall a half-century later that he had opened for Fulbright "the great career with which we are all familiar." In 1985, Leflar took a retrospective look at a 60-year career that included writing a nationally recognized treatise on conflict of laws, working as a Roosevelt administration lawyer during World War II, service as a justice on the Arkansas Supreme Court, and initiating the Appellate Judges Seminars at New York University in the mid-1950s and teaching more than 1,000 appellate judges over a 30-year period. The venerable legal scholar—who was not given to making effusive compliments—bestowed a memorable accolade upon Fulbright, writing: "I have often thought that creating this opening for the future Senator Fulbright may well have been the single most important contribution of my lifetime to the welfare of the state and nation."[39b]

In Fulbright, Leflar and Waterman, the tiny law school in Fayetteville boasted three of the most brilliant minds in the country (and Claude Pepper had taught there a few years earlier). Few, if any, of the nation's small law schools were fortunate enough to have three professors of such intellectual stature. Waterman's career was tragically cut short by his death at a young age in 1943, but Fulbright and Leflar would influence the law for decades to come. In general, the University of Arkansas lagged far behind most of the top universities in the country at the time, largely because the small, relatively poor state lacked the financial resources that the prominent universities from large, more prosperous states could utilize. However, the law school was an exception, at least in the quality of the small faculty. Fulbright was younger than Leflar or Waterman, but as a Rhodes Scholar, honors graduate and later professor of George Washington University Law School, and former Justice Department lawyer, the new addition to the faculty held superb credentials as a legal scholar. Leflar said that he had conducted a detailed study of the nationally prominent law schools in that era and concluded that Fulbright's school, George Washington, ranked with Harvard, Yale and Columbia as among the most impressive in the land. His students considered him to be an excellent teacher who succeeded in making his classes in constitutional law, equity and insurance law interesting.

One of Fulbright's and Leflar's students was Henry Woods, who would become a famous trial lawyer, federal judge and author of a treatise on comparative fault that was cited by lawyers and legal scholars around the country. Woods regarded Fulbright as an excellent, well-prepared scholar in his equity and insurance classes, and was looking forward to taking the Fulbright constitutional law class in his third year when Fulbright suddenly became president of the university. In an assessment of Fulbright that would recur among many Arkansans and other people through the decades, Woods reflected that the students deeply respected Fulbright for his intellect, teaching ability, and his dry sense of humor, but he was not popular with them: "His classes were always interesting and he was an excellent teacher, but he was a patrician who did not mix and mingle with the students."[39c] In that regard, Fulbright contrasted sharply with Waterman, who circulated with the students, invited them to his house, and took a genuine personal interest in them. Moreover, although Fulbright's biting wit could be hilarious at times, he could also be sarcastic to any of his students who were unfortunate enough to have come to class unprepared. In the depths of the depression, the financial gap between the wealthy Fulbright and most of his students—who were generally quite poor and struggling to make ends meet while in law school—also created a certain social distance. Woods remembered Professor Fulbright as somewhat distant and aloof. Of course, the distance that some of his students perceived as the patrician arrogance of the wealthy Rhodes Scholar may simply have been Fulbright's basically reserved personality and his businesslike preoccupation with his scholarly duties. As his later career demonstrated, Fulbright was deeply concerned about providing educational opportunities for low-income people; he would steadfastly support federal aid to education throughout his career regardless of the political consequences of his position. Nonetheless, even if Fulbright did not develop close relationships with most of his students, he was deeply respected by them because of his conscientious success at the task he was there to accomplish—teaching the law.

Fulbright was profoundly influenced by Leflar, whose legal philosophy had been shaped at Harvard Law School by Dean Roscoe Pound, who taught that law is the servant, not the master of the society in which it operates. Leflar's philosophy in this regard reinforced the views Fulbright received from his mother and R. B. McCallum concerning the citizens' duty to make a contribution to the social and political life of society; Fulbright constantly taught his students that politics was a high calling, and service in the arena of public affairs was one of the most impressive accomplishments to which a lawyer could aspire. Leflar's experiences with the various professors at Harvard, where he held an S.J.D., were beneficial for the faculty of the emerging law school in Fayetteville. Leflar was most impressed with the teaching style of the legendary Samuel Williston, whose good-natured yet incisive questioning of students elucidated the legal ideas he was expounding. The young Arkansan at Harvard was impressed not only with Dean Pound's brilliance but with his human qualities and personal concern for students: "[Pound] liked to get acquainted with students, to help them individually, and to join them in their social functions. He remembered them after they graduated, and continued to help them."[39d] Leflar's biggest disappointment as a professor was Felix Frankfurter; his classes largely consisted of conversations between Frankfurter and a few loquacious students who sat in the front rows (Leflar, who was as brilliant as anyone in the class, did not like to raise his hand and thus rarely participated in Frankfurter's class concerning municipal liability in tort law). To a considerable degree, Fulbright benefited from Leflar's conclusions in having studied at the internationally renowned Harvard campus. Fulbright avoided Frankfurter's mistake of having the class monopolized by a dialogue between the professor and a few people, for the young professor made extensive use of the Socratic method of questioning the students. This method involves leading the student through a series of questions until the professor guides the student to the crucial conclusions. With his sharp sense of humor and academic ability, Fulbright's Socratic method was clearly successful. The young patrician was considerably less successful, however, in developing relationships with and empathy for the students after Pound's example. Henry Woods, who was an excellent and gregarious student in Fulbright's classes of 25-35 students, never got to know him well.

Woods recalled Fulbright's teaching as having been somewhat different from that of Leflar, who would devote substantial time to lecturing, and also devote time to questioning the students. For decades, law students and professors have debated the relative merits of lecturing as opposed to the Socratic method. Advocates of the latter method claim that it forces the students to think about the law and provides practice in debate. Critics of the method argue that since the professor has such tremendous advantages over the students in having studied the subject matter for years and knowing the ultimate points he is seeking to reach before the questioning begins, the Socratic method may degenerate into a vehicle for the professor to show off his knowledge and ability rather than a useful pedagogical instrument. The method can waste the class' time and lead to unnecessary embarrassment if a student is unprepared, or is simply nervous at the prospect of being grilled in front of his colleagues (as illustrated, in oversimplified form, in the famous film, "The Paper Chase" many years later). Fulbright's occasional sarcasm and impatience with minds that did not function as rapidly as his did not endear him to some students, although in the great majority of instances Fulbright was carefully polite. According to Woods, most of the students preferred Leflar's teaching style, in which the professor would give a clear lecture summarizing the crucial points for the students, combined with a certain amount of questioning.[39e] Of course, Leflar had been in the legal profession much longer than had Fulbright, who eventually, as it turned out, devoted only a few years of his life to law teaching. Whatever criticisms might be made concerning Fulbright's role as a law professor, it is clear that had

his life not suddenly veered into the political arena, he would have enjoyed a long, rewarding and deeply respected career as a legal scholar.

At home, the Fulbrights bought and remodeled a huge old log house called Rabbit's
Foot Lodge on 150 acres outside town. There Fulbright returned to the idyll of his youth
in his home town, teaching law three days a week and working part-time with his mother.
The Fulbrights' first daughter was born. Betty took to the small town life, to the delight of
her mother-in-law, Roberta, who had liked her from the start, despite some initial concerns
about whether the Philadelphian would adapt to Arkansas. Fulbright said later that Betty
had finally escaped from her dominant mother.[40]

Recognizing Fulbright's academic prowess, the law school asked him to become an
associate professor of law, a full-time position he was to assume in the fall of 1939. For all
he knew, he would spend his life as a scholar (and a rich one) in a university that was beginning to escape from its mediocre origins. The Fulbrights were satisfied. In the summer of
1939 life was good and the living was easy. Then, in September, the president of the
University, John C. Futrall, was killed in an automobile accident, a tragic event that ironically would set the stage for Fulbright to become, through his political connections, the
youngest university president in the country. His elevation to the post drew national attention in academic circles and, in Arkansas, thrust him into the cross-currents of state politics.

For most of his life until 1939, Fulbright had lived in the placid environment of
Fayetteville. One of his fond memories was gazing each day at the beautiful towers of Old
Main—the impressive center of the little campus nestled in the scenic Ozarks—as the faithful, melodious chimes of the clock rang out, always keeping right on time. Bill Fulbright
had flourished under the shadows of Old Main's venerable clocks and towers, but the peaceful years and setting of his early life would soon be over. He did not know it then, but he
was on his way to Congress.

II. THE ROAD TO THE SENATE

Fulbright was not the obvious choice nor even a logical choice to become president of the University of Arkansas. He was only 34 and had just become an associate professor. Deans and department heads were the likely candidates for the succession, and the thought of becoming president did not at first cross his mind. But politics reared its head, this time fortuitously for the University: Governor Carl Bailey and Roberta Fulbright, the editor, were good friends and political allies, in the sense that the *Daily Democrat* had supported him in his campaign and Roberta Fulbright approved of him as a progressive who was not satisfied with the old-style conservative Democratic politics. Clearly Governor Bailey wanted to change things in the University, which was the flagship in the state's fledgling college system, and he was willing to disregard convention and seniority.

The governor was able to direct the appointment, through the Board of Trustees, which he controlled. So the normal course of filling the vacancy was dismissed and Fulbright was offered the position. In the preliminary conversations, he demurred, contending that his mentor, Julian Waterman, was the correct choice. Waterman, however, didn't want the job and Fulbright finally took it, accepting the persuasions of his mother and his wife, but he was embarrassed about it and then somewhat insecure in the presidency because of his unfamiliarity with the byzantine processes of running a college. Characteristically, Fulbright used his dry wit to relieve the tension, commenting in his first speech as president that many remarks had been made about his youth, but "I really mean no offense by it and I am confident that definite progress is being made every day to correct it." He also paid appropriate tribute to the late President Futrall, acknowledging that "I realize that to many of you, long accustomed to the formal, dignified and thoroughly competent presence of Dr. Futrall, my appointment came as a shock... I confess that it surprises even me." As president, Fulbright's wit, youth, and reputation as the Razorback football-star-turned-Rhodes-Scholar made him popular with the undergraduate students, probably much more than he had been in the more restricted role with the law students. In a speech in early 1940, he sounded what would become a familiar theme later in his career, in his sympathy for the idealism of the younger generation as opposed to the staid conservatism of their elders: "It has been suggested that I am too young to be the president of a great institution, but that is one thing for which I do not apologize. One might be too stupid, but never too young. I find that I am more at home with young people and with those who are interested in young people than some of the more sophisticated of our citizens."[40a]

As Fulbright grappled with the myriad problems of leading a university in one of the poorest states, he increasingly came to address the broader social, economic and political issues of the day. In an address to the Chamber of Commerce in Little Rock on October 18, 1940, he was skeptical of businessmen who loved to boast of the state's abundant natural resources in bauxite, oil, lumber, poultry, cotton and rice, for even with all this natural abundance, "both natural and human... Arkansas has the highest per capita debt and the lowest per capita income of any state in the Union." He felt that the state legislature would not deal constructively with these problems, for it was dominated by wealthy special interests. The young president also had a populist vein that showed in his conviction that the powerful northeastern corporations owned many business interests in Arkansas and other Southern states and wielded an inordinate economic influence from outside the state. Having been impressed with the success of federal aid through many of the New Deal policies to the poorer states, he regarded federal action as an effective strategy for breaking the cycle of economic underdevelopment. Unlike many university presidents whose speeches were primarily intended to raise funds and pacify influential alumni, Fulbright troubled his Chamber of Commerce audience with a dire prediction of the problems that would persist if Arkansas' educational system did not improve: many students came to the university with only $20 or so in hand, and "It is pitiful to see how eager they are for an education, but how often they are not prepared for it... It is a terrific economic and human waste to let our best brains settle down to picking cotton or tending a filling station when, with an investment of $1,000 each, they could be made leaders in industry and the professions."[40b]

As an academic figure, his mind turned naturally to education as the primary solution to the challenge of building a better society. He wrote his congressman, Clyde Ellis—a former law student of Fulbright's who had taken his professor seriously on the need for lawyers to go into politics—to make an impassioned plea that Congress restore appropriations for the New Deal's National Youth Administration (NYA) program for college students that had been recently reduced. Congressman Ellis commended President Fulbright's appeal in a speech in the U.S. House of Representatives—the first time Fulbright's name was mentioned in Congress. Fulbright had written Ellis that in light of the concentration of wealth in the eastern states, many privately endowed universities could assist their students, and students in the poorer states deserved the same assistance. "Educational opportunities are obviously out of balance in this country," Fulbright wrote, "when Harvard University can spend $14,000,000 in 1938-39 and many of the state universities of the South and West, serving millions of people, only get $1,000,000 or less." In urging Congress to restore the NYA funds, Fulbright warned that "If democracy is to continue in this country, it must be supported by education of the people, and no more efficient way than NYA has been evolved to accomplish this."[40c]

In the end the experience as head of the university was important for what was to become his real career. He attracted national attention for the first time, as a sort of academic boy wonder, and he gained forums that allowed him to promulgate ideas he had formed on foreign policy and the ideals of public service. As a law professor, he had urged lawyers to go into government as a proper place for their talents and training. Now he returned to this theme—how satisfying it would have been to Cecil Rhodes, who wanted his scholars to become leaders in government; how satisfying it was to Roberta Fulbright, who wrote so much in her columns about the duty of educated people to serve their country!

"It is a mistake to sneer at the word, 'politician,'" Fulbright told a Fort Smith audience, adding: "We should transfer to the politician some of the honor and the reverence which we have so generously bestowed upon the Lindberghs, the Fords, the Edisons, the Morgans and the Babe Ruths."[41]

Even more important, Fulbright used his new-found forums to articulate his ideas on world affairs, including a fierce opposition to Nazism that was ahead of national opinion. This emergence of his views will be treated further in this book, in considering the development of his principles in foreign policy. His job as president of the University of Arkansas lasted less than two years, but it was prelude to his career in Washington.

Fulbright got his appointment as the University president through politics, although it was clearly good for the University. He lost the job less than two years later through politics, after an old enemy, Homer Adkins, was elected governor. Adkins defeated Governor Bailey in the latter's bid for renomination to a third term. Upon his inauguration in January 1941, Adkins got the legislature to reorganize the University Board of Trustees to give him immediate control by appointing six of ten members. He reconstituted the board and on June 9 Fulbright was asked to resign. He refused, forcing the board to dismiss him.

It turned out to be bad politics for Homer Adkins, for Fulbright was a popular president. He was a dashing figure on the campus. The students regarded him as one of them but were impressed by his background as a Rhodes Scholar and Justice Department lawyer. They staged a mass protest meeting on the eve of his dismissal and he won a rousing ovation in his commencement speech. The arrogance of Adkins was not well received in the state. In an editorial, the *Arkansas Gazette* warned of the consequences of such an action:

> The very word "shakeup" is disturbing to the people of Arkansas when it is used in connection with their state university. A university is peculiarly a state institution that should be immune, so far as is humanly practicable, from changes that many state agencies sustain, with change in statehouse administrations...

The *Gazette* was the leading newspaper in Arkansas, with a statewide circulation. The editorial went on to declare:

> Long persisting reports now apparently foreshadow the removal of the president of the University, the dean of agriculture and the assistant extension director... It must be realized that if three men in key positions are to be ousted for successors more acceptable to the present Board of Trustees, those will not be all the changes in teaching and administrative staffs. And it must be plain that every shakeup at the University of Arkansas will make future shakeups easier as one state administration succeeds another.

Subsequent elections suggested that Homer Adkins' high-handed treatment of Fulbright was damaging to the governor. Nevertheless, Fulbright was left jobless in the summer of 1941, and it was the following spring before he saw his next course of action.

He ran for Congress, for a seat in the House of Representatives held by his old friend, Clyde Ellis, who had decided to run for the Senate. Ellis urged Fulbright to seek the House seat. The Fulbright women, wife and mother, concurred. Bill Fulbright was at the threshold.

In the spring of 1942 the United States was engaged, since December 7 of 1941, in a war that would determine the fate of nations for the rest of the century and end forever the kind of American isolation that Fulbright had been preaching against while he was president of the University. Franklin Roosevelt was halfway through his third term. The war was about to stir the national economy out of the Great Depression, at last. There were great themes to be developed in national debate, but great ideas might not win elections in a rural congressional district like the Third District of Arkansas. Bill Fulbright had never run for public office before, but he realized that his splendid education did not prepare him for practical, campaign politics. He had some casual experience with political races, but now he had to learn how to win an election, and in a short time. On a Tuesday before the qualifying deadline for entering the Democratic primary, Clyde Ellis came to him and invited him to run for the seat that Ellis was about to vacate. Fulbright took the issue home, and both Betty and Roberta thought it was a grand idea. Why not? Betty was more excited about it than he was, and so he filed his papers for the campaign. The circumstances of the race were fairly favorable, but what counted most was Fulbright's readiness to work 18 hours a day and his willingness to learn the political art, listening to its practitioners and trekking through the back country, over the dusty, mountainous roads.

Fulbright entered the race as the underdog, opposing a state Supreme Court justice named Karl Greenhaw who had the blessing and support of Governor Adkins. The role of underdog carries with it in Arkansas, and elsewhere, a compensating factor of sympathy for the man running against the odds. Fulbright also found that his candidacy was "buoyed by the area's sympathetic reaction to his ouster at the university." The public had not responded kindly to the rough treatment of the boy wonder of higher education.[42]

The young candidate cultivated the local politicians in every town and at every crossroads, asking for their ideas and, in the process, flattering them about their knowledge and experience. One thing he learned was the kind of campaigning that suited the district best and suited him best personally; at first he would schedule a speech and arrive with his loudspeaker to find only a handful of people on hand. Once there was just one listener. He turned to the much more practical system of visiting stores and homes and courthouses informally, and talking to individuals.[43] Fulbright was always best at dialogue—questions and answers were his best format then and throughout his career. He was a great conversationalist on serious issues, as his constituents learned over the next 32 years. He could listen closely and talk at length on almost any subject.

One of Fulbright's greatest political assets was Betty's natural skill as a campaigner. She tended to get to know people better than he did, and she removed all doubts about whether a Philadelphia socialite could relate to the practical concerns of people in northwest Arkansas. Fulbright would later recall the political abilities of Mrs. Fulbright: "It is exceedingly helpful to have a wife who can go into the kitchen and visit with the women of the family while you engage the men in a discussion. In the conservative rural communities, it is not good manners to discuss politics in the presence of the women. Just why this should be so, I am not quite certain. But in any case, it is an asset to have a wife who likes people." [43a] Although the rural folk had attitudes about gender roles that are regarded as backward in the 1990s—and of course were probably regarded by the Fulbrights as backward at the time—the Fulbrights dealt with the voters successfully. Betty's sharp mind and outgoing personality were tremendously valuable to her husband's political career.

Back in Fayetteville, Roberta Fulbright was keeping quiet, reluctantly, in her newspaper, now named the *Northwest Arkansas Times*. Her son convinced her that it would be better to let the resentment over the University affair ferment on its own without agitation by the candidate's mother. The newspaper's printing plant did turn out a four-page, full-size newspaper called The Victory News, which was mailed to every boxholder in the district. It was folksy, full of pictures and trivia on the Fulbrights, complete with jokes and information about items ranging from flood control to health care.

The governor and his candidate, Justice Greenhaw, were heavy-handed and inept. At one point the State Highway Department sent crews through the district taking down every Fulbright sign. [44]

Young Fulbright's first campaign was a great success. In the first primary he polled about 1,400 more votes than Greenhaw, but lacked a majority because there were 3,876 votes for a third candidate. In the runoff two weeks later, Fulbright won easily, 12,304 votes to 8,426. The general election would be a formality. In those days the Republicans were even weaker in Arkansas than they were in the 1960s and 1970s, and so the Fulbrights prepared to sell Rabbit Foot's lodge and move back to Washington where, more than incidentally, Betty's mother was finally beginning to admit that her daughter hadn't done so badly marrying the Arkansas yokel after all.

As a first-term congressman, Fulbright had swift and stunning successes. He became the author of the resolution committing the United States to a postwar organization dedicated to keeping the peace. It was called the Fulbright Resolution and it passed the Congress by an overwhelming vote. In 1944 he was chairman of the London conference on postwar educational and cultural reconstruction. His emergence as a foreign policy figure was sensational for a freshman in the House, and it will be treated further in the next chapter of this book on the development of his foreign policy positions. His triumphs included a fierce debate with Clare Booth Luce, the good-looking wife of the *Time* magazine publisher who had become a national figure in her own right as a writer and as a militant and flamboyant nationalist. Mrs. Luce was the best-known member of Congress in the class of 1942, and surprisingly, the young Arkansan was considered the clear winner in the press coverage of the debate.

Fulbright, in his later years, related why he had chosen to confront Clare Luce: " . . . even with party differences aside, I felt I could not ignore her remarks. Her idea of a 'postwar order' took into account very little of the rights of other nations and recognized only the right of the stronger nations to do as they pleased. It was full of imperialistic demagoguery." [45] In these circumstances Fulbright proceeded to propose his own plan for peace, abandoning isolationism and "America First" ideology and emphasizing collective security among the nations. He got a grand reception and it emboldened him to introduce what became the Fulbright Resolution.

The phenomenal success of the freshman congressman from Arkansas helped set the stage for his decision to run for the Senate in 1944, reaching for the top rung in the legislative ladder. Hattie Caraway had never been much of a senator and her passive role was catching up with her. She was regarded, correctly, as doomed in her bid for another term. Roberta Fulbright and Hattie Caraway were friends, but Mrs. Fulbright and former governor Carl Bailey were determined to prevent the embarrassment of having Homer Adkins represent Arkansas in the United States Senate. The early favorite to succeed her was Governor Adkins, who was finishing the traditional two two-year terms in the statehouse. Fulbright knew he was in for a bitter, hard fight, but the thought of having to serve in a delegation including Adkins, as senator, was too much. Adkins was not only a personal enemy, his views were distasteful to Fulbright, who proceeded then to test the opinions of his friends and found them encouraging. Fulbright met with local leaders throughout the state in late 1943 and discovered considerable support for his potential candidacy. Adkins was a formidable political foe because of the governor's power over patronage and his political organization. The governor also enjoyed support from powerful interests, especially Witt Stephens of Arkansas Louisiana Gas; later in his career Stephens would become a staunch supporter of Fulbright, but he was in the Adkins camp in 1944.

Even so, Fulbright also had powerful backing. From the beginning, many of the most prominent of the state's business and professional people—including William Darby of National Old Line Insurance, Bailey, Charles Murphy of Murphy Oil in El Dorado and others—were his supporters.[46] John Erickson, who was one of Fulbright's top aides, emphasized relying upon the network of the University of Arkansas alumni community. Fulbright had previously antagonized the conservative Arkansas Farm Bureau because of his support in Congress for the Farm Security Administration (FSA), the agency that had provided long-term, low-interest loans and free technical advice to tenants. In the 1944 Senate race, however, Fulbright cultivated some of the prominent east Arkansas planters, partly because Fulbright was a member of the Arkansas aristocracy just as they were, and also because he was able to convince some of them that Fulbright's role as an internationalist meant lower tariffs and expanded markets for Arkansas rice, cotton and soybeans. Adkins attempted to capitalize on considerable anti-union sentiment in Arkansas by assailing Fulbright as pro-labor. Regarding labor issues, Fulbright acknowledged that he supported the workers' rights to organization and collective bargaining, but stressed: "I do not believe in the radical or racketeering efforts of certain elements within the ranks of organized labor to shackle business or to deprive industry of the essential function of management." When Adkins charged him with being a "New Dealer," he said that while he supported the Agricultural Adjustment Act, the Securities Exchange Commission, and other New Deal reforms, he carefully added that "I do not acquiesce in the continuation of unnecessary bureaus, bureaucratic control, and regulation by bureaucratic fiat."[46a]

Fulbright made preparations for the race by developing his organization and venturing out into the countryside at every opportunity. He started out, again, as the underdog, ranked behind both the governor and the incumbent senator. This time, a surprise candidacy was unsettling to the Fulbright camp. A millionaire industrialist named T. H. Barton got into the race with lots of money and hillbilly entertainers, including the Grand Ole Opry and Minnie Pearl. In the early stages, the auguries turned formidable. Adkins unloaded all manner of unprincipled accusations. The Fulbright Resolution was portrayed as a scandalous giveaway, "worse" than the New Deal. The young congressman was portrayed as an

overeducated egghead who couldn't represent Arkansas in the way a successful businessman or practical politician could. Anonymous circulars called him a "nigger lover" and inte-
grationist. Everywhere they called him "British Billy" and he was accused of being a draft
dodger as well.

Fulbright fought back, and he was helped by a sympathetic state press and a strong
University of Arkansas alumni organization. Adkins' campaign literature howled that the
Rhodes Scholar had announced for Congress after Pearl Harbor, when he was 36 and the
draft age was from 21 to 45. Regarding the draft, Price Dickson, head of the Washington
County Draft Board, wrote a letter that was reprinted in newspapers across the state. The
board had reviewed Fulbright's file in mid-1942, but to prevent any problem of favoritism,
the case was transferred to Russellville. The draft board in Russellville returned the file with
a III-A classification (deferment due to dependents). Fulbright had never written any letters
to the board. As for the "British Billy" charge, the congressman countered that the British
had been valiant fighters against Hitler, and critics of the British were isolationists. Many of
Adkins' most vicious attacks concerned race. In full-page newspaper advertisements, he
attacked the congressman for having been the only member of the Arkansas Congressional
delegation to have voted to reinstate William Pickens, a black Treasury Department employee who had been accused of communist associations by Congressman Martin Dies (D-
Texas) and the House Un-American Activities Committee. Fulbright believed that Dies had
never proved any charges against Pickens, and the congressman had been a stalwart opponent of the Un-American Activities Committee, having voted against renewing appropriations for its redbaiting activities (on a smaller scale, in fact, Dies was a forerunner to the
much more dangerous witch hunts of Senator Joe McCarthy in the 1950s). Fulbright
responded on the racial issue by declaring that he was against social equality and against
letting Negroes vote in the primary elections.[47] He strongly opposed such "noble experiments" as the Fair Employment Practices Committee. His response foreshadowed his future
weak civil rights record in signing the notorious Southern Manifesto in 1956 and his early
votes on civil rights issues, although not his later votes in the late 1960s and early 1970s.
In defending his reaction on the issues of civil rights, Fulbright always thought of himself
as accommodating his constituents in their primary concerns in exchange for their accommodation of his own primary interests; the merits and flaws in Fulbright's justifications
would be discussed at length through the decades, and after his death, by his critics, supporters, and analysts of Arkansas politics.

Both Adkins and Barton appealed to the lowest denominator of popular views and they
failed. Fulbright not only resolutely counterattacked against the mudslinging; he also pointed to his role at the 1944 conference of Allied ministers of education in London. Fulbright
had been appointed chairman of the American delegation by Secretary of State Cordell Hull,
and his visit included a luncheon invitation from Prime Minister Winston Churchill. Many
Arkansans were becoming sensitive about improving the state's image, and such improvement could be achieved by sending to the Senate the Rhodes Scholar and author of the
Fulbright Resolution supporting the establishment of a United Nations Organization. The
outcome was a smashing victory for Fulbright. In the first primary he won 62,000 votes to
47,000 for Adkins; Barton was a close third, Caraway a distant fourth. Now the coalition of
progressives and moderately conservative Arkansans faced their showdown with the former

KKK member and leader of a political machine.

The runoff wasn't much of a contest; Fulbright made a few speeches and a statewide radio broadcast. He won by 117,000 votes to 85,000 for Adkins. His victory attracted immediate national attention. The *Atlanta Journal* commended Arkansas voters, proclaim-. ing that the selection of Fulbright over Adkins meant that "democracy is gaining. The people, especially we Southern people, are voting more intelligently." The Scripps-Howard newspapers contended that the Fulbright victory at the same time that the demagogue, Senator "Cotton Ed" Smith of South Carolina, was defeated, "should raise the level of the U.S. Senate." Arthur Krock wrote in the *New York Times* that the people of Arkansas elected "a higher type of legislator than the South has been sending to Washington in recent years." The campaign established Betty Fulbright as his secret weapon, for she was naturally gregarious and her aristocratic connections in Pennsylvania only dramatized her natural ability to get along with people and win votes. For the next 30 years she was regarded as a major asset to Fulbright the senator.

Henry Woods' impression of Fulbright as the distant, aloof patrician was destined to be a viewpoint that many Arkansans would share over the years. To some extent, this view was inaccurate; although Fulbright could be abrupt when he had important work to do, he could also be quite amiable and charming to those he knew, especially in a calm, unhurried setting. Unfortunately, as his later years in Congress would demonstrate, the periods of calm for a senator would become increasingly scarce. Nonetheless, when Fulbright's supporters in political campaigns praised him as "good old Bill, the candidate who can relate to the common man," it was not purely campaign sloganeering. Fulbright had grown up in a small town, just as most of his constituents had, and he was personally interested in small business and agriculture, just as they were. Late in his career, one of the top aides to a prominent member of Congress would recall his excitement when he learned that he would be sitting next to J. William Fulbright at a Washington dinner party. The aide thought he would get a profound seminar on American foreign policy from the senator, but instead, Fulbright talked for two hours about the huge watermelons, bountiful rice and cotton crops, and other agricultural wonders of Arkansas. He loved the beautiful scenery in the Ozarks, as well as Arkansas' architectural landmarks, including Old Main in Fayetteville and the state capitol in Little Rock. Moreover, his status as an Arkansas Razorback football star made him a folk hero among most Arkansans, for whom following the Razorbacks was the most popular recreational activity. This became politically useful for Fulbright, as the Razorback football team became a national powerhouse in the late 1950s and 1960s. When he came back home to visit or campaign, he could talk football down at the corner store with real interest and knowledge about the game. Despite his ability to charm people in small groups, he could never pursue the back-slapping style of many politicians who were adept at working a crowd. Politicians of a later era, especially Dale Bumpers and Bill Clinton, would master the art of making each individual they talked to become the center of attention. In contrast, Fulbright had difficulty with patiently meeting large numbers of people and displaying interest in each one.

The authors of this book knew from personal experience that Fulbright could be quite engaging and witty in certain settings. For example, when Lee Powell would come to his office for interviews as a student in the 1970s, he would engage in lengthy discussions in which the young fellow was treated as an equal in a debating society, rather than as the neophyte come to sit at the feet of the master. Once, when Powell arrived early for an appointment with a rather hefty suitcase in hand, Fulbright spotted him at the entrance and exclaimed, "Land's sakes, Lee, let me help you with that," and then carried the suitcase up to his office. Fulbright was notably candid in those interviews, perfectly willing to admit error on virtually any subject, with the exception of civil rights. In fact, in the hours and hours that James Powell and Lee Powell spent talking to Fulbright over the decades, the senator only became defensive when the controversial issue of civil rights entered into the discussion. Even concerning the race issue, Fulbright never cut short the conversation or suggested that the *Gazette* editor or the undergraduate, law student or young lawyer did not have the right to take him to task on his positions with which they disagreed. Fulbright's self-deprecating sense of humor was refreshing. Far from the stereotype of the arrogant intellectual often depicted by his enemies, Fulbright was not pretentious regarding his intellect in small groups of people. Once, when Lee Powell had extended the time allotted to the debating society far too long and another, older person was impatiently waiting to get in to see the Rhodes Scholar, Fulbright told the man amidst howls of laughter in his office that "Well, Lee's been in here for a good while trying to pick my brain, but he's found that it's slim pickin's."

The senator's competitive instincts occasionally abraded people. For example, James Powell played golf with the senator at the Burning Tree course in Washington and a course in Little Rock, yet despite the editor's considerable prowess as a golfer, Fulbright always vanquished him. Fulbright's superb athletic ability persisted on the golf course into an advanced age; once when Fulbright was in his late 50s and still superb as a golfer, Powell expressed admiration for the fact that the senator always managed to beat him. Fulbright replied, "Oh, that's because you're so lousy." Powell was rather wounded by the remark and considered protesting, but then thought better of it, not wishing to burden the chairman of the Foreign Relations Committee with the tribulations of his golf swing. On another occasion in the 1970s, Lee Powell and Fulbright attended a Razorback football game together in Little Rock. The Razorbacks, then a national power, trounced a mediocre opponent but were sloppy in doing so. While everyone else was reveling in the home team's victory, Fulbright was rather annoyed that the Hogs had incurred so many penalties and frequently critiqued what he regarded as the poor execution of the offense. He chatted about politics, noted that "it's always crowded in War Memorial [stadium]," and then was the first person of the 56,000 in attendance to leave the game after the Razorbacks built a four-touchdown lead (Hog fans traditionally stay until almost the end, even in blow-outs). Betty Fulbright did not attend the game that night, but it is a certainty he would have been less critical of the Razorbacks had she been there.

Another fundamental character trait of the senator was his equanimity. He was certainly one of the most unflappable politicians this country ever produced. His deep self-confidence and stability were essential in explaining his resilience in facing some of the most bitterly controversial trials in recent American politics, notably his dissent against Joe McCarthy's demagogy in the 1950s and his willingness to stand up to President Lyndon Johnson at the height of the Vietnam War. He simply did not seem to feel that his sense of self-worth was riding on the outcome of his political career. When it finally ended, the authors were impressed by his memorable aplomb as Fulbright, Lee Williams, and the Powells relaxed at his suite at Little Rock's Sam Peck Hotel, watching as the election returns revealed a landslide victory for his opponent, Dale Bumpers. He dissected the electoral debacle with the coolness of a professor drafting an essay. He was naturally displeased with Bumpers, but he was also perfectly capable of accepting the reality of defeat. At one point, as the television showed the returns that ended his 32-year career in Congress, he gently motioned toward the screen with his hand, and said in a philosophical tone, "Well, there it is."

With Bill Fulbright's reserved personality, Betty Fulbright's gregarious nature was invaluable to him, in the 1944 Senate campaign and thereafter. The 1944 race launched Fulbright on his central career, of course, and destined him to become a maker of history. It was received nationally with a good press and general applause. In 1959 he would become chairman of the Foreign Relations Committee, and in the following year he would be John F. Kennedy's first, tentative choice for Secretary of State, only to be passed over for Dean Rusk, another Southerner and Rhodes Scholar who was not encumbered by having signed the Southern Manifesto.

Whatever the forces that would shape his career, the general election of November, 1944, formally confirmed his earlier nomination by the Democratic Party as a United States senator. The crucial test in the primary that year had revealed, in the Arkansas popular majority, a sense of judgment, a perspective, that would serve the Republic well over the next half-century in most of the state's major popular choices. There was the aberration in the notorious Orval E. Faubus, who earned a place as an international symbol of racism, but J. William Fulbright was one of several progressive national figures to rise out of Arkansas, including: Congressman Brooks Hays, the moderate who valiantly if unsuccessfully sought to oppose the racial extremists in Arkansas during the massive resistance era; Governor Winthrop Rockefeller, who led the state government out of the reactionary abyss of the Faubus years; Congressman Wilbur Mills, the legendary chairman of the House Ways and Means Committee; Congressman Bill Alexander, who as a member of the national House Democratic leadership staunchly opposed President Reagan's profligate budgetary policies and interventionism in Central America in the 1980s; the two progressive and able members of the U.S. Senate, Dale Bumpers and David Pryor; and, above all, Fulbright's protege, President Bill Clinton. Fulbright influenced all of these figures, directly or indirectly, either as colleague, friend, mentor, or through his public statements; even Bumpers, who would defeat Fulbright in the 1974 Senate election, admired the Rhodes Scholar's intellectual prowess and foreign policy leadership, once stating that Fulbright had convinced him to oppose the Vietnam War "before he even knew my name."

The 1944 Senate election in Arkansas was prescient in a context even broader than Fulbright's. It was a harbinger of great things to come for a fascinating, often brilliant, and always controversial group of Arkansas political leaders.

Book Two:

THE EARLY YEARS OF THE COLD WAR AND McCARTHYISM

I. THE EARLY YEARS OF THE COLD WAR AND MCCARTHYISM

Introduction

In his first Senate speech of March 1945, Fulbright juxtaposed his bewilderment and dismay at the American fear of the Soviet Union with his hope that the creation of the United Nations would inaugurate a new peaceful world order in the postwar era. Fulbright believed that the most destructive of all the American xenophobias was the hatred of the Soviet Union. Why, he asked, are we so hostile to the Russians when "the Russian experiment in socialism is scarcely more radical, under modern conditions, than the Declaration of Independence was in the days of George III?"[1] In Fulbright's view, emotional super-patriots who constantly played upon popular fears and hatred of communism and Russia only revealed the weakness of their faith in the American system; he concluded that "We must demonstrate the superiority of individual initiative under capitalism by our results, by the provision of a superior way of life, not by the violence of our oratory."[2] Despite his concerns over the damaging effects of extreme anticommunism, the prevailing spirit of the March 1945 speech was a resilient optimism. Only two years earlier the House of Representatives had apparently embraced the principle of collective security by passing the Fulbright Resolution, a declaration of support for the creation of and American participation in an international peace-keeping organization; and now the United States seemed willing to adopt the Charter of the United Nations.[3] The senator appealed to the nation's leadership to avoid repeating the tragic error of 1919-1920, when the rejection of U.S. participation in the League of Nations had "left our people divided and unable to agree upon any policy." In the closing passage of his address, Fulbright reminded the Senate that America now held an opportunity to play a crucial role in establishing a powerful United Nations organization and averting another world war: "By the greatest good fortune, and enormous sacrifice, we have earned a second opportunity to help save the world and ourselves from self-destruction."[4]

Seven months later the explosion of the atomic bomb at Hiroshima, the failure of the United States to embrace the axiom that all nations must accept United Nations supervision of armaments, and the emergent hostility between America and Russia had transformed Fulbright's earlier optimism into a pessimism that essentially lasted for much of the remainder of his career in the Senate.[5] In his speeches during the autumn of 1945, he deplored the reality that instead of cooperating with the Soviet Union in the United Nations, the United States had "already fallen to quarreling with Russia like two dogs chewing on a bone."[6] Fulbright predicted that America would not be able to retain exclusive control over the atomic bomb, for "any one of several industrial nations probably can produce bombs in from three to five years."[7] He vigorously advocated the effective international control of nuclear weapons by the United Nations. The young senator lamented the fears and uncertainties that the terrifying new force of atomic weapons had engendered, comparing contemporary men to primitives living in the darkness of caves and jungles who faced "elemental and infinite forces which we do not understand, forces which threaten to snuff out our lives as one does a candle between the fingers."[8]

In that first year of his Senate career, Fulbright advised his colleagues to play their proper role in the formation of American foreign policy: if the Senate "cannot consent to the measures presented by the Executive it seems to me imperative that it offer our nation and the world an alternative."[9] By the autumn, it was clear that Fulbright could not consent to the basic foreign policies of the Truman administration, and it was equally clear that the executive did not intend to adopt Fulbright's alternative of basing U.S. policies upon the creation of a U.N. with adequate power to curb the Soviet-American arms race. In late 1945, the Arkansan criticized the Truman administration for claiming to support the U.N. while insisting upon the veto provision for the Security Council, for demanding exclusive control of military bases in the Far East while asserting the right of American participation in eastern European affairs, and jealously guarding atomic secrets "under the guise of a self-appointed sacred trusteeship." According to Fulbright, if the President did not adhere to the concept of an international security community, then he should understand that a rigid anti-Soviet posture would lead to a policy of imperialism in which America would have to incessantly enlarge its military establishment and expand its domination of strategic areas throughout the Atlantic and Pacific.[10]

Fulbright's speeches of 1945 foreshadowed his later critique of postwar American policy. He had established his renowned themes of opposition to rigid anticommunism and conventional nationalism, his plea for an amelioration of Soviet-American relations, and his concern for maintaining the Senate's role of advising, consenting, or offering alternatives to the policies of the executive branch. In 1972 he was to write that the foreign policy of the United States from the final months of World War II until President Richard Nixon's journey to China in February 1972 was shaped by two fundamental perspectives on international relations: first, the idea of founding an international security community through the United Nations, and then the belief in a relentless global ideological struggle between "freedom" and "communism."[11] The ephemeral ascendancy of those who advocated the establishment of a powerful United Nations was already weakening by the latter stages of World War II, as nationalistic sentiments, anticommunism, disillusionment with the prospects for cooperating with the Soviets in the U.N., and other forces shattered the hopes for a genuine international security community. After Stalin's ruthless consolidation of Soviet domination in eastern Europe and the Chinese communists' triumph over Chiang Kai-shek, there emerged a generation of American political leaders who were dedicated to the proposition that the Soviet Union and China could be prevented from executing their alleged designs for world conquest only by the intimidating effect of American military power.[12]

In the late 1960s, Fulbright would agree with John Kenneth Galbraith that a third generation of Americans had now recognized "that in fact limited areas of common interest are developing between us and, above all, that the survival of civilization requires at least a tacit understanding among the nuclear powers."[13] This new generation recognized the diversity of the communist bloc and no longer regarded international communism as an aggressive and monolithic conspiracy to rule the world. The third generation, Fulbright would write in 1967, "advocates a creative competition between the communist countries and the West to see who can build the stronger and more prosperous society at home, who can more effectively help the world's less developed nations, who can build better schools and raise healthier children, who, in Khrushchev's colorful phrase, can provide more and better goulash." These advocates of creative East-West competition appeared to enjoy successes in 1963 with the passage of the Nuclear Test Ban Treaty and a general relaxation of Soviet-American tensions. Yet at precisely the moment, in Fulbright's view, when the third generation "seemed about to take full control of America's affairs," a tragic regression to the earlier dogmas occurred: "The Vietnamese war is a manifestation of second-generation attitudes toward communism. It is basically an ideological war." The senator would conclude that "underlying"" the crusade in southeast Asia was the discredited dogma that the United States was fighting the centrally directed, global communist monolith, a force so evil that America must search for and destroy it in every corner of the world.[14] In 1965, the hopes for a realistic and moderate American foreign policy would be dashed.

In the latter years of his career, Fulbright was deeply troubled that the "second generation's" anticommunist ideology had portrayed the Soviet-American relationship as a universal conflict between freedom and the alleged system of international "terror and oppression" directed from Moscow; to the senator's mind, this attitude led the American public and politicians to respond to the actions, statements, and policies of communist states not on the basis of their varying and specific merits, but in terms of the ideological clash between eastern communism and western democracy.[15] The decisive moment in world history had arrived, the anticommunist crusaders proclaimed, when all nations must choose between diametrically opposed "ways of life," communist oppression or democracy. As Illinois Senator Everett Dirksen explained in 1967, such a regime as the corrupt and despotic Greek military dictatorship was democratic because it was attempting to "shove back the communist influence." Given such a world view, it was pedantry for Congress to conduct thorough investigations before extending U.S. aid to a particular regime, for the crucial criterion for that aid was simply whether the regime was sufficiently vehement in its anticommunism. As Fulbright responded to the Illinois Senator's preachments, if America followed the guidelines Dirksen and other Cold Warriors established for choosing the allies of the United States, then the chaotic and authoritarian government of South Vietnam "would also seem to qualify as one of the democracies for whom the United States is resolved to make the world safe."[16]

In his 1972 volume *The Crippled Giant*, Fulbright would regret that the Cold Warriors in Congress had often seemed to prefer the spectacular and the stirring in policy presentations by the executive instead of more pedestrian but more accurate statements.[17] To illustrate this tendency, Fulbright cited the example of the Truman administration's effort to gain Congressional support for its plan to aid Greece and Turkey. At a meeting with Congressional leaders shortly before the famed Truman Doctrine speech in 1947, Secretary of State George Marshall's concise summary of the realities of the Greek civil war left the

leaders singularly unimpressed, whereas Under Secretary of State Dean Acheson immediately captivated the imagination and support of the gathering by warning theatrically that
once the communist virus had infected Greece it would inexorably spread to Europe
through Italy and France, to Africa through Egypt, and to "all the east" through Iran.[18]
According to Fulbright, Acheson may have viewed the decision to state the Truman
Doctrine in sweeping ideological terms rather than in precise strategic terms as a domestic
political tactic to arouse the public's combative spirit and thus solidify Congressional support for the funds involved in U.S. assistance to Greece and Turkey; but whatever Acheson's
views were, his successors in the State Department literally interpreted the Doctrine as a
manifesto for global anticommunist interventions. "I believe that it must be the policy of the
United States," the President pronounced in one of the crucial phrases of the Truman
Doctrine, "to support free peoples who are resisting attempted subjugation by armed
minorities or by outside pressures." In the analysis expressed in *The Crippled Giant*, postwar
American leaders urgently needed to re-evaluate their policies toward the communist
world, yet they felt themselves absolved from having to rigorously analyze the actual statements and actions of the communist states and insurgencies by the Truman Doctrine's
chimera of the universal communist conspiracy against freedom. The interpretation of the
senator's 1972 work is not that Truman's inflated language caused the anticommunist crusade, but that Truman's heated anticommunist rhetoric was a "symbolic and seminal event"
that powerfully influenced popular American thinking on the Cold War in the years after
1947.

Fulbright's 1972 argument held a substantial measure of validity, especially when one
considers the popular and erroneous opinions that the Truman Doctrine's thesis explained
the outcome of the two famous civil wars that were decided in the late 1940s. By the spring
of 1949, Chiang Kai-shek's forces had collapsed on the Chinese mainland, and in October
the communist guerrillas in the north of Greece had been defeated. According to the
Truman Doctrine, America must assist any nation that was battling communism, which was
always based upon "the will of a minority forcibly imposed upon the majority." On the basis
of the antic-ommunists' logic, American aid had been primarily responsible for the triumph
of the anticommunist forces in Greece, while the anticommunist "majority" in China had
disintegrated because it had not received sufficient support from the free world. In actuality, the Greek and Chinese conflicts bore no real similarity to each other, and the "lesson" the
Cold Warriors had learned from the Chinese civil war was palpably false. As Fulbright concluded in *The Crippled Giant*, "Whatever merit the Truman Doctrine may have had in the
circumstances of early postwar Europe, the bond with reality became more and more
strained as the Doctrine came to be applied at times and in places increasingly remote from
the Greek civil war."[19]

America had supplied the corrupt and inefficient Kuomintang of Chiang Kai-shek with
substantial amounts of aid, but the Chinese revolution was determined by indigenous forces
in China that were essentially beyond the control of the United States. Yet the pathological
sense of guilt and failure at having forfeited an opportunity to deliver China from the depredations of the communists continued to plague American political leaders throughout the
1950s and 1960s, culminating in the obsession with preventing a similar communist pen-
etration into southern Asia. President Lyndon Johnson would grimly announce shortly after

his inauguration that he would not be the President who would allow Ho Chi Minh's legions to gain control of Vietnam as Mao Tse-tung had triumphed in China, as if the United States might somehow compensate for the world's most populous nation's "loss" to communism by a rigid and unceasing application of the Truman Doctrine to the small, underdeveloped lands of southeast Asia.[20]

Fulbright's opposition to America's global ideological crusade was not the only issue he emphasized in his dissent against postwar U.S. diplomacy, but it was the single most important issue. As he would concede late in his career, he had frequently not opposed American foreign policy in the earliest period of the post-1945 era.[21] It would require many years and many crises before Fulbright would arrive at his warning to America to avoid the "arrogance of power."

A Young Internationalist's Views in 1940

In the years before 1945, Fulbright had closely studied the central issues of international relations throughout World War II. During the period before the U.S. entry into the war, Fulbright (then the young president of the University of Arkansas) advocated intervention against the Nazis. He supported William Allen White's Committee to Defend America by Aiding the Allies.[22] In 1940, the 35-year-old university president delivered a series of speeches repudiating isolationism and pleading with Americans to recognize that Hitler's relentless career of conquest posed a dire threat to American security. As he argued in a July 1940 address at the University of Oklahoma: "Too often today we hear the profound pronouncement by an isolationist senator that this country does not want war. Of course, we do not want war, just as Austria, Czechoslovakia, Poland, Norway, Holland, Belgium, France, and England did not want war. The fact is, the world has war, and the question is what should we do about it?" Fulbright contended that America should fight to defend the "Atlantic highway" and approvingly quoted a 1917 New Republic article by Walter Lippmann in which the famous journalist had written, "On the two shores of the Atlantic Ocean there has grown up a profound web of interest which joins together the western world. Britain, France, Holland, the Scandinavian nations, and Pan-America, are, in the main, one community in their deepest needs and their deepest purposes. They have a common interest in the ocean which unites them." The young Arkansan regarded the 1917 New Republic essay as even more poignant for the 1940 crisis than it had been in 1917, and concluded that "it is far better to fight for and to lose than to meekly acquiesce." Throughout the pre-Pearl Harbor period, Fulbright reiterated his conviction that Nazi Germany was a uniquely dangerous and insatiably aggressive force that must be crushed.[23]

For the first time in his career, Fulbright's foreign policy statements in 1940 attracted a certain amount of national attention. A noteworthy controversy occurred after his July 1940 Oklahoma address, when the University of Missouri invited the president of the University of Arkansas to give the summer commencement address. Fulbright initially accepted the invitation and sent to Missouri a copy of his speech, which resounded with a bitter attack upon the isolationists: "The weasling, timid and fearful policy of the isolationist senators is one of the greatest dangers to our true interests." The Missouri officials were expecting the famous isolationist, Senator Champ Clark of Missouri, to appear at the commencement, and therefore they asked Fulbright to delete the reference to "the weasling, timid and fearful policy." He refused to alter his words, with the eventual result that he did not deliver the address at Missouri; and Senator Clark was able to attend the ceremonies undisturbed by the ideas of the young internationalist from Arkansas.[24]

A quarter of a century later, the apologists for the Vietnam war would charge that Fulbright was guilty of "appeasement" because of his opposition to the U.S. intervention in southeast Asia. President Lyndon Johnson would compare the threat of Hitler's expansionism to the alleged threat of Ho Chi Minh in the 1960s; as he once succinctly explained to Doris Kearns, "Someone had to call Hitler and someone had to call Ho."[25] Supporters of Johnson's escalation policy in Vietnam would allege that Fulbright was a starry-eyed pacifist who had no conception of the realities of power politics, or that he was an "appeaser" who was following in the tradition of Neville Chamberlain in failing to resist aggression. These condemnations of Fulbright were distorted. First, Fulbright had not been an "appeaser" in 1940, as his speeches of that year clearly demonstrated; in fact, he had advocated resistance to Hitler earlier than the great majority of Americans had (as a young university president in 1940 he was not, of course, as nationally prominent as he later became). The Arkansan understood that the nation had to resort to its military power to protect itself against the limitless expansionism of a Hitler, and he would have deeply preferred that American intervention against the Nazis had occurred much earlier than it did. During the Vietnam War, he was convinced that Ho Chi Minh's small nation of North Vietnam could not possibly represent a threat analogous to Nazi Germany. In both World War II and the Vietnam War, Fulbright argued that U.S. foreign policy should be based upon a realistic analysis of how to defend America's vital interests: in his view, the danger posed by a fascist conqueror leading a powerful, industrialized Germany demanded a military response from the West, but in the post-World War II era Ho Chi Minh's quest to win a civil war in a small third-world nation in southeast Asia did not endanger any important American interests and should have required no American intervention. Fulbright's opposition to the Vietnam War would involve a wide variety of complex issues; but there was nothing inconsistent about his support for resistance to Hitler and his later dissent against the U.S. intervention in Vietnam.

In the early Cold War, hard-line anticommunists would frequently contend that Ho Chi Minh was an agent of the Kremlin; according to the Cold Warriors, the Soviets were similar to Hitler in conspiring to dominate the globe. As will be shown in later chapters, Fulbright and other critics of U.S. involvement in southeast Asia would demonstrate that the extreme anticommunists ignored Ho's nationalism and other indigenous forces in Vietnam. The Arkansan and his intellectual allies would later elaborate upon the argument that the fundamental pattern of Soviet foreign policies did not display the Nazis' insane thirst for destruction and endless military conquest. Over a period of a few years, Hitler had conquered or warred upon the majority of the world's most advanced nations in western, central, and eastern Europe, Russia, North Africa, and upon the high seas. While Fulbright disapproved of many Soviet foreign actions, especially in eastern Europe during the Stalin era, he later concluded with George F. Kennan and other Soviet experts that the U.S.S.R. and Nazi Germany were basically different as far as their foreign policies were concerned; and Fulbright appropriately responded to them differently during the course of his career.

1943-1946

Fulbright's support for the creation of the United Nations was his crucial interest in the realm of diplomacy during his first and only term in the U. S. House of Representatives after his election to Congress in 1942. In 1943, when he served as a freshman member of the House of Representatives Foreign Affairs Committee, he had sponsored the first Congressional Resolution advocating a postwar international organization. The Fulbright Resolution stated that the House of Representatives "hereby expresses itself as favoring the creation of appropriate international machinery with power adequate to establish and to maintain a just and lasting peace and as favoring participation of the United States therein." Secretary of State Cordell Hull, Undersecretary of State Sumner Welles, and Harry Hopkins supported the Fulbright Resolution. In June 1943, President Franklin D. Roosevelt wrote to Hull inquiring about the prospects for "pushing" the Resolution. "It seems to me pretty good," the President maintained, "and if we can get it through the House it might work in the Senate." Roosevelt displayed much less enthusiasm for the Resolution than Hull did, and the President informed Fulbright that he would endorse it provided the Resolution acquired widespread Congressional and popular support. By the fall of 1943, such support had clearly emerged. In July, 1943, a Gallup Poll reported that 78 per cent of the American public favored the Fulbright Resolution. On September 21 the House passed the Resolution by a vote of 360 to 29. Hull believed that the overwhelming margin of the Resolution's passage improved the American position in subsequent negotiations with the British and the Soviets concerning the postwar world, for it suggested that the American people approved their country's participation in a postwar international organization.[1]

During the debate on the House floor shortly before the Fulbright Resolution's passage, Fulbright was careful to avoid exaggerating its impact: "I have no illusions that this resolution is the panacea for all international afflictions. It is the first small step in the process of building a foreign policy which I hope may have better results than that which we have followed in the past." George Mahon of Texas lauded the Resolution as historic, for "Today we propose to pass a resolution which serves notice to the world that when we have won this war we shall try to keep it won. Never before has such action been taken by Congress." The most poignant address in the debate was delivered by a Republican, Congressman Charles A. (Doc) Eaton of New Jersey, the ranking Republican member of the Foreign Affairs Committee. Eaton, a Baptist minister, informed his colleagues with a sad, emotional voice that "I have seven sons. One died of war wounds July 30. Another was killed over Nuremberg August 10. By God, I will vote for any measure which carries some hope of the future abolishment of war's wholesale murder." The dominant response to the Resolution throughout the country was similar to the views of Mahon and Eaton. However, a minority of isolationists assailed the Resolution. During the House debate, Ms. Jessie Sumner of Illinois denounced the Fulbright Resolution as "the most dangerous bill ever presented to an American Congress," for it would furnish "internationalists with all power they ask to rob Americans of their independence." In the *Chicago Tribune*, the diehard isolationist Col. Robert (Bertie) McCormick's editorial page denounced Congressman Fulbright as "a first-termer from Arkansas, who in his formative years was sent as a Rhodes Scholar to Oxford to learn to betray his country and deprive it of its independence. In this instance, as no doubt in many others, Mr. Rhodes appears to have got his money's worth."[1a]

Between September 1943, and January 1945, Fulbright continued to support the establishment of a powerful United Nations. On November 5, 1943, the Senate followed the House's example and passed the Connally Resolution, which advocated an international authority to prevent aggression. Many internationalists regarded the Senate document as weaker than the Fulbright Resolution, since the Connally Resolution specifically endorsed national sovereignty. Nevertheless, in late 1943 and 1944 Fulbright remained optimistic about the strength of internationalist sentiment. He implored Americans to maintain the wartime spirit of cooperation with the Soviet Union into the postwar period. Fulbright did not, however, espouse the extreme pro-Russian perspective exemplified by Joseph Davies, the former Ambassador to Moscow; Davies averred that "to question Stalin's good faith was bad Christianity, bad sportsmanship, bad sense." In Fulbright's view, after the war Russia might become a friend or it might become an enemy of the United States, depending upon how diligently the great powers supported the forthcoming United Nations organization. In a typical speech of late 1943, he asserted that "Either we cooperate with Russia and other nations in a system to preserve peace" after the war, or America might confront the dangers of competing with an industrialized Russia of 250 million people or a China of 450 million in a chaotic world of warring nations."[2]

In the spring of 1944, Fulbright became the chairman of the London conference on postwar educational and cultural reconstruction. The Allied ministers of education from 17 nations attended the London conference, which many internationalists envisaged as an important "steppingstone" in the formation of the U. N. The delegates to the conference drafted a tentative plan for a United Nations agency that would reconstruct the war-ravaged educational institutions of the world; however, later in 1944 American officials decided to postpone the establishment of any such educational organization pending the actual creation of the United Nations.

During his visit to England Fulbright enjoyed a luncheon appointment with Prime Minister Winston Churchill. As the Arkansan later recalled his conversation with Churchill, the Prime Minister did not express any criticisms of the Soviet Union and seemed to regard the Soviets as invaluable military allies; he did, however, consider General Charles de Gaulle an abrasive character who pugnaciously insisted upon a prominent French role in Allied wartime planning. Churchill briefly discussed a wide range of topics, including the preparations for the D-Day invasion, which occurred two months later. Fulbright recalled that the Prime Minister was concerned about extensive but unexplained German military preparations across the Channel; a few weeks later, the British learned that the activity had been preparations for the buzz-bombs assault on London. Churchill also discussed American politics and was interested to learn that Fulbright planned to run for the United States Senate in 1944. Referring to the incumbent, Hattie Caraway, Churchill motioned toward a serving bowl with a large hen decorating the top and said, "So, you're trying to unseat the sitting hen." The Arkansan was also impressed by the Prime Minister's capacity to absorb wine and brandy. The conversation with Churchill was, of course, very brief, but Fulbright's chairmanship of the London conference and his appointment with the Prime Minister reflected the surprising prominence that the Arkansas congressman had acquired by 1944. Despite the tentative nature of the conference's proposal for an international education agency, his journey to England pleased Fulbright. During his 1944 Senate campaign, he publicized his central role at the London conference. Generally speaking, in peacetime many people from Arkansas tended to lack interest in foreign policy, but in the midst of World War II, Fulbright's prestigious and important activities on the international stage strengthened his position at home. Arkansans were clearly proud to be represented by a Rhodes Scholar who had met Winston Churchill and otherwise played a prominent role in Allied planning for the postwar world. His work at the conference enhanced his stature with the Roosevelt administration, and this fact further magnified Fulbright's standing among Arkansans; the 1944 Fulbright Senate campaign would publicize a letter the senator received from Cordell Hull, who wrote: "I continue to receive most favorable reports about the work of yourself and your associates in London. I consider the country exceedingly fortunate to have had a man of your statesmanlike qualities to head this delegation."[3]

Fulbright ended his trip to England with a radio broadcast to the English people over the British Broadcasting Company. In the B.B.C. speech he repeated his theme of the need to reform the system of international politics as it had existed before World War II: "Call it what you will—fascism, democratic decadence, general ignorance—the fact remains that something was wrong with that old world" which the war had destroyed, and "some new machinery with adequate powers must be created now, if our fine phrases and noble sentiments are to have substance and meaning for our children." He closed the B.B.C. address by informing the British public that he was "returning home to campaign for a seat in our Senate, and thereby an opportunity to contribute further, perhaps, to our mutual understanding." During his 1944 Senate campaign he reiterated his ideas for postwar international relations, although his positions on domestic issues were crucial for his electoral victory in Arkansas. Upon entering the Senate in January 1945, Fulbright persuaded 15 freshman Senators to join him in sending a bipartisan letter to President Roosevelt that urged vigorous and prompt action in creating a United Nations organization.[4]

As the debate over the U. N. intensified, Fulbright sought the advice of an old friend and mentor. During 1945 and throughout Fulbright's career, the Oxford scholar R. B. McCallum exerted an important influence upon the Senator's thinking. A British Liberal Party supporter, McCallum had championed the League of Nations and in 1945 endorsed the United Nations. In a January letter to McCallum, Fulbright asked the Oxford sage for his ideas on the "present state of the world," and congratulated him for the flattering reviews of McCallum's book Public Opinion and the Last Peace, which analyzed the British public's response to the Versailles Treaty. McCallum replied to Fulbright by briefly expressing concern over potential international controversies that might destroy the wartime friendship between the United States and the Soviet Union. Although he advocated continued cooperation between the great powers, he warned that America and Russia might become embroiled in conflicts over the internal disputes of the smaller countries of the world, where the Russians would support the communist factions while the Americans and British supported the non-communist factions. He also suggested that the Russians did not respect the Anglo-American tradition of support for free elections. McCallum described future Soviet actions on their pledges at the February 1945 Yalta conference as the "real test" of their intentions. At Yalta Joseph Stalin had accepted Soviet membership in the forthcoming United Nations organization and agreed to promote free elections in Poland. In Public

Opinion and the Last Peace, McCallum emphasized his hope that the "mutual sympathy and respect bred in this war" would facilitate amicable relations between America, Russia, and Great Britain after the war. The Oxford scholar's book espoused the internationalist viewpoint that he had impressed upon his pupil Fulbright many years before: security against future warfare depended upon "the disposition of the peoples to avoid war" by moderating their conduct and uniting to prevent aggression. In 1945 Fulbright did not devote his primary attention to the controversies over Soviet expansion into eastern Europe: he regarded the creation of an effective U. N. and later the question of international control over atomic weapons as the two central issues of Soviet-American relations.[5]

In his maiden speech in the Senate on March 28, 1945, Fulbright had stressed his themes of opposition to anticommunism, support for the U.N. and concern for the Senate's proper role in foreign policy. He had also decried the efforts of certain newspapers and politicians to arouse hatred of the British, the Russians, and other foreigners. The United States had an interest, he argued, in the preservation of a strong Great Britain: "In this troubled and violent world is it not true that we would feel quite alone in the world if the British Commonwealth of Nations had been subjugated by the tyranny of the Nazis, and its resources directed against us?" Fulbright admonished the Senate that a lasting foundation of peace could not be established solely by the defeat of the Nazis and Japan and the signing of the U.N. Charter. In his view, American leaders should inform the people that "the price of peace is high," for "The making of peace is a continuing process that must go on from day to day, from year to year, so long as our civilization shall last. Our participation in this process is not just the signing of a charter with a big red seal. It is a daily task, a positive participation in all the details and decisions which together constitute a living and growing policy." The senator believed that statesmen should not promise the people utopian benefits from any American policies, for the preservation of peace was an onerous and never-ending burden.[6]

When President Roosevelt died two weeks after Fulbright delivered his speech, the freshman senator became distressed over the prospects for creating a viable international organization under the inexperienced leadership of Harry Truman. Fulbright was, of course, saddened by Roosevelt's death, but his quiet, restrained response at the time contrasted sharply with the profuse outpouring of grief from his Texas colleague, Congressman Lyndon Johnson. While being interviewed in the Capitol by a *New York Times* reporter, Johnson wept openly and said: "He was always like a Daddy to me, always... I got my first great desire for public office because of him—and so did thousands of other men all over the country. God. God how he could take it for us all."[6a] Fulbright experienced no such emotional attachment to Roosevelt. The Arkansan had an extended meeting with FDR at the White House when he was a member of Congress and was "of course greatly impressed by the old boy's personality." Fulbright stated to his constituents that Roosevelt's death was a great loss "particularly to those of us who have been devoting so much of our time to an organization for maintaining the peace."[6b]

Fulbright met with Truman immediately after Roosevelt's death in an attempt to reassure the new President. Truman sent him a cordial note thanking him for the visit. "It was a pleasure to see you at the Senate today, and I hope I will have that privilege often." Only two weeks later delegates from fifty nations gathered at San Francisco to draft the U.N.

Charter. Truman's July 2 address to the Senate temporarily heartened Fulbright, for the President implored the senators to approve the U. N. Charter, and he recalled that the Congress had participated in the founding of the Charter through the passage of the Fulbright and Connally Resolutions.[7]

In the spring of 1945, there was considerable speculation in Washington about the selection process for a new Secretary of State—just as there would be 15 years later in an entirely different set of circumstances when John F. Kennedy became President. Media reports asserted in May that President Truman wanted to replace Secretary of State Edward R. Stettinius. Drew Pearson boldly predicted in a radio broadcast at the time that he knew who President Truman's new Secretary of State would be: the brilliant young Rhodes Scholar and senator from Arkansas, J. William Fulbright.[7a] The Arkansan was immediately deluged with correspondence regarding his alleged future career as Secretary of State. In one response, he wrote: "I am glad to have your comments about the Secretary of State. I hoped that it wouldn't do any harm in the sense that anyone would think I was trying to give up my present office, which I am not. As a matter of fact, I have done nothing and do not intend to do anything toward it and would hesitate like anything if it were offered. Besides, I have a distinct feeling that I had better settle down in one place for a while."[7b] The speculation ended soon, as Truman appointed James F. Byrnes to succeed Stettinius.

During the Senate debate on the United Nations in 1945, Fulbright and his friend Senator Claude Pepper of Florida questioned the prevailing belief that the Charter would provide genuine collective security. In late July the Senate overwhelmingly approved the Charter. Fulbright voted for the U.N. Charter, but he criticized its principle of the sovereign equality of all members in the General Assembly. No document, he asserted, could transform the tiny states of Nicaragua and Luxembourg into the equals of the United States and the Soviet Union. The senator did not expect nations to immediately renounce their nationalism, but he wanted the Charter to begin placing limits on national sovereignty. In the fall of 1945, he contended that the Charter did not curb extreme nationalism, and he focused his criticism on the U.N. Security Council veto. He described the veto as a "hopeless" principle in any governmental organization, because he regarded it as "another way of saying that we shall go along and abide by the rules if it suits us in each particular instance." In Fulbright's view, the fundamental American foreign policy should not have been merely to praise or oppose Russia or any other nation, but to obtain its assistance in the formation of a bona fide peace-keeping organization. Since 1943 Fulbright had argued for a powerful United Nations, but he did not believe the U. N. Charter created an effective organization, for it endorsed the Security Council veto and the principle of national sovereignty. He based his vote for the Charter on the assumption that advocates of genuine collective security might gradually strengthen the United Nations in future years.[8]

During the autumn, Fulbright was sharply critical of the Truman administration in speeches to the Foreign Policy Association in New York City in October and in a nation-wide address over N.B.C. Radio in November. He continued to stress that the Soviet Union would develop atomic weapons within a few years and that a U.N. system of inspection and control of atomic weapons needed to be established.[9] The senator did not pretend to have a definitive answer to the problem of how to prevent some future aggressor from unleashing an atomic war upon the world, but he argued that one indispensable requirement for an effective U.N. program of inspection and control would consist of all nations' acceptance of an important infringement on their sovereignty by delegating to the U.N. their powers over atomic armaments. No system of effective international law could be established if the principle of absolute national sovereignty continued, for "There is no law in the real sense between sovereign nations." Fulbright urged the United States to support a system whereby any disputes regarding international control of the atom would be submitted to the compulsory jurisdiction of the U.N., with the judgment against any recalcitrant member (and here again Fulbright stressed that the Security Council veto should be abolished) to be enforced by all other members of the organization. In making these suggestions, the Arkansan was simply fulfilling his duty of offering alternatives to the administration's policies, for he was fully aware that Truman was not following the approach he advocated. The senator believed that Truman's policies too often displayed a "get tough" attitude toward the Soviet Union, and that the President frequently "improvised on the spur of the moment." Fulbright's criticisms infuriated Truman. At a press conference after the senator's N.B.C. speech, the President abruptly rejected Fulbright's views, and then declined further comment.[10] In terms of Fulbright's direct personal relationships with other major critics of Truman's diplomacy, the senator was much closer to Claude Pepper than to Secretary of Commerce Henry A. Wallace. Twenty years earlier, young Fulbright had enrolled in Pepper's law course at the University of Arkansas and engaged in lengthy philosophical discussions with his brilliant, loquacious teacher. In 1945 their relationship remained cordial. Pepper had also criticized Truman for failing to cooperate with the Soviets in the U.N. and endorsed international control over atomic energy, although the Florida senator espoused a more fervent anti-Cold War perspective than did Fulbright. A minor example of this difference occurred in early 1946, when Fulbright chose not to endorse Pepper's proposal that the United States destroy its arsenal of atomic bombs and the machinery for producing them.[11]

By the spring of 1946, Fulbright had begun to adopt a more favorable attitude toward Truman's diplomacy and a more critical view of Soviet foreign policy. In an important speech at New York City in May 1946, he sharply criticized the Soviets for the first time, concluding with profound reluctance that recent Soviet policies contradicted the desire to bring peace to the world under the aegis of the United Nations. The senator's positive response to the Acheson-Lilienthal Report (a proposal for international control of atomic weapons) and his increasing abhorrence of Soviet actions in eastern Europe, Manchuria, and elsewhere were the central reasons for the transition in his position. He wondered if Russia would ever submit to "rules of conduct in any field," and asked "is it the purpose of Russia to dominate the world or is she only seeking security?" He did not give a definite answer, and he suggested that Americans should consider the extent to which Stalin may have based his actions upon the legitimate and ancient Russian quest for warm-water ports. Yet he deplored as acts of aggression the Soviet annexation of the Baltic states and Polish territory, the Soviets' stripping of factories in Manchuria, the demands for bases in the Dardanelles, and the violation of pledges to establish free governments in eastern Europe.

At the same time, however, Fulbright pointed to the flaws in American diplomacy. In his May 1946 address, he alleged that U.S. policy before the Acheson-Lilienthal Report was often indecisive or negative, and he cited the excessive haste in terminating lend-lease aid to Russia as an example of the earlier negativism. The Acheson-Lilienthal Report proposed that no nation should manufacture atomic bombs or the materials for them, and that an international authority of atomic scientists should carry on all dangerous atomic energy activities. Fulbright commended the Report and predicted that Soviet acceptance of it might end the vicious cycle of suspicion and hostility between the two great powers; but, if the Soviets rejected it, their rejection "will provide a very significant clue as to her future policy, and we should shape our own policy accordingly."[12]

Fulbright, the International Scholarship Program, and the Truman Administration, 1946

In the summer of 1946, the United States presented an altered version of the Acheson-Lilienthal Report called the Baruch Plan to the United Nations. The Baruch Plan deeply disappointed many of the experts who helped to prepare the Acheson-Lilienthal Report. The Atomic Development Authority, which Bernard Baruch's proposal would have established, provided for an inspection system over which the Soviet Union could not exercise its Security Council veto. The Baruch Plan assumed that the United States would hold a monopoly of atomic weapons for an indefinite period. Moreover, by controlling a majority within the Atomic Development Authority, the United States could have controlled the development of industrial uses of atomic energy within the Soviet Union. Fulbright failed to observe that the Baruch Plan significantly weakened the Acheson-Lilienthal Report. The Soviets rejected the Baruch Plan, and Fulbright, true to his position in the May 1946 speech, became increasingly critical of Soviet diplomacy and increasingly sympathetic to the Truman Cold War policies. He supported the President during the 1946 congressional campaign.[13]

The administration's endorsement of Fulbright's effort to establish the international scholar-exchange program contributed to the Arkansan's more favorable assessment of the Truman administration. Assistant Secretary of State William Benton and Democratic Senator Elbert D. Thomas of Utah assisted Fulbright in passing the legislation creating the Fulbright program. On August 1, 1946, Truman signed the Fulbright Act, which permitted the sale of U.S. surplus property abroad to finance the international exchange of scholars. Fulbright eventually considered the exchange program as the greatest achievement of his long career (1942-1975) in politics.[14]

Fulbright began thinking about the exchange program in September, 1945, when he had private conversations on the subject with Oscar Cox, the former counsel of the Lend-Lease Administration, and Herbert Elliston, editor of the *Washington Post*.[14a] On September 27, 1945, Fulbright stated on the Senate floor: "Mr. President, I ask unanimous consent to introduce a bill for reference to the Committee on Military Affairs, authorizing the use of credits established through the sale of surplus properties abroad for the promotion of international good will through the exchange of students in the fields of education, culture, and science."[14b] His interest in the exchange program was based upon his Rhodes scholarship and his participation the year before in the London conference on restoring Europe's educational system. A few days after President Roosevelt's death he stated on a radio broadcast that he advocated "the exchange of students, the exchange of professors, the translation of books, and the dissemination of books among all the nations... to persuade the various nations to treat their own histories in a more truthful manner." An exchange program could contribute "as much to the preservation of peace as the control of violence." The difficulty was in overcoming the prejudice among many American politicians against the idea that a fellowship program, education and a higher level of international understanding were vital in international affairs. Fulbright believed that American surplus trucks, jeeps, and bulldozers were rusting away overseas, and foreign countries would be happy to purchase them, but they lacked the money to do so; if they were allowed to pay for them in their own currency, the proceeds could finance an exchange program, and the Arkansas senator contended that the surplus equipment abroad meant that the United States actually had a substantial amount of currency frozen abroad.[14c] Fulbright explained to his Senate colleagues that "Most of the nations desiring to purchase our trucks, railroad equipment and so forth, abroad, do not have American dollars, or even the goods, to pay, and it will, therefore, be necessary for our government to establish credits for this purpose. These debts may never be paid in full and might, like the war debts after World War I, become a source of irritation." The Arkansan later reflected that he had decided not to risk an appeal to the Senate's idealism: "Indeed, it occurred to me that the less attention the matter got the greater would be the chance of victory for idealism."[14d]

Some officials from the executive branch were doubtful about the idea. State Department officials thought foreign policy should be determined by the Department, not by the Congress. Fulbright sought bipartisan support for his initiative, and received an endorsement from former President Herbert Hoover, who wrote, "I am indeed glad of such a proposal," remembering his creation of the Belgian-American Education Foundation after World War I.[14e] The low-profile, quiet strategy succeeded, as the public hearing on his proposed legislation in February 1946, attracted little attention. This strategy may have been fortunate; one member of Congress, at any rate, later privately remarked that had he known of the contents of the legislation at the time, he would have tried to kill it: "I don't want our impressionable American youths to be infected with foreign 'isms."[14f] The Chairman of the Surplus Property Subcommittee of the Senate Military Affairs Committee, Senator Joseph O'Mahoney, presided over a hearing in which the committee's members did not attend, and only Fulbright and four supporters of the legislation testified. Fulbright and Assistant Secretary of State William Benton testified in support of the proposal, and two weeks later, Chairman Elbert Thomas of Utah presided over the reporting of the bill to the full Senate. On April 12, the bill passed by unanimous consent, without debate. On August 1, 1946, President Truman signed the bill into law as P.L. 584, 79th Congress. The Fulbright Act provided that up to $20 million could be used for educational exchanges with any nation that bought surplus property, and up to $1 million could be spent annually in any country where an agreement was made.[14g] The Act included provisions for numerous educational activities. American students could obtain grants for higher education or research abroad, American professors could receive grants to lecture abroad, and foreign students could obtain funds to study at American institutions overseas such as the American University in Beirut and Robert College at Istanbul, or they could obtain money to travel to the United States to attend American universities.[14h] The Act gave the Secretary of State authority to make agreements with foreign governments for exchange programs, and the legislation was wisely drafted to free it of governmental or partisan political influence: the program would be supervised by a group of academic and cultural leaders appointed by the President to serve on a Board of Foreign Scholarships.[14i] The creation of the Board was an essential step in preventing the program from being vulnerable to political influence.

The program would ultimately dwarf the Rhodes Scholarship program. By the mid-1960s, educational exchanges were being executed with 110 countries. The scope of the program was enormous: by 1968, more than 82,000 people received Fulbright Fellowships, about 12 million school children in America and abroad were taught by exchange teachers, and about 88,500 American and almost 12,500 foreign schools took part by gaining teachers or sending them abroad. Michigan State University made a study of more than 5,000 Fulbright Scholars in America. While overseas, they had spoken to more than 250,000 people; they had written more than 4,000 books, more than 2,000 professional papers; and they had written roughly 500 articles about their experiences abroad.[14j] In later years, additional legislation expanded the Fulbright program. The Fulbright-Hays Act of 1961 brought together all the exchange legislation. As the Arkansas Senator would later summarize his achievement in international education:

> Americans and Europeans are prone to thinking of their own societies as the center and source of world civilization, forgetting that the West is only one of the World's great cultures, and forgetting also that some of the most barbarous physical and intellectual slaughters of all history have taken place in the West within our lifetime. It follows, I believe, that man's struggle to be rational about himself, about his relationship to his own society and to other peoples and nations, involves a constant search for understanding among all peoples and all cultures—a search that can only be effective when learning is pursued on a worldwide basis. The educational exchange program is built on this premise, which, stated in another way, holds that America has much to teach the world but also much to learn and the greater our intellectual involvement with the world beyond our frontiers, the greater the gain for both America and the world...
>
> Its [the exchange program] purpose is to acquaint Americans with the world as it is and to acquaint students and scholars from many lands with America as it is—not as we wish it were or as we might wish foreigners to see it, but exactly as it is—which by my reckoning is an `image' of which no American need be ashamed.[14k]

Hence, President Truman had signed into law the program that President Kennedy would later praise as "the classic modern example of beating swords into plowshares." In reality, Fulbright would support the majority of Truman's fundamental foreign policies—the Marshall Plan, the Berlin airlift, the North Atlantic Treaty—far more than he did future Presidents' policies. Ironically, although Fulbright's differences with Truman were celebrated, he basically admired the President. He would state on the Senate floor in the midst of Truman's confrontation with General MacArthur in 1951: "I am not in his [Truman's] good graces. I have spoken with him only once in several years. This, however, does not blind me to the fact that he has made decisions on a number of occasions that equal in imagination, courage, and effectiveness any ever taken by an American President" [referring to the Marshall Plan, the Berlin airlift, sending troops to Europe in peacetime and later to Korea, NATO].[14m]

Political pressures may have influenced Fulbright's 1946 transition from a critic to a supporter of Truman's foreign policy. Truman enjoyed considerable popularity in Arkansas, and Fulbright knew that it was politically dangerous for a freshman senator to continue criticizing a President of his own party. During the 1940s some of the senator's opponents darkly hinted that he had displayed a sympathy for communism, but these charges were infrequent. However, in Arkansas in the late 1940s domestic issues usually attracted more attention than foreign policy questions. As long as Fulbright vigorously supported the economic development of the state and maintained a conservative stance on civil rights, most of his constituents tended to grant him extensive freedom of action concerning his foreign policy positions. His controversial ideas in foreign policy may have occasionally damaged his political position in Arkansas, but the damage was not fatal to his political career. Concern over the potential political liabilities of criticizing Truman's foreign policy probably played only a secondary role in Fulbright's increasing tendency to support the President. The senator's genuine belief that the Baruch Plan represented a magnanimous proposal and his antipathy toward Soviet behavior in eastern Europe, Manchuria, Iran, and the Dardanelles constituted the most important reasons for the change in his perspective on the Cold War.[15]

Fulbright's responses to the early Cold War were not unique, for on the question of atomic secrets his views resembled those of Secretary of War Henry L. Stimson. Fulbright and Stimson had known each other during World War II, although they were not close friends and probably arrived independently at their opinions on U.S. diplomacy. In the fall of 1945 Fulbright, Stimson, several other foreign policy analysts, and many scientists had believed that the Soviets would acquire atomic bombs within three to five years, and therefore the United States should have immediately shared atomic information with the Soviets and established definite agreements for international control of the atom. General Leslie R. Groves and Secretary of State James F. Byrnes had contended that the Russians would require approximately 10 years to develop atomic weapons, but Stimson's prediction of relatively rapid Soviet acquisition of atomic bombs proved correct; the Soviets exploded an atomic weapon in 1949. In Stimson's famous September 1945 memorandum to the President, he had maintained that Soviet-American relations "may be perhaps irretrievably embittered by the way in which we approach the solution of the bomb with Russia. For if we fail to approach them now and merely continue to negotiate with them, having this weapon rather ostentatiously on our hip, their suspicions and their distrust of our purposes and motives will increase." After the delays in presenting the American atomic plan to the U.N., controversies over eastern Europe, and the Soviet rejection of the Baruch Plan, Stimson changed his position. By the fall of 1946, the now retired Stimson advised Secretary of the Navy James V. Forrestal that ""the way things had now developed we should not delay in going forward with the manufacture of all the atomic missiles we can make."[16]

Fulbright perhaps did not reverse his position from 1945 to 1946 quite as drastically as Stimson; however, in a typical speech of late 1946 the senator complained that "Russia has become affected by the fervor of expansion." He averred that if the United States could "impress" Russia with measures such as the extension of the draft, then a relatively stable

relationship with the Soviet Union might continue through a "breathing period," and then in the next 15 to 20 years the exchange of scholars and business connections with the Soviets might gradually remove the suspicions and hostilities from Soviet-American relations.[17]

Despite Fulbright's support for the administration, a curious episode after the 1946 elections led many people to regard the senator as a bitter enemy of the President. During a fall 1946 luncheon with his friend Senator Scott Lucas of Illinois, the reporter Ann Hicks, and others, Fulbright repeated a statement he had made publicly in March 1945. In the 1945 statement, Fulbright had warned that dangerous deadlocks between the president and Congress could jeopardize world peace and domestic prosperity. He advocated a change in the American government to end the adversary relationship between the legislative and executive branches that inevitably arose when one party controlled the Presidency while the other party controlled Congress. Citing the examples of partisan furor in Woodrow Wilson's experiences with the League of Nations after the 1918 elections and Herbert Hoover's difficulties with Congress after the 1930 elections, he asserted that the President should possess the authority to dissolve the government in cases of stalemate between the legislative and executive branches and precipitate a general election. The proposal clearly reflected Fulbright's admiration for British parliamentary procedures. In his 1946 conversation with Lucas he predicted that if the Republicans won the elections, the Democrats in the White House and the Republicans in Congress would engage in incessant and acrimonious debates, and "each party will place the blame for the inevitable stalemate on the other party." He remarked to Lucas that if the Republicans won, Truman should appoint a Republican Secretary of State and then resign, thus making the Republican the new President (since there was no Vice President at the time) and preventing another anomalous adversary relationship from arising. Fulbright suggested Michigan's Republican Senator Arthur H. Vandenberg, the symbol of bipartisanship, as the most logical choice for Truman's successor.[18]

After the Republicans captured both Houses of Congress in the 1946 elections, the reporter who had listened to the Fulbright-Lucas conversation published an article on Fulbright's remarks and thus detonated a furor. Former Secretary of the Interior Harold Ickes, the journalist Walter Lippmann, the *Atlanta Constitution*, and the *Chicago Sun* endorsed Fulbright's idea. Truman refused official comment, although his aides dismissed the quixotic proposal as "'utterly fantastic." Truman did not appreciate the niceties of Fulbrightian political philosophy, despite the Rhodes Scholar's statement on November 10 that "In urging this proposal there was no intention to reflect in any way upon the character or capacity of President Truman." At an off-the-record dinner a few days later, Truman disparaged Fulbright as an "overeducated Oxford SOB," although many years later he denied having made the statement. In 1960, the former President wrote Fulbright in an effort to clarify the matter; he said this was promoted by his having done some background reading "of various things that had happened in the past." Truman told the senator that "some reporter, as they have a habit of doing, did some misquoting of you and me. This report said I had made the same remark about you as I had about Drew Pearson [whom the President had called an "SOB"]. Truman recalled that in talking to reporters at a Press Club dinner shortly after the Republican Congress was elected in 1946 he had not called Fulbright an "overeducated Oxford SOB," although he was widely quoted at the time as having made that remark. "I made the remark," Truman wrote, "that if you had attended a land-grant college in the United States instead of Oxford, you would never have made that statement [about the superiority of parliamentary government, and that Truman should resign]. I never made any reflection on your personal character nor on your mother." Fulbright cordially replied to the former President, saying, "I willingly accept the explanation which you have made." He corrected the President's error about his educational background, however, informing Truman that "I did attend a land-grant college, the University of Arkansas, in my home town."[18a]

After the fiasco of the 1946 resignation proposal, Fulbright became more cautious in pressing his ideas for eliminating governmental deadlocks (although he later made a similar remark when President Eisenhower was confronted with a Democratic Congress); he had learned his lesson, he recalled many years later, about "tilting at windmills." However, throughout the late 1940s and early 1950s, memories of the resignation controversy seriously weakened Fulbright's ability to exert an important influence upon the administration's diplomacy or to work constructively with the President, who thenceforth harbored a hostility toward the senator until after he retired from the Presidency.[19]

The Cold War and McCarthyism

From late 1946 until early 1951 Fulbright's importance as a foreign policy analyst declined. During this period the senator devoted most of his time and energy to the development of Arkansas agriculture and other domestic affairs. His disenchantment with the failure of the great powers to create a powerful United Nations may have contributed to his lessened activity in foreign affairs. Much of his concentration on domestic issues resulted simply from his position within the Senate, where his major committee assignment was on the Banking and Currency Committee. He did not obtain a position on the prestigious Foreign Relations Committee until 1949. From the summer of 1949 to early 1951 he devoted much of his energy to another domestic issue: a Banking and Currency subcommittee's investigation of administration officials' use of favoritism and unethical influence in the Reconstruction Finance Corporation (see Book Three, Chapter Two). The R.F.C. investigation reinforced Truman's bitterness toward Fulbright that had been engendered by some of his criticisms of Truman's foreign policy in 1945, and, more importantly, the 1946 resignation proposal.

Fulbright's R.F.C. inquiry was not related to the Cold War, except in one respect: Walter Lippmann, Ernest K. Lindley, and other political analysts pointed out the contrast between Fulbright's careful, responsible conduct of a Congressional investigation, and the "witch-hunting" of Wisconsin Senator Joseph McCarthy's investigations. Lippmann described Fulbright's conduct of the R.F.C. inquiry as "an example, all the more impressive because its sincerity has been so effortless, of how a good senator can behave."[20]

To the limited extent that the Arkansan involved himself in foreign affairs from late 1946 to early 1951, he continued to support the basic Truman policies. In early 1947 Fulbright commended Truman's appointment of George C. Marshall as Secretary of State after James F. Byrnes resigned in January. A few weeks after the Marshall appointment

Fulbright wrote a letter to the President congratulating him for "making extraordinarily good decisions and appointments." The senator regretted that the press often "put me in a belligerent attitude," for in reality "it is my intention to support you in every way I can."[21]

Fulbright supported Truman's March 1947 request for $400 million in economic and military aid for Turkey and for Greece, where leftist revolutionaries waged guerrilla warfare against the government. In the President's March 12, 1947 speech to Congress he presented his Truman Doctrine, which committed the United States to "support free peoples who are resisting attempted subjugation by armed minorities or by outside pressures." Beyond the specific request for aid to Greece and Turkey, the Doctrine constituted a vague and indeterminate promise to support governments under communist attack. Although Fulbright voted for the specific appeal for aid to Greece and Turkey, he displayed little enthusiasm for the global anticommunist rhetoric of Truman's speech. Throughout his later career Fulbright affirmed that in 1947, given the paralysis of the western European economy, Stalin's expansion into eastern Europe, and the virtual disarmament of the United States in conventional forces, the decision to aid Greece and Turkey represented an intelligent action. But the Arkansan later objected to Truman's inflated rhetoric publicizing the concept of a global ideological conflict between western freedom and Moscow's system of "terror and oppression." Whether the senator privately held these views at the time was debatable, for he failed to offer any public criticisms of the Truman Doctrine. He did propose an alternative strategy for the management of disputes with Russia. He asserted that the "balance of power" should govern American policy in the Cold War and that the United States could restore the European balance by promoting the political and economic federation of Europe as a counterweight to Soviet power. One week after the Truman Doctrine speech, Fulbright and Elbert Thomas of Utah introduced a resolution stating that "Congress favors the creation of a United States of Europe within the framework of the United Nations." The administration as well as the Senate did not accept the resolution.[22]

In March 1947, Truman dealt with another issue that would have profound implications for the preservation of constitutional freedoms in America: the question of responding to allegations that the United States government had been infiltrated by disloyal employees. Upon assuming control of the Eightieth Congress, the Republicans publicized their determination to end what the new Republican Speaker of the House, Joseph Martin, decried as "boring from within by subversionists high up in the government." Truman was particularly concerned about the rabid new chairman of the House Committee on Un-American Activities, J. Parnell Thomas (R.-New Jersey). According to Clifford Durr, a member of the Federal Communications Commission, Truman privately remarked that he created the Temporary Commission on Employee Loyalty "to take the ball away from Thomas." Fulbright opposed the demagogical activities of the Un-American Activities Committee, a red-baiting body that was the precursor to the even more dangerous witch hunts of Joe McCarthy in the early 1950s. Truman charged the temporary commission on loyalty to consider whether existing procedures adequately protected the government against the alleged dangers of hiring disloyal persons, and after hastily conducted hearings, the Commission reported to the President in February 1947 that while it did not know how far-reaching the problem was, "a problem of such importance must be dealt with vigorously and effectively." The Commission advocated a new loyalty program with greater uniformity and "effectiveness." The reality that the Commission had been unable to discover any large number of "disloyal" employees was not considered significant for some of the more zealous anti-communists within the administration. Attorney General Tom Clark warned that "I do not believe that the gravity of the problem should be weighed in the light of numbers, but rather from the viewpoint of the serious threat which even one disloyal person constitutes to the security of the government of the United States."[22a]

In the beginning, Truman held mixed feelings about the "loyalty" controversy. In a letter to an old friend, he said: "People are very much wrought up about the Communist 'bugaboo' but I am of the opinion that the country is perfectly safe so far as Communism is concerned—we have far too many sane people. Our Government is made for the welfare of the people and I don't believe there will ever come a time when anyone will really want to overturn it."[22b] On the other hand, he ultimately accepted Attorney General Clark's hypothesis, for he also stated that "I believe the issue has been blown up out of proportion to the actual number of disloyal persons we may have. But the fact is that one disloyal person is too many." F.B.I. Director J. Edgar Hoover became a driving force behind the new loyalty program, advising the Commission that "subversive" people might recruit fellow employees into disloyal organizations, or they might influence the formulation of domestic or foreign policy in a way that "might favor the foreign country of their ideological choice." On Truman's agenda, passage of aid to Greece and Turkey and the monumental Marshall Plan ranked as his priorities; how could he persuade a hostile Republican Congress to accept such programs for resisting communism in Europe while appearing "soft on communism" at home? The presidential election of 1948 was 20 months away, and the question of who was "tougher on communism" exerted a burgeoning political impact on American politics. Ultimately, nine days after delivering the Truman Doctrine speech, the President promulgated Executive Order 9835, "Prescribing Procedures for the Administration of an Employee Loyalty Program in the Executive Branch of the Government."[22c]

During the McCarthy era, Fulbright would decry the assault upon traditional constitutional freedoms perpetrated by the McCarthyites. Later in his career, he would argue that the Truman administration had prepared the way for the later rigidity of America's Cold War policy through its overblown anticommunism, beginning with the Truman Doctrine speech. While Truman, of course, never agreed with Fulbright's later criticisms of the Doctrine, Truman eventually conceded that the loyalty program was "not in the tradition of fair play and justice."[22d] Truman lamented that he had not realized that once a person had been cleared by a loyalty board, his name was not included in the general file kept on employee loyalty matters, and thus every time a cleared employee transferred to another job he was subjected to yet another investigation. Truman's Executive Order establishing the program had taken the unprecedented step of creating in peacetime a mechanism for affording "maximum protection against infiltration of disloyal persons into the ranks of its employees." The Order required a loyalty investigation of every person entering a civilian job in the federal government and made all agency heads responsible for assuring that currently employed "disloyal" persons were dismissed. Investigators were required to consult such sources of "information" as FBI files, the files of the House Un-American Activities Committee, as well as local law enforcement files. A few years later when the FBI was investigating a minor State Department official, Fulbright refused to turn over his files regarding the official to the FBI, since the senator believed that the FBI allowed redbaiting senators (of whom Joe McCarthy had by then become the most notorious) access to its files, and McCarthy would use the files for an anticommunist smear of the official's patriotism.

The loyalty program eventually became the saddest chapter in the history of the Truman administration from the viewpoint of civil libertarians, who were deeply concerned about preserving the values of constitutional democracy. A person who was accused of disloyalty did not have the right to confront his accusers and cross-examine witnesses. There was no definition of "disloyalty" in the Order. All civilian employees—and there were roughly two million of them—were to be listed with the FBI for a check of their names, even those who were not employed in jobs with national security concerns. Any derogatory information unearthed by the FBI would require an investigation, and the Attorney General now published a lengthy list of "subversive organizations," thus establishing a doctrine of imputing guilt by association. The lower-level loyalty boards and the higher "Loyalty Review Board," which could hear appeals, were administrative bodies, not judicial bodies. These administrative bodies could pass judgment upon the ideas or opinions of private citizens who were employed or seeking employment in the government. Truman was worried about the power of the FBI in controlling the program and for a time tried to channel power to conduct investigations into the Civil Service Commission. But the superior facilities of the FBI, its historic role in investigative activities, as well as Hoover's support from Congress, Attorney General Clark, and Truman's trusted friend and adviser, Clark Clifford, ultimately carried the day. Truman privately expressed concern about an internal "Gestapo" and wrote to Clifford, "J. Edgar will in all probability get this backward-looking Congress to give him what he wants. It's dangerous."[22e] Truman was correct, as Congress expanded the President's budget request for the FBI in the program while drastically reducing the request for the Civil Service Commission's role to one-fifth of what Truman had requested. Although Truman always claimed that he tried to administer the program in such a way as to avoid violating individual rights, the grave flaw of the program remained: it elevated the perceived need for national security above the traditional constitutional rights of individual Americans. Under the succeeding administration, especially during the McCarthy era, abuses became much more frequent. As Fulbright would later lament, in the zeal to combat communism, the Cold Warriors had undermined many of the traditional values they were seeking to preserve; if such authoritarian tendencies continued unchecked in the future, "we may find some day, without quite knowing when or how or why it happened, that we have destroyed our own constitutional democracy—in order to save it."[22f]

While Fulbright consistently opposed the most pathological forms of domestic anticommunism, at times in his analysis of foreign policy issues during the late 1940s Fulbright indulged in the Cold War rhetoric characteristic of the era. When Henry Wallace charged that aid to Greece amounted to American imperialism, Fulbright complained to an Arkansas newspaper reporter that Wallace's statement "sounded just as though it had been written in the Kremlin." Fulbright's remark was a heated criticism, especially since he had frequently praised Wallace (and other Roosevelt advisers) during the Roosevelt administration. The senator might have refuted Wallace's view with a temperate, well-reasoned explanation of the need to strengthen the weak Turkish government or to fill the power vacuum in the eastern Mediterranean that the recent British withdrawal from Greece had created. Instead, he merely denounced Wallace's opinion by complaining that it "sounded just as though it had been written in the Kremlin." Since Fulbright made his criticism in an impromptu interview with a reporter, he may not have reflected upon the derogatory tone of his remark; nevertheless, the published statement represented a harsh effort to disparage the former Vice President and Cabinet official. Wallace's views suffered from a pro-Soviet bias, but his ideas deserved more temperate criticism.

On another occasion in the late 1940s Fulbright differed with Wallace in a more restrained fashion; in 1948 he delivered an address at Southwestern University at Memphis in which he offered a restrained critique of Wallace's third party Presidential candidacy. "Multiple parties in other countries," he argued, "have usually resulted in unstable and ineffective governments." In the Memphis address, Fulbright did not employ any heated anticommunist rhetoric in opposing the Wallace third-party movement.[23]

In 1947 Fulbright demonstrated more enthusiasm for the Marshall Plan than for the Truman Doctrine's global anticommunism. The senator praised Secretary of State Marshall's June 5 speech at Harvard, in which the Secretary announced the administration's plan for economic aid to Europe. The Marshall Plan differed in purpose and tone from the Truman Doctrine, for it committed the United States to the economic rehabilitation of Europe and not to a crusade against communism. In July, Marshall wrote to Fulbright thanking him for his approval of the Harvard speech. The Secretary informed Fulbright that the favorable domestic and foreign responses to the address augured well for the success of the Marshall Plan. Marshall had invited the Soviet Union and its Slavic satellites to join in the economic recovery program. The Soviets eventually rejected the American offer and denounced the program as an American plot to gain control of the European economy. The Soviet repudiation of the Marshall Plan accelerated Fulbright's tendency to attack Soviet diplomacy. In responding to the Soviet rejection, Fulbright charged that the Russians did not desire the rehabilitation of any European country unless "it is communist-controlled and isolated by an iron curtain."[24]

In 1948-1949, Fulbright continued to support Truman's Cold War policies in Europe. The Arkansan endorsed Truman's 1948 presidential campaign and rejected the third-party movement of Henry Wallace as well as the Dixiecrats under Strom Thurmond. During the 1948 Berlin blockade, Fulbright and Senator Scott Lucas traveled to Berlin, where they conferred with General Lucius D. Clay and approved of Clay's handling of the crisis. In June the U.S.S.R. had attempted to prevent the organization of Germany's three western zones into a West German state by blockading West Berlin. Britain and the United States responded with the Berlin airlifts, which supplied the city so effectively that Stalin ended the blockade in 1949 and acquiesced in the subsequent creation of the West German Republic. Stalin countered the Western triumphs in the victory of the anti-guerrilla forces in Greece and the Berlin airlift by establishing the East German Democratic Republic. After the Fulbright-Lucas journey to Berlin, the Arkansas senator stated that "there's little likelihood of war," provided the United States maintained a firm stance against Soviet actions. In 1949 Fulbright voted for the North Atlantic Treaty Organization Pact, through which the United States provided a shield of air and atomic power for western Europe. He demonstrated especial enthusiasm for Truman's Point Four program of technical assistance to underdeveloped countries. As a freshman senator who devoted much of his time to domestic issues,

Fulbright did not play a central role in the N.A.T.O. and Point Four programs, although he supported them wholeheartedly.[25]

In 1949 Fulbright defended the administration against the extreme anticommunists who denounced Truman for "losing" China to communism. Upon Marshall's recommendation, Truman had rejected a direct military intervention in the Chinese civil war. He felt he could not immediately desert the Chinese Nationalists because of Chiang Kai-shek's many influential friends within the United States, and therefore he decided to provide the Nationalists with a moderate amount of aid. In the 1940s the United States supplied the corrupt and inefficient Nationalist Chinese with military equipment and around $2 billion in aid, air-lifted entire Nationalist armies at critical junctures during the war, and seized and held vital Chinese seaports for the Nationalists. A few months before the Nationalists collapsed and fled to Formosa, Truman raised the question of terminating military aid to the Kuomintang. Democratic Senator Pat McCarran of Nevada thereupon introduced a bill to lend $1.5 billion to Nationalist China for economic and military purposes. Republican Senator William F. Knowland of California called for an investigation of America's China policy. Fulbright and Senator Tom Connally of Texas defended Truman and the State Department and blocked McCarran's attempt to continue and deepen the American involvement in China. Later in the year Secretary of State Dean G. Acheson, who succeeded Marshall in 1949, and Ambassador-at-Large Philip C. Jessup supervised the preparation of a State Department white paper on China. The white paper accurately portrayed the Chinese revolution as an indigenous uprising beyond American control.[26]

Fulbright won re-election in 1950, the year Joseph McCarthy charged that 205 communists had infiltrated the State Department. A McCarthyite candidate defeated the conservative Senator Millard Tydings of Maryland, who had thoroughly investigated McCarthy's allegations against the State Department and declared them unfounded. Ohio Senator Robert A. Taft gained re-election after blaming Truman and Acheson for the "loss Of China," while the vociferous anti-communist Richard M. Nixon defeated a liberal in California. Three of Fulbright's closest friends in the Senate, Claude Pepper, Elbert Thomas, and Majority Leader Scott Lucas, lost their 1950 campaigns for re-election. In all three cases McCarthyite allegations contributed to the electoral results, although George Smathers in Florida and Everett Dirksen in Illinois also used other issues to defeat the incumbents.[27]

Fulbright seemed another likely target for a McCarthyite onslaught. In the 1944 Senate campaign Governor Homer Adkins and other right-wing candidates had denigrated the Rhodes Scholar as a "New Dealer" who had displayed a softness toward communism. They cited as "evidence" for their charges the facts that Fulbright had served as an Anti-Trust division lawyer during the New Deal and as a member of the House of Representatives had voted for an unsuccessful effort to abolish Representative Martin Dies' Special Committee on Un-American Activities. Adkins publicized the Congress of Industrial Organizations' endorsement of Fulbright in the effort to smear him as a tool of socialism. Some observers of Arkansas politics speculated that Fulbright might face a similar right-wing challenge in 1950. Throughout late 1949 and much of 1950 the senator conducted an exhaustive campaign of speaking engagements in Arkansas. Fulbright had amply demonstrated his anti-communist credentials in the late 1940s through his bitter criticisms of Soviet rejections of the Baruch Plan and the Marshall Plan. His vigor in encouraging Arkansas' economic devel-

opment and conservatism in civil rights deprived potential opponents of any domestic
issues to use against him. Moreover, although many of his constituents may not have cared
deeply about the specifics of his foreign policy positions, they understood and admired the
prestige Fulbright enjoyed as the author of the Fulbright Resolution, the Fulbright
Fellowships program, and as a new member of the Senate Foreign Relations Committee.

The right-wing threat to end his career did not materialize. Fulbright ran unopposed
and in 1951 emerged with a strengthened position in the Senate.[28]

After the 1950 election Fulbright led the Democratic opposition to Republican condemnations of Truman's Asian policy. Republican senators escalated their attacks on the
State Department after the outbreak of the Korean War in 1950. In November Fulbright
wrote Acheson a brief letter assuring the Secretary that the American people would ultimately grow weary of the Republicans' "carping." On December 19, the New York Times
reported that Fulbright and other Democrats had rallied to a "rare demonstration of solidarity" in opposing Republican suggestions that Truman ask for Acheson's resignation. In a
Senate debate on December 18, Senator Knowland provided the Republican rebuttal by
claiming that his party had simply fulfilled its duty to lambast Acheson for "having closed
the door to communism in Europe while leaving it wide open in Asia." Fulbright decried
Republican criticisms as character assassination of administration officials. To his mind, the
Republican assault on Acheson's patriotism resembled a fascist appeal to prejudice and emotionalism. The Arkansan argued that the Republican attacks might eventually disrupt the
confidence of U.S. allies in the American ability to follow a responsible foreign policy.[29]

Fulbright vacillated in his early responses to the Korean War. For months after the
North Koreans launched their offensive in June 1950, Fulbright had remained silent. After
33 full Chinese divisions ravaged the over-extended American lines south of the Yalu River,
the senator called for an immediate withdrawal of U.S. troops from Korea. In early 1951,
he endorsed Truman's original decision to oppose the "direct and unambiguous aggression"
of North Korea, but he asserted that any risk of involvement in a protracted land war with
China was unacceptable. When China entered the war, he averred, the dangers of fighting
on the Asian continent became militarily "untenable." He followed this assertion with one
of the most harsh anticommunist statements he ever uttered: "We must not forget that the
Kremlin is the primary enemy and China merely a satellite." During the early stages of the
Korean War Fulbright and the Assistant Secretary of State for Far Eastern Affairs, Dean
Rusk, expressed equally distorted evaluations of the strength of Chinese nationalism,
Fulbright describing China as a Russian "satellite," Rusk labeling the Chinese a "colonial
Russian government." The context of the Fulbright and Rusk statements differed greatly.
Rusk contended that since the Peking regime constituted a Soviet colony, the Nationalists
on Formosa were the authentic representatives of the Chinese people, while Fulbright's
description of China as a Soviet satellite occurred in the context of his appeal for an
American withdrawal from the Korean military engagement against China. Nevertheless,
Fulbright's allegation that China was a Russian satellite revealed his lack of knowledge of
the Far East. He possessed a vast store of knowledge concerning Europe, but in the early
1950s he frequently failed to grasp the complexities of Asian affairs.[30]

While Fulbright stressed the importance of Europe for American vital interests, in
December 1950 former President Hoover advocated the removal of all American ground

forces not only from Asia, but from Europe as well. In Hoover's view, the United States should withdraw to island outposts including Japan, the Pacific islands, and Great Britain, and use its naval and air power to defend its interests. Senator Robert Taft of Ohio endorsed his position. Fulbright replied in a Senate speech of January 22, 1951, by rejecting both the hard-line Cold Warrior approach and the new isolationism of Taft and Hoover. The Arkansan summarized three basic approaches to foreign policy that were then being debated in Washington: first, the reliance upon air and sea power and limitation of American commitments to the Western Hemisphere; second, "the so-called Truman Doctrine of opposing aggression in every area where it appears"; and third, American participation in bolstering ground forces in Europe, combined with defense of the Western Hemisphere. Of the latter strategy he said, "One may perhaps call this the Truman Doctrine with limitations." Important strategic areas—such as Japan, Greece and Turkey—other than Europe could be assisted with arms and material, but not ground troops. Fulbright contended that the new isolationist policy was dangerous to America's vital interests, while the Truman Doctrine approach "is beyond our capacity to carry out." The senator contended that by limiting American commitments to "Europe and certain additional strategic areas as I have indicated, we can bring about the unity of the free world."[30a]

During 1951, the radical right's attack on Truman's Asian policy increasingly led Fulbright to turn his attention to the Far East. In the spring he engaged in an acrimonious public debate with General Douglas MacArthur when the general entered the political arena to advocate the escalation of warfare against China. MacArthur delineated his strategy for crushing the Chinese in a speech before Congress on April 19, 1951, shortly after Truman relieved him of command in Korea for publicly defying the President's decision to stalemate the war and seek a truce. The general declared that "military necessity" demanded the bombing of Manchuria, the "unleashing"" of Chiang Kai-shek to invade China, the massive reinforcement of American forces in Korea, and the blockade of the Chinese mainland. The powerful U.S. Representative Joseph Martin and other ultra-conservatives in Congress jubilantly publicized and endorsed MacArthur's appraisal of the military situation in the Far East. On May 16 a Gallup Poll reported that 66 per cent of the American public favored MacArthur's war strategy, while only 25 per cent favored Truman's limited war strategy.[31]

Although Fulbright had often played the role of the skeptical gadfly of the administration in earlier years, he vigorously defended Truman against the avalanche of verbal abuse the President sustained for the dismissal of MacArthur. A week after the general's address to Congress, Fulbright delivered a speech to the Senate in which he denounced the proposal to expand the Korean War as almost certain to precipitate a Third World war. He began his speech by condemning MacArthur's challenge to the venerable American principle of subordination of the military to the civilian authority, stating that only a constitutional amendment could abrogate the President's authority to remove commanders in the field. Fulbright proceeded to discuss the strategic consequences of MacArthur's plan. In a passage that foreshadowed his analysis of American involvement in Laos and Vietnam in later years, he argued that even if the general's critics granted the doubtful contention that Russia would remain passive while Chiang's armies and American bombers invaded China, the Soviets would relish nothing more than the prospect of watching as the United States dissipated its resources in interminable and debilitating conflicts on the periphery of the Soviet empire.[32]

Fulbright contended that MacArthur's strategy represented an ineffable danger, for he believed that the Soviet Union almost certainly would intervene once the bombing began. The senator regarded any lack of specificity in the 1950 Sino-Soviet treaty as irrelevant, because if the U.S.S.R. "should stand idly by and see her Chinese ally knocked to pieces," such inaction would inflict irrevocable damage upon Soviet prestige and security. Finally, although MacArthur commanded the first United Nations army in history, he had not consulted or even mentioned America's allies fighting in Korea. The general proposed that the United States unilaterally reach a decision likely to commit American allies throughout the globe to total warfare. Fulbright raised the possibility that MacArthur's drastic plan (if America accepted it) might drive the western Europeans into making an accommodation or even an alliance with the Soviet Union rather than meekly acquiescing as the United States determined their destinies.[33]

In May, MacArthur testified at joint hearings of the Senate Armed Services Committee and Foreign Relations Committee. At the hearings Senators Fulbright and Wayne Morse of Oregon exposed the glaring inconsistencies in MacArthur's allegation that a land war in continental China would not follow the proposed bombings. Fulbright questioned MacArthur as to whether the primitive economy of China, which possessed thousands of widely dispersed handicrafts industries but no heavily industrialized areas, did not constitute a formidable defense against aerial devastation of its productive capacity. In the senator's opinion, the United States could not have crippled the Chinese war effort by destroying the Manchurian munitions factories, because the Chinese manufactured only small arms for themselves and received the bulk of their military equipment from the Soviet Union. MacArthur evaded Fulbright's questions by stating that a blockade of the mainland would produce a famine that might kill 15 million Chinese and that a failure to adopt his program would signify the degradation of the American "moral tone."[34]

During the MacArthur hearings Fulbright charged that the general's view of the military realities suffered from an erroneous assumption of American omnipotence. The Japanese in World War II had never been able to starve China into submission. Considering the enormous difficulties Japan encountered in attempting to subdue China during the eight years of warfare before Pearl Harbor, when the Japanese commanded virtually complete control of the air, the Arkansan dismissed MacArthur's prediction that the United States could subdue the Chinese through naval and air power alone. In Fulbright's view, the air strikes were the inevitable prelude to the commitment of combat forces in China. Fulbright argued that Soviet military power might represent a threat to U.S. security, but communist ideology alone could not harm America. The general disagreed vehemently, identifying the fundamental threat to American interests as "communism wherever it exists," both within the United States and throughout the world. Fulbright concluded that MacArthur's appeal for a "total victory" had distorted American perspectives on the Cold War by dividing policy alternatives into the absolute polarities of "appeasement" or an utter obliteration of Asian communism, which the general imagined would serve as a panacea for the failures of recent American diplomacy.[35]

The temporary hysteria that accompanied the general's return to the United States gradually abated. The administration's strong defense of its actions and the Senate hearings helped to puncture the legend of MacArthur as the dethroned and noble warrior. However, to many Americans the general remained a hero, and his program of building future policy around Chiang Kai-shek and U.S. sea and air power exerted a pernicious influence on American foreign policy. Truman did not reverse his Far Eastern policy under pressure of the general's assault; but the combined fears and pressures of the Korean War, MacArthur's Asia-first strategy, and McCarthy's attacks on the State Department influenced the Truman administration to adopt a more rigid stance in favor of Chiang and to accelerate aid to the Nationalists on Formosa.[36]

In October 1951, Fulbright resisted McCarthy's onslaught against Ambassador-at-Large Philip Jessup, the former editor-in-chief of the China White Paper. Truman nominated Jessup to fill the post of representative to the U.N. General Assembly. Jessup had previously served at the U.N., where his record as an ardent Cold War orator had often led Fulbright to criticize him for abetting the Soviet attempt to transform the Assembly into a forum for exchanging insults. Yet McCarthy and former Minnesota Governor Harold Stassen questioned Jessup's patriotism because of his association with Acheson and his membership in the Institute for Pacific Relations. The Institute included among its members Owen Lattimore, the former adviser to Chiang Kai-shek who now led the organization's vociferous criticism of Chiang. During a Senate Foreign Relations subcommittee's hearings on Jessup's nomination, Fulbright pressed McCarthy to document his claims that Jessup held a "great affinity for communist causes." At one juncture of the hearings, McCarthy virtually conceded that he had not yet made a convincing case against Jessup, but he urged the senators to wait and weigh the evidence in its totality. Fulbright responded, "A number of zeros doesn't make it amount to one if you put them all together." McCarthy ranted that "men of little minds" were trying to make communism a political issue, whereupon Fulbright sarcastically replied, "You would not do anything like that, would you?"[37]

Despite McCarthy's failure to substantiate his accusations, only Fulbright and Senator John Sparkman of Alabama among the members of the Foreign Relations subcommittee voted in favor of Jessup. Republican Senator H. Alexander Smith of New Jersey explained his crucial vote against the Ambassador-at-Large by conceding that he held absolute confidence in the ability, loyalty, and integrity of his old friend Jessup, but that Jessup had embraced a "group attitude toward Asia" that brought disaster in China. After Jessup's defeat, McCarthy exulted, "This is a great day for America and a bad day for communists." At the time of Fulbright's clash with McCarthy at the Jessup hearings, the Arkansan confided to his friend Senator William Benton of Connecticut that he "hadn't imagined that the man could be as bad as he turned out to be."[38]

In 1952, Fulbright contended that McCarthy was vilifying the Democratic Presidential nominee, Governor Adlai E. Stevenson of Illinois. McCarthy directed a series of scurrilous charges against Stevenson. He "exposed" Stevenson's membership in the Institute for Pacific Relations and charged that the *Daily Worker* had endorsed the governor, which was not true. McCarthy's charges disgusted the Arkansas senator. Fulbright and Stevenson had met when they were New Deal government lawyers and remained friends until Stevenson's death. In October 1952, the *St. Louis Post-Dispatch* reported that Fulbright had sent Stevenson extensive information concerning the techniques the McCarthyites had used in defaming earlier opponents, such as their use of a "faked" composite photograph of Millard Tydings supposedly conversing with the communist leader Earl Browder. The Stevenson organization invited Fulbright to come to Springfield and act as an adviser to the governor during the final stages of the campaign. Fulbright and George W. Ball, Executive Director of the National Volunteers for Stevenson, publicized the similarity between McCarthy's allegations against Stevenson and the McCarthyite campaign against Tydings in 1950. The Arkansas senator and Ball helped mobilize the Democratic counter-attack against McCarthy. Truman criticized Republican presidential nominee Dwight D. Eisenhower's reluctant endorsement of McCarthy as a desertion of the general's former comrade in arms, George Marshall, since McCarthy had frequently denounced Marshall's role in Asian policy. Fulbright played a prominent role in the latter stages of the Stevenson campaign, as he helped raise funds, attempted to persuade other Southern politicians to support Stevenson, contacted Democratic officials across the country, and urged Stevenson to counter the mudslinging attacks of such right wing Republicans as Nixon. Unfortunately, Stevenson's perfectionism in always being late with drafts of speeches and his disregard for the more practical side of politics made the campaign inefficient. Most important, Fulbright had great difficulty persuading Stevenson to respond to the McCarthyite attacks. The Senate electoral results in Wisconsin and Connecticut discouraged many of McCarthy's opponents. McCarthy gained re-election, although he won only 54 per cent of the vote. McCarthy's most vocal antagonist in the Senate, William Benton, lost his campaign for re-election.[39]

In November 1952 R. B. McCallum wrote a letter to Fulbright analyzing Eisenhower's election to the Presidency. "As an English Liberal I have always been pro-Democrat," McCallum observed, "but in many ways it was becoming very dangerous to have the Republicans excluded from office for so long." If the Republicans had again lost the Presidency after 20 years in opposition, he believed they would have vented their frustrations and bitterness on Stevenson and thus placed the Democrat in an untenable position. He thought Eisenhower might become a good President. In Fulbright's February 1953 reply to McCallum, he described Eisenhower as a "good man," although he expressed uncertainty about the President's political astuteness. He regretted that McCarthy and Senator William Jenner of Indiana "are having their way at the moment" and hoped "their day of glory will be short-lived." Fulbright thought Eisenhower must provide the leadership in beginning the repudiation of McCarthy.[40]

In an early 1953 letter to William Benton, Fulbright elaborated upon his views concerning the proper strategy to employ in opposing McCarthy. According to the Arkansan, the Republicans would rally around McCarthy and accuse the Democrats of partisanship if a Democrat made the initial move to condemn the Wisconsin senator. The President or a leading Republican must first "take the curse of partisanship off the matter" before a Democrat could present some type of formal condemnation against McCarthy. He believed that the "political overtones" of McCarthyism were extremely difficult to diagnose, but he assured Benton that he would continue to study the issue of condemning McCarthy. In an early 1953 letter to Fulbright, Benton urged his former colleague to act aggressively in opposing McCarthy. "I was one of eleven Senatorial candidates who ran ahead of Stevenson," he informed Fulbright, "which would not seem to indicate that the McCarthy affair hurt me noticeably—there is no doubt that it hurt, but a good case can be made for the fact that it helped in other directions even more than it hurt." In explaining these "other directions" that helped him, Benton observed that he had received over a thousand contributions to his 1952 Senate campaign from people all over the country who had applauded his dissent against McCarthyism. He predicted that if Fulbright would lead a movement to publicly repudiate the Wisconsin senator, he would receive a "tremendous response" from the legal profession and from people throughout the United States. Benton had accurately analyzed his 1952 defeat. His opponent, William Purtell, may have gained a few thousand votes from McCarthy's endorsement, but his 88,000-vote margin over Benton primarily resulted from Eisenhower's ability to generate support for the entire Republican ticket in Connecticut. As the New York Times summarized it, Benton "got caught in the Eisenhower landslide."[41]

During early 1953, Fulbright erred in depending upon Eisenhower to commence hostilities against McCarthy. The President refused to openly challenge the Wisconsin senator and expected the Senate to discipline its miscreants. Nor did McCarthy's opponents receive any encouragement from Eisenhower's Vice President, Richard Nixon, who had earlier competed with McCarthy in vilifying the Democratic "traitors in the high councils of our own government who make sure that the deck is stacked on the Soviet side of the diplomatic table." By the summer of 1953 Fulbright began to realize that the Eisenhower administration would not assume leadership of the movement to repudiate McCarthy.[42]

At the July 1953 Senate Appropriations Committee hearings concerning funds for the Fulbright Fellowships, Fulbright launched the counteroffensive that culminated in McCarthy's censure in December 1954. McCarthy threatened to terminate the educational exchange program through his charges that it awarded scholarships to communists. He requested that the Senate Committee place in the record of the hearings several statements that Fulbright Scholars had allegedly made "praising the communist form of government." Fulbright revealed that he had come prepared to insert into the record thousands of statements concerning Fulbright Scholars that would refute McCarthy's assertions. Fulbright's response startled McCarthy. The Republican senator gesticulated, raised his voice, and derisively referred to Fulbright as "Halfbright," but he eventually withdrew his demand and never again challenged the exchange program. A State Department official, Francis Colligan, and the scholar Walter Johnson believed that Fulbright's performance in the July 1953 hearings represented the first successful resistance to McCarthy within the U.S. government since McCarthy had launched his anticommunist crusade with the 1950 "Communism in the State Department" speech.[43]

In early 1954 McCarthy, as well as many of his enemies outside the Senate, portrayed the imminent decision on appropriations for his Permanent Investigations subcommittee as a test vote of confidence in the senator. On February 2, the Senate overwhelmingly approved the $214,000 appropriation. McCarthy's margin of victory was 85 to 1, with Fulbright casting the lone dissenting vote. The Arkansan's dissent shocked some of the influential leaders of the liberal bloc in the Senate, especially Senator Herbert H. Lehman of New York, into more vigorous support for the movement to condemn McCarthy. Even before the appropriations vote, Lehman had been one of McCarthy's important critics. On February 4, Lehman paid a visit to Fulbright's office. He said he admired Fulbright's vote, apologized for not having voted with him, and promised that he would not fail to join him in opposing McCarthy in the future.[44]

A few weeks after his vote to terminate the funds for McCarthy's subcommittee,

Fulbright rejected a Federal Bureau of Investigation request for information concerning an anonymous minor State Department official who had known the Arkansan. The F.B.I. was investigating the official as a possible subversive. Fulbright explained his refusal by observing that F.B.I. Director J. Edgar Hoover granted McCarthy access to F.B.I. files, and that McCarthy misused the F.B.I.'s information to defame responsible citizens. The Associated Press reported on March 13 that "the Arkansan is the first Senator to refuse to give information to the F.B.I." The A.P. report stated that Fulbright had "declined any further dealings with the F.B.I." after the initial request. Fulbright affirmed that his report on the State Department official "would have been favorable" if he had given it, but he chose to withhold information from the F.B.I. rather than allow McCarthy to twist the words of his report into an anticommunist "smear" against the official. [44a]

Throughout the early months of 1954, Fulbright broadened his dissent to charge that McCarthyism exerted a destructive impact not only on American foreign policy, but upon the entire social and intellectual environment within the United States. He elaborated upon the theme that the extremists of the radical right were unwittingly acting in league with communists to undermine the foundations of democracy. In his view, McCarthyism fostered the stifling of dissent, the attack on American social institutions and "the swinish blight of anti-intellectualism" that strengthened the international appeal of Soviet propaganda depicting the decadence of American society. Fulbright quoted a passage from the works of V.I. Lenin to buttress his argument in a February speech to the Senate. In analyzing the post-World War I anticommunist hysteria in western Europe and the United States, Lenin had written: "They [the western capitalists] are hunting down bolshevism with the same zeal as did Kerensky and Company; they are overdoing it and helping us quite as much as did Kerensky."[45]

Fulbright especially lamented the pernicious impact of McCarthyism upon the Eisenhower administration's Asian policy. In his opinion, "The current hysteria and fear generated by recent attacks upon the Foreign Service and the State Department" had prevented State Department officials from objecting to unwise ventures, such as a recent decision to ship arms to Pakistan. Fulbright alleged that many State Department Asian experts understood that the U.S. arms shipment to Pakistan risked the alienation of India. The administration delivered the arms in the hope that the Pakistanis would employ them in defense against Asian communists, but many experts feared that the Pakistanis would eventually use the weapons against India. Yet the experts' "mouths are closed," Fulbright lamented in a Senate speech, "simply because criticism of the proposed alliance and arms program might be interpreted by some—unjustly, I believe—as being soft toward communism." The Pakistan arms shipment was one among several examples Fulbright cited to demonstrate the destructive McCarthyite impact on U.S. Asian policy. After the U.S. arms shipment, the Pakistanis agreed to join the Southeast Asia Treaty Organization, an attempted anticommunist coalition that Secretary of State John Foster Dulles created after the Vietnamese communist Ho Chi Minh's forces had defeated the French at Dienbienphu.[46]

Many years later, Fulbright wrote in *The Arrogance of Power* that the initial American involvement in the Vietnamese civil war was conditioned by two extraneous factors: McCarthyism and the Korean War. In the late 1940s Truman had cultivated the belief that only a resolute American will to aid anticommunists was necessary to forestall communist revolutions. A failure to have supported the non-communists in Vietnam would have contradicted his logic and subjected the President to another barrage of vilification from McCarthy and the other extremists. Thus by 1951 the United States was financing 40 per cent of the French military effort in Vietnam. The Truman administration considered Vietnam peripheral to Europe, which Acheson regarded as the epicenter of the struggle against communism. Acheson viewed American support for French colonialism in southeast Asia as a necessary concession to be granted the French in order to secure France's position as the cynosure of the anti-communist coalition in Europe. After war erupted in Korea the Truman administration had virtually ignored Vietnamese nationalism and anti-colonialism and interpreted the Viet Minh's resistance to the French as being analogous to the blatant aggression of the North Korean communists in 1950.[47]

During the Truman and Eisenhower administrations Fulbright regarded Vietnam as peripheral to America's vital interests, and he usually did not devote significant attention to Vietnamese affairs. However, he briefly focused his attention on Indochina after the French collapse at Dienbienphu. In April he made an off-the-cuff comment to an Arkansas Gazette reporter's question as to whether he would send American troops to Indochina if it became necessary. He replied: "There isn't any other option unless we want to join up with the Communists."[47a] The comment revealed that Fulbright could occasionally make statements fully consistent with the Cold War viewpoints prevalent in that era; however, after he had time to reflect on the situation, he began raising questions about the assumptions of American policy in the Far East. He would later voice doubts about the Eisenhower administration's over-emphasis on the alleged menace of China, saying: "China is only a mass of humanity and won't be a power potential until it becomes industrialized."[47b] In the summer of 1954 he questioned American policy in southeast Asia for the first time. At a Foreign Relations Committee hearing with Dulles in June, Fulbright opposed any direct U.S. intervention to uphold French colonialism in Indochina. Dulles had proposed such an intervention earlier in the year. Fulbright suggested that Ho Chi Minh was a Vietnamese nationalist as well as a communist, and therefore might not act as a Soviet puppet. He was particularly concerned about the lack of flexibility in the administration's southeast Asian policy. At one juncture of the hearings he urged Dulles to scrutinize the "background" of the Indochinese situation in order to prevent a "frozen" American attitude:

Senator Fulbright: Is it true that at one time Ho had been allied with Chiang Kai-shek? Was he ever in the employ of Chiang Kai-shek?
Secretary Dulles: Well, he was operating in China; as I say, he worked there primarily with Borodin, and there was a period when Chiang Kai-shek was working himself rather closely with the left-wing elements in China, was himself somewhat of a revolutionary figure, and I think it is probably that period you are referring to.
Senator Fulbright: I do not know that it is particularly important, except that some knowledge of the background of these situations sometimes will help to develop a policy. It at least prevents us from freezing our attitude with regard to some of these people, where there is no possibility of any alternative.
Secretary Dulles: Yes.
Senator Fulbright: It might permit us to develop a more flexible policy when we real-

ize that even in Ho Chi Minh's case he from time to time might have been allied with
people on the other side of the fence. I vaguely remember that at one time Ho Chi
Minh was financed by funds which we supplied through [General Joseph] Stilwell.
I have read things about it from time to time, but I believe you will find that he had
been on both sides of the fence.
Secretary Dulles: I expect he has taken money from both sides of the fence.
Senator Fulbright: Yes, but it could be interpreted, and I am not interpreting it that
way because I do not know, but it could be interpreted that he tried to lead the independence movement without Communist help. Having failed, he took Communist
help. That is a possible interpretation, is it not?

Dulles conceded that Fulbright's conjecture was possible. but he contended that Ho's
earlier training and indoctrination in Moscow was much more important than his commitment to the Vietnamese independence movement, which he thought "was always a communist plot." The tentative nature of Fulbright's brief questioning was typical of his statements on Vietnam in the 1950s and early 1960s: he constantly confessed to his scant
knowledge of Vietnamese affairs and displayed a lack of confidence in pressing his suggestions concerning southeast Asia.[48]

Fulbright demonstrated more assertiveness when he asked Dulles to explain why the
British displayed uncertainty regarding America's Far Eastern policy. Dulles replied, "I do
not get terribly worried by those matters... I would not want to make an answer which
would seem to suggest that we concede that the United Kingdom has a veto power over
anything we might want to do." Fulbright opposed a "solitary policy" of acting unilaterally
in the Far East regardless of British actions. He believed that the United States should be
seriously concerned over British misgivings regarding the rigid American hostility to China.
The senator again decried the impact of McCarthyism upon American diplomacy. He
attempted to elicit from Dulles an admission that McCarthy's witch-hunting obstructed the
administration's ability to conduct a constructive foreign policy, but Dulles dismissed this
suggestion. One should emphasize that Fulbright's questioning concerning southeast Asia
and China at the hearing was one very brief episode in the summer of 1954. At the time
Fulbright was preoccupied with his role in the Senate opposition to McCarthy's redbaiting
campaign.[49] He did not fully analyze all the details of the 1954 Geneva conference and
Dulles' policies in Vietnam until much later in his career.

In a series of public statements during the summer of 1954, Fulbright rebuked the
extreme anticommunist attitudes of Senators McCarthy and Knowland for causing
America's European allies to "question our capacity to lead and to manage our own affairs."
Fulbright argued that "McCarthy's effect in Europe was largely responsible for recent foreign
policy differences between the United States and Britain." The issue of Chinese admission
to the United Nations was the specific difference Fulbright discussed; the Eisenhower
administration was adamantly opposed to Peking's entry, while the British and French were
more favorably inclined toward China's admission. Fulbright rejected Knowland's assertion
that the United States "should walk out of the United Nations if Red China were admitted."
The Arkansan also disagreed with the opinion (similar to Knowland's) of Senator Lyndon
Baines Johnson of Texas that most of the American people would support a U.S. withdraw-

al from the U.N. if China became a member. In two brief public statements in July, Fulbright pointedly informed Senator Johnson that to support such a withdrawal "would be evidence of political immaturity." As an alternative to Knowland's belligerent anticommunist attitude, Fulbright endorsed Winston Churchill's plea for "peaceful co-existence" with the communist states. The Arkansan believed that ultimately the only alternative to Churchill's approach was war, and he observed, "We have coexisted in this same world with them ever since there has been a communist group." "I think it is a mistake," Fulbright warned, "for us to give to other nations the impression that we are now making up our minds that at no time in the future will we ever change our relationship with China."[50]

Fulbright's disagreement with Senator Johnson concerning China policy was a brief episode that attracted little attention in 1954. The Arkansan and the Texan usually did not criticize each other and often assisted each other during the 1950s. It was somewhat unusual for Johnson to actively encourage the far-right-wing Republicans as he did in the particular episode regarding China and the U.N. Fulbright's relationship with Johnson would improve after the Texan supported the censure of McCarthy later in 1954. Yet this early disagreement between the two men was interesting. Johnson seemed primarily concerned with demonstrating his zeal in helping to shackle China as a pariah nation. In contrast, Fulbright was concerned with fostering reflections as to whether a frozen anti-Chinese policy would serve any interests of the United States.

Fulbright stopped short of advocating American support for Chinese entry into the U.N. In light of his general reluctance to approve of the bellicose anti-Chinese attitudes that were prevalent in the early 1950s, his refusal to endorse U.S. support for Chinese entry might appear inconsistent; however, the political difficulties of challenging basic Cold War policies in Asia should be considered in order to place Fulbright's position in the proper perspective. During the course of the year 1954, Fulbright had publicly rebuked a series of powerful right-wing political figures. He had criticized Republican Senator John Bricker of Ohio for attempting to pass an amendment denying the President's power to commit the nation with executive agreements and rejecting the broad interpretation of the President's constitutional authority in foreign affairs. When Bricker first introduced his amendment, it enjoyed extensive support in the Senate. Fulbright and other senators successfully opposed the Bricker Amendment as an isolationist effort to obstruct the President's "duty of conducting our foreign relations by and with the advice of the Senate." The Arkansas senator had advanced, of course, a series of controversial foreign policy positions throughout 1954 in addition to his vigorous opposition to the Bricker Amendment. He sharply criticized Vice President Nixon for continuing to blame former Secretary of State Acheson for current problems in Asia. In Fulbright's opinion, Nixon's carping "made it almost impossible to have a bipartisan or non-partisan policy." During a year in which he had publicly challenged Bricker, Knowland, McCarthy, and Nixon, rejected the F.B.I. request for information on a State Department official, and questioned the Eisenhower administration's Asian policies, it was perhaps understandable that Fulbright did not wish to assume the additional burden of advocating American encouragement for Communist China's entry into the U. N. Fulbright was certainly not immune to the anticommunist pressures of the early Cold War, and even his mild and tentative suggestion that the United States should not permanently "freeze" its negative attitude toward China was a controversial statement in 1954.[51]

Fulbright's support for the movement to censure McCarthy represented his crucial endeavor in 1954. Fulbright encouraged the senior senator from Arkansas, John McClellan, to change his position regarding McCarthy. McClellan had a reputation as a staunch anti-communist and was the ranking minority member of the Permanent Investigations sub-committee. In earlier years he had usually not opposed McCarthy. By 1954, McClellan increasingly tended to believe that no American institution, including the Senate and the U.S. Army, was safe from McCarthy's attacks. McClellan exerted a crucial influence in assuring that the Army-McCarthy hearings were televised, so that the American people could witness firsthand McCarthy's demagogical methods. The Army hearings from April to June marked the turning point in McCarthy's career. Many leaders of the Republican Party had tolerated and encouraged the McCarthyites when they attributed the defeat of Chiang Kai-shek to treason within the Truman administration and waved spurious lists of communists in a Democratic State Department. Fulbright wrote in 1972 that, in retrospect, the Republican electoral defeat in 1948 was probably a misfortune for the country. In their desperate search for a winning political issue the Republicans seized upon the threat of foreign and domestic communism with a ferocity born of having been denied the Presidency for the fifth successive campaign. Thus McCarthy's slander concerning "twenty years of treason" under Democratic Presidents was an immensely powerful political weapon for the Republicans during the early 1950s. But in the 1954 hearings, McCarthy began to destroy himself by his attacks upon a Republican State Department and the U.S. Army. The Wisconsin senator probably sealed his political doom by making these charges and merci-lessly badgering witnesses before the national television cameras at the Army-McCarthy hearings. The most memorable moment of the hearings came when Joseph N. Welch, a mild-mannered lawyer from Boston, stood up against McCarthy for viciously attacking the honor of Welch's young legal assistant: "Until this moment, senator, I think I never really gauged your cruelty or your recklessness...Let us not assassinate this lad further, senator. You've done enough. Have you no sense of decency, sir, at long last? Have you left no sense of decency?"[52]

Fulbright rapidly capitalized on the public's revulsion against McCarthy during the hearings. In the summer of 1954, he persuaded the Republican Senator Ralph Flanders of Vermont to introduce a censure resolution against McCarthy, thereby emphasizing its bipar-tisan nature. Republican Senator John Sherman Cooper of Kentucky also provided impor-tant assistance to the censure movement. The most important of the 33 counts against McCarthy charged that he had publicly incited government employees to violate the law and send him classified information regarding national security, he had made unwarranted attacks upon General George Marshall, he had injured the morale of the Army, and he had brought disrepute upon the Senate. Flanders and Fulbright recommended a condemnation of McCarthy for his contempt of the "Senate, truth, and people." The Senate Select sub-committee on the censure deleted "truth" and "people" from the document in order to assure its passage. The majority of McCarthy's most ardent opponents, including Fulbright, Flanders, and Wayne Morse, did not gain positions on the Select subcommittee. The con-servative Senator Arthur Watkins of Utah headed the subcommittee. The final version of the resolution simply censured McCarthy for his contempt of the Senate.[53]

McCarthy condemned the censure resolution leaders for presenting "scurrilous, false charges" on the Senate floor. He bellowed that "Flanders, Cooper, Lehman, Morse, Monroney, Hennings, and 'Halfbright'" should testify under oath concerning their charges against him. "I assure the American people," McCarthy charged, "that the senators who have made the charges will either indict themselves for perjury or will prove what consummate liars they are, by showing the difference between their statements on the floor of the Senate and their testimony in the hearing." Shortly after the Wisconsin senator finished his remarks, Fulbright took the Senate floor to answer McCarthy's diatribes:

> Mr. President, we have already had a very slight example of what we can expect. I think the junior senator from Wisconsin is a great genius. He has the most extraordinary talent for disrupting and causing confusion in any orderly process of any body of men that I have ever seen.... I am interested in that kind of character as a psychological study. But I think it is doing incalculable harm to the work of the Senate. I know it has already done tremendous harm to the relations of the United States with all the rest of the world, because the people of the other countries think we have lost our minds if we are willing to follow such a leader.[54]

During the censure debate Fulbright received an avalanche of abusive mail from McCarthy's admirers. The tremendous volume and the obscenity of the letters so appalled Fulbright that he inserted a number of them into the *Congressional Record* to publicize the irrationality of "McCarthyism." McCarthy, he asserted, "has so preyed upon the fears and hatred of uninformed and credulous people that he has started a prairie fire, which neither he nor anyone else may be able to control." *Time* magazine observed that all public men occasionally received offensive letters, but conceded that Fulbright "had a point to make last week about the character of what has come to be known as McCarthyism." Fulbright read a few of the less abusive McCarthyite letters to the Senate: "You refused to vote one dollar to the McCarthy committee. A fine dirty red rat are you... Who were the birds that voted not to allow Senator McCarthy time off to recover from his illness? I'll tell you: it was red-loving Fulbright and the rotten Jew, Herbert Lehman." Another letter denounced Fulbright as a "dirty, low-down, evil-minded traitor," while yet another urged the Arkansan to "do the country a big favor and drop dead." In Fulbright's view, the thousands of letters he had received revealed "a great sickness among our people, and that sickness has been greatly enhanced and increased during the course of the past year." He hoped that the censure of McCarthy would help to repudiate "the reckless incitement of the hatreds and fears of people who are suffering from a lack of information or a lack of understanding."[55]

The anti-McCarthy movement inexorably gained strength in late 1954; Lyndon Johnson belatedly endorsed the censure, thus ensuring widespread Democratic support for the resolution. Nevertheless, 22 Senators voted against the censure, with John F. Kennedy of Massachusetts (Kennedy was in the hospital at the time) and several others abstaining. In the early 1950s Kennedy privately explained his silence on McCarthyism to Arthur Schlesinger, Jr.: "Half my voters in Massachusetts look on McCarthy as a hero." Despite the many frustrations Fulbright encountered during the censure struggle, the 67-22 vote against McCarthy in December encouraged the Arkansan. After the Senate action, McCarthy possessed no power to challenge the President or any other citizen. The political leadership of the United States had officially disassociated itself from the Wisconsin demagogue. Flanders later stated, "I could not have accomplished censure" without Fulbright's assistance. Well before the final vote in December, William Benton had congratulated Fulbright on his leadership in the censure movement. He asserted not only that Fulbright's opposition to McCarthy would be "vindicated," but that the Arkansan had now established himself "to a far greater degree as one of the great leaders of the Democratic Party."[56]

Fulbright had displayed adroit manuevering in guiding the censure resolution through the Senate, and he had delivered many eloquent orations in pleading with his colleagues to revive the spirit of free discussion. But the shrewd parliamentary tactics and the eloquence of the censure leaders did not precipitate the fall of Joe McCarthy. In 1954, McCarthy wrought his own destruction because of his political ineptitude and his profound contempt for human dignity. The nation's abhorrence of McCarthy's performance at the Army hearings focused upon his abrasive demeanor, his boorish methods of interrupting and browbeating witnesses, and the pathetic appearance of his victims. To a certain extent, the precipitous decline in McCarthy's prestige and power after 1954 signified a revulsion against his personality rather than a definite repudiation of the blind and counterproductive hostility to communism that he embodied.

The virulent anticommunism of the early 1950s frequently echoed in the positions of some Americans in later years. The Republican nominee for President in 1964, Barry Goldwater, publicly accepted MacArthur's philosophy of war, which held that once hostilities had begun the civilian authorities could place no restraints on the use of force until a total victory had been achieved. Clearly there is an affinity between MacArthur, who declared that his proposal involving the possible starvation of 15 million Chinese would strengthen the "moral" fiber of the United States, and the American officer who explained during the Vietnam War that the Vietnamese town of Ben Tre had been destroyed "in order to save it" [from the communists].[57] At the Vietnam hearings of 1966, Dean Rusk justified the bombings of North Vietnam with a rationale similar to MacArthur's arguments for the proposed air raids against China in 1951. And the anticommunist crusaders' 1951 vision of America as the omnipotent anticommunist gendarme, unilaterally exorcising all the communist devils from Asia, was to find its most concrete and powerful expression in Lyndon Johnson's 1966 Asian Doctrine, which Fulbright described as an effort to "make the United States the policeman and provider for all non-communist Asia."[58]

The extreme anticommunism of the McCarthy era inflicted almost irreparable damage upon many Americans' ability to think rationally and objectively about Asian communist insurgent movements throughout the 1950s and early 1960s. The McCarthyite denial of the legitimacy of the Chinese revolution crippled the American capacity to recognize the genuine patriotism and vigor of Asia's incipient nationalism. McCarthyism disseminated the belief in a monolithic communist conspiracy against democracy, while it inculcated in many politicians fear of the "soft on communism" charge. In 1963, President John F. Kennedy privately remarked that he planned to order a military withdrawal from Vietnam, but "I can't do it until 1965—after I'm reelected. In 1965, I'll be damned everywhere as a Communist appeaser. But I don't care. If I tried to pull out completely now, we would have another Joe McCarthy red scare on our hands, but I can do it after I'm re-elected." Shortly after he became president, Lyndon Johnson declared, "I am not going to be the President who saw southeast Asia go the way China went." In addition to his belief in the insatiably aggressive nature of communism, Johnson maintained that a failure to check the expansion of communism in Vietnam would precipitate a debate over "who lost Vietnam" that would have exceeded in vituperation the controversy over the Chinese revolution.[59]

McCarthy, Nixon, McCarran, and other red-baiters were primarily responsible for inflaming the extreme anticommunist sentiments of the early Cold War; but the Truman administration bore part of the responsibility, for the Truman Doctrine encouraged many Americans to envisage international relations as an arena of universal conflict between western democracy and Moscow's totalitarianism. The years roughly from 1946 to 1950 represented the period of Fulbright's career during which he adhered to a basic anticommunist position that did not differ markedly from most other leaders of the time. But even in that era he was not an extremist. As early as 1949 and 1950 he had vigorously defended the administration against the McCarthyite charges that Truman had "lost" China to communism. In the early years of the Cold War and throughout his career he believed that the Truman Doctrine's application to Asia was vastly more destructive than its application to Europe. A quarter of a century after the Truman Doctrine speech, Fulbright argued in his book *The Crippled Giant* that the specific decision to aid Greece and Turkey was logical; it was the universalism of the Doctrine that he opposed: "The Truman Doctrine, which made limited sense for a limited time in a particular place, has led us in its universalized form to disaster in Southeast Asia and demoralization at home." John Foster Dulles and Dean Rusk would interpret the Doctrine as the charter for the incessant military interventions and global ideological warfare of the next two decades.[60]

Fulbright had shared many of the Cold War assumptions in the late 1940s and early 1950s, as he demonstrated with his denunciations of Soviet eastern European policies and the Soviet rejections of the Baruch Plan and Marshall Plan. Yet he had opposed the red-baiting of the McCarthyites and received a series of accolades from Benton, Lehman, Flanders, and others for his role in the anti-McCarthy movement. By 1954 he was beginning to advance beyond criticisms of McCarthy's methods to reject the Cold War myth that all Third World communists acted as puppets of Moscow. There was obviously a divergence between some of Fulbright's anticommunist statements during the early Cold War and his dissenting views in later years. Some analysts might consider this disparity as inconsistency on Fulbright's part, but the senator's increasing tendency to question American foreign policy might more accurately be considered evidence of flexibility. During the early 1950s he witnessed the destructive effects of extreme anticommunism and was flexible enough to begin changing his position. He was becoming increasingly skeptical of American efforts to fashion anticommunist allies out of politically unstable, underdeveloped Asian nations that did not possess the skilled manpower and industrialized bases that had enabled the western European nations to successfully utilize America's Marshall Plan aid. Fulbright emerged from the McCarthy era with a determination to repudiate the extremism that had ravaged the nation's intellectual environment as well as its foreign policy. The senator was certainly not alone in his nascent role as a dissenter; a minority of politicians and foreign policy analysts including Herbert Lehman, Wayne Morse, and John Kenneth Galbraith resisted the anticommunist hysteria of the 1950s. The record of Fulbright's opposition to McCarthyism confirmed William Benton's prediction that dissent against extremism would ultimately strengthen a senator's prestige. His experience in challenging McCarthy reinforced the Arkansan's conviction that in foreign policy, a politician should not merely react to his constituents' whims, but that he held a responsibility to influence and educate public opinion. In the late 1950s and 1960s, he displayed a burgeoning inclination to return to his earlier critiques of excessive anticommunism within the United States, and eventually led a powerful challenge to the Cold Warrior mythology that dominated America's postwar diplomacy.[61]

II. FROM JOHN FOSTER DULLES
TO THE BAY OF PIGS

A basic corollary of the anticommunist ideology centered upon the belief that Congress' role in foreign policy was restricted to helping create a national consensus in support of the President in order to present an image of unity to international communism. Through a series of what were represented by the postwar administrations as national emergencies arising from allegedly imminent threats of communist aggression, the Congress became habituated to acquiescing to the presidential will, usually after only the most perfunctory debates.[1] Fulbright stated in 1972 that in the period from Truman's waging of the Korean conflict without a Congressional declaration of war to the invasion of Cambodia in 1970, the executive virtually usurped the war and treaty powers of Congress and reduced the "advise and consent" function of the Senate to the privilege of attending ceremonial briefings about decisions that had already been made.[2]

The notion that Congress should not challenge the President's judgment in an emergency and the tendency of American political leaders to confuse nationalism and communism in the Third World seem to have been the determining characteristics of American policy in the Middle East crisis of the mid-1950s, leading to the Eisenhower Doctrine of 1957. President Eisenhower presented this Doctrine (as it came to be known) to Congress in January 1957, claiming that Russia had "long sought to dominate the Middle East."[3] If Congress accepted Eisenhower's (or Dulles') plan, it would be authorizing the President to extend economic and military aid to any Middle Eastern country re-questing help "against overt armed aggression from any nation controlled by international communism."[4] Fulbright opposed the Eisenhower Doctrine, arguing that it was an attempt to eliminate debate through an emotional appeal to patriotism and to stampede Congress into giving the President an unrestricted grant of power over the Armed Forces and American economic resources.[5] Senate Majority Leader Lyndon Johnson disagreed with Fulbright, concluding that Congressional disunity would create an impression of weakness around the world and might inspire further communist adventurism.[6] Johnson controlled enough votes to frustrate Fulbright's opposition and save Dulles' policy.[7]

Beginning in January 1957 Fulbright directed an inquiry by a Senate subcommittee into American diplomacy in the Middle East. The study was cancelled in July 1957 when Fulbright decided that the limitations upon research imposed by the State Department's secrecy requirements had rendered it almost impossible to arrive at a definitive assessment of all the intricate details of the recent Middle Eastern policies.[8] Fulbright delivered a speech to the Senate in August in which he summarized the incomplete results of the subcommittee's seven-month investigation.

He began his address by discussing the $54.6 million grant to Egypt that had been proposed in December 1955 to help finance the initial stages of construction of the Aswan Dam.[9] In his view, the United States had offered this contribution to the project because a Nile River development program was vital to the future of the Egyptian economy, and economic instability would lead to social and political unrest in Egypt and thus endanger the unstable peace in the Middle East.[10] When the administration withdrew its offer in July 1956, it indefinitely postponed "the day when the Egyptian people might seek to build a democratic government upon a solid economic base."[11] The administration's contention that Egypt's ability to devote adequate economic resources to the project had deteriorated between December 1955 and July 1956 was not true, Fulbright concluded. There was no radical worsening in Egypt's economic condition in 1956, since the primary drain on Egypt's resources—the mortgaging of part of her cotton crop in exchange for communist arms—had occurred prior to the U.S. offer.[12]

Fulbright did not elaborate upon the specifics of the meeting between Egyptian Ambassador Ahmed Hussein and Dulles at which the American aid proposal was withdrawn. The Secretary of State had already been disturbed by Egyptian leader Gamal Abdel Nasser's diplomatic recognition of mainland China in the spring of 1956. Hussein pleaded with Dulles at their meeting not to retract the American assistance plan for the Aswan project, because he said the Egyptians had "the Russian offer to finance the dam right here in my pocket."[13] From Dulles' Manichean world view, Hussein's plea was apparently seen as an invitation to the capitalist forces of light to engage in a bidding contest with the communist forces of darkness, and the American offer was peremptorily withdrawn.[14] Fulbright deduced from the Aswan papers that Dulles had considered President Nasser to be a Soviet puppet, despite the judgment of able State Department career officials that Nasser was fully aware of the dangers of aligning too closely with the Soviet Union.[15] In Fulbright's view, Dulles had confused communism with Egyptian neutralism and nationalism, which were forces that could promote political freedom and halt the expansion of communist influence in the Middle East.[16]

In his August 1957 speech Fulbright described the ruinous concatenation of events set in motion by Dulles' decision not to grant the funds for the Aswan project. The withdrawal had been the direct cause of Nasser's nationalization of the Suez Canal, which had led to the Israeli-British-French attack on Egypt, severe oil shortages and economic dislocations in Europe and the United States, and serious damage to relations within NATO when America cooperated with the U.S.S.R. in forcing the British and French to accept a cease-fire in November, 1956 and to evacuate the Canal area.[17] Moreover, the senator argued that if the Western powers had not been divided over the Suez crisis, they might have been able to use diplomatic pressure to at least mitigate the severity of the Soviet repression of the Hungarian revolutionaries after their abortive revolt against the Russians in October 1956.[18] As far as the costs of the administration's blunder were concerned, Fulbright noted that the expenditures authorized by the ultimate American response to the chaotic Middle Eastern situation, the Eisenhower Doctrine, had already reached a figure ($174 million by the summer of 1957) over three times greater than the original contribution for the construction of the dam would have been.[19]

Fulbright ended his report to the Senate on the subcommittee's findings by criticizing the administration's failure to appreciate the tremendous emotional significance the entire Arab world attached to American assistance for the Aswan project as a symbol of America's "willingness to help them help themselves."[20] Dulles' rash withdrawal had immeasurably strengthened the Soviet propaganda that the United States was interested in assisting the economic development of other nations only insofar as its aid could place the recipient nation under U. S. political bondage.[21] In so doing, Fulbright concluded Dulles had greatly facilitated the consolidation of Soviet influence in the Middle East.[22]

Fulbright prepared a thorough indictment of the Eisenhower administration's foreign policy in the summer of 1958. He challenged Dulles' doctrine of mutual deterrence in a Senate speech in June. This doctrine held that since the United States would never start World War III, peace could be assured if the American capacity to carry out a massive nuclear retaliation against communist aggression were maintained.[23] Fulbright considered this doctrine "irrational because of the very degree of rationality it requires" in assuming that the supreme political authorities of the two superpowers, the hundreds of direct custodians of the nuclear weapons systems in both nations, and the allies of the superpowers could always be expected to act upon the basis of reason and attempt to prevent "the war of the millennium."[24] Rather than continue an arms race that no one could win, he suggested that the United States should re-evalute its preoccupations concerning military assistance programs and its vast network of overseas military bases. Perhaps some of the 1,400 American overseas bases (many within short range of the Soviet Union) could be traded for armaments control agreements.[25] The Soviet anxiety over these bases was not unreasonable; Fulbright confessed that "I might find myself plagued by an obsession against Soviet bases if their ballistic- launching facilities were in the Caribbean or Mexico."[26]

In fairness to the Eisenhower administration, the logic of Fulbright and his intellectual allies was at least considered in the highest councils of the executive branch. Secretary of State Dulles had worried constantly—as did all educated people of the era—about the danger of a nuclear exchange, and his views on the subject may have progressed late in his life. In a highly secret memorandum that was unknown to the American public in the 1950s and only became declassified decades later, Dulles wrote that "Atomic power was too vast a power to be left for the military use of any one country." Therefore, the Secretary of State proposed to the President the idea of universalizing "the capacity of atomic thermonuclear weapons to deter aggression" by transferring control of nuclear forces to "a vetoless Security Council."[26a] Of course, the administration did not decide upon this course of action, and the Eisenhower Cold War military policies persisted.

Fulbright emphasized the injurious consequences of America's foreign military assistance program in a Senate speech of August 1958. The speech was given shortly after Eisenhower had, in effect, honored the principle of his Doctrine by sending the Marines to Lebanon to counter an alleged threat of communist subversion.[27] Fulbright did not attack Eisenhower's decision at the time, but he felt that the current troubles in the Middle East were symptomatic of a fundamental flaw in American diplomacy.[28] "We have," he believed, "on a grandiose scale provided peoples of the underdeveloped nations with the weapons of destructive warfare, and have been miserly in providing them weapons to wage war on their own poverty, economic ills and internal weaknesses."[29] Governments that parroted an anticommunist line were lavishly rewarded, primarily with military aid, while governments that persisted in following a neutral course were aided reluctantly or not at all.[30]

Fulbright proceeded to demolish Dulles' argument that armaments proliferation did not endanger international peace and security since all weapons destined for other countries were accompanied by specific stipulations against their aggressive use.[31] American military equipment furnished to the Chinese Nationalists to fight Mao's communists had eventually been used to kill Americans in Korea.[32] And recently the pro-Western regime in Iraq had been overthrown by the Iraqi army, which had received its weapons from the West.[33] Dulles' "specific stipulations" were clearly meaningless.

In one of the most frequently quoted passages in all of Fulbright's writings, the senator advanced the central point of his August 1958 speech: "If there is a single factor which more than any other explains the predicament in which we now find ourselves, it is our readiness to use the spectre of Soviet communism as a cloak for the failure of our own leadership."[34] Vice President Nixon had been spat upon and stoned during his Latin American tour, but this was rationalized by saying that only a handful of communists had been responsible.[35] If violence erupted or a pro-Western government fell in any corner of the globe, the comforting American formula for the evasion of reality was immediately applied: it was simply more of the Soviet Union's insidious machinations.[36]

Fulbright urged the Senate to renounce the belief that the Soviet Union was the sole source of America's troubles.[37] In the fear of the deviltry of communism, America had "cast itself indiscriminately in the role of the defender of the status quo throughout the world."[38] This fearful attachment to the status quo ultimately derived from the popular misconception that the Chinese Nationalists had been defeated because the United States had not supplied them with sufficient military aid.[39] Fulbright concluded that the opposite was true, that America had become too deeply involved with a corrupt and reactionary government that never could have inspired the loyalty of the Chinese people.[40] "Those tragic events in China seem to have set a rigid pattern which has been followed almost unbrokenly ever since."[41] Unless American policy were drastically revised to concentrate foreign aid in the economic rather than the military sphere and to avoid identifying America with the status quo in a revolutionary epoch, Fulbright predicted that the errors in American diplomacy of the 1950s would become the disasters of future years.[42]

Fulbright's sharp criticisms of Dulles in the late 1950s attracted substantial attention in the media. James Reston observed in the *New York Times* that "these two highly intelligent men have established a relationship roughly equivalent to the chemical reaction of dogs and cats. When Mr. Dulles talks, Mr. Fulbright growls, and when the senator talks, the Secretary arches his back." William Hale described Fulbright as "Dulles' severest critic on the Hill and today his most implacable foe." Although some reporters unfortunately dwelled on the personal clash between the senator and the Secretary of State, the differences between their basic approaches regarding foreign policy were substantial. Fulbright sought to base policy upon a sober, realistic assessment of American vital national interests. In contrast, Dulles' approach embodied an evangelical, crusading spirit that did not serve America's long-term interests, as Fulbright had eloquently contended in his memorable Senate speeches in the late 1950s.[42a]

One of the Eisenhower administration's most costly mistakes was its inept performance during the U-2 crisis. Fulbright conducted a Foreign Relations Committee investigation in the summer of 1960 into the flight of the U-2 that was shot down over Russia on May 1, 1960. As had been the case after the Suez crisis, Fulbright encountered difficulties in gaining access to all the facts regarding the flight, but presented the Committee's report along with his personal views on the controversy in a Senate speech of June, 1960.[43] The administration claimed that the May 1 flight had been seeking information that would never again have been available.[44] Since the Senate was not told, "even under conditions of the utmost secrecy," what that information was, Fulbright described the administration's justification as a "cover story" for its incompetent handling of the episode.[45] Several Republican senators accused Fulbright of giving aid and comfort to the enemy after his June speech, although at least one subsequent monograph (*The U-2 Affair*, by David Wise and Thomas Ross) vindicated his position.[46] Fulbright believed that Eisenhower's reaction to the U-2 flight's failure was essentially a reversion to the rigid anticommunism of the Dulles, who had died in 1959. The traditional impersonal diplomatic forms were abruptly cast aside in dealing with the Soviets in the aftermath of the U-2 incident. It was unfortunate that Eisenhower had taken personal responsibility for a covert intelligence operation, for one of the reasons for the CIA's existence was to serve as a "whipping boy" in such incidents.[47] Fulbright criticized the alibi for the flight (NASA's statement that it had been a weather plane that strayed off course) as having made the United States appear foolish when the Russians produced the U-2's surveillance equipment and the pilot, Francis Gary Powers, who admitted that he was on an espionage mission.[48] The administration had inexcusably assumed the self-righteous attitude that the Soviet Union should be blamed for the U-2 flights, because if the Soviets had not been so secretive and threatened to "bury us" with nuclear missiles, America would not have been forced to spy on them.[49]

The disastrous timing of the U-2 debacle inflicted grave damage upon Soviet-American relations for the remainder of the period Khrushchev was in power (until 1964). Fulbright was deeply disturbed that in the spring of 1960 the apparent relaxation of Soviet-American tensions of 1959 had already vanished. At the September, 1959 Camp David meeting, Eisenhower and Khrushchev had jointly declared a willingness to negotiate existing disputes.[50] Khrushchev briefly visited the Senate Foreign Relations Committee shortly before the Camp David conference and was cordially received by Fulbright, who became chairman of the Committee in 1959.[51] On that occasion Khrushchev had vehemently denied that his "We will bury you" slogan was a threat of nuclear devastation, saying that he had been referring to economic competition.[52]

At a Foreign Relations Committee coffee in Khrushchev's honor, the Russian leader grandly autographed the place cards of all the senators, including an absent junior Committee member, John F. Kennedy. Fulbright mailed Senator Kennedy his autographed card, jovially remarking, "Dear Jack: Maybe this will enable you to get out of jail when the revolution comes." (The Foreign Relations Committee in 1959 was far less active than it would become several years later, and one of the least active members in the Committee's affairs was Kennedy, who was vigorously campaigning for the Presidency and rarely attended Committee meetings. The Arkansan would have preferred that Kennedy's attendance had been better, and the Fulbright-Kennedy relationship at that time was not close.) The pleasant atmosphere of Khrushchev's 1959 visit had not been followed by any major improvements in Soviet-American relations, and Russian and American officials had maintained conflicting positions on Berlin and most other issues on the eve of the scheduled conference at Paris in May 1960. The U-2 incident had occurred two weeks before the Paris summit meeting, at a time when Khrushchev was trying to convince the ultra-conservatives in the Kremlin that all Americans were not arrogant imperialists and that Eisenhower was a reasonable man.[53] Charles E. Bohlen, an adviser to Eisenhower at the Paris summit, viewed the "plane incident" as largely responsible for Khrushchev's hostility at Paris.[54] Fulbright carried this critique even further, stating that the administration's ineptitude had "forced Khrushchev to wreck the Paris conference."[55]

The Bay of Pigs

Undaunted by the failure of its aerial espionage over Russia, the CIA began plotting during the final months of the Eisenhower administration to overthrow Fidel Castro's regime in Cuba. Fulbright had become increasingly concerned about newspaper stories predicting an invasion. Long before the debate over Cuba in early 1961, Fulbright had been a staunch believer in the principle of nonintervention. In July 1959 he advised a constituent that while he agreed that adequate and prompt compensation for the expropriated property in Cuba should be provided to American nationals, he warned: "What particularly troubles me is how we can effectively insist on this if the Cuban government proves obdurate. I think any kind of intervention in the manner of Teddy Roosevelt would only be self-defeating, not only in Cuba, but elsewhere in the hemisphere."[55a] In early 1961, the President was planning to spend Easter weekend in Palm Beach and invited the senator to travel on the plane with him to Florida. On the trip Fulbright warned the President that the invasion "would be a great mistake." Fulbright gave to Kennedy a memorandum arguing against an invasion of Cuba. Fulbright contended that the idea represented by Castroism, the program of radical social reform with anti-Yanqui overtones, could not be destroyed by overthrowing Fidel Castro.[56] If the CIA ousted Castro behind a facade of American-trained and equipped Cuban exiles, the United States would be denounced as an imperialist power throughout Latin America.[57] A successful invasion would burden America with the costs of rehabilitating a war-ravaged nation in an advanced state of political and economic disorder.[58] If the exiles unexpectedly encountered formidable resistance, the United States could not conceal its role in the enterprise by refraining from direct military involvement, for the fact that the CIA had been training the exiles in Guatemala had been such a poorly kept secret that the press had almost daily carried detailed accounts of the leaders, equipment, and possible strategy that would be used in the invasion.[59] An American intervention would nullify "the work of 30 years in trying to live down earlier interventions," the senator warned.[60]

Fulbright concluded that for the administration to provide even clandestine support for the CIA's plot would be "of a piece with the hypocrisy and cynicism for which the United States is constantly denouncing the Soviet Union in the United Nations."[61] Moreover, it would be an entirely unnecessary action, since Castro's regime was not a grave threat to the military security or the vital national interests of America unless the

Soviets attempted to install nuclear weapons in Cuba.[62] Removal of Castro would not exclude communist agitation from the Western Hemisphere as long as the Soviets retained their embassies in Mexico, Montevideo, and elsewhere, and, more importantly, as long as the social and economic causes of Latin American political unrest remained.[63] Fulbright averred that it should always be remembered that Castro was "a thorn in the flesh, but not a dagger in the heart."[64]

President Kennedy received the Cuban memorandum in late March 1961. The President and Fulbright flew back to Washington together on April 4, and the President invited the senator to attend a meeting at the State Department that turned out to be the last major policy review before the Bay of Pigs invasion, although the President had mentioned it rather casually to him. Thus the importance of the meeting was unknown to Fulbright until he actually entered the room and found virtually all the major administration officials present. Secretary of State Dean Rusk, Secretary of Defense Robert S. McNamara, three members of the Joint Chiefs of Staff, CIA Director Allen Dulles, State Department Latin American expert Thomas Mann, and most of the other high-level advisers of the administration were present at the April 4 strategy session.[65] The historian William A. Williams (whose views differed from those of Fulbright on many issues) has written that Fulbright displayed "magnificent personal and political courage" at that meeting.[66] The Arkansan elaborated upon the basic points of his memorandum on April 4: that if the invasion succeeded, a Cuba that was an American puppet, an American Hungary, would be a liability to the United States both financially and in the forum of world opinion.[67] The CIA's proposal would violate the principle of nonintervention enshrined in the Charter of the Organization of American States, "the keystone of all Latin American policies toward the U.S."[68] Fulbright was also not convinced that the conquest of Cuba would be such a simple undertaking from the military standpoint, rejecting Dulles' claim that the Cuban people were able and willing to assist any invasion from the outside.[69] No one else openly opposed Dulles' plan at the April 4 meeting.[70]

It required objectivity, but not any great prescience on Fulbright's part to recognize that Dulles' vision of a massive internal revolt against Castro was erroneous, given the overwhelming evidence of Castro's popularity in the early period of his power. One of the book's authors, James O. Powell, visited Cuba before, during and after the revolution; as an editor of the *Tampa Tribune*, Powell visited Cuba at the time of Castro's triumphant acquisition of power. Witnessing those events, the American editor was struck by the revolutionary's passionate delivery of one of his hours-long orations to a jubilant throng in downtown Havana in 1959. What was equally striking was observation of the kangaroo trial of Major Sosa Blanco, a former leader of the Batista regime who was convicted in proceedings that made a mockery of Western principles of justice. The Florida journalist's conclusions were abundantly confirmed by other objective observers who were present in Cuba at the time. Clearly, it should have been obvious at that early date that Castro was no defender of democracy and freedom; but it was just as obvious that after decades of oppression under the decadent, corrupt Batista, the charismatic revolutionary held emotional sway over the masses of Cubans.

Allen Dulles contended at the administration's strategy meeting that if America did not execute the Cuban invasion plan the administration would create an impression of being "soft on communism," and the anticommunist movement in Latin America would wither.[71] According to Dulles, the Cuban exiles would have adequate air support, and even if they were unable to immediately capture Havana they could easily escape into the Escambray Mountains and continue fighting as guerrillas.[72] The fiasco at the Bay of Pigs two weeks later proved all of Dulles' arguments to have been totally inaccurate. Castro quickly gained control of the air, and the CIA had deliberately refrained from informing the exiles that dispersing into the mountains was an alternative strategy. It would have been exceedingly unlikely that the exiles could have initiated guerrilla warfare, for they had been trained as conventional Army units using World War II infantry tactics.[73] Moreover, the "escape hatch" into the mountains lay across 80 miles of virtually impassable swamps and jungles. Attorney General Robert F. Kennedy and other administration figures analyzed the Bay of Pigs shortly after the debacle occurred. Kennedy contended that the Joint Chiefs of Staff had been negligent in its study of the situation and that the chance of the exiles becoming guerrillas "was practically nil." The Chiefs, Kennedy wrote in a June 1, 1961 memorandum, "didn't make any study whether this country was proper guerrilla country. It was proper guerrilla country, but it was guerrilla country between 1890 and 1900. Now, with helicopters, it is no longer guerrilla country and there was no way these men fighting in here in this swampy area could possibly supply themselves." The Attorney General emphasized the importance of the CIA's distorted advice to the President that anti-Castro uprisings in support of the exiles' landings would erupt. But there was no internal revolt against Castro at the time of the Bay of Pigs.[74]

The false allegations presented by the CIA at the final strategy review before the Bay of Pigs partially explains the near unanimity with which administration officials supported the plan. The Kennedys, for obvious reasons, tended to place the major share of the blame for the Bay of Pigs upon the CIA and the military (in their private analyses; in public the President accepted full responsibility); but the egregious advice of Dulles and his allies was not the only reason for the administration's decision. The President also had to consider the political dangers that would have been involved if he had disbanded his predecessor's Cuban liberation phalanx in the face of the "experts'" advice that the project would be a triumph; Robert Kennedy claimed that "If he hadn't gone ahead with it, everybody would have said it showed he had no courage because... it was Eisenhower's plan, Eisenhower's people all said it would succeed, and you turned it down."[75] To some extent the explanation for the President's decision may lie in the precedent set by the events in Guatemala in 1954, when the CIA engineered the overthrow of a leftist government with the approbation of President Eisenhower.[76] The Guatemalan coup was accomplished so easily that it became the model for the Bay of Pigs.[77] But perhaps the reality that John F. Kennedy and the intelligent group of men gathered in the State Department that April evening in 1961 could have expected a tiny band of 1,500 men to wage a powerful assault on a nation of seven million inhabitants can best be explained by Fulbright's belief that an ideological obsession concerning communism beclouded the judgment of American political leaders in the postwar period. The administration's reasoning seems to have been subtly conditioned by a basic precept of the Truman Doctrine. Administration officials failed to meticulously analyze the facts of the internal situation in Cuba, for communist governments were by the Doctrine's definition imposed upon the oppressed majority by the ruthless communist minority. Thus, because of the opinions of a few over-emotional and highly imaginative Cuban dissidents, the administration envisaged a massive sympathy uprising sweeping the emigres to power in Cuba, when the evidence had clearly indicated that Castro was strengthening and consolidating his dictatorial control over the island in 1960-1961.[78]

On April 19, Kennedy resisted Vice President Lyndon Johnson's pressure to "will the means to victory" by ordering air strikes by American planes against Cuba.[79] Apparently this was the only time during the crisis that Kennedy followed the advice of Fulbright's Cuban memorandum. Castro had moved 50 anti-aircraft guns to the area shortly after the invasion began. Even if the proposed American air strikes had been tactically successful in spite of Castro's anti-aircraft arsenal, the CIA Cubans would still have been stranded on the beachhead, surrounded by a vengeful enemy army 200 times its size.[80] Kennedy's wise decision in avoiding direct U.S. military participation obviously does not alter the reality that the Bay of Pigs invasion was a disaster. At a meeting with several Cabinet members, generals, and other major administration officials and Congressional leaders on April 19, Kennedy turned to Fulbright and said grimly but loudly enough for those present to hear, "Well, you're the only one who can say I told you so."[81]

Although McNamara had supported the Bay of Pigs invasion at the final strategy session, in his memoirs in 1995 the former Secretary of Defense was deeply appreciative of Fulbright's wise dissent and apologetic about his own blindness in not seeing the futility of the adventure at the time. The President "called his advisers—perhaps twenty of us in all—to a meeting at the State Department and asked what to do," McNamara wrote, and then Kennedy "went around the table and asked each person's opinion. With one exception—Sen. J. William Fulbright (D-Ark.), who dissented vigorously—everyone in the room supported the action." McNamara's post-mortem analysis of the glaring flaws in the plan read as if it could have been written by Fulbright 34 years earlier. In his apology, the former Secretary of Defense admitted that he had entered the Pentagon with a limited grasp of military affairs, and he tended to be deferential to the CIA and the Joint Chiefs, at one point passing along to the President "without comment, an ambiguous assessment by the Joint Chiefs that the invasion would probably contribute to Castro's overthrow even if it did not succeed right away... The truth is I did not understand the plan very well and did not know the facts. I had let myself become a passive bystander."[81a]

After the debacle in Cuba, McNamara went to the Oval Office and told the President that before the decision to launch the invasion was made, "I was in a room where, with one exception [Fulbright], all of your advisers—including me—recommended you proceed. I am fully prepared to go on TV and say so." Kennedy graciously declined McNamara's offer, accepting responsibility for the blunder and declining to blame McNamara, Eisenhower, or anyone else.[81b]

Kennedy's aides recalled the administration's blunder with deep regret and great appreciation for Fulbright. Before he made the decision, Kennedy had harbored doubts about the plan and wondered if Fulbright might be correct. Theodore Sorenson, special counsel to the late President, later wrote that Kennedy "should have paid more attention to his own politically sound instincts and to the politically knowledgeable men who did voice objections directly—such as Fulbright and Schlesinger—on matters of Cuban and Latin American politics and the composition of a future Cuban government, instead of following only the advice of Latin American experts Adolf Berle, Jr. and Thomas Mann."[81c] Arthur Schlesinger, a White House aide, praised Fulbright's dissent at the final policy review meeting: "He gave a brave, old-fashioned American speech, honorable, sensible and strong; and he left everyone in the room, except me and perhaps the President, wholly unmoved."[81d]

A few days later, Fulbright appeared on "Meet the Press," but he was careful to avoid criticizing Kennedy and declined to indicate whether he had advised Kennedy not to order the Bay of Pigs invasion. On the news program, he was sharply critical of American intervention in Laos, where the pro-Western government was being threatened by the Pathet Lao; but he declined to criticize Kennedy at a moment of weakness for the President, especially since he believed that the young leader would learn from his mistakes and had the potential to become a constructive foreign policy leader. The White House was temporarily irritated when Walter Lippmann wrote a column divulging and praising Fulbright's advice to the President before the abortive invasion: Fulbright "foresaw what would happen, he warned the President that the right policy was not to attempt to oust Castro but to contain him while we worked constructively in Latin America... Senator Fulbright was the only wise man in the lot." Fulbright quickly visited the White House and had an hour-long conference with the President, afterward telling reporters that he was in strong agreement with the President. The next day, JFK commended Fulbright at a press conference: "I think his counsel is useful. I think he should say what he thinks. If he had indicated disagreement on occasions, he has indicated general support on a good many other occasions."[81e]

Fulbright later stated that the Bay of Pigs seriously aggravated many of the ills that beset American foreign policy throughout the early 1960s. One of the reasons Khrushchev attempted to intimidate Kennedy at the Vienna conference of 1961 and later gambled on the installation of Soviet missiles in Cuba in 1962 was, in Fulbright's opinion, that he misjudged Kennedy as inexperienced and perhaps weak after the Bay of Pigs.[82] Conversely, Kennedy became determined to prove that he could be as "tough" as any leader; in Fulbright's words, (in 1978) that "he was a man, not a little boy." Shortly after the Bay of Pigs, Kennedy bolstered American forces in Berlin and Saigon and dispatched Lyndon Johnson to South Vietnam. When Johnson returned he reported that the decisive moment had arrived when the United States would either have to uphold the cause of freedom in southeast Asia or "pull back to San Francisco and a Fortress America concept." A failure to "move forward promptly with a major effort to help these countries defend themselves" would demonstrate to the entire world that America did not honor her treaty commitments, according to the Vice President.[83]

Fulbright had been at once the only dissenter and the only member of Congress consulted at the final strategy review before the Bay of Pigs (Chester Bowles, Arthur Schlesinger, and a few others privately opposed the CIA plan, but they were either absent or remained silent at the April 4 strategy session). Yet the atrophy of Congress' role in foreign policy, which was to have such pernicious consequences for American policy in Vietnam, accelerated rather than abated in the years after 1961.[84] One year and six months after the Bay of Pigs, Fulbright was not included in any meaningful fashion in the administration's deliberations during the Cuban missile crisis. Kennedy and his advisers had already decided to blockade Cuba when they briefed the Congressional leadership on October 22, 1962, immediately before Kennedy informed the nation of his decision on television. Fulbright and Senator Richard Russell of Georgia argued that an invasion of Cuba that would pit American soldiers against Cuban soldiers and allow the Russians to stand aside would be less likely to provoke a nuclear war than a blockade, which might involve a forcible confrontation with Russian ships. There was an obvious problem with Fulbright's contention: air strikes probably would have killed some of the 43,000 Russian soldiers in Cuba (Fulbright did not know at the time that the number was anywhere near that large). In this respect, Fulbright was hampered by the inaccuracy of American intelligence estimates regarding the number of troops in Cuba, for the CIA had erroneously concluded that there were only 10,000 Soviet troops in Cuba. Only many years later did it became public knowledge that the actual number was more than four times that great.[85] The Arkansan later reconsidered his recommendation; in 1966 he wrote that if the administration had advised him at the time of all the facts that were later made public he might have recommended a different course of action. In later years the senator emphasized that the administration did not give the Congressional leaders any time to consider alternatives or reflect about the crisis, since the President's nationally televised address was to be delivered only two hours after Kennedy briefed Fulbright and his colleagues. More importantly, the executive branch did not provide the Congressional leaders with all the relevant data concerning the emergency. From beginning to end of the entire crisis, Fulbright was excluded from the small group of advisers who determined the nation's course during the October, 1962 crisis.[86]

After Khrushchev withdrew the missiles from Cuba, Fulbright praised the President for having "proved to the Soviet Union that a policy of aggression and adventure involved unacceptable risks." Khrushchev, who was faced with a clear American military superiority in 1962, agreed to remove the missiles in return for a U.S. guarantee not to invade Cuba; and in a private agreement unknown to Fulbright and almost everyone else until many years later, Robert Kennedy had verbally assured the Soviet ambassador that the obsolete American Jupiter missiles would be removed from Turkey in four or five months, provided that the Soviets did not make any public mention of the private understanding about the Turkish missiles. The Turkish arrangement was secret because the Kennedys felt that American hawks would have lambasted the administration if it had appeared to be granting concessions under duress. Moreover, Khrushchev could point to the American "no-invasion-of-Cuba" guarantee as well as the Turkish arrangement in his efforts to justify Cuban missile withdrawal to the hard-liners in the Kremlin.[88] The Jupiter missiles were removed from Turkey in the spring of 1963. Although the Kremlin hawks were angered by Khrushchev's performance during the crisis, they did not prevent the relaxation in Soviet-American tensions that occurred in 1963. Fulbright enthusiastically supported the ephemeral post-missile crisis detente: in particular, he led the fight for the ratification of the Nuclear Test Ban Treaty, which was designed to slow the arms race by eliminating atmospheric testing.[89]

Arthur Schlesinger alleged in *The Imperial Presidency* that if Fulbright had participated directly in the administration's decision-making process during the Cuban crisis of 1962, he would probably have agreed with the strategy Kennedy decided upon; considering Fulbright's later approval of Kennedy's performance and his re-evaluations of the advice he gave on October 22, Schlesinger's argument is plausible. Yet, as Schlesinger aptly observed, the very brilliance of Kennedy's handling of the emergency "appeared to vindicate the idea that the President must take unto himself the final judgments of war and peace," and thus one of the tragic legacies of the missile crisis was "the imperial conception of the Presidency that brought the republic so low in Vietnam."[90] The Arkansas senator's exclusion from the inner councils of the administration in October, 1962, did not damage U.S. diplomacy in the specific case of the Cuban missile crisis, but there would be other crises in the Caribbean and in Asia when the executive branch desperately needed the genuine participation of Fulbright and other Congressional leaders in making crucial decisions. But later presidents would attempt to maintain their exclusive grasp of the nation's destiny in the international arena, just as John F. Kennedy had in that legendary autumn of 1962.

Years after the President's assassination on November 22, 1963, Fulbright came to believe that Kennedy had not fully recognized that Khrushchev was immersed in an internal power struggle with the Soviet military in the early 1960s. The senator did not assert that he had the definitive explanation for Khrushchev's Cuban blunder, and indeed the Soviet leader's motivations have been a subject of intense scholarly debate. But a number of Soviet specialists would agree that a theory Fulbright described in 1972 as "plausible" held a substantial measure of validity. According to this perspective, Khrushchev placed the missiles in Cuba as a desperate gamble to counter the domestic pressures emanating from the coalition of generals and ultra-conservatives who opposed his program of decreased military spending and his rejection of the Stalinist form of totalitarianism. Kennedy contributed to the deterioration of Khrushchev's position by expanding both American conventional forces and the American nuclear missile arsenal, even though the United States enjoyed an enormous strategic superiority by 1962.[91] As Fulbright phrased it in *The Crippled Giant,* the placement of missiles in Cuba was largely an effort to "narrow the Soviet missile gap in relation to the United States, without forcing Khrushchev to concentrate all available resources on a ruinous arms race."[92]

In retrospect, the senator argued that especially during the early Kennedy Presidency the United States had not understood that "Khrushchev was a world statesman with whom business could be done" and that Khrushchev's Cuban adventure was not simple, flagrant aggression, but was influenced by the American military build-up of 1961-1962 as well as by internal pressures. By 1972, Fulbright regretted the aftermath of the Cuban crisis within the U.S.S.R.; the Kremlin hawks resented the October, 1962 episode as a resounding diplomatic defeat for the Soviet Union, and thus the long-term effect of the missile crisis complemented Eisenhower's errant policy during the U-2 affair in hastening the downfall of Khrushchev, who for all his excesses was still the Soviet leader who "repudiated the Marxist dogma of the inevitability of war between communist and capitalist states."[93] The senator always believed that the prospects for negotiating armaments control agreements and a political settlement in southeast Asia received a setback when Khrushchev fell from power in 1964.[94] Khrushchev's successors escalated the arms race and brought the Soviet Union to a rough strategic parity with the United States by 1972, ended Khrushchev's de-Stalinization policies, and greatly increased Soviet aid to the Vietnamese communists in response to the American escalation in southeast Asia.[95]

In reflecting upon the Kennedy administration a decade later, Fulbright would lament the President's basic misunderstanding of Khrushchev in 1961. To his mind, Kennedy had misinterpreted Khrushchev's endorsement of the communist doctrine of "wars of national liberation" as a formal declaration of a Russian intention to sponsor subversion, guerrilla warfare, and revolution in southeast Asia and throughout the globe.[96] Khrushchev's outrageous rhetoric was largely a response to the Chinese communists' accusations that the U.S.S.R. was betraying the cause of communist revolution by some of the recent, relatively conciliatory Soviet policies toward the United States. If Kennedy's judgment in 1961 had not been distorted by a residual belief in the myth of the global communist monolith, he might have been able to correctly analyze the effects of the internal divisions in the communist world. He initially interpreted Khrushchev's verbal support for "wars of national liberation" as being essentially analogous to the communist threat in Europe in the late 1940s.[97] By 1963, Kennedy was beginning to re-evaluate many of the dogmas of the Cold War, although whether or not he was definitely planning any fundamental changes in Vietnam policy in the months before his death remains unclear. But in 1961-1962, the Kennedy administration concluded that the containment policy of the Truman administration had frustrated Stalin's alleged expansionist designs; now a similar containment policy in the 1960s must demonstrate to the Chinese as well as to the Russians that "indirect aggression" through subversion and guerrilla warfare was not a relatively safe and inexpensive method of expanding communist power.[98]

In dissecting the errors of those years, Fulbright did not claim that he had been immune to many of the intellectual fallacies that were the conventional wisdom in the early 1960s. When he remembered the inflated anticommunist rhetoric of Kennedy's speeches in 1961, the senator would reflect, "I do not recall these words for purposes of reproach; they represented an assessment of Communist intentions which most of us shared at that time." At several junctures of that era, notably his dissent from the Bay of Pigs adventure, Fulbright had demonstrated an unusually lucid ability to perceive and warn against the emotional and ideological biases that afflicted U.S. foreign policy. That experience would serve him well during the even more troubled era in the later 1960s, when the senator would play a historic role as America's conscience.

Book Three:

FULBRIGHT, DOMESTIC POLITICS, AND CIVIL RIGHTS

I. DISTORTIONS IN THE ARKANSAS POLITICAL PROCESS IN THE 1950s

While Senator Fulbright preferred to devote most of his time and energy to foreign affairs and to domestic issues such as aid to education, in the 1950s he was confronted with the dilemma of responding to the crisis over racial issues that enveloped Arkansas and much of the nation of that era. For the rest of his life, he would look back upon those events with sadness. Regarding his own political strategy, he would reflect at length upon the shocking results of the 1958 congressional election in Arkansas: in the fall of that year, Fulbright's friend, the moderate Congressman Brooks Hays, narrowly lost his campaign for reelection against an extreme segregationist who condemned Hays for having advocated compliance with *Brown v. Board of Education* during the Little Rock desegregation crisis. Many political and legal analyses have cited Hays' defeat and the Little Rock Central High crisis of 1957-58 as evidence that the adamant segregationists dominated Arkansas politics to the extent that no politician could appeal for moderation and survive politically. Charles C. Alexander's history of the Eisenhower era portrayed the President as having allegedly provided steadfast support for *Brown* in the face of racist hysteria: "School desegregation could come to Little Rock in 1957 only at bayonet point."[1] Similarly, Robert Bork contended in *The Tempting of America* that "At one point President Eisenhower had to send in airborne troops to guarantee compliance with the Court's rulings."[2] While it is true that Governor Orval Faubus played upon segregationist sentiments in dominating the staunchly conservative delta region of eastern Arkansas, such observers as Bork or Alexander were inaccurate in depicting Eisenhower as valiantly upholding the rule of law against an allegedly monolithic force of reaction throughout Arkansas. In reality, Eisenhower's reluctance to support *Brown* played into Faubus' hands at several critical junctures throughout the massive resistance period. Moreover, in regions outside the delta the moderates were not as impotent as Bork and Alexander suggest; Hays, one of the South's most eloquent spokesmen for racial moderation, lost by only 1,200 votes in a central Arkansas election flawed by numerous electoral irregularities at the height of Faubus' popularity.[3]

Given Hays' narrow margin of defeat, Fulbright was inaccurate in his later analysis of that election as providing definitive evidence that any position of public moderation would spell political doom for Arkansas politicians of that era. A more convincing interpretation of the 1958 election would stress that if Hays had received more support from moderates who were not by any means liberal on racial matters but at the same time would not countenance extremism and resistance to the rule of law–and Fulbright was, of course, one of the classic examples of these "moderates" who remained silent in the face of Faubus' demagogy in 1958–then Hays might have been able to survive the election. Ironically, Fulbright's political concessions in the Southern political arena probably cost him an opportunity to serve in the foreign policy realm as Secretary of State in the Kennedy administration; Arthur M. Schlesinger and other knowledgeable analysts of the selection process for Kennedy's Secretary of State in late 1960 have emphasized that the President-elect initially preferred Fulbright for the chief State Department post, but ultimately decided that he could not appoint him because of the Arkansas senator's weak civil rights record.

Even some scholars and political analysts who stressed the strength of the moderate faction in the earlier period from roughly 1950 to 1958 have embraced the view of the Hays loss as proof of extreme segregationist domination by 1958. For example, Tony Freyer's *The Little Rock Crisis* concluded that "Hays' defeat indicated the level of pro-segregationist sentiment that had engulfed Little Rock."[4] Freyer failed to refer to the narrow margin of victory and the extraordinary circumstances regarding Hays' battle with a pro-Faubus write-in candidate, Dale Alford. In the July Democratic primary, Hays had defeated Amis Guthridge, leader of the Capital Citizens Council that had been one of the most vociferous groups in inciting racist sentiments during the Central High crisis in 1957.[5] Hays was then unopposed until a few weeks before the November election, and scheduled a series of speaking engagements out of state and naturally made no effort to campaign; the announcement of the Alford write-in candidacy thus emerged as a complete surprise to the Hays forces. Utilizing the Faubus political organization, Alford suffered none of the organizational problems write-in candidates normally face; in fact, the nature of his candidacy facilitated his victory, especially through the use of prefabricated "Alford write-in stickers" with a check mark after Alford's name. In a clear violation of election laws, the Alford stickers were distributed not only by the candidate's campaign workers, but at several polling places by election officials.[6] Since Democratic primaries were then considered tantamount to reelection, turnout at the general election was much smaller than in the primary, and Hays actually received a larger total number of votes in the primary than Alford won in November. At least several thousand of the Alford votes involved distribution of the stickers and other dubious methods; but even had there been no irregularities, the 1,200-vote margin out of 61,000 votes cast belies Freyer's notion that central Arkansas was "engulfed" by the Alford forces in November 1958. Fulbright's political situation was different from that of Hays, for the congressman's district did not include the delta, which was the most heavily segregationist region in the state. Since the senator, of course, was elected by all the state's voters, he did have to campaign in the delta. On the other hand, Fulbright also campaigned in northwest Arkansas, where race issues were not as crucial as in the delta or in central Arkansas. Nonetheless, Fulbright's frequent justifications for his silence in the Little Rock crisis overlooked the reality that Hays won the Democratic primary and waged a fierce political battle in the general election, despite the widespread irregularities in the write-in campaign.

Congressman Thomas "Tip" O'Neill (D.-Mass.), John Dingell (D.-Mich.) and other liberal Democrats were outraged by the apparent fraud and objected to Alford's seating in the new Congress, but ultimately Democrats from the Deep South threatened a vendetta of challenges against the electoral results of black Northern members of Congress if Alford's victory were challenged. Hays himself had not contested the election out of concern for appearing bitter at the "loss," and Speaker Sam Rayburn eventually decided that the political costs of a fratricidal conflict among Democrats were too great to justify a bona fide investigation into the election.[7] The House Administration Committee reported a perfunctory whitewash that avoided offending states' rights sensibilities by not questioning Arkansas officials' certification of the electoral results as valid. Thus, the Deep South bloc, which was dominated by the extreme segregationist factions, reinforced the Faubus administration's efforts to eliminate the moderate congressman who had steadfastly argued that regardless of Southern opinions of *Brown*, it would have to be obeyed as the "law of the land." Hays had unsuccessfully attempted to mediate between Eisenhower and Faubus during the Central High crisis in an effort to assure a peaceful beginning to desegregation; as early as the mid-1940s Hays had maintained a moderate stand on racial issues, advocating abolition of segregation in all forms of interstate travel, federal fair employment practices legislation aimed at eliminating job discrimination based on race, and an amendment initiated by Congress to repeal the poll tax. The loss of Hays' leadership was clearly a severe blow to the supporters of racial moderation in Congress.[8] Fulbright was saddened by the loss. "It was a great and painful surprise to see him removed," the senator would recall.[8a]

The obvious question arises as to how Arkansas could have given Faubus a landslide victory in 1958 while Hays still retained the support of almost half his district's voters, even after the electoral irregularities. Much of the explanation focuses on the much greater strength of the moderates in Hays' central Arkansas district than in the delta, where the extreme segregationists dominated. More broadly, the Arkansas political process in that era suffered from severe distortions that prevented electoral results from being legitimate indications of the full range of public opinion in the state; the most serious of the distortions concerned black voting in the delta. Aside from repeated problems of voting irregularities throughout the state in which the Faubus political machine was involved, such as those in the Hays-Alford election, the black vote in the delta was systematically manipulated. In the 1940s, most of the east Arkansas political leaders had decided to abandon explicit, formal disfranchisement of blacks, and in the late 1940s and early 1950s blacks were voting in substantial numbers. Most blacks lived in the delta, where the planter oligarchy controlled their votes through a system of influence over employment, credit, payments to black precinct leaders for alleged "campaign work" and to cover poll tax expenses, patronage to local black leaders, in some instances outright fraud, and other forms of socioeconomic and political pressures.[10] This led to results in the delta in which black precincts overwhelmingly were counted as voting for the segregationist positions of the planters. For example, a state constitutional amendment drafted by the racist politician Jim Johnson stated that Arkansas could nullify Supreme Court decisions until Congress acted; that amendment passed in a black ward of West Memphis by a margin of 521 to 41 in November 1956.[11]

In contrast, blacks were gradually migrating to Little Rock and Pine Bluff (the other central Arkansas city of substantial size) and demonstrating burgeoning political independence by the 1950s, buoyed by the stronger white moderate element in the larger urban areas and the growth of a black middle class. With a number of successful black businesses creating independent sources of black economic power, and a black professional elite including several prominent lawyers such as the NAACP leader, Wiley Branton, blacks in central

Arkansas voted with their white moderate allies, helping keep some local officials and Hays in office until the 1958 debacle.[12]

The Arkansas leadership had engaged in debates in the 1940s that in some respects were somewhat similar to the Southern political struggles of the late 19th century, albeit with an opposite outcome. Some oligarchs contended that it would be better to control the black voters than to persist in denying them the franchise altogether, just as Wade Hampton of South Carolina had argued in favor of suffrage for the emancipated slave on the grounds that the black man "naturally allies himself with the more conservative of the whites."[13] The advocates of disfranchisement had ultimately prevailed by stressing that if blacks could vote, there would always be the potential that "radical" forces could win their votes. Repugnance for corrupt elections played an important rhetorical role in rationalizations for disfranchisement in Arkansas and throughout the South.[13a] Half a century later, a small band of liberals argued in favor of enfranchisement on the grounds that a reasonably well-educated, more prosperous black community was now emerging in Little Rock that would not be vulnerable to electoral corruption. One member of this group argued in 1934 in a Little Rock newspaper that "since the necessity for maintaining a strictly white man's party no longer exists, politicians should stop appealing to race hatred and qualified Negroes should be permitted to vote."[14] This view was in a distinct minority in the 1930s, but would expand rapidly after World War II. In contrast to the Little Rock supporters of enfranchisement, conservatives in the delta supported black voting for a diametrically opposed reason: to control the black votes and use them to augment the power of the local oligarchy. The conservative arguments won the day in the Arkansas delta, and the oligarchy in the late 1940s and 1950s succeeded in controlling the black vote; although unlike Hampton's benign picture of blacks "naturally" allying themselves with the planters, their votes were subject to various forms of intimidation and fraud. Consistent with the general amelioration of race relations wrought by World War II throughout the country, moderates in central Arkansas and in the mountainous northwest Arkansas region argued that blacks should vote because of their wartime service to the country and the revulsion against the racism of Nazi Germany. The Truman administration exerted a profound impact in Arkansas, as a Truman protégé, Sid McMath, rode the crest of moderate sentiment into the governor's mansion in the late 1940s and early 1950s. McMath's progressive administration focused on industrial development, improved educational opportunities, and elimination of racial strife, largely as a means of attaining the economic and educational objectives.[15] The strength of McMath and the political independence of the Little Rock blacks posed long-term dangers to the oligarchy's power; if similar independence ever emerged in the agricultural regions of southern and eastern Arkansas, the east Arkansas planters' powerful influence in the state's politics would be broken.

Over the long term, the reactionaries of the late 19th century as well as their ideological heirs in the 1940s were correct in arguing that as long as blacks could vote there remained the potential that some white factions might bid for their support; Hays and McMath performed that feat in central Arkansas as early as the 1940s, with the black vote tipping the scales for Hays in an area where rival moderate and conservative white factions were relatively evenly matched. By the 1960s Winthrop Rockefeller would finally generate enough financial power, combined with growing black political activism, to break the manipulation of the planters over the black vote in eastern Arkansas. Indeed, by 1968, black voters could exercise the suffrage relatively free of intimidation or fraud, and would propel probably the most liberal congressman in Arkansas' history, Bill Alexander, into Congress from the east Arkansas district. But for the short term in the 1950s, the political process in east Arkansas was temporarily malfunctioning even more than it had in the earlier era, when blacks were disfranchised, for the black votes now actually augmented the power of the planters.[16]

In 1958, for example, blacks in the delta "voted" overwhelmingly for Faubus, but where blacks were relatively free to cast ballots without socioeconomic intimidation or fraud—i.e., in Little Rock—blacks voted overwhelmingly against Faubus, and, of course, in favor of Hays in the congressional race.[16] To cite one comparison, in black precincts in Little Rock Faubus received less than 20 percent of the vote, while in Lee County, a delta county with a black majority of 61 percent of the population and a high overall voter turnout, Faubus won more than 70 percent of the total vote, with similar landslide margins in other black belt counties.[17] About 64,000 blacks voted in the state in 1958 out of a total statewide vote of 563,000; the black vote potentially could become decisive in a situation where relatively even factions competed with each other.[18] In Little Rock, the newly independent black vote was frequently a crucial swing element in some elections. In some counties, the old patterns of actual disfranchisement still persisted and the local county leaders' socioeconomic and political coercion was directed at preventing the black vote altogether, but the dominant trend in most of the black belt counties increasingly centered on the power structure assisting blacks in payment of the poll tax and close "supervision" of their voting. The poll tax, of course, had a racially discriminatory impact, although it was not used as extensively as in the Deep South; about 50 percent of the Arkansas white voters did not pay the poll tax and thus were ineligible to vote, while about 70 percent of black voters did not pay it.[18a] Faubus could draw comfort from the reality that his largest potential source of opposition in the delta either was disfranchised in a few areas or was effectively pressured, coerced or simply fraudulently recorded as voting in his favor. Black voting was gradually increasing throughout the state, and slowly in the largest northeast Arkansas town of Jonesboro and a few of the larger east Arkansas towns an independent black political force, allied to a much weaker and smaller white moderate element, began in embryonic form to replicate the Hays coalition in central Arkansas.[19] But this coalition in eastern Arkansas was not yet a significant political factor in the late 1950s. Fulbright's perception of the relative weakness of the moderates, especially in eastern Arkansas, would play a major factor in his analysis of Arkansas politics in that era.

Another factor in explaining Faubus' high vote total in the state in the late 1950s was the intensity of the segregationists regarding *Brown*. Moderates agreed with arguments that the Supreme Court must lay down the "law of the land," and therefore were willing to comply with desegregation. The moderates displayed little enthusiasm for desegregation, but in contrast to the extremists they tended to be more concerned about a range of issues such as economic development and educational improvement that ranked higher in their priorities. Since racial strife interfered with these objectives, moderates were willing to accept *Brown*. By the early 1950s, the planters looked with disdain on the rise of the moderates led by Hays, McMath, and—initially—Faubus, whose political career began as a McMath-appointed highway commissioner and populist from the northwest Arkansas region, where there were very few blacks and race was not a burning issue.[20] After *Brown*, the east's antipathy to the moderates became increasingly virulent, and the delta's leaders made it abundantly clear to Faubus that they would not support him unless he "defended the Southern way of life" on the race issue.[21] After calling out the Arkansas National Guard to obstruct the entry of black students into Central, Faubus became the hero of the east Arkansas segregationists, whose intensity on the race issue obsessed them virtually to the exclusion of all other issues. In northwest Arkansas where few blacks lived and racial issues were secondary, Faubus could still retain the support of some moderates based upon his record in issues other than race, such as his relatively progressive record in raising teachers' salaries, improving social services and increasing benefits to the elderly.[22]

After Eisenhower dispatched federal troops to Little Rock, some Arkansans who were not particularly extreme on racial matters were also attracted to the Faubus banner on the question of federal intervention in local Arkansas affairs. This segment of moderate opinion was a minority, but it has often been misunderstood; it is clear that the most extreme elements in Arkansas led by Jim Johnson or Amis Guthridge merely used states' rights as a cover for their racist agenda. But there were others who might have held relatively moderate views on race who were simply offended by the notion of "outsiders" telling Arkansas how to conduct its business. While Hays acknowledged some need for a careful federal role in certain racial matters, even he was offended by the Eisenhower administration's record of vacillation and refusal to support *Brown* for a lengthy period before 1957; he was also offended by what he regarded as the administration's inept, heavy-handed use of combat paratroopers; federalizing the Arkansas National Guard, in Hays' view, would have been sufficient to deal with the crisis.[23] After the administration's interminable failure to act and the racist agitation of Faubus and other fire-eaters, in Hays' analysis, the situation had degenerated to the point where the need for restoring order by some federal action was inescapable; but the congressman was convinced that decisive action in federalizing the National Guard at an earlier date was one critical action that might have greatly lessened the magnitude of the crisis.[24] Regardless of whether Hays' analysis of the administration was correct, it is clear that Faubus greatly enhanced his popularity by playing upon the memories of Reconstruction after the paratroopers entered Little Rock.

Segregationist forces also succeeded in silencing some of their potential critics through such aggressive strategies as boycotts of businesses owned by advocates of desegregation, so that in Little Rock and the delta there would be social and economic costs to opposing Faubus. The most spectacular instance was the Faubus-supported boycott against the *Arkansas Gazette*, then the state's largest newspaper and a consistent proponent of desegregation. Although the *Gazette* never wavered in its resistance to Faubus in the post-Central High period, the boycott enabled its hitherto weak conservative competitor in Little Rock, the *Arkansas Democrat*, to greatly expand its circulation, even surpassing the *Gazette* briefly in 1959.[25]

The harsh reality that Faubus and his right-wing allies triumphed in the political struggles of 1957-58 was powerfully influenced by the failure of certain rational, responsible leaders within and outside Arkansas to support the efforts of Hays and others in calling for compliance with *Brown*. Although Faubus seems to have preferred avoidance of controversy on race before 1957, when it became impossible to evade the issue at the time of the Central High controversy he embarked on his campaign of racist demagogy largely to alleviate his principal political problem of the eastern Arkansas reactionaries' opposition to his campaign for a third term.[26] After it became painfully clear that Faubus had abandoned his earlier alignment with the moderates and joined forces with the segregationists, the Hays faction desperately needed help. The crucial leaders who might have aided in a peaceful transition toward desegregation were the Eisenhower administration officials and some of the Arkansas moderates, notably Senator Fulbright, who knew that Hays, McMath and the *Gazette* were in dire need of support; but an important group among the "moderates" led by Fulbright ultimately decided not to take the risks involved in standing against the segregationist onslaught. Bereft of the allies they had hoped would aid them, the moderates were temporarily vanquished, and Arkansas, the state that had previously boasted a relatively enlightened record in race relations, became a symbol of racist hatred as the images of white adults shouting epithets at black students entering Central High were broadcast around the world. The crisis and its denouement in Hays' defeat and Faubus' unprecedented third-term victory posed a classic example of the dilemma that Harry Ashmore, executive editor of the *Gazette*, lamented in *An Epitaph for Dixie* in 1958: "It would seem that those who resolutely turn away from the future would at least be able to read the first lesson of the South's past: When responsible men default, irresponsible men take power."[27]

II. THE LATER TRUMAN YEARS:
THE RFC AND DOMESTIC POLITICS

During the last years of the Truman administration, Fulbright's relationship with the White House deteriorated because of conflict between the senator and the President over certain domestic issues, especially the question of favoritism and questionable influence within the Reconstruction Finance Corporation. Fulbright had already antagonized the President, of course, by his widely misunderstood suggestion after the 1946 elections that the President resign and appoint a Republican Secretary of State— a suggestion, as previously discussed in this book, that was based upon the Arkansan's theoretical preference for parliamentary government. Some political observers believed that there was friction between Fulbright and an informal "Arkansas brain trust" of Truman's advisers who were from Arkansas: Leslie Biffle, secretary of the Senate and a Truman confidante; John Steelman, a special assistant to the president; John Snyder, Secretary of the Treasury, who had been in banking in Arkansas before moving to Missouri; Frank Pace, an Arkansas native who was Secretary of the Army; and the senior senator from Arkansas, John McClellan, a powerful Arkansan from the standpoint of dispensing patronage favors.[1] In 1948, another major Arkansas figure would be added to the circle of influential Arkansans close to the Truman administration, as the young progressive politician Sid McMath was elected governor. Fulbright was not a member of the inner circle of the "Arkansas brain trust," and some observers speculated that this was an additional source of tension between Fulbright and the President. Actually, such speculation was largely Washington political gossip, for Fulbright generally maintained amicable relations with McClellan, and in the late 1940s and early 1950s Fulbright was a friend of McMath. He always tended to remain somewhat aloof from the "club" of political insiders in Washington.

Fulbright's investigation into the RFC was the principal source of the senator's tensions with the administration in the early 1950s. In 1949, Fulbright had been presiding at a hearing of a Senate Banking and Currency Subcommittee when he learned that a witness and RFC official, John Haggerty, had accepted a lucrative job with a company that had previously borrowed $6 million from the RFC. Fulbright thought this action improper, and questioned the RFC directors about it; he was not satisfied by the answers, and in February 1950, received approval from the full Senate to conduct an investigation into the entire agency.[2] The Banking and Currency Committee appointed a subcommittee chaired by Fulbright for the investigation. The RFC had been created by President Hoover in 1932 to battle the depression by lending money at low interest to financial, industrial and agricultural institutions. In World War II, the agency financed construction of defense plants. After the war, the Truman administration had been concerned about the possibility of a new depression, and the scope of the agency's lending was widened; subsequently several large loans went into default.[3]

When Fulbright first entered Congress, he had been concerned about the inexorable shift of power from Congress to the White House and the executive agencies. Staff members in the huge agencies were drafting an increasingly large percentage of all the legislation enacted by Congress. With the tremendous manpower and specialization of the executive departments, Fulbright felt that many members of Congress were overwhelmed by the sheer volume of legislation. The permanent bureaucrats were acquiring ever more power, and they often tended to regard elected officials as amateurs who would only be in Washington temporarily. Referring to the condescending attitude of the executive officials, Fulbright observed that "It is quite irritating to be regarded as a pork-barrel politician who would sacrifice the public good for a favor for a friend."[4] His concern about the expansion of executive power was a fundamental issue in his career, and the RFC hearings would place him in the national spotlight in a role—one that would become familiar to him later in his career—of acting as a check on abuses of influence emanating from the executive branch.

One relatively brief episode in the RFC inquiry centered upon an official in the legislative branch: Joe McCarthy. At one point during the subcommittee's investigation, Fulbright briefly turned his attention to the Lustron Corporation, which was financed with government money; it developed that Senator McCarthy had accepted $10,000 from Lustron for compiling a pamphlet on housing. Fulbright believed it was a conflict of interest, since McCarthy at that time was a member of the Banking and Currency Committee, which had jurisdiction over Lustron's affairs. The Arkansan would later reflect that the episode convinced him McCarthy "was a boodler." Yet, McCarthy had not violated any law, so that Fulbright had only his ethical criticisms; McCarthy escaped the episode relatively unscathed, and the subcommittee focused its attention on the primary affairs and officials involved in the RFC and the administration.[5]

In the early stages of the investigation, Truman submitted a plan to reorganize the RFC, an independent agency, and transfer it to the Department of Commerce. The Senate rejected the plan. As the subcommittee's inquiry continued, Fulbright and his colleague, Paul Douglas of Illinois, became concerned about the conduct of two of the five members of the RFC Board of Directors; the two Democratic senators made a visit to the White House with Charles Tobey of New Hampshire, a Republican. This effort was typical of Fulbright's initial attempts to achieve reform by private conferences, and, as would happen with future disputes with Presidents, the private strategy proved ineffective. Fulbright and his two colleagues met with Truman privately, made suggestions for reforming the RFC and strengthening it, and expressed concerns about the conduct of two directors: William Willett, a Democrat, and Walter Dunham, a Republican. The meeting itself was amicable, and the senators were temporarily pleased. Yet, two weeks later, without any further communication with the senators, Truman announced the renomination of Dunham and Willett at the expiration of their terms as directors.[6] The private approach had failed, and now Fulbright concluded that he must make public the subcommittee's preliminary conclusions.

The preliminary subcommittee report in February 1951, entitled *Study of Reconstruction*

Finance Corporation: Favoritism and Influence, indicated that RFC policy and loans had been affected by favoritism and political influence from the administration and the Democratic National Committee.[7] Truman publicly condemned the report as "asinine," whereupon Fulbright's subcommittee held public hearings. Reporters asked Truman at a press conference whether the Fulbright report provided any basis for criticism of the RFC directors or other administration officials, and Truman snapped: "No, I haven't . . . The objective of this report seems to have been a reflection on the President himself. And I am sorry for that, because I have never in my life brought pressure on the RFC or any other agency of the government to do anything except in the public interest." Truman was overreacting and distorting the report, which clearly made no such attack on the President himself, and was restrained in its discussion of the influence peddling and apparent favoritism within the agency. As was his wont, Truman also personalized the dispute, accusing Fulbright of ducking him, saying "he left town when he found out I wanted to see him."[8] Actually, in January Fulbright had tried to contact the White House to discover what the President was planning to do, and there had been no response. Fulbright had "left town" to make a long-scheduled speech in Florida, where he replied to Truman's blast: "As to whether the report is asinine, I am willing to let the report speak for itself. According to the press dispatches, the President states that I had left town when I found out that he wanted to see me. I do not want to seem disrespectful to the President but this statement of the President is not true."[9]

On another occasion during the hearings, Truman again erred in making an erroneous attack upon the integrity of some members of Congress, an attack that he later retracted. The President made a call to Senator Tobey in the midst of the hearings to say that the real "crooks and influence peddlers" were members of the committee, referring to members of Congress who had allegedly accepted fees for promoting RFC loans. There was no basis for the charge that members of Congress were "crooks," and Truman himself later realized it and recanted the accusation.[10] It was another revelation to Fulbright and Douglas, however, of how far Truman was overreacting against the investigation.

The RFC hearings revealed an atmosphere of questionable influences within the agency, one of the most celebrated examples of which was the disclosure that an $8,540 mink coat had been given to a White House employee by her husband, Merl Young, who was a former RFC employee and a friend of Donald Dawson, an administrative assistant to Truman. After Young left the RFC, the coat was bought for him by an attorney who represented applicants for RFC loans; the disclosure at the hearings implied that the coat was a gift to Young in return for past favors at the RFC.

Mrs. Young's coat was destined to become the most famous mink coat in American history. The next presidential campaign was only a year and a half away. The Republicans looked forward to recapturing the White House after 20 years of Democratic domination and successfully transformed the mink coat into a symbol of alleged corruption in the Truman administration. Richard Nixon would refer to it in his famous "Checkers" speech of September 1952, defending himself against charges of corruption by contrasting the mink coat of Mrs. Young with his wife Pat's: Mrs. Nixon "doesn't have a mink coat. But she does have a respectable Republican cloth coat."[11]

Truman's advisers later recalled that in private discussions at the White House, the President would predict that the controversy over the RFC would soon abate. Joseph Short, then Truman's press secretary, advised the President that the episode was making a deep impression upon the public and would not simply "blow over." Another Truman adviser, Roger Tubby, noted in his journal at the time that the President and some of his senior advisers privately spoke in a "rather disparaging and lighthearted way" of both the Fulbright investigation and another inquiry undertaken in the same period by Senator Estes Kefauver into Truman's appointment as Ambassador to Mexico of William O'Dwyer, who as mayor of New York had appointed to office people with underworld connections. (Despite the Kefauver investigation, Truman refused to change O'Dwyer's status as ambassador.) One of Truman's biographers, Robert J. Donovan, concluded that the President was strangely complacent and reluctant to offer leadership in eliminating unethical conduct and removing doubts about the rectitude of government agencies.[12] Truman's code of tenacious loyalty to his veteran lieutenants such as Dawson also affected his dogged reactions to the investigations and the negative media coverage. At the time, he wrote to Clark Clifford (then practicing law) that "There have been only two or three presidents who have been as roundly abused and misrepresented in certain sections of the press as I have. I call your attention to Washington, Jefferson, Jackson, Lincoln and particularly to Grover Cleveland."[13] Truman protested too much, and his historical assessment was overstated; certainly he had received more criticism than Washington and Jefferson (with the major exception of the Federalist press in New England[14]), and Lincoln had faced criticisms in the unique context when the nation was in danger of tearing itself asunder from within. Truman indeed faced world crises of a different dimension, but it should be mentioned that along with the criticism, there was also a tendency during the Cold War for the nation to rally around the President whenever a foreign crisis erupted. Yet, it was certainly true that by the time of the RFC hearings, Truman had absorbed years of public criticism, and his decision not to run again may have made him less concerned about the political consequences of the Fulbright and Kefauver investigations. One of the Arkansas "brain trusters," John Steelman, later reflected that Truman resented what he regarded as exaggerated media reports of corruption in his administration, feeling that reporters constantly placed the worst possible "spin" on controversies; Steelman felt, however, that Truman did not believe that all the charges of corruption were unjustified.[15]

Throughout the RFC investigation, Fulbright was careful to acknowledge that the line between discharge of duty by a public official and an exertion of improper political influence can sometimes be difficult to ascertain. Figures including William Boyle, the Democratic National Chairman, and others involved were not federal employees at the time. Mrs. Young, a White House stenographer, committed no crime in accepting the coat from her husband. No incumbent government official was ever indicted in the entire investigation. However, Mr. Young was later indicted for perjury and sent to jail. Most of the publicity centered on Dawson, who had once been the RFC director of personnel. Dawson's friends included RFC officials Dunham and Willett, as well as borrowers from the RFC. In 1947, Dawson had moved from the RFC to the White House, where he handled personnel and patronage for Truman and hence could influence appointments and promotions at the RFC. He was also a principal liaison between the White House and the Democratic National Committee. Despite calls—some from concerned Democrats—for Dawson's resignation as part of a "housecleaning" to neutralize the political damage caused by the investigation,

Truman stood doggedly behind his old friend, thus intensifying the impression that he was insensitive to the problems of unethical conduct.

The Fulbright hearings dealt with numerous instances of indiscriminate patronage, use of public office to grant favors to partisans and friends, and acceptance of gifts from businessmen. The investigation further revealed insensitivity to connections between some local Democratic leaders and underworld figures, cheating on tax returns, conflict of interest, and laxity by the Department of Justice in prosecuting alleged wrongdoings by some Democrats. Although these were undoubtedly serious matters, they were also unquestionably vastly less serious than other notorious executive branch scandals of the 20th century, such as the massive plunder in the Harding administration and Teapot Dome, the abuse of legal powers by the highest officers in government revealed in the Watergate scandal, or the illegality and contempt for Congress revealed in the Iran-Contra affair. Despite Fulbright's resolve in pursuing the investigation in the face of administration pressure and the clear damage to his own party that the adverse media coverage caused, the Arkansan did not play to the headlines or exaggerate the extent of the problem. At the hearings, Dawson testified that he had not tried to influence RFC decisions. He admitted, however, that he had stayed for no charge at a hotel in Miami Beach that had received a large loan from the RFC, and under grilling from the committee promised not to accept any such favors in the future.[16] Senator Douglas, who took a tough stance against the administration's questionable conduct during the affair, later conceded that Dawson was a good witness "and only minor peccadilloes were proved against him."[17] Fulbright and Douglas, however, did not feel that this excused Dawson's "minor peccadilloes"; they felt that as a presidential assistant, Dawson's conduct should have been above reproach. At the close of the hearings, Fulbright told Dawson he did not believe "that you were out throwing your weight around in seeking and attempting to dominate the RFC. What we are saying is that whether you sought to do it, or attempted to do it, you did influence them."[18] The chairman stated that the testimony had revealed that the directors, especially Dunham and Willitt, were anxious to do anything to curry favor with Dawson. Dawson denied this, and then attempted to torture Fulbright's statement into an exoneration of Dawson's behavior. Fulbright explicitly rejected this construction of his statement, and reserved judgment as to Dawson's motives.[19] The full Senate Banking and Currency Committee issued a final report stating that the public hearings had substantiated Fulbright's preliminary report. The former directors had habitually discussed RFC activities with persons who had no responsibility in it, and "It became accepted practice, in many instances, for loan applicants to seek introduction to the directors of the RFC or to some of them through officials of the Democratic National Committee." A separate report by the Republican minority called for Dawson's firing and alleged that the RFC had become a victim of the White House staff, "minor employees, political hangers-on and self-proclaimed cronies."[20]

President Truman belatedly capitulated. In a decision that was tantamount to a concession that the subcommittee's criticisms of RFC mismanagement were correct, the President submitted a reorganization plan providing that the RFC would be placed under the direction of a single administrator rather than a board of directors. Congress approved the plan. Then Truman appointed the highly respected Stuart Symington, then of the National Security Resources Board, as the new RFC administrator.[21]

The episode was a case study in the damaging repercussions that can flow from obstinate over-reactions to criticism, followed by belated reforms that eventually concede the merit of the criticisms. Had Truman acceded to the Fulbright-Douglas criticisms in the beginning, much of the political damage might have been spared the administration. The reality was, however, that Presidents wielded vast power in the era in which Fulbright served in the Senate, and they tended to discount or only become angered at criticism; in many political controversies, only major public dissent backed by public indignation could influence the executive powerhouse to change its policies.

Fulbright's general conduct of the hearings was widely applauded. Walter Lippmann wrote that "Senator Fulbright has set an example, all the more impressive because its sincerity has been so effortless, of how a good senator can behave."[22] The questioning was judicious, the staff research was thorough. A Buffalo, New York reporter who covered the hearings wrote: Fulbright "has a quiet manner with an almost impish grin that leads witnesses on until they become entangled in their own efforts to avoid a flat answer. He frequently sums up the apparent meaning and significance of a whole series of answers in one statement and asks the witness if that is the impression he wants to leave with the committee."[23] In sharp contrast to Joe McCarthy's abusive treatment of witnesses, Fulbright was respectful to them; as the Buffalo reporter wrote, "Thus, browbeating tactics which so infuriate witnesses and lead them to the belief that they have been made the 'goats' of congressional inquiries have been eliminated. The new system seems sure to leave a much better taste in the mouth of the public."[24] Of course, it was over-optimistic to speak in 1951 of the triumph of the "new system" of conducting congressional hearings, for some of McCarthy's worst abuses were yet to come. Some observers at the opposite end of the spectrum felt Fulbright should have been more aggressive in criticizing the administration. Fulbright's reluctance to lecture Dawson or the other witnesses, or to seek sensational publicity for the hearings, led him to be criticized at the time for not lambasting Truman. Senator Douglas did not agree with that criticism in assessing Fulbright's aloof demeanor: "He's a child of the 18th century. He's a throwback to the age of enlightenment, trust in reason, temperate argument, and slightly aristocratic tendencies. That, I think explains why he seems a little aloof, a little different from the rest."[25]

As a former constitutional law professor, Fulbright was faced in the RFC hearings with issues that were not, for the most part, explicitly addressed by the letter of the law. In a major Senate speech in the latter stages of the RFC controversy, Fulbright lamented the "moral deterioration of democracy":

> When confronted with an evil, we Americans are prone to say, 'There ought to be a law.' But the law does not and cannot apply effectively over wide fields of men's activities. It cannot reach those evils which are subtle and impalpable . . . The law cannot prevent gossip. It cannot prevent men from bearing false witness against their neighbors. It cannot restrain a man from betraying his friends. In short, it cannot prevent much of the evil to which men are, unfortunately, prone.
>
> What should be done about men who do not directly and blatantly sell the favors of their offices for money and so place themselves within the penalties of the law? How do we deal with those who, under the guise of friendship, accept favors

which offend the spirit of the law but do not violate its letter? . . . What of the men outside the government who suborn those inside it? Who is more at fault, the bribed or the bribers? . . . Who are the bribers? They are often men who walk the earth lordly and secure, members of good families; respected figures of their communities; graduates of universities. They are, in short, the privileged minority, and I submit that it is not unreasonable to ask of them that high standard of conduct which their training ought to have engendered.

I wonder whether in recent years we have unwittingly come to accept the totalitarian concept that the end justifies the means, a concept which is fundamentally and completely antagonistic to a true democratic society. Democracy is, I believe, more likely to be destroyed by the perversion of, or abandonment of, its true moral principles than by armed attack from Russia.[26]

Fulbright proposed that Congress appoint a commission of prominent citizens to analyze the problem of ethical conduct in public affairs, in the context of the investigations such as the RFC inquiry, the Kefauver hearings on O'Dwyer, and similar investigations. The senator suggested that such widely respected figures as former Supreme Court Justice Owen Roberts, Judge Learned Hand of New York, Reinhold Niebuhr of the Union Theological Seminary, and Robert Hutchins of the University of Chicago should be appointed to the commission. The commission would serve as a catalyst to draw conclusions and generate preventive measures from the mass of data then being unearthed by the investigations. Fulbright acknowledged that he would be lampooned as naive for making this proposal: "To expect, or even hope, for an improvement in the moral climate of Washington is, in the eyes of the boys who know, I am sure, thoroughly utopian."[27]

The commission idea provoked some discussion in academic circles, but otherwise came to naught. His overall conduct of the RFC investigation, however, magnified Fulbright's stature as a national political leader. Senator Douglas publicly endorsed Fulbright for the Democratic presidential nomination in 1952; Governor McMath of Arkansas stated that Fulbright's candidacy was more serious than that of a "favorite son."[28] Most political observers then assumed that Truman would not run again, and Fulbright was ultimately pleased by the choice of his old friend, Adlai E. Stevenson, as the party's nominee. Fulbright was shrewd enough as a politician to know that he had no chance for the nomination, and he encouraged his supporters to refrain from doing anything more than placing his name in nomination as a traditional "favorite son" candidate. Fulbright's admirers complied with these requests, resulting in a routine "favorite son" nomination of the Arkansan at the Democratic Convention in Chicago. Fulbright's conservative civil rights record would have offended Democratic liberals, while his thoughtful, independent stands on foreign policy positions had alienated the Cold Warriors. He had antagonized many of the Democratic professionals with his celebrated disagreement with Truman in the RFC affair, compounded by the earlier misunderstanding about his statement after the 1946 elections that Truman should resign.

In many respects, Fulbright held some of the same views about the nation's economic development as did many other Southern members of Congress. Once in 1948, when he was opposing the appointment of a Philadelphia banker to the Federal Reserve Board,

Fulbright revealed a strain of populism in his thinking:

> The people of the North are extremely solicitous of our welfare and progress. They assure us that if we will furnish better schools and abolish poll taxes and segregation that strife will cease and happiness reign. They are critical of our relative poverty, our industrial and social backwardness, and they are generous in their advice about our conduct. Their condescension in these matters is not appreciated . . . because these people . . . have for more than a century done everything they could to retard the economic development of the South. It is no secret that the South was treated like a conquered territory after 1865. Since that time, the tariff policy and the freight rate structure were designed by the North to prevent industrial development in the South; to keep that area in the status of a raw material producing colony. Above and beyond these direct restrictions, the most insidious of all, the most difficult to put your finger on—is the all-pervading influence of the great financial institutions and industrial monopolies. These influences are so subtle and so powerful that they have in many instances been able to dominate the political and economic life of the South and West from within those states as well as from Washington.[29]

Fulbright's historical assessment was awry in stating that the South was treated like a conquered territory for a lengthy period after 1865. The harsh period of Reconstruction was not lengthy, and the late 19th century was notable more for Northern acquiescence in allowing Southern states to conduct their racial policies after the end of slavery as the South saw fit, rather than any condescending meddling in Southern race relations.[30] Fulbright's hostility toward powerful Northern financial and industrial institutions, however, was understandable and not altogether inaccurate, although he might have admitted more fault on the people of the South themselves for some of their economic failures.

In 1955, when Fulbright became Chairman of the Banking and Currency Committee (his chairmanship of that committee continued until 1959, when he became Chairman of the Foreign Relations Committee) he undertook a "study" of the erratic behavior of the stock market. Market prices had risen dramatically during the previous 15 months. The Eisenhower administration was worried that the Fulbright hearings on the stock market would ignite concerns that Republican pro-business policies might lead to another stock market crash reminiscent of 1929. John Kenneth Galbraith testified before the Banking and Currency Committee in March, and he recalled that the Republican Presidents of the 1920s had lauded the virtues of America's business leaders at a time when such euphoria was unjustified, promoting skyrocketing stock prices; the Eisenhower administration was similarly exaggerating the virtues of big business. Other prominent economic experts also testified. The report that emerged from the Fulbright hearings was restrained and did not engage in any headline-seeking bashing of New York financiers, but Fulbright's committee had at least sent a message to the market that Congress was scrutinizing Wall Street. Fulbright's restrained study of the stock market was well received in Arkansas. At the end of the hearings, Fulbright announced that the committee had not discovered any severe problems in the market, although the prices of certain securities such as in mining, uranium, and nuclear power, had escalated far beyond their value. The committee had not uncovered any illegal activity, but it would continue to observe activities in the market. The Eisenhower administration criticized the hearings as allegedly improper meddling with the hallowed market, although the Federal Reserve Board did boost margin requirements for its member institutions to 70 percent.[31]

The 1948 speech about Northern economic power, whatever its exaggerations, clearly revealed Fulbright's deep concern for promoting the economic development of Arkansas. Ironically, Fulbright would later be criticized for allegedly "neglecting" Arkansas' domestic issues because of his international profile as Chairman of the Foreign Relations Committee. It was not true that Fulbright neglected Arkansas' local economic affairs. Fulbright led a battle in Congress to repeal federal taxes and license fees on margarine, which is made almost entirely from soybeans and cottonseed. When asked about the relevance of foreign policy to Arkansas, one of Fulbright's standard responses was to point out the great importance of foreign markets for the state's rice, cotton, chickens, and other agricultural products. He supported the Dixon-Yates power combine, thus offending more liberals outside the South, and his sponsorship of the 1955 natural gas bill (along with Rep. Fred Harris of Oklahoma) led to a break with his old friend, Paul Douglas of Illinois. If Northern liberals were antagonized by Fulbright's action, the Arkansan had solidified his support among southwestern oil and gas producers, notably Witt Stephens. When Douglas charged that the bill would impose great hardships on the urban masses, Fulbright countered that it was time for the South to gain its fair share of the nation's wealth. The North and East had long exploited the natural resources of the rest of the country through domination of Congress and the Interstate Commerce Commission, Fulbright alleged. "The issue," the Arkansan proclaimed, "is whether the poorest section of our land shall continue to be exploited as it has been exploited throughout our history, in order to enrich the great urban centers which have the power to impose their will." The Eisenhower administration was initially impressed by the free enterprise rhetoric behind the bill and thought it could strengthen its political appeal in the Southwest through its support for the bill. Senator Lyndon Baines Johnson provided powerful support for the bill, which passed the Senate easily. However, Republican Senator Francis Case of South Dakota disclosed that a lawyer for the gas interests had offered him a bribe, and the President handed down a veto.[32]

In his positions on the natural gas bill and labor, he reflected the influences in his family business and his patrician background. On many other domestic social and economic issues, he was unpredictable, leading those who insisted upon thinking in terms of ironclad categories of "liberal" or "conservative" to be confused. He opposed a minimum wage bill, thus displeasing the unions. He was not a Keynesian in economic policy and consistently was suspicious of deficit spending; of course, much of his criticism of excessive government spending focused on the massive military spending that consumed such a large share of the budget. On some domestic issues, he voted in a manner that Democratic liberals could approve. He consistently fought for passage of federal aid to education legislation throughout his career, and supported federal housing, job training and anti-poverty programs. These policies would attack the source of social unrest, in the senator's view, but during the Cold War such policies were starved by the exorbitant costs of defense spending.

When Fulbright faced the greatest domestic movement of his era—the civil rights movement of the 1950s and 1960s—he was carrying a heavy political burden from his numerous controversial stands on a wide variety of issues. The racial extremists regarded him as suspect on the subject of segregation, for such positions as having opposed the Dixiecrats and for his conspicuous failure to engage in racial oratory, as Jim Johnson and later, Orval Faubus, would do with such fervor, to their lasting discredit. The theoretical call for Truman's resignation and the RFC controversy had angered many Democratic professionals in the Truman administration. Indeed, Haynes Johnson would go so far as to write in his 1967 biography that "In the end, Fulbright would contribute greatly, [because of the RFC hearings and his speeches about governmental ethics] though unintentionally, to the failure of his party to maintain control of the White House, and the subsequent beginning of the Eisenhower era."[33] Actually, this statement exaggerates the significance of the RFC hearings, which weakened the Democrats somewhat in the 1952 campaign but were certainly not crucial to Eisenhower's resounding victory. Fulbright's foreign policy positions had antagonized the Cold Warriors, while his unpredictable stands on many other domestic issues had at times irritated other interest groups. The senator also lacked the back-slapping political skills of a Faubus or other traditional Arkansas politicians. The Rhodes Scholar and law professor would enter the fateful era of massive resistance with a substantial burden of political problems, although the problems remained largely under the surface in the 1950s. Many Arkansans took pride in the fact that a brilliant intellectual represented them in the Senate. In the coming years, the Supreme Court's decision in *Brown v. Board of Education* would present him with the greatest domestic political challenge of his life.

III. INITIAL RESPONSES TO BROWN V. BOARD OF EDUCATION, 1954-1956

Arkansas political leaders had displayed a relatively progressive attitude toward racial issues in the late 1940s and early 1950s. Fulbright had used his influence as a former constitutional law professor and president of the University of Arkansas in Fayetteville to work quietly for the desegregation of the law school, and blacks were admitted beginning in 1948.[28] The graduate schools were desegregated shortly thereafter. Fulbright and McMath had resolutely opposed the Dixiecrats and facilitated Truman's victory in Arkansas in the 1948 election. In a widely publicized speech in Memphis during the presidential campaign, Fulbright had condemned "the threatened revolt of the South" and warned that "the effect of multiple parties on our traditionally two-party system can be extremely serious to the future of our constitutional system of self-government."[29] Characteristically, Fulbright avoided any specifics concerning civil rights issues, but the fact of supporting Truman against the Democrats in 1948 was nonetheless significant; Truman had incurred the wrath of Southern segregationists for his resolute positions regarding racial justice. The President's executive order in July, 1948 had required equality of treatment for all military personnel, and by the time of the Korean War racial segregation had been eliminated in the Navy and the Air Force. Demands for manpower after the military conflict began led to dramatic progress in integrating the Army, and the last all-black Army units were ended by 1954. The findings of the Civil Rights Commission's landmark report, *To Secure These Rights*, had revealed shocking racial injustices, and such revelations clearly hounded Truman's conscience. In the 1948 campaign, Truman fought for an end to the poll taxes that still existed in seven Southern states, federal anti-lynching legislation, an end to discrimination in the armed forces, and the establishment of a Fair Employment Practices Committee with authority to stop discrimination by employers and labor unions, and an end to discrimination in interstate travel. Truman's biographer, David McCullough, would describe Truman's 1948 civil rights message to Congress as "a brave, revolutionary declaration, given the reality of entrenched discrimination and the prevailing attitudes of white Americans nearly everywhere in the country, but especially in the South, where the social status and legal 'place' of black citizens had advanced not at all in more than half a century... Asked at a press conference a few days later what he had drawn on for background, he replied, the Constitution and the Bill of Rights." Truman had not entirely outgrown his Missouri background—some of his ancestors had been Confederates—and in private conversation he often reverted to the crude segregationist chatter of the region where he had grown up; but his leadership in the civil rights arena by 1948 was unmistakable. As Clark Clifford ably summarized the President's progress regarding racial issues: "The wonderful, wonderful development in those years was Harry Truman's capacity to grow."[29a]

Unlike McMath, Fulbright had been careful not to antagonize the powerful Southern segregationists. In 1943, he had voted against a bill to outlaw the poll tax. In 1945, Fulbright opposed the nomination of Aubrey Williams for a 10-year term as head of the Rural Electrification Administration. Williams, an Alabama native, had formerly been an able administrator in directing the National Youth Administration, and had been a valiant advocate of racial justice. In particular, he had advocated legal abolition of discriminatory hiring practices. The Alabama progressive had incurred the wrath of the Southern racists: Theodore Bilbo of Mississppi ranted that "We do not want this Negro-lover on the job." In 1946, Fulbright took part in a filibuster against continuation of the Fair Employment Practices Committee. Fulbright pontificated that the FEPC could not transform public morals by legislative decree: "Do you think that you can make people hire those whom they regard as unfit for any reason?... In theory no one approves of discrimination of any kind," but laws could not change human nature. Proponents of the FEPC could not muster the two-thirds vote needed to force cloture, and the legislation renewing the FEPC died. In response to the Truman administration's program in *To Secure These Rights*, Fulbright and Senator Richard Russell of Georgia discussed a compromise: Southerners would support anti-poll tax and anti-lynching legislation, but the North would not disturb Southern segregation and employment discrimination. Fulbright was disturbed by the radical Southerners who abandoned the Democratic Party and supported the Dixiecrats under Strom Thurmond in 1948, and he sought to develop some compromise that would ease the strains within the Democratic coalition. Harry Ashmore of the *Arkansas Gazette*, Mark Ethridge of the *Louisville Courier-Journal*, Congressman Brooks Hays of Arkansas, Senator Carl Hayden (D-Arizona) and other moderates championed the compromise, which became known as the "Arkansas Plan." Ashmore contended that Southerners would accept anti-poll tax and anti-lynching laws, but for many years they would persist in rejecting desegregation and fair employment legislation. Fulbright was so cautious about the issue that he would only lobby in private for the Arkansas Plan, but made no public endorsement of it. Truman rejected the Arkansas Plan. Again in early 1949 the Southern bloc engaged in a filibuster against the Truman administration's support for the program embodied in *To Secure These Rights*. In 1948, Truman had become the first presidential candidate from one of the major parties to campaign in Harlem. He reminded his Harlem audience that he had already issued two executive orders to establish equal opportunity in the armed services and in federal employment, and he promised to persist in his commitment to equal opportunity. In a famous campaign replete with huge crowds and enthusiastic applause, the ovation Truman received in Harlem was the most deafening of all.[29b]

Truman's courageous position risked antagonizing the powerful Southern Democratic bloc, although his civil rights positions won tremendous support from the black community, which was crucial in some Northern areas. In Arkansas, Truman found a stalwart ally in Governor McMath, who had backed enfranchisement of blacks, appointed several blacks to previously all-white state commissions, and opposed the disparity in funding for white schools over black schools.[30] These were limited measures, but were great improvements over the state's previous leaders who had usually ignored race except to inflame segregationist prejudices during elections. McMath's position was in contrast to that of Fulbright, who had carefully avoided offending the segregationist bloc–with the exception of his stout loyalty to Truman in the 1948 campaign–with such votes as his opposition to an appropriation for the Fair Employment Practices Committee. McMath's campaign to win a third term failed in 1952, but race had little to do with the outcome; the crucial issues that led to the defeat were revelations of financial improprieties among some of McMath's aides in the Highway Department, and an Arkansas tradition against any governor serving more than two terms.[31] Despite these setbacks, in 1954 McMath challenged the conservative Senator John L. McClellan, and missed forcing him into a runoff by the narrow margin of 5,000 votes.[32]

Brooks Hays had advanced a series of moderate initiatives in the period just before Brown. In early May 1954, he testified at a congressional hearing to endorse legislation against segregation in interstate transportation. Hays said the bill he backed would end the patchwork patterns of handling seating and accommodations for passengers in interstate commerce. "Still fixed in my memory," Hays recalled, "was a train ride I had taken as a boy when the Negro passengers had been crowded into the rear of the car while there were still many vacant seats in the white section." The congressman reminisced that "I had often wondered what the effect would have been of removing the rope dividing the sections or at least moving it forward so that all passengers could ride in comfort." Hays agreed with arguments that requiring passengers to move from one coach to another when crossing state lines into the South violated the Equal Protection Clause, and then argued that Supreme Court decisions in this field were correct in making "non-segregation" a national policy. He felt that "It is wise for the Congress to make clear that there is a policy of the national community and that interstate travel must be governed by that policy of non-segregation."[33]

As a member of the House Foreign Affairs Committee, Hays emphasized in his testimony that it was important in the Cold War struggle for the sympathies of the Third World to impress upon foreign black visitors American strides toward progress in racial justice. Hays commended the previous "ground-breaking" decisions of the Supreme Court in invalidating segregation in this area, and added that he spoke "for this proposed legislation to enable the government to assume the burden and expense of prosecuting cases."[34] Interstate transportation was far less controversial and important than education, but Hays was nonetheless assuming a forthright stand in favor of ameliorating Southern race relations.

Initial responses to Brown in 1954 were temperate. Hays set the tone by contending that "the people of Arkansas always had accepted the principle that ours is a government of laws and not of men," and that he was confident "the state's leadership will apply itself with diligence to the ways and means of meeting standards set out in the Court's decision."[35] Congressman James Trimble from the northwest Arkansas district observed that "Arkansas will meet the problem with its usual common sense." Trimble and Congressman Oren Harris, whose district included part of the delta, were pleased that Brown might lead to increased federal aid to education in the South.[36] Governor Francis Cherry, in the midst of his reelection campaign against Faubus, emphasized that "We will not approach the matter from the standpoint of being outlaws," and promised not to follow if other Southern leaders threatened to ignore the Court's rulings.[37]

In 1954-55 Fulbright emphasized to his constituents that the South must refrain from extreme resistance to the *Brown* decision, and that a few school districts in the state were proceeding toward desegregation without incident. In April 1955, a constituent from the northwest Arkansas town of Charleston told Fulbright that the integration of schools in that small town was advancing without racial strife.[38] Fulbright replied to the Charleston constituent that "the result of integration in the Charleston schools was extremely interesting. I think that the same situation has prevailed at Fayetteville where Negroes are also attending school with Whites."[39] Fayetteville was not typical of Arkansas since its citizens claimed that their town was one of the first in the South to integrate its schools, and the black population was tiny in the mountainous northwest.[40] A limited amount of desegregation took place without mishap in northwest Arkansas from 1954 to 1957, and by early 1957, 10 school districts were integrated.[41]

The moderates were also encouraged in May 1955, when the Supreme Court handed down *Brown v. Board of Education of Topeka (Brown II)*, 349 U.S. 294 (1955). In correspondence with constituents, Fulbright commended the Court's decision that the school desegregation cases "arose under different local conditions and their disposition will involve a variety of local problems," and that courts would have to consider whether the action of local school authorities constituted good faith implementation.[42] The senator was particularly pleased with the language stating that "the courts will require that the defendants make a prompt and reasonable start toward full compliance with our May 17, 1954 ruling. Once such a start has been made, the courts may find that additional time is necessary to carry out the ruling in an effective manner."[43] In a letter to a constituent in the summer of 1955, Fulbright related that "I was pleased to see that the court recognized the many difficulties which their decision will bring about," and expressed confidence that "educational leaders in Arkansas are giving this matter a great deal of thought and study and will arrive at some workable solution as to how the court's decision can be equitably carried out."[44] Of course, *Brown II* left myriad issues unanswered, but the clear early response of moderates in Arkansas was appreciation for the Court's understanding that historic social changes could not be achieved "immediately," as Fulbright phrased it.[45]

Fulbright was similarly restrained in communications with segregationist constituents in the plantation belt. Despite the Court's restraint in *Brown II*, extremists in the delta began agitating the race issue in response to the ruling. The extremists had initially pinned their hopes on the conservative Southern federal district judges who would decide whether local school authorities' actions constituted good faith implementation "because of their proximity to local conditions." But in 1955 and early 1956, while many district judges embraced a lenient view of the amount of time required for desegregation, others emphasized the "prompt and reasonable start" requirement and began to set dates for compliance. In early 1956 Judge J. Skelly Wright would deliver a resounding opinion declaring that "the magnitude of the problem may not nullify the principle."[46] By the summer of 1955, the NAACP had filed desegregation petitions signed by local blacks in 170 school boards in 17 states.[47] These developments sent the extreme right wing leaders in the delta into paroxysms of rage against the Warren Court. In 1955 several prominent east Arkansas businessmen expressed their outrage against *Brown II* and demanded that Fulbright should exert his influence in an attempt to reverse the *Brown* decision.[48] "There is no way," Fulbright informed the extremists, "under our Constitution, that a legislative act can affect a decision of the Supreme Court."[49] Fulbright advised the east Arkansas constituents that Arkansans would have to comply with the Supreme Court's ruling regardless of their opinions concerning desegregation.[50]

Faubus had similarly declined to inflame racist sentiment in 1955, resisting pressure to abet the efforts of Jim Johnson and other firebrands to obstruct the desegregation of Hoxie, a small town in northeast Arkansas near the area where the hill country ends and the delta begins.[51] In another decision strengthening the moderates in 1955, Faubus appointed Winthrop Rockefeller to head the Arkansas Industrial Development Commission, which led the effort to attract new industry to the state. Rockefeller was a vigorous proponent of the view that Northern capital could not be attracted and a healthy climate for business could not be developed if Arkansas developed a reputation for racial strife.[52]

Fulbright did not regard Faubus as a demagogue in 1954-55. The moderates in the Democratic Party shared that assessment and were on amicable terms with Faubus at that time. In December, 1955, Adlai Stevenson, Fulbright and Faubus ventured on a duck hunt in Arkansas together, with a famous photograph in the *Arkansas Gazette* capturing the three leaders in a jovial mood. Two short years later, it became apparent that Faubus differed drastically from Fulbright and Stevenson in the Arkansas governor's blatant willingness to inflame prejudices of the voters in order to advance his political career. Fulbright had a sympathetic attitude toward people who grew up in small towns and later achieved positions of prominence. In this context, Fulbright spoke positively of Faubus in an interview at Columbia University in 1956 (Fulbright stipulated that the interview was not to be made public until after his death). High among Fulbright's values were the virtues of small-town America and the lightly populated states, like Arkansas. In the Columbia interview and other occasions, the senator revealed an innocent faith in inner America, its people and its leaders. He spoke of Faubus in the interview as one of the governors from small states who were serving splendidly. In 1956—before Faubus revealed himself as a demagogue in the Central High crisis—Fulbright and many other Arkansans had a regard for Faubus that was lost forever in 1957.[52a]

While Faubus maintained a reasonably circumspect record on racial issues in 1954-55, it should be emphasized that even in his "moderate" period he never demonstrated the deep sensitivity for racial justice displayed by Rockefeller, Hays, or McMath. Faubus' campaign against Governor Francis Cherry in 1954 basically did not focus on racial questions, but upon Faubus' criticisms of the governor for being too closely aligned with the state's big business interests, especially the Arkansas Power and Light Company.[53] However, at one point Faubus experimented with the use of school segregation as a campaign tactic, inserting advertisements in the *Gazette* and *Democrat* claiming that the principal issue in the current campaign was segregation. He proposed a local option solution, which would allow whites to control Arkansas public schools but would provide for the possibility of some desegregation in the future. The plan's emphasis on local control would have entrenched segregation, and the *Gazette* sharply criticized Faubus for attempting to inject race into the campaign.[54] The *Gazette* was basically supportive of Faubus at the time because of his reputation as a progressive in the McMath tradition, and Faubus avoided any references to the segregation issue for the remainder of the campaign. His upset of Cherry was largely based on the governor's blunder in hurling McCarthyite charges against Faubus as a communist sympathizer for his connections as a youth with Commonwealth College, which was later designated a communist-front organization by the Justice Department.[55] This was a sensitive issue for Faubus, whose father was a well-known radical political activist in Arkansas who had been a longtime admirer of Eugene V. Debs. The Arkansas moderates at the time regarded red-baiting tactics with disdain; Fulbright's leadership was critical in that regard. At one point in early 1954, Fulbright had cast the lone dissenting vote in the Senate against the appropriations for Senator Joseph McCarthy's anticommunist witch hunts, with the Senate voting in favor of McCarthy by 85 to one.[56] Although Fulbright initially suffered a storm of abuse from the right for his opposition to McCarthy, his condemnation of McCarthy's demagogy increasingly came to be seen as courageous as time passed; the Arkansan filed the bill of particulars that formed the basis of the Senate's censure of McCarthy later in the year.[57] By launching the McCarthyite attack on Faubus, Cherry lost all credibility with the moderates and ran afoul of a general antipathy among Arkansas voters for "mudslinging" tactics.

Faubus similarly benefited from his opponent's mudslinging charges in the 1956 gubernatorial election against the segregationist, Jim Johnson, who condemned Faubus for being "soft on integration" because of the governor's appointment of six blacks to the Democratic State Committee.[58] Faubus countered these charges in 1956 by denouncing Johnson as "a purveyor of hate" in race relations, and pleading for "the cooperation of all the people in upholding the law and order and in preserving . . . peace and harmony."[59] Faubus eventually won reelection, with comfortable margins of victory in regions outside the delta, winning 180,000 votes to 83,000 for Johnson, with minor candidates winning about 45,000. However, much of the Faubus landslide in 1956 emanated from the strong Arkansas tradition that a governor should be given two terms but not more, barring extraordinary circumstances. Johnson was a dynamic, eloquent orator who became the champion of the right wing and attracted the highest vote of any runner-up in a race against an incumbent governor in the state's recent history. Fulbright regarded Johnson as the extremist and Faubus as the relatively "moderate" candidate in the race. Fulbright's impression at the time was widely shared; as C. Vann Woodward would write in *The Strange Career of Jim Crow*, "Governor Orval E. Faubus of Arkansas had been elected over an all-out segregationist and had earned a reputation for moderation."[59a] If Faubus wished to run again in 1958, two severe political problems loomed: the staunch resistance against allowing a governor to serve more than two terms, and the burgeoning opposition to Faubus from the extreme segregationist faction. Moreover, it was not clear that public sentiment in the state would continue in the relatively moderate mode characterized by the initial responses to *Brown*, for Johnson and his allies were diligently attempting to inflame anti-Supreme Court opinion, combining segregationist prejudice with states' rights sentiment and animosity toward "'outsiders'" attempting to influence the resolution of Arkansas' affairs. The conflict between the competing forces would culminate at Central High.

IV. THE EMERGENCE OF
MASSIVE RESISTANCE, 1956-57

Responses to *Brown* began to change in late 1955 and early 1956. Extremists escalated their rhetoric against the Supreme Court, and Eisenhower refused to support *Brown*, effectively undermining the Court with such platitudes as "I don't believe you can change the hearts of men with laws or decisions." Richard Russell of Georgia, Harry Byrd of Virginia, and other powerful senators began organizing the Southern congressional bloc to foment resistance to desegregation.[60] Moderates in Arkansas had hoped that the conservative, patrician Byrd would respond in a manner similar to the conservative Governor Francis Cherry. Cherry had no affection for integration, but his conviction that the rule of law must be upheld trumped his status-quo beliefs regarding segregation. The reality that Byrd, Russell, and the other patriarchs of the Southern bloc were instigating massive resistance to *Brown* exerted a powerful impact on some of the Arkansas leaders, particularly Faubus and Fulbright. In a harbinger of his later role as racist demagogue, in January 1956, Faubus sent five east Arkansans to Virginia to study "legal" methods of obstructing desegregation. Faubus concluded that moderate sentiment was still strong enough to justify a platform portraying himself as the temperate alternative to Johnson, but the mission to Virginia to study massive resistance from the "experts" demonstrates his uneasiness about the threat posed by the "massive resisters."[61] In early 1956, leaders of the Southern bloc in Congress exerted immense pressures on wavering Southerners to endorse a polemic against *Brown*, creating severe problems for moderates such as Hays and Fulbright, who were up for re-election.

Russell, Strom Thurmond of South Carolina and three other Southerners drafted a document entitled the "Declaration of Constitutional Principles," later known as the Southern Manifesto. The first draft of the statement condemned *Brown* as a "flagrant and unjustified abuse of judicial power" and upheld the states' rights to nullify the Court's ruling.[62] Fulbright, Hays, Senators Albert Gore and Estes Kefauver of Tennessee, Senator George Smathers of Florida, and Senator Price Daniel of Texas privately opposed the Southern Manifesto; Lyndon Johnson advised the Southern leaders he would not be able to sign it because of his national political position as majority leader, rather than any disrespect for the other Southerners.[63] It was a crucial episode for Fulbright, who contemplated publicly breaking with the Southern bloc over the issue. The senator drafted and circulated among his colleagues a statement which he planned to deliver in justifying his dissent, warning: "I fear the statement holds out the false illusion to our own southern people that there is some

means by which we can overturn the Supreme Court's decision. Our duty to our own people in their hour of travail is one of candor and realism. It is not realistic to say that a decision of the Supreme Court is illegal and unconstitutional, and to imply, thereby, that it can
be overturned by some higher tribunal."[64] Fulbright objected that the Manifesto could be
interpreted as endorsement of several nullification and interposition measures that the legislatures of several Southern states had passed, and concluded, "I do not wish to be in the
position of giving any such blanket endorsement and commitment, particularly since my
own state has taken no such action."[65] In early 1956 the Alabama legislature declared the
Court's school decision "null, void, and of no effect," and the legislatures of Georgia,
Mississippi, South Carolina, and Virginia passed similar anti-desegregation resolutions.[66] At
that time Arkansas had refrained from such actions. Fulbright warned his colleagues that "I
do not wish to hold out any false hope that such measures will be successful, especially
those which envision recalling the ghost of nullification."[67]

Despite Fulbright's rejection of the interposition resolutions, he did not question the
Southern antipathy to federal "intrusion" upon state authority; but he contended that the
most effective way to avoid such intervention would be "to convince many persons of good
will in the rest of the nation that we ourselves have been making rapid progress in the
improvement of race relations and in the welfare of the Negro minority in the South."[68] In
the Arkansan's view, Southern invective against the Court would alienate public opinion in
the North and encourage extremism: "It is a false assumption that the nation will support
us in defiance or castigation of the Supreme Court. In the end this problem will be solved
by the good will, tolerance, understanding and moderation of all the people–North and
South." Fulbright's conclusion caused considerable consternation in the Byrd camp, as he
warned, "I fear the statement will give aid and comfort to agitators and trouble makers within and without the South."[69]

Byrd and Russell were deeply concerned over the schism within the Southern ranks. It
was imperative, in their view, that the South come as close to unanimity as possible; with
Fulbright, Hays, Smathers and Daniel threatening to join the Tennessee senators in dissent,
and perhaps attracting other dissenters in their wake, the statement could attract criticism
in a significant section of the South. In their private negotiations with the dissenters, Byrd
and Russell pursued a two-pronged strategy of wielding pressure against them to conform
to the basic Southern position while promising minor, legalistic concessions to Fulbright's
viewpoint.[70] One of this book's authors, James O. Powell, was Smathers' administrative
assistant at the time. The aide remarked to the senator that the Manifesto was an extreme
document—of the sort that the celebrated Arkansas trial lawyer and later federal judge,
Henry Woods, would subsequently describe as efforts "to renegotiate Appomattox."
Smathers replied to his aide, "Hell, you should have seen it before Fulbright and I toned it
down."

Fulbright and Hays were in a vulnerable position. Although the moderates could be
politically viable when they took the position of reluctantly acquiescing in gradual desegregation on the grounds that the rule of law must be respected, and that other goals such as
economic development and educational improvement ranked higher than segregation, it
was also abundantly clear that no Southern politician could have survived if he had taken
a "liberal" position of enthusiastically endorsing widespread, immediate integration as an

essential goal in itself by 1956. If their opponents had been able to portray Fulbright and Hays as actual race "liberals" at the time, they would have had little or no chance of surviving the 1956 election. In an emotional atmosphere, moreover, the distinction between the liberal and moderate positions might have been obscured by their opponents. In planning the break with the Byrd-Russell faction, Fulbright and Hays were mapping out a strategy that could at once oppose the extremists and avoid being tarred as left-wing radicalism; it was a precarious effort. McMath was privately encouraging Fulbright to make his dissent public, advising the senator that he could become the leader of a viable moderate coalition if he would forcefully drive home the points of his memorandum against the Manifesto.[71] At the time Fulbright was popular and did not have any opposition, although he believed an opponent might emerge if he opposed the Manifesto. Hays, Little Rock Mayor Woodrow Mann, the *Gazette*, Rockefeller, and other moderates stood ready to aid him; most of the congressional delegation consisted of members who were not then identified with the hardline segregationist wing of the party, such as Harris, Trimble, and Wilbur Mills. And Faubus was still closer to the moderate camp than to the Johnsonites.

For a brief interlude, it appeared as though Fulbright might publicly deliver his eloquent critique of the Manifesto. In February, Fulbright wrote to Theo Epperson, a black labor leader in Pine Bluff: "I had hoped that this matter could be gradually worked out without bitterness and violence being stirred up, and I still hope that this can be done in Arkansas."[72] Fulbright referred to the mob violence that had erupted in Alabama that month when the black student Autherine Lucy attempted to enroll at the University of Alabama, and remarked to Epperson that "I am sure you have read of the difficulty in some of the other Southern states, and by all means, we want to avoid this in Arkansas."[73] Epperson implored the senator to stand firmly behind the Supreme Court's authority: "We the colored people are American citizens and we feel we are entitled to all the things all other people are. Do you think that? Colored and White children going to school together. We are depending on you to support the action [*Brown*]. Can we depend on you? Because you can depend on us."[74] Mrs. L. C. "Daisy" Bates, leader of the Little Rock NAACP, thought she had received the answer to Epperson's question from friends of McMath and Fulbright who knew about the behind-the-scenes discussions and prematurely informed the NAACP that Fulbright had definitely accepted McMath's entreaties and was preparing to oppose the Manifesto.[75] When Fulbright ultimately decided against the break with the Southern bloc, black leaders, and especially Daisy Bates were bitterly disillusioned by Fulbright's failure to oppose the extremists.[76]

Severe pressures militated against Fulbright taking the plunge against the Southern Senate bloc. Not only did he risk having his opposition to extremism distorted by opponents into a radical left-wing stance, but even if he survived the election, his future in the Senate would be undermined by destroying his relationship with the powerful Southern patriarchs who wielded great influence within Congress. Byrd made it clear that a failure to sign would be "disloyalty" to the region, and Fulbright's bright future, with the chairmanship of the Senate Foreign Relations Committee looming just a few years away if he could continue to ascend in the hierarchy, would fade. Fulbright genuinely respected and held affection for his Southern colleagues, especially Russell, a man Fulbright argued would have made a great President had he not suffered from a tragic rigidity on the racial issue. It was ironic that Fulbright uttered that regret about Russell, for many progressives found the same flaw in the Arkansas senator.[76a]

The plight of Russell's colleague Senator Walter George of Georgia held poignancy for Fulbright, because George had the inherent disadvantage of being chairman of the Foreign Relations Committee and was thus vulnerable to the criticism that he devoted too much time to foreign affairs, to the alleged neglect of his constituents' local concerns. Fulbright, as a senior member on Foreign Relations and noted foreign policy leader in the Congress, had similar problems, although they were not as serious in 1956 as they became after the Arkansan assumed the chairmanship in 1959. George was also confronted with an attack from the extreme right on the race issue in Georgia, where the extremist Herman Talmadge was accusing George of being weak in defending the Southern way of life; indeed, part of Russell's motivation in supporting the Manifesto was to give George a way of demonstrating his commitment to segregation in order to parry the Talmadge onslaught. The Talmadge strategy ultimately succeeded in forcing George to retire in spite of his signing of the Manifesto, but George's moribund political fate was already evident by late February and March, when the discussions over the Manifesto took place.[77]

Fulbright and Hays eventually concluded that dissent would create serious opposition to their re-election chances and only lead to their replacement in Congress by segregationist hotspurs. In addition to political pressures, Byrd and Russell made concessions to the moderate position. Language referring to "nullification and interposition" was stricken from the Manifesto, and some of the inflammatory rhetoric was deleted.[78] Fulbright and Hays may have believed at the time that they had won a significant victory in making clear that only "lawful" criticism of the Court was being countenanced by the Manifesto, and Fulbright's supporters would later attempt to defend his eventual signing of the Manifesto by emphasizing his "moderating" role.[79] But his attempts to restrain the Southern attack on the Court obviously ended in failure, since many inflammatory passages remained in the final version of the document, and the moderate position Fulbright had previously taken in advocating respect for the Court was now seriously undermined. The Manifesto condemned Brown as a "clear abuse of judicial power" and commended the motives of the states "which have declared the intention to resist forced integration by any lawful means."[80] The Southerners assailed the Court for encroaching upon states' rights and planting racial hatreds and suspicions where there had been racial understanding. The decision was unwarranted and "contrary to the constitution," since the Supreme Court possessed no power to demand an end to segregation, a power only the states held, according to the Manifesto.[81] In the end, 101 members signed, and 27 Southerners refused to sign; but in the Senate only Johnson, Gore and Kefauver declined, and so the names of Fulbright and Daniel were published next to those of Thurmond, Eastland, and Byrd.[82]

The Southern Manifesto debacle dealt a devastating blow to the moderate cause in the South and to their potential allies elsewhere in the country. Ashmore, who was on leave from the *Gazette* in order to serve as an adviser to Adlai Stevenson in the 1956 presidential campaign, argued that the Southern Democratic support for the Manifesto weakened Stevenson's campaign by antagonizing blacks and racial moderates throughout the nation. "The Manifesto was a final disillusionment," Ashmore wrote, for black Democrats everywhere, adding: "They had been able to make a distinction between moderates and extremists of the South; they could recall 1948 when the majority of the Southern leaders refused to follow Strom Thurmond under the Dixiecrat banner; they could disassociate men like Fulbright, Hill and Sparkman from Eastland, Talmadge, and Ellender." But now, the Southern senators all stood together, Ashmore recalled, "and where they stood, no Negro could stand."[83] C. Vann Woodward accurately analyzed the Southern responses to *Brown* from 1954 to early 1956: "The border states gave early indication of compliance, and the so-called mid-South states—Tennessee, Arkansas, Texas, and Florida—appeared to be inclining toward the example of the border states rather than in the opposite direction."[84] But the Manifesto symbolized a turning point; as Woodward observed, "Among the signers were several political leaders who had previously spoken in tones of moderation and from whom better leadership was expected."[85] The entire episode left the moderate faction demoralized and exhausted. As Fulbright wrote in a discouraging letter to former Undersecretary of State Will Clayton in the aftermath of the Manifesto controversy: "The rising tension in the South threatens to weaken the educational system in the various Southern states. Senator Byrd is asserting very strong leadership in stirring up the resistance of the South, which as you know, is sometimes difficult to control once it is underway." Fulbright advised Clayton that the Manifesto "was reluctantly signed by a number of Senators, but the alternative [a break with the Southern bloc] was unacceptable. All in all it is not an encouraging picture."[86] Moderate constituents expressed their profound disillusionment to the senator; as one Little Rock woman lamented, "I am afraid you have given encouragement to the up-to-now small but vocal hate groups of White America, White Citizens' Councils and other such 'hate' groups existing in the state."[87]

Hays was similarly melancholy in the aftermath of the Manifesto's signing, observing shortly afterward that "while it contained items which to me would have been better omitted and expressed some sentiments in language not to my liking, I believed the declaration was an honest reaction to the injury the South believed had been done to its way of life."[88] Hays argued that since it was known that the moderates had secured the deletion of all references to nullification and interposition, the statement was largely a rhetorical barb that reflected the majority of the Southerner's right of dissent without "advocating measures which might do violence to the Constitution."[89] Given the Manifesto's inflammatory rhetoric against the Court, however, the congressman was clearly troubled by his concession to the segregationists, despite his efforts at justification. The political pressures some of the Southern moderates were facing were amply demonstrated in the 1956 North Carolina elections, in which two congressmen who refused to sign were defeated.[90] On the other hand, Albert Gore, Sr., would survive the episode and continue another 14 years in office, as did a number of other dissenters.

Massive resistance at the congressional level created problems for the moderates in central Arkansas who were trying to devise a desegregation plan to comply with *Brown*. Yet the Little Rock moderates remained relatively resilient. In November 1956, almost half of the city's voters opposed a White Citizens Council-sponsored constitutional amendment nullifying *Brown*. White supremacy advocates directly attacked the Little Rock School Board's "gradualist" desegregation plan in March 1957 in the school board elections, and extremists were soundly defeated by moderate candidates.[91] The Little Rock School Board had instructed Superintendent Virgil Blossom to draw up a compliance plan one day after the May 17,

1954 decision was handed down. After prodigious study of the situation, Blossom developed the Little Rock Phase Program in 1955, which provided for nine black students to begin attending Little Rock Central High in 1957, with increasing numbers being integrated into white schools in succeeding years and elementary school desegregation to begin in the early 1960s.[92]

While the Little Rock School Board won praise among moderates for developing a plan immediately after *Brown* was announced when most Southern school officials made no effort to do so, Blossom's plan was in fact seriously flawed. Blossom was a local school administrator who meant well but had never faced the virulent opposition that he now encountered from the Guthridge and Johnson forces. The superintendent wanted to begin progress toward desegregation while simultaneously avoiding unduly antagonizing the Capital Citizens Council and the League of Central High School Mothers, well-organized segregationist groups that engaged in letter-writing campaigns to Faubus and otherwise publicized their adamant opposition to desegregation.[93] The membership of these groups was not large, but the intensity of their opposition was simply unsettling to the superintendent. Blossom engaged in the Sisyphean task of trying to appease these groups, who would not have been satisfied by anything less than total segregation.

The initial glaring flaw in the plan was its selection of only one high school to begin desegregation, allowing segregation to continue at the all-black Horace Mann High School and all-white Hall High School, the latter located in the socially prestigious Pulaski Heights area of the city where many of Little Rock's business and professional elite lived.[94] Designing the plan this way inflicted double-barreled wounds on desegregation: first, it meant that Central was left with pupils drawn primarily from the city's white lower and working classes, precisely the groups that were historically most likely to hold strong racial prejudices. Blossom tended to spend almost all his time consulting with people of higher socio-economic standing, and thus many lower class people felt that desegregation was being imposed upon them without consultation, while the wealthier classes from the Heights could continue to attend a lily-white school.[95] Secondly, many of the professional and business people who lived in the Heights were the moderates who were most likely to support desegregation at Hall, so that most of the people who would have supported sending their children to school with blacks had no direct involvement.[96] Since this was a local matter, Fulbright, of course, was not initially involved in it; but the controversy that later ignited over Little Rock school desegregation eventually involved all the major Arkansas politicians, willingly or not.

Blossom mistakenly believed that the way to mollify the Citizen Council forces was to promote the Phase Program as quietly as possible. Thus, despite the reality that Little Rock had a powerful moderate community, Blossom actually discouraged Rockefeller, Hays, the progressive Arkansas Council on Human Relations, McMath, the *Gazette* and others from discussing the plan publicly; at one point the Greater Little Rock Ministerial Alliance offered to endorse publicly the plan, but Blossom prevented them from doing it.[97] School authorities discouraged media coverage concerning the plan, and the *Gazette* had to give what favorable coverage it could without Blossom's cooperation. In his fears of antagonizing public opinion, Blossom allowed the uninformed views of parents to overrule the professional assessments of experienced educators, who had emphasized that it would be more beneficial to begin desegregation on the grade school level, where scholastic deficiencies and race consciousness were negligible. However, a public opinion poll Blossom commissioned revealed that white parents with elementary school children seemed more committed to segregation than those with high school children.[98] There was no program for preparing teachers for adjusting to a biracial student body. Finally, in order to avoid confrontations with segregationists at the more than 200 speeches he delivered concerning the plan from 1955 to 1957, Blossom apologetically said he believed the Supreme Court was moving too fast on desegregation, but there was no alternative to compliance. Given this negative, fearful approach, the school board had no reservoir of support when the crisis erupted in September 1957.[99]

One of the myths that Jim Johnson, Faubus and others would later propagate centered on the notion that local people of all races were happy with the status quo, but outside agitators came to Little Rock and fomented "extremist" pressures toward immediate integration. Actually, the reality was just the reverse; segregationists from the Deep South and the Arkansas delta came to Little Rock to fan the flames of massive resistance, but Northern liberals had little impact on the local situation until after it became a nationally publicized controversy. The Arkansas NAACP leaders initially supported Blossom's plan, and fashioned their responses to it without significant advice from the national NAACP office in New York. The national office had a tremendous number of items on its agenda, of course, and Little Rock did not initially rate at the top of its priorities. In August 1954, the local NAACP did not seem inclined to challenge the Little Rock School Board. Chairman Wiley Branton of the Legal Redress Committee wrote to School Board President William G. Cooper emphasizing that the NAACP had no intention of filing a suit against the board, and Daisy Bates announced in 1954 that there would be no litigation in areas where school boards moved toward integration and consulted with the NAACP.[100] However, in 1955, divisions within the local NAACP developed, with one group arguing that given the relatively moderate mood of race relations in the state, litigation should focus on school districts making no effort whatsoever to desegregate. This group was at first dominant, but the mood began to change when Blossom started hedging on his initial efforts, particularly when it became clear that the new Horace Mann High School would open in early 1956 as a segregated school. The local NAACP eventually decided to challenge the Blossom Plan, and advised the NAACP national office of its decision, in which the national officers played virtually no role.[101]

After a number of black children were turned away in an effort to register at several Little Rock schools in early 1956, *Aaron v. Cooper* was filed in the U. S. District Court for the Eastern District of Arkansas. The nature of desegregation in Little Rock would change dramatically by the time the issue reached the Supreme Court in different form in 1958, and by that time Fulbright would become involved in the case, drafting an *amicus curiae* brief in support of the school board's position. Presiding at the District Court level was Judge John E. Miller, a pillar of the Arkansas political and legal establishment who had formerly served as a U.S. senator, Roosevelt appointee to the federal court and close ally and friend of Senator Joseph T. Robinson, who as Senate Majority Leader had been responsible for guiding much of the New Deal legislation through Congress in the years from 1933 to 1937. Miller philosophically disagreed with *Brown*, but had a reputation even within NAACP circles for handing down decisions that were good faith implementations of the Court's May 17, 1954 ruling. An internal memorandum in the New York NAACP Legal Defense Fund office observed of Miller: "the rather consistent trend of Judge Miller's decisions on integration has caused many white Southerners to see the handwriting on the wall . . . a factor which will keep down violent expression."[102]

Blossom and Cooper testified that Blossom's Phase Program had been developed voluntarily before *Brown II*, and that it was reasonable in light of local conditions to make a gradual transition toward integration. The local NAACP was hampered in the case by the lack of enthusiastic interest of the out-of-state NAACP; a Dallas-based LDF lawyer, U. Simpson Tate, had not displayed any great interest in the Little Rock desegregation issue, although he would ultimately argue the case before Judge Miller. Tate had engaged in only perfunctory consultations with Branton and other Arkansas NAACP leaders beforehand. Branton had wanted a precise argument focusing on the limited nature of the Blossom Phase Program and the hardships it created for black children, many of whom lived near Central and had to walk by it and go two miles away to Horace Mann. Tate's argument, in fact, ran counter to the local NAACP's purpose, which was essentially to return to the original outlines of the Blossom Phase Program that had envisaged gradual desegregation at all the schools (this was the version Blossom developed before he began caving in to the pressure from the segregationists). Tate's argument was long on generalizations about the broad constitutional issues involved in desegregation, and short on the precise details for which Miller prided himself in deciding cases.[103]

Miller found that the Blossom Plan was a "prompt and reasonable start," and that there must be no interference with the plan, "so long as defendants move in good faith, as they have since immediately after the decision of May 17, 1954, to inaugurate and make effective a racially nondiscriminatory school system." The NAACP lost an appeal of this ruling to the Eighth Circuit in the spring of 1957. The quality of Tate's work may not have made a difference, and at the appellate level Thurgood Marshall and Branton handled the case and did a thorough, careful job. However, the various internal complications of the NAACP both at the local level and in the interaction between local and national levels illustrate the great difficulty of deciding upon the most effective legal strategies. Miller retained jurisdiction of the suit in order to deal with questions that might arise later as the school board carried out its program. When the decision was handed down in mid-1956, it was thought to be a defeat for the NAACP; ironically, the forces of reaction would alter the situation so drastically by late 1957 that the plan Miller upheld would become the rallying point for the supporters of desegregation.

Miller's decision was greeted with support by the majority of the moderates. The *Gazette* editorialized that "the Blossom Plan might well set a pattern for the Upper South and point a way out of the dilemma that now faces many Southern communities," adding: "It takes into account the social problems inherent in any such transition, and the emotional climate in which school officials must function. But it turns away from the futile course of defiance of the legal process . . . which is being urged across the Deep South."[104] Yet the decision was obviously troubling. Critics could ask at what point did "gradualism" become tokenism intended as obstruction of real desegregation. Certainly, delay would become the essential strategy elsewhere in the South several years later. Some of the moderates were saddened by the failure of the national NAACP to provide effective aid (since Tate's performance was less than first-rate), the internal disagreements within the local NAACP, and the school board's failure to build on its promising beginnings in 1954.

The absence of leadership from the school authorities was exacerbated by chaos in the city government. Mayor Mann was clearly a moderate in his political philosophy and sympathetic to the Rockefeller-McMath faction, but for reasons unrelated to race he had simply proven to be an inept administrator, and in 1956 the voters chose to dismantle the mayor-alderman form of government and replace it with a city manager form of government. The transition to the new form of government was not to begin until November 1957, so that Little Rock would have a lame-duck, discredited mayor at the time of the crisis.[105] Mann turned over the administration of the desegregation arrangements to Blossom, who was not a person inclined to accept responsibility for a controversial matter. Blossom in turn tried to lateral the responsibility to Faubus, urging him to make a statement promising to maintain order and permit no obstruction to desegregation. Faubus refused, asserting that it was a local problem that should be solved on the community level.[106] In mid-1957 the Capital Citizens Council and its allies escalated its propaganda campaign, which included leaflets, advertisements, out-of-state speakers, and a letter writing campaign to Faubus spreading and originating rumors about impending violence that threatened to erupt if desegregation proceeded as planned. One of the rumors held that a secret society of Ku Klux Klan-like fervor would descend upon the capital and engage in acts of terrorism if the Phase Program were not stopped. Neither FBI investigations (undertaken at the time and later made public) nor scholarship ever subsequently substantiated any of the rumors.[107]

One Arkansan's recollection of the summer of 1957 again strengthens the view that there was no real threat of an eruption of violence in Little Rock before Faubus' actions in calling out the National Guard and otherwise inciting racial tensions. Billy Roy Wilson, a high school football star from Scott County in western Arkansas, came to Little Rock for the High School all-star football game in August, and Virgil Blossom was his "sponsor" for the all-star festivities. Blossom took Wilson—whose parents were teachers in Waldron, Arkansas—to a couple of schools to show him some construction projects. Blossom told young Wilson and another student that he was working carefully with Governor Faubus behind the scenes, and that he and the Governor "felt sure that there would be no violence when token integration commenced" in a few weeks. Billy Roy Wilson would later emerge from his chrysalis to be transformed from football star into Vanderbilt Law School graduate, distinguished trial lawyer, and finally into United States District Judge William R. Wilson, Jr., an appointee by President Clinton to the federal court in Little Rock. Wilson vividly recalls that Blossom told him that they were keeping a close watch on the gun stores and pawn shops, and no unusual numbers of weapons were being sold.[107a] Wilson's strong impression from his conversation with Blossom was that the superintendent was confident that there was no actual threat of violence in early August 1957.

If Faubus provided no constructive leadership, it is nonetheless true that his political machinations were masterful. He continued to drift into the east Arkansas world on segregation, but extracted benefits from the oligarchs in return. Faubus' increasing political strength in the late 1950s would generate speculation that he would become a threat to defeat Fulbright for the Senate in 1962. To get the eastern Arkansas planters to support

Faubus' $22 million reform package for raising teachers' salaries and expanding benefits for the elderly, Faubus agreed to support a series of laws designed to delay desegregation. By making both the reform package and the segregation laws part of the same political compromise, Faubus secured passage of both when either one by itself might have encountered difficulty in passing.[108] The northwest Arkansas moderates were pleased by the reform elements of the package and not deeply concerned about the racial issue that did not affect most of their constituents directly; the eastern Arkansas conservatives were delighted by the segregation laws; and because Faubus declined to implement the segregation laws throughout much of 1957, even some of the Little Rock moderates could be somewhat mollified and reflect upon Faubus' achievements in fields other than race. However, this was a balancing act that would have to be resolved one way or the other when the September 1957 date for implementation of the Phase Program arrived.

Pressures on Faubus culminated in August when Governor Marvin Griffin of Georgia delivered a fiery speech to the Capital Citizens Council in Little Rock assuring his audience that Georgia would not allow integration, and that Faubus similarly had the power in Arkansas to cancel school desegregation under the sovereign power given to him by the state of Arkansas.[109] Griffin conferred with Faubus at the governor's mansion during his sojourn in Little Rock, which proved to be the Citizens' Council's most effective propaganda ploy. Shortly afterward, Faubus stated, "People are coming to me and saying if Georgia doesn't have integration, why does Arkansas have it?"[110]

With political tensions mounting, Faubus decided to delay the desegregation of Central. He privately arranged for a suit to be filed on August 27 in Pulaski County Chancery Court in which Mrs. C. Thomason, secretary of the Mothers League of Central High School, asked for a temporary injunction against the school board. Plaintiff argued that there might be violence if the Phase Program was implemented on schedule, and asked the Court to enjoin the school board from integrating Central. Simultaneously, Attorney General Bruce Bennett began litigation intended to harass the NAACP, based on legislation passed in the omnibus compromise package a few months earlier. On August 29, Faubus testified in the *Thomason* case that violence was likely if integration proceeded as planned, but he did not cite any specific facts for this concern. Blossom testified that he did not expect violence. Based on Faubus' testimony, the court granted the injunction against Blossom's plan. The school board then went before the federal district court requesting an injunction against the chancery court's order. Judge Miller asked to be relieved of further involvement in the case, so that Roland N. Davies, who was from North Dakota, was temporarily presiding. Unlike district judges from the South elsewhere who had allowed political interference to render their rulings ineffective, the North Dakota judge granted the school board's request and reaffirmed the court's order that the Blossom Plan must be carried out.[111]

The Eisenhower administration's failure to support compliance with *Brown* in other Southern states did not bode well for the moderates' plight in Arkansas. The President clearly had his eyes on the prize of Southern electoral votes for the Republican Party; in 1952 he carried Texas, Virginia and Florida, and in 1956 he carried those states and Louisiana. Southern Republicans were concerned that if they were perceived as liberal on civil rights issues this would endanger the Party's inroads into the white Southern vote.[112] In 1956, the Supreme Court had ordered the University of Alabama to admit its first black graduate student, Autherine Lucy, but violent mobs threatened her and the university's trustees suspended her for her own safety and "the safety of the students and faculty members."[113] A federal district judge had ordered the university to reinstate Lucy, but the trustees expelled her for allegedly making "outrageous" charges against them. Eisenhower responded by saying, "I would certainly hope that we could avoid any interference." The federal government failed to act, and the University of Alabama remained segregated for another seven years.[114] Subsequently, Governor Allan Shivers of Texas used the Alabama incident to rationalize his deployment of state police to prevent the court-ordered integration of Mansfield High School. Shivers ordered the Texas Rangers to arrest anyone who threatened to disturb the peace, which was interpreted to mean the black students who were trying to comply with the federal court order, and the federal judge in that case did not press the issue.[115] Amis Guthridge and other Arkansas extremists taunted Faubus with the Texas episode; Guthridge ran a newspaper advertisement noting that Shivers had used the Rangers to prevent desegregation in Texas, so why could not Faubus do the same in Little Rock?[116] Lest anyone miss the point about the Eisenhower administration's attitude, the President declared in the summer of 1957 that "I can't imagine any set of circumstances that would ever induce me to send federal troops . . . into any area to enforce the orders of a federal court, because I believe that the common sense of America will never require it."[117] Again at a press conference at the time the Central High crisis erupted, Eisenhower reiterated his favorite homily that "You cannot change people's hearts merely by laws."[118]

Nor were Faubus' contacts with the Eisenhower administration confined to observations from afar of the executive's responses to developments in other states, for the governor held a series of private discussions with Justice Department officials. Arthur B. Caldwell, an Arkansas native and the head of the Justice Department's Civil Rights Section, met with Faubus, the school authorities, Ashmore, and Judge Miller in the summer of 1957. The school authorities warned Caldwell of the segregationist clamor incited by the extremist fringe groups, such as a Little Rock speech by Rev. J. A. Lovell from Dallas at one of the Capital Citizens Council meetings in which he warned that "there are people left yet in the South who love God and their nation enough to shed blood if necessary to stop this work of Satan."[119] Caldwell gave no encouragement to the school officials that the administration would play any forceful role. On August 28, Faubus met with Caldwell and asked him what action the federal government intended to take to insure that desegregation proceeded peacefully in Little Rock.[120] Caldwell told Faubus that unless some major incident occurred, the federal government would take no action.[121] In August, Faubus at times still sounded like he was committed to respecting the rule of law, stating at one press conference a few weeks before Governor Griffin's speech that "Everyone knows that state laws can't supersede federal laws," and he would not attempt to nullify federal authority with state legislation.[122] Fulbright maintained a careful silence as these events were unfolding.

Governor Griffin's Little Rock speech and Faubus' favorable reception of it exploited the confusion regarding "the law of the land." Initially, the moderates had regarded respect for the rule of law as the greatest weapon in their arsenal; regardless of what we think of *Brown*, they would solemnly intone, we must obey the law. But by 1957 many people in Little Rock were befuddled as to what "the law" was. Fulbright and their other representatives in Congress had informed them in the Southern Manifesto that *Brown* had disregarded ancient legal precedents and was "contrary to the Constitution," the President did not seem to be enforcing the decision, and now the chief executive of one of their sister states had advised them that they need not acquiesce in desegregation with resignation. Although the most well-educated and well-informed were not duped by the Griffin tirades, some people in Little Rock were now unsure as to the legal standing of the *Brown* decision in Arkansas, and Faubus skillfully played upon the confusion, especially in the working class white areas where understanding of the issues was lower, Central was the school their children would attend, and racial prejudices tended to be stronger than in the higher-income, more well-educated areas in the Heights.

In a dramatic televised speech on September 2, the day before school opened at Central, Faubus blamed Blossom, the school board, and the federal courts for forcing integration on the people against their will in violation of "the time-honored principles of Democracy." Faubus claimed that until the Griffin speech people in Little Rock had been willing to accept desegregation, but now the climate had changed and the people were uncertain about legality issues. In a masterpiece of Faubusian obfuscation, the Arkansas governor cited recently passed state interposition statutes (which vaguely regarded *Brown* as of uncertain legality until Congress acted on school desegregation issues) as reflections of Little Rock's will, saying it was uncertain whether *Brown* or the state statutes were the "law of the land." Actually, Faubus' argument was a distortion even of states' rights ideology, which held that policy decisions are supposed to be made by local bodies; in this instance, the 1957 school board elections had already given a clear local mandate to the moderates to proceed with the Blossom Plan.[123] This important fact was omitted from the Faubus oration. He stated that he was bound to enforce the state statutes until "the proper authority" determined their constitutionality; who the "proper authority" might be at that point, no one listening to Faubus' speech knew for sure, since the governor did not explain it. He may have meant Congress or the state courts, or more plausibly he may have intended to leave the legality question confused. As the crisis escalated in the following days, he would adopt an increasingly extreme anti-Supreme Court, states' rights stand. Faubus proclaimed that until the alleged "legal uncertainty" was cleared up, state law was in force, and to prevent violence against the black children, units of the Arkansas National Guard would be stationed around Central High. The black students would not be permitted to enter Central. Faubus insisted that he was neither defending segregation nor opposing integration, but only preserving the peace.[124] He asserted that he was not relying on interposition and claimed that he was not defying the federal court order.

When black students were barred from entering Central on September 3, Judge Davies ordered the governor to remove the National Guard units and stop interfering with the desegregation plan, but afterward the Guardsmen once again turned the blacks away, this time with a crowd of angry whites milling about outside the school. Faubus' defiance of a court order confronted the Eisenhower administration with a federal-state conflict so blatant that the President would ultimately be unable to evade it.[125] Even after Faubus' speech, Eisenhower reiterated that he opposed the use of federal troops to enforce court orders, and for three interminable weeks the administration permitted the controversy to worsen before even taking the modest action of federalizing the National Guard and changing its orders.[126]

On the question of Faubus' intentions during the crisis, Fulbright would later write: "I have little doubt that his motivation in opposing the integration of Central High School was political."[126a] Some scholars have depicted Faubus as a "trapped" politician in the fall of 1957, a man with no racist inclinations who felt that the threat of mob violence forced him into obstructing desegregation. Numan V. Bartley, for example, wrote that Faubus "feared a leaderless city was slipping into violence. He felt that political considerations and past commitments prevented his underwriting peaceful desegregation."[127] Bartley contended that by the fall of 1957 Faubus had "only one alternative, even this not an enviable one for a cautious politician who had never shown a desire to fan racial discord nor to alienate Negro voters." There are several questions that could be raised about Bartley's depiction of Faubus. First, if there was a threat of violence, Faubus' duty was to escort the blacks to school safely and protect them, not to allow the mob to veto their entry.[128] Moreover, the notion that Little Rock was on the verge of being engulfed in racist violence at that time simply has no basis in the evidence. The lack of any factual basis for Faubus' lurid picture of events has been attested to by a diverse variety of analysts across the political and academic spectrum: scholars such as Harvard Sitkoff and Carl Brauer, *Gazette* reporters who were covering every story regarding Central, and Justice Department officials citing FBI investigations (based on interviews of more than 500 people) that did not uncover any threat of violence.[129] An analysis more accurate than Bartley's was aptly summarized by the historian Carl Brauer: "Although no threat to public safety had existed when the governor first sent the Guard, he had helped to create one by the time he removed it." Davies based his order to proceed with desegregation in part on Mayor Mann's statement that neither he nor the police had received any notice of impending trouble.

Possibly Bartley may have meant that Faubus honestly but mistakenly believed that violence would erupt; but given Faubus' failure to ever provide specific details backing up his allegations, this seems implausible. Even if one assumed, arguendo, that Faubus did honestly misunderstand the situation, that would not excuse his negligence in acting on the basis of preventing massive violence when in reality there was no such threat. Considering Faubus' acute grasp of what was happening in Arkansas, it is incumbent upon Bartley to adduce evidence that Faubus either misunderstood the situation or that there was some factual basis for the imminent violence theory. Of course, after the governor's incendiary actions in calling out the National Guard and inflaming sectional, racial, and anti-federal sentiments, Faubus exploited a tense atmosphere that eventually led to mob intimidation and thus created a real threat of violence.[131] With his skill in confusing issues, Faubus later justified his actions by pointing to the mobs that materialized around Central; but the mobs formed after the Griffin and Faubus speeches and the Guard units took up positions around the school. As Ashmore described the first day of the crisis: "Little Rock arose [on September 3] to gaze upon the incredible spectacle of an empty high school surrounded by National Guard troops called out by Governor Faubus to protect life and property against a mob that never materialized." At the least, it is safe to say Faubus greatly exaggerated whatever threat there may have been, and there is substantial validity to Mayor Mann's complaint that Faubus "perpetrated a hoax on the people of Arkansas" by his impending-bloodshed theory.[130]

Bartley is also inaccurate in depicting Faubus as a cautious man who had "never fanned racial discord" nor sought to alienate black voters. Faubus was certainly cautious whenever his own political fortunes were threatened, and a more accurate analysis of Faubus' record would focus on his constant tendency to base his policies on political expediency in any given era. Although many of Fulbright's contentions regarding the massive resistance era were inaccurate and defensive, he was accurate in depicting Faubus' actions in the Central crisis as having been based upon political opportunism. When the moderates were ascendant in the Truman administration and during the initial responses to *Brown* in 1954-55, Faubus had utilized moderate rhetoric, made a few appointments of blacks, and otherwise cultivated a moderate image. It should be recalled that in 1956, Faubus found it politically expedient to portray himself as the voice of restraint and amiable relations between the races, yet it was easy to appear "moderate" in comparison when his opponent was the extremist Jim Johnson. On the other hand, Faubus saw the climate begin to change at the time of the Southern Manifesto and carefully marked reports of Johnson's popularity in the plantation belt; in that period he began making overtures to the right, in such actions as the mission of the Arkansans to study massive resistance in Virginia and a statement in favor of segregation that won him praise from White America, Inc. He was gradually moving toward the segregationist camp from early 1956 to mid-1957. Bartley was correct that Faubus began his political career aligned with the moderate faction, and continued to be perceived in that light until the Central High crisis; but the dominant strand in his conduct was political expediency. It was true that Faubus was not an ideological racist, and in fact never revealed any deep philosophical commitment either way on the issue of segregation. In this regard he provided a sharp contrast to the racists such as Amis Guthridge, who fervently believed that segregation was politically and morally correct. Even after the Central crisis Johnson and Guthridge, in fact, always looked upon Faubus with distrust as one who was not a true believer but "hit the jackpot with our nickel."

Numan Bartley's assertion that Faubus did not seek to antagonize black voters was true in the sense that the governor tended to make sweeping, sometimes even contradictory appeals to all segments of the electorate; but Bartley's statement ignores the reality that in the delta, most blacks either did not vote or had their votes manipulated through the various methods of socio-economic intimidation or inducements, or outright fraud. In Little Rock, where the black vote was genuinely free, Faubus had soundly trounced Jim Johnson in 1956 but in 1958 would lose by a landslide in black precincts (gaining less than 20 percent in all the predominantly black areas of the city) after his demagogy in the Central High crisis. Afterwards, Faubus continued to throw occasional rhetorical sops to blacks, such as his statement at the height of the crisis in September in which he noted Arkansas' earlier progress in race relations and boasted that "my only child . . . is now attending classes in a state-supported integrated college."[131] But such statements became increasingly rare after September 1957, as Faubus completed his metamorphosis into champion of the plantation belt. Faubus would have preferred that responsibility for desegregation could have been removed from his shoulders and placed elsewhere–upon the school board–but with the high profile actions taken by Governors Shivers of Texas, Griffin of Georgia, and others of his Southern brethren, there was no way to escape responsibility. By August 1957, most of Faubus' chief political advisers were privately advising him that it would be "political suicide" if he were perceived to have "allowed" desegregation in Little Rock. There were others with whom he was still on good terms before September–Rockefeller, McMath,

Hays—who also discussed the matter with him privately and advised him not to obstruct compliance with *Brown*. All three later reported that Faubus had told them that Johnson or a like fire-eater would "tear him to shreds" in his planned bid for a third term if he did not try to block desegregation, although Faubus retorted that the three were lying in their reports of the conversations.[132] Since Faubus was not a man characterized by deep moral or constitutional convictions, his resolution of the issue turned on his analysis of the political equation.

A segregationist stand would enable Faubus to solve his earlier problem in the 1956 election of weak support in the conservative eastern and southern regions of the state, chiefly agricultural areas with substantial black populations of roughly 25 percent or more in most counties. These regions constituted about half the state's vote, with the central Arkansas area dominated by Little Rock and Faubus' home territory of the mountainous northwest making up the rest. Because of the appeal of his regional "favorite son" advantage and the reform package in education and senior citizens' issues, Faubus won by wide margins in the northwest. There was little or no rabid racist sentiment in the northwest but race was not considered of great importance, since the region was 99 percent white. Northwestern voters would not be likely to base their votes on handling of desegregation in Little Rock. Voting fraud was not confined to the delta; Faubus once won 102 percent of the vote in his home county of Madison near the Missouri border. The governor explained this apparent fraud by reference to a large number of "maiden voters" whose names had not yet been placed on the voter registration rolls. More skeptical observers attributed the vote to a heavy Faubus turnout from people who were then residents of Missouri or of graveyards. With the northwest vote added to the delta, with its fraud and manipulation of the black vote—Faubus would not have to be concerned with his showing in central Arkansas to win re-election by a landslide, something that was exceedingly difficult to do in a state where there was such a strong tradition against three terms for a governor.[133] As Fulbright would recall with understatement, "Faubus very much wanted a third term."[133a]

In central Arkansas, Faubus would now confront the independent black voting bloc and a substantial moderate white faction. Of Little Rock's population of 107,000 at the time, 25,000 were black and 82,000 were white.[134] There was also a substantial segregationist faction, along with a number of nonideological, unpredictable voters who could swing either way depending on the circumstances at a given election. The moderate-black coalition was usually evenly matched against the conservatives at most elections, although the moderates suffered from the problem that a number who usually voted with the Hays faction occasionally defected to the conservatives in extraordinary circumstances. Faubus' most effective arguments for these unpredictable, mildly conservative members in the moderate group were the emotional appeals pitched to the visceral Arkansas antipathy to federalism or "outsiders" interfering in Arkansas' affairs.

Potentially the most influential political leader for the centrists was Senator Fulbright, who in 1956-57 was an entrenched, powerful incumbent, rivaling Faubus in popularity before the Central High crisis. The senator had made his fundamental decision on how to respond to racial issues at the time of the Southern Manifesto, and from that time until the mid-1960s he gave no meaningful support to the moderate faction, essentially evading the issue to the fullest extent possible, and acquiescing to segregationist pressures in those instances where it was impossible to avoid taking a position. Predictably, he had voted against the Civil Rights Act of 1957, contending that it was not a meaningful measure that would improve the welfare of the black minority, but merely a "legislative declaration of equality."[135] This was an unfair description of the bill, which in its original version would have allowed the Attorney General to sue for school desegregation. Senator Lyndon Johnson worked out a compromise in which the Southern bloc succeeded in deleting the provision regarding the Attorney General and school desegregation, in return for allowing a diluted version of the bill to become law. The final version authorized Justice Department investigations of voting rights violations, and created a bipartisan Civil Rights Commission and a Civil Rights Division within the Justice Department. Although the civil rights movement had thus won the symbolic victory in the first civil rights legislation in the 20th century, the compromise was well received throughout much of the South. Senator Russell lauded as the "sweetest victory" of his 25-year career the ability "to confine the federal invasion of the South to the field of voting and keep the withering hand of the Federal Government out of our schools."[136] Fulbright supported the Russell bloc concerning the legislation.[137]

At one point early in the crisis, Fulbright had considered criticizing Faubus and urging his constituents to support the rule of law. Fulbright wrote to a relative in October, 1957, that the Central High fiasco was "a great tragedy for the state... There was no excuse whatever for the action taken by the governor, but we will all have to pay for it, nonetheless." The senator's sister, Anne Teasdale, wrote him a poignant letter, reminding him that "ever since you've been in public life you have represented, to many people in this country, and others, too, I'm sure, the moderate, rational, thoughtful unprejudiced point of view. Your exchange program implies feelings about the importance of understanding and appreciation of other cultures and the necessity of learning to live together." Thus, she had found it exceedingly difficult to accept "your not speaking out against the lawlessness, violence and hatred shown in Arkansas." Nonetheless, many other influential friends advised him that Faubus had already captivated majority public sentiment in the state, and he could only destroy himself politically by opposing Faubus. Fulbright was in Europe when the Central High crisis erupted. Fred Pickens, a wealthy Fulbright supporter from Newport, Jim Neal, a West Memphis lawyer, and others advised the senator after his return from Europe that Arkansas was already solidly in the Faubus camp; it was too late to make any realistic stand against him, in their view.[137a]

Fulbright never actively exploited racial sentiments for his advantage, but he nonetheless acquiesced to the white Southern majority's position. He remained silent about the Little Rock question. In September 1957 he was in Great Britain working on foreign policy issues and delivering a speech at Oxford. The senator called Harry Ashmore at the *Gazette* shortly before he left for England. Ashmore and Fulbright were still friends, although the senator's signing of the Southern Manifesto had strained their relationship. Fulbright had not consulted Ashmore for political advice since the Manifesto, but he now did so; Ashmore suggested that he should call Faubus and urge him to make state forces available to maintain law and order.[137a] It was predictable that he would receive an unsatisfactory answer from Faubus, Ashmore said, but he could publicly announce the result of his efforts. Fulbright replied that he was leaving for England that afternoon to deliver a lecture at Oxford, and he thought he should avoid any statement until his return.[137b] Days later, after federal troops had stabilized the situation, Fulbright's aide John Erickson called Ashmore to report that the senator would be coming home, and he could no longer avoid making a statement about the Little Rock crisis; Fulbright had asked Erickson to find out whether Ashmore had any suggestion. Ashmore responded that at that point, Fulbright might as well enroll for the second semester.[137c]

Although in many ways they were at opposite ends of the spectrum, the cerebral, patrician Fulbright and the earthy, former lumberjack and small-town newspaperman Faubus developed similar analyses of Arkansas politics in some respects. Fulbright could also roll up huge majorities in the delta by acquiescing to the segregationist position, although he could avoid the issue more easily than Faubus since he was not governor. Also like Faubus, he was a moderate on issues other than race who enjoyed strong support from his home area of the northwest. Finally, before the Central High crisis he had enjoyed strong support in central Arkansas, but the Little Rock crisis would prove to be an issue that he could not evade by silence. The political implications of the situation were clear: if Faubus could win the delta by becoming the champion of the segregationists, his political position would become virtually impregnable. And a powerful Faubus leading the staunch segregationists would pose alarming political problems for Senator Fulbright.

V. "A SMALL MAN FROM THE HILLS" AND COOPER V. AARON

With officials at all levels, from Superintendent Blossom, to Mayor Mann, Governor Faubus, Senator Fulbright, and President Eisenhower all wishing in various ways and for various reasons to avoid responsibility for the desegregation of Central, into the vacuum of leadership stepped Congressman Hays. Little Rock's congressman hardly suffered from a martyrdom complex; he had been willing to sign the Southern Manifesto when 100 of his colleagues did so and when he regarded it as a matter of survival. But unlike Fulbright, the pangs of conscience for having engaged in that distasteful affair hung heavily upon Hays, and he would redeem himself in the eyes of the civil rights community during the greatest domestic crisis America faced during the Eisenhower years.[138] Hays argued in favor of federalizing the Arkansas National Guard so that the Eisenhower administration could regain control of the situation and enforce the federal court order. In an effort to promote this resolution of the crisis, he arranged a conference between Faubus and Eisenhower, who was on a golfing vacation in Newport, Rhode Island. At the time, former Governor McMath and the prominent Little Rock lawyer, Henry Woods, were talking on the telephone with Vice President Nixon, in an effort to persuade President Eisenhower not to meet with Faubus. Woods and McMath believed there was no reason for Eisenhower to hold the meeting: Faubus was completely in the wrong, and Eisenhower was completely right in enforcing the law. The meeting would only appear to give legitimacy to Faubus, in the McMath-Woods view. As Woods and Beth Deere would write in the *Arkansas Law Review* in 1991, "This conference was a great mistake because it appeared to the people of Arkansas, and indeed to the entire South, that the surrender at Appomattox was about to be renegotiated. Faubus became the darling of the segregationists, states' righters, interpositionists, and nullifiers."[138a] Ironically, the conservative Nixon agreed with McMath and Woods and attempted to persuade Eisenhower to follow their advice, but the Vice President was unsuccessful in his efforts.

When Hays, Faubus and Eisenhower finally gathered in Newport, Hays tried to persuade Faubus that if the administration took over responsibility, the governor would be relieved of any political burden in the issue. Surprisingly, Faubus privately agreed with Hays' suggestion regarding federalization of the Guard, although of course he made no public statement on that matter.[139] Ashmore, who was a friend and admirer of Hays, would later write that Hays was naive in thinking that he could persuade Faubus not to take an extreme stance at that point. Even at the late date of September 14, however, Eisenhower was still reluctant to assume any responsibility. Presidential adviser Sherman Adams opposed the Hays proposal, and after that Faubus terminated the discussions.[140]

Hays privately warned the governor at Newport that he was becoming a carbon copy of Jim Johnson. The warning had no real effect, except a rhetorical scrap Faubus gave the moderates in a press conference statement with Eisenhower and Hays at Newport in which the governor proclaimed, "I have never expressed any personal opinion regarding the Supreme Court decision of 1954 which ordered integration. That is not relevant. That decision is the law of the land and must be obeyed."[141] This was a temporary foray into verbal restraint from Faubus, who within a few weeks back in Arkansas began proclaiming that Supreme Court decisions are not valid expressions of national law.[142]

School board officials asked the Justice Department for federal marshals to supervise the return to Central of the black students, who under the advice of the local NAACP had decided to stay home temporarily. The Justice Department rejected this request. If there had been little threat of mob violence on September 2, by later September the threat had become real. Faubus finally withdrew the Guard on September 20 in nominal compliance with the federal court order, but when blacks entered Central on September 23-24 a mob at the school resulted in their departure after a few hours. While the confrontation between Faubus and Eisenhower attracted national publicity as the weeks of September passed, racists from across the South flocked to the city to help obstruct desegregation.[143] The mob that gathered at Central consisted of about a thousand people, some from out of state, some from east Arkansas, and some organized by the Guthridge faction in Little Rock. Photographs of white racists shouting at the well-behaved black students were broadcast around the world. The image left an indelible impression on millions of people who previously had little knowledge of Little Rock, and for years afterward the city would be remembered by many people as a symbol of racism. Mayor Mann this time requested federal intervention, and at last, the administration had no alternative but to act.

After months of inaction, the administration careened to the opposite extreme and took actions that not even most of the liberals in Little Rock thought necessary. The President not only federalized the 10,000 Arkansas National Guardsmen, an action that Hays had earlier promoted as sufficient to assure the blacks could enter Central peacefully; he also ordered 1,000 combat paratroopers of the 101st Airborne Division into Little Rock, with bayonets fixed. Even Hays was horrified by the notion of soldiers with fixed bayonets in Little Rock, and for a time actually spent much of his energy negotiating with the administration to take the bayonets off the rifles. It was a source of no little frustration to the congressman that the only proposal he suggested during the crisis that the administration accepted was his entreaty to have the bayonets removed. The people taking part in the mob were not, to put it mildly, emotionally stable, and Hays was afraid of a violent confrontation between the paratroopers and the rednecks. With Hays mediating between all the various forces, federal and state, military and civilian, of both races, at least enough reason returned to the situation to put an end to the threat of physical violence. The avoidance of deaths or serious injuries was surprising, given the level of hysteria into which the city had descended by late September. Order was restored within a few days, although latent tensions remained.[144]

The troops remained at Central for two months, and then the federalized Guard units took over for the rest of the academic year. The administration had decided to use the paratroopers because of General Maxwell Taylor's conclusion that the Guardsmen were disloyal, and therefore federalizing them would not by itself solve the situation. It is difficult to disprove this assertion, although many moderates like Hays, as well as the liberal Ashmore, found it preposterous. But in any event, the notion that disloyalty was that rampant in Little Rock was deeply insulting to the community. Resentment against federal intervention became the dominant sentiment in the white community, and the moderates became fragmented and demoralized. Faubus, sensing no restraints on his burgeoning power, escalated his attacks on desegregation, the federal government, and the courts. In yet another demonstration of the administration's feebleness, the Justice Department decided against any efforts to prosecute the most notorious rabble rousers among the mob in the Central incident, and then essentially retired once again from the entire Little Rock desegregation issue.[145] By early 1958, Faubus reversed his earlier acceptance of the principle that federal court decisions were binding as "the law of the land," and now charged that the Supreme Court's decisions were merely the political opinions of nine liberals in Washington and were not valid expressions of law. Only Congress or "the people" could make law. Evoking images from Reconstruction, Faubus portrayed Arkansas as "under military occupation," and ranted against the fixed bayonets, warning about "the warm red blood of patriotic citizens staining the cold, naked, unsheathed knives."[146]

While Faubus had unquestionably reached the apogee of his power, he also received severe criticism from a minority within the state. Ashmore advanced the dissenters' views in front-page editorials in September 1957, and throughout the crisis. Little Rock had devised a plan for gradual desegregation that the federal courts had accepted, "but now Mr. Faubus and the angry, violent and thoughtless band of agitators who rallied to his call may well have undone the patient work of responsible local officials."[147] The President's use of military authority was essential to restore order, the *Gazette* contended. A Faubus-led boycott of the newspaper cost it over a million dollars and thousands of subscribers turned to the second largest paper in the state, the *Democrat*, which supported Faubus.[148] The *Democrat* briefly passed the Gazette circulation in the late 1950s, but by the early 1960s the *Gazette* regained its traditional status as the state's dominant paper. In 1957-58 the *Gazette* was supported by the other major moderate leaders, including McMath, Henry Woods, McMath's former aide and then a prominent trial lawyer in Little Rock, former Arkansas Supreme Court Justice Edwin Dunaway, Rockefeller, Hays, Mann and the NAACP.

The *Arkansas Gazette's* role in the Central High crisis earned applause throughout the country, except in the Deep South. One of the most important progressive leaders in the confrontation was Hugh B. Patterson, Jr., publisher of the *Gazette*, son-in-law of John Netherland Heiskell, the owner. Patterson, a native of Mississippi, and his wife, Louise, saw their family institution and inheritance imperiled by the tide of unreason, yet they stood strong against Faubus' demagogy. The Pattersons were steadfast liberals, and their influence was essential upon J. N. Heiskell—himself a stout believer in the rule of law—in the *Gazette's* resolute stand. The Pattersons were deeply disappointed by Fulbright's silence throughout most of the crisis.

Fulbright returned to the United States from England in late September, but declined to respond to media questions regarding Little Rock. Faubus blasted Fulbright for not backing up Arkansas' stance–which the governor equated with his own actions–when the state was being oppressed by "federal interference."[149] Sensing Fulbright's fear of race-related issues at the time and thereafter, Faubus' instincts as a bully came to the forefront in his relationship with Fulbright. He would taunt the senator for allegedly spending too much time on foreign affairs, deriding him as "the senator from Timbuctoo."[150] He would criticize Fulbright's aristocratic lineage as a son of one of northwest Arkansas' wealthiest families. "If I'd lived in Fayetteville, the Fulbrights wouldn't have let me in the country club."[151] Fulbright concluded that his jugular would be vulnerable to Faubus if he adopted anything resembling a liberal stand on the race issue, and he was determined not to give the governor anything to use against him for an oft-discussed, possible Faubus run for the Senate. Fulbright's only public statement regarding the crisis in the fall of 1957 came in October, in the form of a statement to the press in three sentences: "It is regrettable and it is tragic that Federal troops are in Little Rock. The people of Little Rock and of Arkansas do not deserve this treatment. The citizens of Arkansas are, and always have been, law-abiding citizens."[152]

Fulbright's cryptic statement was interpreted by most observers as a criticism of Eisenhower and a defense of Faubus, although Fulbright later attempted to deny it. For example, Charles Johnston, a Little Rock banker, advised Fulbright that "if you meant what was inferred in the popular mind that the President had no right or business sending the troops here then I think you are wrong."[153] Johnston argued that the federal government was left with no choice but to intervene after Faubus "constantly issued statements calculated to encourage the mob." In an appeal frequently urged by the more restrained constituents, Johnston urged Fulbright: "Give us a chance to rally behind a statesman. The mob can only survive if respectable people are kept quiet. It will take courage on your part, but we are here and will be counted—try us and see."[154] In defending his October statement, Fulbright told Johnston that "What I was trying to say was that Arkansas, and Little Rock in particular, has had a fine record for many years in the field of race relations." Fulbright referred to the desegregation of the University of Arkansas in Fayetteville that had begun at the graduate school level in the late 1940s with his support, describing it as "far superior to that of any other Southern state, and just now to receive the publicity which we have is, it seems to me, undeserved by the people of the state. . . . We have not been a narrow-minded or bigoted people, and yet the rest of the country now looks upon us as such. To me, this is an undeserved tragedy."[155] What Fulbright's response failed to acknowledge was that regardless of the state's earlier progress in race relations, the earlier record could not justify obstructionism in the *Brown* era. The senator failed to address Johnson's argument that it was imperative for all of the rational leaders in the state to provide public, resolute support for compliance with court orders.

In responding to a constituent in eastern Arkansas who was critical of Faubus in October 1957, Fulbright revealed sentiments that would become crucial in his political strategy. The senator derisively compared the governor, "a small man from the hills," to Joe McCarthy, and lamented that "The most discouraging thing is that I believe the Governor now senses that he has a vehicle for publicity and notice, and that he will not permit it to be solved or even calmed down until after the next election."[156] Fulbright predicted that Faubus would eventually be repudiated, but it would take time: "When the facts begin to become apparent, there will be a reaction just as there was with McCarthy, but it will take time for that to develop." In a statement that summarized the basic political strategy he followed regarding race issues until the latter part of his career, Fulbright concluded, "I am not going to make any speeches until the circumstances are a little quieter, and the people are more likely to be willing to reason about the matter."[157] Fulbright's letter failed to recognize that it was precisely when "circumstances" were in turmoil that the South was most in need of rational leadership. The senator would not publicly criticize Faubus until 1959, when it was too late to make a difference. At the time, many moderates had privately encouraged Fulbright to take a public stand against Faubus. Fulbright would later acknowledge that "People—including my elder sister, whose views I greatly respected—criticized me for not opposing Faubus publicly and taking a stand. I can't imagine what I could have done to oppose Faubus successfully; he went on to be elected four more times."[157a] Yet, from Fulbright's experiences in battling the Dixiecrats and especially in his widely acclaimed battles against McCarthy, he had always emphasized that it is essential in opposing extremists to take the initiative and attempt to lead public opinion rather than sitting back and waiting for some indeterminate time in the future when "the people are more likely to be willing to reason."

In belittling Faubus as a "small man from the hills" of Greasy Creek, Arkansas, who thirsted after adulation, Fulbright had discerned a central insight into the governor. For a man who had never enjoyed significant success before his upset run for the governor's mansion in 1954, Faubus now soared into regional prominence as one of the most legendary figures in recent Southern history. He became the toast of the Southern governors' conferences, and was greeted with standing ovations in speaking engagements in the Deep South. In December 1958, Faubus' name appeared on a national Gallup organization list of the 10 people most admired by Americans along with Winston Churchill, Charles de Gaulle, and former President Truman, because of the Southern respondents' overwhelming praise for the Arkansan.[157a] It was not merely the numbers of Arkansas segregationists that attracted Faubus, then, it was their incredible zeal, and the reality that their segregationist brethren in Deep Southern states provided him with the kind of admiration that Faubus coveted but would never receive among the intelligentsia and the national audience that had recently elevated Fulbright to a role of national prestige on other issues.

The senator received a massive volume of correspondence during 1957-58 concerning the Little Rock crisis. Most of the constituents supported Faubus, although a substantial and vocal minority of constituents like Charles Johnston implored the senator to oppose the governor. In a typical example of the right wing arguments, a constituent asked the senator, "I am shocked and surprised at your silence. Must you give the Federal Government and the Republicans everything they ask for, and sit idly by while they cram integration down our throats?"[158] In a reference to the minority of vocal critics of Faubus in the state, the constituent asked, "How can you sit by and see the choice of the people, Governor Faubus, harassed and humiliated?"[159] To the right-wing constituents, Fulbright frequently began to use his signing of the Southern Manifesto as a shield to deflect segregationist criticism, replying to myriad letters over the late 1950s with clipped, two or three-sentence responses citing his signature on the Manifesto.[160] By 1957, Fulbright was unique among Arkansas politicians in that he maintained communications with almost all factions of the political spectrum, from the NAACP to Faubus, but his evasion of the issue during the Little Rock crisis strained his relations with groups on both sides. While Fulbright's communications to moderates did not directly contradict those with the segregationists, the stark difference in issues he chose to emphasize in communicating with different audiences led most black leaders and progressive whites to regard his positions as inconsistent and disingenuous. Black leaders particularly felt a deep sense of betrayal. Daisy Bates, recalling the assurances the Little Rock liberals had erroneously given her that Fulbright would not sign the Southern Manifesto, and then his silence in the school crisis, would later ask, "Why does he have to sell his soul and his people like that? . . . I'll listen to Faubus more than I'll listen to Fulbright."[161]

Faubus received a torrent of criticism from the white moderates and supporters of the NAACP. Ben Jordan, a minister and leading figure in the nascent moderate faction in Jonesboro, condemned the governor in a letter to him at the time of the Central crisis: "You have done what all demagogues do. You have preached violence until you have actually incited it."[162] Hammering on one of the familiar themes of the progressives—that racism damaged America's image in the Cold War struggle for the sympathy of the Third World— Jordan charged that "Not only have you blackened the name of Arkansas in the eyes of the nation, but what is more tragic you have shamed America before the world."[163] Jordan terminated his former support for the governor, lamenting that "I am terribly ashamed that I voted for you in both of your campaigns for Governor," and vowed to do everything possible to oppose him in possible future races for governor or the U. S. Senate (meaning Fulbright's seat, for McClellan was a formidable, staunch segregationist and was not vulnerable to a Faubus candidacy).[164]

In spite of the steady stream of dissent from the Jordans and pro-Hays forces, Faubus received a substantially larger volume of correspondence from admiring segregationists. A classic example of such praise came from one of Guthridge's admirers in Little Rock who commended Faubus' "intestinal fortitude in taking the stand that you have against the Carpetbag Edicts that has [sic] been imposed upon the whole United States of America by a packed Supreme Court."[165] The constituent predicted Faubus would ultimately emerge victorious because the Supreme Court "forgot to take the people into consideration when they threw away principle of the constitution and used a book called American Dilemma wrote by some Swede." [sic][166]

If Faubus could temporarily feel secure that the Jordans and Johnstons were outnumbered by those who would condemn the "Carpetbag Edicts" based on the ideas of "some Swede," (the constituent who wrote to Faubus condemning the Court was obviously making a befuddled reference to Gunnar Myrdal's monumental *An American Dilemma: The Negro Problem and Modern Democracy*, two volumes, 1944) there was a much more unsettling force emerging from the criticism of his prize appointee, Winthrop Rockefeller. With his family's imposing connections in the national business community, no one in Arkansas' history had ever matched his record in attracting Northern investment into the state. Conservatives who were indifferent to Hays' appeal to the rule of law or the *Gazette's* eloquent appeals for racial justice were deeply concerned when Rockefeller began warning that Faubus' demagogy was damaging the state's hitherto promising ability to attract Northern capital. A disturbing example Rockefeller cited was a letter he received at the height of the Central crisis from Harold Caplin, an executive of Seamprufe, Inc., a New York garment corporation that had become a major employer in the Little Rock area.[167] Caplin began by congratulating Rockefeller on his efforts to promote Arkansas as a site for investments from the New York business community, but then warned, "It is difficult to express to you, however, our disappointment in the actions taken by Governor Faubus. . . . We believe the steps that the Governor has taken will undo much of the good your office [Arkansas Industrial Development Commission] has done in promoting Arkansas."[168] In a warning that Seamprufe's opening of new plants in Arkansas might not continue in the prevailing climate of racial turmoil, Caplin advised Rockefeller that "We, at Seamprufe, would like to be able to point with pride to the people and the state in which we operate. We believe your office and the people of Arkansas should exert every effort to do the right thing towards all people regardless of race, color, or creed."[169]

Rockefeller inveighed against the segregationist legislation that the General Assembly began churning out at the height of the Faubus era. He blasted a newly created state sovereignty commission possessing investigative powers as a "dangerous" bill that threatened to become an "Arkansas Gestapo." No organization "would be safe from embarrassment of an investigation, and behind closed doors, too."[170] Other legislation required the NAACP to register and make public reports of its activities. The local NAACP concluded in a private memorandum that the courts would eventually declare these laws unconstitutional, but before the litigation could be concluded, the Faubus forces would be able to generate substantial obstruction and deflect the organization's time, money and resources in battling the harassment litigation.[171]

Rockefeller's criticism of Faubus did not tarnish his status as a prestigious, rising political star in the state, principally because of his economic service. But unfortunately for the history of race relations in the state, in early 1958, Fulbright and a significant number of other "moderates" did not follow the example of Rockefeller, McMath, Hays and the other assertive moderates. Some had been driven into a defensive stance by the Faubus onslaught. The Little Rock School Board retreated from its gradual desegregation plan and petitioned the district court for a delay of two and a half years until "tempers had cooled."[172] With Judge Davies' temporary duties ending in March, the presiding judge was J. Harry Lemley, another moderately conservative Arkansan from the Roosevelt era.[173] The school board argued that the governor and legislature had incited so much hostility that for the immediate future a sound educational program with blacks attending was not possible.[174] Lemley granted the delay, but the Eighth Circuit reversed on August 18, staying the order 30 days to permit the School Board to petition for certiorari. The black students then filed a motion in the Supreme Court to stay the Eighth Circuit's postponement. Since the school term for the new school year was set to begin on September 2, 1958, Chief Justice Warren ordered a Special Term to convene in order to have a decision in time to permit arrangements for the 1958-59 academic year.[175] Fulbright would file an *amicus curiae* brief supporting the Little Rock School Board's plan for delay.

Warren would later reflect that "There was but one event that greatly disturbed us during my tenure, and that was . . . the Little Rock case [*Cooper v. Aaron*] which gave Governor Faubus the national spotlight."[176] The Chief Justice was outraged by Faubus' contention that a governor's statement could control the action of the courts. Unbeknownst to the public, there was actually division within the Court, not over how to decide the case but whether to make symbolic gestures to the school board commending its members for their good faith efforts. Felix Frankfurter, John Harlan and Tom Clark tended to be sympathetic with the plight of the school board members and their lawyer, Richard C. Butler, who were often critical of Faubus. The school board had directly defied Faubus in deciding to delay the school term's beginning until September 15, in order to assist the Supreme Court in its efforts to resolve the issue before the school year began. Frankfurter wrote to Warren shortly before the case was decided that "the *Washington Post* was right the other day in its editorial in characterizing the action of the School Board as courageous." Since the Board "showed a good deal of enterprise and courage to stand up to Faubus and Company," Frankfurter suggested to Warren that he should compliment the board's attorney for its action. The ultimate solution of the problem, Frankfurter concluded, "depends on winning the support of lawyers of the South for the overriding issue of obedience to the Court's decision. Therefore, I think we should encourage every manifestation of fine conduct by a lawyer like Butler."[177] Warren disagreed with Frankfurter's view, on the grounds that he would not make a special point to praise a lawyer who was arguing that Southern obstruction justified delay in implementation of black rights.[178]

The School Board and Butler had hoped that the Court might be sympathetic to their arguments in light of their earlier record of having developed an acceptable plan and their disagreements with Faubus. The delay of two and a half years was based on the board's belief that Faubus would no longer be governor by the end of that time, an assumption that turned out to be false. Butler asked Fulbright to submit an *amicus curiae* brief to the Supreme Court supporting the Board's plan for delay, and Fulbright accepted. Fulbright's support added considerable intellectual luster to the Board's position because of the senator's lengthy list of credentials as an academic and legal expert: Rhodes Scholar, honors graduate of George Washington University School of Law, Justice Department attorney in Washington during the New Deal, constitutional law professor at George Washington and the University of Arkansas, and president of the University of Arkansas. His consistent support in Congress for expanded federal aid to education and his founding of the Fulbright Scholar international exchange program had further enhanced his stature as an educator. Before writing his brief, Fulbright discussed the issues with Judge Learned Hand. Judge Hand delivered the Holmes lectures at Harvard Law School in 1958, and he had advocated adherence to the doctrine of judicial restraint. Although Judge Hand had supported the *Brown* decision, he was becoming increasingly disenchanted with the Warren Court's activism. In his private correspondence with Justice Felix Frankfurter—who was also critical of what he regarded as an activist, "result-oriented" inclination by Warren, Black, Douglas and Brennan—Hand disparaged Warren and his allies. "Black and Douglas," the famous federal judge wrote to Frankfurter, "are frankly not judges at all." In Hand's view, "those whom I most dread ... are the men who conceive it to be the chief part of their duty to keep this society in the path of righteousness and high endeavor... They are getting to believe that they are charged with remoulding this sorry scheme of things nearer to the heart's desire. If they keep on they will have their tail feathers clipped. True, the pendulum will swing back; but I don't want it to swing at all."[177a] In addition to his consideration of Hand's criticism of the activist approach, Fulbright also consulted David Cohn, a wealthy businessman, graduate of the University of Virginia and Yale, and former speech writer for Stevenson. Cohn argued that the races in the South coexisted in a labyrinth of social taboos and conventions that would make the process of reform complex and arduous. Racial differences, "except that of social segregation," would yield only gradually through the exercise of patience and wisdom, in Cohn's view.[177b] Fulbright's brief was rare in his career, for it was one of the few times he ever discussed a race-related issue in detail. However, most of his analysis largely consisted of philosophical generalizations based on Edmund Burke's idea that ancient social institutions cannot be reformed too rapidly, and there was little discussion of specifics of the Little Rock case.

Fulbright's brief argued that the people of Arkansas were basically law-abiding, and "until the recent violence, it had been thirty years since racial disorder [a reference to the Phillips County race riot in *Moore v. Dempsey* 261 U.S. 86 (1923)] had troubled the people of Arkansas."[179] Fulbright emphasized that in *Brown II* the Court stated that "because of their proximity to local conditions," district judges could best decide what constitutes good faith implementation. Judge Lemley, in Fulbright's view, was intimately familiar with the local conditions and had found that the School Board had attempted to comply in good faith with *Brown*, "but that conditions are so chaotic that a delay should be granted the Little Rock School Board in order to enable calmer spirits to find a way to conform to the principles enunciated by the Court." Lemley had concluded that "there was bedlam and turmoil in and upon the school premises, outside of the classrooms" and that the disruption interfered with the educational process to an incalculable extent.[180] Fulbright also quoted the dissenting opinion of Chief Judge Archibald Gardner of the Eighth Circuit, who had contended that "the action of Judge Lemley was based on realities, and on conditions rather than theories."[181] Fulbright recalled that the majority of the Eighth Circuit had placed great emphasis on the activities of forces and governments outside the case, but "neither their recollection nor the courts' despair of them affords the school board any solution to the problem of how to conduct public education in an acknowledged atmosphere of bedlam and turmoil." Then he warned: "The Court's refusal to support the good faith position of the board can only intensify the effect of those outside forces." In Fulbright's opinion, the majority opinion displayed no familiarity with the cultural patterns and traditions of the South, in contrast to Judge Gardner, who wrote that fundamental alterations in entrenched social practices "if successful, are usually accomplished by evolution rather than revolution, and time, patience, and forbearance are important elements in effecting all radical changes."[182]

In his concluding passage, Fulbright avoided all specifics and philosophized about the dilemma of Southern race relations:

> The people of Arkansas endure against a background not without certain pathological aspects. They are marked in some ways by a strange disproportion inherited from the age of Negro slavery. The whites and Negroes of Arkansas are equally prisoners of their environment. Certainly, no one of them has ever been free with respect to racial relationship in the sense that the Vermonter, say, has been free. The society of each is conditioned by the other's presence. Each carries a catalog of things not to be mentioned. Each moves through an intricate ritual of evasions, of make-believe, and suppressions. In Arkansas, one finds a relationship among men without counterpart on this continent, except in similar Southern states. All this is the legacy of an ancient and melancholy history.

> In our congenital optimism, we Americans believe, or affect to believe, that social questions of the greatest difficulty may be solved, through the discovery and application of a sovereign remedy that will forever dispose of the problem. Yet all this flies in the face of human experience.[183]

While the rhetoric was elegant, Fulbright failed to answer the fundamental issue posed by the Eighth Circuit in holding that suspension of the plan to integrate "would result in accession to the demands of insurrectionists or rioters." In keeping with his self-image as a moderate, Fulbright and his aide, Lee Williams, were proud of their handiwork and hoped that the NAACP might see some merit in it. Williams met privately with his old friend Wiley Branton, who attended the University of Arkansas Law School with Williams, and Thurgood Marshall. Branton and Marshall cordially received Williams, but other than graciously remarking that the brief was well-written, they were not impressed by the proposal for delay. Marshall summarized their response by telling Williams, "It is a compelling argument, but I am not compelled."[184]

A glaring omission in Fulbright's belief was his failure to discuss Faubus' efforts to manufacture a threat of violence in August and September 1957 when desegregation would almost certainly have proceeded without violence had not the governor intervened.[185] Moreover, the senator exaggerated the "bedlam" at Central over the course of the entire school year; while it is true that the educational process was disrupted in September and October, as the year went on calm was gradually restored. The first black student graduated from Central in May without mishap, with Martin Luther King, Jr., in attendance.[186] However, there was certainly tension at the school agitated by a small group of racists, and Central's normally excellent academic standards had obviously suffered compared to earlier years. The continuing unwillingness of the federal government to remain involved created serious problems. None of these problems could justify Fulbright's rejection of the principle that the mob could not be allowed to obstruct court orders. Moreover, his argument was weak even as an exposition of Burkean philosophy. Burke's preference for gradualism obviously did not contemplate allowing political leaders to countenance disrespect for the law. Burke had stressed that "There is no pleasure in holding office if one does not reflect one's own views." The political leader was obligated to make the most enlightened choice he or she could rather than slavishly following their perception of current popular opinion.[187]

Unfortunately for Fulbright and Butler, the Justices were in no mood to brook Southern delay. The Court refused to accept Fulbright's *amicus* brief. Fulbright had expected his brief to have some favorable impact on the Court and was surprised by their rejection of it. The Justices clearly expected better leadership from Fulbright because of his background in the law, as well as his national and international reputation as a foreign policy leader in the Senate. But if Fulbright felt personally offended by the Court's firm attitude, he was fortunate that he did not have Butler's role of arguing for the Board before Warren. A polished Southerner who had developed great poise and equanimity through many years of practice, Butler apparently expected to get sympathetic treatment from the Court, because of the Board's earlier compliance and its occasional, if largely unsuccessful efforts to criticize Faubus. Butler's strategy was to emphasize the early development of the Blossom Plan, blame Faubus for the fiasco and contend that "the School Board is placed between the mill-stones . . . in a conflict between the state and the Federal government." Had Butler confined his argument along those lines, he would have still lost the case but might not have incurred Warren's wrath.

What outraged the Chief Justice was Butler's contention that "if the governor of any state says that a United States Supreme Court decision is not the law of the land, the people of that state have a doubt in their mind and a right to have a doubt." Warren reproved the Little Rock attorney, literally shouting at him that he had never heard such an argument in all his years in the law: "I never heard a lawyer say that the statement of a governor as to what was legal or illegal should control the action of any court." Butler then compounded his error by alluding to Warren's experience in having to deal with controversial issues as governor of California, but the Chief abruptly stopped him: "But I have never tried to resolve any legal problem of this kind as governor of my state. I thought that was a matter for the courts, and I abided by the decision of the courts."[188] The Court rejected the notion that there was a crucial distinction between the Board and the state government: "Whether it's the school board or whether it's the Governor or whether it's the legislature, whether it's the militia, whatever agency of the state government, if it did frustrate the rights of these children, it's a violation of the Constitution."[189]

Butler had no answer to Warren's central question: "Can we defer a program of this kind because elements in a community will commit violence to prevent it from going into effect?" The attorney tried to argue that "social turmoil and other pressures" would calm down in two and a half years. And if the climate three years hence was no more tranquil than in 1957, would they ask for another delay? There was no satisfactory response. In reality, the specious reasoning behind asking for the delay was abundantly demonstrated by subsequent history. Although Butler's references to the governor in court remained at a relatively generalized level, the Board privately based its reasoning on the premise that Faubus would not run for a fourth term, but in fact he continued to serve as governor until deciding not to run in 1966. Moreover, the Board was operating on the faulty premise that no desegregation was possible in Little Rock for however long Faubus remained governor. For the short term, this was correct, since after *Cooper v. Aaron* Faubus closed the Little Rock schools for the 1958-59 year; but by 1959-60, many Little Rock parents who had originally supported Faubus in the crisis began to grow weary of the deterioration in the city's once fine educational system, and the gradual desegregation plan at the local level was resumed, in direct contradiction to Faubus' position. Faubus, moving as always with the political winds, backed off the issue.

By the 1962 gubernatorial campaign, Faubus had come full circle to his original strategy of portraying himself as the moderate alternative to the "extremes" of the reactionary Dale Alford and the liberal McMath. In that year, Faubus would win only 52 percent of the vote, narrowly missing being forced by his former mentor McMath into a runoff, which was almost always fatal to incumbents in Arkansas. Faubus' personal popularity was so legendary that even some voters who disagreed with him on most issues would continue to vote for him; in this respect his political talents at the statewide level were somewhat similar to President Reagan's personal popularity in the 1980s. Butler could not have prophesied Faubus' future career in 1958, but the episode demonstrates the error in contentions that at some point in the future, a "prompt and reasonable start" toward desegregation could be made, but not today.

The internal disagreements within the Court at one point threatened the solidarity with which it had previously decided the desegregation cases. In a note to Harlan, Frankfurter observed: "Butler's advice to his School Board was much wiser than the views which Bill Brennan tells me the Chief Justice expressed to you fellows at luncheon last Friday [Frankfurter was referring to Warren's view that there should be no statement to Butler complimenting the Board's various actions taken in defiance of Faubus]. Of course Faubus has been guilty of trickery, but the trickery was as much against the School Board as against us." Frankfurter concluded that "in any event the fight is not between the Supreme Court and Faubus, tho apparently this is the way it lay in the C.J.'s mind." In a final dig at the Chief Justice, Frankfurter lamented that Warren's actions more closely resembled those "of a fighting politician than of a judicial statesman."[190] Frankfurter at one point planned to announce a concurrence simultaneously with the main opinion in *Cooper v. Aaron*, but in service to the unanimity principle, the Justices resorted instead to the unique decision of having all nine Justices sign their names to the opinion.[191]

Justice Clark was similarly disturbed by the Court's conduct, especially in the extraordinary decision to convene a special term to handle the case. The Texan wrote a draft dissent in which he argued, "As I understood *Brown*, integration was not to be accomplished through push button action but rather by 'deliberate speed.'" Clark contended that the Court should not allow "massive resistance" to influence its procedures: "The case should be considered in its regular course, not by forced action. Of all tribunals this is one that should stick strictly to the rules." Clark argued that it would make no difference whether the petitioners entered integrated schools in September or in October, when the Court was scheduled to convene its next term. However, Clark quickly realized the importance of maintaining the Court's solidarity on this issue, and dropped the idea of dissenting.[192] Faubus exacerbated his defiant stance by calling a special session of the legislature after oral arguments in the Supreme Court on August 28. The governor secured passage of a series of segregationist laws giving him the power to close the schools and to transfer public school funds to private segregated schools. At conference, the Chief appealed for a decision upholding the Eighth Circuit with a firm reaffirmation of the duty for all state officials to obey the law as laid down by the Supreme Court, and all the Justices agreed.

Yet the *Brown* tradition of unanimity was in fact broken in *Cooper v. Aaron*, because Frankfurter remained wedded to his idea of combining a rejection of the Board's request for a delay with an acknowledgment that the Butlers, Fulbrights and Blossoms of the South were making a good faith effort to deal with a traumatic situation.[193] Frankfurter engaged in a sympathetic dialogue with Butler at oral argument. The former Harvard law professor kept up a steady correspondence with a network of his former students across the South, and because of this fancied himself as being particularly influential in the Southern legal community. Frankfurter signed the Court's opinion, which seemed to speak with one voice when it was announced on September 29. But Frankfurter also delivered a separate concurring opinion on October 6 in which he wrote, in language similar to the thrust of the Court's opinion, that "Whatever sophisticated explanations may be devised to justify such a request, they cannot obscure the essential meaning that law should bow to force."

Frankfurter reiterated that "To yield to such a claim would be to endorse lawlessness, and lawlessness if not checked is the precursor to anarchy."[194] The concurrence contained language complimenting Little Rock for its progress before 1957: "The process of the community's accommodation to new demands of law upon it, the development of habits of acceptance of the right of colored children to the equal protection of the laws guaranteed by the Constitution, had peacefully and promisingly begun."[195] Since there were similar passages in the majority opinion, this language did not make a substantive contribution to the opinion.

Given Frankfurter's vigorous work in helping to insure unanimity in the original *Brown* decision, Warren, Brennan and Hugo Black were infuriated by his decision to file a concurrence.[195a] Black and Brennan at one point were planning to file another concurrence emphasizing that the Frankfurter concurrence should not be interpreted as diluting the force of the Court's opinion in any way. Harlan wisely pointed out that this would only call further attention to the divisions within the Court on the issue, and Black and Brennan withdrew their concurrence. In later justifying his concurrence, Frankfurter said that his opinion was directed to a "particular audience, to wit: the lawyers and law professors of the South, and that is an audience which I was in a peculiarly qualified position to address in view of my rather extensive association, by virtue of my twenty-five years at the Harvard Law School, with a good many Southern lawyers and law professors."[196]

There is little evidence that the Frankfurter concurrence elicited the grateful response from Southern lawyers that the Justice had hoped. Frankfurter did know the University of Arkansas Law School Dean, Robert Leflar, Sr., a Harvard Law School graduate who was a nationally prestigious legal scholar in his own right and a revered figure in all but the most reactionary quarters of the Arkansas legal community. But Leflar needed no encouragement; he had already thundered against the lawlessness of Faubus' demagogy and the need to avoid caving in to such hysterical forces. Frankfurter had, indeed, taught Leflar at Harvard, but as Leflar would reveal many years later in his memoirs, he had regarded Frankfurter as rather disappointing as a law professor.[196a] Many Arkansas lawyers saw Frankfurter as a Harvard egghead with no particular ties to or understanding of Arkansas affairs; his kind words for the Butler group were not, to put it mildly, much of a political asset. Some lawyers even responded disdainfully; one Southerner wrote to Frankfurter calling on him to resign because of the concurrence.[197] The concurring opinion added no substance to the Court's opinion, and essentially underscored the accuracy of the position Warren and Frankfurter had taken at the time of the Court's internal deliberations on *Brown* that it would be damaging if the Justices did not speak with one voice on this vital question. However, the main concern to avoid any dissenting opinions was realized and the central reality of *Cooper* was its resounding affirmation of *Brown*; since Frankfurter emphasized his complete agreement with the majority and there were no dissents, it did not undermine *Cooper's* fundamental achievement. The concurrence did not attract major notoriety in Arkansas.

The Court's internal discussions were further complicated by Harlan's suggestion to add to Brennan's original draft of the opinion language stressing that since the first *Brown* opinion three new Justices had come to the Court: "They are at one with the Justices still on the Court who participated in the original decision as to the inescapability of that decision." Brennan was deeply opposed to the Harlan addition on the grounds that "any such reference to the three new members would be a grave mistake. It lends support to the notion that the Constitution has only the meaning that can command a majority of the court as that majority may change with shifting membership." Brennan contended that whatever truth there might be in that notion, "I think it would be fatal in this fight to provide ammunition from the mouth of this Court in support of it."[198] Brennan's argument was rejected and the Harlan language was adopted.

Brennan was probably correct in the debate, although he may have stated his point more starkly than was necessary in describing the Harlan language as "fatal." The differences within the Court regarding desegregation focused on finding the best strategy to implement *Brown*, and unlike some other crucial constitutional issues *Cooper* did not involve fundamental philosophical conflicts among the Justices. The reference to change in the Court's composition, combined with the Frankfurter concurrence, might focus attention on the views of those who wondered whether the Justices were merely deciding the cases based on the policy preferences of the dominant group on the Court, namely Warren, Black, Douglas, and Brennan. Candid acknowledgments that the shifting composition of the Court influenced decisions might be admirable on other issues involving close decisions, but it was unnecessary to call attention to that question in a line of cases that had been unanimous. Given the unprecedented resort to having all the Justices sign the opinion individually, the Harlan suggestion seemed at best superfluous. In spite of Harlan's unnecessary language, the final version of the Brennan opinion became, as Professor Bernard Schwartz has aptly observed, "one of the classic statements of the rule of law under the Constitution."[199]

The Court concluded that the petitioners stood in this litigation as agents of the state of Arkansas, and could not assert "their good faith as an excuse for delay in implementing the respondents' constitutional rights, when vindication of those rights has been rendered difficult or impossible by the actions of other state officials."[200] The Court acknowledged the constructive activities of the School Board in the face of the state government's obstructionist actions, such as the passage of an amendment to the state constitution requiring the Arkansas General Assembly to oppose "in every Constitutional manner the unconstitutional desegregation decisions." In summarizing the chronology of events, the Court stated that even after such damaging actions by the state, "the School Board and the Superintendent of Schools nevertheless continued with the preparations to carry out the first stage of the desegregation program" in September 1957. In another passage of the opinion, the Court stated, "One may well sympathize with the position of the Board in the face of the frustrating conditions which have confronted it." But none of this justified the Board's legal position. "The constitutional rights of respondents," the Court concluded, "are not here to be sacrificed or yielded to the violence and disorder which have followed upon the actions of the Governor and Legislature, and law and order are not here to be preserved by depriving the Negro children of their constitutional rights."[201] Thus did the Court resoundingly reject the various arguments offered by Fulbright, Butler and other lawyers on the Board's behalf.

Cooper admonished the states that *Brown* cannot be nullified openly by any state officials, nor nullified indirectly through evasive schemes. At Black's request, Brennan added a statement that "State support of segregated schools through any arrangement, management, funds, or property cannot be squared with the Amendment's command that no State shall deny to any person within its jurisdiction the equal protection of the laws."[202] The Court thus rejected Faubus' scheme to set up a private school corporation to keep running segregated schools if the public schools were closed down. This passage was one of the few unfortunate statements in the *Cooper* opinion, for the issue of public support of private segregated schools was not directly before the Court in this case, so the Court was prejudging the issue and arguably violating the prohibition against advisory opinions.[203] An NAACP suit challenging the private school corporation was in progress, but it would be months before a decision was handed down.[204]

In addressing the premise of the governor's actions that they were not bound by the holding in *Brown*, the Court recalled "some basic constitutional propositions which are settled doctrine." Citing *Marbury v. Madison*, the Court observed that the Constitution is the paramount law of the land and the federal judiciary is supreme in its exposition: "It is emphatically the province and duty of the judicial department to say what the law is." It follows from this that "the *Brown* case is the supreme law of the land" and the supremacy clause makes it binding on the states. All state officers are bound by oath under Article VI to support the Constitution, and the Court cited Chief Justice Taney's statement in *Ableman v. Booth* that this provision reflected the Founding Fathers' "anxiety to preserve it [the Constitution] in full force, in all its powers, and to guard against resistance to or evasion of its authority, on the part of a state." Citing Chief Justice Hughes in *Sterling v. Constantin*, the decision stated that if a governor had power to nullify a federal court order, then "it is manifest that the fiat of a state Governor, and not the Constitution of the United States, would be the supreme law of the land."[205]

For the short term, *Cooper* was subjected to a torrent of abuse. The tough stand the Court took had advantages, however. It placed unassailable pressure on Eisenhower to speak up for the Court, which he belatedly did. The President issued a statement appealing for public support of the decision: "All of us know that if an individual, a community or a state is going to defy the rulings of the courts, then anarchy results."[206] Supporters of the decision were momentarily encouraged, until Eisenhower diminished most of the effect of his statement when he replied to a reporter's question about the statement by conceding that desegregation could be "slower." That, of course, was precisely the argument of Fulbright and the School Board.[207] After he sent in the federal troops, Eisenhower had reverted to his policy of "hands off" the South and never again enforced the Court's desegregation decision after the Little Rock crisis.[208] Justice Black was indignant at the President because of his diffidence in enforcing *Brown*. No one in public life had suffered more public condemnation because of *Brown* than had Black, who had once been an admirer of Eisenhower; he now said that "Ike" was a nice fellow who would have made a good probate judge in Alabama.[208a]

Faubus closed the public schools in response to *Cooper*. The tough stance taken by the Court was actually beneficial to the moderates, for the long term, for they could now argue that the Court meant what it said and "prompt and reasonable start" did not mean endless delay. The moderates could also point out that even a conservative administration such as Eisenhower's might act decisively in extraordinary circumstances such as the Central High crisis, although these arguments were weakened by the President's dilatory responses to the controversy before September 1957, and the continuing evidence of the administration's desire to avoid the issue. If the views of such scholars as Charles Alexander were correct in arguing that Faubus had destroyed any possibility of rational activity concerning desegregation, which in Alexander's view could come to Little Rock at the time "only at bayonet point," one would expect to find landslide victories for the Guthridge faction in Little Rock in 1958. Yet in December 1958, several moderate candidates were persuaded to run in the Little Rock School Board elections by that most radical of organizations, the Little Rock Chamber of Commerce. The Chamber's position was that the schools must be opened on a basis consistent with minimal integration that had been laid down by the federal courts. The basic reason for the Chamber's position centered on the alarming reality, to the business community, that the crisis had wielded a pernicious impact on the previously booming business climate in Little Rock.[209] The election results were split down the middle, with the moderates winning three seats and the segregationists winning three.

The three segregationists on the Board voted not to renew the contracts of 44 teachers in the Little Rock School District whom they assailed as "integrationists." *Little Rock School District v. Pulaski County Special School District*, 584 F.Supp. 328 (E.D.Ark. 1984)(opinion of Judge Henry Woods). A majority of the School Board had to renew the contracts, and as Judge Woods would write in an eloquent opinion a quarter of a century later:

> Dismissal of these teachers, many of whom were the best and most experienced teachers in the district, galvanized a few leading citizens into activity and brought into being an organization, the Women's Emergency Committee, which would spearhead the movement to retain the dismissed teachers and to reopen the schools. The leadership and commitment of this group of dedicated women made possible the first victory for the moderate forces since the controversy had begun over integration of the Little Rock School District. The Women's Emergency Committee became the active and front-line component of a broader movement called STOP (Stop This Outrageous Purge) which determined to force the teacher dismissal issue by recalling the segregationist members of the School Board. . . . A coalition composed of representatives from the Chamber of Commerce, labor, parent-teacher associations and black groups, organized and spearheaded by the Women's Emergency Committee, was victorious in the recall election. The segregationists were recalled; the moderates were retained. Act 4, the school closing legislation, was declared unconstitutional by a three-judge federal court on June 18, 1959 and the way was thus cleared to reopen the closed school for the 1959-60 school term. *Aaron v. McKinley*, 173 F.Supp. 944 (E.D.Ark. 1959)(cited in *Little Rock School District, supra*, 584 F.Supp at 334).

The STOP campaign enlisted the energetic and brilliant efforts of many of Arkansas' most distinguished citizens—Woods, Mrs. Adolphine Fletcher Terry, Mamie Ruth Williams, Sarah Murphy, Pat House, Irene Samuel, Jane Mendel, Vivian Brewer, the Pattersons, and the other leading moderates—who were already socially prominent at the time and would attain heightened political prestige in Arkansas in the future. Mrs. Terry was a classic example of the social and intellectual prestige enjoyed by the moderates; a graduate of Vassar, she was the sister of Pulitzer-Prize winning poet John Gould Fletcher, daughter of a prominent Little Rock banker and businessman, and the wife of former Congressman David D. Terry. Another example was the advertising executive, Ted Lamb, who was elected to the School

Board in December, 1958, and then lost 21 out of his 26 advertising accounts because of a Faubus campaign of harassment against his clients. Lamb persevered, retrained as a lawyer, and continued as a forceful advocate for integration.[209a] The moderates had begun their campaign as a courageous minority, but ultimately succeeded. This group displayed a lasting and in many cases a bitter disappointment in Fulbright for evading the civil rights issue.

In early 1959, the Chamber ran an opinion poll asking first if people were in favor of continuing with closed schools, and secondly, "Do you now favor the reopening of Little Rock's public high schools on a controlled minimum plan of integration acceptable to the Federal Courts?" Of the responses, 632 said no to continued school closing, while 230 said yes and 285 did not respond; 819 respondents said yes to the second question, to only 245 opposed and 83 not responding.[210] The poll was not scientific, but the central reality of the situation was that many Little Rock parents were tired of having their children's educations disrupted.

Faubus' diatribes continued to degenerate. Once a victim of red-baiting charges himself in the 1954 campaign, he now began to charge that advocates of integration were communist sympathizers. As luck would have it, although most of the NAACP members were middle class professionals who were the soul of moderation, one of its local members turned out to be a bona fide communist. Dr. Lee Lorch had been a committed advocate of racial justice for many years, but his communist affiliation caused serious political problems for the local organization. The NAACP warned him of injecting extraneous issues into the cause of integration, and by the end of 1958 the Lorch family had moved to Canada.[211] Faubus may have gained somewhat politically by exploiting the communist issue, although some people in Little Rock were offended by his berating of the harmless, idealistic Dr. Lorch.

When Faubus suggested not rehiring a number of administrators and teachers who favored compliance, he was widely criticized in the city for damaging the educational system. In an April speech at Little Rock University, he compared massive resistance to the American Revolution: "Suppose it is the law of the land; that does not mean it has to be obeyed. The orders of George III were the law of the land for the colonies, but they didn't have to be obeyed."[212] A backlash against such extremism began to crystallize. The moderate board members resigned over the issue of the purge against the teachers and administrators, and when new recall elections were held in May 1959, the segregationist members were removed. Opposition to Faubus in the black wards and the higher income wards of the professional and business elite in the Heights led to the victory. The spring, 1959 elections broke the power of Faubus over the Little Rock school system.

Federal court rulings striking down the state school closing law and the private school incorporation scheme followed in June, and the Supreme Court affirmed this decision later in the year. *Aaron v. McKinley*, 173 F.Supp. 944 (E.D. Arkansas, 1959); unanimously affirmed, *Faubus v. Aaron*, 361 U.S. 197 (1959). In the Eighth Circuit's ruling in *Faubus v. United States*, 254 F.2d 797 (8th Cir.1958) upholding an order enjoining Faubus from using the Arkansas National Guard to obstruct or interfere with court orders, in *Faubus v. Aaron*, and in *Cooper v. Aaron*, the federal courts had repudiated all of Faubus' assaults upon the rule of law. Faubus once against tried to conjure up the specter of a special legislative session to devise another stratagem for evasion, but in light of *Cooper*, this time not even the statewide body would agree to it. The Board publicly challenged the governor to devise a plan that could provide for segregated schools and yet withstand the courts' scrutiny. The governor could only vaguely sputter that he was preparing such a plan, but it was never forthcoming. To Faubus' chagrin, the Little Rock high schools reopened in August 1959, with a small number of blacks attending two previously all-white schools—Hall as well as Central—so as not to needlessly inflame class tensions. City police maintained order without mishap and no federal assistance was asked for or needed.[213] The worst period of the Faubus era had ended at last. Although civil rights issues would remain controversial for the remainder of Fulbright's career, never again would Fulbright and other political leaders in Arkansas be subjected to the dilemma of dealing with an internationally notorious racial crisis in their home state. Yet, in his silence during the crisis, Fulbright had seriously tarnished his standing among many thoughtful Americans who had hoped for leadership from the Rhodes Scholar who had made so many contributions in arenas other than civil rights to America's public life in education, international relations, and rational solutions to social and political controversies. Charles Johnston's unsuccessful plea to Fulbright at the height of the crisis might serve as an epitaph to the hopes of the moderates: "Give us a chance to rally behind a statesman. The mob can only survive if respectable people keep quiet. It will take courage on your part, but we are here and will be counted–try us and see."[213a]

VI. "NO DESIRE FOR MARTYRDOM"

By the late 1950s and early 1960s, Faubus was even criticized by Fulbright, who joined a consensus for restraint in civil rights issues after others had taken the lead in creating it. His first indirect criticism of Faubus occurred in May 1958, when he delivered a Senate speech praising the *Gazette* when it won two Pulitzer prizes for reporting and front-page editorials criticizing Faubus during the Central crisis.[214] The senator praised Ashmore as a "great editor and writer," and complimented the *Gazette's* contributions to the "very real progress my state has made." Fulbright approvingly quoted the Pulitzer's citation of the paper: "The *Gazette* showed the highest qualities of civic leadership, journalistic responsibility, and moral courage in the face of an attempt at mob rule stimulated by the highest authority in the state."[215] Yet, the senator avoided all direct discussion of Faubus. The speech appeared intended to mollify the Pattersons and Ashmore, yet avoid assuming a controversial position on *Brown*.

By August 1959, weariness with Faubus' extremism had reached the level that Fulbright criticized him directly. Fulbright was asked on "Face the Nation" if he thought "the governor handled Little Rock's school desegregation crisis wrong," and answered: "I do. There's no doubt about that." He argued that most people in Little Rock no longer agreed with Faubus' actions at Central. "I think, as people must do in our system," Fulbright said, "they are trying to adapt themselves to this decision and they are proceeding to do it in a dignified and intelligent way." He described *Brown* as the "law of the land" and disparaged extreme Southern actions and statements denouncing it as "ridiculous . . . I have deplored the unwise decision, but it's erroneous to say that the Court doesn't have the power."[216] The *Gazette* described Fulbright's statement as "an offhand endorsement of the *Brown* decision," although considering Fulbright's criticism of the decision as "unwise," the report was overly generous.[217]

Faubus was meanwhile disparaging Fulbright as an "addle-brained visionary" and warning him "he'd better make his scheduled hand-shaking tour of the state this fall."[218] However, Fulbright's statement came late enough that it did not call down the torrent of abuse upon him that it would have a year earlier; while his signing of the Manifesto, his *Cooper* brief, and his votes against civil rights legislation were sufficient to protect his civil rights flank against a Faubus candidacy. Faubus ultimately never ran for the Senate, although the threat of his doing so cast a shadow over virtually the entire remainder of Fulbright's career. In 1962 and 1968, it was frequently assumed that Faubus would run against Fulbright. The senator would argue that it was his position in *Cooper* and other concessions on civil rights issues that kept Faubus out of the Senate, and this may have had some truth in it. At the same time, Fulbright had several years to repair any political damage that making a pro-law and order statement in 1957-58 would have entailed. The central rationalization he would cite endlessly for the next 35 years centered on the shocking defeat of Hays, his political ally and friend since the 1920s. "Look what happened to Brooks," he would say; "I had no desire for martyrdom."[219]

Fulbright's depiction of the Arkansas political climate centers on the alleged inevitability of segregationist domination of the 1958 elections. The senator's interpretation has unfortunately been repeated in many scholarly accounts, like Freyer's oversimplified statement that Alford's defeat of Hays showed that pro-segregationist views had "engulfed Little Rock." What the senator always omitted from his analysis was the surprising strength Hays demonstrated in 1958. In the July Democratic Primary his opponent was none other than the hero of the Little Rock racists, Amis Guthridge himself. The sentiments in favor of respect for the law, educational progress, and economic development were simply too strong, especially when consistently advanced by the indefatigable, self-assured Hays. Defusing the tension of the situation with his homespun humor, Hays often rejected the notion that everyone in central Arkansas was agitated by the race issue; the South was in reality "a hotbed of tranquillity," he said. The congressman's deep religious convictions also helped him, (although he made no effort to directly connect religion and politics) as he was a national Baptist leader and the 1957-59 president of the Southern Baptist Convention. Fulbright's contention that Hays suffered from a martyrdom complex was inaccurate; Hays had in fact made some rather distasteful political concessions to survive the storms of the massive resistance era, chiefly in signing the Manifesto. But some concessions he would not indulge in. His advisers informed him that all he had to do to win by a landslide was to make one statement endorsing segregation. This he would not do. In the Guthridge race, this decision seemed to be a triumph for both political courage and sagacity as he won by a 3-2 margin of roughly 11,000.[220] Hays stressed that he was running on his record, "and at the top of it I place the efforts I made to solve the problem of Central High School at Little Rock." Guthridge fired a series of predictable charges against Hays for "selling out Arkansas" to the federal government and the Northern liberals.[221]

Faubus fumed at Hays' resiliency. The congressman was buoyed by his defeat of Guthridge and the positive responses he received from many Arkansans. As one constituent wrote to Hays after an October 1958 speech, "I wish to commend you for your speech in defense of a moderate position on the integration issue . . . I cannot help but have a feeling that if a man like you can say this often enough the intelligent people of Arkansas will soon begin to respond."[222] The Democratic Primary was tantamount to reelection, there was no Republican opponent, and Hays naturally disbanded his campaign organization and made no further efforts in campaigning until the fall. When given time to explain his case, Hays had demonstrated a talent for getting people to calm down and reason about the situation; thus the Faubus camp concluded that they should wait until a few weeks before the election to spring a surprise write-in candidate on the incumbent. In September, Hays suffered from an accident of bad timing when he was the guest speaker of the predominantly black National Baptist Convention in Chicago on the day *Cooper v. Aaron* was announced. Photographs of Hays at the convention were later reprinted and distributed by the thousands shortly before the election on a circular accusing Hays of spending his time with Northern blacks and liberals to the detriment of Arkansas, and alleging that *Cooper* involved a conspiracy in which Hays had known of the decision in advance and had arranged to be at the convention of black Baptists on that very day to begin propagandizing for the decision.[223]

The conspiratorial charges concerning Hays and the *Cooper* decision did not convince any voters except the most adamant segregationists who already detested Hays. Support of the Faubus organization removed any organizational difficulties that otherwise would have been faced by Dale Alford, the last-minute candidate. Since it had been widely assumed since July that Hays was assured of re-election, the turnout was unusually low, except in the lower class white neighborhoods, where turnout was usually low in most election years. Again, the intensity of the segregationists on race-related issues became an important factor in the outcome as the most heavily segregationist areas produced an unexpectedly high turnout, unlike the black and more highly-educated pro-Hays areas, where the Hays forces faced a problem of getting their supporters to recognize that the congressman faced a serious challenge. The eventual victory of a congressional write-in candidate was unique in Arkansas history.

Alford praised Faubus as a "defender of the Southern way of life," and ranted that "not one time have we heard Congressman Hays say a single word in praise of our great and wonderful governor. . . . I am a Faubus Democrat, and Hays is a Paul Butler [DNC chairman] Democrat who is selling Arkansas out." Hays also lost a number of votes on non-race related issues, such as his vote in favor of rent controls on landlords. However, segregation was clearly the key issue in the campaign. Hays was caught off-guard by the unexpected opposition and never got his organization into its normal array. Use of preprinted Alford stickers with the check by Alford's name was illegal, since write-in votes were supposed to be written in by hand. The election officials also assisted "illiterate" voters regarding how to vote in the congressional race.[224] But the most brazen Faubus tactic was the dissemination of Alford stickers by election officials at several voting places.[225] This tactic was utilized at places where the Faubus supporters thought they were sure of the loyalty of the officials involved. But they erred in judging several of the officials, and some of them publicly criticized the fraudulent tactics. At least one submitted an affidavit in early 1959 to the congressional committee that was supposed to investigate the election, stating that in her precinct the Alford stickers were passed out with the ballots by one of the other Arkansas election officials.[226] A conservative estimate of the number of stickers passed out was several thousand. Fulbright and others later argued that substantial numbers of people who voted against Hays "were just showing their disapproval, to sort of slap him down even though they really liked him. Even the people who voted against him were shocked by what happened."[227] Fulbright's reminiscences in his memoirs 30 years later were conjectural, but the narrow margin of victory and the clear electoral irregularities were facts. Alford's alleged margin of victory was 1,200 out of 61,000 votes cast; since in 1959 Southern Democrats in Congress blocked any meaningful investigation of the election, the question of who really won will never be decided.

Fulbright omitted most of these details from his analysis of the 1958 election. Moreover, if Hays came that close to surviving under extreme duress without assistance from his longtime friend Bill Fulbright, the additional unpleasant question arises as to what he might have done had Fulbright made statements in support of Hays. No "liberal" endorsement would have been required, only a statement that Hays performed a useful public service in working to maintain calm during the crisis. None was forthcoming from Fulbright. Even in Fulbright's memoirs, in which he was generally complimentary of Hays, he persisted in portraying the history of that era as if it were strictly a question of political strategy. "If I had criticized Faubus or issued a statement," Fulbright would reflect, "I wouldn't have altered his course—other than to give him a reason to challenge me in the 1962 primary and destroy me politically." In contrast, Hays' "timing" had been off—"If you do it too soon, as Brooks did, you're out. And once he was out, he couldn't do any more educating. He couldn't do anything about it. After that, he played no significant or interesting role in Arkansas affairs."[228] This was a distinctly ungenerous view of Hays, and it missed the reality that Hays gained far more in 1957-58 from his courageous stance, in spite of the defeat, than he ever could have by remaining silent and staying in office. Before, he had been a respected but not particularly well known congressman outside of Arkansas. After his efforts to solve the Central High crisis and subsequent defeat, he became famous, a legendary figure in the civil rights community. He received myriad letters of regret for his defeat from throughout the nation, and would receive an appointment from President Kennedy as a White House aide. In the 1960s Hays would become a moral symbol for the civil rights leaders. The simplest but most moving accolade to Hays was delivered by Martin Luther King, Jr., who would introduce him on a few occasions in the 1960s when they gave speeches together by saying, "This is Mr. Hays. He has suffered with us."[229]

Fulbright was genuinely shocked by Hays' defeat at the time, writing to him shortly thereafter, "You probably will live much longer as a result of this sad development. I say sad, because I really do feel sorry for the people of Little Rock who have been caught up in this emotional hysteria and seem now to have an urge toward self-destruction."[230] Some of the emerging progressive leaders in northeastern Arkansas became dedicated to follow Hays' example and revive the state from its political nadir; as Bill Penix, a Jonesboro lawyer wrote to Hays at the time, "I have an abiding faith that there are prospective leaders in the state with a few sparks of decency left in them, and that these people will come out of hibernation somewhere near the bottom of the cesspool and guide us back upward."[231] In the 1960s, Penix would become the campaign manager for Bill Alexander, the moderately liberal Democrat who would forge a black-moderate white alliance after the model of Hays' coalition in central Arkansas, finally breaking the oligarchy's historic stranglehold over the delta congressional district. But Penix's voice was still in the minority in 1958 in the east.

The Hays defeat brought national notice to the triumph of the Arkansas segregationists, although there was little or no national media coverage of the electoral irregularities. Eisenhower expressed regret, saying Hays had "served the country well and loyally, and I hope will continue to do so for a long time."[232] Curiously, one of the most effusive tributes came from Hays' longtime political opponent, Vice President Richard Nixon: "There was no more tragic result of this election, from the standpoint of the nation, than your defeat in Arkansas." Nixon told his former adversary that "When statesmanship of the type you represent in such an exemplary way becomes the victim of demagoguery and prejudice, it is time for men of good will in both of our major parties in all sections of the country to exert more positive leadership in developing the public understanding on the issue of civil rights which is essential if America is to continue to be a nation of responsible laws rather than irresponsible men." Nixon may have been angling for black votes in looking ahead to the 1960 Presidential election. At any rate, whatever Nixon's motivation in writing the letter, he made no secret of it, releasing the entire two-page text to the *New York Herald Tribune*, which printed it verbatim on its front page.[234]

Hays' defeat represented an example of the problem of voting fraud that was widely decried by Faubus' opponents. The charges of fraud were not confined to his liberal or moderate opponents; Jim Johnson had charged that his 1956 electoral totals had been reduced by the Faubus political machine in several counties. An examination of the voting patterns in the 1958 elections reveals the fundamental malfunctioning of the Arkansas political process regarding the black vote. Predictably, Faubus won in a landslide, although it should be noted that the heavyweights among the moderates–McMath and Rockefeller–decided not to run and Faubus thus enjoyed an election against weak opponents. Presumably even the heavyweights would not have been able to defeat Faubus at that time, but his 69 percent of the vote came against unknown candidates. There is no question that Faubus was the most popular Arkansas politician in 1958, but some scholars have drawn erroneous conclusions from the elections of that year. Freyer has contended that "Officials in Washington must have been bewildered by the fact that blacks in Little Rock and across the state voted overwhelmingly for Faubus, presumably because of his impressive record of accomplishments in improving Arkansas' economy and social services."[235] It is true that Faubus won landslide victories in black precincts in the delta, but Freyer's statement that blacks in Little Rock voted for Faubus is simply erroneous. Despite the relative obscurity of his two opponents, Lee Ward and Chris Finkbeiner, Pulaski County returns from predominantly black precincts show a landslide vote *against* Faubus.

To give a few examples: Box 1B, 557 for Ward, 73 for Finkbeiner, 104 for Faubus; Box 2B in North Little Rock, 542 for Ward, 17 for Finkbeiner, and 83 for Faubus; and Box 3C, 490 for Ward, 82 for Finkbeiner, and 123 for Faubus.[236] The percentages in these black precincts were roughly 69 percent for Ward, about 19 percent for Faubus, and 12 percent for Finkbeiner. In these same areas in the fall, Hays defeated Alford, 83 percent to 17 percent. Freyer does not cite any statistics on the Little Rock vote. On the other hand, Freyer is correct that blacks in the delta overwhelmingly voted for Faubus. For example, Faubus won predominantly black precincts in Mississippi County, adjacent to the river, by a 7-to-1 margin.[237] An accurate analysis of the Arkansas political system would indicate that the blacks and their moderate allies were financially and politically strong enough to exercise an independent, free vote in Little Rock, but in the delta their votes were manipulated in a manner somewhat similar to what had been done in the 1880s.

The conclusion that Freyer draws is even more baffling than his erroneous assertion that Little Rock blacks overwhelmingly voted for Faubus: "What was most evident was that Arkansans of both races had apparently endorsed segregation, for in his campaign Faubus had appealed to the emotions, fears, and prejudices that had been aroused among whites since the preceding fall."[238] Daisy Bates, Wiley Branton and numerous other black leaders who had fought segregation across the state would be dumbfounded to know that they and their supporters had "apparently endorsed segregation." Bates and Branton were pillars of the black community, and were increasingly respected among all races as time passed.

Contemporary whites often promoted the dream that blacks were content with the segregationist regime, but this had little basis in reality for the great majority of blacks. Freyer's assertions regarding 1958 contradict arguments he made elsewhere in his monograph on the Little Rock crisis: that is, blacks in the delta had their votes manipulated through socioeconomic pressures, payments on election day, threats about termination of employment, outright fraud or other means of control. Freyer cites the results in predominantly black Ward 4 of West Memphis, just south of Mississippi County, where the pupil assignment law passed by a vote of 545 to 17. Such landslide margins for purely segregationist measures could hardly be explained by an unconstrained, freely exercised vote, as Freyer acknowledges in that context. The basic point that Freyer was attempting to make in that passage–that 1958 was the high tide of the segregationists, with Jim Johnson winning a race for the Supreme Court–certainly held considerable validity. But he carried the argument much too far in minimizing Hays' strength and trying to argue that Faubus even won the Little Rock black vote.

An additional force obstructing blacks' political participation emanated from the persistence in some of the smaller rural counties of the old explicit disfranchisement methods. In most counties, the plantation owners arranged to pay the poll taxes for the blacks when they "voted them," and most blacks in Little Rock managed to pay the poll tax, but there were still a few counties where blacks were disfranchised.[239] The system of manipulating black votes was in place in the most heavily populated black counties: Phillips, Mississippi, and Crittenden. In most areas of the plantation belt, the oligarchs felt it was old-fashioned and foolish to deprive the power structure of a substantial augmentation in votes by disfranchisement, so the more "modern" system was to "vote the blacks"; hence the results such as the 7-to-1 Faubus landslide in Mississippi County. Fulbright's awareness of the oligarchy's grip on the voting process in the delta was, of course, one of the important reasons behind his political calculations.

Ironically, Faubus' ultimate undoing would be wrought at the hands of a progressive who suffered from two major political liabilities that were unrelated to race: Winthrop Rockefeller was a Republican in a state dominated by Democrats, and a multimillionaire Yankee who had only recently moved to Arkansas from the Frozen North. The malfunctioning of the political process regarding blacks was the most serious obstacle to Rockefeller's political future in the late 1950s, but as the black vote became independent, it eventually propelled him into the governor's mansion. Rockefeller was uniquely qualified to challenge the planters' system of manipulating the black vote. In any area where the votes were controlled by payments at election time for poll taxes or for campaign work—whether for actual work or using money to manipulate votes—Rockefeller was the only candidate whose bottomless campaign coffers could surpass those of all the plantation owners combined.[240]

Moreover, the rise of black political activism would make it increasingly difficult for the legacy of oppression to intimidate blacks from voting. Blacks came to realize that threats to fire employees if they voted against the oligarchy were ultimately idle if blacks voted as a bloc. Where blacks were a majority or a substantial minority, white employers were obviously dependent on them as a labor supply. Sid McMath waged a spirited campaign against Faubus in the 1962 gubernatorial race, with the *Gazette* and other moderate and liberal forces vigorously supporting McMath. The *Gazette's* impact on the race was difficult to judge; the paper's liberal editorial stance had clearly antagonized the hard-core right wing, yet the paper's thoughtful analyses of the race issue inescapably elevated the public discourse in the state and influenced the moderate voters. Although the Faubus machine was still too strong to be defeated in that year (and the reactionary Dale Alford was also a candidate, although he was by then not a threat to win) Faubus narrowly averted being forced into a runoff—a dangerous situation for an incumbent. The situation might have been politically fatal for Faubus had it not been for the surprising decision of yet another candidate—Marvin Melton—to withdraw from the race. Melton was a popular eastern Arkansas real estate developer and implement dealer, and he privately contacted McMath with the proposal that they both run in the primary and then join forces behind the candidate who gained the runoff spot against Faubus. Melton would have siphoned off votes precisely in the area—east Arkansas—where Faubus had become politically powerful. Unfortunately, soon after McMath entered the race, the anti-Faubus forces received a severe blow; as the former governor and Henry Woods were driving to a political rally, they were stunned by an announcement that Melton had mysteriously withdrawn from the race.[240a] The McMath forces wondered if the Faubus camp had privately brought pressures to bear upon Melton to gain his withdrawal, although the Jonesboro candidate's decision remained a mystery. John Troutt, editor of the *Jonesboro Sun*, the largest northeast Arkansas newspaper, recalled later that Melton "got cold feet and did not feel driven enough to do it." McMath and Faubus had attracted most of the available campaign funds, so that Melton's race would have lacked financial resources in competing against the incumbent governor and the former governor. Melton was a middle-of-the-road candidate and certainly no liberal on racial issues, but he was also noticeably free of Faubus' demagogy on civil rights, and he believed in upholding the law. His withdrawal justifiably depressed the McMath forces. Troutt—who was known as a shrewd analyst of Arkansas politics—believed that McMath's chances of defeating Faubus in a runoff would have been excellent, considering the fact that incumbents who became involved in runoffs in Arkansas were usually vulnerable. In light of the blow the anti-Faubus forces suffered by Melton's unexpected withdrawal, it is even more remarkable that they came within two percent of the vote to forcing a runoff.

Meanwhile, from 1960 to 1962, Fulbright had faced the prospect of a Faubus bid for the Senate. Fulbright tried to encourage McMath to run against Faubus for the gubernatorial nomination in 1960, and the senator enlisted former President Truman and Averell Harriman in the effort to persuade McMath to challenge the governor. McMath decided not to run, and four lesser candidates entered the Democratic primary. Fulbright worked behind the scenes for Faubus' opponents, but the governor still prevailed. Late in 1961, the senator made a vigorous tour of the state speaking to small groups of Arkansans, strengthening his political base before the 1962 Senate election. W.R. Stephens, founder of a major Little Rock investment firm and one of the wealthiest and most influential people in the state, privately exerted a major influence in Fulbright's favor. Stephens' political positions were often determined by personal loyalty and faithfulness rather than ideology, and surprisingly, he had friendships with both Fulbright and Faubus. Stephens advised Faubus not to run against Fulbright, and although Stephens' role was not publicly known at the time, his influence was undoubtedly a significant factor in dissuading a possible Faubus senatorial bid. Other wealthy Arkansans who were friendly to both Fulbright and Faubus—such as Bill Darby and Jack Pickens, took the same position as Stephens. The Kennedy administration privately warned Faubus not to run against Fulbright. In addition, Faubus had little knowledge of national issues and no meaningful knowledge of international affairs; probably, Faubus was smart enough to realize that he would have been out of his element in the United States Senate. Moreover, Fulbright had protected his political flank on the civil rights issue, of course. In the end, Faubus did not run for the Senate.[240b]

By 1963, Fulbright was becoming more aware of pressures to turn away from the old racial politics of reaction in the South. Faubus had narrowly avoided a runoff. President Kennedy and Attorney General Kennedy were in constant communication with some of the Southern senators in that year. The President hoped for the emergence of a "Southern Vandenberg," meaning a Southerner who would have the courage to break with the politics of his region just as Republican Senator Arthur Vandenberg had broken with Midwestern Republicans who were wedded to isolationism; Vandenberg instead had worked with the Truman administration in forging a bipartisan foreign policy. Fulbright and Lister Hill of Alabama were Kennedy's favorites for the role of the "Southern Vandenberg," but they both rejected the challenge. Kennedy would also taunt his close friend in the Senate, George Smathers, about when he was going to cast "that really courageous vote" on civil rights. Smathers also declined the historic opportunity, being more concerned—as were Fulbright and Hill—with his immediate political survival.[240c]

After doing extensive polling in the South, Kennedy's friend Louis Harris advised the President that the outstanding development in the South was related not to race, but to the region's rapid economic growth. "You can well go into the South throughout 1964 not to lay down the gauntlet on civil rights," Harris advised the President, "but rather to describe and encourage the new industrial and educational explosion in the region." Kennedy began implementing that approach in October, 1963, on an early campaign swing through Arkansas. At Little Rock, the President praised Arkansas' imposing congressional delegation, led by Congressman Wilbur Mills, Fulbright and McClellan:

> ...They are forward-looking men, and their contribution to the welfare of this country may come as a surprise to those whose view of the South may be distorted by headlines and headline-seekers. The old South has its problems and they are not yet over, nor are they over in the rest of the country. But there is rising every day, I believe, a new South, a new South of which Henry Grady spoke about 80 years ago, and I have seen it in your universities, in your cities, in your industries. The new South I saw this morning on the Little Red River, the dams and reservoirs through the White River and the Arkansas River Basin in a sense symbolize the new South, for they mean navigation for your commerce, protection for your cities, opportunity for your people.

Kennedy's emphasis upon economic development won a warm reception from a state tired of lagging behind in the prosperity enjoyed by much of the rest of the nation. Of course, it was ironic that Kennedy had spoken in such glowing terms of Henry Grady's "new South," for Grady had indeed spoken of the new era 80 years before, and the South was still waiting to experience the dawn of the long-awaited new era of economic plenty. Fulbright was pleased by Kennedy's visit to Arkansas and the potential it demonstrated for Democratic prospects in the 1964 election; the only depressing note was Fulbright's concern about the President's upcoming visit to Dallas, Texas. Fulbright himself had been subjected to extreme verbal abuse from zealous right-wing elements that were strong in Dallas, and the senator privately advised Kennedy that Dallas was dangerous and that he should not go there. In general, however, Fulbright was greatly encouraged by the President's favorable impression in his state.[240d]

Part of Kennedy's success in Arkansas could be attributed to his famous grace and charm. Fulbright remarked at the time that Kennedy "had an unusual courtesy in small ways with people." One episode revealing the President's human touch took place when Mrs. James O. Powell, the *Gazette* editorial editor's wife, had a chance to meet the President, and asked him to reach down and shake hands with her son, Lee Powell, who was then a kindergarten graduate and considerably shorter than he would later become. Bad back and all, the President stooped over and gave the tyke a warm handshake and a broad grin, leaving an impression on the lad that would last a lifetime. For a refreshing change, the *Gazette* assumed a position that, at least temporarily, reflected the views of a majority of Arkansans: John F. Kennedy's enthusiastic reception in Arkansas, predicted editor James O. Powell, could well mean that "the Republicans may be counting prematurely in adding up all those electoral votes for 1964 from a Solid Republican South."[240e]

Kennedy's increasing determination to push for civil rights legislation had not weakened his overall political strength in the fall of 1963. In October, a Gallup poll showed him leading Fulbright's old rival, Barry Goldwater, by 55 to 39 percent, and he led Nixon in the same poll by a slightly larger margin of 58 to 37 percent. A poll conducted on November 20 indicated that most whites believed that Kennedy was pushing too fast for civil rights, but their concern was not sufficient to outweigh his overall positive ratings, since he enjoyed a 59 percent approval, according to Gallup. However, there were nascent signs of the white backlash that would help Nixon gain the White House five years later. One example was the hostility to civil rights displayed in some areas of Boston, led by Louise Day Hicks, who received substantial white support in winning reelection to the committee that controlled that city's schools. George Wallace publicly speculated about entering the Democratic primaries for President to demonstrate what he regarded as national resentment over Kennedy's stance on civil rights.[240f]

In late October, 1963, Fulbright suffered from his customary ambivalence regarding the race issue. In late August, he had watched Martin Luther King's televised "I Have a Dream" speech at the Lincoln Memorial, and was impressed by the peacefulness of the 200,000 people of both races who took part in the "March on Washington" demonstration. In contrast, the senator was deeply troubled by the violence of the Southern extremists. When four young black girls were killed in the bombing of a church in Birmingham, Fulbright called the White House and offered his help for a new civil rights bill. He was impressed with Kennedy's growth as President by that stage, yet he was always wary of a backlash. Late in October, a group of senior Southern senators gathered and decided that their most effective strategy was to delay action on the legislation that would eventually become the historic Civil Rights Act of 1964. Most of the Southerners thought they detected a growing disenchantment with civil rights across the country, although they misread the public mood; many Americans were becoming increasingly sensitive to the need to remove the blight of racial discrimination from their society. Fulbright decided to help the Kennedy administration by at least keeping them advised about Southern political strategy; one of Fulbright's aides, with the senator's knowledge, privately informed the White House about the meeting and the political conclusions of the majority of Southern senators.[240g] However, Fulbright could never bring himself to become the Southern Vandenberg and cast "that really courageous vote;" he would vote against the Civil Rights Act of 1964, in yet another bitter disappointment for many of his admirers.

With the emerging black vote in Arkansas, an additional political force was developing that could have supported a shift by Fulbright or other politicians toward a moderate position on race. Rockefeller would give Faubus a strong race in 1964, while Faubus chose to retire in 1966 with a rematch against Rockefeller looming. Even before the Voting Rights Act, the black voting bloc in Arkansas had become a potent force. Blacks provided the crucial margin of victory for President Johnson's victory in the state in 1964 in a campaign in which the Civil Rights Act of 1964 was a major issue for Arkansas.[241] Once again, Fulbright was willing to take whatever political risks were involved in supporting the Democratic national ticket. Rockefeller would defeat Jim Johnson in the 1966 governor's race by 50,000 votes, with the black vote making the difference.[242] Rockefeller received about 18,000 less white votes than Johnson, but won a 67,000-vote margin among blacks. [243] In some black boxes in West Helena that had reported landslide totals for Faubus in 1958, Rockefeller won 98.2 percent of the vote.[244] But in a disturbing indication of how arduous the process of ending the informal intimidation methods had been, an internal memorandum written by Ben Grinage, a black aide in the Fulbright campaign organization (which was actively courting black votes by 1966) stated after the election that in some counties blacks "were free to vote as they wanted to for the first time in many areas. This is probably the most significant factor in the voting pattern of the Negroes."[245] Rockefeller would similarly defeat a candidate of the Faubus machine in 1968. Thus would Faubus' one-time appointee engineer the demise of the governor's lengthy domination of the state's politics. But the long-awaited era of reform would blossom only after a concatenation of missed opportunities, lack of leadership from Fulbright and a number of "moderates" who were otherwise respected for their statesmanship, and a distorted political system had combined to ignite an era of massive resistance that set back Arkansas' racial progress by years, and inflicted scars on the state's reputation that would be decades in the healing.

Conclusion

One school of constitutional thinkers has portrayed *Brown* as a "political" triumph that wrought profound change in the South despite virulent opposition. In *The Tempting of America,* Robert Bork contended that *Brown* "had prevailed despite the fact that it had ordered a change in an entrenched social order in much of the nation." The Court believed that it had departed from original understanding in *Brown,* in Bork's view, yet nevertheless "triumphed over intense political opposition despite that fact. . . . We remember the television pictures of adult whites screaming obscenities at properly dressed black children arriving to attend school."[245] Behind this picture of a politically triumphant Court, in Bork's depiction, stood the valiant Eisenhower, who dispatched to Little Rock "airborne troops to guarantee compliance with the Court's ruling." Far from having damaged its authority by "acting politically," Bork concluded, "the Court is virtually invulnerable, and *Brown* proved it." A historical analysis of massive resistance would indicate that this is an oversimplified assessment of *Brown's* political impact: the Supreme Court wields a limited capability to engineer rapid social change without the support of the political branches; by 1964, only 123 blacks out of 7,000 students attended desegregated schools in Little Rock. [246] Significant desegregation would occur only after the executive branch and a majority of the legislative branch began supporting desegregation, culminating in passage of the Civil Rights Act of 1964. However, *Brown* unquestionably played a vital role in preparing the foundations for the achievements of the civil rights movement, and the gradual progress in race relations that took place over the years was greatly assisted by the Supreme Court's historic decision in 1954.

Arkansas exemplified the regional pattern after passage of the Civil Rights Act, with its especially significant provision prohibiting racial discrimination in any program receiving federal assistance, and authorizing federal agencies to cut off funding upon noncompliance. With the new HEW guidelines promulgated in the mid-1960s, the percentage of Southern blacks in desegregated schools expanded from 2.3 percent in 1964 to 44 percent in 1971.[247] Central would become a model of successful integration by 1981, with a black student body president and a reputation as one of the finest academic high schools in the South.[248] Most of the other schools did not boast such an impressive record and problems emerged in some areas because of residential patterns; but public education in Little Rock had nonetheless undergone extensive change since the regime of Jim Crow. *Brown* played a vital long-term role in initiating support for the civil rights movement and providing moral and legal authority for advocates of integration, but Bork's depiction of it as a political triumph backed up by the Eisenhower administration was ahistorical. With the exception of the one belated decision to use military authority in Little Rock, the Eisenhower administration hindered the civil rights movement through its silence mixed with homilies about not changing the hearts of people through law. Major progress in civil rights required an administration with an affirmative commitment to civil rights, and a Congress altered by the 1964 Congressional elections that smashed the Republican-Southern Democrat alliance that had obstructed civil rights legislation in the 1950s.[249]

The limited nature of the Court's ability to produce social change is further revealed by the Court's generally excellent performance in the desegregation cases. It is clear that the Court brilliantly predicted the future consensus that would emerge in favor of integration in following decades. In *Brown II*, the Court demonstrated that it understood the need to avoid attempting to move in an unrealistically rapid rate toward changing entrenched social traditions. In *Cooper*, the Court had made clear that endless delay did not constitute a prompt and reasonable start toward desegregation. In reality Hays and several other moderates were privately pleased with the ruling and thought it ultimately strengthened their hand; the moderates could then make their case to the people that the Court was so adamant on the issue that desegregation was inevitable, and the South might as well begin complying.[250] *Cooper* did not clarify the confusion concerning the specifics of what *Brown* required, and the Court did not begin to delve into systematic oversight of the desegregation process until the 1960s; yet it might have been damaging to make such an attempt prematurely, and in any event *Cooper* stood as a landmark against outright defiance.[251] Despite the blend of moral vision, practical wisdom and firmness displayed by the Court, it could wield only a limited impact in fashioning major social change without support from the national political branches.

As for Bork's argument that the *Brown* opinion's reasoning did not rest on original intent, originalism is hardly the only valid justification for the opinion. Of course, legalistic arguments were not prominent in the public debate of the 1950s. As a former constitutional law professor, Fulbright was steeped in the Reconstruction era debates, and was well aware that while some radicals had expressed egalitarian sentiments, the floor manager of the Civil Rights Bill that was the forerunner to the Fourteenth Amendment had stated in a House speech that "civil rights do not mean that all children shall attend the same school," and Congress continued school segregation in the District of Columbia at the time. [252] A narrow originalist theory—one that focused on specific statements of most of the Framers and ignored the broad interpretation that the Framers chose expansive language to allow for future growth and flexibility—should have led inexorably to the conclusion that *Brown* was wrongly decided. Such views were not widely discussed in the Arkansas political debates in the 1950s, for people were understandably concerned about their contemporary activities and not particularly interested in what the Reconstruction era Framers had intended a century before. Indeed, the originalist theory that Bork espoused decades later should logically have led to the conclusion that *Brown* was wrongly decided; given the widespread conviction that *Brown* was one of the great decisions in the Supreme Court's history, such an analysis could easily lead to the further conclusion that originalist theory has profound weaknesses. As the conservative legal scholar and judge, Richard Posner, would write in 1990, Bork's arguments claiming to be supportive of *Brown* prove that Bork "is not a practicing originalist."[253]

Of course, *Brown* had become such a moral and constitutional icon decades later that neither Bork nor anyone else wishing to gain a wide forum for their views could criticize it. But in the Arkansas of the 1950s, it is interesting that despite the possible criticisms that might have been hurled against the *Brown* reasoning on the original intent score, such criticisms were not prominent in the debate. This was partly because of the realism of Fulbright, who, from his days as a New Deal attorney, was all too familiar with activism from the Court—then from the opposite end of the spectrum—and found nothing surprising about a Court whose dominant figures were racial liberals turning out racially liberal opinions that might not rest on original intent. With his lawyerly background, Fulbright was inclined to be respectful even toward a Court he felt was moving too fast, although political passions from empowered constituents trumped his professional inclinations in practice. In general, in the midst of contemporary political controversies, legalistic arguments concerning the Reconstruction era were not part of the usual vocabulary in public debate.

Since the Arkansas political process was not functioning fairly in the 1950s, it was an appropriate situation for the Supreme Court to intervene, since the state government did not fairly respond to all the people in the state and had a self-interest in maintaining the status quo. As the moderates were able to cite *Brown's* moral and legal force over the years, the decision seized upon the momentum in changing racial attitudes that had begun in World War II. Even in the 1940s, the court's decision in *Smith v. Allwright* invalidating the all-white primary faced no major resistance in Arkansas. The question arises as to whether school segregation would have been challenged without Supreme Court intervention. The avoidance of meddling from federal outsiders would have removed a major phobia of Southerners that Faubus was able to exploit to such devastating advantage in the Central crisis.

In central Arkansas, where blacks were voting freely, results were already in motion. Black policemen patrolled black areas in Little Rock, integration of the city's public transportation system began in the early 1950s and was completed by 1956, department stores ended segregation of fountains. Blacks frequently served on juries in federal courts, and to a lesser extent in state and local courts. In many areas of the city, blacks and whites lived in close proximity to each other without conflict. [254] Hays was naturally a staunch advocate of black voting rights since he would owe his seat to the black bloc in a close election; he had advocated integration in other areas such as in interstate transportation before *Brown*, and taken a series of other progressive positions on race. As Numan Bartley aptly pointed out, "Of all southern cities, Little Rock was among the least likely scenes for a dramatic confrontation between state and federal power."[255] Paradoxically, the moderate city became the site of the historic confrontation because the moderates and the NAACP were strong enough in Little Rock to fashion a desegregation plan that ignited the racist reaction, ultimately causing the crisis that led to the federal intervention. In a Deep Southern state where progressives were weaker, the Eisenhower administration could more easily stand aside. Results roughly similar to those in Little Rock could reasonably have been expected in the delta if blacks had been allowed to vote freely there; the whites were more staunchly segregationist there and lacked the substantial white liberal and moderate factions existing in Little Rock, but the black population was much larger, making up a majority in some counties and a third or more of the population in others.

Given the progress made in Little Rock after blacks acquired the vote, even in the era before *Brown*, it seems safe to argue that some of the worst features of Jim Crow would likewise have been ameliorated in the delta had blacks possessed free voting rights. The old regime was so powerfully entrenched in the delta, however, that a judicial role was essential in intervening in a political system that functioned unfairly. Even in Little Rock, progress toward school desegregation would have been much slower without moral and legal pressure from the Supreme Court, for whites were much more tolerant of blacks serving on juries or riding desegregated public transportation than they were of desegregation in the schools.

Faubus' domination of the state's politics did not reflect the full spectrum of opinion in the state. The emergence of an independent black vote not only would produce a 20 percent bloc of the entire Arkansas electorate that would adamantly oppose him, but it would strengthen the resolve of the white moderates who would become viable opponents of the segregationists when the black votes joined theirs. The black vote in the late 1950s was less than 10 percent of the total electorate, with much of that total being subject to manipulation or corruption in the delta. With the zeal of the massive resisters, their determination to resort to boycotts and other aggressive tactics, an additional obstacle to a coalition of blacks and moderates developed in the form of intimidation of dissent. Of course, when blacks emerged as a free voting force, their intensity would at times match that of the most extreme segregationists. The moderates' appeals for the support of the rule of law tended to be constructive when they were coupled with arguments advancing beyond reluctant admissions that the South must bow to superior federal authority. Arguments linking desegregation to avoidance of educational or economic stagnation were particularly helpful, but arid assertions that the Court must be obeyed even though its decisions were deplorable tended to undermine the moderates' position. As a final barrier to opposition, a certain amount of outright fraud in voting also swelled the Faubus totals. For any of those who felt disaffected by the racial appeal, Faubus would often emphasize his role as defending Arkansas' prerogatives against federal encroachment. Finally, in the northwest, race was not at the top of Faubus' agenda, as he could push for education or senior citizens' issues and avoid race in the virtually all-white region.

In analyzing the Faubus era, what Alexander and a number of other scholars have emphasized was the governor's alleged utter domination throughout the state exclusively through racial politics. According to these accounts, for the entire period until the mid-1960s he was allegedly representing the views of the great majority of Arkansans. While there is no doubt that Faubus exploited a combination of racist and anti-federal prejudice, and that he symbolized a tragic era in the state's history, it is doubtful that support for his extreme segregationist positions of the 1957-58 period ever reached more than 55 percent of the state's citizens. Blacks and moderate whites constituted roughly 45 percent of the population, even at the height of the reaction in the late 1950s. Rather than being mesmerized by Faubus' command of the majority of the whites, what seems equally striking in retrospect was how forcefully the minority of dissenters opposed the governor in the teeth of the reaction, and how powerful the anti-Faubus coalition would clearly have been had blacks been able to vote freely up to their 20 percent of the population. The black vote concentrated in the delta would have transformed Faubus' greatest post-1957 bastion into a hotly contested region, while it would have given the Fulbrights and other vacillating "moderates" a reason to stiffen their resistance to the Faubus machine. One of the keys to Faubus' success in his heyday from 1957-61 was in fostering the illusion of his own invincibility; by so doing he was able to avoid attracting any serious opponents in the 1958 and 1960 elections and thus run up landslide victories against weak candidates. With his relatively narrow victory in 1962 against the eloquent, talented McMath, Faubus won only one more election, and then after toning down his segregationist rhetoric and running in 1964 as the hometown, country boy Democrat against the rich Yankee Republican.

Some observers have also argued that because of Faubus' political talents, initial ties to the moderate camp and his origins in the northwest, he was uniquely situated to dominate the state's politics through a move toward the racist camp after Brown. McMath, for example, emphasized Faubus' curious ability to hold together seemingly contradictory elements under his banner in different parts of the state, and the shocking nature of his initial plunge into the Johnson camp. As McMath recalled it, "The last man I would have expected to have called out the National Guard in defiance of court orders was Orval Faubus."[256] As the historian David Wallace noted, the other candidates backed by the east Arkansas oligarchy tended to have political liabilities for the rest of the state on social issues, unlike Faubus, whose tenure saw teachers' salaries more than double from $2,264 to $5,100, and monthly welfare payments to the elderly rise from $30 to $75.[257] However, just as Faubus cast his lot with conservative forces on race, in the later period of his administration he would also develop closer ties to big business interests that had been the target of Faubus' populist attack back in 1954. Such views emphasizing Faubus' uniqueness hold some plausibility, but they neglect the reality that in his handling of the desegregation issue Faubus was responding to larger social and political forces within the state. Had not Faubus led the massive resisters, it is entirely plausible to believe that some other politician would have attempted it, and the moderates would have been confronted with a somewhat similar dilemma from a different politician. Nonetheless, it is true that Faubus was the leader who occupied the crucial role in the critical state of Arkansas in 1957; had he not taken the path he chose, massive resistance might not have assumed the crisis of international proportions that it did in Little Rock.

It was crucial in the sad culmination of massive resistance in the Central High crisis that a section of the state's reasonable people chose to depart the fray. Fulbright was the most famous and important of these, but it was not simply his own role that was important— Fulbright symbolized an entire group of moderates who had no sympathy for Faubus' demagogy, but also rationalized their silence as a question of survival. Congressmen Oren Harris and Jim Trimble were others from the relatively moderate camp who also acquiesced to the Faubus regime. It was easy to follow Fulbright's example. Yet, despite the malfunctioning of the Arkansas political process, it was not inevitable that Fulbright and other moderate leaders were trapped into silence in the face of Faubus' defiance of the Court. The aura of inevitability in which Fulbright has cloaked his silence has been accepted by many scholars as well as politicians in subsequent decades, but in reality, had the moderates maintained solidarity against the Faubus onslaught, the state's history might have been substantially different. Arkansas at least might not have plummeted as deeply into the abyss as it did in the Central crisis. There was a most unpleasant fact against Fulbright's thesis of fatalism: that in the 1958 Democratic Primary Hays had campaigned and won on the "moderate" platform of upholding law and order in calling for compliance, and emphasizing the educational and economic advantages of doing so, and that he almost won in the general election in spite of the extraordinary circumstances of that election. This has been neglected not only in accounts by Fulbright, but by many scholars and by such writers as Alexander who stress Arkansas' intransigence against integration. The position of the Fulbright group had a self-fulfilling prophecy, for if such influential figures never lifted their voices against extremism, this contributed to the eventual somber result.

Fulbright himself was quite popular in 1958 and might have assisted Hays but chose not to do so; whether his influence might have made that small change that would have meant the difference between losing Hays' leadership and elevating an extremist to Congress can never be known. Hays' defeat had a chilling effect not only in Arkansas, but on the moderates throughout the South. As Congressman Frank Smith of Mississippi later recalled, Hays' loss inflicted a disheartening impact on all those Southern politicians who were secretly hoping to mount an effective resistance to the massive resisters: "Hays thus reaped his reward for trying to avoid violence when Central High School at Little Rock was integrated."[258] Such was the lesson imparted by the 1958 election. In less chaotic times in the mid-1960s as a Kennedy White House aide and then assistant secretary of state in the Johnson administration, Hays would be restored to a statesmanlike stature in Arkansas' public estimation, but for several crucial years moderates would be deterred from attacking Faubus because of the memory of the Hays debacle. In fairness to Fulbright, the pressures to conform to the racial status quo could be virulent. James O. Powell, the *Gazette's* new editorial editor in the late 1950s, would later recall the vicious letters, telephone calls, and other abuse the *Gazette* received in the late 1950s and early 1960s, as the newspaper advanced from the position it had advocated in the mid-1950s—that *Brown* should be obeyed as the "law of the land" and gradual desegregation should proceed, to the even more controversial argument that full racial integration was vital to fulfill the promise of democracy. At one point Powell received in the mail a rifle scope's bullseye, which he promptly turned over to the FBI. At the rhetorical level, Faubus had a field day lambasting the *Gazette's* "flaming liberal" editorials, while Jim Johnson would paint Powell as a radical "to the left of Mao Tse-tung." Nevertheless, it should also be stressed that there were rewards for adopting the liberal position at that early stage: the conviction that the liberal position would be vindicated in the long term as the voice of reason and justice, as well as the deeply appreciated approval at the time from stalwarts such as Sarah Murphy, Edwin Dunaway, Henry Woods, and Winthrop Rockefeller.

The history of the era is rife with episodes of political leaders avoiding the racial debate, from the silencing of the potential dissenters at the time of the Manifesto, to the President's evasion of the issue, to the well-intentioned but often bungled efforts of local officials to devise an acceptable response to *Brown*. Fulbright would argue that all this turmoil was inescapable, given the South's entrenched allegiance to segregation. With the customary theoretical bent of a constitutional law professor, the senator devised a theory that attempted to justify his silence in the Faubus era. "The average legislator," he wrote, "early in his career discovers that there are certain interests, or convictions, of his constituents which are too dangerous to trifle with." In his view, the legislator was justified in "humoring" his constituents' desires on issues that were "not of fundamental importance to the welfare of the nation." Under his theory, he would rely upon his own judgment in those issues, such as foreign policy, in which he regarded his knowledge as superior to that of his constituents, but in matters directly related to the daily lives of his constituents—segregation—his actions would conform to the majority's will.[259]

From the theoretical perspective, critics have suggested that problems immediately arise with the theory: the legislator himself is the one responsible for judging which issues were vital and which were secondary under this view, and will naturally tend to devise self-serving definitions of the "vital" and "secondary" categories. On the other hand, it is obvious that no theory can escape the reality that the legislator himself must decide which issues he is willing to risk his career in fighting for. Certainly, however, no reasonable observer could deny that respect for the rule of law and opposition to extremism are "vital" issues. Fulbright's interpretation of his theory led him to conclude that he would be responsible for voting his conscience in foreign policy, which was then much less controversial than race. The crucial flaw with Fulbright's rationalization flowed from its omission of any potential that the senator might have influenced public opinion in Arkansas rather than reacting as a passive observer to his constituents' wishes. On the other issues, including controversial ones such as federal aid to education and McCarthyism, Fulbright had demonstrated an impressive capacity to influence and lead public opinion. The conclusion that integration was not of fundamental importance was obviously weak. No one expected a "liberal" embracing of integration, but had he delivered such a statement as his memorandum against the Southern Manifesto opposing extremism, and reminded his compatriots that *Brown* would not be reversed, it might have influenced some indecisive Arkansans toward compliance. When such decisions not to speak out were multiplied frequently through the years, the South's plunge toward massive resistance quickened.

In reality, one of the great ironies of the Little Rock crisis centered on the truth that those who chose to enlist with the forces of reaction, or to remain silent, earned the profound disapproval of posterity on this issue, while the minority who withstood prejudice to stand in favor of racial tolerance eventually earned everlasting fame—*even within Arkansas*—in so doing. Fulbright would constantly assure his critics for the rest of his career that he would have been consigned to oblivion had he spoken up for the rule of the law in the context of the Central High crisis; yet the careers of all of Faubus' famous critics contradict his position. Woods would become a highly respected federal judge; Hays would be elevated from a position as a solid, if relatively unknown member of Congress to a position of national renown; the *Gazette* earned a chapter in the history of courageous American journalism; Rockefeller went on to lead the state into a more progressive era as governor in the mid-1960s. The federal judiciary in Arkansas, in particular, became a bastion of progressives on racial issues in later decades, including Woods; Garnett Thomas Eisele (an aide to Governor Rockefeller); Chief Judge Richard Arnold of the Eighth Circuit; William Overton; William R. Wilson, Jr.; black judges including U.S. District Judge George Howard and U.S. Magistrate Judge Henry Jones; and others. There were simply other opportunities–such as service as a Secretary of State or other high-level foreign policy adviser to the President–that would have remained open for him. Indeed, the prospects for such service would have been greatly enhanced had he taken a moderate stance in 1957; as discussed elsewhere in this book, John F. Kennedy might have appointed him Secretary of State had it not been for his civil rights record. While being sympathetic to the tremendous pressures upon Fulbright in 1957, objective observers would conclude, in retrospect, that Fulbright had erred in his contention that any other choice than the one he took at the time would have rendered him an obscure figure with no future in public life.

Ironically, the segregationist Amendment 44 that was passed by a vote of 185,374 to 146,064 in 1956 met its unlamented demise in Judge Woods' courtroom. Amendment 44 stated that "the General Assembly of the State of Arkansas shall take appropriate action and pass laws opposing in every Constitutional manner the Unconstitutional desegregation decisions of May 17, 1954 and May 31, 1955, including interposing the sovereignty of the State of Arkansas to the end of nullification of these and all deliberate, palpable and dangerous invasions of or encroachments upon rights and powers not delegated to the United States nor prohibited to the States by the Constitution of the United States . . ." Judge Woods found the amendment void *ab initio* [from the first act], observing that the doctrine of nullification "has attracted little attention since 1833 and none since Appomattox, except in Amendment 44." *Dietz v. Arkansas*, 709 F.Supp. 902, 904 (E.D. Ark. 1989). Amendment 44 flagrantly challenged principles "which are the bedrock on which this republic was founded. They are the principles under which we have flourished—that the rule of law prevails over the rule of men." *Id.* at 905. Woods' stress upon the fundamental principle of upholding the rule of law was the central idea that was missing in Fulbright's justifications for his decision in 1957. Fulbright would later argue that the relative progress in race relations that had been made since the 1950s, the strengthening of the moderate faction in Arkansas politics, and the general acceptance of the ideas expressed in such opinions as *Dietz*, did not signify that he had erred in his decisions. Racial problems persisted, Fulbright would point out, noting that litigation over Little Rock integration persisted for decades. It was true that problems continued. The Little Rock school case had been profoundly frustrating. Judge Woods had ordered the consolidation of the city's three school districts in the mid-1980s; it was a bold and definitive remedy for Little Rock segregation, which was not as formidable as it had been a quarter of a century earlier, but nonetheless was still extensive. Judge Woods' order set off furious opposition in the school districts and the opponents prevailed in the Eighth Circuit, which substituted a timid remedy that changed the district lines but left the fundamental problem in a balkanized school system unresolved. For a time Woods tried to implement the Eighth Circuit's order, but encountered further interference. Finally, he recused himself and turned the case over to another judge–Susan Wright–who also has been unable to prevail over the Byzantine intrigues of the three school districts. The Little Rock school case would drag on, interminably, unresolved even at the time of Fulbright's death in 1995. Judge Woods' decision of a decade earlier appeared more and more as the wisdom of a prophet. Before Fulbright's death, the senator would point out the persistence of such problems as the Little Rock school case as justification for his fatalistic approach to racial problems.

In judging Fulbright's overall responses to the plight of race relations in the South, the senator could make plausible arguments regarding his compromises. Fulbright already carried a heavy political burden of accusations that he was too "liberal" for supporting increased federal aid to education and progressive stands on a variety of social and economic issues; a legislator will naturally develop priorities and expertise in certain areas, and his critics may have set an unrealistic standard in expecting the senator to provide courageous, thoughtful leadership in every arena. The conservative strategy on civil rights helped prevent Faubus from replacing Fulbright in the Senate, and by remaining in power Fulbright could work effectively behind the scenes, as he did in privately influencing the University of Arkansas Board of Trustees to begin the gradual desegregation of the university in the late 1940s. As Senator Albert Gore, Sr. observed, Fulbright regarded his concessions on civil rights as his "admission ticket" to the Senate to achieve his goals in education, diplomacy, and other policies.[260] Finally, the senator's defenders could argue that the liberals were imposing their values on Fulbright, whose "gradualist" approach differed sharply in principle from the belief of such critics as the *Gazette* editors that integration was long overdue by the late 1950s and should proceed forthwith.

By surviving the Faubus era, Fulbright in his later career would cast one of the few Southern votes for Thurgood Marshall's appointment to the Supreme Court in 1967. Unlike many other Southerners such as Richard Russell who abandoned the national Democratic ticket in 1964 after the Civil Rights Act was passed, Fulbright would resolutely campaign for Johnson. He would be the only Southern senator to vote against William Rehnquist's nomination in 1971 in what was primarily seen in Arkansas as a racial issue of Rehnquist's opposition to integration earlier in his career; and he would play a vital role in defeating the nomination of the segregationist Harold Carswell's nomination to the Court in 1970. He frequently reminded critics that had he not survived the massive resistance era, he would not have been in the Senate to bring about these accomplishments. The classic example of his debate with liberals took place at the height of his dissent against the Vietnam War, when Fulbright privately confronted ADA leader Joe Rauh and asked him, "Joe, do you admit now I was right on my stand on civil rights [in the massive resistance era] so that I could stay up here" and provide leadership in the antiwar movement? Rauh was startled by the blunt nature of the question, and could only reply that it was "an unanswerable proposition—to do wrong in order to do right."[261] The senator's criticism of the Vietnam War's impact on the promising era of race-related reforms that had begun in 1964-65 was commended by Martin Luther King, Jr., who wrote to him in 1965: "Yours is one voice crying in the wilderness that may ultimately awaken our people to the international facts of life. I trust that you will not let any pressure silence you."[262] In that crisis, Fulbright would remain true to his creed of reason, and perhaps the burden he carried with him from the earlier painful era buoyed him through a series of resolute, thoughtful dissents in the later years of his career.

While Fulbright's justification thus possesses some merit, it ultimately runs aground on his record in the Central High crisis. The senator was inaccurate in denying any possibility of alternatives to remaining in the Senate, for he had been one of the principal prospects as a Democratic foreign policy adviser ever since he was first elected to the Senate in 1944. Congress was not the only possible realm for service, since he could anticipate a high-level appointment–much higher than Hays could have expected–to the executive branch when the Democrats next captured the White House. In fact, President-Elect John F. Kennedy initially considered Fulbright as his top choice as Secretary of State in December 1960, but ultimately decided that he could not appoint him because his civil rights record in the massive resistance era would create problems in the Cold War struggle in the Third World. As Robert Kennedy later explained it, "Jack always wanted William Fulbright" for Secretary of State, but eventually concluded he could not appoint him because the Arkansan suffered "from this terrible impediment of having signed the Southern Manifesto."[263]

The moderates were not as politically impotent as Fulbright depicted them, although it is clear that some concessions to public sentiment–such as the vote against the Civil Rights Act of 1957–were necessary to remain in power. Beyond the Arkansas political question or the alternative of service in the executive branch, critics would ask the more profound question about the price of his silence as Arkansas, previously so proud of its reputation for moderation, became a symbol of racism in 1957 throughout the nation and much of the world. He was not up for re-election for five long years in which he could have repaired the damage from a pro-law and order stand; and it will never be known whether Faubus' power could have been checked by a statewide figure who wielded substantially greater political power than did Hays. The rationalization that domestic race relations and foreign policy could be sealed off into two isolated compartments was pure fantasy; the Central High crisis was a major propaganda boon to the Soviet Union in the Cold War, as Fulbright was painfully aware.

Fulbright's defense founders on his failure to support Hays' efforts to stand for obedience to *Brown* as the law of the land when Faubus incited an atmosphere conducive to mob violence in the Central crisis, for this issue transcended his attempt to portray the matter as a "liberal-versus-conservative" political question. His silence in the 1957 Central crisis—far more poignantly than any of his other compromises on civil rights controversies—contradicted values that were undeniably central to Fulbright's profound convictions on a senator's duty to oppose extremism, uphold respect for the law, and support nonviolent methods of resolving political and social conflict. In a thousand similar decisions by "moderates" across Florida, Texas, and other Southern states, the quest begun in 1954-55 for a racially tolerant response to the *Brown* decision collapsed, strangled by a distorted political system, failure of the national political branches to lead, and the understandable, if tragic reluctance of many otherwise thoughtful Southerners to risk their careers over the cauldron of race relations. While the region's views on race had begun to change in the late 1940s and early 1950s, massive resistance demonstrated that the history of Southern politics was notoriously volatile, replete with brave new predictions that the "New South" of the millennium had at last arrived, only for the hopes to be dashed within a short season, delaying once again the arduous movement toward racial justice.

A future United States senator, James William Fulbright, is two years old and is being held by his maternal grandmother, Lucy Frances Waugh, circa 1907. (Fulbright Papers)

Arkansas Razorback triple threat Bill Fulbright, photographed here kicking the winning field goal against the Razorbacks' arch-rival, Southern Methodist University, 1922. Hogs 9, Mustangs 0. (Fulbright Papers)

Bill Fulbright (seated at lower right), Rhodes Scholar, on the Oxford lacrosse team. (Fulbright Papers)

Roberta Fulbright, Bill Fulbright, and Betty Fulbright. (Fulbright Papers)

Bill Fulbright, the young president of the University of Arkansas. (Fulbright Papers)

President Harry S. Truman signs the Fulbright Act on August 1, 1946, creating the Fulbright Program, as the senator and Assistant Secretary of State William Benton look on. (Fulbright Papers)

One among many expansions of the Fulbright Program: Austrian Ambassador Keinwaechter signs an exchange program agreement between the United States and Austria in the presence of Secretary of State Dean Acheson and Fulbright. (Fulbright Papers)

The pride of Arkansas: the magnificent Hope water-
melons. (Also pictured are the state's two senators,
J. W. Fulbright and John McClellan.) (Fulbright
Papers)

Fulbright, Senator Scott Lucas of Illinois and Governor Adlai Stevenson of
Illinois. (Standing are Steve Early, Senator Joseph O'Mahoney of Wyoming,
Senator Elbert Thomas of Utah, Senator-elect Clinton Anderson of New
Mexico, and Senator Carl Hatch of New Mexico.) (Fulbright Papers)

President Eisenhower, Senator Fulbright, Vice President Nixon, and other Washington officials enjoy a jovial moment in July, 1954. (Photo by Abbie Rowe, courtesy of National Park Service, Fulbright Papers)

President Eisenhower, Fulbright, and the Board of Foreign Scholarships of the international scholar exchange program, meeting at the White House, June 15, 1959. Left to right are Elmer Ellis, president of the University of Missouri; John Andrews of the Veterans Administration; Hurst Robins Anderson, president of American University; Daniel Hofgren, Columbia Law School student; Robert Storey, dean of the law school, Southern Methodist University; President Eisenhower; Senator Fulbright; Ms. Bernice Cronkhite, dean of the graduate school, Radcliffe College; Robert Thayer, special assistant to the secretary of coordination of international educational and cultural realtions; Felton Clark, president of Southern University; George Benson; president of Claremont College. (Fulbright Papers)

1955: Avant le deluge. Before massive resistance exploded onto the nation's political scene, Fulbright and Adlai Stevenson regarded Governor Orval Faubus as a moderate young governor. Fulbright, Senator John Sparkman of Alabama, Governor Orval Faubus, and Adlai Stevenson were photographed at a duck hunt in El Dorado, Arkansas. (*Arkansas Democrat-Gazette*)

Fulbright and Congressman Brooks Hays in the fall of 1957. Hays was an old friend of Fulbright, and was defeated for re-election a year later by a vociferous segregationist, Dale Alford. Hays spoke at a Congressional Forum at the Hotel Marion in Little Rock and proposed a "breather" for the South to re-evaluate the *Brown* decision. When a reporter asked him how the Supreme Court could be prevented from "legislating," Hays replied that he respected the Supreme Court and warned that "we lose something precious by flouting its decisions." (*Arkansas Democrat-Gazette*)

J. William Fulbright becomes chairman of the Senate Committee on Foreign Relations, 1959. Senator Theodore Green hands over the chairman's gavel to Fulbright in the presence of Senator John F. Kennedy of Massachusetts and Senator Lyndon Baines Johnson of Texas. (Fulbright Papers)

Fulbright and President Kennedy at a bill-signing ceremony (Fulbright Papers)

Fulbright and Attorney General Robert Kennedy in March, 1962. RFK talked with JWF before going into a closed meeting of the Senate Foreign Relations Committee in which Kennedy briefed senators on his recent trip around the world. Although RFK had initially advised President Kennedy not to select Fulbright as his Secretary of State in 1960, he later repented his decision. By the later 1960s, Fulbright and then-Senator Robert Kennedy became the two most influential critics of the Vietnam War in the Senate. (Associated Press/Wide World Photos, worldwide rights)

Fulbright, President Kennedy and a choral group from the University of Arkansas (Fulbright Papers)

Fulbright and Secretary of State Dean Rusk discussing the Nuclear Test Ban treaty of 1963. Fulbright and Rusk worked closely together in promoting the passage of the Test Ban Treaty. A couple of years later they would become adversaries regarding American policy in the Dominican Republic and Vietnam. (Fulbright Papers)

President Kennedy's visit to Arkansas, fall of 1963. Congressman Wilbur Mills, Fulbright, Senator McClellan, Governor Faubus, and JFK. (Fulbright Papers)

Fulbright and Johnson at bill signing (Fulbright Papers)

Fulbright and Johnson, with map of southeast Asia in the background (Fulbright Papers)

Fulbright and Johnson—with Washington Monument in the background
(Fulbright Papers)

Fulbright and McNamara, eyeball to eyeball, and Fulbright just blinked.
(Fulbright Papers)

Fulbright stands at the door of his Senate office, decorated with the AP poll rating the Arkansas Razorbacks as the Number One team in the land. (Fulbright Papers)

Chairman Fulbright presiding at the famous Vietnam hearings in 1966. (Associated Press/Wide World Photos, worldwide rights)

One of the most well-known campaign photographs of Fulbright in an informal moment. (Fulbright Papers)

One of the big guns in Fulbright's campaign arsenal: Betty Fulbright, hitting the campaign trail in Arkansas. (Fulbright Papers)

Fulbright campaigning in Arkansas. (Fulbright Papers)

Fulbright and Johnson greet each other as Clark Clifford becomes Secretary of Defense, 1968. Clifford exerted an important influence in Johnson's decision to stop escalating the war in 1968. (Fulbright Papers)

Congressman David Pryor (later a U. S. senator) of Arkansas, Fulbright, and Stuart Symington of Missouri in 1968. (*Arkansas Democrat-Gazette*)

Congressman John Paul Hammerschmidt of Arkansas, Governor Winthrop Rockefeller, President Richard Nixon, Senator McClellan, Fulbright, and the young Republican political star, George Bush, watch as No. 2 Arkansas plays No. 1 Texas in football in 1969. (Fulbright Papers)

Congressman Bill Alexander of Arkansas, Fulbright, Governor Dale Bumpers, and Senator John McClellan, testifying at Senate hearings on Public Works regarding a major bridge project on Norfork Lake in Arkansas. The Arkansas Congressional delegation of that era was famous for its ability to secure federal funding for public works projects in Arkansas. (Files of Bill Alexander)

Fulbright, Senator Mike Mansfield of Montana, and Henry Kissinger. (Fulbright Papers)

Fulbright and Congressman Wilbur Mills, Chairman of the powerful House Ways and Means Committee, in 1972. (Fulbright Papers)

Fulbright and Senator Robert Byrd of West Virginia, at Little Rock in April,
1974, during the Senate campaign. Byrd defended the value of Fulbright's
seniority and experience for Arkansas as well as for national policy.
(*Arkansas Democrat-Gazette*)

Fulbright greets Senator Mike Mansfield at the Little Rock airport. The two
senators held similar views on the southeast Asian conflict, although they
frequently differed on the most effective strategy to employ in opposing the
war, especially during the Johnson administration. (Fulbright Papers)

Fulbright talks to a labor union member on the campaign trail in Arkansas. (Fulbright Papers)

The young governor of Arkansas, Bill Clinton, and his mentor, former Senator Fulbright. Clinton is a former Fulbright staff member, Rhodes Scholar, Yale Law School graduate, and law professor. Fulbright had also been a Rhodes Scholar, graduate of a prestigious law school (George Washington University) and law professor earlier in his career. (Fulbright Papers)

Fulbright and Clinton at the rededication of Old Main. (*Northwest Arkansas Times*)

President Clinton with Lee Powell in the Oval Office at an informal gathering of the Powells and a few of Fulbright's former aides, shortly after the memorial services for Fulbright in Washington in February, 1995. The President delivered the eulogy at the services for the senator.

President Clinton awards Fulbright the Presidential Medal of Freedom, as Mrs. Harriet Fulbright looks on. (Associated Press/Wide World Photos, worldwide rights)

Book Four:

FULBRIGHT AND THE PAX AMERICANA

I. FULBRIGHT AND PRESIDENT KENNEDY, 1961-1963

Fulbright and the Selection Process for Secretary of State: "The Best Man for the Job"

Senator Fulbright's melancholy performance, or nonperformance, on civil rights in the civil rights confrontations of the 1950s clearly cost him the opportunity to become John F. Kennedy's Secretary of State in 1961. It is fascinating to consider how Fulbright as Secretary of State might have kept Kennedy from blundering into the Bay of Pigs, or how he might have influenced the prosecution of the Cold War in other ways, on its several fronts. In any case, as chairman of Foreign Relations, he did not extend his public critique of the anticommunist prejudice in American diplomacy to Vietnam to encompass the Kennedy and Johnson administrations' policies on Vietnam until 1966. During the early 1960s the attention of Congress was primarily focused upon Cuba and Europe, and Indochina appeared to be an area of peripheral concern. More importantly, from 1961 to 1965, Fulbright basically accepted his contemporaries' ingenuous view of the inordinate power the Presidency had acquired by the 1960s. He was convinced that the individuals who served as President during those years would use that power with wisdom and restraint. Fulbright, Kennedy, and Johnson generally supported efforts to emasculate the political influence of the extreme right in the United States. The fact that Kennedy's and Johnson's policies seemed moderate when juxtaposed with the radical rightists' demand for a "total victory" over world communism tended to obscure for Fulbright the militancy of the administration's strategy in Vietnam.

Lyndon Johnson's influence upon Fulbright was one of the reasons that some of the senator's statements on Vietnam and the Cold War in the early 1960s exhibited a somewhat hostile attitude toward the communist powers. On March 5, 1960, Fulbright delivered a Senate speech in which he denounced the Eisenhower administration for neglecting federal aid to education, defense research, and missiles in its obsession with balancing the budget. Fulbright stated that it was then being argued whether the Soviet missile superiority was "three to one or maybe only two to one."[1] This statement was a remarkable departure from Fulbright's longstanding opposition to any issue that might accelerate the arms race. Fulbright apparently based this speech to some extent on information given to him by Johnson (who had obtained the information through leaks from the Air Force) which indicated that Eisenhower's budget-cutting economies had created a "missile gap" between the Soviet Union and the United States.[2] The "missile gap" was, of course, later discovered to have been nonexistent, though after (in David Halberstam's words) "many God-fearing [sic], Russian-fearing citizens had cast their votes to end the gap and live a more secure life, only to find that they had been safe all along."[3]

There has been much speculation concerning the close Fulbright-Johnson relationship in the late 1950s and early 1960s.[4] Fulbright admired Johnson's political skills and his ability to manage the Senate as Majority Leader. Probably Fulbright concluded that Johnson at least partially approved of his general critique of U.S. foreign policy, since Johnson referred to Fulbright as "my Secretary of State" in the late 1950s and early 1960s. Actually there is little evidence that Johnson agreed with Fulbright's foreign policy positions in the 1950s. The Majority Leader had supported Dulles while Fulbright was frequently critical of the Eisenhower administration's foreign policy.[5] During his first 15 years in the Senate, Fulbright had frequently been in an adversary relationship with the executive branch, and he understandably relished the prospect of playing a more creative role in politics, possibly as Johnson's Secretary of State.[6] But he did not publicly display any great eagerness for the Secretary of State post; he was content to remain in the Senate as a supporter and counselor to Kennedy and Johnson.

Perhaps Johnson's choice of Fulbright as "my Secretary of State" was similar to John F. Kennedy's selection of Chester Bowles as his foreign policy adviser for the 1960 Presidential campaign. In order to receive the nomination of the Democratic Party, the central political difficulty of a centrist candidate such as Kennedy or Johnson was to conciliate the Stevenson wing of the Party.[7] This could be achieved by associating the name of a political figure who was closely identified with Stevenson, such as Fulbright,[8] or Bowles, with the centrist candidate's campaign. When Kennedy and Johnson became President, in turn, each considered one of his major political problems to be the necessity of preventing a right wing backlash against his administration's policies.[9] Johnson was preoccupied with the fear that he might be vilified for "losing" Vietnam as Truman had "lost" China.[10] Thus Dean Rusk, the friend and admirer of John Foster Dulles, the chosen candidate of Robert Lovett,[11] (and hence an unlikely target for any charges of being "soft on communism") and the author of the description of Mao Tse-tung's regime as a "colonial Russian government" in 1950, became the most congenial choice for Secretary of State by the two presidents who in 1960 had grandly displayed the names of Chester Bowles and J. William Fulbright.

Early in 1960, Fulbright had further antagonized blacks and liberals by his vote against the Civil Rights Act of 1960. In an editorial on March 3, the *Washington Post* rebuked the senator for participating in the Southern filibuster against the Civil Rights Act. During the filibuster Fulbright had repeated the arguments he had advanced in his *Cooper v. Aaron* brief. The Arkansan had stated that blacks in Arkansas "voted freely and without coercion," and went on to make a statement virtually calling into question the logic of universal suffrage for all races: "I do not know what proof there is that the greater the vote the better the result." In a scathing criticism of Fulbright entitled "No Colossus of Rhodes," the *Post* editorial epitomized the liberal disenchantment with the senator's civil rights record. The *Post* doubted that Fulbright was sincere when he vaguely asserted that protections for blacks' voting rights in the South were already adequate in 1960.[10a] In its final version the Civil Rights Act of 1960 authorized federal judges to appoint referees to register black voters in areas where registration was denied them, but the Southern opponents of the bill succeeded in eliminating provisions that would have awarded federal aid to communities struggling with the problems of school desegregation. In the *Post's* view,

> The onus [for obstructing civil rights legislation] falls most heavily upon the chairman of the Foreign Relations Committee, Sen. J. William Fulbright of Arkansas, because more is expected of him. Mr. Fulbright is a Rhodes Scholar and a former university president. By virtue of his role in foreign affairs he is looked to for sane comment and leadership above sectionalism.[10b]

The *Post* charged that Fulbright was inflicting an injustice upon himself and upon the Senate by "joining in this cabal of know-nothingism."

In the early period of Fulbright's career in Congress, Fulbright had been admired by the elite on the east coast. In the spring of 1945, Drew Pearson and others had publicly discussed Fulbright as a possible Secretary of State to replace Edward R. Stettinius, although Truman's choice, of course, was James F. Byrnes. Later in 1945, after the passage of the UN Charter, a special faculty committee of Columbia University had unanimously chosen Fulbright to succeed President Nicholas Murray Butler. Fulbright had declined the invitation, pointing out that he "was already off to a good start in the powerful United States Senate." The man who ultimately succeeded Butler was General Dwight D. Eisenhower; given Eisenhower's later career many political observers would later discuss where Fulbright's career would have led him had he accepted the Columbia presidency. Many liberal intellectuals on the east coast, however, had believed that Fulbright would eventually become a leader for the civil rights movement in the South. When these hopes came to naught in later years, the earlier effusive admiration turned to bitterness in the minds of a substantial number of those intellectuals. The classic example of the liberals' criticism of Fulbright's positions on segregation was the dissent against President-Elect Kennedy's consideration of the senator as a possible Secretary of State. In November and December, 1960, the Americans for Democratic Action leader Joe Rauh encouraged liberals to oppose Fulbright's nomination as Secretary of State. Supporters of Chester Bowles–who was also under consideration for the State Department post–began agitating black and Jewish organizations against Fulbright, although they acted without the knowledge of Bowles. On December 8, the editorial page of the *Washington Post* reiterated the theme of its "No Colossus of Rhodes" editorial, maintaining that the vast majority of blacks and liberals in the nation opposed Fulbright's elevation to the Cabinet. Recalling Fulbright's failure to oppose Faubus in 1957, the Post argued that in the opinion of many civil rights progressives Fulbright acted "as a reactionary in Arkansas and a liberal in Washington." Robert Kennedy stressed the importance of civil rights issues in the context of the 1960 election, in which the landslide Democratic victory among black voters had been crucial in JFK's victory. Fulbright had supported Lyndon Johnson–a man Robert Kennedy detested–for the Democratic nomination. The Arkansas senator had not attended the Los Angeles convention because he was at odds with Governor Faubus, the head of Arkansas' delegation; but in the general election Fulbright had campaigned vigorously for Kennedy in Arkansas, despite the political difficulties presented by Kennedy's civil rights plank in the Democratic platform, at the time the most resolute and progressive plank in the party's history.

Executive Secretary Roy Wilkins of the NAACP urged the President-Elect to remove Fulbright from consideration. The NAACP took the position that American foreign policy with respect to African and Asian nations would be "hampered" if the Secretary of State "has, as Mr. Fulbright has, repeatedly upheld segregation as a way of life." Robert Kennedy privately pressed similar arguments upon the President, stressing Fulbright's signing of the Southern Manifesto.[10c]

John F. Kennedy was still inclined to appoint Fulbright as Secretary of State when the President-Elect discussed the Cabinet selection process with Arthur Schlesinger on December 1. Some of the negative publicity may have decreased whatever enthusiasm Fulbright had for the job, and he told his brother-in-law, Hal Douglas, his aide Jack Yingling, and Senator Richard Russell that he would accept the position if offered, but did not seek the job. Russell later told Fulbright that he had relayed to the President the message that Fulbright had doubts about being offered the post. Nonetheless, in early December the headline of a front-page news report in the Washington Post declared, "Fulbright Is Still Front-Runner for Secretary of State Post," despite the criticisms of his civil rights record and complaints from the Jewish community that Fulbright was pro-Arab. The Israeli embassy and numerous American Jewish people urged the administration not to appoint Fulbright. Vice-President Elect Lyndon Johnson strongly supported Fulbright. The New York Times and Washington Post reported in November that Johnson would be influential in the selection of Cabinet members, primarily because his campaigning in the South during 1960 had been crucial in gaining Southern support for the Democrats. At one point, Gene Farmer of Life magazine called Fulbright to say that he had heard directly from Kennedy advisers that the Arkansas senator would be the next Secretary of State, and he wanted to come to Fayetteville for an interview; Fulbright replied that it was premature, that he had not received any word from Kennedy. Fulbright had provided stalwart support for the Kennedy-Johnson ticket during the campaign. Kennedy admired Fulbright's erudite, cosmopolitan mind, and he appreciated Fulbright's critique of John Foster Dulles' rigid Cold Warrior policies. In a private conversation with the renowned journalist Walter Lippmann on December 6, Kennedy discussed the problem of Fulbright's civil rights record. Lippmann was supportive of Fulbright, claiming that he had to vote with the segregationists if the senator intended to be re-elected. Kennedy replied, "I know that, but the Africans and our own blacks will raise a terrible howl if I appoint him, even though he's probably the best man for the job."[10d]

Of course, Fulbright had no thought of campaigning for Secretary of State, as Dean Rusk was campaigning for it at the time. On November 28, the senator had announced that he was "not a candidate for Secretary of State." In December of 1960 the widespread speculation over a possible Fulbright appointment to the most prestigious Cabinet office was causing great excitement in Arkansas. At Little Rock, the Arkansas Gazette's editorial editor had breakfast with Fulbright one morning at the Sam Peck Hotel, where Fulbright always stayed in Arkansas' capital.[11b] Fulbright's comments about the appointment to State were speculative and noncommittal but the idea was pleasing to him; the senator was clearly intrigued by the thought. If the President had asked him to take the position, how could Fulbright have refused, given his belief in the obligation to public service? Fulbright acknowledged later that if the President had publicly offered him the State Department post he would have accepted it.

The contrast between Fulbright and Rusk was clear at the time. They were both Southerners and Rhodes Scholars, but Rusk was a Cold War hardliner whose few discourses in the past were not closely examined by the Kennedy aides. On November 22, 1960, Rusk went out of his way to write Kennedy remarking that he (Rusk) wanted to heal the scars of racism, a way of reminding Kennedy that Rusk had no signature on the Southern Manifesto to complicate his own appointment.[11c]

Over the next eight years, Rusk was one of the most militant Cold Warriors in the Cabinet, but his militancy was out of place in a Secretary of State, who is supposed to take the more restrained diplomatic view, in contrast to the roles of the Pentagon or the NSC. Fulbright and Rusk became fierce adversaries and after both had left office their dislike continued. In 1976 the *Gazette* editorial editor, James Powell, encountered Dean Rusk in Atlanta at a highly publicized reception for Deng Xiao-peng, China's head of state replacing Mao. The two exchanged pleasantries and Rusk was solicitous about the health of Betty Fulbright, who, he said, laughing, always had more sense than the senator all those years he served as chairman of the Foreign Relations Committee. This was a put-down in the timeless genre that President Clinton's detractors used decades later in comparing him with Hillary Clinton. As always, the inky wretch had the last word, referring in an editorial shortly thereafter to Rusk's "interminable" career as a Cold Warrior in the State Department. The encounter had no particular significance in itself, but it revealed Rusk's incredible tenacity and rigidity in adhering to the dogmas of the hard-line anticommunist creed. In sharp contrast to McNamara, Rusk would never admit error in Vietnam and always maintained that the United States had been right to intervene in Indochina.

Although there were several considerations in Kennedy's ultimate decision not to appoint Fulbright Secretary of State, the civil rights issue was clearly the most important. The Arkansan's position during the Suez crisis and his opposition to a belligerent anti-Egyptian policy had offended many Jewish leaders, who charged that Fulbright was pro-Arab. In truth, Fulbright advocated then and later an evenhanded policy regarding the Arab and Israeli forces in the Middle East, but his views were anathema to the pro-Israeli lobby in the United States. Fulbright had supported the creation of the state of Israel in the 1940s, but he had been critical of the high-pressure lobbying strategy of pro-Israeli political groups. Moreover, Henry Luce, founder of the *Time-Life* empire and undaunted champion of Chiang Kai-shek, warned the administration that Fulbright would be unacceptable as Secretary of State because the senator was not an advocate of unceasing hostility to Mao's China. Luce was one of the partisans for the selection of Dean Rusk, and he let it be known that Rusk was blessed with impeccable credentials as a knight-errant against Asian communism.[11d]

Another Cold Warrior who opposed Fulbright as Secretary of State was Dean Acheson. When Kennedy conferred with Acheson shortly after the election and told him that Fulbright could become Secretary of State, Acheson objected vigorously. Fulbright, in his view, was "not as solid and serious a man as you need for this position. I've always thought that he had some of the qualities of a dilettante. He likes to criticize—he likes to call for brave, bold new ideas and he doesn't have a great many brave, bold new ideas."[11d] For whatever reason, Kennedy persisted in his preference for Fulbright, even after his conversation with Acheson. Possibly, he may have taken into consideration the strained relationship between Fulbright and the Truman administration officials, or that Acheson disapproved of some of Fulbright's controversial dissenting ideas concerning the Cold War.

Yet another criticism of the senator was his alleged "laziness." This charge was based upon the senator's tendency to focus upon a relatively small number of vital issues, sometimes to the exclusion of other matters. Some of his critics pointed out that he had not managed a large organization since he was president of the University of Arkansas. Fulbright did not care for the more mundane details of a senator's work, and was particularly annoyed by requests from constituents for favors. To some extent, there was some justification for this criticism; some of the constituent requests he found so bothersome emanated from people with legitimate arguments, or from genuinely talented people seeking a career in public service rather than hackers seeking political patronage. In the larger sense, however, there was merit to the approach of focusing on the crucial issues and trying to adopt a long-term point of view. One anecdote was typical: a constituent came to his office to see the senator, but found him on a couch, not busily engaged in any apparent activity. The constituent remarked later that Fulbright was "not doing anything," but of course, he had been engaged in that most constructive of activities: he was *thinking*. Many members of Congress might have profited from a similar determination to avoid getting bogged down in minutiae and to attempt to focus on fundamental issues. The allegations of Fulbright's "laziness" were essentially unjustified accusations hurled by the senator's critics who were primarily opposed to his nomination on other grounds.

In a February, 1961 memorandum, Robert Kennedy explained the most important reason for John Kennedy's decision: "Jack always wanted William Fulbright" for Secretary of State, but the Kennedys were concerned that the senator's appointment would offend many Africans and American blacks because of his conservative civil rights record. Another problem with Fulbright's nomination concerned his place in the Senate: while he would be highly influential sitting right where he was as chairman of the Foreign Relations Committee, if he had left the Senate his successor probably would have been Orval Faubus or a pro-Faubus politician. A November editorial in the *Arkansas Gazette* summarized the "Faubus problem": "It is doubtful that the national Democratic leadership is anxious to give Orval Faubus a Senate seat by default." Had Faubus won the Senate election scheduled for 1962, he might have become an entrenched incumbent similar to Jim Eastland or Strom Thurmond; had he done so, he obviously would have caused major long-term political problems for the national Democrats in Washington. In years after the early 1960s, Fulbright's claim that he prevented Orval Faubus from gaining a seat in the U.S. Senate was one of the senator's crucial justifications for his civil rights record. The President's decision was ultimately based upon Robert Kennedy's analysis of Fulbright's "terrible impediment of having signed the Southern Manifesto."[11e]

Kennedy vacillated in the selection process, rejecting Adlai Stevenson, David Bruce, Chester Bowles and Fulbright. Bowles had political problems regarding civil rights that were just the opposite of Fulbright's: Bowles had been an author of the Democratic civil rights plank, and Southern Democrats consequently were adamant in opposing his nomination (although in Bowles' case there were crucial issues other than civil rights).[11f] Finally, Kennedy decided upon what appeared at the time to be the least controversial choice: thus,

Dean Rusk, the man Kennedy barely knew and had met only a few days before, the moderate Southerner in the realm of race relations, and the disciple of John Foster Dulles in American diplomacy, became the Democratic nominee for Secretary of State.

In reflecting upon the consequences of Rusk's elevation to the State Department, it might be recalled that Arthur Schlesinger was always convinced that the President would have canceled the Bay of Pigs adventure if only one Cabinet official had opposed it in early 1961; Rusk and the others did not do so. The divergence between Fulbright's views and Rusk's hard-line anticommunist stance concerning the Far East was already significant by 1960; and the divergence would become a chasm in later years. Of course, the senator had no strong ambition to be Secretary of State, and opinions as to what he might have accomplished in the Cabinet are only speculation. It will never be known whether Fulbright might have changed the American diplomatic history of the 1960s if he had served as Kennedy's Secretary of State instead of Dean Rusk.

The Arkansas senator did not object to Rusk's appointment in 1960, and he was able to influence the selection of several secondary level advisers. Fulbright played a crucial role in persuading Kennedy to appoint as Under Secretary of State George Ball, who would later gain fame as one of the few administration officials who advised Kennedy and Johnson not to escalate the American military involvement in Vietnam. At one point, Kennedy had virtually decided to appoint William C. Foster, a progressive Republican businessman who had held posts in the Truman administration. There had been concern about Kennedy's consideration of Republicans for top administration posts; at one point Robert Kennedy had worried that the appointment of Douglas Dillon as Secretary of the Treasury could create major problems if the Republican Dillon resigned after only a few months and then blasted the administration's financial policies. A Republican would have no reason to be loyal, RFK argued. In Dillon's case, his later service in the Treasury Department proved these fears to be unfounded. But at the time, many Democrats were worried about the prospect of Foster's appointment coming right after Dillon's. Adlai Stevenson asked Fulbright to speak to Kennedy about the issue, whereupon Fulbright suggested to the President in Palm Beach that giving Republicans so many top posts in State, Treasury and Defense was manifestly unfair to Democrats who had fought valiantly for his election. The policy of appointing so many Republicans, Fulbright added, could create the impression that the Democratic Party lacked people of sufficient stature to serve in the highest levels of government. Kennedy found Fulbright's arguments persuasive, withdrew his tentative offer to the Republican Foster, and appointed Ball.[12]

The President had invited Fulbright to visit him in Palm Beach in early 1961, apparently because Kennedy thought that Fulbright had been deeply hurt by the publicity concerning the selection process, or the fact that Rusk won the appointment, or both. "He thought it was a terrible blow, I guess," Fulbright would later recall. The President "more or less apologized for the publicity, which he regretted, he said, but he couldn't help it." The President's father, Joseph Kennedy, told the senator in Palm Beach that liberals, the NAACP, and the Jewish lobby had "just raised hell" in opposing Fulbright as Secretary of State. The elder Kennedy sent him a case of scotch when the senator returned to Washington. Fulbright was profoundly impressed by President Kennedy's sensitivity: "I don't think I've ever seen a man of such importance, with more consideration, more sympathy for another politician than this man was," Fulbright reflected, adding that "I think he was the most tolerant and sympathetic person I've ever known."[13]

In contrast to Kennedy, Lyndon Johnson's reaction to the entire affair was one of irritation at Fulbright for not having actively campaigned for the State Department post. Of course, Fulbright may have simply been realistic enough to know that the coalition of forces opposing his nomination was simply too strong and that in the end "it wasn't in the cards." Johnson, with characteristic hyperbole, accosted Carl Marcy of the Foreign Relations Committee staff a few days later and asked, "What's the matter with your boss? He could have been Secretary of State. I was for him all the way. I got Jack to agree to take him, and then he turned it down. What the hell's the matter with him?"[14]

Fulbright, U.S. Foreign Policy, and Vietnam, 1961-63

In January, 1961, Fulbright reflected about the profound problems the Democrats were inheriting. He advised his mentor, R.B. McCallum, that "Our economy shows signs of a serious recession, our national payments continue to show a large deficit, and of course trouble has broken out in Africa, South Asia, and Latin America. I do not believe that the problems inherited by Roosevelt in 1933 were anything like as ominous and difficult as the ones now confronting Kennedy." Observing that the President-elect had chosen many of his top advisers from Harvard and a few other distinguished universities, the senator told McCallum that he thought their conduct in office would be better than the businessmen who had filled the higher echelons of the Eisenhower administration; yet, "how much better remains to be seen."[15] Fulbright had overstated the challenges confronting Kennedy in his assertion that they were much more serious than FDR had faced in 1933. The senator had confidence in the Democratic administration, however, and he was prepared to support a more powerful Presidency in dealing with the difficult problems looming ahead in the 1960s.

Fulbright delivered two speeches in April and May of 1961 in which he virtually subscribed to the notion that the Cold War and nuclear technology had rendered the traditional constitutional balance between the legislative and executive branches of government almost obsolete. He was at least partially influenced by his personal respect for Kennedy. The senator did not criticize the young President in the aftermath of the Bay of Pigs, arguing that Kennedy would learn from his errors and mature as a world leader. In an address at the University of Virginia, he contended that "we now have the kind of President" who can impart to the people "that zest of action so greatly needed if we are to win the contest of will which engages us today." "My question," he continued, "is whether we have any choice but to modify and perhaps overhaul the eighteenth century procedures that govern the formulation and conduct of American foreign policy. I wonder whether the time has not arrived, or indeed already passed, when we must give the executive a measure of power in the conduct of our foreign affairs that we have hitherto jealously withheld." It is especially revealing that Fulbright complimented Johnson for his support of the Eisenhower administration's foreign policy. Although Johnson may have erred on particular issues, Fulbright noted, the Texan had correctly followed the "proper long-term procedure" of the Senate, which should be to support the administration's basic policy while offering judgments on how best to execute that policy. This view is almost diametrically opposed to Fulbright's statement in 1966 that the Senate should attempt to exert influence "not on the day-to-day conduct of foreign policy but on its direction and philosophy as these are shaped by major decisions."[16]

The discrepancy between Fulbright's praise for Johnson in 1961 and his criticism of the Majority Leader in 1957 goes beyond the fact that Johnson had been, in one writer's words, "Capitol Hill's chief flag-waver for Dulles," whose policies Fulbright had execrated. Johnson had been a champion of the Eisenhower Doctrine in 1957, and to eulogize his record as Majority Leader is to espouse a theory of Congress' role in foreign affairs through which Congress bestowed unrestricted grants of power upon the executive in order to counter alleged threats of communist aggression. Fulbright reconsidered his position only after he helped to guide the most infamous of these resolutions through Congress: when the Johnson administration portrayed the incidents in the Gulf of Tonkin in 1964 as incontrovertible evidence of North Vietnam's deliberate and systematic campaign of aggression, Fulbright reacted almost exactly as had Johnson in 1957, immediately endorsing the administration's effort to acquire unrestricted authority to oppose the communist "conspirators."

In the summer of 1961, Fulbright cooperated with Kennedy and McNamara in alerting the nation to the dangers of the "strategy for survival conferences" that attempted to propagate the belief that internal communist infiltration represented the principal, if not exclusive, peril to America's freedom and security.[17] Right-wing orators and military personnel dominated those conferences, which were based upon a 1958 National Security Council directive authorizing the U.S. government to enlist the military's assistance in arousing the public to the menace of the Cold War.[18] Fulbright suggested that the administration should cease reprimanding military personnel who engaged in propaganda activities on an individual basis, and issue a general directive reaffirming the principle of the military's subordination to the civilian authority.[19] McNamara issued such a directive shortly afterwards, and the National War College indicated at least nominal acquiescence in the reform by applauding a speech given by Fulbright at the College in August.[20] Fulbright concluded in a memorandum to McNamara in August that the radicalism of the "strategy for survival conferences" could be expected to have considerable mass appeal during the "long twilight struggle" (in Kennedy's phrase) with international communism.[21] In Fulbright's view, the primary task of leadership in the republic "is to restrain the desire of the people to hit the communists with everything we've got, particularly if there are more Cubas and Laoses. Pride in victory and frustration in restraint during the Korean War led to MacArthur's revolt and McCarthyism."[22]

Senator Strom Thurmond was incensed when he learned from Pentagon sources that Fulbright had sent his memorandum to McNamara and the President. In a Senate speech, the South Carolinian railed that "there is a concerted attack under way against the anticommunist indoctrination of the American people and our troops in uniform and particularly against participation in this effort by our military officers." Thurmond quoted an article from a communist newspaper that had commended Fulbright's position on the radical right and the strategy for survival conferences. Thomas Dodd (D-Connecticut) and other zealous anticommunists joined in the attacks. Governor Faubus complained that "It appears to me that a man in uniform should be able to speak against what he is expected to shoot against. I see no indication that the military has any desire to participate in partisan politics." Members of the John Birch Society across the country wrote letters condemning Fulbright to their representatives and senators, while right-wing evangelists such as the Rev. Billy James Hargis denounced the Rhodes Scholar for weakening America's defenses against the communist menace. Fulbright responded by inserting his memorandum to McNamara into the *Congressional Record*. In early August, 1961, President Kennedy resolutely supported Fulbright, advising reporters that the Arkansan had been correct in sending McNamara the memorandum on political activities of the military. The President endorsed Fulbright's concern about preventing military officers from being used for political objectives. The Arkansan received further support at an Armed Services Committee hearing in September, in which McNamara and the senators discussed the case of General Edwin Walker, a decorated combat veteran of World War II and Korea who had distributed John Birch Society materials to his troops and attempted to influence results in the 1960 Congressional elections. Senator Thurmond lambasted McNamara for Walker's reprimand, ranting that it was a disgrace that a war hero was rebuked for warning his troops about communism. Chairman Richard Russell and Senator Harry Byrd of Virginia then asked if Walker had commanded the federal troops in the Little Rock Central High crisis, and McNamara said "Yes." Russell thereupon criticized Walker's allegedly arbitrary and intimidating methods in the Little Rock incident. Senator Russell was a staunch anticommunist, but he knew that there was no dire threat of communists subverting America from within, and he was solid in support of Fulbright in the controversy. The eventual outcome of Fulbright's battle with Thurmond was a victory—both politically and on the merits—for the Arkansan, who had successfully pointed out the dangers of collaboration between the military and the radical right.[22a]

Fulbright's investigative activities were not confined to the problems presented by the Thurmonds, Walkers, and Birchites. In the early 1960s, he hired Walter Pincus, earlier a reporter, to investigate the activities of unregistered foreign agents. Pincus uncovered evidence that eventually led to the indictment of Igor Cassini, a man who had engaged in lobbying efforts regarding American policy toward the Dominican Republic that violated the Foreign Agents Registration Act. Regarding other foreign lobbying activities, Pincus discovered that roughly 20 members of Congress had taken money from unregistered foreign agents. The Foreign Relations Committee investigation also turned to the activities of the Jewish Agency for Israel. Fulbright was disturbed by what he regarded as the bias in aid toward Israel. Indeed, U.S. aid to Israel exceeded aid to all the Arab states. Some particularly zealous pro-Israeli lobbyists even accused Fulbright of anti-Semitism, although the idea to investigate the Israeli lobby originated with Pincus, who happened to be Jewish. The outcome of the investigation ordered by Fulbright and engineered by Pincus was a reform of the Foreign Agents Registration Act: Fulbright and other senators passed amendments to the act that outlawed political contributions by foreign governments or corporations through their agents, mandated registration by foreign agents with the Justice Department, and required them to state for whom they were working when they communicated with members of Congress.[22b]

Israel was one among an increasing number of countries in which Fulbright was concerned that the foreign aid program was flawed. For example, Fulbright received a disturbing letter from Iran, where an American living in Teheran advised him that the Shah and his government oppressed the people and took for themselves the extensive American aid upon which his regime depended for its survival. Liberal Democrats developed misgivings about the aid program to such countries as Iran, combining with the traditional conservative critics of foreign aid to produce, in Arthur Schlesinger's words, "a congressional mood that cut the President's 1962 request from $4.9 billion to $3.9 billion and reduced development loans by more than 20 percent."[22c]

Cuba, Europe, the radical right, foreign aid and other international problems occupied a more prominent role on Fulbright's agenda than did southeast Asia in 1961, for that far-off region appeared at the time as one of many trouble spots around the globe. In the spring of 1961, Kennedy met with Fulbright before announcing that he was sending Vice President Johnson to Saigon to "assess" the situation. Such Vice Presidential missions tend to be indications that an administration is already close to making a decision; as Henry Kissinger would later contend, no Vice President could possibly have made an independent analysis of a 10-year-old war on the basis of a visit that lasted only a few days. "Vice presidential overseas missions," in Kissinger's view, "are generally designed to stake American prestige, or to supply credibility for decisions that have already been made." Of course, this particular Vice Presidential mission was more important than usual, since Johnson would become President a few years later and the trip deepened Johnson's conviction that the United States should hold fast in South Vietnam. Kennedy advised Fulbright before Johnson's mission that American troops might have to be sent to Vietnam at some point in the future. Fulbright immediately expressed concern about the people who would be America's allies in the region: had they requested American assistance? The question was a crucial one, for as the United States would learn in later years, one of the key reasons for the eventual quagmire in southeast Asia was the absence of a dependable, politically and socially stable ally in South Vietnam. Nonetheless, Fulbright indicated to the President that he would be supportive of the administration's policy, provided that the question about American allies was resolved.[22d]

Johnson's mission was indeed an indication that the Kennedy administration had descended deeper into the southeast Asian morass. At the same time of his departure, a National Security Council directive stated that the prevention of a communist conquest in South Vietnam was a national objective of the United States. America would create in that country "a viable and increasingly democratic society" by political, economic, psychological and covert actions. Johnson returned from Saigon to publicly announce that Ngo Dinh Diem was an admirable leader, if remote from his people, so that the only alternative to supporting Diem was withdrawal. Johnson, of course, opposed the latter alternative, and predicted that Vietnam could be saved as long as the United States moved quickly and decisively on two fronts: the Americans would simultaneously eradicate hunger, ignorance, poverty, and disease in South Vietnam, while aiding Diem in waging guerrilla warfare against the communist forces. Johnson failed to explain how the United States could at once build a society after America's image—a process that would take decades to achieve in many ways, and in other respects could never be achieved given the cultural differences that exist-ed between Vietnamese and Americans—and wage war against a bitter enemy that had already fought savagely for a decade and was now stronger than when the war began.[22e]

When Fulbright analyzed the problem of communist expansion in southeast Asia in a Senate speech of the summer of 1961, he was preoccupied with his confrontation with the radical right and the larger question of the impact of the Cold War upon international pol-itics. There is more material in this speech on the American-Soviet competition for political influence in the Third World, the aftereffects of the Bay of Pigs misadventure, and the com-munist threat in Laos than there is on the Vietnam controversy, which did not appear to be of overwhelming significance at that time. Fulbright began his discussion of Vietnam in a somewhat theoretical fashion, interpreting the collapse of the French empire in Indochina as a demonstration of the validity of Mao Tse-tung's principle that if guerrillas have the sup-port of the civilian population in subverting a reactionary social and economic structure, they will "multiply and flourish like fish in warm water."[23] According to Fulbright, France wasted seven billion dollars, eight years, and the lives of 100,000 French and Vietnamese soldiers in its abortive effort to defeat the Vietminh.[24] "But France bore the heavy burden of its colonial record and its unconcern with political and social reform. Inevitably, France lost."[25]

Fulbright proceeded to criticize American policy in Laos. America had recently failed in a quixotic venture to transform Laos into an armed anticommunist bastion.[26] Fulbright stat-ed that there was neither procommunist nor anticommunist motivation in Laos, a remark-ably primitive country even by regional standards.[27] This passage is consistent with Fulbright's tendency throughout his career to emphasize the irrelevance of ideology to poor, peasant populations.[28] The people of Laos were interested in their village, family, and reli-gious life and were totally apathetic about the question of whether the ruling faction in their distant capital labeled themselves socialist commissars, royalty, or a military junta.[29] The illusion that the United States could inspire the Laotians to become staunch democrats and anticommunist zealots resulted in a cost of $300 million and an immeasurable blow to American prestige.[30] Fulbright considered American policy in South Vietnam to be heavily prejudiced in favor of military assistance. In his view, economic and social progress would ultimately determine the outcome of South Vietnam's "struggle for independence," yet there had been no evaluation of Vietnam's long-range economic weaknesses, nor any coherent attempt to measure aid programs against specific economic targets.[31] Paramilitary operations within Vietnam could not assure South Vietnam's independence, and neither could a pro-tracted and inconclusive military conflict in Laos.[32] President Ngo Dinh Diem's regime was "of necessity authoritarian," but Fulbright felt that Diem had been excessively severe.[33] The South Vietnamese government should begin the process of social and political reform—which would eventually thwart communist infiltration tactics by desisting from its present policy of suppressing all internal opposition to its rule, including anticommunist elements.[34]

Fulbright's fundamental argument in the June 1961 speech was reminiscent of what he had said in 1958 concerning the popular misconception that the Chinese Nationalists had been overthrown because the United States had not vigorously supported them. He believed that many Americans were drawing the wrong conclusion from the "lesson in Cuba" (the Bay of Pigs): that inadequate methods had been employed to achieve a worthy objective and that America must "beat the communists at their own game" of subversion, saturation propaganda, and terror.[35] In Fulbright's view such a strategy would not only violate America's traditional moral values, but would "draw the United States into costly commitments of its resources to peripheral struggles in which the principal communist powers are not directly involved."[36] Senator Barry Goldwater denounced Fulbright's address as advocating a dangerous doctrine of "nonintervention".[37] In the same speech (also in the summer of 1961) Goldwater pronounced it to be astounding that the Kennedy administration had not declared its purpose to be a total victory over the tyrannical forces of international communism.[38]

The June 1961 address by Fulbright seems prescient if only the above passages are cited. Fulbright did not, however, apply the logic of what Goldwater had called a doctrine of "nonintervention" to Vietnam. American policy in Vietnam had been a classic example of the tendency in American diplomacy that Fulbright had abhorred since the 1950s, for the primary objective had not been to assist in the creation of viable political institutions or a sound economy in South Vietnam but to prevent communist expansion beyond the 17th parallel.[39] Approximately 90 percent of American aid throughout the Diem era was concentrated upon developing the South Vietnamese army and military bureaucracy.[40] Fulbright had attacked this bias in the aid program but had nevertheless described both American policy in Vietnam and the performance of the Diem regime as "qualified successes."[41] Diem had been "courageous, diligent" and "strong in a situation where strength has been essential."[42]

It was strangely out of character for Fulbright to defend any dictator, and particularly one as brutal and inept as Ngo Dinh Diem. Apparently Fulbright accepted the view popular in Washington in the early 1960s that Diem was a capable Asian strongman whose authoritarian methods would be necessary during an interim period until the communist guerrillas could be defeated. Such an opinion was based upon a lack of knowledge of Vietnamese affairs. Frances Fitzgerald has written that the "Saigon government bore no resemblance to a strong, Asian-style government" but rather "resembled nothing so much as an attenuated French colonial regime."[43] Diem had ignored every article of the constitution he had so ostentatiously promulgated, incarcerated thousands of critics of his government in concentration camps, and by distributing the bulk of U.S. relief aid to Catholic villages, he perpetuated the French policy of rewarding Catholics at the expense of the majority of the population.[44] The Vietnamese courts continued to follow the French colonial code, there were no substantive changes in the French administrative system, and over a third of the Diemist administrators had formerly collaborated with the French.[45] Diem claimed to be a proud Vietnamese nationalist, but the fact that his regime was tainted by vestiges of colonialism was an almost insurmountable disadvantage in its struggle with the Vietnamese communists led by Ho Chi Minh, the leader of the resistance against the French and Japanese and perhaps the only authentic Vietnamese national hero.[46]

The most surprising error in Fulbright's June 1961 speech was the fundamental distinction he drew between the communist dangers in Laos and Vietnam. Laos emerges in this address as a country where a "peripheral struggle" must be avoided at all costs; Vietnam does not. It would be absurd, he argued, to commit thousands of American troops to interminable warfare in the jungles of primitive Laos, where the simple, peace-loving peasants had no understanding of what the terms "communism" and "capitalism" signify. The United States must search for a political settlement in Laos, even if it meant the participation of communists in a coalition government.[47] But in Vietnam, Fulbright confidently declared that "the people are anticommunist."[48] Therefore, America should redouble its efforts to develop the economic infrastructure of South Vietnam, while continuing its support for the South Vietnamese army.[49]

The image of the South Vietnamese people as resolute anticommunists was as erroneous as the conception of Diem as a strong and competent dictator. It is probable that there were as many anti-Diemists as there were anticommunists at that time. Diem was conducting an increasingly violent campaign of terrorism against both communist and noncommunist opponents to his rule, and thereby alienating all factions within the country except possibly the Catholics and those who could derive some private advantage by currying favor with his venal administration.[50] By late 1961 the communist guerrillas had extended their influence to over 80 percent of the rural population in South Vietnam.[51] The American officials in Saigon supported Diem in his refusal to adopt a system of electoral democracy, for all intelligence estimates indicated that the communists would have won a majority of the votes in normal elections.[52] (It should be added that since Vietnam possessed no real democratic tradition, there would have been difficulties in insuring that the elections were free and fair.)

Fulbright's distorted view of the prospects for a noncommunist state in South Vietnam can be explained partially by the problem that the executive branch was the major source of information concerning Vietnam during the first six years of Diem's dictatorship.[53] American journalists generally did not travel to Vietnam until 1961. By 1966 Fulbright had detected a pattern in which a professional reporter from a newspaper such as the *New York Times* or the *Washington Post* would write an article saying that the communists were inexorably gaining strength, that the South Vietnamese government had failed to inspire the loyalty of the people, and that the difference between American anticommunism and French colonialism was not recognized by the South Vietnamese.[54] The Kennedy and Johnson administrations would then dismiss the journalists' accounts as irresponsible.[55] Two or three years later Fulbright would discover that the reporters had been correct, at which time the administration would respond with a new set of optimistic evaluations contending that only a few thousand more troops or more extensive air raids for a few more years would assure the final victory of America's stalwart ally.

The fact that a senator is often absorbed by the interests and opinions of his constituents must be considered in order to place Fulbright's statements concerning southeast Asia in the early 1960s in their proper perspective. This was especially true of Fulbright in late 1961 and 1962. Senators John Tower, Barry Goldwater, and Strom Thurmond came to Arkansas to campaign against Fulbright, and there was widespread speculation that Governor Orval Faubus might be able to defeat Fulbright in the 1962 primary election.[56] Thurmond delivered a speech in Memphis attended by some east Arkansas ultraconservatives in which he challenged Fulbright's patriotism and advocated his defeat. In late 1961 Fulbright traveled throughout Arkansas speaking to small groups of Arkansans, and by early 1962 had demonstrated enough political support to eliminate the possibility of a Faubus candidacy for the Senate. Fulbright ridiculed the notion that "there's a communist under every bed";

at one speech, he drew an appreciative response from the crowd when he asked: "I don't have any doubt that there are some of those [communists] in New York. It may well be; you can find almost anything in New York, but how many communists do you know in your hometown?" One reporter rejected the notion that "a onetime Razorback halfback [could] be soft on communism." After thus dismissing the hysteria of the Thurmonds and Birch Society, Fulbright focused much of his speaking tour in Arkansas upon down-to-earth matters of direct concern to his constituents: he emphasized his work in reducing foreign trade barriers against Arkansas poultry and other farm exports, his work for river navigation, flood control, power generation, and other local issues. President Kennedy and Attorney General Kennedy privately but explicitly warned Faubus that if he ran against Fulbright, as RFK phrased it to Faubus, "you will not get one damn thing out of us for patronage." The powerful Oklahoma Senator Robert Kerr gave a similar warning from the legislative branch: "If you come to Washington, I promise that you will not get anything for Arkansas out of the Senate." The senator was aided by a network of powerful political allies in Arkansas, foremost of whom was Witt Stephens, who (as discussed previously) privately advised Faubus not to run against Fulbright.[57] Fulbright eventually received about 70 percent of the total vote in the 1962 general election, defeating an obscure candidate named Kenneth Jones.[58]

It was unfortunate that Fulbright was at least partially preoccupied with Arkansas politics in late 1961 and 1962, for in October of 1961 the President's Special Military Representative, Maxwell Taylor, and Walt Rostow (then the chairman of the Policy Planning Council) were reporting to President Kennedy after their mission to southeast Asia that combat troops and advisory units would be necessary to check the expansion of communism in South Vietnam.[59] Rostow was particularly enthusiastic about the potential military impact of American air power in Vietnam.[60] Kennedy resisted the pressure to authorize a massive, systematic bombing campaign or the direct commitment of combat troops, but endorsed the proposal to increase the number of advisers to the South Vietnamese army.[61] Within 15 months after the Taylor-Rostow mission, Kennedy expanded the contingent of advisers from 500 to 10,000, allowed these advisers to engage in combat, promised continuing assistance to Diem, ordered U.S.A.F. units to attack Vietcong strongholds in South Vietnam, and attempted to pacify the countryside by approving a Strategic Hamlet program that uprooted and alienated the South Vietnamese peasantry.[62] Thus, during much of the period when Kennedy was making the fateful decisions escalating the American commitment in Vietnam, Fulbright was traversing the delta and hill country of Arkansas, cultivating the support of the local power structure, defending his controversial August 1961 memorandum to McNamara by referring to the American tradition of strict subordination of the military to the civilian authorities, and discussing the significance of U.S. economic aid in developing foreign markets for Arkansas cotton, rice, soybeans and chickens.[63]

In 1963, Fulbright continued to devote the majority of his time and energy to issues other than Vietnam; but an exception occurred in September, 1963, when Fulbright appeared on CBS' "Face the Nation." Fulbright spoke shortly after Senator Frank Church had introduced a resolution calling on Diem to reform his government or face the prospect of an American withdrawal from South Vietnam. Assistant Secretary of State Roger Hilsman had privately asked Church to introduce the resolution, although the President later made

a public rejection of any American intention of withdrawing from Vietnam. The administration apparently envisaged the resolution as an instrument for exerting more pressure on
Diem to institute reform. On "Face the Nation," Fulbright endorsed the spirit of the Church
resolution, but the Foreign Relations Chairman also opposed an American withdrawal "at
this time." He stated that "Vietnam is the most serious crisis at the moment, obviously it is;
and what we do there is very, very important." The senator stressed that unless the Diem
regime inaugurated a program of internal reform, the South Vietnamese government was
destined to fall regardless of the extent of aid from the United States.[63a]

In October, the Senate Foreign Relations Committee listened to a briefing by Secretary
of Defense McNamara and General Maxwell Taylor, who had recently returned from
Vietnam.[64] After the briefing Fulbright told reporters that McNamara and Taylor had reported "impressive progress" in the military situation and that the Vietnamese countryside
would be pacified by 1965 unless "political unrest" complicated matters.[65] As Fulbright was
speaking of impressive military progress while remaining concerned about political instability, events were unfolding that epitomized the futility of the American involvement in
Vietnam.

By October 1963 Kennedy had sent 16,000 American soldiers to be advisers to the
South Vietnamese army, increased military aid to South Vietnam, and authorized a CIA-
sponsored program of clandestine sabotage operations in Laos and North Vietnam.[66] Having
accepted defeat at the Bay of Pigs and agreed to a compromise neutralization formula for
Laos, the President was not prepared to accept a communist triumph in South Vietnam.
However, the administration became increasingly impatient with Diem's failure to institute
reforms and effectively fight the guerrillas. After the Diem government perpetrated the massacre of 30 Buddhist monks at a Saigon pagoda in August, the administration rapidly lost
confidence in Diem. With the knowledge if not the approval of Washington, the Vietnamese
generals plotted a conspiracy against Diem and assassinated him on November 1, 1963.
(Kennedy had known of the coup and had doubts about it, but he did not know of the
assassination attempt beforehand and was shocked by the South Vietnamese leader's murder.)[67] The inept dictator the United States had supported for eight years had finally been
eliminated, and yet the overthrow of Diem apparently exacerbated the problem of political
instability in South Vietnam.[68] It was not until 1965 that Nguyen Cao Ky and Nguyen Van
Thieu, with massive American support, terminated the succession of South Vietnamese
coups and counter coups that followed Diem's fall.[69]

In the early 1960s Fulbright accepted the nominal American objective of securing the
independence of South Vietnam. As he later came to realize, American policy was working
against the independence of Vietnam. The continuation of the war weakened the ability of
North Vietnam to pursue the traditional policy of all the smaller states of the Far East, which
was to remain independent of China.[70] American aid for South Vietnam created a total
dependency on the United States. An American economist who visited Vietnam in 1961
concluded that the aid program represented a gigantic relief project rather than an economic development program, and consequently withdrawal of the aid would produce both
political and economic collapse.[71] When the former Pentagon official Daniel Ellsberg testified before the Senate Foreign Relations Committee in 1970, he described the political systems of Diem and Thieu as "Diemism."[72] Ellsberg defined Diemism as a government based

upon the military, Catholics, bureaucrats, landlords, and businessmen. The Diemists rigidly excluded the Buddhists and other religious sects, students, trade unions, and the smaller political factions from participating in the exercise of power.[73] The basic characteristics of
Diemism were the use of police state methods to suppress freedom of speech or other political activities, a total unwillingness to negotiate with the communists, and an extreme
dependence on the United States.[74]

By 1963, Fulbright had become increasingly concerned that the United States could
become entangled in a military involvement in southeast Asia from which it would be difficult to extricate itself. In his speech on southeast Asia in 1961, he had warned about the
dire consequences of repressive policies by the South Vietnamese government, and he had
been concerned about the dangers of repeating the French military intervention in Vietnam.
By 1963, the internal chaos within South Vietnam had risen to alarming proportions.
Within the administration, Robert Kennedy and McNamara were raising the issue whether
withdrawal was the wisest course. In the fall, RFK had wondered aloud whether, if the
United States could not win a war with Diem, the American military presence should be
withdrawn. Rusk immediately bristled at the Attorney General's suggestion, vaguely
responding that "we would be in real trouble" if the Viet Cong took over South Vietnam. In
October, McNamara recommended to the President that 1,000 of the American advisers be
withdrawn, and that a training program for the Vietnamese be carried out so that essential
functions then performed by U.S. military personnel could be conducted by Vietnamese by
the end of 1965, when the United States should withdraw the rest of its forces. After
McNamara had briefed the Foreign Relations Committee in closed session on October 10,
Fulbright had told reporters about this timetable that envisaged no need for an American
military presence by December, 1965, provided that the problem of political unrest had
been solved. McNamara was acutely conscious of pressures from Fulbright and others in
Congress to avoid a military quagmire in southeast Asia, and in his major report to the
President in October, he explicitly referred to Fulbright's concerns

> The advantage to taking [the 1,000 advisers] out is that we can say to Congress
> and the people that we do have a plan for reducing the exposure of U.S. combat
> personnel to the guerrilla actions in South Vietnam—actions that the people of
> South Vietnam should gradually develop a capability to suppress themselves. And
> I think this will be of great value to us in meeting the very strong views of Fulbright
> and others that we're bogged down in Asia and will be there for decades.[74a]

McNamara's report to the President stressed that South Vietnam's government should
be closely monitored "to see what steps Diem takes to reduce repressive practices and to
improve the effectiveness of the military effort," but the Secretary of Defense carefully rejected the idea of supporting a coup against Diem. As events degenerated in the following
weeks, the latter suggestion faded. McNamara's view at the time was also flawed by the characteristic optimism concerning the military situation. He said: "The military campaign has
made great progress and continues to progress," while acknowledging that the Diem-Nhu
government was becoming increasingly unpopular. McNamara would later speculate in his
memoirs that had Kennedy lived, he would have concluded that the South Vietnamese were

incapable of defending themselves, and that Saigon's fatal political weaknesses rendered it futile to try to compensate for the limitations of the South Vietnamese military by sending in U.S. combat troops on a massive scale. The conditions that the United States could not win their war for them and that they needed internal stability in order to fight could not be met. McNamara asserted that "Kennedy would have agreed that withdrawal would cause a fall of the `dominoes' but that staying in would ultimately lead to the same result, while exacting a terrible price in blood."[74b] McNamara's speculative argument obviously did not come from an objective source, since the former Secretary of Defense was deeply attached to JFK.

An analysis of the record of the President's actions and public statements in late 1963 does not yield any definitive answer to the question McNamara posed. Kennedy had decided to withdraw the 1,000 advisers, and the administration official he trusted most–Robert Kennedy–was beginning to have profound doubts about the war. In contrast, during the Johnson administration RFK would have an adversarial relationship with President Johnson. Fulbright was deeply impressed with the President's capacity for growth and his much greater knowledge of Cold War issues by 1963 as opposed to 1961. In contrast to such blunders as the Bay of Pigs early in his Presidency, Fulbright would point to Kennedy's wisdom in the Test Ban Treaty and the post-missile crisis detente. Such flexibility and growth augured well for the President's future decision-making in Vietnam, had he lived, although what he would have done is not a question that historians or anyone else can answer. Some of the President's statements repeated the familiar Cold War dogmas about southeas Asia, although he consistently hammered on the theme that it was South Vietnam's war to win or lose.

In a televised interview with Walter Cronkite in September, JFK had rejected withdrawal, which would have been a politically explosive position to take at the time, but stressed that "I don't think that unless a greater effort is made by the [South Vietnamese] government to win popular support that the war can be won out there. In the final analysis, it is their war. They are the ones who have to win it or lose it." The President said that the United States could help them, "we can give them equipment, we can send our men out there as advisers, but they have to win it." On the other hand, Kennedy endorsed the "domino theory" in an interview with Chet Huntley and David Brinkley a week later: "China is so large, looms so high just beyond the frontiers, that if South Vietnam went, it would not only give them an improved geographic position for a guerrilla assault on Malaya, but would also give the impression that the wave of the future in southeast Asia was China and the communists." Yet, other important statements by the Kennedy administration in its last few weeks reiterated the theme that it was South Vietnam's war. In late September, McNamara stated on CBS that instability was increasing in South Vietnam and that unless the government and the populace could work together, the Viet Cong would win the war. "It's important to recognize it's a South Vietnamese war," McNamara emphasized, and "we can advise and help, but they are responsible for the final results." In the President's last public comments on Vietnam at a news conference on November 14, Kennedy stated that the object of American policy was "to bring Americans home, permit the South Vietnamese to maintain themselves as a free and independent country... I don't want the United States to have to put troops there."[74c]

One of the crucial differences between Kennedy and Johnson would be their choice of advisers and their ability to tolerate dissenting viewpoints. Johnson preferred the hard-liners Rusk and Walt Rostow, and also tended to push his advisers to devise ways of winning the war. Kennedy respected Fulbright and gave serious thought to his foreign policy ideas–even when he disagreed with them–whereas for Johnson, Fulbright was seen as a committee chairman whose support could be politically useful. Johnson would arrange meetings of high-level advisers in which one of the dissenters would be present, but most of those present would be interventionists. Rather than a real consideration of dissident ideas, Johnson's strategy was more an effort to make a record of having consulted all viewpoints. Cold Warriors like Rusk and Rostow flourished in the Johnson administration, whereas dissenters such as Fulbright were basically considered as obstacles to be overcome, especially in restricting their dissent to private advice and memoranda. When Fulbright began publicly speaking out against the war later in the Johnson Presidency, LBJ was outraged and terminated his long friendship with the senator.

Kennedy was planning to replace Rusk as Secretary of State in his second term, and preferred the more flexible, capable views of McNamara. Although by his own admission, McNamara was "terribly wrong" in his assessments concerning Vietnam, he clearly had demonstrated a much greater understanding of the complexities involved, whereas Rusk's reaction to crises was to apply the tired dogmas of the Cold War. Above all, unlike Rusk, McNamara could admit error. Kennedy also greatly valued the advice of Walter Lippmann, who would become another major critic of the war. A President who would genuinely listen to the views of a Fulbright, a Lippmann, or a Robert Kennedy clearly held a greater prospect of avoiding disaster in Vietnam than one who relied much more upon Rusk and Rostow. In any event, we will never know whether JFK would have led America into the Vietnamese abyss had he lived.

The End of Camelot

Later in the 1960s, the Arkansas senator would investigate the U.S. Vietnam policy in exhaustive detail; but in the summer and fall of 1963 Fulbright regarded the American dilemma in southeast Asia as peripheral to the fundamental issue of Soviet-American relations.[75] In the early Kennedy administration, Fulbright had been concerned about the confrontation between the President and Khrushchev at the Vienna conference, where the Soviet leader took a hard line regarding Berlin and set a deadline of six months for deciding the city's permanent condition. Fulbright suggested to Rusk the neutralization of Berlin through the placement of token NATO and UN forces there, while the West would be guaranteed free access into the city. Fulbright was consulting with Lippmann, as he usually did, and both men agreed that Washington should not risk continuing confrontations with the Soviets by refusing to sign a treaty recognizing the German Democratic Republic. The GDR was a reality, Fulbright argued, and "we should have conferences at the ministerial level to avoid a showdown leading to nuclear war." Kennedy was cautious at the time about taking any action that would lead to accusations of "appeasement," but in the aftermath of the

Cuban missile crisis, his strategy regarding Soviet-American relations began to change.[75a]

Fulbright approved of President Kennedy's nascent efforts to reduce Cold War animosities in 1963, and he was especially pleased with Kennedy's eloquent speech at American University in June.[76] Both the United States and the Soviet Union had a "mutually deep interest," the President had declared at American University, "in a just and genuine peace and in halting the arms race. . . . If we cannot end now all our differences, at least we can help make the world safe for diversity."[77] Fulbright held Senate Foreign Relations Committee hearings on the Nuclear Test Ban Treaty. A series of administration officials and scientists appeared before the committee and made a compelling argument that the treaty would drastically reduce atmospheric fallout, was enforceable, and would not threaten American security. Although the nuclear physicist Edward Teller and a few other notable figures opposed the treaty, the ban eventually attracted powerful, bipartisan support. The debate had a beneficial impact, as public opinion polls revealed a strong increase in support to 80 percent by September. After the Nuclear Test Ban Treaty was signed in Moscow, Kennedy had not attempted to exaggerate its significance. He conceded the treaty would not resolve all conflicts with the U.S.S.R. or reduce nuclear stockpiles, but it would eliminate atmospheric testing and represent an "important first step toward peace."[78] He quoted a Chinese proverb in summarizing the importance of the treaty: "A journey of a thousand miles must begin with a single step."[79] On September 24 the Senate ratified the Treaty 80 to 19 with Fulbright's vigorous support.[80] Kennedy praised the Senate's action as "a welcome culmination of this effort to lead the world once again to the path of peace."[81]

A few days after Kennedy's assassination on November 22, Fulbright eulogized the fallen leader's willingness to listen to dissenting opinions: "He was the most approachable President. I never had the slightest hesitancy in saying anything I thought to him. I never thought he might take offense at any idea I might have contrary to his own." The senator was especially complimentary of Kennedy's diplomatic skills with people from other countries, saying, "I think he had a sensitiveness to foreign people that no other President had... Every time I went to a White House dinner, or any kind of ceremony, I was very proud of the way he represented me and my country."

Fulbright was able to make a lasting legacy to President Kennedy's memory through his work on legislation that culminated in the establishment of the John Fitzgerald Kennedy Center for the Performing Arts. The senator had an instinct for recognizing and sponsoring developments of great import to education and culture. On February 24, 1958, he had introduced in the Senate a bill to establish a National Culture Center in Washington, D.C. In the House of Representatives, the bill was introduced by Congressman Frank Thompson of New Jersey.[81a] In September 1971, the center was opened as the John F. Kennedy Center for the Performing Arts; it was to become one of the great cultural institutions of the country.[81b] Originally the legislation called for the Center to be built on the Mall, opposite the National Gallery of Art, but later the site was changed to a location in the Foggy Bottom area. After introduction, the bill swiftly caught the fancy of notables in the world of society and the arts, including Perle Mesta and John Brownlee, the opera star, as well as a formidable array of figures representing national music organizations. All turned out for the Congressional hearings on Fulbright's bill. Fulbright showed that on occasion he could employ Cold War arguments for a worthy cause: in March 1958 he made a speech to opera producers and managers in New York calling for a national opera and ballet center at Washington so that Americans would not "hang their heads in shame whenever people tell us about the Bolshoi Theater."

After the assassination of President Kennedy, Fulbright introduced in the Senate on November 26, 1963, an amendment to the legislation for the Culture Center, appropriating the "last $5 million" for its construction and changing its name to honor the fallen President. The senator was immensely proud of his part in establishing the Kennedy Center, and he was also proud of a letter of appreciation he received from Mrs. John F. Kennedy. In January, 1964, he replied in a letter: "Dear Jackie: Nothing I can do could ever begin to express my appreciation and gratitude that this country was privileged to have had such a President, even for so short a time."[81c]

In late 1963, Fulbright believed that Lyndon Johnson would listen sympathetically to his ideas concerning foreign policy. On the evening of November 22, President Johnson arrived at the Executive Office Building in Washington, where he conferred for more than two hours with intimates and political leaders. The first person he consulted was his old friend J. William Fulbright. In the early days of his presidency, Johnson frequently invited the senator to lengthy personal conferences, and Fulbright regarded himself as an influential foreign policy counselor to the new administration. The senator attempted to encourage Johnson in the weeks after the assassination, publicly stating that his former senate colleague would probably become a great President. In a January 1964 letter to Will Clayton, Fulbright was somewhat less effusive: "The Texas President is doing a fine job under difficult circumstances. . . . He will come out all right, I think." The cordial relationship between Fulbright and the new President was symbolized by a famous photograph of the two men aboard Air Force One in December 1963. The President autographed the picture with the words, "To J. William Fulbright, than whom there is no better. Lyndon B. Johnson."[82]

"I thought," Fulbright would later reminisce concerning the America of January, 1964, "we were on the verge of entering our golden age." The senator was especially enthusiastic that Johnson would divert America's energies away from the Cold War and concentrate upon solving the nation's domestic problems.[83] Despite the frustration and the tragedy of the previous years, the early Johnson presidency was a season of euphoria for many progressive political analysts, who expected Johnson to lead the nation in domestic affairs while relying heavily upon the advice of Fulbright, Lippman, Mansfield, Ball, and other moderates in foreign policy. For many enlightened Americans of that day, 1964 promised to be the dawn of an era of greatness for the Senate, the Presidency, and the nation.

II. 1964:
THE YEAR THE MODERATES LOST

In 1964 Senator J. William Fulbright was one of the principal Congressional apologists for President Lyndon Johnson's foreign policy in southeast Asia. Fulbright delivered two important analyses of the Vietnam War during the first year of Johnson's Presidency: in a major Senate address on March 25, 1964, he endorsed the President's policy of supporting the noncommunist regime in Saigon, and in August he praised the administration's Gulf of Tonkin Resolution. Yet Fulbright did not devote great attention to Vietnam in 1964, for he was primarily concerned with opposing the presidential candidacy of Arizona Senator Barry Goldwater. Fulbright later asserted that until the early 1960s he had considered the American military and economic aid to South Vietnam as "a very small operation. I wasn't at all concerned. I was entirely preoccupied with Europe. I don't recall we ever had a hearing on Vietnam."[1] The Arkansas senator tended to rely on the administration for information concerning southeast Asia, largely because he was not particularly knowledgeable about Vietnam in 1964.[2] Thus, in March he accepted the administration's contention that the United States should not seek an immediate negotiated settlement in Vietnam, and five months later he did not challenge the President's allegations of flagrant North Vietnamese aggression in the Gulf of Tonkin.

Fulbright briefly analyzed American policy toward Vietnam in a passage of his March 25, 1964, Senate speech entitled "Old Myths and New Realities." The only "realistic options" in Vietnam, he declared, were "the expansion of the conflict" or a "renewed effort to bolster the capacity of the South Vietnamese to prosecute the war successfully on its present scale."[3] In Fulbright's view, "Whatever specific policy decisions are made, it should be clear to all concerned that the United States will continue to meet its obligations and fulfill its commitments with respect to Vietnam."[4]

Fulbright opposed an immediate negotiated settlement, arguing that it was exceedingly difficult for a party to a negotiation to achieve by diplomacy "what it has conspicuously failed to win by warfare."[5] He expressed the idea that later became the Johnson administration's private justification for expanding the American military involvement in southeast Asia: the United States would intervene in order to substantially alter the military "equation of advantages" in favor of the anticommunist forces, and thus establish the existence of an independent, noncommunist South Vietnam as a precondition for any diplomatic conference.[6] The senator did not speculate about the future duration of the American military presence in South Vietnam. He did not indicate whether he recommended expanding the conflict, although he approved of the first air strike against North Vietnam a few months later.

Fulbright did not elaborate upon what would be required in a "renewed effort to bolster" the South Vietnamese military capacity, nor did he define America's obligations and commitments to South Vietnam. His ambiguity was typical of the perennial difficulties that Johnson's supporters experienced in presenting specific, cogent justifications for the American intervention in Vietnam.[7] When Fulbright expanded the March 25 Senate speech into his book entitled "Old Myths and New Realities" later in 1964, the only "evidence" he offered to demonstrate the alleged threat to American security in Vietnam was a vague and inaccurate charge of Chinese and North Vietnamese aggression.[8] In 1964 he believed that the Congress must rely upon the thousands of experts in the State Department and the Central Intelligence Agency for expertise in the realm of diplomacy, largely because the half-dozen staff members of the Senate Foreign Relations Committee could not comprehensively analyze all the myriad controversies of America's foreign relations.[9] Fulbright's dependence on the administration for information was unnecessary, as he eventually realized. During the late 1960s he employed a larger number of Congressional investigators, sought the ideas of journalists and scholars, conducted frequent Foreign Relations Committee investigations, and diligently attempted to acquire independent sources of information concerning American foreign policy in Vietnam and elsewhere. But it was only after the massive military interventions in Vietnam and the Dominican Republic that Fulbright would become wary of depending on the executive's evaluations in foreign affairs; in 1964 he accepted the administration's judgment on the southeast Asia crisis.

The lack of detail in Fulbright's passage on Vietnam in "Old Myths and New Realities" may be partially explained by the fact that the speech was a general review of American diplomacy, and the Vietnam policy was only one of many controversial issues that Fulbright discussed on March 25. His analysis of the Vietnam War constituted less than one-tenth of the material in the address. The brevity of the section on Vietnam was characteristic of his inattention to southeast Asia in the early 1960s.

Fulbright's views on Vietnam in "Old Myths and New Realities" were similar to those outlined by McNamara in a major speech in Washington on March 27. The Secretary of Defense acknowledged that the situation in Vietnam had unquestionably deteriorated, and that "the picture is admittedly not an easy one to evaluate and, given the kind of terrain and the kind of war, information is not always available or reliable." McNamara warned that "the large indigenous support that the Viet Cong receives means that solutions must be as much political and economic as military." Despite these concessions concerning the profound difficulties in Vietnam, McNamara still regarded it as a "test case": "Success in Vietnam [by the Viet Cong] would be regarded by Peiping as vindication for China's views in the worldwide ideological struggle." The new President had entered office determined to succeed in South Vietnam. In one of his first meetings as President with high-level advisers on November 24, 1963, Johnson discussed Vietnam with Rusk, George Ball, Ambassador to South Vietnam Henry Cabot Lodge, and McNamara. The President lectured his advisers that the administration would win the war in Vietnam. Johnson had inherited a terrible dilemma. As Vice President, he had opposed the coup against Diem, and in the first 90 days of the Johnson administration two governments in Saigon briefly held power and then disintegrated, and four more South Vietnamese regimes would similarly crumble in the next nine months. In the early weeks of his Presidency, Johnson made clear to McNamara his conviction that

China was bent upon attaining hegemony in the Far East, and that the United States had not been doing all it should in South Vietnam.[9a]

Ironically, in spite of the inaccurate analysis of Vietnam in "Old Myths and New Realities," the rest of Fulbright's speech was one of his most famous critiques of the Cold War mentality. He urged the United States to renounce "the master myth of the Cold War that the communist bloc is a monolith composed of governments all equally resolute and implacable in their determination to destroy the free world."[10] According to Fulbright, some communist states, such as Yugoslavia and Poland, posed no threat to the West, while China allegedly posed an immediate threat.[11] Nikita Khrushchev's diplomacy was much more prudent than the aggressive Stalinist foreign policy of the early postwar period.[12] Communist imperialism and not communism as a doctrine represented a danger to the West, Fulbright asserted.[13] He concluded that as long as any nation was content to practice its doctrines within its own frontiers, regardless of how repugnant its ideology appeared to be to Americans, the United States should have no quarrel with that nation.[14]

The most controversial passages of "Old Myths and New Realities" dealt with Latin America. The senator challenged the conventional wisdom by observing that Panama's desire to change the terms of the 1903 treaty regarding U.S. control of the Panama Canal was in America's interest to pursue. Even more importantly, Fulbright stated that American policies designed to overthrow Fidel Castro in Cuba had been failures. Neither military invasion nor an American trade ban had succeeded in the past, and such aggressive policies would not succeed in the future.[15] The United States should accept the reality that the Castro regime was a "distasteful nuisance but not an intolerable danger" and stop flattering "a noisy but minor demagogue by treating him as if he were a Napoleonic menace."[16]

Many liberal politicians and journalists praised Fulbright's March 25 address before the Senate.[17] Walter Lippmann eulogized the senator in an article written for Newsweek in early April: "He says what he believes is true rather than what is supposed at the moment to be popular. He is not listened to on the floor of Congress until he has been heard around the world. He has become the leading witness to the present truth, but it is not a fatal mistake to be right too soon."[18] The Johnson administration, however, was more critical of the speech.[19] Rusk insisted that Castro was much more than a nuisance, and reiterated that the embargo must persist. The Secretary did blandly acknowledge the presence of change in the communist world. In two successive press conferences after March 25, President Johnson denied any connection with the ideas expressed in "Old Myths and New Realities."[20]

The President's response to Fulbright's address was a significant indication of Johnson's intolerance of even mild dissent. Fulbright's views concerning American diplomacy in the Far East were not sharply different from those of the administration; the March speech may have been influenced by Rusk's conception of the relationship between North Vietnam and China. Senator Fulbright wrote in 1972 that Rusk adhered to a modified version of the communist conspiracy thesis.[21] In the late 1940s and 1950s, many foreign policy analysts had imagined international communism to be a global conspiracy, with the head of the "octopus" in Moscow and its tentacles reaching out to the farthest corners of the earth.[22] Fulbright contended that after the Sino-Soviet break became obvious in the 1960s, Rusk professed to be scornful of the conspiracy thesis. Yet Rusk defended the Vietnam War with references to a "world cut in two by Asian communism," the only difference between the earlier and later perspectives being, in Fulbright's opinion, that Rusk had discovered a second "octopus" in Peking.[23] When Fulbright was writing in 1972, Rusk's specter of "Asian communism" seemed farcical. But in 1964 Fulbright may not have clearly understood that North Vietnam was not a Chinese puppet. He spoke of preventing South Vietnam from being dominated by "Peking and Hanoi" as if North Vietnam and China were practically indistinguishable.[24]

Fulbright probably thought his treatment of China in "Old Myths and New Realities" was moderate, since he clearly hoped for an eventual amelioration of Sino-American relations at some unspecified date in the future.[25] A reduction of tensions in the Far East, he hypothesized, might "make it possible to strengthen world peace by drawing mainland China into existing East-West agreements in such fields as disarmament, trade, and educational exchange."[26] He commended the recent French recognition of China, which might "serve a constructive long-term purpose, by unfreezing a situation in which many countries, none more than the United States, are committed to inflexible policies by long-established commitments and the pressures of domestic public opinion."[27] The French initiative, he speculated, might facilitate a re-evaluation of American foreign policy toward China.[28]

Despite the senator's favorable response to the French recognition of China, there were no specific differences between Fulbright and the administration with respect to America's China policy. He contended that the United States should not recognize China or acquiesce in Chinese admission to the United Nations, for "there is nothing to be gained by it so long as the Peiping regime maintains its attitude of implacable hostility toward the United States."[29] China represented an "immediate threat" to the West, according to Fulbright, yet he did not explain what the threat was. Fulbright's rhetoric concerning China in 1964 was sometimes conciliatory and never as abrasive as the administration officials' statements, but the fact that his views were influenced by the belligerent anti-Chinese position of the executive branch was revealed in August 1964, when he described the Gulf of Tonkin Resolution as a device to "deter aggression on the part of the North Vietnamese and Chinese."[30]

In 1966 Fulbright would characterize the Gulf of Tonkin Resolution as a blank check signed by the Congress in an atmosphere of urgency, which seemed to preclude debate.[31] On August 5, 1964, Johnson summoned Fulbright and other Congressional leaders to an emergency meeting at the White House and advised them that North Vietnamese naval vessels had flagrantly violated the principle of freedom of the seas by attacking American destroyers in the Gulf of Tonkin.[32] Without questioning Johnson's version of the Tonkin incidents, Fulbright cooperated closely with the administration in guiding the resolution through the Congress.[33] The Senate Foreign Relations Committee and the Armed Services Committee held a joint executive session hearing that lasted an hour and a half on August 6. Fulbright was the floor manager for the resolution, which proclaimed that the United States was "prepared, as the President determines, to take all necessary steps, including the use of armed force, to assist any member or protocol state of the Southeast Asia Collective Defense Treaty requesting assistance in defense of its freedom."[34] The resolution was adopted on August 7 by a vote of 416 to 0 in the House of Representatives and 88 to 2 in the Senate. Senator Wayne Morse of Oregon and Senator Ernest Gruening of Alaska cast the only dissenting votes.[35]

During the August 6 joint hearing Rusk, Secretary of Defense Robert McNamara, and

Chairman of the Joint Chiefs of Staff Earle G. Wheeler defended the resolution and an August 5 air strike against North Vietnam.[36] Rusk emphasized the President's desire to continue closely consulting with Congress: "As the southeast Asia situation develops, and *if it develops in ways we cannot now anticipate, of course there will be close and continuous consultation between the President and Congress* [emphasis added]." The Secretary of State did not employ John Foster Dulles' domino theory to justify the resolution of the bombings. This theory had been explained by President Eisenhower in 1954, when he averred that if the noncommunists in Vietnam were overthrown, communist expansion into Burma, Thailand, the Malay peninsula, Indonesia, Australia, New Zealand, Japan, Formosa, and the Phillippines would inevitably follow.[37] The Johnson administration's rhetoric may have differed from that of Eisenhower and Dulles, but the policy of supporting the noncommunist regime in Saigon persisted. Rusk described the domino theory as unnecessary, for "it is enough to recognize the true nature of the communist doctrine of world revolution and the militant support that Hanoi and Peiping are giving that doctrine in southeast Asia."[38] According to Rusk, the two attacks on American destroyers in the Gulf of Tonkin were not isolated events but were part of North Vietnam's systematic and deliberate campaign of aggression in southeast Asia.[39]

The August 5 air raid was a retaliation against North Vietnam for the alleged attacks on August 2 and August 4, which had inflicted no damage upon the American destroyers.[40] The bombings destroyed several shore facilities, approximately two-thirds of the North Vietnamese navy (which consisted of patrol boats), and the largest petroleum storage depot in North Vietnam.[41] Senator Russell Long of Louisiana asked McNamara at the August 6 hearing if the American planes had achieved a "surprise attack" against the North Vietnamese naval bases that was similar to the Japanese surprise attack upon Pearl Harbor; McNamara replied, "Yes, that's exactly true."[42] Almost all the senators congratulated the administration on the promptness and moderation of the decision to bomb North Vietnam. Fulbright commended Rusk, McNamara, Wheeler, and President Johnson for the "restraint with which overwhelming power in the area was used, a new attitude on the part of a great power."[43]

Wayne Morse was the only senator who opposed the administration's Vietnam policy at the August 6 hearing. Morse criticized not only the resolution but the premise of North Vietnamese aggression upon which the administration's policy was based. He denied that the executive branch had produced a "scintilla" of evidence to prove that regular North Vietnamese army and navy units were engaged in aggressive acts against South Vietnam.[44] The Oregon senator specifically questioned the validity of the administration's version of the Tonkin incidents, asserting that the American destroyers had committed a provocative act by cruising so close to the North Vietnamese shore.[45] (When the transcript of the secret hearing was finally published in 1966, the State Department deleted the exact distance, although McNamara later admitted that the administration had authorized the American vessels to cruise within four miles of the North Vietnamese coastline.)[46]

McNamara and Rusk answered Morse with the rather lame rejoinders that the American-equipped South Vietnamese sea patrol had searched 130,000 junks in 1963 and discovered 140 Viet Cong, and that North Vietnam was infiltrating parties of 100 to 200 guerrillas into South Vietnam through Laos.[47] The administration officials' statements were ambiguous and were not relevant to Morse's questions, for they did not specify the frequency with which the alleged infiltrations occurred and they failed to demonstrate that North Vietnamese regular units were fighting in South Vietnam. However, there is no doubt that North Vietnam was providing increasing levels of military support for the Viet Cong.

During the brief Senate debate over the resolution Senator George McGovern of South Dakota asked Fulbright about the South Vietnamese operations in the Gulf of Tonkin on July 30, 1964. Fulbright answered McGovern by saying the administration had assured him that the destroyer patrol "was entirely unconnected or unassociated with any coastal forays the South Vietnamese may have conducted."[48] At the August 6 secret hearing, Secretary McNamara had claimed that "our Navy played absolutely no part in, was not associated with, was not aware of any South Vietnamese actions, if there were any."[49] McNamara stated that the commander of the American destroyer, the *Maddox,* "was not informed of, was not aware, had no evidence of, and so far as I know today had no knowledge of any possible South Vietnamese actions in connection with" two islands close to the North Vietnamese coast that South Vietnamese patrol boats had attacked in a 34A operation. Four years later in testimony before the Foreign Relations Committee, McNamara contradicted his earlier assertion when he admitted that the American warships had been cooperating with South Vietnamese naval raids against North Vietnam in July and August 1964.[50] The *Maddox* had been engaged in a DESOTO patrol, which was part of a system of global electronic reconnaisance conducted by specially equipped American vessels. In his memoirs, McNamara conceded that the *Maddox* commander had known about the 34A operations, and admitted, "My statement was honest but wrong."[50a]

During the August 1964 debate in the Senate, Senator Gaylord Nelson of Wisconsin attempted to clarify the meaning of the resolution. When Nelson asked Fulbright if the resolution was "aimed at the problem of further aggression against our ships," Fulbright replied affirmatively.[51] Nelson offered an amendment to the resolution declaring it to be the policy of the United States to avoid a direct military involvement in the southeast Asian conflict, and Fulbright indicated that the amendment was "an accurate reflection of what I believe is the President's policy, judging from his own statements."[52] Throughout 1964, Johnson assured the Arkansas senator that he intended to avoid a massive, direct military intervention in the Vietnam War.[53] Fulbright, as floor leader, did not accept Nelson's amendment because it would have required further consideration by the House of Representatives and thus delayed the Gulf of Tonkin Resolution's passage. The Foreign Relations Committee chairman was under pressure from the Johnson administration to pass the resolution immediately in order to emphasize America's unity in opposing potential aggressors.[54]

At one juncture of the debate Fulbright conceded that "the language of the Resolution would not prevent" the Commander in Chief from landing large American armies in Vietnam or China.[55] But he also maintained that "I have no doubt that the President will consult with Congress in case a major change in present policy becomes necessary."[56] Fulbright believed he was summarizing the general sentiment of the Senate (which was also expressed by McGovern, Frank Church of Idaho, John Sherman Cooper of Kentucky, and others) when he concluded: "I personally feel it would be very unwise under any circumstances to put a large land army on the Asian continent."[57]

Fulbright supported the Gulf of Tonkin Resolution because he did not suspect the

President's version of the alleged incidents was untrue and because he did not wish to cause any political difficulties for Johnson during a campaign in which the alternative candidate was Barry Goldwater, a man whose election Fulbright envisaged as a disaster for the United States.[58] At one point during the campaign Goldwater replied to a question about what policy he would follow in Vietnam by saying, "I would turn to my Joint Chiefs of Staff and say 'fellows, we made the decision to win, now its [sic] your problem.'"[59] He had spoken of defoliating the jungle trails in Vietnam with "low-yield atomic bombs."[60] In contrast, Johnson skillfully played the role of the man of peace, declaring: "We are not about to send American boys 9,000 or 10,000 miles away from home to do what Asian boys ought to be doing themselves."[61] Fulbright was convinced that Johnson would use the resolution with wisdom and restraint.

During the Senate's deliberations over the resolution Fulbright assured his colleagues that Johnson did not intend to expand the war. Many senators thought of the resolution as a typical Johnson political ploy.[62] An anonymous source later quoted Fulbright as having remarked in the Democratic cloakroom at the time that, "This resolution doesn't mean a thing. Lyndon wants this to show he can be decisive and firm with the communists too."[63]

The Johnson administration eventually would refer to the Gulf of Tonkin Resolution and the Southeast Asia Treaty Organization Treaty as constituting the "functional equivalent" of a declaration of war.[64] The language of the resolution included no restrictions upon the authority of the President to "take all necessary measures to repel any armed attack against the forces of the United States and to prevent further aggression."[65]

The 1964 Fulbright was far more disturbed by the threat of Goldwater's Presidential candidacy than he was by events in southeast Asia. He believed that Goldwater essentially advocated a policy of "co-annihilation."[66] When the administration requested Fulbright's support during the Tonkin Gulf crisis in August, he was influenced by a partisan desire to help repudiate the extremist Republican and ensure the triumph of the "moderate" candidate, Lyndon Johnson.[67] He interpreted the administration's request for passage of the resolution as not only an appropriate response to the alleged attacks on American ships, but also as a device to deprive Goldwater of the "soft-on-communism" charge against Johnson.[68] The resolution and the retaliatory air raids against North Vietnam could demonstrate Johnson's determination to oppose communist aggression. From the standpoint of domestic politics, the administration's handling of the Tonkin affair was brilliantly successful. A Louis Harris poll showed the President's positive rating skyrocketing from 42 percent before the crisis to 72 percent after his responses to the alleged incidents in the Gulf.[69] Fulbright's support for the Gulf of Tonkin Resolution had helped Johnson to eliminate the Vietnam controversy as an issue in the campaign, a fact which contributed to Johnson's overwhelming victory in November.[70]

During the summer of 1964 the senator from Arkansas believed that Johnson's account of the events in the Gulf was honest and accurate. It was not until 1966 that he would fully realize his error of substituting his personal trust in the President for a proper institutional balance between the legislative and executive branches, a balance that might have been achieved by holding extended hearings on Vietnam in August 1964, as Senator Morse advocated.[71] Fulbright later wrote in The Arrogance of Power that if the Senate had thoroughly debated the resolution, or if a careful investigation of the alleged attacks on American ships had been conducted, then "we might have put limits and qualifications on our endorsement of future uses of force in Southeast Asia, if not in the resolution itself then in the legislative history preceding its adoption."[72] But in 1964 he believed that if the administration ever contemplated a massive expansion of the war his old friend Lyndon Johnson would consult him and weigh his advice thoughtfully.[73] He still relished his role as senior Senate foreign policy partner to the President.[74] It was not until 1966 that he held the hearings Morse had called for in 1964. And only then would he become convinced that in the allegation of unprovoked aggression on the high seas in August 1964, the administration had deliberately deceived the American public and the Congress.

Johnson's actions during the Tonkin Gulf controversy produced a temporary political triumph, as the Harris poll indicated. But the long-term consequences of the administration's mendacious performance during the affair weakened the President politically, for Congress and the public began to question Johnson's veracity after the facts of the Tonkin episode became public knowledge in the late 1960s. In the middle and later 1960s, Fulbright's realization that the administration had deceived him during the Tonkin crisis helped to galvanize the Senator into an adamant opposition against the Vietnam War. Fulbright began to investigate the Tonkin incidents in 1966, after his exhaustive analysis of the 1965 American intervention in the Dominican Republic demonstrated that the administration had justified its Dominican policy through false allegations of communist aggression.[75] He would then begin to suspect the administration's accusations of communist aggression in the Gulf of Tonkin had been similarly distorted. His investigations eventually revealed the executive's duplicity during the Tonkin controversy and facilitated the emergence of a "credibility gap" in Washington—a widespread belief that the Johnson administration perennially failed to present candid explanations for its policies.[76]

In 1966 Fulbright investigated the August 1964 incidents in the Gulf of Tonkin. Cyrus Vance, one of McNamara's chief assistants in the Defense Department, had explained shortly after the first North Vietnamese attack that "We assumed it was brought about by mistake," or by confusion created by the activity of South Vietnamese vessels in the Gulf.[77] Fulbright accepted this view of the first incident.

His doubts about the administration's account of the second attack began when Rear Admiral Arnold True advised Fulbright that the American destroyers probably could not have detected whether the North Vietnamese patrol boats were in attack formation at their reported distance on the night of the second incident.[78] A study by the Foreign Relations Committee staff in 1967 showed that the American destroyers were on an intelligence-gathering mission on August 4, not on a "routine patrol" as the administration claimed.[79]

The executive branch never adduced evidence to prove that the North Vietnamese gun boats committed hostile acts; in fact, the effects of stormy weather on the radar and sonar of the Maddox, as well as over-enthusiastic sonar men, may have accounted for the reports of torpedo attacks.[80] Fulbright received "top secret" briefings from the Pentagon in 1966 and 1967, at which the only "evidence" produced to substantiate the administration's version of the events in the Gulf was one machine-gun shell said to have been fired from a North Vietnamese gun boat.[81] He became convinced that the second alleged attack had never occurred, and that the administration had falsely represented the Tonkin incidents as acts of blatant aggression in order to generate public support for military action in Vietnam.[82]

In the later 1960s, the Tonkin Gulf controversy became a focal point of Fulbright's increasingly vitriolic critique of the Johnson administration's disingenuousness. Fulbright would also criticize the Gulf of Tonkin Resolution as presidential usurpation of Congress' constitutional authority to initiate war (the constitutional arguments are discussed in Chapter 7).

One should emphasize that Fulbright's public opposition to the American involvement in the Vietnam War began roughly 18 months after the August 1964 incidents in the Gulf of Tonkin. The obvious question arises: Why was Fulbright so dilatory in challenging the Vietnam policy? The administration's attempt to mislead the Senator concerning the alleged attacks on American destroyers is only a partial explanation, for Fulbright clearly erred in failing to hold extensive hearings to examine the President's account of the incidents as well as the basic policies in Vietnam. Fulbright's fear of the Goldwater threat, his conviction that China was an aggressive power, and his view of Johnson as a "moderate" were probably crucial in leading him to support American policy in Vietnam during 1964. His lack of knowledge about southeast Asia and his belief that the Foreign Relations Committee staff could not compete with the executive branch in the realm of intelligence-gathering also contributed to his tendency of relying upon the administration's judgment regarding American diplomacy in the Far East.

Fulbright's notion that President Johnson was restrained and prudent in foreign policy was not unusual in 1964; many politicians and foreign affairs analysts believed in Johnson's "moderation" at the time. Walter Lippmann concluded in an August 6, 1964, column in the *Washington Post* that the President intended to exercise American power "with measure, with humanity, and with restraint."[83] The vast majority of the Congress regarded Johnson's actions during the Gulf of Tonkin crisis as prudent. "At that time," Fulbright later admitted in discussing the Gulf of Tonkin Resolution's passage, "I was not in a suspicious frame of mind. I was afraid of Goldwater."[84] Thorough Foreign Relations Committee hearings on Vietnam might have embarrassed Johnson in the midst of the presidential campaign, with the Democratic National Convention scheduled to begin on August 24.[85]

Despite Fulbright's anxiety over the Goldwater candidacy, the Arkansas senator held a genuine conviction that the Chinese were in a belligerent and resentful mood in 1964 and 1965. In the spring of 1965, months after Goldwater had been decisively repudiated at the polls, Fulbright continued to refer to the Chinese as imperialistic in his private communications with the President.[86] Thus, Fulbright's fear that public criticism of Johnson's Asian policy would strengthen Goldwater and precipitate a recrudescence of extreme anticommunist sentiment in the United States was not the sole motive for his support of America's Far Eastern policy. He vaguely perceived the danger of alleged Chinese aggression as the threat of a conventional imperialism,[87] and he never endorsed Rusk's notion that the Chinese were plotting a uniquely nefarious conspiracy to banish freedom from the earth. Nevertheless, Fulbright's belief that the Chinese were resentful and hostile toward the West facilitated the administration's efforts to convince him that there was a coordinated North Vietnamese-Chinese campaign of aggression in southeast Asia. The senator would clarify his thinking about the Far East in 1965-1966, after the military escalation in Vietnam became the central controversy in American foreign policy.

In addition to the reasons cited above for Fulbright's support of the Johnson administration's Vietnam policy, the senator had maintained throughout the early 1960s that the

Presidency must be the dominant institution in the formulation of American diplomacy. According to Fulbright, members of Congress had to devote most of their time to the study of domestic affairs, and hence their "advise and consent" function must be secondary to the President's role in foreign policy.[88] In the early 1960s, Fulbright would recall several episodes of American diplomatic history in which the Senate obstructed the President's endeavors in foreign affairs, notably the defeat of the Versailles Treaty and American membership in the League of Nations, and the Senate's opposition to full American participation in a World Court.[89] He frequently cited the demagogical investigations of former Wisconsin Senator Joseph McCarthy as the classic example of the potentially pernicious consequences inherent in "senatorial excursions into foreign policy."[90] Whatever the merit or lack of merit in Fulbright's historical interpretations, it is clear his plea for a strong, activist President was the standard position of the intellectuals in the Democratic Party during 1964.[91] His favorable perception of the individual who held the Presidential Office in 1964 obviously influenced his theoretical justifications for an increasingly powerful Presidency.

Fulbright would later advocate a much more assertive role for the Senate in foreign policy. "The Senate," he wrote in *The Arrogance of Power*, "has the responsibility to review the conduct of foreign policy by the President and his advisers, to render advice whether it is solicited or not, and to grant or withhold consent to major acts of foreign policy."[92] The fiasco of American policy in southeast Asia was the catalyst that led Fulbright to reassess his perspective on the proper institutional balance between the executive and the legislative branches of government. In his 1972 work, *The Crippled Giant*, he confessed: "I myself was among those who took an ingenuous view of Presidential power until the disaster of Vietnam compelled me to reevaluate my position."[93]

Fulbright was basically an enthusiastic supporter of President Johnson in 1964, but several of his ideas in "Old Myths and New Realities" and in the Senate's Gulf of Tonkin debate foreshadowed his future dissent. In "Old Myths and New Realities" he had criticized the administration's belligerent anticommunist stance in its Cuban policy. His attack upon the myth that all communist states were relentlessly expansionist was not congenial with Johnson's Weltanschauung.

The March 25, 1964, Senate speech had not questioned American policy in Vietnam, but Fulbright's decision to publicly analyze the southeast Asian crisis was disturbing to the President, who did not desire a thorough public discussion of Vietnam during the election year.[94] Johnson's basic strategy was to delay the crucial decisions in Vietnam until after the election.[95] Thus, he merely expanded American assistance and increased the number of American advisers in South Vietnam, for he feared a direct, large-scale intervention would jeopardize his cherished domestic program and his prospects for being elected.[96] Johnson was pleased, of course, that Fulbright did not follow "Old Myths and New Realities" with an effort to generate a public dialogue on Asian policy in August 1964.[97]

In 1964 Fulbright was harboring private doubts about the American involvement in Vietnam.[98] He sent a newspaper photograph of South Vietnamese soldiers torturing a suspected communist guerrilla to Secretary of Defense Robert McNamara in May, writing: "I have been gravely concerned over the situation in Vietnam even without reports of tortures and indiscriminate bombing."[99] This letter did not have a significant impact on the thinking of the executive branch, and it was largely forgotten after the turmoil over the Gulf of

Tonkin crisis and the Presidential campaign. The President privately assured Fulbright that he would not "send in the Marines a la Goldwater," for his administration's Vietnam policy consisted only of "providing training and logistical support of South Vietnamese forces."[100] During the latter half of 1964 and early 1965, Fulbright came to believe that the danger of being confronted with a stark choice between immediate withdrawal and massive escalation in Vietnam was not imminent.[101] He believed that the President was sincerely interested in a political settlement of the war.[102]

In later years, Fulbright would regard his decisions not to hold comprehensive hearings on the Gulf of Tonkin Resolution in 1964 as the fundamental error in his responses to America's Vietnam policy from 1964 to 1966.[103] When the Foreign Relations Committee belatedly conducted its 1966 investigation of the Vietnam War, there were approximately 200,000 American soldiers in South Vietnam.[104] At that late date, the administration would successfully exert pressure on the Congress to continue the appropriations for the war by presenting the issue not as a choice of approving or disapproving of the Vietnam War, but of either supporting or abandoning "our boys out there on the firing line."[105] When the Congress allowed the alternatives to be defined in these terms, there could be little doubt of its vote for the appropriations in the late 1960s.

Despite his failure to foster a thorough public debate concerning Vietnam in August 1964, several of Fulbright's statements during the Senate deliberations over the Gulf of Tonkin Resolution adumbrated his later role as an adversary of U.S. policy in Asia. He clearly did not envisage the resolution as a mandate for an expanded war, since he constantly referred to Johnson's declarations that he sought to avoid a massive military intervention in Vietnam. (It should be acknowledged that the President was uncertain about the degree of military power that would be required to defeat the Vietnamese communists, although he always underestimated their will to fight for a unified Vietnam under Ho Chi Minh).[106] Fulbright also asserted that the President should closely consult with Congress regarding its Vietnam policy in the future.

Most importantly, Fulbright had unequivocally rejected the strategy of deploying American armies on the continent of Asia, for air and sea power were the foundations of America's strength.[107] His response to the administration's decisions during the Tonkin controversy was similar to that of his old friend Walter Lippmann. Lippmann endorsed the President's actions in the belief Johnson was signaling that American involvement in the Vietnam War would be limited to naval and air support for South Vietnam.[108] "The lasting significance of the episode," Lippmann predicted in August 1964, "is the demonstration that the United States can remain in Southeast Asia without being on the ground."[109] Fulbright concluded in the Senate's August 6, 1964, debate that he would "deplore" the landing of a large American army on the Asian mainland, for "Everyone I have heard has said that the last thing we want to do is become involved in a land war in Asia."[110]

In McNamara's analysis of the Gulf of Tonkin crisis in his memoirs, he agreed with some of Fulbright's arguments but denied that the administration had been dishonest during the Tonkin episode. McNamara adamantly repudiated the notion that the administration had deliberately provoked the attacks in order "to justify an escalation of the war and to obtain, under a subterfuge, congressional authority for that escalation." However, many of the statements McNamara made in his extended analysis of the crisis weakened or even contradicted his denial that the administration misled Congress. For example, consider his statement that he made an "honest" mistake in erroneously telling the Armed Services and Foreign Relations committees at the August 6 executive session that the *Maddox* commander did not know about the clandestine 34A operations. It is far worse for one branch to engage in deliberate deception of the other, and the former Secretary of Defense could be commended for his candid admission of error. On the other hand, the reality remains that McNamara—inadvertently or not—had misinformed the Congress. It was McNamara's responsibility to make sure that he did not mislead the senators, who needed reliable information from the executive, especially in the atmosphere of haste and crisis in which the administration enveloped the entire episode. Moreover, the former Secretary of Defense acknowledged that if the action in the Gulf of Tonkin had not taken place, the Gulf of Tonkin Resolution (or a similar resolution under a different name) would have been submitted to Congress within a matter of weeks. The administration had been concerned about delaying presentation of the southeast Asian resolution to Congress until after the Civil Rights Act of 1964 passed the Senate in September. Such a resolution would probably have passed, McNamara stated, "but the resolution would have faced far more extensive debate, and there would have been attempts to limit the President's authority."[110a]

More importantly, in one passage McNamara conceded that Fulbright had been misled by Johnson and Rusk, although the former Cabinet member stressed that he personally had not deceived Fulbright. This is a rather lame defense; if the President and the Secretary of State were not truthful to the Chairman of the Foreign Relations Committee, it is hardly exculpatory for the administration as a whole that the Secretary of Defense's comments were the product of honest error. As McNamara admitted:

> *Senator Fulbright, in time, came to feel that he had been misled—and indeed he had.* [emphasis added]. He had received definite assurances from Dean [Rusk] at the August 6, 1964, hearing (and I believe privately from LBJ as well) that the President would not use the vast power granted him without full congressional consultation.

McNamara also pointed out that at a later hearing in 1968 called to re-examine the entire episode, Fulbright had graciously absolved him of the charge of intentionally deceiving Congress.[110b]

In fairness to McNamara, there indeed was legitimate confusion about what happened regarding the alleged second attack on the American vessels. On a cloudy, moonless night in the Gulf beset with thunderstorms, visibility was extremely difficult. McNamara himself conceded that he was puzzled by the apparently irrational nature of North Vietnamese attacks on American destroyers, for such action carried the risk (from the North Vietnamese viewpoint) of American intervention in the war. Ironically, long before the Gulf incidents, McNamara and many other administration officials had recognized that the 34A operations were virtually worthless. The South Vietnamese agents who were sent into North Vietnam were either captured or killed, and the South Vietnamese patrol-boat attacks on North Vietnamese shore and island installations "amounted to little more than pinpricks," in McNamara's phrase. In retrospect, some of the arguments McNamara cited to prove that the attack had actually occurred seemed highly speculative. Admiral Sharp's conclusion that there had been an attack was cited as "evidence," but a commander's opinion by itself was not necessarily evidence of an attack; what were crucial were the facts upon which Sharp based his conclusion. McNamara cited the facts that a decoded North Vietnamese message apparently indicated that two of Hanoi's boats were sunk. It is unclear why the sinking of two North Vietnamese boats could be considered as conclusive evidence that the North Vietnamese had deliberately attacked American vessels again. The *Maddox* commander, Capt. John Herrick, sent an immediate "flash" message to Washington at the time that read: "Review of action makes many reported contacts and torpedoes fired appear doubtful. Freak weather effects on radar and overeager sonar men may have accounted for many reports. No actual visual sightings by *Maddox*." Other facts cited by McNamara were more plausible but not conclusive as supporting his position: one of the destroyers had observed PT boat cockpit lights, anti-aircraft batteries had fired on American planes flying over the area, and the *Turner Joy* had allegedly been illuminated by fire from automatic weapons (not the thunderstorms, in McNamara's view).[110c]

In a larger sense, McNamara's microscopic view of the details of the incident loses sight of the larger problem of the administration's lack of candor in 1964. The former Secretary of Defense rejected the notion that the second attack never occurred; but even writing at the late date of 1995 McNamara could not say for certain that the second alleged attack ever occurred, although he stated that it "appears probable." The details about the second alleged attack are not the crucial issues regarding the Gulf of Tonkin Resolution. More importantly, the President and Rusk not only deceived individual senators about their basic intentions, but Johnson's constant messages portraying himself as the moderate candidate of peace who would not send American boys to die in the jungles of Asia strengthened the views of Fulbright and others who could not believe that the Gulf of Tonkin Resolution would be used to justify a massive land war in Asia.

Some passages of McNamara's treatment revealed the natural tendency to defend the administration against charges of dishonesty. Yet, regarding the profound constitutional issues posed by the Gulf of Tonkin Resolution, McNamara delivered a resounding confirmation of the views that Fulbright had expounded upon for many years. The senator passed away a few weeks before McNamara's memoirs were published; undoubtedly, Fulbright would have been gratified by his former adversary's admissions. McNamara stressed that Congress recognized the vast grant of power in the language of the Resolution, although he agreed with a 1967 Foreign Relations Committee report concluding that Congress, under the Constitution, did not have the authority to abdicate its war power to the executive by a resolution. Moreover, Congress did not conceive of the Resolution as a declaration of war:

> [Congress] did not intend it to be used, as it was, as authorization for an enormous expansion of U.S. forces in Vietnam—from 16,000 military advisers to 550,000 combat troops. Securing a declaration of war and specific authorization for the introduction of combat forces in subsequent years might well have been impossible; not seeking it was clearly wrong...
>
> Was the Johnson administration justified in basing its subsequent military actions in Vietnam—including an enormous expansion of force levels—on the Tonkin Gulf Resolution?

Answer: Absolutely not. Although the resolution granted sufficiently broad author-ity to support the escalation that followed, as I have said, Congress never intend-ed it to be used as a basis for such action, and still less did the country see it so.[110d]

A quarter of a century later in December 1990, McNamara would testify before the Foreign Relations Committee about the possible use of American forces in the Persian Gulf War. Secretary of Defense Richard Cheney had previously testified that President George Bush had the authority to commit large-scale American forces (ultimately there would be 500,000 American troops in the war) to combat in the Persian Gulf region under his powers as Commander in Chief. Senator Paul Sarbanes (D-Md.) asked McNamara for an assessment of Cheney's position. McNamara replied that the senator had asked the wrong question, for the issue was the fundamental one: "should a President take our nation to war (other than to repel an attack on our shores) without popular consent as voiced by Congress?" The former Secretary of Defense emphatically stated that a President should not do so, and McNamara praised Bush's handling of the debate in 1990: "Before President Bush began combat operations against Iraq, he sought–and obtained–Congress' support (as well as that of the UN Security Council). President Bush was right. President Johnson, and those of us who served with him, were wrong."[110e] The Iraqi aggression against Kuwait, of course, differed sharply from Vietnam in hav-ing been a clearcut invasion of one nation by another; aside from the separate issue of whether mistakes in the Bush administration's policy contributed to the problems that led to the Iraqi attack on Kuwait, it is clear that President Bush's actions in seeking Congress' support and the UN Security Council's support were vast improvements over the Johnson administration's fail-ure to obtain real, fully informed support from Congress and the UN. Clearly, at least from the standpoint of the imperative of gaining popular and congressional support for going to war, McNamara had candidly and correctly admitted that the Johnson administration was wrong.

During the fall of 1964, Fulbright was predominantly concerned with his appeal to the nation to reject Goldwater's vague proposals for gaining a "total victory" in the Cold War. He frequently delivered speeches criticizing Goldwater's militant anti-Soviet attitude. As the histo-rian Lloyd Ambrosius has observed, Goldwater failed to propose a peaceful, positive program for winning a "total victory" in the Cold War. Throughout the early 1960s, Goldwater's sugges-tions for a victorious Cold Warrior policy were almost entirely negative: the United States should withdraw diplomatic recognition from the Soviet Union, avoid negotiations with com-munist states, eschew disarmament, abolish the cultural exchange program with the Soviet Union, and terminate all trade with communist nations. The Arizona senator's only positive, nonmilitary proposal was his plea that the administration should announce to the world America's determination to achieve a total victory over communism. But such an announce-ment would have been a statement of purpose rather than a program for achieving the goal.[111] Yet Goldwater still promised a "total victory" without nuclear war.

In responding to Goldwater's foreign policy positions during the early 1960s, Fulbright stressed the absence of specific methods in Goldwater's recommendations:

It would be beneficial and instructive, I think, if those who call for total victory would spell out for us precisely how it might be achieved . . . Is it to be won by nuclear war—a war which at the very least would cost the lives of tens of millions of people on both sides, devastate most or all of our great cities, and mutilate or utterly destroy a civilization which ha been built over thousands of years?[112]

In contrast to Goldwater's opposition to negotiations with the communist world, Fulbright enthusiastically supported such agreements as the Test Ban Treaty. The Foreign Relations chairman endorsed increased trade and expansion of the cultural exchange program with the Soviet Union as policies that could reduce the tensions of the Cold War and introduce "a degree of normalcy into our relations with the Soviet Union and other communist countries." On September 8, 1964, Fulbright delivered a Senate speech repudiating the Arizona senator's belief in American omnipotence:

> The senator's assumption that the Russians can be counted on to accept humiliation rather than war is a dangerous delusion. It is based on the fantastic premise that the American people will prefer the destruction of their cities and perhaps a hundred million deaths to an adjustment of interests with the communists, but that at the same time, the Russians will surrender to an ultimatum rather than accept the risk of nuclear war. . . . The simple point which Goldwater Republicans seem unable to grasp is that no nation can be expected to acquiesce peacefully in its own 'total defeat.'[113]

Fulbright was convinced that the President agreed with him on the need to ameliorate Soviet-American relations, as well as on the necessity of avoiding a military entanglement in the jungles of Indochina. In Fulbright's opinion, only the Goldwater movement and a minority of right-wing Democrats advocated escalation of the American commitment to South Vietnam. Decades later, it would become painfully clear that the foreign policy moderates had in reality lost the debate over Vietnam in 1964, for LBJ was bent upon gaining a victory. The chairman of the Senate Foreign Relations Committee would not have believed that President Lyndon Johnson would begin to implement many of Goldwater's proposals for the Vietnam War within a year after the Gulf of Tonkin crisis.

III. THE DECLINE OF CONFIDENCE
IN JOHNSON'S LEADERSHIP

In the final weeks of 1964 Senator Fulbright was optimistic about the prospects for ameliorating America's relations with the communist nations of the world. The senator's old antagonist and the principal spokesman for the radical right in the United States, Barry Goldwater, had been repudiated at the polls in November. The Republican won only 52 electoral votes, as opposed to 486 electoral votes for the Democratic ticket. Fulbright had repeatedly denounced Goldwater for proposing a radical policy that envisaged the total destruction of communism and the imposition of American ideas of democracy upon the entire world. In contrast, President Johnson proposed a "conservative policy" of preventing communist expansion while negotiating limited agreements with communist nations that would reduce the danger of nuclear war. Fulbright conducted an unusually strenuous campaign of speaking engagements during the Presidential race, and competent observers of Arkansas politics attributed Johnson's victory in Arkansas primarily to Fulbright's vigorous efforts on the President's behalf.[1]

The senator was exuberant after the electoral triumph of the politician he had praised so profusely in his speech at the 1964 Democratic Convention:

> The same understanding of human nature which enabled him to lead the Senate so effectively during a difficult period in our history will enable him to find a way to resolve differences which exist among nations. I commend Lyndon Johnson to this convention and to all our people as a man of understanding with the wisdom to use the great power of our nation in the cause of peace.[2]

Given the later animosities that developed between President Johnson and Fulbright, it is difficult to recall the enthusiasm with which virtually all forces within the Democratic Party viewed the Johnson administration in 1964. The progressive forces in the Party believed that the new President would combine his political skills with the intellectual brilliance of the Kennedy advisers, and the result would be a historic era of reform. In contrast to the later hostility, depression and suspicion Johnson demonstrated in his Presidency as the Vietnam conflict escalated, the new President was often amiable in his relationships with people in the early days of his administration. The Fulbright and Johnson families were on the most cordial of terms. Moreover, in contrast to his later strained relations with the press, the President enjoyed a heightened reputation among many journalists, who regarded him as the voice of moderation in comparison to the dangerous radical, Goldwater. And the

President often turned on his Texas charm in those days. To cite one amusing example, at the 1964 American Society of Newspaper Editors convention in Washington, Mrs. James O. Powell, wife of the *Arkansas Gazette* editor, exclaimed to the President as the editors were leaving the White House that she had not been able to dance with him at the ball that evening. LBJ, ever the can-do President, replied, "Well, we'll dance right here, Mrs. Powell." And so, without music, the President and the Little Rock editor's wife twirled around the foyer, to the delight of the other editors. The Texan's gallantry was reported on the front page of the *Washington Post* society section the next day. Mrs. Powell thus won the distinction of being the only member of the Powell family ever to have been featured on the *Post* society page or to have danced with a President, a family record that still stands. The Powells and the Fulbrights agreed that Johnson could become a great President. Those days appear in retrospect almost as in a fairy tale; a few years later, the *Gazette* (on the smaller stage of Arkansas) would follow Fulbright's lead in bitterly criticizing Johnson for allowing America's lost crusade in Indochina to devour the promise of the Great Society.

Fulbright continued to support the President despite the fact that he was beginning to have private anxieties over the administration's Vietnam policy. During 1964 Fulbright discussed the Vietnamese dilemma with Walter Lippmann, who reinforced the senator's doubts concerning the American military involvement in southeast Asia.[3] But Fulbright's doubts were mitigated by his conviction that Johnson would give a fair private hearing to dissenting views concerning Vietnam. Fulbright's friendship with Johnson strengthened his belief that the President would carefully listen to his ideas. A telegram the senator and Mrs. Fulbright sent to the Johnsons immediately after the election revealed the cordial personal relationship between the two men and their families: "What a team you are!! Heartfelt congratulations to both of you from both of us, and all best wishes for happy and fulfilling years ahead."[4] Many years later, Fulbright would admit that he had been dilatory in challenging the military escalation policy "primarily because I misjudged the intentions of President Johnson and because I was not informed about Vietnam and China," but he added, "my friendship with the President also contributed to my reluctance to take issue with him publicly."[5] The warm Fulbright-Johnson relationship in 1964 was perhaps an unfortunate example of the tendency David Halberstam has decried, whereby "key congressmen like William Fulbright, rather than playing their true constitutional roles, were often handled as friends of the White House family."[6] The senator thought the President was sincerely interested in achieving a political settlement in Vietnam, and that by refraining from public criticism of Johnson's policies he could retain the ability to exert a powerful influence on the administration privately.

As Fulbright later admitted, the belief that he was privately persuading the President of the futility in expanding the military commitment to South Vietnam was an "illusion."[7] In *The Arrogance of Power* Fulbright would excoriate the policy of the executive branch to notify Congress of decisions that had already been made rather than genuinely consulting it.[8] This policy continued in 1964-1965, though he was not fully cognizant of it at the time. A memorandum in the Pentagon Papers, written by Assistant Secretary of State for East Asian and Pacific Affairs William Bundy in November 1964, exemplified the administration's attitude toward Congress as one among many external "audiences" to be manipulated in the desired direction (the news media, the American public, and international opinion were the other principal audiences).[9] Bundy wrote that Fulbright and other "key leaders" of Congress should be consulted, but "perhaps only by notification if we do a reprisal against another Bien Hoa."[10] The assistant secretary argued that guerrilla assaults, such as the recent Bien Hoa attack, might be repeated at any time and would "give us a good springboard for any decision for stronger action."[11] The memorandum listed Fulbright as one of 15 Congressional leaders who were to be notified of "stronger action" in Vietnam, but it did not assign any particular importance to the chairman of the Senate Foreign Relations Committee.[12]

Fulbright was not aware of the cavalier attitude represented by the Bundy memorandum in late 1964. During November 1964 he had rarely held more confidence in an administration. Shortly after the election he departed for Yugoslavia to confer with Marshal Josip Broz Tito and preside over the signing of an agreement inaugurating Yugoslavia's participation in the Fulbright fellowship program.[13] This assignment was especially rewarding for Fulbright, not only because he regarded the student exchange program as the greatest achievement of his career and was always pleased by its expansion, but also because Yugoslavia was the first communist nation to join the program.[14] In Fulbright's view, the new exchange agreement was a classic example of the Johnson administration's "conservative" policy of gradually reducing tensions with the communist world and eroding the ideological prejudices against communism that had plagued American diplomacy since the 1940s.[15] He was highly impressed with Tito after his conversation with the Yugoslav leader.[16] Fulbright's favorable perception of Yugoslavia subtly and significantly influenced his thinking on the dilemma in southeast Asia. If Yugoslavia was a communist state that was not aligned with the Soviet bloc and pursued policies often friendly and seldom harmful to U.S. interests, then he began to speculate that a communist but independent and nationalistic Vietnam would serve American interests in southeast Asia far better than a corrupt, unstable regime dependent on American manpower and financial aid.[17] He persistently emphasized his ideas concerning the value of a "Titoist buffer state" for Vietnam in conversations with Johnson during the months after his visit to Yugoslavia.[18]

The senator delivered a speech at Southern Methodist University a few weeks after he returned to the United States in which he advocated the "building of bridges to the communist world."[19] Fulbright observed that there was a general tendency among communist countries toward more liberal domestic policies and less aggressive foreign policies. Yugoslavia had demonstrated the most outstanding progress by adopting a neutralist diplomacy and permitting certain liberties for its people. The United States should encourage the independence of Tito's government by engaging in cordial political relations and signing educational exchange agreements with the Yugoslavs, and by according them most-favored-nation treatment in trade.[20] Similarly, Fulbright argued that Brezhnev and Kosygin were basically pursuing a prudent strategy abroad and had not resurrected the Stalinist apparatus of police terror at home.[21] This increasing moderation of Soviet policy in the preceding decade should be rewarded by arranging limited accommodations that lessened East-West hostility and thus reduced the danger of war. Hence, the United States should continue to negotiate constructive agreements with the U.S.S.R. such as the test ban treaty, the prohibition against placing nuclear weapons in orbit around the earth, and the sale of surplus American wheat to the Russians.[22]

The fundamental assumption of the Southern Methodist address seemed to be that change was virtually an inalterable law of human existence that did not cease to exist when nations became communist. Although Fulbright was disturbed by China's "ideological fanaticism," he believed that Peking might eventually follow the progressive evolutionary pattern of the Soviet Union and assume a more moderate attitude toward the West.[23] He approvingly quoted a recent article by George Kennan in which the distinguished diplomat had stated that Americans should not interpret the current Chinese antipathy toward the United States as absolute and permanent. Kennan wrote:

> Neither these men in Peiping nor the regime over which they preside are immune to the laws of change that govern all human society, if only because no single gen- eration, anywhere, ever sees things exactly the same as the generation that went 10 years before it.[24]

Fulbright concluded that China's admission to the United Nations was inevitable.[25]

The passage quoting Kennan was the only point in the speech in which Fulbright indi- rectly questioned the view of China as an unchanging and malevolent aggressor. Despite the fact that he thought China's admission into the U.N. was inevitable, he said the United States would have to oppose its entry if that occurred in the near future; the Chinese should not be extended diplomatic recognition or allowed into the U.N. because of their "aggres- sion and subversion."[26] Fulbright referred to Chinese aggression frequently in the address, but he failed to cite any specific instances of this alleged Chinese imperialism. The lack of evidence to support his contentions concerning China was in sharp contrast to the passages where he enumerated specific examples of American cooperation with Yugoslavia and the Soviet Union to buttress his arguments for improving relations with those nations. Apparently Fulbright considered Chinese imperialism in the Far East as so flagrant and obvious that it was unnecessary to adduce evidence to prove Peking's aggression. He was unable to cite any evidence to demonstrate China's alleged imperialism simply because China was not an expansionist power, as he eventually realized.

Fulbright entirely avoided any discussion of the controversy over Vietnam. The senator as well as several historians later felt that his inaccurate perspective toward China weakened the logic of his critique of the American involvement in Vietnam.[27] Since he accepted the prevailing contemporary view of China as a relentlessly expansionist power, President Johnson could believe in late 1964 and early 1965 that Fulbright agreed with Rusk, McNamara, and the other major advisers on the basic necessity of containing China, and differed only in thinking the existence of a noncommunist South Vietnam was peripheral to American interests.[28] The President would decide that Fulbright was wrong, that "the experts knew the facts" about South Vietnam's alleged crucial relevance to American secu- rity.[29]

The December 1964 speech at SMU, entitled "Bridges East and West," was the subject of a brief set of remarks delivered on the Senate floor by Senator Frank Church of Idaho on January 6, 1965. Senator Church placed "Bridges East and West" in the *Congressional Record* declaring, "I have never read a more impressive statement outlining the goals, methods, and policies our Government should have in mind in our dealings with the Communist world."[30] Church was particularly complimentary of Fulbright's analysis of the communist nations as representing a panoply of change and limited progress rather than a monolithic and belligerent bloc. The Idaho senator also praised Fulbright for his belief in the futility of total military victory as a panacea for all American difficulties in the international arena.[31] Church did not comment upon the section of the address dealing with China.

A week after Frank Church's tribute to "Bridges East and West" Fulbright identified himself with a mild dissent against Johnson's Vietnam policy by placing in the *Congressional Record* a *Ramparts* magazine interview with Church that Fulbright described as "an excellent statement with regard to what our policy should be in southeast Asia."[32] Church strongly opposed escalation and advocated the neutralization of southeast Asia, although he did not endorse an immediate American withdrawal.[33] He speculated that the United Nations might be able to help maintain the territorial integrity of the states in the region. According to Church, the conflict in South Vietnam was a civil war, basically an indigenous revolution against the existing government that only the people of South Vietnam could suppress. America could not "win their war for them," especially in a country where most of the populace associated all Western nations with imperialism.[34] The South Vietnamese did not recognize the distinction between white soldiers in French uniforms fighting to preserve a French colony and white soldiers in American uniforms fighting to arrest communist expansion.[35] In Church's opinion, the people of Vietnam were not confronted with a choice between the tyranny of the North and the freedom of the South, because South Vietnam was a military despotism just as North Vietnam was. Finally, he asserted that if the military situation in the South drastically deteriorated, the United States should find the maturity to accept the unpleasant reality of a communist Vietnam and eventually withdraw.[36]

Fulbright's insertion of the *Ramparts* interview with Church into the *Congressional Record*, along with several editorials approving of Church's position, was a significant departure from his complete avoidance of the Vietnam issue in the December address at Southern Methodist University. If he was determined by early 1965 to refrain from direct public criticism of the Johnson administration, he was equally determined to publicly offer alternatives to Johnson's policies. Fulbright's alternative suggestions would lead him to assume the precarious position in early 1965 of professing support for President Johnson while endorsing proposals that contradicted the administration's view of the war in Vietnam. His approbation of Church's perspective on the war in the *Ramparts* article may have been the first of these contradictions, since Johnson and Rusk obviously did not agree with such ideas as Church's assertion that the Vietnamese conflict was a civil war.[37]

It should be acknowledged, however, that Fulbright's endorsement of Church's *Ramparts* article was only a mild and oblique questioning of America's course in Vietnam, for Church avoided mentioning Johnson or the presidential advisers and made several comments favorable to the administration's position. Dean Rusk certainly would not have argued with Church's claim that the United States must continue its massive military and economic assistance to Saigon and that the interdiction of the Ho Chi Minh trail in Laos would substantially alleviate the Vietcong's pressure on the South Vietnamese army.[38] Fulbright did not elaborate upon his opinions concerning Laos or aid levels to Saigon, his only remark on Church's article being the general observation that it was excellent. Fulbright's attitude was indirectly expressed by the editorials he placed in the Record, which extolled Church's neutralization proposal and his warnings about the folly of escalating the direct American military involvement in Vietnam.[39]

During January Fulbright began to clarify his thinking about American policy in Vietnam. On January 14, he revealed considerable uncertainty in his letter to an acquaintance, stating, "Like everyone else I am more than a little disturbed by the situation in southeast Asia, and more than a little perplexed as to what our proper course should be."[40] Again, in correspondence a few days later with Frank Stanton, president of the Columbia Broadcasting System, he was unsure: "I have just read the report [a transcript of a CBS documentary on Vietnam]. A classic dilemma if I ever saw one. I confess I have not been able to arrive at a conclusion."[41] By late January Fulbright was becoming more decisive, stating in a letter to a Little Rock constituent, "I agree with your son's idea that we are trying to do the right thing, but the difficulties seem to be beyond our capacity to handle." The letter ended with words that adumbrated his future dissent: "I have been perfectly willing to go along with the efforts of the past, but I am not willing to enlarge this into a full-scale war."[42]

Fulbright's increasing determination in late January to oppose expansion of American military operations in Indochina was expressed publicly as well as in private correspondence. At the end of January a *Time* newsman asked Fulbright a hypothetical question concerning what he would do if given the choice of escalation or withdrawal from Vietnam through negotiations.[43] Fulbright replied that he would withdraw.[44] He firmly rejected arguments in favor of escalation through bombing, contending in the *Time* interview that "You can't selectively do a little bombing."[45] In his opinion, once the bombings began it would be impossible to predict how massive the involvement might become, because "you can't see down the road far enough."[46] The senator persisted in his belief, however, that the time of the ultimate decision on America's proper strategy in southeast Asia was not imminent.[47]

Late January and early February actually constituted one of the crucial junctures in the administration's deliberations on Vietnam, although in public the President and his aides consistently and disingenuously denied that any major changes were being contemplated.[48] On January 27 Secretary McNamara and Special Assistant for National Security Affairs McGeorge Bundy delivered a memorandum to President Johnson that declared that the fundamental decision could not be delayed any longer and an expanded use of force in Vietnam was necessary.[49] Bundy and McNamara suggested that Bundy should travel to Saigon in early February for an investigation "on the ground." The skeptics within the bureaucracy associated with Under Secretary of State George Ball, who knew of Bundy's inclination to use force, were pessimistic about the prospects for his mission's impact upon American policy.[50] Fulbright was not thoroughly informed of the top-level discussions in the administration, although Johnson attempted to reassure him by arranging for Dean Rusk to have frequent breakfasts with the senator. The secretary would report to the President that Fulbright's views remained unchanged by these meetings, whereupon Johnson would prescribe more Rusk-Fulbright breakfasts, which would have similar results.[51] Fulbright was still able to meet with Johnson personally, but their conversations were often dominated by Johnson's monologues on his valiant efforts to resist extremist pressures for escalation.[52]

The euphoria Fulbright had experienced after the electoral triumph in November had not dissipated by January, despite his concerns over Vietnam and his limited consultations with the President. His enthusiasm for Johnson's domestic legislation was one of the important reasons for his continuing favorable assessment of the President. Fulbright argued forcefully in a January 16 speech at Miami that the United States should renounce its self-appointed role as global anticommunist gendarme and instead direct its talents and economic resources toward solving domestic problems.[53] The money that had been devoted to the military demands of the Cold War in the previous two decades could have been used to build myriad schools, housing facilities, and hospitals and to combat poverty at home.[54] Fulbright strongly implied that the Johnson administration would at last reverse the American obsession with opposing communism and channel the nation's energies into domestic affairs.[55] The senator described Johnson's proposal for federal aid to education, which was presented to Congress a few days before Fulbright's January 16 address, as "a work of high political creativity," and he was confident that "the American people and their leaders are prepared to launch new and creative programs in various areas of our domestic life."[56]

Fulbright was a staunch supporter of most of LBJ's Great Society reforms, despite the political difficulties that position engendered among the rigid conservative bloc. The Arkansan praised the Office of Economic Opportunity (OEO), a domestic peace corps called Volunteers in Service to America (VISTA), Head Start and the other initiatives in Johnson's War on Poverty. In a Senate speech in 1964, he informed his colleagues that the Economic Opportunity Act "is designed to help those people–and particularly those children–who did not have the wisdom and foresight to be born of the right parents or in the right place." Fulbright cited dismal statistics in Arkansas in illustrating the dimensions of poverty: 60 percent of Arkansas families had incomes under $4,000, and 14 percent had to struggle through with less than $1,000 a year. Fulbright was critical of Johnson for expanding the budget of the National Aeronautics and Space Administration in the quest to put a man on the moon by the end of the decade; he thought the moon race with the Russians smacked of jingoism and there were far more pressing needs on earth. The billions that were devoted to the space program could have been spent far more profitably, he felt, on federal aid to education, the exchange program, or other more practical and constructive policies. Overall, however, he was deeply enthusiastic about the conduct of the Johnson administration in its early period. In 1965 Fulbright backed the Public Works and Economic Development Act, providing funding for water and sewer projects, roads, and industrial parks in underdeveloped areas.[56a]

Even in the bitterly controversial realm of civil rights, Fulbright was impressed with Johnson's leadership. Lee Williams and other members of his staff held progressive views on racial issues and encouraged him to change his position on civil rights issues. A series of forces bestowed powerful momentum upon the civil rights movement: Kennedy's strong support for civil rights legislation in 1963, the President's assassination, the revulsion against racial extremists, President Johnson's political ingenuity, and the ability and eloquence of Martin Luther King and other prominent leaders in the movement of that day. The Civil Rights Act of 1964 prohibited discrimination in hotels, restaurants, theaters, unions, employment, and voting. The act authorized the Attorney General to institute suits on behalf of aggrieved people in desegregation or discrimination cases and allowed federal agencies to stop funds for projects that allowed racially discriminatory practices. In June, 1964, the Senate took the unprecedented step of voting for cloture on the bill. Fulbright's vote was not needed for cloture, but he seriously considered voting for the bill. Ultimately, he decided to deliver statements to the South appealing for acceptance of the law, but voted against it. After its passage, he implored Southerners to remain calm and assured them that President Johnson would administer the law fairly and with an understanding of local opinions. Johnson wrote the senator praising him for helping to prevent a fratricidal quarrel within the Senate and for asking his colleagues and constituents to accept the act. During debate on the bill, Fulbright's comments had been restrained; he pointed out the progress made in desegregation in Arkansas, since 123 blacks now attended integrated schools. Of course, this was only a tiny amount of desegregation. Moreover, Fulbright's compromise on civil rights legislation was more difficult to defend at the late date of 1964 than it had been in 1960 or 1957, since the growing strength of moderates, politically active blacks, and the state's general revulsion against the excesses of the earlier era of massive resistance had now modified the political equation. Many prominent Arkansans were disgusted by the humiliating publicity of the Central High crisis, and sought to move from the fixation on racial issues to more constructive matters such as educational and economic development. By 1966, the political climate would change enough for the progressive Republican, Winthrop Rockefeller, to win the gubernatorial race. It is clear that his vote was not needed for passage, with the act passing easily, 73 to 27. In concluding that he had more to fear from the right and once again voting with the segregationists despite the reform movement so powerfully assisted by the Johnson administration, Fulbright inflicted another black mark upon his already tarnished civil rights record.

The theme of Fulbright's January 16, 1965, speech urging a renewed focus on domestic reform was almost identical with the central idea of Walter Lippmann's February 2 column in the *Washington Post*. It was not surprising that the opinions of Fulbright and Lippmann were similar, for Fulbright had been a confidant of Lippmann for many years and the two men were communicating frequently in early 1965.[57] The Lippmann article was even more optimistic than the Fulbright address about the prospects for diverting American energies from the Cold War to domestic affairs under the Johnson administration.[58] Analyzing in retrospect the administration's performance in January, Lippmann wrote that for the first time in the quarter of a century since World War II began, the fundamental attention of the President of the United States was focused not upon the dangers abroad but upon the nation's problems at home.[59] The columnist affirmed that "the state of the world today permits and justifies the preoccupation with American domestic affairs."[60] He eulogized Johnson's domestic proposals, writing, "we have rarely, if ever, seen at the beginning of a new administration such a coherent program, such insight and resourcefulness."[61]

It would be facile to condemn Fulbright's January 16 speech and Lippmann's February 2 column as exercises in wishful thinking; but it should be considered that in earlier articles Lippmann had warned against foreign entanglements that could destroy Johnson's reforms,[62] and Fulbright's *Time* interview had delineated his dissent against bombing. Moreover, the administration's plans for escalation in Vietnam were enveloped in secrecy, while the Johnson agenda for domestic reform was attracting an enormous amount of generally favorable publicity in Washington.[63] It seemed unlikely that a Great Society and a war in southeast Asia could be launched simultaneously. And it had only been a few months earlier that Johnson had dramatically portrayed himself as the "man of peace" in the 1964 campaign, proclaiming his absolute refusal to send American boys 10,000 miles away from home to fight a war Asian boys must fight for themselves. Both the renowned *Washington Post* columnist and the chairman of the Senate Foreign Relations Committee had been assured in conversations at the White House that the Vietnamese conflict would not be expanded.[64] Thus, at the end of January Walter Lippmann and J. William Fulbright imagined broad vistas of time looming ahead, time for the Great Society of Lyndon Johnson to arise and flourish, and time for the gradual termination of America's anticommunist crusade.

The increasing campaign of aerial devastation in February dealt a severe blow to the hopes of those who had counseled restraint in Vietnam. The administration emphatically denied that the February bombings of North Vietnam represented a major policy change, justifying the air raids as retaliatory measures for the February 6 Vietcong attacks on the American army barracks at Pleiku in which nine Americans were killed.[65] In reality, the initiation of regular bombing attacks advanced well beyond the limited reprisal strikes during the Tonkin Gulf crisis of August 1964.[66] As the historian George C. Herring has observed, the Pleiku incident provided the auspicious occasion, not the cause, for implementing the program of air strikes that many administration officials had been advocating for more than two months.[67] Pleiku was not unprecedented. There had been a Vietcong assault on the Bien Hoa air base in November that had resulted in four American deaths; again in December the Vietcong exploded a bomb at Saigon's Brink Hotel, killing two Americans. Yet no retaliatory actions had been taken in late 1964, primarily because of fears of provoking a Vietcong offensive against the rapidly weakening South Vietnamese regime.[68] By the end of January there was an overwhelming consensus within the bureaucracy that the Saigon government was so feeble that only bombing would revive it.[69] William Bundy's November memorandum on Congressional opinion had maintained that "Bien Hoa" might be repeated at any time and would "give us a good springboard for any decision for stronger action."[70] McGeorge Bundy expressed this attitude more icily in February when he averred, "Pleikus are like streetcars" (i.e., one comes along every ten minutes.)[71]

McGeorge Bundy returned from Saigon in February recommending a policy of steadily intensifying air attacks. Fulbright was not invited to the crucial National Security Council meetings on Vietnam escalation in early 1965.[72] Senator Mike Mansfield of Montana was asked to attend the NSC conference immediately after the Pleiku attack, however, and Mansfield's views were quite similar to those of Fulbright.[73] Years later Fulbright would remember Mansfield as the one senator with whom he was cooperating most closely in his efforts to prevent a disastrous enlargement of the southeast Asian conflict.[74] At the NSC meeting after Pleiku Mansfield stated his concern that the retaliatory policy might lead to Chinese intervention, or that it would eventually cause China and Russia to draw closer together and perhaps heal the growing Sino-Soviet split.[75] He offered the general suggestion that the United States should begin negotiations on the Vietnamese controversy. President Johnson responded that we had disregarded provocation in the past but now communist aggression had become too outrageous, and he was certainly not going to be the President to preside over another "Munich."[76]

Mansfield had been the only critic of the retaliatory policy at the NSC meeting, and Fulbright and Mansfield were the only opponents of bombing when the Congressional leaders were summoned to the White House to be informed of the President's decision.[77] McNamara and other principal administration officials demonstrated to the Congressional leadership why the sole reasonable course of action was to expand the air war.[78] During these February meetings Johnson would first ask for the opinions of the leaders whose support could be expected, such as Everett Dirksen and John McCormack.[79]

Johnson would ask Fulbright and Mansfield for their views last, after a strong majority seemed to be coalescing in support of the President's position.[80] Fulbright repeated the arguments he and Mansfield had been presenting to Johnson in early 1965, that escalation of the bombing would entrap the United States in a quagmire everyone wanted to avoid.[81] The dissent of the Foreign Relations Committee chairman at that time was largely based upon an instinctive reaction against the excessive use of violence in foreign policy, for he had few facts and figures with which to counter the plethora of intelligence reports and statistics resonating through the phrases of Robert McNamara in the White House conferences of February.[82]

Fulbright did not profess to have a comprehensive knowledge about Vietnam in early 1965. He had always been primarily knowledgeable about European and to a lesser extent Latin American affairs.[83] Throughout 1965 he frequently engaged in lengthy conversations with journalists who had been to Vietnam, and he began to read extensively in the writings of Jean Lacouture, Han Suyin, Philippe Devillers, Bernard Fall, and other experts on China and southeast Asia.[84] Later in the year the Foreign Relations Committee attempted to develop additional independent sources of information on the war by employing two former members of the Foreign Service to travel to Vietnam and send back reports to the committee.[85] By December many competent observers of the Senate felt there were few senators who had so rigorously studied the history, culture, and politics of southeast Asia as had Fulbright in the course of the year.[86] But it would require considerable time for the senator to educate himself thoroughly about a region of the world he had considered peripheral to American interests. In early 1965 his opposition to expanding the war was founded on his suspicion of zealous anticommunism and his reluctance to use force, precepts that were derived from his 22 years' experience in Congress of analyzing American foreign policy.

On February 12, 1965, Fulbright once again attempted to offer an alternative to the retaliatory policy by endorsing United Nations Secretary General U Thant's proposal for negotiations. The senator asserted that "I think it is always wiser to talk than to fight when you can get the parties together."[87] On February 12 U Thant proposed that both sides enter into discussions aimed at preparing the ground for "formal negotiations for a settlement."[88] The Secretary General's plea was essentially a reiteration of his July 1964 proposal to reconvene the 1954 Geneva Conference on southeast Asia.[89] U Thant did not try to summon the Security Council because of "its past history and the fact that some of the principal parties are not represented in the U.N.," presumably referring (according to a *Washington Post* report) to the facts that North Vietnam and China were not members of the U.N. and the Security Council meetings after the Tonkin crisis had not led to a diplomatic conference.[90] In applauding U Thant's plan of reconvening the 1954 Geneva Conference Fulbright observed that it was quite proper for the Secretary General of the U.N. to urge that negotiations be initiated immediately.[91] The administration's response was diametrically opposed to Fulbright's suggestion.[92] Both the State Department and the White House refused to com-

ment on U Thant's specific proposal, although they definitively rejected the idea that negotiations were in order at that moment.

During the weeks following Fulbright's approval of the February 12 U Thant recommendations, important columnists began referring to him as one of the Senate's prominent
critics of military escalation in southeast Asia. On February 21 Drew Pearson stated that
Johnson's Vietnam policy was receiving panegyrics from former critics of the President such
as Richard Nixon, Barry Goldwater, and Everett Dirksen, while Democratic leaders "Mike
Mansfield of Montana, Frank Church of Idaho, and even Bill Fulbright of Arkansas are
either openly critical or privately unhappy."[93] Pearson did not elaborate upon his opinions
concerning the substance of Fulbright's criticism.

A column by John Chamberlain in the *Washington Post* was explicit in its treatment of
Fulbright's critique of American involvement in Vietnam. In an admiring article on Senator
Thomas Dodd of Connecticut entitled "The Churchillian Voice of Tom Dodd," Chamberlain
maintained that in the early days of the Cold War the Truman Doctrine had committed the
United States to protect small nations being threatened by Communist aggression. Tom
Dodd was courageously upholding the Truman Doctrine tradition by defending the
Doctrine's application to South Vietnam, the columnist opined, but Chamberlain lamented
that "Morse of Oregon, Gruening of Alaska, Fulbright of Arkansas have all sidled away from
the Truman Doctrine tradition."[94] There was a distinct implication in John Chamberlain's
column that if Tom Dodd was the heir of Winston Churchill and valiant resistance to aggression, then Morse, Gruening, and Fulbright were the legatees of Neville Chamberlain and
"appeasement."

Pro-administration journalists and several Republican senators, especially Everett
Dirksen, were criticizing Fulbright in early 1965 for hampering Johnson's foreign policy by
advocating cooperation with the communist world.[95] The Foreign Relations Committee
chairman eschewed direct criticism of Johnson, despite the fact that his endorsement of U
Thant's proposal and his public skepticism in January on the efficacy of bombing had contradicted the administration's views of the war. He still clung to the illusion that he might
privately dissuade the President from expansion of the conflict, and he regarded his public
professions of loyalty to the administration as strengthening his private influence at the
White House.[96]

In conversations with the President during March and April he again stressed the value
of a Titoist buffer state for Vietnam. A March 3 Fulbright letter to Johnson revealed that the
senator's favorable perception of Yugoslavia continued to influence his thinking about
American relations with the communist world.[97] In the March 3 letter he related his belief
that Tito was an unusually attractive and intelligent leader, and that Tito had requested in
their November 1964 discussion that the senator convey to Johnson his wishes for a "further strengthening of friendly relations between our countries."[98] Tito had also mentioned a
desire for Johnson to visit Yugoslavia in 1965.[99] The senator persistently argued in private
conversations with the President that a unified, communist Vietnam would be similar to the
Yugoslavia of Tito in its nationalism and independence, that like Yugoslavia it might eventually engage in amicable relations with the United States, and that a unified, communist
Vietnamese state would not represent a mere extension of Communist China.[100]

In early March Fulbright made only the most oblique references in public to his belief that the strength of nationalism, and not communist ideology, was central to the struggle in Vietnam.[101] He stated in an address at Johns Hopkins University that "I think we ought to ask ourselves hypothetically whether a communist regime that leans away from China is worse or better from the viewpoint of our political and strategic interests than a noncommunist state, such as Indonesia or Cambodia, that leans toward China."[102] He did not elucidate the significance of this statement for American policy in southeast Asia. The speech avoided discussion of Vietnam, in keeping with the senator's strategy of refraining from public criticism of the President.[103] Fulbright's Johns Hopkins address did not attract significant attention.[104]

Fulbright clarified his public position on March 14, 1965 when he appeared on NBC's *Meet the Press*. On the N.B.C. program Fulbright doubted that southeast Asia was vital to American security "from a long-term point of view," but he conceded that U.S. interests were involved in Vietnam at that moment simply because of the American military presence in that country.[105] He was pessimistic about the prospects for improving the military situation through the large-scale introduction of American ground forces.[106] The senator was asked for his opinion concerning the recent proposal of Everett Dirksen for a "no concession-no deal policy on further agreements and trade with the communists until they halt aggression in Vietnam and elsewhere."[107] Fulbright dismissed the Dirksen suggestion, saying, "This so-called hard line, I think, leads nowhere."[108] He regretted that the Vietnamese conflict was an obstacle to the amelioration of Soviet-American relations, but he maintained that the United States should continue to negotiate constructive agreements with the U.S.S.R. such as the 1965 Test Ban Treaty.[109] Fulbright reiterated the theme of his January 16 Miami address, calling for a policy of cooperation with the communist world and a reorientation of American priorities toward solving domestic problems.[110]

In recalling the thesis of the Miami speech, repudiating Dirksen's belligerent ideas, and questioning the wisdom of sending U.S. ground forces to southeast Asia, Fulbright was remaining consistent with his earlier positions on Vietnam. But the general tenor of his remarks contradicted his previous opposition to bombing and his February support for immediate reconvening of the Geneva Conference. He expressed theoretical approval of negotiations, but through the circuitous logic that the air strikes would impress upon the North Vietnamese the "seriousness of the situation" and eventually lead to negotiations.[111] The air raids were appropriate, in Fulbright's opinion, because "the objective of these strikes is to bring about a negotiation."[112] Fulbright accepted the administration's claim that the bombing campaign was a tactic designed to avoid the introduction of American ground troops.[113] He thus reversed the perspective of his public as well as private views in January and February, when he had envisaged bombing as the precursor of a debilitating and inexorably expanding American military involvement in Vietnam.

On the March 14 edition of *Meet the Press* Lawrence Spivak observed that there were contradictory reports concerning Fulbright's analysis of President Johnson's course in Vietnam. Some reports held that Fulbright supported Johnson's Vietnam policy, was being consulted constantly by the President, and wielded immense power within the administration's foreign policy councils.[114] Other reports, notably a recent *New York Times* story, contended that Fulbright did not support the February retaliatory policy, did not exert significant influence in the administration's deliberations on Vietnam, and was not being adequately consulted by the President.[115] The *New York Times* report was obviously closer to reality, for Rusk's frequent breakfasts with Fulbright and Johnson's monologues to the senator on his moderation and his need for Fulbright's help can hardly be considered adequate consultation. But Fulbright answered Spivak's request for a clarification of which reports· were accurate by affirming his support for Johnson's policy in Vietnam and stating that he had been adequately consulted.[116] He did not speculate on the extent of his influence. The Foreign Relations Committee chairman asserted that it would be improper for the Committee to conduct public hearings on the war "while conditions are so critical in Vietnam."[117] The program ended on a melancholy note, with Fulbright concluding that he would be deeply disillusioned by a massive deployment of American ground forces in southeast Asia, but "when we are in this critical a matter we have to support our President, you know that, in our system."[118]

The notion that Congress must dutifully support the President in time of crisis constituted the most glaring flaw, during early 1965, in Fulbright's campaign to prevent a disastrous American intervention in Vietnam. As long as Fulbright was competing with Robert McNamara, Dean Rusk, Maxwell Taylor, and McGeorge Bundy for the private attention of the President his protests were ineffective; he had been arguing for months that the existence of a noncommunist regime in South Vietnam was not crucial to American security, and his reasoning never had any significant impact on the administration. The Vietnam hearings of 1966 would demonstrate that Fulbright was most influential when he was revitalizing the public dialogue on American foreign policy that had become quiescent during the years of Cold War diplomacy in the 1950s and early 1960s. But in 1964 and 1965 Fulbright rejected Wayne Morse's plea for hearings on Vietnam.[119] The President professed to be fearful that a public debate would ignite a recrudescence of extreme anticommunist sentiment in the country, and in hopes of strengthening his influence with Johnson the Arkansas senator did not attempt to foster such a dialogue in early 1965.[120] Thus,·Fulbright averred on *Meet the Press* that a public debate on the war led by the Senate Foreign Relations Committee would hamper the President's execution of foreign policy during the southeast Asian crisis.

Fulbright had initiated tentative efforts to develop an open discussion of the Vietnam policy in January and February 1965. He had publicly denied that bombing was a solution to the conflict and endorsed U Thant's proposal for a diplomatic conference on southeast Asia. His criticism of bombing occurred before the air attacks were escalated, and his endorsement of U Thant's recommendation was announced before the administration's rejection of negotiations was clear. By March he was forced to either follow the logic of his previous statements and openly criticize the President's decisions for escalation, or confine his dissent to private conversations. His comments in the *Meet the Press* appearance revealed his choice of the latter strategy.

It proved to be virtually impossible for the senator to adhere consistently to this strategy. He would deliver indirect critiques of the administration's foreign policy even when he was attempting to publicize his loyalty to the President. On the Spivak program he had expressed disenchantment with the massive introduction of ground forces into southeast Asia during the month when Johnson was ordering Marine battalions to South Vietnam.[121]

For a President as intolerant of dissent as was Lyndon Johnson, no public criticism could be allowed. By the summer of 1965, Fulbright concluded that if the President's anti-communist consensus was so stifling that only secret dissent could be tolerated, then the restoration of the proper constitutional balance between the executive and Congress was imperative.[122] That balance might be restored by a public challenge to Johnson's foreign policy. Fulbright's challenge would occur when he became convinced that Johnson had justified the 1965 American intervention in the Dominican Republic through distorted claims of communist infiltration into that diminutive nation.[123] The administration's distortions of the communist threat in the Caribbean reinforced Fulbright's suspicion that the dangers of Asian communist aggression had been similarly exaggerated, that China was not Nazi Germany reincarnate.[124] Thus, by the end of 1965 he was prepared to conduct the comprehensive public investigation of America's Asian policy that the President had feared and skillfully delayed.

An analysis of Fulbright's responses to Johnson's foreign policy initiatives in late 1964 and early 1965 is largely the story of the waning of the senator's optimism about the President. Fulbright was confident in late 1964 that many communist states, especially Yugoslavia and the Soviet Union, were displaying a more cooperative attitude toward the United States. In his praise of George Kennan's November 1964 article on China there was even the hope that the Chinese might become less hostile toward the West, despite the senator's inaccurate perception at the time that China was imperialistic. Fulbright believed that Johnson would capitalize on this nascent reduction in Cold War animosities by channeling American energies into domestic affairs, consequently redoubling the nation's vitality. The war in Vietnam had all but destroyed Fulbright's optimism by the spring of 1965. He began to fear that the President would not only fail to build bridges to the communist world, but would lead America on a violent crusade into the depths of the ominous Vietnamese labyrinth.

IV. THE PRELUDE TO FULBRIGHT'S DISSENT
SPRING 1965

Senator Fulbright was becoming increasingly disillusioned with the American foreign aid program in the mid-1960s. Since the late 1950s he had argued against utilizing foreign aid to support corrupt, reactionary regimes whose only merit was their zealous anticommunism. In late 1964 he notified Dean Rusk of his refusal to manage the foreign aid bill in 1965.[1] The *Washington Post* columnist William S. White denounced Fulbright's decision as "an unexampled abdication of the traditional responsibility of a chairman of the Foreign Relations Committee."[2] Walter Lippmann's column in early March 1965 expressed a less heated and more logical view of Fulbright's refusal to manage the bill. The fundamental issue concerning foreign aid, in Lippman's opinion, was the dispute between Fulbright and most members of the House of Representatives, who resisted expansion of economic aid programs but consistently supported massive military assistance to oppose communism throughout the world. Lippmann believed President Johnson could not support Fulbright because of the House's adamant opposition to the senator's position, but that the administration basically agreed with Fulbright's arguments for reduced military assistance and expanded economic assistance.[3] The columnist concluded that Fulbright "is doing wonders to make the country and the Congress begin to re-examine the encrusted deposit of ideas and ideology and prejudices under which our foreign policy labors and groans."[4]

Fulbright eventually acquiesced to administration pressures and agreed to manage the foreign aid bill in 1965. He had proposed the division of military and economic aid into two separate bills, the substitution of multilateral for bilateral assistance, and long-term instead of annual aid authorizations.[5] The administration did not incorporate any of Fulbright's innovations into the aid program.[6] This rejection of Fulbright's proposals, as well as his disagreements with administration officials during the foreign aid hearings in March and April, revealed that the administration's perspective on foreign aid was much more similar to the House of Representatives' view than Lippmann had believed.

David E. Bell, the administrator of the Agency for International Development (AID), appeared before the Foreign Relations Committee on March 12 to discuss the foreign aid bill. At the March 12 hearing Fulbright enumerated fourteen small nations that were receiving American aid, including South Vietnam, and asked Bell if the United States had vital interests in all of those nations. Bell delivered two contradictory responses, replying first that American interests were certainly not involved in all of the countries.[7] When Fulbright pressed him to justify aid to countries in which U.S. interests were nonexistent, the AID administrator replied that American interests were served whenever a nation preserved its independence of communist domination.[8] Fulbright rejoined: "Now you have come to the crux of it. We are so fascinated with communism that we are just going to keep out the communists all over the world."[9]

Fulbright rejected Bell's contention that anticommunism was a legitimate reason for extending foreign aid to a nation and thus involving the United States in its affairs.[10] He doubted that the United States had any vital interests in South Vietnam. In Fulbright's opinion, economic aid had gradually led to the burgeoning military commitment to South Vietnam, so that American pride and prestige had become inextricably entangled with the campaign to preserve the South Vietnamese regime.[11] He asserted that Americans assumed the nation's interests were involved in South Vietnam simply because of the massive economic and military commitment to that nation. But, in Fulbright's view, it was primarily the nebulous and emotional concept of America's "honor, pride, and prestige" that was involved in Vietnam. Bell defended his evaluation of South Vietnam as crucial to American security by quoting President Eisenhower's 1954 statement to the South Vietnamese: "We support you, we want to help you, we think it is important that your independence be sustained."[12] Fulbright responded that if the United States defined its vital interests in terms of maintaining other nations' independence, then no region of the globe was exempt from American responsibility.[13]

Fulbright continued to question the administration's assumptions concerning Vietnam when Under Secretary of State George W. Ball testified before the Foreign Relations Committee on April 7. The Committee's chairman was gravely concerned by the negative Japanese reaction to the American military escalation. He observed that Shunichi Matsumoto, a senior Japanese diplomat, had recently challenged Washington's allegation that the Vietcong insurgency was predominantly a communist movement.[14] Premier Eisaku Sato had sent Matsumoto to survey the situation in Vietnam. In his report to Sato, Matsumoto stated that the Vietcong had no direct connection with China or the Soviet Union. The Vietcong insurgents were basically nationalistic and would not renounce their political and military objectives in the South because of the bombing of North Vietnam.[15] Fulbright inserted in the record of the hearings a *New York Times* article that attributed great significance to the Matsumoto report, partly because of Matsumoto's stature as the special envoy of Sato, but fundamentally because his ideas seemed to confirm a skepticism about America's role in Vietnam already evident in Japan. The *New York Times* news story concluded that despite the support for the U.S. position in the official rhetoric of the Sato government, Japanese public opinion was overwhelmingly negative in its response to President Johnson's Vietnam policy.[16]

George Ball responded to Fulbright's pessimistic statements concerning Japanese public opinion by emphasizing the Sato regime's steadfast verbal support for the American position.[17] Fulbright proceeded to ask Ball why the two largest Japanese newspapers were so hostile to American policy, especially the newspaper *Asahi*, which had published an article by Matsumoto summarizing his Vietnam report. Ball and Assistant Secretary of State for Congressional Relations Douglas MacArthur II attempted to denigrate the Japanese criticism by arguing that the two huge Japanese newspapers were infiltrated by communists.[18] Fulbright interrupted this argument to assert that Matsumoto was certainly not a commu-

nist, and Premier Sato had authorized his mission. The senator questioned Ball about the
validity of Matsumoto's contention that the Vietcong would not cease their military operations because of the bombing of North Vietnam. Ball rejected Matsumoto's analysis, claiming the Vietcong were commanded by North Vietnam and encouraged by China. The bombing would bring about a cessation of the North's infiltration and control of the southern
guerrillas, according to Ball, thus rendering the South Vietnamese insurrection "quite manageable."[19]

Fulbright continued to elaborate upon the adverse foreign reaction to American policy
in Asia. The chairman sardonically commented on Canada's failure to share Washington's
perception of China as a malevolent aggressor: "The Canadians, as you know, among our
friends have probably the best representation and best reception in China than any, and we
usually don't consider the Canadians Communists."[20] Fulbright observed that a recent article from the *Toronto Globe and Mail* had failed to support American assumptions about the
war in southeast Asia. The *Toronto Globe* described the escalation of the war as a "perilous
course" that risked a Chinese retaliation against the inexorably expanding American intervention.[21] Fulbright also fostered a brief discussion regarding Canadian Prime Minister
Lester Pearson's critique of Johnson's Vietnam policy, apparently referring to Pearson's
appeal for a termination of the U.S. bombing campaign and an immediate effort to conclude
a peaceful settlement.[22] He avoided endorsing Pearson's controversial position, but he felt
the Canadian Prime Minister's proposals at least deserved serious consideration rather than
an irascible dismissal. Ball averred, however, that communist propaganda had indirectly
influenced the thinking of the Canadians, the French, and other peoples who were critical
of American policy in Vietnam.[23]

George Ball was probably the most eloquent and vigorous private critic of the military
escalation in Vietnam,[24] yet his statements at the foreign aid hearings revealed no intimation
of his private dissent. He replied to Fulbright's questions concerning Japanese and Canadian
opposition to the U.S. intervention by denouncing North Vietnam's aggression and by
stressing the support the United States was receiving from the great majority of its allies. He
recounted the Sato government's firm verbal support for the American cause in Vietnam.
The NATO Council had endorsed the American position a week earlier and would regard
any American withdrawal as catastrophic, according to Ball.[25] He did concede that the
French government disapproved of the U.S. military involvement in southeast Asia. But the
French disapprobation, no less than that of Lester Pearson, was influenced by the communist propaganda falsely portraying the Indochinese war as an indigenous revolt. Ball regretted that the complexity of the Vietnamese situation facilitated the dissemination of this communist propaganda throughout the world.[26]

During the course of the hearings, Fulbright had generated a limited amount of constructive debate by trying to elicit from David Bell and G. W. Ball a definition of American
interests in Vietnam and an explanation of the burgeoning international opposition to
President Johnson's foreign policy. It was unfortunately an atrophied debate, for there were
only a half-dozen passages in the entire 650 pages of testimony in which administration witnesses were compelled to defend the Vietnam policy. Only Fulbright, Morse, and
Republican Senator George Aiken[27] of Vermont (there were 19 members of the committee)
asked a substantial number of questions about Vietnam, and much of the testimony dealt

with less important issues connected with the aid program.

The 1965 foreign aid hearings might have provided an excellent opportunity to conduct a thorough investigation of the Vietnam dilemma; one year later Rusk's testimony for a foreign economic aid authorization to South Vietnam developed into the celebrated 1966 Vietnam hearings, and again in 1968 when Rusk testified for that year's foreign assistance bill the Foreign Relations Committee subjected him to a lengthy and rather hostile interrogation.[28] But in early 1965 few members on the committee were adversaries of the executive branch. Fulbright was still attempting to demonstrate his support for President Johnson, despite his disagreements with administration officials at the hearings.

Fulbright developed several ideas during the foreign aid discussion that were central to his critique of the crusading anticommunism of American diplomacy. He recalled a theme he had been emphasizing since the late 1950s when he repudiated the AID administrator's contention that opposition to communism constituted a legitimate basis for extending foreign aid to a government. The senator persistently affirmed in 1965 and the later 1960s that American pride and prestige rather than any crucial national interests were involved in Vietnam.[29] He also maintained that the aid program had acquired a momentum of its own, so that many Americans were psychologically unable to liquidate the commitment and thus admit that the billions of dollars previously channeled into support of South Vietnam had been a fatuous and futile investment. In this perspective, additional billions would have to be expended to insure that the earlier investment was not wasted.[30]

The chairman had revealed briefly at the 1965 foreign aid hearings that administration witnesses experienced immense difficulties in presenting a persuasive defense of their policies when confronted by critical questioning. For example, the only specific argument David Bell could ultimately muster to define a concrete American interest in Vietnam was the need to uphold Eisenhower's 1954 pledge of support to South Vietnam. G. W. Ball's basic refutation of Matsumoto, Pearson, and the French was the sterile assertion that communist propaganda had misled them. Throughout the later Johnson years the voices of dissent were strengthened by the abject failure of administration officials to present a cogent justification for President Johnson's foreign policy when they testified before the Foreign Relations Committee.[31]

The administration was hostile to any intensive discussion of the Vietnam War. Secretary McNamara was especially disenchanted by the prospect of appearing before an open session of the Foreign Relations Committee. He insisted that his testimony should be given at an executive session hearing.[32] A transcript of the foreign assistance hearings was made available to the public later in 1965, but many of the statements by Bell, McNamara, and Ball were deleted "in the interest of national security."[33] At one juncture during the McNamara hearing on March 24 Fulbright asked the Secretary of Defense 10 consecutive questions about Vietnam, and nine of the responses were either evasions or security deletions.[34] When Rusk testified there was little discussion of southeast Asia. Thus the dialogue on Vietnam at the foreign aid hearings of March and April 1965 receded into obscurity, emasculated by the President's antipathy toward public debate and the Senate Foreign Relations Committee's reluctance to challenge the administration.

In the spring, Fulbright was becoming increasingly disturbed by Soviet reactions to the American bombing of North Vietnam. Fulbright conferred at length in March with

Ambassador Anatoly Dobrynin at the Soviet embassy. Dobrynin told Fulbright that the air war was causing deep concern in the Kremlin, and the Soviets would be forced to increase military aid to Hanoi. The senator was appalled at the idea that the remote involvement in southeast Asia could provoke a crisis with the Soviet Union, and after his discussion with Dobrynin he became determined to support a halt in the bombing. He privately advised Rusk that the United States could halt the bombing in return for Soviet efforts to persuade Hanoi to reduce its flow of military aid and men southward; then the great powers could convene an international conference, with all involved agreeing to abide by the results of internationally supervised elections throughout Vietnam.[34a]

Fulbright was especially careful to avoid vehement public disputes with the President's advisers in late March and early April, for he believed Johnson was finally beginning to see the validity of his arguments for a negotiated settlement. On one occasion at the end of March Fulbright privately conferred with Johnson at length, and in contrast to their earlier conversations the President seemed to be attentive and sympathetic.[35] When the administration announced another escalation of the American military effort a few days later, Fulbright eschewed definite criticism of the decision.

The President had decided at an April 2 National Security Council meeting to intensify the air attacks against North Vietnam, dispatch several thousand additional troops (28,000 American soldiers were in Vietnam at the time) to South Vietnam, and provide assistance for a major expansion of the South Vietnamese military forces.[36] The administration would also increase economic assistance to Saigon.[37] Maxwell Taylor, the Ambassador to Saigon who had recently arrived in Washington to attend the NSC meeting, appeared later on April 2 before a closed joint session of the Senate Armed Services and Foreign Relations Committees.[38] Fulbright told reporters after the joint session that he was unhappy and apprehensive about Vietnam because the war "can always escalate beyond control."[39] He precluded an interpretation of this comment as an indictment of Johnson's policy by adding that Ambassador Taylor was "unhappy and apprehensive, too."[40] The senator was concerned that the administration had not defined its views of an "acceptable" political settlement, but he continued to profess his general support for the President.[41]

In early April Fulbright attempted to persuade Johnson that a Titoist buffer state in Vietnam would be compatible with American interests. He summarized his ideas about Vietnam in a memorandum to the White House on April 5, two days before the President was scheduled to deliver an important address at Johns Hopkins University.[42] Fulbright's Vietnam memorandum consisted of six basic propositions. First, it would be a disaster for the United States to engage in a massive ground and air war in southeast Asia.[43] A prolonged war in Vietnam would be extremely costly and would revive and intensify the Cold War, which had begun to ease after the Cuban missile crisis.[44] A large-scale air war would not defeat the Vietcong and would risk an intervention by the North Vietnamese Army or even by China.[45] Fulbright predicted that "the commitment of a large American land army would involve us in a bloody and interminable conflict in which the advantage would lie with the enemy."[46]

The memorandum's second point held that Chinese imperialism, and not communist ideology, represented the primary danger to peace in Asia.[47] Fulbright's perception of China as an imperialistic power was the only serious flaw in the memorandum.[48] A year later he would effectively refute his earlier views by writing that the Chinese tended to be intro-spective and were vastly more concerned with their domestic objectives of industrialization and social transformation than with supporting foreign revolutions.[49] In 1966 Fulbright asserted that despite the ferocity of China's official rhetoric, the Chinese had made no effort to subjugate the weak and non-aligned nation of Burma, had voluntarily withdrawn from North Korea, and had failed to intervene in Vietnam.[50] The second argument of his April 1965 paper was accurate in its contention that Chinese ideology could not harm the United States, and the following point of the document correctly stressed the resiliency of Asian nationalism. Fulbright's third proposition stated that the smaller Asian nations were histor-ically afraid of–and independent of–China.[51] Thus, a communist state in Vietnam independent of China, as Tito was independent of Russia, would be far more valuable for world security than a feeble anticommunist regime dependent on American dollars and manpower.[52]

The three remaining proposals of the memorandum dealt with Fulbright's appeal for a negotiated settlement. In order to end the war, the United States should declare a morato-rium on the bombing, clarify its intentions, and initiate a campaign to persuade the Vietnamese people, north and south, of the economic and political advantages of a free, independent Vietnamese state.[53] The United States could make its wishes known through Great Britain or Russia that it would accept an independent Vietnamese regime, regardless of political makeup, and that it would cooperate with the other great powers in guarantee-ing the independence of Vietnam and the rights of minorities.[54] America should join with the great powers in assuring that the new unified regime would not be the pawn or satel-lite of any great power.[55] Finally, it would be advantageous for international stability to have a government in Vietnam oriented more toward Russia rather than exclusively toward China, since at least for the moment China was in a belligerent and resentful mood.[56] The inaccurate perspective on China again weakened this final point, but it should be noted that there was an assumption in Fulbright's Vietnam memorandum, as there had been in his 1964 "Bridges East and West" speech, that the Chinese were not immune to the laws of change and their "resentful" attitude was not absolute or permanent.[57]

On the day after President Johnson received the senator's written recommendations for a diplomatic settlement, he invited Fulbright and Mansfield to the White House to discuss the draft of his Johns Hopkins University speech.[58] Fulbright's influence was partially responsible for the passage in Johnson's address proposing "unconditional discussions."[59] After President Johnson delivered his speech at Baltimore on April 7, Fulbright compli-mented the President's conciliatory tone.[60] The Johns Hopkins address was crucial in con-vincing Fulbright that he was persuading Johnson of the futility of escalating the Vietnam War[61] Fulbright's response to the speech was too sanguine, for Johnson reiterated at Baltimore the fundamental goal of three previous administrations: "Our objective is the independence of South Vietnam and its freedom from attack."[62] Johnson regarded the American bargaining position as much too precarious to begin serious negotiations in the spring of 1965; thus, the dramatic peace initiative at Johns Hopkins was primarily designed to silence international and domestic critics of U.S. foreign policy.[63]

If the Johns Hopkins address temporarily muted Fulbright's criticism of President Johnson, it failed to prevent the senator from offering alternatives to the escalation policy and publicly disagreeing with the President's advisers. It was not illogical for Fulbright to have made a crucial distinction between Johnson and the President's immediate entourage, because Johnson was assiduously cultivating an image of himself as a "dove" surrounded by "hawkish" advisers, particularly in his communications with Fulbright, McGovern, and Church.[64] Fulbright provoked a brief but acrimonious dispute with Rusk and McNamara on April 18 when he advocated a cessation of the air strikes against North Vietnam in order to· open an avenue toward peace negotiations.[65] While the White House refused to comment, Dean Rusk rebuked Fulbright for proposing an action that "would only encourage the aggressor and dishearten our friends who bear the brunt of battle."[66] Secretary McNamara declared that terminating the bombing of North Vietnam would discourage the South Vietnamese people in their struggle to oppose Hanoi's campaign of terror, which was dependent upon the daily flow of men and military equipment from the North.[67] Republican Senator Jacob Javits of New York joined Rusk and McNamara in rejecting Fulbright's proposal, and Senator John Stennis of Mississippi asseverated that far from halting the bombings, the United States must prepare to fight an expanded war for an indefinite period.[68]

It was remarkable for Fulbright's mild criticism (which was expressed in an interview with Jack Bell of the Associated Press) to have provoked such vituperation from the Cabinet officials. Fulbright had merely hypothesized that a temporary cease-fire would be advisable "in the near future before the escalation goes too far" in order to allow all of the belligerents time to calmly reflect upon the situation in Vietnam.[69] He preferred a cease-fire for all combatants, but if that couldn't be obtained then the United States should unilaterally stop the bombing.[70] In Fulbright's opinion, the air war against the North Vietnamese might galvanize them into more determined resistance to the U.S. military effort.[71] The North Vietnamese might react to aerial devastation as Great Britain did in World War II, when the German air raids only strengthened British resolve to defeat Hitler.[72] Furthermore, the Foreign Relations Committee chairman felt that the Russians might cooperate in bringing about a diplomatic conference on southeast Asia if the air strikes were suspended, but would resist negotiations while the bombing continued.[73] Fulbright approved of Johnson's proposal at Baltimore for a Mekong River Valley economic development program, but essentially his approbation was based on the belief that peace would have to be established as a precondition for inaugurating such a program.[74] He did not think the Mekong River development project was feasible while the war continued.[75]

Fulbright's Associated Press interview was followed by a series of speeches delivered by dissenting senators in late April. On April 28 Senator Church praised the contributions of Fulbright, Mansfield, and Aiken to the Vietnam debate by inserting into the *Congressional Record* Arthur Krock's column in the April 22 *New York Times*. Krock complimented the three members of the Foreign Relations Committee for responsibly fulfilling their constitutional role in advising the President on foreign affairs.[76] In Krock's opinion, Fulbright had received "unwarranted abuse" from the President's advisers for recommending a temporary suspension of the bombing.[77] He considered the "hysterical attacks on Senator Fulbright" to be evidence that the administration refused to even consider Fulbright's idea.[78]

Krock was complimentary of Mansfield's April 21 speech in the Senate, in which he had proposed the reconvening of the Geneva Conference on the limited basis of guaranteeing the neutrality of Cambodia.[79] Mansfield hoped a Cambodian neutrality agreement would be the preliminary to a diplomatic solution for Vietnam. The Montana senator's response to the

Johns Hopkins address was similar to that of Fulbright in extolling the President's call for unconditional discussions. But Robert McNamara announced another expansion of the war on the same day of Mansfield's speech, prompting Arthur Krock's foreboding conclusion: "Continued escalation of the Vietnam War on a steadily rising scale is our only policy for the restoration of peace in southeast Asia."[80]

Senator Church characterized Joseph Kraft's columns as unusually perceptive analyses of the Vietnam crisis, and placed Kraft's April 23 *Washington Evening Star* article in the *Record*.[81] Kraft maintained that the United States must achieve a negotiated settlement immediately, before the great communist powers became directly involved in southeast Asia. He viewed the substantial reduction in Vietcong attacks during early April as a propitious development. "Taken together with the expressions of such figures as the Pope, Senator J. William Fulbright, Democrat, of Arkansas, and Prime Minister Lester Pearson, of Canada," he said, the nascent decline in Vietcong military activity presented excellent prospects for a cease-fire and discussions.[82] Kraft warned that if the opportunity was missed, a vicious circle of reciprocal escalation would ensue that might lead to general war. In response to the American bombing of North Vietnam the Russians had just begun to provide the North Vietnamese with antiaircraft missiles, whereupon China attempted to surpass the Soviets in demonstrating their support for Hanoi by officially recruiting volunteers, a policy the Chinese had not followed since they intervened in Korea in 1950.[83]

On the same day that Church lauded the recommendations of Fulbright and Mansfield, the Foreign Relations Committee chairman delivered a brief set of remarks on the Senate floor. Fulbright approved of Senator Aiken's recent speeches advocating a vigorous role for the United Nations in extricating the United States from the tragic predicament in Vietnam.[84] He inserted a *New York Times* editorial into the *Record* that eulogized the "dean of Senate Republicans."[85] The *Times* editorial criticized the State Department's refusal to encourage U.N. Secretary General U Thant in his campaign to initiate negotiations on the southeast Asia crisis.[86] The April 28 Senate statements by Fulbright and Church, as well as the other dissenting speeches and interviews in April, offered a definite alternative to the Johnson administration's course in Vietnam. In the critics' view, the United States should suspend the air war against North Vietnam as an initial step toward reconvening the Geneva Conference. They believed Secretary General U Thant should be encouraged in his efforts to arrange a diplomatic conference on southeast Asia.

It was clear in late April that an expansion of the war was opposed by several senior members of the Senate Foreign Relations Committee, the columnists Joseph Kraft and Walter Lippman, the *New York Times* editorialists, U Thant and other Asian statesmen, the Pope, Prime Minister Pearson, and Charles de Gaulle. And in addition to this rather formidable array of world leaders, there were other prestigious statesmen who were privately advising the President against escalation in Vietnam, notably Adlai Stevenson and George Ball.

The senators and foreign policy analysts associated with Fulbright, Mansfield, and Lippmann could not match the powerful influence exerted on American diplomacy by a bipartisan political coalition that was rapidly coalescing in support of the escalation policy during the spring of 1965. William S. White, a Johnson intimate, described this "new coalition" in a *Washington Post* column at the end of April. White extolled the leadership of the Republican Party for forming an alliance with the Democratic administration and rallying to the aid of "a country called the United States of America in its terrible and thankless task of standing up all over the world against creeping Communist aggression."[87] Senate Republican Leader Everett Dirksen and House Republican Leader Gerald R. Ford of Michigan were providing invaluable assistance for the President's resolute opposition to communist expansion. Dwight Eisenhower, Richard Nixon, and Barry Goldwater were dutifully aiding the Republican Congressional leadership in this indispensable concert for the survival of America. In contrast to White's panegyrics of the Republicans and the Johnson administration, the journalist lamented that "the chief foreign policy spokesman in the Senate, J. William Fulbright," and Senate Majority Leader Mike Mansfield were "hampering rather than supporting this Government in its all-national policy to resist Communist aggression in South Vietnam."[88] According to White, Fulbright and Mansfield were the leaders of "a thin but vocal fringe of the Democratic Party" that invariably opposed American military actions in the Congo, Latin America, Vietnam, or any region of the globe where American power was honorably employed.[89]

The Vietnam War was temporarily eclipsed during late April by an American military intervention in the diminutive and impoverished isle of Hispaniola in the Caribbean Sea. The eastern half of that island, the Dominican Republic, was being ravaged by a rebellion against the pro-American regime of Donald Reid Cabral.[90] By April 28, Reid had been overthrown and civil war was being waged between the regular Dominican military leaders and the supporters of Juan Bosch, the former president.[91] Ambassador W. Tapley Bennett sent a series of cables to Washington, the first emphasizing the need to protect American lives, the later cables predicting "another Cuba" if the military junta's forces collapsed.[92] CIA reports of communist support for the Bosch movement began to alarm Washington officials, especially Thomas C. Mann, the administration's principal Latin American specialist and a zealous anticommunist.[93] President Johnson briefly conferred with Thomas Mann and then instructed McNamara to order U.S. Marines to the Dominican Republic.[94]

A few hours after Fulbright delivered his April 28 Senate remarks on the U.N. and Vietnam, he was summoned to an emergency meeting at the White House. Fulbright and other members of Congress were informed of the administration's decision to land Marines in Santo Domingo for the sole purpose of protecting the lives of Americans and other foreigners.[95] Johnson said nothing of communist infiltration.[96] Fulbright did not express any disapproval of an intervention to save American lives.[97] Later that evening Johnson appeared before national television cameras to report the Congressional leadership's endorsement of his actions in the Dominican crisis.[98] He told the American people the Marines had landed "in order to give protection to hundreds of Americans who are still in the Dominican Republic and to escort them safely back to this country."[99] Again there was no mention of communism.[100] Yet in another televised address on May 2, the President abruptly reversed the justification for his decision and represented the intervention as a campaign to prevent communist expansion in the Caribbean: "The American nation cannot, and must not, and will not permit the establishment of another Communist government in the Western Hemisphere."[101]

Fulbright, Morse, and Senator Eugene McCarthy of Minnesota were privately disturbed by the apparent metamorphosis of the intervention from an evacuation of American citizens to a crusade against Caribbean communism.[102] Johnson had actually been agitated by the threat of communism on Hispaniola since late April. John Bartlow Martin, the former ambassador to the Dominican Republic, later recounted a conversation at the White House on April 30 in which Johnson proclaimed he did not "intend to sit here with my hands tied and let Castro take that island. What can we do in Vietnam if we can't clean up the Dominican Republic?"[103] Fulbright was perplexed in late April by the conflicting reports on the revolt in Santo Domingo. The chairman and Senator McCarthy contended that the Foreign Relations Committee should conduct a thorough classified investigation of the Dominican intervention. Dodd, Frank Lausche of Ohio, Karl Mundt of South Dakota, and other members of the committee were disgruntled at the prospect of an exhaustive analysis regarding the administration's actions, but at the insistence of Fulbright and McCarthy the Dominican hearings began in the summer of 1965.[104]

In the beginning Fulbright was not certain that the administration had committed an egregious error in landing more than 20,000 American troops in Santo Domingo. But he began to doubt Johnson's judgment in May. His misgivings were intensified by the administration's failure to demonstrate that communists dominated the Dominican revolt. Fulbright became more determined to hold extended hearings after he listened to CIA Director William F. Raborn's briefing shortly after the President decided to intervene. The Foreign Relations Committee chairman asked Raborn to specify the number of communists who were definitely involved in the Dominican revolution. Raborn replied, "Well, we identified three."[105]

Rusk appeared before the committee on April 30 to discuss the Dominican crisis, but Fulbright also brought up Vietnam at the hearing, indicating that he was displeased with developments in Vietnam and that the administration was not working to obtain a settlement. He reminded Rusk that when the Gulf of Tonkin Resolution was passed, the administration had not stated any intention to land massive U.S. ground forces in Indochina. With American troops expanding in number, Fulbright suggested that the administration might need to gain a fresh mandate from Congress:

> This operation in Vietnam has obviously become quite controversial. A lot of us have been quiet. We do not want to embarrass the administration. We have not discussed it in public. Some have, some have not. I am quite sure some would like to have, but they did not wish to embarrass the administration, because we realize this is a very difficult situation.
>
> However, I would think it would be wise if the administration could make up its mind to present the matter to this Committee and at least to the Congress, as to how much and how far they are contemplating going.

Rusk's answer was clearly not responsive: "Well, Mr. Chairman, it is very hard to look into the future."[105a]

In a letter to a man who had asked the senator why he had not publicly opposed the Vietnamese or Dominican interventions, Fulbright replied that he had attended many executive meetings on these issues, but he had not believed it appropriate to "take issue in public with the government's policy at this time...Personally, I have not believed that my making public statements about it would result in any beneficial change. I have always made the distinction between an immediate critical situation and long-term policy in indulging in public discussions."[105b] These conclusions were in error, as Fulbright would later admit.

Fulbright devoted much of his attention to Vietnam and Europe (as well as to domestic affairs) in the six weeks following the initial deployment of Marines in the Dominican Republic. In early May the President requested from Congress a $700 million supplemental appropriation, explaining that the passage of this appropriation would be considered a vote of confidence in his entire Vietnam policies.[106] The $700 million was primarily intended to cover military expenditures for Vietnam. The Senate passed the measure by an overwhelmingly pro-administration vote on May 6, with only Morse, Gruening, and Gaylord Nelson of Wisconsin in opposition.[107]

Fulbright was in Europe at the time of the May 6 vote, delivering speeches before the Consultative Assembly of the Council of Europe in Strasbourg. At a Strasbourg news conference on May 5, Fulbright advocated a Vietnam settlement based on the 1954 Geneva agreements.[108] The senator called for the United Nations to supervise the elections envisaged by the Geneva accords. He believed the elections would lead to a nationalist regime that would be determined to maintain its independence of China.[110] A week later in a speech at Vienna he stated that the emerging reconciliation between East and West "can be arrested and reversed at any time by the spreading impact of such occurrences as the tragic war in Vietnam."[111] In the Strasbourg and Vienna statements, Fulbright did not deviate from his earlier professions of support for President Johnson,[112] despite his appeal for a negotiated settlement.

The Johnson administration suspended the bombing from May 12 until May 18, prompting Arthur Krock to disparage the previous Rusk-McNamara invective against Fulbright's proposal for a bombing halt.[113] Three weeks earlier Fulbright's recommendation had provoked a deluge of fiery rhetoric from the Cabinet officials portraying a bombing pause as a betrayal of America's friends and an encouragement of aggressors. Now in May the administration was experimenting with a temporary cessation of the air raids against North Vietnam. In a May 18 *New York Times* column, Krock observed, "The reason why this swift turnabout has embarrassed the Administration is the round of shooting-from-the-hip which the highest officials engaged in, with Fulbright's suggestion as their target."[114] The air strikes were resumed a few hours after the Krock column was written.[115] Fulbright initially responded to the bombing suspension with mildly favorable comments, but in an October 1965 *Meet the Press* appearance he argued that a bombing pause must continue much longer than six days to represent a genuine peace initiative.[116] For Fulbright, suspension of the air attacks should have been the prelude to negotiations; for the administration, the ephemeral bombing halt of May was essentially a stratagem in the campaign to silence its critics.[117]

Fulbright delivered his last speeches in support of the Johnson administration during the first half of June. Johnson requested an additional $89 million of economic assistance to South Vietnam, Thailand, and Laos in a June 1 special message to Congress.[118] Fulbright endorsed the proposal for expanded economic assistance in a Senate address of June 7 entitled "Political and Economic Reconstruction in South Vietnam."[119] The June 7 speech was Fulbright's first important Senate discourse concerning Vietnam in 1965. He had been relatively quiet in the aftermath of his confrontation with Rusk and McNamara in April. Earlier in the year he had expressed his views on Vietnam in press conferences, interviews, occasional references to southeast Asia in speeches on foreign affairs, and insertions of articles and editorials into the *Congressional Record,* such as Frank Church's January *Ramparts* interview and the April *New York Times* editorial advocating a vigorous role for the U.N. in southeast Asia. But Fulbright had eschewed major Senate addresses on Vietnam until June 7, partially in order to refrain from direct public criticism of the President.

"Political and Economic Reconstruction in South Vietnam" dealt with two basic issues: Johnson's June 1 request, and the nascent nationalism of underdeveloped countries in Asia, Latin America, and Africa. Fulbright maintained that in Vietnam, as in the other emerging nations, nationalism was a far more powerful force than communist or capitalist idealogy. "Communism" or "democracy" would be successful "in the underdeveloped world to the extent–and only to the extent–that they make themselves the friends of the new nationalism."[120] In Fulbright's opinion, the Vietnamese people were not concerned with the ideological struggle between communism and democracy. He believed the Vietnamese were principally interested in tending their rice crops, educating their children, building a viable economy, and ending the violence that ravaged their land. The meeting of their human needs was "the only meaningful objective of the war and the probable condition of success in the war."[121] Fulbright regretted that American efforts to stabilize South Vietnam's political and economic structure had been dwarfed by American expenditures for war in southeast Asia.

On June 7 Fulbright also enumerated Johnson's recommendations for additional economic assistance to South Vietnam, Thailand, and Laos. Approximately half of the $89 million would be used to finance Saigon's imports of iron, steel, and other materials necessary for industrial expansion, and another $25 million would provide electrical, agricultural, and medical services. The remaining $19 million would be utilized for the development of the Mekong River Basin.[122] It was ironic that Fulbright was endorsing the Mekong project, for in 1965 he had been scathingly critical of such bilateral assistance programs during the foreign aid debate. He had argued that economic aid should be multilateral rather than bilateral in order to attenuate charges of American "neocolonialism" and to help prevent the United States from becoming increasingly entangled in the internal affairs of other nations.[123] He had denied that vital American interests were involved in many of the underdeveloped nations receiving American aid, including South Vietnam.[124]

Fulbright's June 7 endorsement of the President's Baltimore proposals for a Mekong River Basin project was partially inconsistent with his April Associated Press interview, in which he had doubted the feasibility of inaugurating the Mekong program while the war continued. Even during the June 7 Senate debate Fulbright was ambivalent about the Mekong project. Shortly after he praised Johnson's Baltimore proposals in his speech, he became engaged in a dialogue with Senator Gruening in which he said, "So long as the war is continuing as it is, what we can do in this respect [the Mekong River Basin development] will be limited."[125] Fulbright's fundamental position was probably summarized a few moments later when he reiterated his support for a negotiated settlement as a precondition for the economic development of southeast Asia. He concluded: "What appeals to me the most about the proposal is the possibility–at least, I hope it is a probability that the emphasis will be changed from escalating the war into construction or reconstruction and development of this area."[126]

An unlikely coalition formed on June 7 to oppose the President's request for expanded economic assistance to South Vietnam. Wayne Morse and Ernest Gruening, the two most radical opponents of Johnson's Vietnam policy,[127] were aligned with a group of senators who had enthusiastically endorsed expenditures for military escalation in Vietnam, including Bourke Hickenlooper of Iowa and Strom Thurmond of South Carolina. The improbable Hickenlooper-Morse alliance acquired 26 total votes.[128] Johnson's recommendations were supported by the majority of the dissenters against escalation, including Fulbright, Mansfield, McGovern, Nelson, and Church. Dirksen and several fervent anticommunists also voted in favor of the administration. Jacob Javits and Robert Kennedy of New York, as well as Edward Kennedy of Massachusetts and one-third of the entire Senate, abstained. The economic aid passed the Senate by a vote of 42 to 26.

An understanding of the June 7 debate might be enhanced by analyzing the arguments of Hickenlooper, Fulbright, and Morse. Hickenlooper asserted that the Senate did not have sufficient information concerning the economic assistance proposal. In contrast, the Iowa Senator considered the military requests to have been quite specific. When Fulbright pressed him to define exactly what the military appropriations would be used for in Vietnam, the most specific explanations Hickenlooper could offer were "for war," "for military activity," and finally, for "victory."[129] Fulbright challenged Hickenlooper's statements, maintaining (in a reference to the May 7 passage of Johnson's military appropriation request) "the Senate even more precipitately authorized and appropriated $700 million, and no one knew whether that was to be used for nuclear bombs for Peiping, or what it was to be used for."[130] According to Fulbright, the senators associated with Hickenlooper had complete trust in the military leaders and allowed them to spend billions of dollars as they pleased, but this pro-military Senate bloc would subject any meager request for economic assistance to the most rigorous and pedantic examination.

Wayne Morse represented the smallest faction in the Senate. He did not oppose all economic aid to South Vietnam, but he did oppose the addition of $89 million to the foreign aid bill, wryly observing: "We had better get the war settled first. I have a little difficulty with the paradox of pouring $89 million of aid into a country and, at the same time, destroying $89 million worth of property."[131] Morse concluded that the Senate could never be adequately informed about the expenditure of the $89 million in a land 9,000 miles from American shores, just as it had not possessed precise information regarding the $700 million military appropriation in May.

The Oregon senator emphasized the fact that the Vietcong would inevitably capture many of the materials sent to rural areas. [132] Morse's perspective was accurate, for the Vietcong dominated many rural areas throughout South Vietnam and had frequently captured American commodities (and American weapons) intended for South Vietnam's development.[133] Hickenlooper's June 7 orations on the merits of military appropriations as opposed to economic appropriations were vacuous, although he was probably correct to criticize the precipitous manner in which Johnson demanded Senate approval of his economic aid request.

During the June 7 debate Fulbright had failed to explain how the United States could effectively begin an enlarged program of economic development in South Vietnam while the level of violence was expanding. Considering his colloquy with Gruening and his earlier doubts about the Mekong project, he may have actually agreed with Morse's analysis of the prospects for economic aid. But Fulbright was determined to encourage any conciliatory gestures toward the Vietnamese communists in 1965, including the Johns Hopkins proposals. In the early period of the escalation it was common for many of the dissenting senators and other critics of the American intervention to hope that the President's Baltimore address would be an initial step toward a negotiated settlement; as late as 1966 the southeast Asian expert Bernard Fall suggested that one component of a diplomatic solution for Vietnam might be to "restate and expand the idea of a flexible area-wide rehabilitation program" on the basis of the Baltimore speech.[134]

Fulbright's June 7 speech had not offered an alternative to the Johnson administration's policy. "Political and Economic Reconstruction in South Vietnam" dealt with the broad philosophical problem of the underdeveloped nations' responses to the West, and it described the technical points of the President's June 1 message to Congress. In a major Senate address on June 15, Fulbright attempted to clarify his position concerning the alternatives confronting American policy in southeast Asia. The June 15 speech, entitled "The War in Vietnam," was unquestionably Fulbright's most important Senate discourse on Vietnam in 1965. Johnson had invited Fulbright to the White House in early June and delivered another monologue on his valiant resistance to the extremists' demands for massive expansion of the war.[135] This conference with the President was a unique occurrence in Fulbright's career, for it was the only time he ever allowed Johnson to read the draft of one of his speeches.[136] The June 15 address would constitute Fulbright's final effort to maintain his precarious strategy of praising the President while opposing military escalation in Vietnam.

On June 15 Fulbright rejected the arguments in favor of an intensified air war. According to the Foreign Relations Committee chairman, the bombing of North Vietnam had failed to weaken the military capability of the Vietcong. An expanded bombing campaign would invite a large-scale intervention of North Vietnamese troops, and this intervention "in turn would probably draw the United States into a bloody and protracted jungle war in which the strategic advantage would be with the other side."[137] A decision to escalate the air war to unprecedented levels of destruction would risk Chinese intervention or nuclear war. Fulbright believed that a military victory in Vietnam could be attained "only at a cost far exceeding the requirements of our interest and honor."[138] American policy should be based upon a determination "to end the war at the earliest possible time by a negotiated settlement involving major concessions by both sides."[139] The senator reiterated his appeal for a return to all the specifications of the 1954 Geneva accords.

Fulbright recited the litany of President Johnson's attempts to end the war through negotiations, above all the Johns Hopkins initiatives. The North Vietnamese and Chinese, he alleged, had repudiated the President's magnanimous offer to enter unconditional discussions for terminating the war.[140] Fulbright admitted, however, that American policy had been characterized by serious errors in the past. In Fulbright's view, the most detrimental mistake had been American encouragement for President Ngo Dinh Diem's violations of the Geneva accords in failing to hold the elections envisaged by the 1954 agreements.[141] He suggested that in contemplating a new diplomatic conference it would be well for both sides to recall the destructive consequences of their past violations of the Geneva agreements. Fulbright contended that American policy had erred most recently by failing to halt the bombing for more than the perfunctory six-day suspension in May 1965.[142]

Despite his admissions of American blunders in the past and his predictions of disaster if the U.S. military intervention expanded, Fulbright urged a restrained "holding action" in Vietnam.[143] He explicitly repudiated a precipitous withdrawal. In a turgid, one-sentence paragraph, Fulbright delineated the justification for American involvement in the Vietnam War, the identical justification he would spend much of the next decade condemning: "I am opposed to unconditional withdrawal from South Vietnam because such action would betray our obligation to people we have promised to defend, because it would weaken or destroy the credibility of American guarantees to other countries, and because such a withdrawal would encourage the view in Peiping and elsewhere that guerrilla wars supported from outside are a relatively safe and inexpensive way of expanding Communist power."[144] It was the most inaccurate statement Fulbright ever uttered on the subject of Vietnam, and it obviously contradicted his earlier views that the Vietnamese conflict was fundamentally a civil war.[145] This sentence of the June 15 speech rendered Fulbright vulnerable to legitimate criticisms that he had vacillated, and it also facilitated Johnson's ad hominem charges that Fulbright's later denunciations of the Vietnam War were based on personal pique.[146] The latter charges were unjustified, but the vague notion that "Peiping" either was supporting or was planning to support the communist guerrillas in southeast Asia seriously weakened Fulbright's analysis on June 15. It is ironic that his opposition to the Vietnam escalation in 1965 was hampered by a perspective on China as an aggressive power, for it is clear in retrospect that one of the greatest achievements of Fulbright's 32-year career in Congress was his contribution to the improvement of Sino-American relations from 1966 to 1972. Early in 1966, Fulbright would begin to use the Foreign Relations Committee as a forum for publicizing dissident ideas about China, Vietnam, and the anticommunist ideology. The historian Daniel Yergin has described the 1966 China and Vietnam hearings as "the crucial beginning step within the United States to making a realistic appraisal of American policy in Asia."[147]

The genesis of Fulbright's criticism of Johnson's Asian policy can be traced to his January 1965 *Time* interview (if not earlier to the "Bridges East and West" speech of 1964). In the *Time* interview, he advocated probing "for areas of peaceful contact" with China, and he expected the Chinese leadership to gradually become less hostile toward the United States.[148] He was reading voraciously in the scholarly literature on Far Eastern politics, economics, and history, and his ideas about the Chinese communists were in flux.[149] But his public statements on China in the first half of 1965 were erratic; at times he would revert to the hoary platitudes of the Cold War concerning Chinese malevolence, and on other occasions he would appeal for an amelioration of Sino-American relations.[150]

Perhaps Fulbright felt that he was significantly qualifying his June 15 statement by specifying "unconditional" withdrawal as being unwise. Many other important critics of escalation opposed immediate abandonment of South Vietnam. Walter Lippmann's June 17 column in the *Washington Post* warned against any desire to "scuttle and run."[151] Lippmann was still trying to avoid direct personal criticism of Johnson,[152] and even complimented him in one passage of the June 17 column:

> In the task of containing the expansion of communism there is no substitute for
> the building up of strong and viable states which command the respect of the mass

of their people. The President, of course, knows this, and has frequently said it.[153]

Nevertheless, Lippmann joined Fulbright in adamantly opposing any expansion of the American military involvement in southeast Asia.[154] The June 15 Senate address and the June 17 column were probably their final major efforts to conciliate the President.

Fulbright's speech fomented a debate that continued throughout the summer of 1965. The Arkansas senator became involved in a discussion with several of his colleagues immediately after he finished speaking on June 15. Stuart Symington of Missouri commended Fulbright's address, especially the passages recounting American peace initiatives. He asked Fulbright to clarify his statement about an American holding action. Fulbright maintained that if a diplomatic conference could not be arranged immediately, then the United States should remain in South Vietnam until October and then negotiate a settlement. He thought the monsoons and the Vietcong offensive would be subsiding in October, thus making that month an auspicious juncture to end the war.[155]

A few moments after Symington's remarks, Ernest Gruening eulogized Fulbright's exposition for opposing escalation, endorsing a return to the Geneva agreements, and reminding the Senate that U.S. policy in Vietnam had been plagued by errors in the past. Gruening observed that official U.S. pronouncements rarely admitted any American mistakes or any American violations of the Geneva accords, and he congratulated Fulbright for demonstrating that both sides had violated the 1954 agreements.[156] No one was surprised when Fulbright agreed with Gruening's accolade of his speech.[157]

The June 15 discussion between Fulbright and Republican Senator Leverett Saltonstall of Massachusetts was much less mellifluous than the Fulbright-Gruening dialogue. Saltonstall was disturbed by the intransigence of "the other side" in rejecting negotiations. According to the Massachusetts Republican, the North Vietnamese had transgressed against agreements in the past and might try to do so again after future negotiations. He felt that Fulbright had not adequately confronted this problem.[158] Fulbright did not deign to repeat his arguments that both sides had violated previous agreements, and responded to Saltonstall by saying he was primarily concerned with preventing an expansion of the conflict "either of worldwide proportions or even as large as the war in Korea was. I do not think that the Korean war was beneficial to the world or to that country."[159]

A few days after the June 15 speech, the Republican Congressional leadership delivered a vigorous indictment of the Arkansas senator's position. House Minority Leader Gerald R. Ford and Senate Minority Leader Everett Dirksen held a joint news conference to attack Fulbright's proposal for a negotiated settlement involving "major concessions by both sides."[160] The Republican doyens averred that far from obtaining a compromise with "the Communists," the United States should specify the concessions which it would refuse to offer.[161]

The controversy between Fulbright and important Republican politicians reverberated through the summer of 1965. In contrast to Fulbright's plea for a bombing halt, on July 7 Representative Ford called for immediate air strikes against antiaircraft missile sites in North Vietnam. Reporters asked Ford at a news conference whether he would make this recommendation if he knew Russian technicians were present at the missile sites. He replied, "If the Soviet Union wants to participate in escalating the war, I'm fearful they'll have to take the consequences."[162] Fulbright described the Ford statement as the precise attitude that would risk a direct confrontation with the Soviet Union and possibly lead to general war.[163]

Richard Nixon launched the most vitriolic Republican attack on Fulbright in September. While he was visiting South Vietnam on September 5, Nixon held a news conference in which he criticized Fulbright's "so-called peace feelers."[164] Nixon accused Fulbright of advocating a "soft line" toward North Vietnam and "a major concession to the Communists in order to get peace."[165] He pontificated that negotiations would only reward aggression, prolong the war, "encourage our enemies, and discourage our friends."[166] The former Vice President complained that military escalation was proceeding too slowly, and a massive enlargement of U.S. ground forces in Vietnam would be necessary. In Nixon's view, the United States must prepare to fight for four more years, if not longer: "We cannot afford to leave without a victory over aggression."[167] Nixon also warned on September 5 that if President Johnson "compromised with the Communists" the Republicans would make Vietnam a campaign issue in the 1966 Congressional elections and the 1968 presidential election.[168]

Immediately following Fulbright's June 15 speech, President Johnson called an impromptu press conference in which he challenged the Congressional critics of his Vietnam policies to repeal the Gulf of Tonkin Resolution.[169] Johnson claimed that virtually all of the dissenting members of Congress had fully approved his policies by passing the Tonkin Resolution and hence could not properly oppose the escalation. Pro-administration senators and journalists seconded the President's assertions. Senator Dodd answered Fulbright by inserting in the *Congressional Record* an endorsement of Johnson's Vietnam policy by AFL-CIO president George Meany.[170] On June 23 Johnson's old friend William S. White denounced the recalcitrant bloc of senators who wistfully dreamed of rendering the communist aggressors more tractable by granting excessive concessions while requesting nothing in return. "The most important of these senators," White affirmed, "is William Fulbright of Arkansas."[171] According to White, the Chinese laughed at America's dissenting senators and did not even attempt to conceal their objective of subjugating South Vietnam. The *Washington Post* columnist bemoaned the pernicious consequences of the Arkansas senator's "appeasement": "Sen. Fulbright demanded a suspension of American bombing of the nests of aggression in North Vietnam. The predictable result was more and more aggression."[172]

On June 16, the front-page news reports in both the *Washington Post* and the *New York Times* interpreted the Fulbright address as evidence that the President was beginning to recognize the wisdom in avoiding any expansion of the southeast Asian conflict.[173] The *Times* reported that an increasing number of senators shared Fulbright's disenchantment with escalation, including McGovern, Church, Morse, Gruening, Albert Gore of Tennessee, and the Republicans Javits, Aiken, and John Sherman Cooper of Kentucky.[174] The *Post* described Fulbright's appeal for "major concessions" as an "authoritative" statement of President Johnson's position, largely because of Fulbright's extended conference with the President the day before the speech.[175] The President's press conference dispelled this erroneous notion. Two weeks later an Evans and Novak column entitled "LBJ and the Peace Bloc" expressed a more accurate view, arguing that Johnson was conducting a June offensive to disarm his critics.[176] He had recently persuaded Senator Church to deliver a speech praising his ceaseless efforts to restore peace to southeast Asia, and he had even convinced the "arch-critic" Wayne

Morse to remain silent during much of June. Finally, Johnson had successfully beseeched Fulbright to extol the presidential peace initiatives on June 15, although the mild criticisms in the Foreign Relations Committee chairman's address were sufficient to incur the President's wrath.[177]

Several senators commended Fulbright's analysis of the Vietnam crisis in the weeks following June 15. Joseph Clark of Pennsylvania endorsed Fulbright's plea for a return to the Geneva accords and placed the June 17 Lippmann column in the *Record*.[178] Mike Mansfield opined that Fulbright's remarks "constituted a most constructive contribution to the consideration of this critical issue and were in the best traditions of the Senate."[179] Mansfield inserted into the *Record* a June 17 *New York Times* editorial approving the Fulbright speech. The *Times* lauded Fulbright for opposing both "unconditional withdrawal" and escalation: "At a time when some military men and some Republican leaders, including Representative Laird, of Wisconsin, are returning to the Goldwater objective of total victory and calling for a stepped-up bombing of North Vietnam, this re-statement of aims is invaluable."[180] Every American, the editorial maintained, should read Fulbright's exposition that military victory could be attained "only at a cost far exceeding the requirements of our interest and our honor."[181] The *Times* was hopeful the President agreed with Fulbright's arguments.

Senator Church addressed the Senate on July 1 and complimented Fulbright's contributions to the Vietnam debate. He placed in the *Record* an address Fulbright had delivered to the Rhodes scholars' reunion at Swarthmore College on June 19. Fulbright's caustic tone on June 19 provided a remarkable contrast to his tortured efforts to praise the President while opposing escalation only four days earlier. The Arkansas senator contended that in the past few months the state of world politics had "taken an ominous turn," and he quoted Mark Twain's bitter "War Prayer" to illustrate the belligerent passions unleashed by the Dominican and Vietnamese interventions.[182] Fulbright advised his fellow Rhodes scholars that "the nations are sliding back into the self-righteous and crusading spirit of the Cold War" essentially because "the crises in Vietnam and the Dominican Republic are affecting matters far beyond the frontiers of the countries concerned."[183] The Dominican intervention threatened to destroy the future of the once promising Alliance for Progress. The Vietnam War, Fulbright charged, was damaging American relations with Eastern European countries and other small nations by disseminating the belief that America was an implacable enemy of nationalism in the underdeveloped world.[184]

Fulbright believed that the most destructive result of the Vietnamese and Dominican crises was the degeneration of Soviet-American relations. The detente that had begun to develop in 1963 was now held in abeyance, largely because of the remote involvements in Indochina and Hispaniola.[185] Fulbright warned against the dogmatism that envisaged international relations as an immense arena of conflict between virtuous Americans and nefarious communists. It would be constructive, he observed, for Americans to realize that the Russians and the Chinese sincerely believed their policies would lead to world peace, the ultimate goals which Americans pursued.[186] The remark about the Chinese was a general philosophical reflection, but it clearly bore no resemblance to Dean Rusk's specter of the Chinese communist conspiracy against freedom.

Fulbright's June 19 address was a harbinger of the senator's increasingly vociferous opposition to the Vietnam War during the next decade. His rationale for giving the June 15

Senate speech was clear; he would offer one last major effort to praise Johnson's diplomacy, and if this failed to magnify his influence he would be forced to become openly critical of the President.[187] Frank Church recognized Fulbright's emerging role as a public dissenter on July 1, when he described the Rhodes scholars' reunion discourse as "stark, but accurate."[188]. These were the ideas, Church asserted, of "a political philosopher and foreign affairs analyst unexcelled among those who have held political office in the modern history of our Republic."[189] The Idaho senator's encomium may have been exaggerated, but he obviously understood and welcomed Fulbright's burgeoning determination to publicly oppose the Johnson administration's foreign policies.

It should be acknowledged that the language of the June 19 Swarthmore address was highly generalized and theoretical. Fulbright did not refer specifically to President Johnson or any official of the executive branch. The Swarthmore address was somewhat similar to *Old Myths and New Realities* in its theoretical tenor, although *Old Myths* was optimistic about the possibility of improving Soviet-American relations, in contrast to the profound pessimism of the June 19, 1965, speech. The March 25, 1964, Senate address had endorsed the policy of supporting the noncommunist regime in Saigon, while the only references to southeast Asia in the Swarthmore speech were reflections about the Vietnam War's pernicious impact upon America's relations with the Soviet Union and the underdeveloped nations of the world.

Fulbright delivered his final effort to praise Johnson's foreign policy in the June 15 Senate discourse in order to exhaust the moribund strategy of hoping to enhance his private influence at the White House by publicly supporting the President. At the time many of Fulbright's aides and several journalists were arguing that he had a responsibility to avoid an open break with the President that could destroy the senator politically.[190] During the next three months Fulbright would conclude that his ultimate responsibility consisted of attempting to educate and marshal the force of public opinion against the crusading anticommunist consensus, which seemed invincible in 1965.

In 1964 Fulbright's fear that public criticism of Johnson's foreign policy would strengthen Goldwater had contributed to the senator's support for the presidential decisions on Vietnam. But in 1965 a resolve to challenge the administration's anticommunist assumptions was replacing his earlier fear that public opposition to the Vietnam policy might ignite an onslaught of McCarthyism from the radical right. During April 1965 he had publicly confronted the Secretary of State and the Secretary of Defense over the escalation of the bombing against North Vietnam, and in his June 19 speech he implied that the contemporary American policies in Vietnam and the Dominican Republic were reviving the crusading anticommunism of the early Cold War and severely damaging the prospects for Soviet-American detente. In 1965, of course, Fulbright no longer had to fear the Goldwater candidacy; but a more important reason for his nascent determination to oppose the President's diplomacy was his realization that the administration's southeast Asian and Dominican policies were displaying the rigid, global anticommunism the senator had excoriated in *Old Myths and New Realities*. There was a vital difference between Fulbright's views in *Old Myths and New Realities* and his perspective in the June 19 Swarthmore address, for in March 1964 he had directed his critique of militant anticommunism against Goldwater and the radical right; by the summer of 1965 he was beginning to direct similar criticisms against the foreign policy of President Lyndon Johnson.

CHAPTER V. CHALLENGE TO THE ANTICOMMUNIST CONSENSUS

Summer to Autumn, 1965

Senator Fulbright's first caustic criticisms of specific Johnson policies dealt with the administration's diplomacy in Europe and Latin America. It was perhaps logical that the senator's indictment of the administration's global anticommunism was initially focused upon these two regions, because before 1965 Fulbright had primarily been knowledgeable about U.S. relations with Europe and Latin America.[1] During July he asserted that the President was failing to resist the efforts of extreme anticommunists to sabotage American relations with eastern Europe. The dispute over eastern European policy was a comparatively minor episode; but Fulbright's opposition to the administration's intervention in the Dominican Republic precipitated an irreparable break between the senator and the President and inaugurated Fulbright's role as a dissenter during the last three and a half years of Johnson's Presidency.

In July 1965, Fulbright criticized the administration for failing to resist extremist pressures against the policy of "building bridges" to the communist world. The most recent example of this failure, in Fulbright's opinion, was the rupture of negotiations between the Rumanian government and the Firestone Company for the design and engineering of synthetic-rubber plants.[2] A Firestone competitor and an extreme right-wing organization called Young Americans for Freedom had conducted an anticommunist crusade against the Firestone-Rumanian agreements, claiming that the Vietcong would eventually use the tires that the Rumanian plants would produce.[3] The opponents of the Firestone contract had denounced it for indirectly supplying the Chinese communists with badly needed technical expertise.[4] Fulbright decried the administration's curious reluctance to support Firestone against the extremists. Such stalwart anticommunists as William F. Buckley, Jr., Strom Thurmond, and John Tower raged at Fulbright and extolled the Y.A.F. for its patriotic stand against the Rumanians, who had recently joined with Russian and Chinese officials in a condemnation of American "open acts of war" in Vietnam.[5] Joseph Kraft, Mansfield, and Morse endorsed Fulbright's position.[6]

George Ball investigated Fulbright's allegations,[7] and in the fall of 1965 the State Department successfully defended a group of American tobacco companies that had purchased eastern European tobacco against another series of attacks from anticommunist pressure groups.[8] Fulbright wrote a letter to President Johnson in October congratulating the

State Department for its handling of the eastern European tobacco purchases in contrast to its weak performance in the Firestone fiasco.[9] The senator was well aware that the Firestone affair and the tobacco purchases were quite insignificant in comparison with Vietnam.[11] But he felt that an important principle was involved, for if extreme anticommunist organizations could influence the U.S. government then there was little hope of conducting a rational foreign policy. Fulbright believed that his criticism during the Firestone episode may have led to the more reasonable State Department response to American trade with eastern Europe in the fall of 1965. This lesson strengthened Fulbright's resolution that he could influence the Johnson administration only by public dissent, and not by private conversations and memoranda.[12]

Fulbright's foreign policy statements in July were highly annoying to President Johnson.[13] The President was increasingly excluding Fulbright and Adlai Stevenson from any significant role in the administration's deliberations on Vietnam.[14] The responses of Fulbright and Stevenson to the Vietnam escalation in early 1965 were somewhat similar. Stevenson was favorably impressed by Johnson's Baltimore speech.[15] The U. N. Ambassador's memoranda to the President in 1965, however, had clearly warned against a precipitous expansion of American military operations in Indochina.[16] Stevenson was disturbed by the bombing of North Vietnam. In a March memorandum to the President, Stevenson predicted that a limited bombing campaign from the 17th to the 19th parallels would not "produce indications of a [North Vietnamese] willingness to negotiate."[17] He speculated that an expansion of the bombing to population centers and industrial targets farther north might lead the North Vietnamese to negotiate, or it might provoke them into more extensive infiltration of North Vietnamese forces into South Vietnam via Laos; regardless of Hanoi's reaction, world opinion would be outraged by massive American bombing of Asian noncombatants. Thus, Stevenson concluded that "the worldwide political consequences of such action [air strikes against major population centers] would very probably outweigh any military advantages it might produce."[18] In his view, the United States should enter negotiations even if the Vietnamese communists did not provide any favorable assurances in advance concerning the results of the negotiations.

Stevenson had been cooperating with U Thant in attempting to arrange negotiations in southeast Asia. In his April 28 memorandum to the President, Stevenson stated that U Thant was "strongly convinced that the continued use of force holds no promise for a settlement but only the ever-increasing danger of wider warfare, as well as a reorientation of Soviet foreign policy from limited detente with the West to close cooperation with Communist China."[19] U Thant proposed a cessation of hostilities in Vietnam, followed by "immediate discussions, in whatever manner the parties prefer, designed to strengthen and maintain the cessation of military activity and to seek the bases for a more permanent settlement."[20] Stevenson argued that a positive American response to the Secretary General's appeal would reinforce the favorable international impression created by the President's Baltimore speech. "The Secretary-General," Stevenson maintained, "by making such an appeal, would become the center of the effort to terminate hostilities in Vietnam, a fact which would facilitate a later move on our part–should we so desire–to involve the United Nations in the role of supervising or policing a negotiated settlement."[21] Stevenson frequently advised the State Department of U Thant's proposal for discussions "with Saigon,

Hanoi, and the Viet Cong seated at the table." On July 7 the Ambassador informed the Department that U Thant had recently "repeated several times that it was only realistic that the discussions of a cease-fire would have to include those [the Viet Cong] who are doing the fighting."[22]

The U.N. Ambassador's occasional vague references to "Chinese expansionist plans" weakened the logic of his private communications to the President. Stevenson did not adduce evidence to support the allegations of Chinese expansionism. His statements on China in his 1965 memoranda were difficult to explain, especially in light of later reports by David Halberstam and other writers of his private opposition to the administration's China policy.[23] Perhaps Stevenson believed that whatever influence he still retained as an official of Lyndon Johnson's administration would vanish if he challenged the President's view of China as an aggressor. Fulbright's private communications to the President may have been more blunt than Stevenson's in describing escalation in Vietnam as a disastrous course, but the senator's April memorandum to the President had also suffered from the reluctance to refute the Cold War hostility toward China. Whatever the explanation for their inaccurate statements on China in 1965, the administration obviously rejected the Fulbright and Stevenson recommendations for a negotiated settlement in southeast Asia.

Stevenson's basic perspective on Vietnam may have been revealed on a July 12 British Broadcasting Corporation television program. BBC correspondent Robin Day asked Stevenson to comment upon a recent exposition by Fulbright in which the senator expressed hope for a "greater emphasis on the political aspects of the problem" in Vietnam.[24] Stevenson replied that all knowledgeable observers of southeast Asian affairs had always regarded the political problems as "uppermost," and "that this isn't a war that can be resolved by military means, nor can we find a solution there except by political means." A few moments later he dutifully defended American policy, reminding his interviewer that "Communist China is doing its very best to destroy the United Nations," while President Johnson had offered unconditional discussions on Vietnam. Many of Stevenson's friends later maintained that he was depressed by having to defend Johnson's Vietnam and Dominican policies and was considering resigning in early July.[25]

During 1965 Fulbright and Stevenson also held a similar revulsion for Johnson's policy in the Dominican Republic. The administration's Dominican intervention strengthened their suspicions that the Vietnam escalation was mistaken and precipitous. In late May, Stevenson privately remarked that "if we did so badly in the Dominican Republic, I now wonder about our policy in Vietnam."[26] Among the major public or private critics of Johnson's foreign policy, Fulbright and Stevenson were probably the two statesmen who were most disturbed by the intervention in the Dominican Republic. Several of Stevenson's associates later said the Dominican crisis troubled Stevenson more than any other incident that occurred during his years in the U.N.[27] The Ambassador thought the American intervention had alienated public opinion throughout Latin America and devastated the principle of peaceful international settlements. David Schoenbrun later publicly reported that Stevenson had described the intervention as a "massive blunder." The President was disgusted by the Schoenbrun story, and instructed his press secretary to dismiss it as a disservice to Stevenson's memory.[28]

The extent of the Fulbright-Stevenson communication concerning Hispaniola is not clear. In June Stevenson wrote a letter to Fulbright, his friend for 30 years, but it dealt with placing restraints on the arms race.[29] Fulbright sent a note to Stevenson on July 13 to forward a constituent's request for an appointment, apologizing for writing about such a mundane matter during a time of crisis in southeast Asia and the Caribbean.[30] "Now you see in action," the senator wryly observed in a poignant admission of his lack of power, "the major function of a Senator."[31] Fulbright's pessimism did not inhibit his determination to challenge the administration's foreign policy, for the Foreign Relations Committee investigation into the Dominican crisis was scheduled to begin in mid-July. The senator's melancholy was deepened when Ambassador Stevenson died of a heart attack on July 14, the day the Dominican hearings began.

The decision to hold the hearings accelerated the decline in Fulbright's influence with the administration. On July 27 Johnson summoned 11 Congressional leaders to the White House to discuss the proposals for increasing the number of American ground forces fighting in Vietnam.[32] In earlier White House meetings the President had asked Fulbright and Mansfield for their expected dissenting opinions only after all the other Congressional leaders had approved of his policies.[33] Now in late July, Johnson's relationship with Fulbright had deteriorated to the extent that the President did not deign to invite him to the July 27 discussions.[34] Historian George Herring has described the July deliberations as "the closest thing to a formal decision for war in Vietnam," and yet the President excluded the chairman of the Senate Foreign Relations Committee from participating in the White House discussions regarding the decision.[35] George Smathers, who ranked 10th on the Foreign Relations Committee but was a staunch anticommunist, was asked to attend rather than Fulbright.[36] Thus the President isolated Mansfield, who alone argued against sending more troops.[37] And even Mansfield declared that he would loyally support Johnson's decision, despite his profound skepticism regarding expansion of the war.[38]

Fulbright met with a group of the most powerful foreign policy leaders in the Senate on the afternoon of July 27. Richard Russell, chairman of Armed Services, Majority Leader Mansfield, John Sparkman of Alabama, and two Republicans—John Sherman Cooper of Kentucky and George Aiken of Vermont—assembled in Mansfield's office. Russell and Sparkman were generally considered hawks on foreign policy, but Fulbright was pleasantly surprised to find that *all* the senators present believed that the bombing never should have begun and that Vietnam was peripheral to America's vital interests. The senators summarized their views and sent them to the President immediately. To give the letter maximum political effect, Fulbright decided not to include signatures on the letter from the most liberal or vociferous critics of the war such as Morse, McGovern, Church, and others, since he knew Johnson regarded them as either starry-eyed idealists or opportunists. But surely, Fulbright felt, the President could not reject such conservative voices as Russell, Sparkman and Cooper. On July 28, Johnson met with the dissenting senators to inform them that the United States was now committed to the war in Vietnam, where the situation was rapidly deteriorating. America would fight to the end, and the war might last six or seven years. Fulbright was shocked.[38a]

The President had decided to increase the number of American troops in South Vietnam from the 75,000 already there to a total of approximately 200,000; nonetheless he publicly announced at his July 28 press conference an increase of only 50,000, although he indicated more troops would be sent to Vietnam later to halt the "mounting aggression":

We did not choose to be the guardians at the gate, but there is no one else.

Nor would surrender in Vietnam bring peace, because we learned from Hitler at Munich that success only feeds the appetite of aggression. The battle would be renewed in one country and then another country, bring with it perhaps even larger and crueler conflict, as we have learned from the lessons of history . . .

I have asked the commanding general, General Westmoreland, what more he needs to meet this mounting aggression. He has told me. We will meet his needs. I have today ordered to Vietnam the Air Mobile Division and certain other forces which will raise our fighting strength from 75,000 to 125,000 almost immediately. Additional forces will be needed later, and they will be sent as requested . . . [39]

Johnson continued to mislead Congress and the public as to the significance of his decisions, denying that he had authorized any change in policy.[40] The United States would have to fight in Vietnam to maintain the credibility of its promises to all other nations, but the President added, "We do not want an expanding struggle with consequences that no one can perceive."[41]

Fulbright was engrossed in his analysis of the Dominican intervention in the six weeks after the July 28 press conference. The senator's doubts about the administration's actions had increased in May, when the executive branch exaggerated the danger of communist infiltration in Santo Domingo.[42] Admiral Raborn had informed Fulbright in April 28 that three communists were participating in the revolt, but in May U.S. officials publicized a list of 58 communists who were allegedly allied with the pro-Bosch forces.[43] Many of the 58 people on the list could not have played a role in the rebellion because they were either in prison or out of the country during April.[44] The administration valiantly attempted to explain why 58 communists represented an ominous threat to a nation of 3.5 million people. Dean Rusk declared that the precise number of communists involved in the revolt was unimportant, for "There was a time when Hitler sat in a beer hall in Munich with seven people."[45]

President Johnson was much more imaginative than Rusk in portraying the hideous specter of aggression on Hispaniola, revealing at a June 17 press conference that "some 1,500 innocent people were murdered and shot, and their heads cut off."[46] This account mystified the President's aides, for the atrocities Johnson described never occurred.[47] Fulbright would eventually regard the falsehood about the 1,500 decapitations as the classic example of Johnson's duplicity.[48] During the Dominican hearings Fulbright asked Thomas Mann to explain the President's macabre assertion on June 17. Mann simply refused to believe that Johnson had uttered the statement, even after Fulbright produced the official State Department bulletin of the June 17 press conference, which reprinted the President's exact words.[49]

The Dominican hearings remained closed to the pubic for many years after 1965, although in 1968 Haynes Johnson and Bernard Gertzman publicized a limited amount of information concerning the hearings from an anonymous source.[50] (The two journalists published a biography of Fulbright in 1968.) The most important administration witnesses were Rusk, Thomas Mann, and Cyrus Vance. The administration spokesmen argued that a military dictatorship was preferable to a communist regime.[51] Mann contended that any popular front that included communists was "per se a dangerous thing."[52] He conceded that Juan Bosch was not a communist, but he considered Bosch a "poet professor type" who could be controlled by the Dominican leftists, many of whom had been trained in Cuba.[53] Mann believed that if the communists established a dictatorship in the Dominican Republic, "Haiti would fall within 30 minutes."[54] During the course of the hearings it became clear that the administration thought the communist threat in the Dominican Republic was related to leftist subversion in Colombia, Venezuela, Uruguay, Argentina, Bolivia, Ecuador, British Guiana, Haiti, Honduras, Panama, and Guatemala.[55]

Fulbright observed that according to Mann's analysis, the United States should intervene against any movement in Latin America that had communist support.[56] The result of such a policy would be to restrict the alternatives for all Latin America to either communist rule or a military junta.[57] In Fulbright's opinion, the widespread dissatisfaction with the status quo in Latin America was justified. If the policy of indiscriminate intervention persisted, then some dissident Latin Americans might conclude that they must become communists in order to change the reactionary character of their pro-United States governments. He hoped the administration would adopt a policy of encouraging changes in Latin America by aiding noncommunist reformist groups. Specifically, he argued that the administration would have been wise to support the noncommunist rebels in the Dominican revolt.[58]

The Foreign Relations Committee was hopelessly divided over the Dominican controversy. Dodd, Lausche, Hickenlooper, and Russell Long assumed an aggressive anticommunist position during the debate.[59] The largest faction on the committee did not support the hawks, but also failed to criticize the President.[60] Only four or five senators supported Fulbright's resolute criticism of the administration's actions.[61] Although the hearings were private, Dodd and others publicly accused Fulbright of being prejudiced against the administration. The dispute within the committee became so acrimonious in August that Fulbright publicly speculated about resigning his chairmanship.[62] The committee never wrote a report on its investigation.

Johnson temporarily reversed his efforts to isolate Fulbright and instructed Rusk to begin another series of private discussions with the Foreign Relations Committee chairman.[63] Fulbright wrote a speech in August elucidating his opposition to the intervention. His administrative assistant, Lee Williams, advised him not to deliver it, because it would precipitate an "irreparable break" with Johnson.[64] The aide told Fulbright, "You practically call him a liar."[65] Fulbright discussed his critique of American policy in Santo Domingo with several foreign affairs analysts, including Carl Marcy, the chief of staff of the Foreign Relations Committee.[66] When Marcy and the others agreed that his analysis was accurate, Fulbright decided to deliver the address.[67]

On September 15, 1965, Fulbright presented his conclusions concerning the Dominican crisis to the Senate. He asserted that the United States intervened in the Dominican Republic not primarily to save lives, as the administration originally contended, but to prevent the victory of a revolutionary movement that was judged to be communist-dominated. According to Fulbright, the Dominican communists did not participate in planning the revolution. Although they quickly joined the revolt after it erupted, the communists never controlled the rebel forces. The fear of "another Cuba" had little basis in the evidence offered to the Foreign Relations Committee; on the contrary, Fulbright maintained that a chaotic situation existed "in which no single faction was dominant at the outset and in which everybody, including the United States, had opportunities to influence the shape and course of the rebellion."[68] In their apprehension lest Santo Domingo become another Cuba, American officials had forgotten that there was a crucial difference between communist support and communist control of a political movement, and that it was quite possible to compete with the communists for influence in a reformist coalition rather than abandoning it to them. The senator argued that the policy followed in the Dominican Republic would have disastrous consequences if applied throughout Latin America:

> Since just about every revolutionary movement is likely to attract communist support, at least in the beginning, the approach followed in the Dominican Republic, if consistently pursued, must inevitably make us the enemy of all revolutions and therefore the ally of all the unpopular and corrupt oligarchies of the hemisphere.[69]

Fulbright criticized the administration's failure to exert a positive influence on the course of events during the early days of the rebellion. On April 25, Juan Bosch's party (the P.R.D. or Dominican Revolutionary Party) requested a "United States presence," and on April 27 the rebels asked for American mediation and a negotiated settlement.[70] Fulbright observed that the P.R.D. entreaty presented an excellent opportunity to encourage the moderate forces involved in the coup, either by providing American mediation or officially indicating that the United States would not oppose a regime controlled by the P.R.D. But both requests were rejected on the basis of exaggerated estimates of communist infiltration into the revolutionary forces and hostility to Juan Bosch's return to power. Pedro Bartolome Benoit, the leader of the military junta, appealed for American military assistance on April 28. Only American intervention, Benoit pleaded, could avert a communist coup.[71] Washington responded that if Benoit would say American lives were in danger the United States would intervene. Benoit then changed his rationale for needing American troops so as to conform to Washington's response, and within hours Marines landed in Santo Domingo. After an exhaustive analysis of W. Tapley Bennett's cables to Washington, Fulbright decided that the fear of communism was the Ambassador's fundamental reason for recommending the military intervention. The senator's conclusion followed: "The danger to American lives was more a pretext than a reason for the massive U.S. intervention that began on the evening of April 28."[72]

On September 15 Fulbright denounced the reversal in American attitudes toward Juan Bosch and the P.R.D. during the period from September 1963 to April 1965. Fulbright recalled that the United States had supported Bosch while he was President of the Dominican Republic during 1963. President Kennedy attributed such importance to the Dominican President's success that he sent Vice President Johnson and Senator Hubert Humphrey to Bosch's inauguration in February 1963.[73] Fulbright reminded the Senate that in December 1962 Bosch had triumphed in the first free and honest election ever held in the Dominican Republic. After Bosch was overthrown by a military coup in September 1963, the United States had not recognized the successor regime for three months. The Johnson administration had finally recognized the government that succeeded Bosch only after it began conducting military operations against a band of alleged communist guerrillas in the Dominican mountains. Fulbright strongly suspected that the successor government exaggerated the threat of the guerrillas in order to secure American recognition.[74]

In Fulbright's view, the administration had erred in opposing the P.R.D.'s return to power after Donald Reid Cabral's regime collapsed in April. The senator conceded that Juan Bosch "was no great success as President," yet Bosch was still "the only freely elected President in Dominican history," and "the only President who was unquestionably in tune with the Alliance for Progress."[75] Bosch himself had not been eager to return to Santo Domingo in April 1965, but Fulbright emphasized that "the United States was equally adamant against a return to power of Bosch's party, the P.R.D., which is the nearest thing to a mass-based, well-organized party that has ever existed in the Dominican Republic."[76] Fulbright summarized the history of American policy toward the Dominican Republic during the Johnson administration with an unequivocal condemnation: "Thus the United States turned its back on social revolution in Santo Domingo and associated itself with a corrupt and reactionary military oligarchy."[77]

Fulbright proceeded from his indictment of the administration's actions in the Dominican Republic to a general critique of Johnson's foreign policy toward Latin America, observing, "one notes a general tendency on the part of our policy makers not to look beyond a Latin American politician's anti-communism."[78] The Dominican crisis had severely damaged America's reputation among "our true friends" in Latin America, who had supported the ideals of the Alliance for Progress.[79] In the opinion of many Latin American reformists, the United States had suppressed a movement that was sympathetic to the Alliance's goals. The landing of Marines in Santo Domingo violated the O.A.S. Charter's principle of non-intervention, which most Latin Americans considered the quintessence of the inter-American system. Fulbright's reference to the O.A.S. Charter was related to his only passage on Vietnam in the speech; he detected an inconsistency in the administration's zeal to uphold the "ambiguous" commitment to South Vietnam while simultaneously violating a "clear and explicit treaty obligation" in the Americas.[80] The passage on Vietnam was brief, however, and Fulbright did not elaborate upon this argument.

In his September 15 address Fulbright attacked the global anticommunism of the Johnson foreign policies. "Obviously," the senator concluded, "if we based all our policies on the mere possibility of communism, then we would have to set ourselves against just about every progressive political movement in the world, because almost all such movements are subject to at least the theoretical danger of Communist takeover."[81] The rigid anticommunist approach contradicted the nation's interests, according to Fulbright. He maintained that diplomacy must be based upon developing "prospects that seem probable" rather than forever attempting to anticipate possible dangers of communism.[82]

Fulbright's final major argument on September 15 dealt with the disingenuous manner in which the administration had justified its actions to the public. "U.S. policy," he charged, "was marred by a lack of candor and by misinformation."[83] Fulbright illustrated the lack of candor and misinformation by referring first to the initial assertions that the United States executed the intervention to save American lives, and second by quoting President Johnson's June 17 statement about the 1,500 decapitations in the Dominican Republic. The senator tersely noted that there was no evidence to support the President's allegation. Fulbright tried to maintain in the speech, and also in a September 15 letter to Johnson, that he was not attacking Johnson personally but only the substance of the President's policies.[84] The distinction was unimportant. As Daniel Yergin has written, "The speech was aimed at the stupidity and what he was soon calling the arrogance of American power but, though he like to pretend it was not directed also at Johnson, Johnson rightly saw that it was."[85]

Fulbright defined his purpose in delivering the address as an effort to develop guidelines for future policies, and not simply to lambast the administration for its previous errors. The decision to hold the hearings had apparently begun to exert a minor impact on U.S. policy by September 14, when General Wessin y Wessin, who had been one of the leaders of the military junta during late April, left the Dominican Republic under American pressure. In his speech Fulbright described Wessin's departure as "a step in the right direction."[86] A year later in *The Arrogance of Power* Fulbright speculated about the effect of his Dominican address. His September 1965 exposition may have been a factor, he wrote, in the administration's subsequent support for democratic government in the Dominican Republic, thus repairing some of the damage wrought by the April 1965 intervention in support of the Dominican military. The senator also conceded that the O.A.S. and the Inter-American Force that remained in Hispaniola until the summer of 1966 had finally restored a degree of order and stability. But Fulbright did not agree that the election of Joachin Balaguer as President of the Dominican Republic on June 1, 1966, vindicated the intervention, for the power of the reactionary military oligarchy remained unimpaired.[87] Fulbright's skeptical attitude was accurate, especially considering the background of events before the election campaign. In December 1965 Dominican army tanks had attacked Colonel Caamano and other leaders of the April 24 revolution while they were attending a requiem mass for one of the colonels killed in the revolt. The offices of a pro-Bosch magazine and some pro-Bosch radio and television stations were bombed. The United States claimed to be neutral during the campaign in early 1966, but actually the enormous U.S. embassy provided strong support for Balaguer, who had held the honorific post of President during the regime of Rafael Trujillo, the cruel dictator who had oppressed the people of the Dominican Republic for 30 years until he was assassinated in 1961. Trujillo had even meddled in the affairs of other Latin American nations, sending his agents to Caracas in 1960 in an attempt to assassinate the progressive leader of Venezuela, Romulo Betancourt; the O.A.S. had imposed sanctions against Trujillo for his role in the unsuccessful assassination attempt against Betancourt. In 1966, the Dominican oligarchy backed the former Trujillist Balaguer. The voting itself was reasonably fair, but the context of American support for Balaguer and the Dominican military's intimidation of some of Bosch's allies strongly influenced the results against Bosch.[88]

In Fulbright's view, the administration's actions during the Dominican crisis had alienated virtually all the reformist movements in Latin America and weakened confidence in America's word and intentions throughout the world.[89] He contended in both the September 1965 speech and in *The Arrogance of Power* that the American anti-revolutionary bias might drive Latin American reformers into becoming anti-American leftists.[90]

The administration's vehement response to his speech in 1965 shocked Fulbright. Secretary of Defense McNamara described Fulbright's criticism of Ambassador Bennett as "an unfair attack" and claimed there was "no question" that American citizens were endangered by the Dominican revolution.[91] McNamara did not answer the senator's assertion that U.S. officials exaggerated the communist threat.[92] Senator Richard Russell of Georgia seconded McNamara's defense of Bennett. Bill Moyers, the President's press secretary, dismissed Fulbright's conclusions as totally unjustified.[93] Tom Dodd led the pro-administration senators in a counterattack against the Foreign Relations Committee chairman. According to Dodd, Fulbright suffered "from an indiscriminate infatuation with revolutions of all kind, national, democratic, or Communist," as well as a general "tolerance of communism."[94] Russell Long rebuked Fulbright's speech by maintaining, "We have information now that the Communists in the Dominican Republic are stronger than Castro was when he started to take Cuba."[95] Senator Smathers congratulated Long for his analysis of the Dominican crisis and added, "Castro proved that it was not necessary to have a large number of communists in order to deliver a country to communism."[96] Representative Ford and Senator Dirksen joined the President's Democratic supporters in condemning the Fulbright speech.

In the first few days after September 15, the debate concerning Fulbright's Dominican address did not focus upon the substance of the analysis. Many of Fulbright's opponents argued that the chairman of the Foreign Relations Committee simply did not have the right to deliver such a scathing criticism of the President's foreign policy. William S. White epitomized this attitude when he averred that

> ...it is not simply with President Johnson and Secretary of State Dean Rusk that Fulbright has broken. He has also broken the unwritten rule of the game, a code which demands of those holding high committee chairmanships—and uniquely the chairmanship of foreign relations—a degree of self-restraint and personal responsibility not demanded of the rank and file.[98]

In contrast to White, Republican Senator Margaret Chase Smith of Maine resolutely defended Fulbright's right to dissent, even though she supported the administration's policy in the Dominican Republic.[99] Similarly, Eric Severeid's article in the October 4, 1965, *Washington Evening Star* commended the Foreign Relations Committee's ex post facto investigation into the Dominican crisis for establishing lessons that would be useful in future policies.[100] Sevareid did not comment upon the substance of Fulbright's conclusions, except to remark that he disagreed with them, but he complimented the senator when he wrote, "the Fulbright speech was a drama simply because it was unique in this period of consensus and a homogenized Congress."[101]

Senator Mansfield also rejected the notion that Fulbright's criticism was irresponsible, although he publicly supported the administration's Dominican policy.[102] Whether Mansfield privately agreed with Fulbright's analysis is uncertain. Mansfield had attended only one of the 13 Dominican hearings, and he was reluctant to become involved in an open confrontation with the executive branch.[103] The Montana senator tended to believe that he could influence Johnson's policies more effectively through private remonstrances rather than vociferous public opposition.[104] Fulbright had agreed with Mansfield's strategy earlier in 1965, but by the autumn he was convinced of his inability to influence Johnson through private communications.[105] After Fulbright became a public adversary of the Johnson foreign policies (including the Vietnam War) in late 1965 and early 1966, he did not cooperate with Mansfield as closely as he had when the two senators were privately advising against escalation in early 1965.[106]

Joseph Kraft, Walter Lippmann, Morse, McGovern, McCarthy, and Joseph Clark were among the small minority who supported Fulbright during the Dominican furor. Kraft aptly summarized Fulbright's position: "With the Dominican case before him, he sensed a new disposition to identify all social protest with Communist subversion, and a connected tendency to shoot first and think later."[107] In Kraft's view, the administration's rancorous attacks on the Dominican address only intensified the doubts Fulbright raised about U.S. policy in Latin America. The administration failed to resist the extreme anticommunists who were condemning the Foreign Relations Committee chairman. In response to the Fulbright speech, the House of Representatives voted overwhelmingly to pass a resolution that endorsed direct American military intervention in Latin America to prevent "subversive action or the threat of it."[108] Armistead Selden of Alabama sponsored the resolution. According to Kraft, Selden was "wrapping himself in the mantle of anti-communism" in order to ensure his re-election.[109] Kraft asserted that the administration had promoted Thomas Mann, Douglas MacArthur II, and other Foreign Service officers within the State Department whose ideas, careers, and reputations were permanently attached to "the era of unsophisticated, monolithic anti-communism."[110] The State Department forces led by Thomas Mann had "practically invited the Selden resolution."[111] Finally, Kraft concluded, "the White House itself seems to be holding anti-communism as a rod to discipline its congressional majority."[112] If Johnson maintained this rigid anticommunist stance, it seemed doubtful that he could respond constructively to the vast social changes sweeping Latin America, Africa, and Asia. Kraft regretted that the President "has gone soft on Goldwaterism."[113]

Walter Lippmann commended Fulbright's Dominican address in his September 28 *Washington Post* column. The amelioration of Soviet-American relations, Lippman wrote, depended upon encouraging "the prudent and the practical to predominate over the ideological and the hot."[114] "In this country," he continued, "the process will require the resumption of public debate—the kind of debate which Senator Fulbright has once again opened up. For the issue which he has posed in his remarkable speech is the essential issue in our attitude and policy toward the revolutionary condition of our time."[115] Lippmann believed there was no definitive formula that could be applied to determine American foreign policy toward all underdeveloped nations. American diplomacy must be flexible in responding to the infinitely varied circumstances present in Latin American, African, and Asian revolutions. Lippmann recommended a conciliatory attitude or "some kind of accommodation" in order to avoid confrontations with the Soviet Union in the Third World. He extolled Fulbright's efforts to revitalize the public dialogue between the administration and its critics. It was imperative to prevent the public debate in America from being monopolized by "the assorted hangers-on, often more Johnsonian than Johnson himself, who are presuming to lay down the rule that only those who conform with the current political improvisations are altogether respectable and quite loyal."[116]

Lippmann had perceived the ultimate significance of the Dominican speech by analyzing it in the global context of Soviet-American relations. Fulbright had criticized far more than the American blunders on a tiny Caribbean island; he had challenged the anticommunist assumptions of an entire era. In evaluating the historical importance of the Dominican address, Daniel Yergin later wrote, "From that moment can be dated the breakup of the Cold War consensus and the beginning of a meaningful dissent."[117] As Haynes Johnson described the September speech, "Not since Borah had criticized the sending of the Marines into Nicaragua in the 1920s had the chairman of the Foreign Relations Committee directly challenged an administration of his own party," although "the circumstances were hardly comparable."[118]

The Dominican furor had a devastating impact on Fulbright's relationship with Johnson. Many years later the senator informed an interviewer, "Never again was I consulted."[119] Upon reflecting a moment, he added that he had never been genuinely consulted, for throughout the first half of 1965 Johnson was simply "trying to keep me in bounds, so I wouldn't take issue and embarrass him."[120] Fulbright wrote Johnson a courteous letter in early October, explaining that his speech was intended "to help you in your relations with the countries of Latin America."[121] "Subservience," he reminded Johnson, "cannot, as I see it, help develop new policies or perfect old ones."[122] The President did not respond to Fulbright's letter.[123]

Fulbright's melancholy was deepened at the height of the Dominican crisis when Betty Fulbright suffered a heart attack. She recovered, but the Fulbrights' social activities were thenceforth reduced. The senator was understandably bitter at the time: "I can't advise them [senators] to speak out, because if you do then everyone jumps down your throat. This country has gotten to where you are not supposed to speak out."[123a]

During the summer of 1965 Fulbright became convinced that the administration's impetuosity, duplicity, and crusading anticommunism were not confined to U.S. foreign policy in Latin America, but were fundamental characteristics of Johnsonian diplomacy.[124] After his Senate discourse of September 15, Fulbright rapidly began to intensify his critique of the military escalation in Vietnam. In an October 24, 1965, *Meet the Press* appearance he reiterated his appeal for a suspension of the air attacks against North Vietnam, arguing that a bombing halt must continue much longer than the six-day pause of May in order to represent a genuine peace initiative.[125] When Peter Lisagor asked him if it was not the function of Republicans to dissent from a Democratic President's foreign policy, Fulbright replied that the great majority of the Republicans endorsed Johnson's actions. "I don't understand," he asserted, "why this consensus has reached such a state that people feel Senators, or particularly this Senator, should not speak about any matter in which he dissents from the current views of the administration."[126]

Throughout the NBC program Fulbright defended his analysis of the Dominican crisis. The Vietnam War was almost totally overshadowing the Dominican intervention by October, and the reports in the *New York Times* and other newspapers concentrated upon Fulbright's recommendations for the Vietnam policy on *Meet the Press*.[127] The White House issued its customary repudiation of Fulbright's Vietnam proposals.[128]

During the fall of 1965, the discussion of Fulbright's dissenting views began to focus on the substance of his ideas rather than the question of whether he possessed the right to openly criticize President Johnson. E. W. Kenworthy's article in the October 31 *New York Times* presented a succinct assessment of Fulbright's foreign-policy positions in the early 1960s. The article was entitled, "Fulbright: Dissenter." Kenworthy recalled that in March 1961, Fulbright's memorandum on Cuba had urged President Kennedy to tolerate the Castro regime rather than attempting to overthrow it.[129] The Cuban memorandum obviously did not deter Kennedy from authorizing the Bay of Pigs invasion. Kenworthy affirmed that Fulbright had enjoyed a minor success in the summer of 1965, when he was "the prime mover in assembling a group of influential senators from both parties—who must be nameless—who are credited with reinforcing the President's growing resistance to those who advocated a call-up of reserve and national guard units last summer."[130] Nevertheless, Kenworthy admitted, Fulbright had been advising Kennedy and then Johnson for five years, yet "much of the advice was, like Robert Frost's road, 'not taken.'"[131] Kenworthy noted the President's hostile reactions to the Dominican address and Fulbright's statement on Meet the Press. The article ended with the somber observation that Fulbright's advice "has more effect after the event than on it. And so it almost certainly will be with policy on the Dominican Republic and Vietnam—if, indeed, it has any effect at all."[132]

In retrospect, it is clear Fulbright's relationship with Johnson had been gradually deteriorating ever since the "Old Myths and New Realities" speech of March 25, 1964. By the fall of 1965, the administration perceived Fulbright as one of the most influential critics of Vietnam policy. In McNamara's view, the reality that the war was assuming more and more of the flavor of an American enterprise led to "some outbreaks of criticism in the United States, but polls continued to show broad public support for President Johnson." As for the Congress, the Secretary of Defense recalled that "approximately 10 senators and 70 representatives could be counted severe critics—including such influential figures as William Fulbright, Mike Mansfield, and Wayne Morse—but, on the whole, the legislative branch remained supportive."[132a] A Newsweek article in late 1965 compared "Old Myths and New Realities" to the Dominican speech, claiming that the latter "echoed his earlier salvo against U.S. foreign policy last year."[133] Actually, there was a crucial difference between the two, for "Old Myths and New Realities" was primarily a theoretical attack on the mythical concept of a relentlessly expansionist, monolithic communist bloc.[134] In contrast, "The Situation in the Dominican Republic" of September 1965 constituted both a critique of America's global anticommunism and a specific denunciation of the 1965 Dominican intervention. The March 1964 Senate address did not, of course, criticize American policy in Vietnam.[135] The most controversial passage of "Old Myths and New Realities" dealt with Cuba.[136] Fulbright argued that the United States should accept the reality of the Castro regime as "a distasteful nuisance but not an intolerable danger" and stop flattering "a noisy but minor demagogue as if he were a Napoleonic menace."[137] Throughout 1964 Johnson and Rusk had carefully disassociated the administration from the ideas expressed in "Old Myths and New Realities."[138] Nevertheless, Fulbright's relations with Johnson had remained outwardly amicable after the March 1964 speech.

Fulbright's objections to the foreign aid bill in late 1964 and early 1965 were a secondary annoyance to the administration. But his dissent against the bombing of North Vietnam in February and his appeal for a negotiated settlement in his April 5 Vietnam memorandum exasperated the President. From March through the June 15 Senate address Fulbright publicly supported the administration, but his proposal for a bombing halt and his resolute opposition to escalation infuriated Johnson. During the summer he began to excoriate the administration's failure to pursue the policy of "building bridges" to the eastern European nations. The process of Fulbright's alienation from President Johnson culminated in his September condemnation of the Dominican intervention. A few weeks after the

Dominican controversy subsided, Fulbright decided to inaugurate an exhaustive Foreign Relations Committee investigation of American foreign policy toward Vietnam and China. There would be a vital difference between the Dominican and the Vietnam hearings, for the latter would be not only public, but nationally televised.

Walter Lippmann was Fulbright's most formidable ally in all of the senator's major confrontations with the Johnson administration. Lippmann and Fulbright had known each other since the 1940s, and the famous columnist had often eulogized the Arkansas senator. In a preface to Karl Meyer's 1963 collection of Fulbright's speeches Lippmann wrote, "The role he [Fulbright] plays in Washington is an indispensable role. There is no one else who is so powerful, and also so wise and if there were any question of removing him from public life, it would be a national calamity."[139] Lippmann delivered a similar accolade to Fulbright after the "Old Myths and New Realities" speech in 1964.[140] He endorsed Fulbright's position during the 1965 foreign aid dispute.[141] The two men had been discussing Charles de Gaulle's neutralization plan for Vietnam at least as early as May 1964.[142]

During the first half of 1965 Fulbright and Lippmann eschewed direct personal criticism of President Johnson, but adamantly opposed military escalation in southeast Asia. At the same time, McGeorge Bundy was having a series of private conferences with Lippmann that were similar to Dean Rusk's discussions with Fulbright. As Ronald Steel has observed, Bundy did not believe that he could convince Lippmann to support military escalation, but he thought Lippmann might be "neutralized," or prevented from publicly opposing the administration's policy.[143] Lippmann was invited to the White House on April 6, a few hours after Johnson had conferred with Fulbright and Mansfield about his Baltimore speech. The President assured Lippmann that "the war had to be won on the non-military side."[144] Bundy hinted to Lippmann that there might a possibility of a cease-fire.[145] Fulbright and Lippmann later asserted that Johnson misled them about his intentions, and both men began to denounce the Johnson foreign policies in late 1965 and early 1966 when the President's duplicity had become palpable. The extensive personal communications Fulbright and Lippmann had earlier experienced with Rusk, Bundy, and Johnson virtually ceased by December 1965.[146]

In 1965 there may have been a minor difference between Fulbright and Lippmann in the sense that Fulbright was incensed by the Dominican intervention, while Lippmann initially argued that the action was defensible, not on the ground that the United States was a "global fire department appointed to stop communism everywhere," but on the "old-fashioned and classical diplomatic ground that the Dominican Republic lies squarely within the sphere of influence of the United States."[147] Later, when it became obvious there had never been a communist threat in Santo Domingo, Lippmann expressed his dismay that Marines had restored the power of a reactionary military dictatorship.[148] After the Dominican address in September, Lippmann congratulated Fulbright for generating a public dialogue concerning American foreign policy.[149]

In evaluating Fulbright's analysis of the Vietnam War in early 1965 Daniel Yergin has written: "history shows that Fulbright's private arguments to Johnson were perceptive."[150] The senator had predicted in his April memorandum that "the commitment of a large land army would involve us in a bloody and interminable conflict in which the advantage would lie with the enemy."[151] It is precisely because Fulbright's prediction was so perspicacious that some foreign policy analysts have criticized him for not being more aggressive in opposing the war. Johnson deceived Fulbright in early 1965, but that does not absolve the senator from the responsibility of exhausting all methods of resistance against a policy he detested, especially in the years 1965 to 1968. Fulbright and the minority of dissenting senators might have introduced an amendment to terminate the funds for the war during the Johnson administration. Albert Gore later contended that such an action would have "destroyed us and the movement politically."[152] Fulbright reluctantly agreed with Gore's argument in the early period of the war, for he did not sponsor legislation cutting off funds for military operations in southeast Asia until the Nixon administration began.[153]

Fulbright would sponsor an amendment to a defense appropriations bill in 1969 that prohibited the President from using American money to support military operations in Laos and Cambodia.[154] The Fulbright amendment did little or nothing to inhibit Nixon's military incursions into those two countries.[155] Yet it served as the model for the McGovern-Hatfield amendment to end the war and the Cooper-Church amendments restricting military operations in Laos, Thailand, and Cambodia.[156] The Fulbright amendment may have been similar to many of the Arkansas senator's foreign policy initiatives; in the beginning it appeared to be a failure, but from a long-term perspective it may have strengthened other dissenters in their determination to oppose the war. One should hasten to add that it was late in the Nixon administration before the Congressional movement to cut off funds for the war in Cambodia succeeded in ending the American military involvement in southeast Asia.[157] Perhaps if the movement had begun in 1965 or 1966 its success might not have been so belated. Senator Gore argued, to the contrary, that opposition to the military expenditures would have simply destroyed the antiwar forces before they could gather political momentum. It is clear that the opponents of the war were a small minority in 1965. But perhaps Fulbright offered the most accurate answer to the question of how to oppose the Vietnam War in his 1972 book, *The Crippled Giant*. "In our system," Fulbright maintained, "withholding funds is a legitimate, appropriate—and, all too often, the only effective—means of restraining the executive from initiating, continuing, or extending an unauthorized war, or from taking steps which might lead to war."[158] Fulbright's conclusion might provide a fitting epitaph for an era of Congressional impotence: "It is not a lack of power which has prevented the Congress from ending the war in Indochina but a lack of will."[159] Many of the opponents of the Vietnam War might have wished Fulbright had arrived at this conclusion in 1965, rather than in the 1970s.

If Fulbright's performance in the arena of direct legislative action was belated, it was nevertheless true that during late 1965 Fulbright began to revitalize the process of public debate concerning American foreign policy. The initial reaction to Fulbright's dissent revealed the potentially repressive nature of the American anticommunist consensus. In the first six months of 1965 Fulbright's efforts to foster an open dialogue with the administration had been sporadic, and his statements had often been inconsistent. During the period when he was largely confining his opposition to private remonstrances, his influence on U.S. foreign policy was negligible. After he became one of President Johnson's foremost adversaries in late 1965, Fulbright's admirers attributed a panoply of magnificent achievements to the senator: supposedly, he had marshaled the forces of public opinion against a disastrous war, he had restrained the crusading anticommunism of American diplomacy, and he had led Congress' struggle to arrest the expansion of the administration's power. It is doubtful that one senator could have immediately produced all of these alleged triumphs, and while his dissent would ultimately deal a devastating blow to the rigid Cold Warrior consensus, his influence was more in the nature of a long-term educational influence rather than an immediate impact. Yet Fulbright's dramatic emergence as a dissenter in late 1965 represented a historic accomplishment, for he had demonstrated that an American statesman could repudiate the dogmas of militant anticommunism and retain, or even enhance, his public prestige.

At the beginning of 1966, Fulbright's burgeoning role as a dissenter was powerfully reinforced by a prescient letter from Clyde Edwin Pettit, an Arkansan who had recently visited South Vietnam as a radio broadcaster and interviewed more than 200 military personnel, businessmen and journalists. Pettit began his disturbing letter (which is discussed further in the section of this book on sources) by warning that "The war is not only not going well, the situation is worse than is reported in the press and worse, I believe, than is indicated in intelligence reports; I have had intelligence officers admit as much to me privately." Pettit acknowledged that morale was exceedingly high among the American troops. but such a "gung ho spirit" and "a messianic attitude of anger...can lead to dangerous complacency and overconfidence." In a sense, Pettit explained, "the number of U.S. military personnel is irrelevant...most are literally confined in closely guarded compounds, protected by moat-like defenses of concertina-wire and incessant barrages of U.S. artillery and 85 and 105-millimeter mortar fire." The overconfident enlisted men and low-to-middle-ranking officers opposed any compromise or cease-fire, and they presented a stark contrast to the colonels in Saigon, "who are infinitely more pessimistic, more cynical, and more realistic. One colonel who is most erudite...told me, 'If there is a God, and he is very kind to us, and given a million men and five years and a miracle in making the South Vietnamese people like us, we stand an outside chance of a stalemate.'" Pettit conceded that these were harsh and bitter words, but he gloomily related that "there is considerable evidence that [the colonel] may be stating the situation realistically." Pettit lamented the

> tragic fruits of generations of French misrule. Vietnam is dotted with magnificent old French colonial mansions which serve as reminders of a dispensation which did nothing but suppress, which provided no education beyond the primary grades, which insulted a national dignity in countless ways. These mansions are inhabited by American officers now...we are now the inheritors of the French mantle. We are Westerners, the outsider, the alien. To the leftists, we are villains; to the rightists, we are fools (even if, out of temporary self-interest, we are allies). Left or right, there are very few South Vietnamese indeed who do not hate the shadows that remain of the Navarres and the Salans, and who do not inwardly cheer at the memory of Dienbienphu... Father Ho is a great leader who I happen to believe with considerable evidence is more admired in the South than any other Vietnamese.

Pettit, who was a confidant of Lee Williams and Fulbright, at first requested that the letter's author remain anonymous, and thus a few weeks later Fulbright would quote Pettit's epistle at the Vietnam hearings without revealing who had written it; a few months later Fulbright would take the floor of the Senate and praise Clyde Pettit's letter as brilliant and prophetic.

VI. FULBRIGHT'S OPPOSITION TO THE VIETNAM WAR, 1966-1968

In the aftermath of the Dominican controversy, President Johnson attempted to ostracize Senator Fulbright from Washington's social and political life. A minor example of the administration's bitterness occurred in December 1965, when the executive branch rejected the senator's routine request for a jet to fly to a parliamentarians conference in New Zealand, causing him to make a tedious four-day journey by a propeller plane.[1] The President no longer permitted Fulbright to engage in lengthy private conversations with him at the White House, and increasing hostility replaced their earlier friendship.[2] In contrast to the President's repudiations of the Foreign Relations Committee chairman's ideas concerning American foreign policy, Johnson began to praise Governor Orval E. Faubus, a zealous anti-communist who was Fulbright's principal critic in Arkansas.[3]

Johnson's efforts to denigrate Fulbright's foreign policy positions did not deter the Senator from fostering a public debate over the Vietnam War in 1966. During early January he reflected upon the most effective strategy to employ in restraining the administration's Far Eastern policy. The President "takes actions," Fulbright informed a constituent in a January 13, 1966 letter, "in the Dominican Republic and in Vietnam of which I do not approve. Under a strict interpretation of the constitution it would appear that he should request a declaration of war or some other form of approval by the Congress."[4] He observed that Congress possessed the "constitutional recourse" of impeaching the President, but he apparently regarded impeachment as extreme and quixotic, and he did not recommend it.[5] His response to the dilemma of how to oppose the Vietnam War constituted an attempt to mobilize public opinion against the escalation policy, an attempt that Fulbright inaugurated with the Vietnam hearings.

The Senate Foreign Relations Committee's nationally televised investigation of the Vietnam War in January and February 1966 was the first organized forum for dissent against America's involvement in the southeast Asian conflict.[6] There had been sporadic antiwar demonstrations, speeches, and teach-ins in 1965, but there was no genuine, sustained dialogue between the administration and the opponents of the American intervention in Vietnam until 1966. During the 1966 Vietnam hearings the Foreign Relations Committee transferred its respectability to the opposition against the Vietnam War and began the discrediting of President Johnson's policies that eventually contributed to his decision not to seek re-election in 1968.[7]

In preparation for the Foreign Relations Committee's analysis of the Johnson administration's Asian policy, Fulbright continued to educate himself about Far Eastern affairs. During the December trip to New Zealand he read Han Suyin's *The Crippled Tree*, a Chinese engineer's poignant critique of Western imperialism in early 20th-century China.[8] He was also reading the works of Jean Lacouture, Philippe Devillers, and Bernard Fall during late. 1965 and 1966. He began to regard China's official anti-Western rhetoric as an understandable reaction to Western intervention in Chinese internal affairs from the Opium Wars to the 1940s.[9] The senator agreed with Lacouture's arguments stressing the autonomy of the Vietcong and deprecating Rusk's perspective on the southeast Asian conflict as "a war of aggression, mounted in the North against the South."[10]

On January 28, 1966, the Foreign Relations Committee scheduled Dean Rusk to testify in support of a bill authorizing a supplemental $415 million in foreign economic aid, most of which would be used in Vietnam.[11] There were 180,000 American soldiers in South Vietnam at the time.[12] Three days earlier the Foreign Affairs Committee in the House of Representatives had responded favorably to the Secretary of State's testimony.[13] Rusk's dialogue with the Senate Foreign Relations Committee was not to be so harmonious. Fulbright's opening statement at the Vietnam hearings revealed that the Senate committee would analyze the central issues of the Vietnam War and would not confine its investigation to the specific proposal for supplemental assistance: "These requests for additional aid cannot be considered in a vacuum, but must be related to the overall political and military situation in Vietnam. I am sure that this hearing will be helpful to the committee and to the public in gaining a better understanding of fundamental questions concerning our involvement in the war."[14]

On the first day of the hearings Fulbright and Senator Albert Gore questioned Rusk's contention that the administration's massive escalation of the war was justified by the Gulf of Tonkin Resolution. Senator Gore claimed that he had voted for the resolution because he had interpreted it as approving the "specific and appropriate response" [the August 5, 1964 air raid] to the alleged North Vietnamese attacks in the Gulf of Tonkin.[15] Rusk replied to Gore's statement by simply reading verbatim the two crucial sections of the resolution. The first section authorized the President to take all necessary measures to prevent aggression. The second stated that since the peace and security of southeast Asia were vital to American national interests, the United States was prepared, as the President determined, to assist any member or protocol state of the southeast Asia Collective Defense Treaty requesting assistance in defense of its freedom.[16]

Fulbright inserted excerpts from the record of the Senate's August 1964 debate over the Tonkin Resolution into the transcript of the hearings in order to show that Congress had not intended the resolution to be a blank check for the expansion of the military effort in Indochina without the consent of Congress. These excerpts included the passage (which is discussed in the chapter on 1964) where Fulbright and Senator Gaylord Nelson had agreed that the resolution was "aimed at the problem of further aggression against our ships."[17] During the August 1964 debate Fulbright and other senators had rejected the strategy of a massive deployment of ground forces in Vietnam. Rusk responded to Fulbright's assertions concerning the Tonkin Resolution with platitudes about the perfidy of the North Vietnamese and the need to uphold the credibility of America's commitments. The sterility and evasiveness of Rusk's answers at the hearings strengthened the administration's adversaries. As David Halberstam has written, "From that time on, dissent was steadily more respectable and centrist," primarily because of "the failure of the Administration under intense questioning to make a case for the war."[18]

Fulbright asked Rusk to explain why the administration's stated reason for intervening in Vietnam and its terms for withdrawing seemed to be contradictory. American forces were fighting in southeast Asia, according to Rusk, to help the independent sovereign nation of South Vietnam resist the foreign aggression of its neighbor to the north, and the Geneva Agreements of 1954 were an adequate basis for peace. The fallacy in Rusk's argument was that the Geneva Agreements had stipulated that the 17th parallel was "provisional and should not in any way be interpreted as constituting a political and territorial boundary."[19] If one accepted Rusk's doubtful assumption that there were two legitimate states in Vietnam, the conflict was still basically a civil war, for even according to Rusk's estimates 80 percent of the Vietcong were South Vietnamese and there were no Chinese soldiers in South Vietnam.[20]

Fulbright's crucial question about the Geneva Accords concerned the provision for holding elections by 1956. The United States had not signed the Accords, but Undersecretary of State Walter Bedell Smith had issued a unilateral declaration stating that the United States would refrain from the threat or use of force to disturb the Agreements, and would seek to achieve the unification of Vietnam through free elections.[21] In 1955 Eisenhower had acquiesced as John Foster Dulles supported Diem's refusal to hold the elections that would have, in the opinion of all knowledgeable observers, unified Vietnam under Ho Chi Minh's rule.[22] Rusk stressed the continuity of the Eisenhower, Kennedy, and Johnson policies and asserted that the United States had failed to honor its commitment with respect to the Geneva Agreements because the prospects for free elections were poor in 1955. Fulbright described this explanation as a "device to get around the settlement" and asked if the prospects for free elections had ever been favorable in 2,000 years of Indochinese history. Rusk then referred to the elections of 1965, which were local elections held only in the areas controlled by the South Vietnamese government and were irrelevant to the provision for national elections of the Geneva Agreements.[23]

The administration blamed the North Vietnamese for the failure to reconvene the Geneva conference and bring about the cessation of hostilities. According to Rusk, China and North Vietnam had repeatedly stated that negotiations would be possible only when the United States recognized the National Liberation Front (the communist political organization in South Vietnam) as the "sole representative of the South Vietnamese people."[24] Fulbright argued that the NLF's statements were conflicting and that on numerous occasions the NLF had called for free elections to create a coalition government. The administration's position was more bluntly affirmed by retired General Maxwell Taylor, the President's Special Consultant, who informed the Foreign Relations Committee in February that the administration intended to achieve sufficient military successes to force the communists to accept an independent, non-communist South Vietnam. When Fulbright asked Taylor if the Vietcong might be included at a diplomatic conference and if a compromise might be reached on the basis of the existing political and military strength, Taylor dramatically replied, "How do you compromise the freedom of 15 million South Vietnamese?"[25]

Thus, the Johnson administration viewed the corrupt, authoritarian regime of Nguyen Cao Ky and Nguyen Van Thieu was a valiant defender of freedom. As the Vietnam hearings began Johnson flew to Honolulu to confer with Thieu and Ky. In part this meeting was a successful effort to dominate the news as the Vietnam hearings were opening.[26] The Honolulu conference was probably Johnson's most spectacular justification for the war; the principal administration officials were present, photographs were taken of Johnson embracing Ky, and Johnson delivered an exuberant declaration pledging America's everlasting friendship to the South Vietnamese people. The South Vietnamese, he pronounced, "fight for dreams beyond the din of battle. They fight for the essential rights of human existence–and only the callous or the timid can ignore their cause."[27] Johnson could not accept the logic of the "callous and the timid that tyranny 10,000 miles away is not tyranny to concern us—or that subjugation by an armed minority in Asia is different from subjugation by an armed minority in Europe."[28] The President proposed a comprehensive program for development of South Vietnam's economy, medical and educational facilities, and agricultural system which Vice President Hubert Humphrey soon began describing as an Asian or Johnson Doctrine that would, in Humphrey's words, realize "the dream of the Great Society in the great area of Asia, not just here at home."[29]

The Honolulu conference caused considerable dismay among the opponents of the war, partly because General Ky had recently expressed his admiration for Adolf Hitler.[30] More importantly, the Honolulu conference created grave doubts about Johnson's sincerity in claiming that the United States was seeking a political settlement, for the President had solidified the alliance between his administration and the government of Ky and Thieu, who were intransigent in their demand that the National Liberation Front be excluded from all negotiations. When the Secretary of State made his second appearance at the Vietnam hearings in February, Fulbright described the administration's attitude as "adamant" and asked Rusk if the U.S. government supported Ky and Thieu in their refusal to accept a coalition.[31] Rusk evaded the question by relating that Ky had called the NLF the "national enslavement front" at Honolulu.[32]

Johnson revealed that he considered the alleged North Vietnamese-Chinese aggression in Southeast Asia to be analogous to the Soviet threat to Europe in the late 1940s by his statement at Honolulu that it was as essential to help "free men" resist "subjugation by armed minorities" in Asia as it was in Europe. "Subjugation by armed minorities" were the famous words of President Truman in the March 1947 Truman Doctrine speech. When Rusk testified at the hearings in January, he elaborated upon the administration's intention of devising a containment policy for Mao Tse-tung and his presumed surrogate Ho Chi Minh in southeast Asia similar to the containment policy directed against Stalin in Europe.

Rusk began his opening statement at the Vietnam hearings by quoting the basic formula of the Truman Doctrine: "I [Truman] believe that it must be the policy of the United States to support free peoples who are resisting attempted subjugation by armed minorities or by outside pressures." "That is the policy we are applying in Vietnam," Rusk proclaimed.[33] For Rusk, the Vietnam War was ultimately a clash of ideologies, in which the Truman Doctrine must triumph over the Chinese dogma of "wars of national liberation." In 1968 the Foreign Relations Committee again held televised hearings on Vietnam and Fulbright then questioned Rusk as to whether China or North Vietnam represented the threat to American security. Rusk replied that the danger emanated from the Chinese doctrine of world revolution. Fulbright responded by stating the fact that Lin Piao, the Chinese theorist and politician who was the author of the doctrine, had written that if a war of national liberation fails to "rely on the strength of the masses, but leans wholly on foreign aid, no victory can be won, or consolidated even if it is won."[34]

Thus the Chinese dogma of supporting wars of national liberation emerges to a large extent as an expression of sympathy for Third World revolutions rather than a declaration of an intent to sponsor worldwide subversion and guerrilla warfare. The absence of a Chinese military presence in Vietnam was palpable evidence of this fact. Yet at one point in the 1966 hearings Rusk asserted that the struggle in southeast Asia was not the United States' war, but "Mao Tse-tung's war" because of China's support for Ho Chi Minh.[35]

George F. Kennan challenged many of the administration's basic assumptions concerning Vietnam when he testified at the hearings in February. Kennan was a former ambassador to the Soviet Union and Yugoslavia, and had been chairman of the State Department's Policy Planning Committee in the late 1940s.[36] In contrast to Rusk's opening statement that the Truman Doctrine must be applied to Southeast Asia as it had been applied to Europe in the 1940s, Kennan began his presentation by calling Vietnam an area of minimal military and industrial importance and asserting that "if we were not already involved in Vietnam I would know of no reason why we should wish to become so involved."[37] Kennan disputed Rusk's contention that a communist Vietnam would be a Chinese satellite, stating that nationalism is a universal human phenomenon and does not magically desert men when they become communists.[38] In the opinion of Fulbright and Kennan, Yugoslavia was an example of a communist country that had followed a neutral course in the East-West rivalry and that certainly was not a puppet of either of the great communist powers. The existence of the Soviet Union as an alternative ally within the communist world rendered it unnecessary for a communist Vietnam to become merely an extension of Chinese power.[39]

The question of whether China was an expansionist state was one of the fundamental issues debated at the Vietnam hearings. Fulbright and Kennan doubted the validity of the popular view of China as a relentlessly aggressive power, observing that there was a significant disparity between the Chinese leaders' violent rhetoric and their actions. Neither Fulbright nor Kennan expressed the opinion that China was not a difficult nation to deal with. Fulbright described Chinese conduct as "outrageous"; Kennan stated that the idea that China was the center of the universe had always presented problems in China's relations with other countries.[40] But the senator regarded the arrogant anti-American statements of the Chinese as an understandable reaction against the century or more of humiliation inflicted upon China by the West from the Opium Wars to the 1940s. In late February General Taylor conceded in testimony before the committee that the Chinese had been justified in their grave concern and military response to the possibility of an American invasion in 1950, when MacArthur was rapidly advancing toward the Yalu.[41] Fulbright noted that according to Taylor the Indian troops had started the brief war with China in 1962 by moving forward into the disputed territory along the Chinese border. Kennan did not excuse the Chinese aggression in seizing Tibet in 1959, but he pointed out that Chiang Kai-shek was fully in agreement with Mao Tse-tung in considering Tibet to be an integral part of China. Thus, in Kennan's judgment, many of the international controversies involving China in the postwar years would have existed even if China had not been a communist country, for the problems originated in traditional emotions of Chinese nationalism and xenophobia.[42]

Kennan's basic critique of the American policy in Vietnam focused upon his conviction that the Johnson administration had "become enslaved to the dynamics of a single unmanageable situation" and had thereby caused a "grievous disbalance" in the entire global structure of American diplomacy.[43] The administration's escalation of the war had violated one of the cardinal precepts of American foreign policy since the Korean War, which was never to risk a military confrontation with China on the Asian land mass. Moreover, the Vietnam War forced Russia to compete with China in vilifying the American imperialists, for Chinese propaganda had consistently accused the Russians of somehow being in collusion with the United States in Southeast Asia.[44] The central issues of international relations, such as nuclear armaments control agreements, the problems of Germany, and the future of the United Nations and China had all been placed in abeyance in deference to this one remote involvement.[45]

Retired General James Gavin presented the "enclave theory" as an alternative to the escalation policy when he appeared at the hearings in February. In 1954 General Gavin and General Matthew Ridgway had helped persuade President Eisenhower to reject the plan of Admiral Radford, Dulles, and Nixon to intervene in Vietnam to rescue the French from military disaster. Gavin had believed that an intervention would have been a tragic mistake because of the difficulties in the terrain and the possibility of a Chinese intervention.[46] The general reiterated his basic argument in 1966.

Gavin suggested that the United States should confine its military activities to enclaves along the coast or other areas where American air and sea power could be decisive, cease enlarging its ground force, and desist from the bombing of North Vietnam as an initial step toward achieving a diplomatic solution.[47] He urged the administration to renounce its infatuation with the air war, for it was in his estimation one of the greatest illusions of modern times that air power could win a war.[48] The bombings were not "psychologically punishing" the North Vietnamese as Chairman of the Joint Chiefs of Staff Wheeler claimed, but were largely only succeeding in seriously damaging America's image before the court of world opinion.[49]

The American bombing campaign had been utterly futile. Johnson began the systematic bombing of North Vietnam shortly after the Vietcong killed nine Americans at the U.S. base in Pleiku in February 1965. Apparently the air strikes galvanized the North Vietnamese into even more frenzied military resistance against the Americans, for North Vietnamese infiltration into the south had increased from 800 men per month in the summer of 1965 to 4,500 men monthly in early 1966.[50] Gavin believed that if the Johnson strategy of aerial devastation combined with ever-expanding ground combat forces continued for a substantial length of time, the Chinese would re-open the Korean front and invade South Vietnam. The Chinese, with their virtually limitless supplies of manpower, could probably only be defeated through the use of nuclear weapons, in Gavin's opinion.[51] Some of the Chinese leaders were saying at the time that even if China suffered 200 or 300 million casualties from a nuclear attack, they would still have several hundred million people with which they could win any war.[52] This was perhaps the ultimate fear of the opponents of the Vietnam War; that America had "become enslaved to the dynamics" of a situation that might lead to a nuclear war with China.

Fulbright believed China would intervene in southeast Asia only if the Chinese political leaders concluded that the United States was planning to expand the war into a conquest of North Vietnam or an invasion of the Chinese mainland. The senator repudiated the view of China as an aggressive power after the pattern of Nazi Germany. The Johnson administration, however, seems to have equated Nazi aggression in Europe with the alleged North Vietnamese and Chinese threat in Southeast Asia; those who called for an American withdrawal from Vietnam were advocating appeasement. Rusk replied to the question of whether the Vietnam War presented a situation different from Hitler's expansionism in Europe by saying, "There are differences but there are also enormous similarities."[53] When Rusk spoke of "this phenomenon of aggression," he did not draw a significant distinction between the Vietnam dilemma in the 1960s and German aggression in the 1930s. At one point during the Vietnam hearings Rusk proclaimed: "Hitler could see the Japanese militarists were not stopped in Manchuria. Now, what happens here in southeast Asia if Peiping discovers that Hanoi can move without risk?"[54] Henry Cabot Lodge, the Ambassador to South Vietnam, sent a telegram to the Foreign Relations Committee as the Vietnam hearings were opening declaring: "We, Vietnamese and Americans, are doing in Vietnam in 1966 what the free nations failed to do in 1936 when Hitler went into the Rhineland."[55]

Fulbright tried to refute the notion that there was a basic similarity between the China of Mao Tse-tung and the Germany of Hitler in his book *The Arrogance of Power*. The book was based on the Vietnam hearings and a series of lectures the senator delivered in April 1966 at Johns Hopkins University. "China," the senator wrote, "is not judged to be aggressive because of her actions; she is presumed to be aggressive because she is communist."[56] The ferocity of Peking's language had obscured the fact that China had allowed her neighbors to remain independent. China had withdrawn her troops from North Korea in 1958 although there was no external pressure to do so, and had not attempted to dominate the weak and non-aligned nation of Burma.[57] Fulbright agreed with Kennan that even though North Vietnam was to some extent dependent on China for economic and logistical support to prosecute the war, North Vietnam remained substantially in control of its own affairs.[58]

Fulbright did not romanticize China. He stated that the Chinese would have to abandon their ancient image of China as the celestial empire in a world of barbarians and their more recent role as the nominal champion of world revolution before an amelioration of American-Chinese relations could occur.[59] But Fulbright depicted the basic American perspective on the Vietnam War as the consummate example of the ideological prejudice that had distorted the judgments of Americans since the 1940s. Ho Chi Minh was the hated tyrant, while Ky and Thieu were valiant democrats fighting for their nation's freedom; North Vietnam was China's puppet while South Vietnam was America's stalwart ally; and China was the true aggressor in Southeast Asia despite the fact that there were no Chinese troops on the soil of China's southern neighbor, whereas the hundreds of thousands (more than 200,000 in 1966, more than 500,000 in 1968) of American soldiers were resisting foreign aggression in a land 8,000 miles from America's shores.[60]

If the United States considered it vital to its national interests to construct a bulwark against the alleged "Chinese imperialism" in Vietnam, Vietnamese nationalism alone could have provided that bulwark. Americans must acknowledge, Fulbright wrote, that Ho Chi Minh and his communist allies in South Vietnam represented the genuine nationalist movement of Vietnam, the only nation in the world that won its independence from colonial rule under communist leadership.[61]

Fulbright argued that the unilateral nature of the American intervention in Vietnam indicated that America's allies did not share the Johnson administration's view of the conflict as a manifestation of international communist aggression. He believed any political settlement would have to be only tolerable and not satisfactory, such as the 1962 Geneva Accords providing for the neutralization of Laos. Fulbright admitted at the Vietnam hearings that it was true, as Rusk never tired of contending, that the North Vietnamese had consistently violated those agreements by infiltrating troops and equipment through Laos to assist the communists in South Vietnam.[62] But as unsatisfactory as the 1962 Accords were, Fulbright asserted that they were diplomatic triumphs in the sense that hundreds of thousands of American soldiers were not engaged in the Sisyphean task of eliminating the communist guerrillas from the jungles of Laos.[63]

The Foreign Relations Committee succeeded in strengthening the opposition to the war in 1966 despite several difficulties during the hearings. Fulbright could not persuade General Matthew Ridgway to testify before the committee. Ridgway held profound doubts about the war and might have powerfully reinforced Kennan's views, but he could not bring himself to publicly criticize a war while American troops were still fighting.[64] Senator Mansfield did not make a significant contribution to the Committee's investigation of the Vietnam policy, attending only one of the six hearings. A minority of "hawks" on the committee continued to praise the administration and disparage Fulbright's foreign policy positions.[65] Nevertheless, Fulbright was receiving far more support from the members of the Foreign Relations Committee in 1966 than he had a year earlier. During the Dominican controversy probably four or five senators supported Fulbright; by the time of the Vietnam hearings and the "Arrogance of Power" speeches of early 1966, approximately 10 of the 19 members of the Committee agreed with Fulbright's critique of America's crusading anti-communism.

The Fulbright hearings gradually produced a crucial and salutary change in television coverage of Vietnam, despite the failure of CBS to carry the Kennan hearing. CBS would have absorbed a financial loss if it had covered the Kennan hearing, and some of the CBS executives were reluctant to publicize the controversial ideas of an intellectual who was not an administration witness.[66] However, NBC televised the Kennan hearing, and CBS televised four of the six hearings, including Gavin's testimony. Before the Vietnam hearings, television had been a reliable ally of the administration, usually reporting pro-war goals and statements without criticism. The fact that administration witnesses, and especially Rusk, delivered the bulk of the testimony legitimized the Vietnam hearings to the public.[67] But it was obvious that Rusk's answers to the difficult questions at the hearings had not been convincing. During the Vietnam hearings, for the first time national television reported in detail the dissenting views of critics such as Fulbright, Morse, and Gore. After the hearings, the television networks exhibited an increasing tendency to report both pro-war and anti-war analyses of the southeast Asian conflict.[68]

If Fulbright provoked mainstream America to think seriously about Vietnam, he again angered the extremists on the radical right. In March 1966 a right-wing terrorist organization called the Minutemen plotted to assassinate Fulbright. The FBI arrested Minuteman Jerry Milton Brooks in Kansas City. Brooks said his orders to shoot Fulbright were called off at the last minute, but the assassination plot was part of a conspiracy designed to intimidate dissident members of Congress into "voting American."[68a]

Opinion polls of late February and early March represented one of the earliest portents of extensive popular discontent with the war. Louis Harris' poll of February 28 reported that the great majority of the American people professed a desire for an early end to the war but were divided over how to achieve it, "with 33 percent favoring an increased military effort and 34 percent favoring an accelerated effort to bring about negotiations." The Harris survey indicated that only 10 percent of the American public favored immediate withdrawal and only 16 percent favored "all-out war against North Vietnam." According to Harris, support for the President's Vietnam policy "has dwindled sharply in the last six weeks–from 63 percent to 49 percent of the public." George Gallup's poll on March 9 revealed findings similar to the Harris survey. Gallup did not attempt to identify the primary catalyst in the decline of Johnson's support, although he noted that the poll just before the Vietnam hearings had shown roughly 60 percent approval for the President's policies, while the poll taken at the end of the hearings indicated a "substantial weakening in Johnson's support."[4]

The administration refused to acknowledge any connection between the decline in the President's support and the opposition senators' publicizing of dissident ideas. In February, Johnson privately warned New York Senator Robert F. Kennedy (who was not a member of the Foreign Relations Committee) that he would destroy politically "you, Fulbright, Church, and every one of your dove friends in six months. You'll be dead politically in six months."[5] In early March, a White House official alleged that "when public opinion polls show a drop in support for President Johnson's policy in Vietnam, it is because the American people do not think he is pressing the war hard enough." "The dove group," the White House contended, "stayed steadily at about 10 percent, and the recent rise in the proportion opposing Mr. Johnson's policies has reinforced the proportion of hawks."[6] The administration carefully omitted mentioning Harris' finding that in addition to the small faction urging immediate withdrawal, 34 percent of the public endorsed an "accelerated effort to bring about negotiations." During March Fulbright cited Harris' February 28 poll to substantiate his view that opinion concerning Vietnam was gradually beginning to change. The senator noted Harris' explanation of the poll's central meaning: the survey revealed "a growing consensus for peace along with a growing division as to how to achieve it and a mounting uneasiness as to the continuation of the war."[7]

The China Hearings

Fulbright envisaged the next political offensive in the anti-Vietnam War movement as an attempt to re-examine Rusk's image of China as an expansionist power akin to Nazi Germany. In early March Fulbright announced that the Foreign Relations Committee would convene hearings on "U.S. Policy With Respect to Mainland China." The Committee intended to analyze the connections between American policy toward China and the Vietnam War, and also to examine the China policy in its historical perspective. In his opening remarks at the China hearings, the chairman asserted: "At this stage perhaps the most effective contribution the Committee can make is to provide a forum for recognized experts and scholars in the field of China." The committee would discuss 3,000 years of Chinese history, the history of Sino-American relations, and the history of the American involvement in Vietnam. The effort to focus on such an enormous range of subjects meant that much of the discussion would remain at a highly generalized level. But Fulbright believed that since almost all Americans, including the members of the Foreign Relations Committee, were ignorant of the Far East, the initial step in educating the nation should be a broad overview of the culture, politics, and society of that region of the globe.[8] He characterized the hearings as primarily "educational, although the ultimate objective must be political, to prevent a war with China."[9]

Professor John King Fairbank of Harvard delivered the most widely publicized testimony at the China hearings. Fairbank, who was probably the most prestigious American historian of China, appeared before the committee to discuss the origins of the hostile Chinese attitude toward the West. In contrast to Rusk's assertion that the Chinese hostility toward the Western powers emanated from communist ideology, Fairbank analyzed the Chinese suspicions of the West primarily in terms of China's unique historical development. The Harvard historian emphasized China's remarkable feeling of superiority as an important source of its hauteur regarding the West. He observed that China was separated from western Asia by the mountains and deserts of central Asia and thus remained "isolated throughout most of its history, preserving a continuity of development in the same area over some 3,000 or 4,000 years."[10] In Fairbank's view, the isolation and longevity of China's cultural development had fostered a "strong tendency to look inward, an attitude of ethnocentrism or Sinocentrism, China being the center of the known world and of civilization, the non-Chinese being peripheral and inferior." The Chinese emperor ruled his vast domain through the Confucian myth of rule-by-virtue: the emperor's virtuous conduct would set an example for the proper behavior of all mankind, including foreigners. According to Fairbank, the Chinese extended their domestic doctrine of rule-by-virtue into their diplomacy by requiring that all foreign relations must be tributary relations, thereby "reinforcing the myth of Chinese supremacy and particularly the myth that foreign rulers were attracted by the emperor's virtue and 'turned toward him' to offer their submission to the center of civilization." The Chinese empire preserved at least the ritual of rule-by-virtue into the early twentieth century, even after China had become weak and dominated by the Western powers; Nepal offered the last tribute mission to the empire in 1908, when Mao Tse-tung was a youth.[11]

In analyzing the modern Chinese hostility toward the West, Fairbank recounted the record of foreign aggression in China during the nineteenth century: "By 1900, the British, the French, and the Japanese had all fought wars with China; the Russians had seized territory; and all of them, together with the Germans, had seized special privileges in spheres of influence." While the British and others "had fought the colonial wars" against China, Americans had also enjoyed extraterritoriality and the other special privileges of foreigners in China. The foreigners destroyed the ancient faith in the superiority of Chinese civilization, and eventually provoked a nationalistic reaction against their hegemony. Fairbank described the Leninist form of party dictatorship as the "doctrine" that proved most effective in the Chinese nationalistic quest to recreate a strong state. Marxism-Leninism offered a devil-theory to explain the catastrophe of the nineteenth century: capitalist imperialism had joined forces with feudal reaction to betray and exploit the Chinese people, thus distorting their otherwise normal development toward socialism. In the Maoist plea for the peoples of the Third World to emulate the Chinese communists' revolution, Fairbank concluded, "we see the continued desire to set a model for mankind, to be the center from which civilization is derived."[12]

In one of the most frequently quoted passages of the hearings, Fairbank dissented from Rusk's allegation that Chinese Defense Minister Lin Piao's call for the underdeveloped countries to overthrow the developed countries was similar to Hitler's vision of world domination in *Mein Kampf*.[13] The Harvard scholar argued that the ancient Chinese preoccupation with the fiction of rule-by-virtue still influenced the pronouncements of Chinese leaders:

> Applying all this background to the present moment, I suggest we should not get too excited over Peking's vast blueprints for the onward course of the Maoist revolution. Some American commentators who really ought to know better have overreacted to the visionary blueprint of world revolution put out by Lin Piao last September in Peking about the strangling of the world's advanced countries or 'cities' from the underdeveloped countries or 'countryside.' This was, I think, a reassertion of faith, that the Chinese Communists' own parochial example of rural-based revolution is the model for the rest of the underdeveloped world to emulate. It was put out mainly as compensation for China's recent defeats in many parts of the globe.
>
> [Later in the testimony Fairbank briefly referred to China's 1965 defeat in failing to organize an Afro-Asian conference excluding the Soviet Union, and the slaughter of the pro-Peking Indonesian Communist Party following an abortive communist coup in 1965.] To compare it to Hitler's 'Mein Kampf' would be quite misleading. Rule-by-virtue required that the rulers proclaim their true teaching, claiming that it will still win the world even if they themselves are too weak to support it in practice.[14]

Mao Tse-tung might consider himself the successor to Marx, Lenin, and Stalin, Fairbank informed the committee, "but he is much more the successor of the emperors who ruled in Peking until 1912 when Mao was already 18 years of age."[15]

Fairbank recommended an American policy of gradually encouraging China's participation in the international community and dispelling Chinese fears and suspicions concerning the West. He opposed the current U.S. policies of a trade embargo and adamant resistance to Peking's entry into the United Nations, advocating American trade with China in non-strategic goods and U.S. support for Chinese participation in the Security Council as well as the General Assembly of the United Nations. China's restoration to the center of the world's councils would redress the balance of the last century's humiliations and eventually lead to a "mellowing" of the Chinese revolutionary attitude. "In short, my reading of history," Fairbank maintained, "is that Peking's rulers shout aggressively out of manifold frustrations, that isolation intensifies their ailment and makes it self-perpetuating, and that we need to encourage international contact with China on many fronts."[16]

Fulbright commended Fairbank for condensing in his statement "a great deal of profound thought about China." The chairman asked him if a parliamentary democracy could have reunified and effectively governed China as the communist regime had succeeded in doing. Fairbank replied, "No. The Chinese tried it at one time. It didn't work. It is a different style." Fulbright proceeded to argue that much of the distortion in American attitudes toward China could be attributed to the unrealistic notion that "it is a terrible tragedy to have communism in that country." China did not possess the "history and traditions" of parliamentary democracy, in Fulbright's view, and Americans were "foolish" to be dismayed that a parliamentary system had not developed in China. Fairbank simply answered, "I agree."[17]

Fulbright approved of all of Fairbank's basic recommendations concerning China. But he emphatically disagreed with Fairbank when the Harvard historian reluctantly supported the administration's policy in Vietnam. Fairbank offered a few tentative criticisms of the American intervention, describing the U.S. "buildup in South Vietnam as so massive it comes very close to a colonial takeover, even though it is firmly intended to be only temporary." The Harvard professor also criticized the administration for being preoccupied with warfare in Vietnam and neglecting the process of "nation building," particularly the creation of viable South Vietnamese economic and political institutions. Despite these criticisms, Fairbank endorsed the basic thrust of the administration's containment policy: "Military containment on the Korean border, in the Taiwan Straits, and somehow in Vietnam cannot soon be abandoned and may have to be maintained for some time." He vaguely asserted that the United States must remain in Vietnam so that the American model of noncommunist nation building "can compete effectively with the Chinese communist model of nation building." Fulbright was exceedingly skeptical about America's prospects for building a nation in South Vietnam. The chairman recalled that he had reviewed the foreign aid program every year for more than 15 years, and even under peaceful conditions the United States had encountered immense difficulties in attempting to construct viable, prosperous democracies in underdeveloped Asian nations whose cultural and political traditions differed profoundly from those of the West. Fulbright reminded the professor that by 1966, the escalation in expenditures, numbers of military personnel, and bombings had only succeeded in demolishing hundreds of South Vietnamese villages, distorting Saigon's economy, and fueling a South Vietnamese inflation rate of 50 percent during the preceding year.[18]

Fulbright proposed the neutralization of southeast Asia as an alternative to the administration's quixotic attempt to fashion a South Vietnamese nation after America's image. In his opinion, the most persuasive argument that might influence the Chinese to support a neutralization agreement would be American assurances that "the United States would not maintain itself permanently in the area militarily." Fulbright advocated a cease-fire, an American withdrawal from the countryside to coastal enclaves where U.S. naval and air power were predominant, and American pledges of an eventual withdrawal of all its military forces from Vietnam.[19] He recommended the convening of a diplomatic conference including China, the Soviet Union, Great Britain, and France designed to formulate a general international agreement for the neutralization of southeast Asia.[20]

Fairbank responded to the chairman's proposal for a neutralization agreement by suggesting that such an agreement might be a constructive idea at some point in the future, but for the present the United States must continue fighting in Vietnam "to make the Maoist model of takeover ineffective and stalemated." The dialogue concerning Vietnam was frustrating for Fulbright, because he thought Fairbank had failed to carry his arguments to their logical conclusion. The professor had conceded that American policies in Vietnam had been heavily prejudiced toward military destruction rather than economic reconstruction, that the American escalation resembled a colonial "takeover," and that no threat of Chinese military expansionism existed. In Fulbright's view the conclusion to be drawn from these statements was obvious: America should at least gradually withdraw from Vietnam. Why Fairbank failed to follow his own criticisms to their logical culmination was never clear from his testimony. He did not clarify why the United States "must stalemate" the Maoist doctrine of Third World revolution in Vietnam, and his comments on southeast Asia were generally desultory and vague. He was reluctant to answer questions concerning Vietnam and once attempted to evade a question about the war by stating, "an expert witness on history is not an expert witness on policy." He was vastly more knowledgeable about China than about Vietnam, and his views on the war were obviously in flux in March 1966. In later years Fairbank became an opponent of the Vietnam War, and in early 1966 he was clearly moving in the direction of dissent. During Fulbright's initial efforts to question Fairbank's reluctant defense of the Vietnam policy, the China scholar replied that the alternative of withdrawing was even worse than the current policies, but as Fulbright continued to press his case against the war Fairbank modified his position. Near the end of the hearing, after Fulbright had reiterated his beliefs that the administration's policy would foment massive disenchantment within the United States and that it was impossible to simultaneously fight a war and create stability in an underdeveloped Asian land, Fairbank answered, "Your statement is very eloquent, and it persuades me that there are great difficulties, and I also think that we may not succeed very well."[21]

The Arkansas senator and the Harvard historian finished the hearing with an amicable discussion concerning the general significance of the committee's sessions on China. Fulbright, Morse, and several other senators were delighted by Fairbank's testimony on China, although they subjected him to a rather difficult interrogation on his position regarding Vietnam. Yet at the end of the grueling five-hour session the professor still praised the Committee's decision to hold the hearings: "There are now enough people who have been working on China and they do have something to offer, and I think it is a marvelous thing to have these sessions." Fulbright congratulated Fairbank for his great contribution to the public discussion of Asian policy. The chairman asserted that the hearings had "brought this subject, which has been taboo for so long, out into the open. It is now respectable, I think, to discuss it."[22]

Fairbank's testimony was representative of the majority of the statements delivered at the China hearings. The testimony of retired General Samuel Griffith, Morton Halperin and Benjamin I. Schwartz of Harvard, A. Doak Barnett of Columbia, and Robert Scalapino of the University of California was similar to the Fairbank discourse. Most of the China scholars agreed that the Chinese tended to "look inward," that China was much more interested in the domestic objectives of industrialization and social transformation than in encouraging Third World revolutions. Scalapino expressed a typical recommendation when he suggested that the United States offer the Chinese diplomatic recognition, support for Chinese membership in the United Nations, cultural and trade exchanges, and commerce in nonstrategic goods. China might reject or accept the offers, Scalapino observed, but these diplomatic overtures would at least confront Peking with alternatives and thus "eventually subject the Chinese leadership to pressures to take the path toward moderation" in their attitude toward the West.[23]

The Fairbank hearing was also typical of the testimony on Vietnam, for the witnesses were reluctant to criticize the American military involvement in southeast Asia, despite their pleas for a reversal in America's China policy. With the exception of Scalapino, who enthusiastically endorsed the administration's Vietnam policy, most of the witnesses presented mild criticisms of American tactics in the war; many of them were critical of the escalation of air strikes throughout Vietnam. The contrast in the witnesses' statements on Vietnam and their views on China represented a recurring theme of the hearings. The scholars would deliver detailed, logical expositions concerning China, but their remarks on Vietnam were often vague and revealed a lack of knowledge of the current crisis in southeast Asia. Griffith, Halperin, and other witnesses admitted that they were not familiar with the details of the situation in Vietnam. Despite their inadequate knowledge of Vietnam and their criticisms of the bombings, the scholars praised the administration's statements claiming that the United States would eventually build a viable, democratic nation in South Vietnam. They accepted the executive's assertions that America sincerely sought a negotiated settlement to the southeast Asian conflict.[24]

The chairman's response to the testimony usually followed the pattern of the Fairbank hearing, for he tended to compliment the witnesses for their astute observations about China while disagreeing with their views on Vietnam. Throughout the hearings Fulbright reminded the witnesses of the absence of American allies' support for the U.S. intervention. He noted that the United States had substantially increased its economic aid to South Korea "in return for their sending troops to South Vietnam," but South Korea was the only American ally that was making a significant contribution to the American military effort in Vietnam. Fulbright asked A. Doak Barnett if he was concerned about the reluctance of Japan, India, and other "important, sophisticated, experienced nations" to endorse the official American assumption that the Vietnamese civil war constituted a threat to world peace. Barnett conceded that the lack of genuine support from America's allies "bothers me," but he opposed either withdrawal to enclaves along the coast or "galloping escalation." Barnett urged "restraint" in the use of force against North Vietnam, and opposed expansion of the air strikes into the urban centers of northern North Vietnam. The Columbia professor joined Fairbank in recommending greater emphasis on economic reconstruction in South Vietnam. He summarized his position on Vietnam by stating, "As I balance all the complex factors, I come out supporting a policy of continued political and military action in South Vietnam, with restraint."[25]

Fulbright, Morse, and other critics of the war were somewhat frustrated and annoyed by the China scholars' support for the administration's Vietnam policy, and in subsequent hearings they focused the discussion more on the strictly Chinese issues. However, it proved impossible to analyze the China policy without discussing southeast Asia, and at each of the seven hearings the dissenting senators reiterated their opposition to the Vietnam War.

The testimony of retired General Samuel Griffith and Harvard professor Morton Halperin was particularly valuable in refuting the administration's image of China as a Nazi Germany reincarnated. Griffith and Halperin were two of the nation's most distinguished experts on the Chinese military posture. The two scholars argued that China did not possess the military capability to embark upon a campaign of conquest throughout Asia. Griffith compared the relative conventional military strength of the United States and China, and concluded that China was a military "paper tiger" except in regional terms, while America was "the greatest military power in the world." The general estimated that the superiority of American military power over Chinese power was "in a ratio of 10 to 1." He described the Chinese People's Liberation Army as a "potent regional instrument," but asserted that "the Chinese cannot yet project conventional power beyond adjacent areas, and they won't be able to for at least another ten years." The Chinese had been exceedingly careful in the recruitment and indoctrination of their soldiers. Contrary to Taiwan's claims that many PLA men were disloyal, Griffith characterized the PLA as a "highly motivated, loyal, and dedicated instrument." But the PLA's lack of motor transport would place it at a disadvantage in confronting a motorized army; moreover, the Chinese had not yet developed a modern air force and were hampered by inadequate training, insufficient jet fuel supply, and other technical problems. Halperin contended that the Chinese were as concerned about the dangers of nuclear war as America and Russia were. The Chinese had exploded their first nuclear device in 1964, but their embryonic nuclear installations were still vulnerable to American air power. Mao Tse-tung had expressed fears that at least 300 million Chinese would be killed in a nuclear war. Halperin interpreted Mao's statement as the result of calculations by the Chinese military staff that reflected China's preoccupation with the problem of nuclear war. Griffith and Halperin urged America to avoid over-reacting to China's quite limited military capability.[28]

Griffith provided a somewhat different defense of America's Vietnam policy than had most of the witnesses. When Fulbright pressed the general to define America's vital interests in South Vietnam, he replied, "We have made a moral commitment in the face of the world in South Vietnam, and I think that if we pulled out of there, that we—our name—would be mud, our promises would be worthless." Fulbright asked rhetorically if America held a superior moral position in injecting its force into Vietnam, and responded, "Did we go there in pursuit of a crusade based on moral principles?" Griffith contended that former South Vietnamese ruler Ngo Dinh Diem had invited the Americans to intervene, and that Diem was a "reasonable" representative of the South Vietnamese people. The general's statement was incorrect, for the Eisenhower administration had established Diem in power after the 1954 French defeat in Indochina. Diem enjoyed good relations with the French plantation owners and drew his most important support among the Vietnamese people from the landlords rather than the masses; yet regardless of his failures to enact social and economic reforms the Eisenhower administration continued to provide Diem with military and economic aid as long as he remained staunchly anti-communist. Fulbright described Diem as a "creature" of the Americans. In the senator's view, Diem had possessed no significant political base in the South in 1954, for he had been living in the United States during much of the early 1950s while Ho Chi Minh was leading the Vietnamese war of independence against the French. The senator observed that Diem "did make some very powerful friends" in America in the early 1950s. He mentioned no names, but Francis Cardinal Spellman, Senator John F. Kennedy, Senator Mansfield, and other prominent Americans had befriended Diem in the 1950s. Fulbright dismissed the idea that Diem had genuinely represented the people of South Vietnam. Griffith ceased his defense of the Vietnam policy at that juncture of the hearing and admitted, "Senator, I am afraid you know a great deal more about Mr. Diem than I do." Halperin also confessed that he had "not read into the background of Vietnam." The Fulbright-Morse interrogation of the witnesses on Vietnam was not as detailed as it had been at earlier hearings, largely because the senators were growing weary of the disagreements over Vietnam. The chairman closed the hearing by remarking, "It is really unfair to press you on Vietnam because you came here to enlighten us on China."[29]

Two difficulties within the Foreign Relations Committee complicated Fulbright's efforts to generate enlightened discussion of U.S. Asian policies. First, Senator Mansfield, who was the Majority Leader and a high-ranking member of the committee, did not attend any of the hearings. Mansfield's absence was unfortunate, for he was one of the most knowledgeable Asian experts in the Senate. He had advised the President that Fulbright's arguments concerning the Far East were accurate; but the hearings were far too controversial for Mansfield, who pursued a cautious political strategy of avoiding any direct confrontations with the administration. Mansfield was constantly concerned about his position as Majority Leader and his sense of a higher loyalty to President Johnson, and in later years Fulbright would refer to him as "Johnson's alter ego." The Majority Leader sometimes obtained information from the administration that was not shared with his colleagues on the Foreign Relations Committee, thus increasing the tensions between Fulbright and Mansfield. The two senators did not cooperate effectively in the later Johnson years, although they would return to a more constructive relationship during the Nixon Presidency.[30]

A second difficulty arose from the complaints of the "hawkish" minority on the committee. Ranking Republican member Bourke Hickenlooper of Iowa led four other senators on the 19-member committee in complaining that the witnesses and the majority of the members were biased against the administration's Asian policy. The right-wing members remained relatively quiet during the first five hearings.[31] Most of the discussion during these sessions consisted of a dialogue between the witnesses and the administration's most vigorous opponents, who were Fulbright, Morse, McCarthy, Frank Church of Idaho, Albert Gore of Tennessee, and Joseph Clark of Pennsylvania. Two Republican members, George Aiken of Vermont and Clifford Case of New Jersey, displayed a burgeoning inclination to agree with most of the arguments of the dominant Fulbright-Morse faction. After some private disagreements with Hickenlooper, Fulbright acquiesced to the senior Republican's request to invite the witnesses for one hearing. Hickenlooper exhumed former U. S. Representative Walter Judd to testify at the hearing on March 28. Judd was an ardent anti-communist who had condemned the Truman administration for failing to provide sufficient aid to Chiang Kai-shek during the Chinese civil war and thus "losing" China to communism. Professor Davie Rowe of Yale assisted Judd in presenting the "hard-line" perspective on China and Vietnam.[32]

During the March 28 hearing Judd and Rowe lamented that the Johnson administration was not exerting sufficient military force against the southeast Asian communists. Judd advocated an intensification of the air strikes against North Vietnam. The former congressman urged the expansion of the bombing targets to include "war plants, power plants, and oil tanks" in the industrial centers of North Vietnam. Professor Rowe advocated the mining of Haiphong harbor as well as escalation of the bombing. Judd and Rowe opposed admission of China to the United Nations and American diplomatic recognition of the mainland regime. Rowe contended that the United States should maintain an attitude of "extreme hostility" toward China for the next 10 to 15 years in order to convince the Chinese of America's determination to oppose aggression. The Yale professor warned Americans against developing the "frame of mind" that had afflicted France before World War II, "when the futility of resistance to aggression was uppermost in the mind of so many people in that unfortunate country."[33]

Fulbright pressed Rowe to specify the means America should employ to change the alleged Chinese appetite for military expansion. Rowe stated that an accommodation between the United States and China would be possible if the Chinese "were militarily defeated and the communist regime was uprooted and destroyed." The Yale professor did not regard a military victory over China as the only means of changing China's supposedly aggressive behavior, however. In his opinion, a hostile American policy of isolating China might eventually lead to a moderation in the Chinese attitude toward the West, thus allowing the United States to accept Chinese membership in the U.N. at some distant point in the future. Rowe did not clarify why he thought a policy of hostility would gradually lead the Chinese to adopt a more friendly posture toward the West. Fulbright dismissed Rowe's remark that a military victory over the Chinese communists might lead to an amelioration of Sino-American relations, and he did not believe Rowe had presented any evidence to substantiate his view of China as an evil aggressor nation. He reminded the professor that a central objective of the hearings was to prevent the growth of bellicose American attitudes toward China. The senator argued that the United States could not encourage a more amicable Chinese policy toward America by treating China as a pariah and excluding it from the international community. The United Nations, he asserted, could not be considered a "gentleman's club" that demanded "gentlemanly" behavior from all its members. Fulbright observed that many current members of the U.N. pursued policies that were even less "gentlemanly" than the Chinese, and the American policies of nonrecognition and opposition to Chinese admission to the United Nations represented a visionary effort to ignore the existence of the most populous nation on earth.[34]

Hickenlooper approved of his witnesses' testimony and joined them in warning Americans to avoid a futile foreign policy of "appeasing" communist aggression. But the general reaction to the Judd-Rowe testimony in the press and the committee was highly unfavorable. With the exception of Hickenlooper, the senior members of the committee rejected the recommendations of Judd and Rowe. The Washington Post reported on March 29 that Fulbright and second-ranking Republican member George Aiken were exasperated by the "hard-liners' statements." Fulbright seemed mystified by the Judd-Rowe viewpoint; "I am very slow-witted," the Rhodes Scholar opined, "in grasping their reasoning." The chairman had "pointedly noted" that Hickenlooper invited the witnesses. The Post's front-page article asserted that the usually sedate Senator Aiken became "visibly riled" when Rowe implied the China hearings were being conducted in the interests of the Chinese communists, since the hearings would supposedly convince the Chinese that America was not united in its resolve to resist aggression. When Aiken challenged Rowe's criticism of the committee's sessions on China, the Yale professor first modified his statement by saying the committee was holding the hearings in the national interest, but then virtually repeated his earlier accusation by claiming that "the results will be exploited by those who want to aid and abet Red China." Most members of the committee dismissed the extremists' statements as reminiscent of the demagogical accusations of Wisconsin Senator Joseph McCarthy in the early 1950s.[35]

Almost all the witnesses at the China hearings maintained that Judd, Joe McCarthy, and other Republicans and right-wing Democrats had irresponsibly blamed President Truman for the rise to power of the Chinese communists. Harvard professor Benjamin I. Schwartz repudiated the notion that the United States could have prevented a communist victory in the Chinese civil war by providing greater military and economic aid to Chiang Kai-shek. Schwartz recalled General George C. Marshall's arguments in 1945-1947 that even a massive commitment of billions of dollars and millions of American troops could not have guaranteed a victory for Chiang. The China scholars were in accord that such a commitment would have been disastrous; Fulbright and Schwartz agreed that the avoidance of a land war with China should be a cardinal tenet of American foreign policy.[36] Schwartz attributed much of Mao's success to the communists' tenacious resistance against the Japanese during World War II and their concern for the indoctrination, morale, and physical well-being of their soldiers. By the later stages of the war, many Chinese patriots admired the communists for their zeal in attempting to expel the Japanese from their homeland. In contrast, Chiang Kai-shek's Kuomintang forces became increasingly obsessed with defeating the communists and assumed a passive posture toward the Japanese. Chiang concluded that it was futile to confront Japanese power before carrying out the military unification of China. The Kuomintang correctly assumed that the Americans would overwhelm Japan. But the Kuomintang's campaigns against the communists during late World War II, according to Schwartz, "provided the unfortunate spectacle of Chinese fighting Chinese rather than the common Japanese enemy."[37]

The Harvard professor asserted that the communists' military policies, program of agrarian radicalism, and above all their nationalistic appeal had facilitated their campaign of gaining the peasants' support and broadening Mao's power base in the countryside. In contrast to the communists' effort to identify with the masses, Schwartz maintained that the Nationalist government became dependent on the "local holders of power and privilege" throughout China. The Kuomintang had unwisely and ineffectively concentrated on urban modernization and "paid little attention to the vast rural hinterland which was hardly affected by the Nationalist rise to power."[38] The other China scholars and most members of the committee accepted Schwartz's conclusions as accurate and clear. In his speeches in the spring of 1966, Fulbright summarized the scholars' conclusions regarding the Maoist seizure of power in China: "Greatly assisted by the incompetence and demoralization of the Kuomintang, the Chinese communists emerged from the Second World War as the proponents of a genuine Chinese nationalism."[39] Fulbright had been a bitter political enemy of Joe McCarthy (although his opposition to McCarthy was not discussed at the hearings) 15 years before; in 1966 he again dismissed as demagogy the McCarthyite charges that America had "lost" China to communism, for the Chinese civil war was decided by indigenous forces that were beyond the control of the United States.[40]

Fulbright continued to explore the question of the political implications involved in changing the China policy in his dialogue with Professor Hans J. Morgenthau of the University of Chicago. The University of Chicago professor delivered the testimony of the final session of the hearings on March 30. Morgenthau was one of the nation's most famous critics of American policies in Asia. Fulbright asked Morgenthau to offer suggestions on the most effective means to employ in promoting a change in American attitudes toward the mainland regime. The chairman recalled the political difficulties involved in challenging the Cold Warrior perspective concerning Cuba. "Yesterday the President commented that these hearings," the senator observed, "had increased the hawkish element in our country." Johnson had not explained how or why the hearings were increasing "hawkish" pressures, he had merely asserted it. The chairman noted the criticisms of the Hickenlooper faction on the committee: "Even our opening up of this discussion of China has brought forth torrents of abuse from members of this Committee as being disloyal merely to suggest it." Morgenthau responded to Fulbright's observations with a vigorous defense of the Committee's decision to provide a forum for the China experts. He asserted that many Americans were beginning to join with "genuine enthusiasm" in the nascent rational discussion of Sino-American relations. The professor cited a recent conference on China held in Chicago in which academics, journalists, religious figures, and "simple people from all over the Middle West" eagerly participated in a candid discussion of America's China policy. Morgenthau's contention that the China hearings should have been held several years earlier represented his only criticism of the committee's effort to generate a public debate on China:

> I have said for fifteen years that our China policy has been the victim of our political leaders' unfounded fears of domestic public opinion. What has happened this year could have happened five or ten years ago if there had been in our government people of insight and courage who would have opened up the problem of China. I remember when President Eisenhower in the fall of 1956 raised in a press conference the possibility of a two-China policy, the next Gallup poll, which formerly had shown as overwhelming majority against having anything to do with Communist China, showed a radical change. I think presidential and congressional leadership is a vital factor in this reformation of public opinion. In truth, it is not so much a reformation of public opinion as an articulation of a public opinion which is already there.[41]

Morgenthau contended that the most common misconception regarding Chinese foreign policy was the tendency "to think in terms of historic analogies and we can't help thinking of China in terms of our experience with Nazi Germany." In his analysis, the expansion of Chinese influence in Asia was primarily cultural and political and bore no resemblance to the Nazis' military expansionism. Morgenthau attributed the enormous influence China had historically exerted upon the Asian mainland to the "unchallengeability" of Chinese civilization; it was inevitable that China's neighbors would be attracted to the modern Chinese renascence, for China possessed the greatest cultural tradition in Asia. The professor conceded that the Chinese rhetorical condemnations of the West were "almost mad," but he interpreted the Chinese xenophobia as a "continuation of an old Chinese tradition which looks at the outside world as being naturally inferior to China."[42]

Morgenthau did not dismiss the significance of the mainland regime's communist ideology, contending that China's efforts to increase its political influence in the Third World "can be explained primarily in terms of her competition with the Soviet Union for the dominance of the world communist movement." The Sino-Soviet rivalry centered upon the issue of communist attitudes toward the United States. The Soviets advocated peaceful coexistence and political, social, and economic competition with the United States, relying upon an eventual demonstration of superior Soviet productivity to facilitate a gradual decline in the international influence of capitalism. Soviet propaganda emphasized the imperative of avoiding nuclear war. China adhered to the classical Bolshevik thesis that all communists must unfailingly support (at the ideological level) the unfolding of the world revolution against American imperialism. The Chinese accused Moscow of using their appeals for the avoidance of nuclear war to conceal Soviet collaboration with America for the purpose of world domination.

Despite this dispute with the Soviet Union, Morgenthau thought Mao Tse-tung's foreign policy had been quite cautious. The professor believed the basic goals of the Chinese communists' foreign policy were "within the nationalistic tradition of China," and were not fundamentally motivated by Marxist-Leninist ideology. In demonstrating the importance of nationalism in Chinese foreign policy, he cited Chiang Kai-shek's agreement with many of Mao Tse-tung's foreign policy objectives over the previous 16 years. Obviously, Chiang and Mao had waged civil war over who should rule China; both considered Tibet and Taiwan to be integral regions of China. Morgenthau did not excuse the Chinese seizure of Tibet in 1959, but he pointed out that Chiang endorsed Mao's view of Tibet as part of China. At the Morgenthau hearing and throughout the Vietnam and China hearings, Fulbright and other senators noted presidential adviser General Maxwell Taylor's admission that India had initiated the Sino-Indian warfare in 1962 by moving its troops forward into the disputed territory along the Chinese border. Morgenthau stressed that Mao and Chiang agreed that the Chinese were justified in seizing control of the strategic route between Tibet and Sinkiang during the 1962 border war with India. "There has been no disagreement," Morgenthau concluded, between Mao and Chiang in approving the nationalistic quest to restore the boundaries of China as they had existed in the early nineteenth century, before the era of Western domination in China. These boundaries included Asian territories that Russia had annexed in the nineteenth century, so that at least one important source of the Sino-Soviet rivalry emanated from the conflicting claims of Russian and Chinese nationalism rather than their ideological dispute over the proper communist stance toward America. Thus, many of the international controversies involving China in the postwar years would have existed even if China had not been a communist country, in Morgenthau's judgment, for the·problems originated in the traditional goals of Chinese nationalism.[43]

Morgenthau's testimony on China was similar to that of Fairbank, Barnett, and most of the other witnesses, although he placed even greater emphasis on Chinese nationalism and ethnocentrism as explanations for China's behavior. However, Morgenthau differed radically from the other witnesses when he proceeded from his analysis of Chinese diplomacy to deliver a devastating dissent against America's entire Asian policy. He was the only witness who sharply criticized both the China and Vietnam policies of the Johnson administration. Morgenthau averred that the American attempt to isolate China by excluding it from the U.N., severing commercial relations with it, and recognizing the Taiwan government as the legitimate government of all China "has been a complete failure." The isolation policy had not only failed to produce a collapse of the communist regime; the policy had actually isolated the United States, since most nations had refused to participate in the "isolation" of China. Admission of the Chinese into the U.N. and cultural exchanges "might improve the international climate of opinion," but Morgenthau defined the decisive problem of Sino-American relations as the need for the United States to recognize the Chinese threat in Asia as cultural and political rather than military. In his opinion, a cultural and political threat "cannot be contained by local military means in Taiwan or Vietnam or elsewhere." The policy of local military containment around the periphery of China was doomed to failure, for China would inevitably exert political influence on its neighbors. If this influence was incompatible with America's vital interests, then the United States must destroy the Chinese communist regime. Morgenthau did not, of course, believe the Chinese political and cultural influence in Asia contradicted any American vital interest and he did not recommend the destruction of the mainland regime, but simply argued that the containment policy would eventually lead to war with China if the administration pursued it to its logical conclusion.[44]

Morgenthau urged the United States to accept the reality that China was the greatest power on the Asian mainland even in its relatively backward state of development in 1966. He predicted that if 700 or 800 million Chinese acquired fully modern technology, then China would become the most powerful nation on earth. He believed the Chinese would become more restrained in their foreign relations as they became more powerful, for if China intended to be a "first-rate industrial and nuclear power, she will have to develop large population and industrial centers, which will then be as vulnerable to attack as ours and the Soviet Union's are already." The threat of nuclear destruction of its industrial centers would have the moderating effect upon China's leaders that "the identical threat has had upon the leaders of the United States and the Soviet Union."[45]

The Fulbright-Morgenthau dialogue was one of the most mellifluous exchanges in the China hearings. The senator asked the professor if he detected any recent changes in the Johnson administration's global anticommunism. "Strangely enough," Morgenthau replied, "there is a gap between our rational recognition that the monolithic character of communism has been replaced by polycentrism, on the one hand, and an almost mechanical application of obsolescent modes of thought and action to the situation in Asia."[46] The Morgenthau analysis of the administration's position was accurate. To official Washington, the communist world remained united on essentials. Rusk once acknowledged that "there is solid evidence of some tensions between Moscow and Peiping," but basically Russia and China were "two great systems of power which are united in general in a certain doctrinal framework and which together have certain common interests vis-a-vis the rest of the world."[47] If Rusk grudgingly conceded that China and the Soviet Union were engaging in what he regarded as minor squabbles, he rigidly adhered to his contention that the "Asian communism" of China and North Vietnam was implacably aggressive and monolithic.[48]

Fulbright and Morgenthau directed their most caustic criticisms against the anti-communist crusade in southeast Asia. The chairman reiterated his belief in the futility of America's efforts to create a viable anti-communist nation in South Vietnam. He felt that the fierce xenophobia of the Vietnamese people presented an almost insuperable obstacle to the American intervention: "It seems to me the very fact that you are supported by a great foreign country compromises you in the eyes of the local people and makes this an impossible undertaking." Morgenthau responded that after World War II the United States had succeeded in reconstructing the economies of nations such as France, Great Britain, and Japan, where viable political and economic institutions had previously existed. But he asserted that American assistance in helping developed nations to recover their political and economic health was "an entirely different matter from creating through outside intervention a nation which doesn't exist yet, and, Mr. Chairman, I fully agree with your negative attitude toward that possibility."[49]

In Morgenthau's analysis, French colonial domination had prevented South Vietnam from arriving at "nationhood" before the American intervention began. In words that epitomized the attitude of the dissenters toward the administration's goal of "political and economic reconstruction" in South Vietnam, Morgenthau decried the Sisyphean objective of simultaneously fighting a war and building a nation:

> So far as South Vietnam is concerned, I think we are falling into the same trap into which France fell in Algeria. With one hand we destroy the enemy and the civilian population and habitations and with the other we try to build them up. I think this inner contradiction cannot be resolved, and inevitably when you are engaged in a war, the exigencies of war will take precedence over humanitarian aspirations.
>
> I remember very vividly having read a couple of months ago a very moving account of an AID official who had lived in a South Vietnamese village for a year, had built a school and other facilities and really done a great deal for the people by way of 'rural reconstruction.' In one night, he said, it was all wiped out.
>
> This is inevitable. But since it is inevitable, it is a delusion to think that you can have it both ways, that you can destroy your opponents in a civil war, to whom at the very least the indigenous population is indifferent if it does not actively support them, and that at the same time you can reconstruct that very same society which you are trying to destroy.
>
> This inner contradiction cannot be resolved by doing justice to both objectives. It is to be resolved in favor of military destruction.[50]

Fulbright and Morgenthau advocated a cessation of military destruction in Vietnam. They questioned the administration's contention that the National Liberation Front was adamantly opposed to any negotiations. According to the senator, the NLF's proposals for possible negotiations were "always shifting. One day they say they will accept a free election, and the next day this acceptance is qualified as meaning only in accordance with the program of the NLF. I think this is a matter for negotiations." Fulbright recalled the NLF's statements endorsing "a return to the Geneva accords which provide for an internationally supervised election." Following the French defeat by Ho Chi Minh's forces at Dien Bien Phu in 1954, the Geneva accords had established a temporary partition of Vietnam at the 17th parallel and provided for elections within two years to unify the country. Western observers agreed with Ho's prediction that he would win a smashing electoral triumph in 1956.[51] Morgenthau agreed with Fulbright that the NLF's statements on the Geneva accords were conflicting, and he speculated that the "political program of the NLF covers only the modalities of a coalition government." Fulbright and Morgenthau believed that the United States should cease quibbling about whether Vietnamese elections would be "free," for there was little or no historical precedent for Western-style "free elections" in Vietnam. The senator and the professor regarded the concept of elections in the 1954 Geneva accords as a "device" intended to end the warfare in Vietnam. 'But the device wasn't utilized," Fulbright observed, since the Eisenhower administration supported Diem's refusal to participate in the national elections envisaged by the Geneva accords. At the end of the China hearings, Morgenthau and Fulbright concurred in urging the United States to support elections or any other "device" that might hasten the cessation of hostilities.[52]

Fulbright stated at the final session on China that the hearings had accomplished the purpose of stimulating "nationwide interest and encouraging widespread discussion of U.S. policy toward China." The senator's statement was accurate, for the China hearings attracted widespread national attention. The committee's sessions on China received extensive publicity in the national television news broadcasts, although they were not televised "live" in their entirety as the Vietnam hearings had been. Many major newspapers in the country devoted front-page coverage to the hearings. Journalistic accounts of the hearings were generally either objective summaries or commendations of the committee. Television had previously been a reliable ally of the administration, usually reporting pro-war goals and statements without criticism. Until 1966, the mass media had tended to depict dissenters as emotional, alienated radicals; in 1966 Fulbright's use of the Foreign Relations Committee as a forum for dissent demonstrated that some of the most distinguished foreign policy analysts (including Fulbright, Kennan, and Morgenthau) in the United States were deeply disenchanted with American policies in Asia. The Vietnam and China hearings played a crucial role in leading the television networks to increasingly portray opposition views as respectable and centrist.[53]

The renowned theologian Reinhold Niebuhr's March 20 letter to the *New York Times* represented an example of the favorable responses to the hearings: "Senator Fulbright has earned the gratitude of all troubled citizens by mounting two hearings, first on the war in Vietnam and then on our attitude toward China. These hearings were exercises in political sanity." Niebuhr encouraged the committee to continue this "process of enlightenment, for we are in a neurotic darkness about China. Our neurosis manifests itself in alternate moods of pretending that China does not exist and terrible fears of Chinese power and malice."[54] Niebuhr's letter to the Times was quite brief and he left his readers to deduce the significance of his remarks. A similarly generalized article by *New York Times* columnist James Reston contended that "out of the lively controversies over Senator Fulbright . . . there is a growing feeling that the present policies will not last, and in this realization there is at least some hope." The columnist noted the inconsistency of official American assumptions about Chinese reactions to the Vietnam War: the United States "would not tolerate Chinese power in the South of Mexico, but assumes that China will tolerate our power in the South of Vietnam." As Reston admitted, "No real changes had been made," but he alleged that the hearings had led many Americans to re-examine the obsolete China policy.[55] Niebuhr's letter and Reston's column were entirely lacking in specifics, but they clearly advocated a general amelioration of Sino-American relations.

In his March 24 column in the *Washington Post*, Walter Lippmann endorsed Fulbright's attempt to change American attitudes toward China. His column, entitled, "The Dead Hand in Foreign Policy," was a caustic indictment of the Johnson administration's diplomacy in Asia and Europe. "By a rather neat coincidence," he wrote, Fulbright was forcing the nation to re-examine America's post-World War II China policy just as Charles de Gaulle was provoking discussion concerning U.S. postwar policy in Europe. Both the European and China policies were "showing all the signs of a breakdown." He believed it was inevitable that any "postwar settlement breaks down, because about 15 years after the end of a war a new generation of men have grown up and taken power." Yet the State Department, in Lippman's view, "is looking only backwards," and merely defending obsolete postwar policies. Instead of fashioning new diplomatic strategies the Johnson administration was constantly complaining that many politicians were criticizing its diplomacy and complicating the task of the knowledgeable State Department experts. Lippmann was especially critical of the administration's efforts to blame its failures upon its political adversaries: "It is a petty and shallow view to think that but for a few dissenting scholars and senators our Asian policy today would be unchallenged, that but for General de Gaulle our European policy would stand intact."[56]

Lippmann contended that the administration was not responding to the changing realities of contemporary Europe and Asia. The fundamental "reality" in both Europe and Asia was the emergence of the Soviet Union as a nuclear, conservative great power "which has a paramount interest in the preservation of peace." For Lippmann, the central reality in the Far East was China's resurgence as a powerful nation, in contrast to the debilitated China that had been ravaged by years of civil war until 1949. Far from being internally feeble allies of the Soviet Union, the Chinese communists were now in the midst of a "fierce conflict" with the Soviet Union, and the Maoist revolution had irrevocably "consolidated its grip on mainland China." Despite the revolutionary changes that had taken place in the Far Eastern power structure since 1949, the administration remained committed to a foreign policy that was based on the premise that China was weak and dependent upon the aggressive Soviet Union that had existed in Stalin's time. Lippmann concluded that President Johnson's vaunted ability to discredit his political opponents was irrelevant to the American dilemma of creating a viable foreign policy: "The President will find all too soon that his problem is not how to get the better of Senator Fulbright or even of General de Gaulle but of how to master the realities which they are talking about." The columnist granted that Johnson was still powerful enough to overcome his domestic opposition. "But the argument," Lippmann predicted, "will not stay won because the realities in Asia and Europe are not under his control. The realities will not yield to his argument and his briefings, and will continue relentlessly on their course."[57]

On a Columbia Broadcasting System evening news broadcast in mid-March, Eric Sevareid approved Fulbright's refutation of the criticisms the administration had initially directed against the committee's public inquiry into American policies in the Far East. During late February and early March administration officials were "privately denouncing" the Foreign Relations Committee hearings for "conveying to the enemy and the world an image of the United States as a divided country." In Sevareid's opinion, Fulbright "made the right answer" when he stated, "since the country obviously was divided, the hearings conveyed not an image but a fact." CBS produced a television seminar on China and Vietnam, with Fulbright and Fairbank appearing as the analysts; this program was another indication that the hearings had opened up public discussion of American diplomacy in the Far East. The senator elaborated upon his defense of the Committee's public investigation of Asian policies in a widely publicized speech at Johns Hopkins University shortly after the hearings:

> I see no merit in the view that at the cost of suppressing the normal procedures of democracy, we should maintain an image of unity even though it is a false image.
> The hearings . . . were undertaken in the belief that the best way to assure the prevalence of truth over falsehood is by exposing all tendencies of opinion to free competition in the market place of ideas. They were undertaken in something of the spirit of Thomas Jefferson's words: `I know no safe depository of the ultimate powers of the society but the people themselves; and if we think them not enlightened enough to exercise their control with a wholesome discretion, the remedy is not to take it from them, but to inform their discretion.'[58]

In his evening news commentary and in magazine articles in 1966, Sevareid commended Fulbright's challenge to American foreign policy in Asia, arguing that when the Senate consented to the decisions of the executive branch concerning Asia, "that's not news. In our 16 years' involvement with Vietnam that is all it has done. But when it advises that is news." Thus, the CBS commentator concluded that Fulbright's advice and dissent regarding Johnson's foreign policy was "the biggest story in Washington." He applauded Fulbright's attempt to halt the "drift" in the administration's thinking "from the idea of war with China as a possibility toward the idea as a probability. The next step would be expectation." Sevareid believed the "expectation" of war with China would increase the likelihood that such a war would occur. The momentum within the administration toward increasing hostility against China had begun to abate after the Vietnam and China hearings, Sevareid maintained. On March 13 Vice President Hubert Humphrey softened his previously militant stance against China, describing the China hearings as "fruitful procedures" and advocating a policy of "containment without isolation." The vague phrase "containment without isolation," in Sevareid's opinion, signified that the administration was at least beginning to accept the need for developing minimal lines of communication with China. He argued that the President's recnt decision to allow American scholars to travel to China—if China would let them in—was further evidence that the administration wanted to establish a modicum of communication with Peking.[59]

Sevareid's evaluation of the executive's response to the hearings was overly sanguine, for the President was not contemplating any important changes in the China policy. Humphrey had briefly modified his anti-Chinese rhetoric in March, but the change in the Vice President's rhetoric was qualified by his observation that China's "aggressive militancy" had caused China's isolation in the international community. A few weeks after the Humphrey statement, Rusk ruled out any change in the administration's diplomacy, since "there is no prospect for improved relations unless we are willing to surrender Formosa." He urged the free nations of the world to tighten their trade restrictions against China, particularly in any trade that might increase the Chinese "sinews of war."[60] Rusk's plea was totally unrealistic, for America's major allies did not support the U.S. embargo and did not follow any trade restrictions with China; the Chinese were able to obtain all essential goods through their foreign trade. The embargo had only succeeded in annoying many American businessmen, who wanted to participate in the China trade that Japan and other nations were then monopolizing.[61]

The President disparaged the hearings with his remark (which Fulbright and Morgenthau mentioned at the March 30 session) that they were increasing the extreme anti-communist pressures within the country. Johnson's criticism reflected his fears of a potential right-wing backlash against any intimation that the U.S. government might be considering a change in America's Cold War posture in Asia. The McCarthyite attack upon the Truman administration for the "loss" of China had left an indelible impression upon Johnson's perception of American politics. The scholars who testified at the hearings (with the exception of Rowe) dismissed the "loss of China" charges as utter vilification, while Fulbright and Morgenthau had contended that most Americans would approve of a reversal in the Cold War policies in Asia. But Johnson ignored these arguments and remained preoccupied with his goal of preventing a neo-McCarthyite assault upon his administration for "losing" Vietnam.[62] As he had announced early in his Presidency, "I am not going to be the President who saw southeast Asia go the way China went."[63] At the time of the China hearings, Johnson told an interviewer: "The hearings, not Lyndon Johnson, have excited all this talk . . . Fulbright says the more you debate, the better. That's a lot of crap." He berated the senator's "pathological defeatism" in Asia and attempted to discredit Fulbright as an irresponsible publicity seeker who was a "frustrated old woman" because he had never been appointed Secretary of State.[64] In Johnson's view, the public debate would only arouse the extreme anti-communists and create dangers of another era of McCarthyite witch-hunting. As late as 1969 he wrote in his memoirs, "A divisive debate about 'who lost Vietnam' would be, in my judgment, even more destructive to our national life than the argument over China had been."[65]

Many of Fulbright's admirers later claimed that he had restrained the Johnson administration from pursuing an increasingly aggressive anti-Chinese posture, which eventually would have led to a war with the mainland regime. Opposition to expanding the Vietnam War into a military conflict with China was certainly the most common opinion expressed at the hearings. The chairman's ally, Albert Gore, later contended that Fulbright "may well have saved us from a war with China." Gore's assertion was impossible to prove, of course; Johnson never advocated war with China and rejected certain military actions, such as a full-scale ground invasion of North Vietnam, which probably would have produced a defensive Chinese military reaction. Yet, as Sevareid argued, the danger existed that the administration might gradually "drift" from a belligerent anti-Chinese position into a military conflict that the President had not desired. The hearings may have reinforced Johnson's concern to avoid war with China, and they may have checked the administration's momentum of increasing hostility toward Mao; in responding to the hearings the administration had made minor concessions to the proposals for modifying the Cold Warrior stance in Asia, such as Johnson's decision to allow American scholars to travel to China. Ultimately, however, the Foreign Relations Committee's dissent did not lead to any alterations in the President's basic policies, and throughout the Johnson years the United States would continue to blame "Asian communism, with its headquarters in Peking."[66]

The basic significance of the hearings consisted of their long-term influence upon public opinion. The Vietnam and China hearings were the crucial beginning movement in a realistic national appraisal of American policies in Asia. Fulbright's committee had forced the nation to re-examine a confrontation in which the world's most populous country and the world's most powerful country, both armed with nuclear weapons, essentially refused to communicate with each other. During the late 1960s and early 1970s Fulbright continued to plead for an amelioration of Sino-American relations. Under the leadership of National Security Adviser Henry A. Kissinger, the executive branch became increasingly sympathetic to Fulbright's arguments. The chairman supported Kissinger's detente policies with China, which culminated in President Nixon's 1972 journey to Peking. Many foreign policy analysts alleged that only the zealous anti-communist Richard Nixon could have traveled to Peking without igniting an era of neo-McCarthyism. Fulbright had argued that the change could have begun earlier, for the American people tended to respond favorably to Presidential and Congressional leadership in foreign policy. Lyndon Johnson had also possessed impeccable credentials as a staunch anti-communist, although presumably he would have been more vulnerable to the extreme right-wing minority's recriminations than a Republican. In any event, whether Nixon was the sole American politician who could have initiated the rapprochement with China was a highly conjectural question. Fulbright praised Kissinger's detente with China, although he warned that a future alliance with the mainland regime would provoke Russian suspicions of a Sino-American alliance against the Soviet Union. John King Fairbank wrote in his autobiography that at the time of the announcement of Nixon's visit to Peking, "Fulbright signalized the triumph of the liberal view by holding a hearing of the Senate Foreign Relations Committee with John Davies, Jack Service, and me to testify."[67] Davies, Service, and Fairbank had served as U.S. government officials in China in the 1940s and had been condemned by the McCarthyites for predicting that the Maoists and not the Kuomintang owned the future of China. Kissinger appreciated Fulbright's contributions in the effort to change American policy toward China, and in his memoirs paid tribute to the senator: "I greatly respected Senator Fulbright across the chasm of our policy differences [a reference to Fulbright's opposition to the Nixon-Kissinger policies of continued U.S. military involvement in southeast Asia] for his erudition, fairness, and patriotism."[68]

Nonetheless, the Foreign Relations Committee's dissent obviously failed to alter the Cold Warrior diplomacy of the Johnson administration. Whether a different approach by the committee would have exerted a greater impact on the executive's policies was another conjectural question. Johnson's biographer Doris Kearns charged that the hearings "merely tugged and hauled at the President" through a series of disconnected statements.[69] There was a certain problem of too many voices examining too many complex issues at the hearings: 14 witnesses and 17 senators participated in the discussion, which covered the history of China and southeast Asia, Sino-American and Vietnamese-American relations, and the history of China's relations with the Soviet Union and Western Europe. Barnett and Fairbank testified alone, but at later hearings two or three scholars appeared simultaneously. At times the committee seemed to be analyzing the history of the world, and occasionally the participants briefly discussed important issues and almost immediately raced to another topic. Considering America's lack of knowledge about the Far East, however, a broad overview was probably necessary as the initial step in the nation's education concerning China and southeast Asia.[70] The Vietnam and China hearings were the two most notable instances of this educational process, but they were only the beginning; Fulbright held "educational" hearings on China and Vietnam throughout the late 1960s and early 1970s, and in many other ways attempted to promote public, thoughtful discussion of U.S. policy in the Far East. Moreover, at the 1966 hearings Fulbright usually succeeded in focusing the discussion on the nature of Chinese foreign policy rather than on Mao's internal program or other issues.

The chairman regarded the Chinese as basically cautious in their foreign policy. He recalled General Maxwell Taylor's admission that the Chinese intervention in the Korean War had been a justifiable and defensive response to General Douglas MacArthur's precipitous drive toward the Yalu in 1950; he noted that the Chinese had removed their troops from North Korea in 1958 despite the absence of any external pressures to withdraw.[71] The chairman did not devote detailed attention at the hearings to China's domestic policies. Fulbright and several witnesses briefly mentioned the Great Leap Forward of the late 1950s as an abortive effort to industrialize overnight. The Great Leap was probably the crucial factor in causing China's severe depression in the late 1950s and early 1960s.[72] The senator was never enamored of the Maoist revolution; he simply believed that a nation that was totally immersed in its domestic problems, as China appeared to have been in the 1960s, was an unlikely candidate for a role as conqueror of all Asia. But he based this position on the evidence of caution in Chinese diplomacy, and not upon any assessment of the domestic situation in China.

Fulbright was fortunate to have refrained from eulogizing Mao's internal policies, for one month after the China hearings ended China became convulsed by the Cultural Revolution, a repressive campaign by the PLA and the Red Guard youth to terrorize any Chinese suspected of deviations from Maoist orthodoxy.[73] As late as 1989, the oppressive nature of the Chinese regime was again shockingly demonstrated in the brutal repression of the student demonstrators in Tiananmen Square. By the 1990s, some observers of China believed that the extreme stages of the Maoist revolution had passed and that there was long-term hope for reform as had occurred in eastern Europe and the Soviet Union. Nonetheless, given the persistent strain of authoritarianism that afflicted China in the domestic sphere, Fulbright was wise to have avoided adopting a romanticized view of the Chinese government in its domestic policies. The senator consistently maintained that Mao's internal policies were beyond the control of the United States, and the proper concern of American foreign policy should be the Chinese conduct of their external relations.

Doris Kearns contended that the hearings were not related to any direct legislative challenge to Johnson's Vietnam policy.[74] Kearns neglected to mention the dissenters' effort to repeal the Gulf of Tonkin Resolution in early March 1966. Fulbright was one of only five senators who voted for the attempt to repeal the Resolution.[75] The Senate rejected the repeal of the Resolution by a vote of 92 to five, and the administration cited this triumph as evidence of Congress' enthusiastic support for Johnson's escalation policy. After the debacle of the 92 to five reaffirmation of the Resolution, Fulbright became determined to devote his energies to the Foreign Relations Committee hearings rather than legislative challenges to the escalation policy.[76]

A valid criticism could be directed against most of the witnesses' testimony on Vietnam. Hans Morgenthau and most of the senators had delivered vigorous indictments of the Vietnam policy, and hence dissenting ideas were publicized at every hearing. Yet most of the scholars had opposed the China policy only after they had amply demonstrated their anti-communist credentials by supporting the Vietnam War. Such stalwart guardians of Cold War orthodoxy as *Time* magazine and Joseph Alsop responded favorably to the hearings largely because Fairbank and the other scholars had not endorsed the Fulbright-Morse analysis of the war. The greatest enigma surrounding the hearings was the support by many of the most brilliant scholars in America for the disastrous intervention in Vietnam. The witnesses demolished Rusk's thesis that Chinese military expansionism threatened to devour southeast Asia, and this thesis was the principal justification for the war in early 1966. Yet each of the witnesses embraced other rationales that the administration offered to defend the intervention. Griffith approved the notion that regardless of one's opinion concerning the wisdom of the original involvement in Vietnam, the United States was committed to the defense of Saigon in the 1960s, and the nation must fight to preserve the credibility of the American promise to uphold its commitments throughout the globe. Fairbank and others had accepted yet another set of justifications: the positive goal of building a viable democracy in South Vietnam, and the negative objective of preventing dissemination of Mao's doctrine that the Chinese revolution was the model for leftists in the Third World to emulate. In practice, Fairbank's public reason for supporting the war differed from Rusk's view only in the professor's belief that the Chinese would not supply direct military assistance to Third World revolutionaries. As he had informed Fulbright, "To make the Maoist model of takeover ineffective and stalemated, I foresee that we have got to keep on fighting. That is the answer." Fairbank never explained how the United States might use armed force to destroy a doctrine.

Reinforcing the ideological justifications for the war, there were obvious pressures to conform and rally to the President's support in a time of crisis. In his memoirs Fairbank explained that he had not wanted to discuss Vietnam when he was supposed to be testifying on China. This statement was not a convincing explanation, for elsewhere he had argued that the Vietnam and China policies were integrally related. Perhaps he provided a more logical elucidation when he stated, "I did not want to be used by the Congress against the Executive." Having suffered through accusations of "softness on communism" during the McCarthy era, he may have been wary of becoming entangled in another political debate involving anticommunism. Fairbank clearly regretted his failure to oppose the war in his testimony. As he later described his appearance at the hearings, "Fulbright led me along toward saying that Vietnam was much like China and our policy equally ill advised." Fairbank resisted his probing, and as the professor recalled a conversation with the senator shortly after hearing, "Fulbright chided me in his gentle way for not making an obvious point. He was right, I should have done so."[77]

In the broad sense, the testimony on Vietnam in the China hearings was a rude awakening for those who believed that academic figures tend to provide brilliant, objective analyses of public policy debates, while members of Congress are political hackers who have little extensive knowledge of serious issues and are largely concerned only for their personal political future. Fulbright and Morse were leagues ahead of the scholars (with the obvious exception of Morgenthau) who testified at the hearings regarding Vietnam policy, not only in their intellectual analysis of the war but in their courage in expressing dissident ideas. On the other hand, the professors were thoroughly disappointing in their timid failure to draw the logical conclusions from their testimony about China and apply them to southeast Asia. The brutal reality, as the testimony on Vietnam painfully indicated, was that professors are not significantly different from any other profession in America from the standpoint of their reluctance to avoid nonconformist, unpopular ideas. This conclusion might be vehemently denied by some American academics, most of whom pride themselves on their profession's stalwart quest for truth. Yet, at the China hearings, as well as throughout most of mainstream academia in early 1966, most of the university community was generally not critical of the war. The conformist climate of opinion in the country was disturbing, and many thoughtful critics dejectedly recalled Alexis de Tocqueville's criticism of American intolerance during the nineteenth century in *Democracy in America*: "I know of no country in which there is so little independence of mind and real freedom of discussion as in America."

A relatively small number of highly prominent professors—notably Morgenthau of the University of Chicago, Norman Graebner of the University of Virginia, John Kenneth Galbraith, and a few others—were beginning to educate their colleagues across the country regarding southeast Asia. Yet it was a slow intellectual process. In February, 1967, two University of Michigan sociologists polled the faculty of their campus and reported that while many professors vocally opposed the war, "the largest single bloc... was not the doves, as the current folklore would have it, but supporters of the administration policy." An extensive survey of 6,000 professors across the country in 1969 indicated that only 18 percent favored immediate withdrawal from Vietnam, another 40 percent supported the establishment of a coalition government, while roughly one third supported gradual de-escalation and the prevention of a communist takeover. As late as 1973, the sociologist E.M. Schreiber concluded that "faculty opinion on the war was not markedly more anti-war than mass public opinion." As Professor David Levy concluded in *The Debate Over Vietnam*, professors in the social sciences tended to oppose the war, followed by humanities professors, and those in the natural sciences. Those in vocational fields such as business, agriculture, engineering and education tended to support the war in greater numbers than did their colleagues.[77a]

While Fulbright was unquestionably gaining powerful intellectual support from a small number of academic figures who were among the most prestigious thinkers in the country—the Morgenthaus and Kennans—he was deeply disturbed by the widespread conformity he saw on too many college campuses. In *The Arrogance of Power*, he implored American universities to return to the ideal that cultivation of the free and inquiring mind was the cardinal responsibility of higher education. The danger of excessive dependence upon government funding in the universities went far beyond the problem of contractual associations with the CIA, for when extensive governmental associations in all forms "become primary areas of activity, when they become the major source of the university's revenue and the major source of the scholar's prestige, then the `teaching of things in perspective' is likely to be neglected and the universality of the university compromised." The professor most valued "in the government-oriented university," Fulbright wrote, "is one, I suspect, who though technically brilliant is philosophically orthodox, because the true dissenter, the man who dissents about purpose and not just technique, is likely to lose a sale."

In Fayetteville, the University of Arkansas had suffered from efforts to stifle expression on campus in the 1960s. When the famous psycotherapist, Dr. Albert Ellis, had delivered a controversial speech about "Sex-Love Relationships," Governor Faubus had called for the firing of Ellis' sponsor, and in 1962, the university even forbade gubernatorial candidates from appearing on campus. Fulbright opposed this climate of censorship, and supported Rev. James Loudermilk when he allowed a speech entitled "Life in Bulgaria" to be given at the Methodist Student Center after the address was banned on campus. Fulbright vehemently objected to the idea that speeches on controversial subjects could not be given at universities, contending that "the right to hear as well as to speak freely about controversial subjects is a basic principle of our democratic society." In the later years of the Vietnam War, support for free speech on campus broadened, and student critics of the war expressed their dissent freely. Fulbright argued that the university cannot separate itself from society, but neither should the community of scholars accept the status quo, as if the scholar's proper function consisted of devising technical means of carrying out policies created by the government. Controversial questions should not be excluded from debate in the name of a spurious patriotism, and Fulbright urged the academic community to return to its calling of promoting uninhibited, free, and necessarily controversial debate:

> It would be a fine thing indeed if, instead of spending so much of their time playing 'war games,' political scientists were asking how it came about that we have had for so long to devote so great a part of our resources to war and its prevention, and whether we are condemned by forces beyond our control to continue to do so. The scholar can ask what is wrong with the 'other side,' but he must not fail to ask as well what is wrong with our side, remembering always that the highest devotion we can give is not to our country as it is but to a concept of what we would like it to be.[77b]

If the majority of professors were not noticeably dissident in 1966, neither were the students. The Young Democrats initially supported the war, although by 1968 many student activists in that organization would become involved in the campaigns of Eugene McCarthy or Robert Kennedy. The Young Republicans had hundreds of thousands of members, roughly a thousand local chapters, and generally supported the war to the bitter end. The well-funded, aggressive and effective Young Americans for Freedom was a militant conservative group that supported the war. As the war progressed, however, the anti-war forces became much stronger in the activist, heavily involved segment of the student population. A few of the groups, such as the Young People's International Party (the Yippies) espoused radical means of dissent that Fulbright found counterproductive. The Students for a Democratic Society (SDS) expanded rapidly in the late 1960s, having roughly 400 campus chapters by 1969. The obvious factor in turning the activists on the campuses against the war was the ominous threat facing male students: they might be drafted and sent to fight and possibly die in Vietnam. While some activist groups were radical, many of them expressed their dissent in moderate ways: through university newspapers, teach-ins, sit-ins, peaceful demonstrations, and campaign work for the Kennedy, McCarthy or McGovern campaigns.[77c]

Fulbright, of course, opposed the radical fringe's methods of dissent, but as for the majority of conscientious, student opponents of the war, he gave the highest praise: the protest movement "is an expression of the national conscience and a manifestation of traditional American idealism."[77d]

Fulbright routinely helped students from Arkansas who requested assistance in getting draft deferments. One student Fulbright helped was Bill Clinton, a bright young Arkansan who had worked on Fulbright's staff while he was a student at Georgetown. Many years later, President George Bush would lambast Clinton in the 1992 presidential campaign for having evaded the draft. Lee Williams had contacted the University of Arkansas ROTC about a deferment on behalf of Clinton; there was nothing unusual about this action, and an effort of a student to avoid the draft in the late 1960s was the rule rather than the exception. Clinton succeeded in avoiding the draft in 1968-69, attending Oxford as a Rhodes Scholar and then the Yale Law School. (The draft episode will be treated in more detail in Book Six.) Fulbright advised Clinton, as well as many other young Americans, to find legal ways of avoiding the draft.

One of the oversimplifications concerning the anti-war movement focused on the notion of a "generational gap," in which the young opposed the war and the older generation supported it. This notion was inaccurate, for there were supporters as well as opponents of the war spread through all age groups. In August 1965, the Gallup organization reported that 76 percent of Americans under age 30 supported the war, 64 percent of those 30 to 49 years old supported it, while only 49 percent of those over 49 supported it. In August 1968, the war was supported by 45 percent of the young, 39 percent of the middle group and 27 percent of the older group. In 1971, support among the young was down to 34 percent, with the other two groups supporting it at levels of 30 and 23 percent, respectively. A careful student of public opinion, John E. Mueller, concluded that "no case can be made for the popular proposition that 'youth' was in revolt over the war.'" In explaining the widespread perceptions that the campuses were in revolt (a Gallup poll in June 1970 found that "campus unrest" was the number one problem in America, according to those polled), the intensity and determination of the anti-war activists must be considered. The student organizations could turn out large numbers for the anti-war demonstrations or the anti-war political candidates, while relatively larger numbers of the status-quo oriented students were not activist. The media extensively reported the views of the dissident students, thus accentuating their profile in the public's mind. Moreover, as David Levy and other analysts of the Vietnam debate have concluded, it is crucial to distinguish between students in general and those who attended the nationally prominent, most prestigious universities that had the most demanding admission standards. Just as the intellectual elite among the professors—the Graebners and the Morgenthaus—tended to oppose the war, on the nationally prominent campuses the student bodies turned against the war sooner than did their colleagues at institutions with only local students and local academic reputations. By the late 1960s and early 1970s, an anti-war consensus had emerged at such universities as Yale, Harvard, the University of Virginia, the University of California at Berkeley, and other nationally prominent institutions. As Levy concluded, "Graduate students at the leading institutions tended to be strong opponents of the war and faculty members at these schools, more critical of official policy in Vietnam than were those at less prestigious colleges."[77e]

Although Fulbright tried to reach all segments of the American public, it is clear that in the beginning he was having more success in reaching the well-educated than others. A Harris poll after the hearings indicated that 37 percent of Americans had followed the hearings, and a majority of those who had were college-educated. About 55 percent were supportive of the Foreign Relations Committee in holding the hearings, while 45 percent were not. Unfortunately, Senator Morse's strident tactics had not been helpful; 60 percent felt that he had been more harmful than constructive at the hearings, and 45 percent classified him as "radical". While Morse was a courageous and brilliant dissident, apparently his abrasive demeanor was not beneficial politically; in this respect, Fulbright's more restrained approach was more successful in the tasks of education and communication.

Fulbright unquestionably exerted a powerful impact upon the growth of dissent in the universities. He had long enjoyed a strong reputation in academic circles because of his status as a Rhodes Scholar, constitutional law professor, university president, and founder of the Fulbright Scholar program. Many intellectuals were influenced by Fulbright's warning that the conformity of thought that de Tocqueville had observed was worsening, "among other reasons, because more and more of our citizens earn their livings by working for corporations and other large organizations, few of which are known to encourage political and other forms of heterodoxy on the part of their employees." Not only were his views extensively reported in the *New York Times* and other major newspapers, the national television networks, and other news organizations, but *The Arrogance of Power* was one of the most well-known books of its time. By June 1967, it had sold 100,000 copies, and eventually it would be translated into Spanish, German, Italian, Japanese, and Swedish editions, selling more than 400,000 copies worldwide. It enjoyed a particularly wide distribution on college campuses and was sometimes used in the required reading lists in courses; Professor Henry Kissinger at Harvard, for example, required it in one of his classes. Many professors were influenced by Fulbright's warning that universities should not become sycophantic to the government and must avoid conformity of thought.[77]

The Arrogance of Power, of course, followed the vital opening of discussion initiated by the Vietnam and China hearings. For all the disappointments of the scholars' testimony on Vietnam, the China hearings were nonetheless highly beneficial. Several witnesses—notably John King Fairbank—were clearly in a transitional period, were becoming more critical of Vietnam policy, and would become clearcut critics of the war. Above all, in refuting the myth of China as a Nazi-like expansionist power bent upon world conquest, the hearings challenged the intellectual foundations of the Vietnam policy and strengthened the burgeoning doubts about the war that were beginning to emerge in the minds of millions of Americans.

The Arrogance of Power

In Fulbright's "Arrogance of Power" speeches of April 1966, the Senator intensified and elaborated upon his indictment of the Johnson administration's foreign policy. The speeches formed the nucleus of his book *The Arrogance of Power* (published several months later) in which Fulbright summarized the basic foreign policy proposals he had advocated in 1964, 1965, and 1966. One part of the book reiterated the theme of his "Old Myths and New Realities" and "Bridges East and West" speeches of 1964 in appealing for the policy of "building bridges" to the communist world. Another chapter reiterated the thesis of Fulbright's September 1965 Dominican address. The most detailed sections of the book dealt with the controversies over America's Asian policy, which Fulbright, Rusk, Taylor, Gavin, and Kennan had debated at the Vietnam hearings.

In *The Arrogance of Power* Fulbright delineated a program for the eventual restoration of peace in Vietnam. The initial point in his program was a recommendation that the South Vietnamese government should seek negotiations with the National Liberation Front. The United States should remind the contemporary regime in Saigon, the senator maintained, that America would not become committed to the objective of complete military victory for the government of Ky and Thieu or any successor government. "At the same time," he continued, "as the Saigon government makes direct overtures to the National Liberation Front the United States and South Vietnam together should propose negotiations for a cease-fire among military representatives of four separate negotiating parties: the United States and South Vietnam, North Vietnam and the National Liberation Front."[69] While the United States was inaugurating these peace initiatives, it should terminate the bombing of North Vietnam and pledge to withdraw American military forces from Vietnam.

According to Fulbright, the four principal belligerents should direct their negotiations toward organizing a national referendum acceptable to the South Vietnamese government and to the National Liberation Front. The United States should commit itself explicitly to accept the results of the national referendum in order to allay suspicions that America and the South Vietnamese government would repeat the error of 1956, when the Diem regime failed to hold the elections envisaged by the Geneva Agreements. In Fulbright's opinion, "the outcome of a referendum in South Vietnam cannot be predicted," but he observed that elections might reveal "the full diversity of South Vietnamese society, with the National Liberation Front emerging as a major political force in the country but with the Buddhists and Catholics, the Cao Dai and the Hoa Hao also showing themselves to be important forces in their respective zones of influence."[70]

After the principal belligerents arranged a cease-fire and a national referendum for South Vietnam, Fulbright proposed that "an international conference should be convened to guarantee the arrangements made by the belligerents and to plan a future referendum on the reunification of North Vietnam and South Vietnam."[71] All of the great powers, including the Soviet Union and China, should participate in this conference. In addition to the plans for the reunification of Vietnam, the international conference should negotiate a multilateral agreement for the neutralization of all southeast Asia.

If the negotiations failed, Fulbright conceded that the United States should retire to General Gavin's "enclave theory" (discussed above), although the senator did not refer to Gavin's theory by name. One should emphasize that Fulbright proposed the coastal enclave strategy only if determined, constant, and sincere American efforts to negotiate a peaceful settlement failed.[72] The administration, of course, repudiated Fulbright's peace program.

The senator concluded his plea for the restoration of peace in southeast Asia by quoting a speech Charles de Gaulle delivered in Cambodia on September 1, 1966. De Gaulle predicted a triumph for American diplomacy if the United States followed a course of accommodation and neutralization in Vietnam: "In view of the power, wealth, and influence at present attained by the United States, the act of renouncing, in its turn, a distant expedition once it appears unprofitable and unjustifiable and of substituting for it an international arrangement organizing the peace and development of an important region of the world, will not, in the final analysis, involve anything that could injure its pride, interfere with its ideals and jeopardize its interests. On the contrary, in taking a path so true to the Western genius, what an audience would the United States recapture from one end of the world to the other, and what an opportunity would peace find on the scene and everywhere else."[73]

In a memorable passage of *The Arrogance of Power*, Fulbright defended the right of a patriot to advocate dissident ideas concerning American diplomacy. "Gradually but unmistakably," he wrote, "America is showing signs of that arrogance of power which has afflicted, weakened and in some cases destroyed great nations in the past. In so doing we are not living up to our capacity and promise as a civilized example for the world. The measure of our falling short is the measure of the patriot's duty of dissent."[74] Fulbright urged Americans to eschew "the arrogance of power, the tendency of great nations to equate power with virtue and major responsibilities with a universal mission."[75]

In reminding the republic that foreign adventurism had frequently wrought the decline of great nations in the past, Fulbright often compared the American crusade in Southeast Asia to the disastrous Athenian expedition against Syracuse in ancient history. At a hearing during the spring of 1966, the Senator reflected:

> It seems to me the best we could get out of it, if we were to have a total victory, would be another authoritarian regime, which would not be much to show for billions of dollars and thousands of lives, and, I think, the loss of the confidence of our important allies.
>
> I keep having this persistent thought that some historian in the year 3000 will be comparing our exploit in southeast Asia to Athens' attack on Syracuse. It is the classic case of a misjudged situation . . .
>
> I have made a suggestion, a very feeble one, for which I am sure I will have very few followers. I think it was in accordance with the views of General Ridgway, General Gavin, and Mr. Kennan, that we should de-escalate this war and seek a conference in the nature of a compromise, because it is not an issue which warrants enormous sacrifice of life and money. I said it reminded me of Syracuse. In that case they also had a debate, and there was a great division of opinion, and the side that finally decided it won by a very narrow margin, but it was a disaster and a catastrophe that we have been paying for ever since. [75a]

President Johnson interpreted the senator's "arrogance of power" rhetoric as a personal attack upon his administration. Fulbright continued to argue that his criticisms were directed against the substance of Johnson's foreign policy, and were not accusations that Lyndon Johnson was an arrogant politician. In a May 1966 letter to the President, Fulbright attempted to clarify the thesis of his speeches: "Greece, Rome, Spain, England, Germany, and others lost their pre-eminence because of failure to recognize their limitations, or, as I called it, the arrogance of their power; and my hope is that this country, presently the greatest and the most powerful in the world, may learn by the mistakes of its predecessors."[76] He added that he was confident America would not succumb to the "arrogance of power" under President Johnson's leadership. This additional comment was not consistent with some of the more critical passages in Fulbright's speeches; it was part of a forlorn effort to deter Johnson's tendency to personalize their conflict. The senator had written a somewhat similar letter to the President in March 1966, requesting that the administration should at least devote careful study to his proposal for the neutralization of Vietnam "before it is discarded as unreasonable."[77] The Department of State, he observed, had recently rejected the neutralization idea "as being quite unthinkable."[78] He respectfully recommended that the Policy Planning Staff conduct a thorough investigation of the neutralization proposal.

In a May 1966 speech at the Democrats' annual fund-raising dinner in Washington, Johnson noticed Fulbright a few steps away from the speaker's platform, glanced in Fulbright's direction, and said, "I'm glad to be here among so many friends—and some members of the Foreign Relations Committee." Privately, Johnson would charge that Fulbright's alleged "racism" led him to oppose the war, because the Arkansan simply did not care about the plight of yellow people. The President's public remarks at a Chicago fund-raising dinner in mid-May 1966 delineated his response toward Fulbright's attempt to restore a modicum of direct communication between the Foreign Relations Committee chairman and the administration. Johnson disparaged the opponents of the Vietnam War with the following animadversions: "I do not think that those men who are out there fighting for us tonight think that we should enjoy the luxury of fighting each other back home. There will be Nervous Nellies and some who become frustrated and bothered and break ranks under the strain and turn on their leaders, their own country, and their own fighting men."[79]

Fulbright and four other senators displayed impressive political courage by voting in favor of an attempt to repeal the Gulf of Tonkin Resolution on March 1, 1966. After the Senate rejected the repeal by the margin of 92 to five, the administration cited this triumph as evidence of Congress' supposedly enthusiastic support for Johnson's escalation policy. Fifteen Senate critics of the war failed to vote for such a politically dangerous, direct confrontation with the administration. The five senators in dissent were Fulbright, Morse, Gruening, Eugene McCarthy, and Stephen Young of Ohio. In their biographies of President Johnson and Fulbright Doris Kearns and Haynes Johnson neglected to mention the dissenters' effort to repeal the Gulf of Tonkin Resolution. This omission was unfortunate, because the abortive repeal attempt was an important demonstration of Fulbright's relentless determination to oppose the escalation policy. Haynes Johnson and Kearns do not seem to have known about the March 1 Senate vote on repeal. Kearns contended that the Foreign Relations Committee hearings were not related to any direct legislative challenge to Johnson's Vietnam policy, but this contention was incorrect, for the repeal movement clearly constituted a direct challenge to the administration's policy and it was related to the hearings, which were constantly referred to during the Senate debate over repeal. The Vietnam hearings ended a few days before the vote, and other hearings on the war and U.S. policy in Asia resumed a few days after the March 1 vote. After the debacle of the 92 to five reaffirmation of the Resolution, Fulbright did not advocate any additional attempts to obtain repeal until the dissenters could expect to gain substantially more than five votes; in 1966 such attempts had no chance of winning a majority, and the administration publicized such results in the March 1 vote as endorsements of escalation. Nevertheless, Fulbright had shown that he was not afraid to publicly repudiate the Gulf of Tonkin Resolution.[79a]

By the spring of 1966, a pattern had emerged that would persist, with minor variations, for the remainder of Johnson's Presidency. Throughout the interminable period of American military escalation during 1966, 1967 and early 1968, Fulbright repeatedly urged a cessation of the military intervention and pleaded for the neutralization of Vietnam. The administration incessantly reiterated its position and dismissed the Foreign Relations Committee chairman's recommendations.

While Johnson was often personally bitter at Fulbright, at times he carefully made efforts to avoid any charge of a personal vendetta against the chairman. On May 27, he wrote to Fulbright, complaining that "statements can be taken out of context and interpretations can draw a different meaning than you meant from your words. It's happened to me!" Unfortunately, Johnson demonstrated that none of Fulbright's ideas had made any meaningful impact, since he said the "Munich analogy" should have been included in his analysis in his "Arrogance of Power" speeches. Fulbright, of course, regarded Munich as an entirely different historical setting from Vietnam. Johnson was determined to strike a friendly tone, however: "I cannot believe our differences over policy have erased the friendship we have shared for so long. I have a fondness for Betty and you that is real... I am sorry that careless people have appeared to paint another picture."[79b] The uglier side of Johnson's persona also revealed itself at the time; the President ordered Fulbright and several other Senate dissidents placed under FBI surveillance.[79c]

The propaganda machinery at the disposal of the administration was immense, not only through normal channels, but also through the CIA. The CIA reported to the "secret seven"—a special subcommittee of the Armed Services Committee. Fulbright sought to have three members of the Foreign Relations Committee added to the "secret seven." Chairman Russell refused, whereupon Fulbright persuaded the Foreign Relations Committee to report a bill changing the secret seven subcommittee into a Full Committee on Intelligence Operations, a new body with members from Foreign Relations, Appropriations and Armed Services that would oversee the intelligence activities of all government agencies. In the course of the debate, Fulbright discovered that the CIA had even exploited the Fulbright Program as part of its intelligence activities, and the chairman extracted a pledge from the agency to desist from such activities. Fulbright also revealed that the CIA had penetrated many other organizations, including the National Student Association and the American Newspaper Guild. Senator Russell joined forces with the White House to charge that Fulbright had leaked information affecting the national security during the Dominican controversy and the debates over Vietnam policy, and the full Senate ultimately supported Russell, thus leaving the "secret seven" as the exclusive preserve of the Armed Services Committee. Despite Fulbright's disclosures of the massive scope of CIA activities, the administration would later misuse the agency in attempting to stifle antiwar dissent. In 1967, Johnson ordered the CIA to place leaders of the Students for a Democratic Society (SDS) and several other dissident groups under surveillance, allegedly to prove that foreign governments were directing them. This program violated the CIA's charter, which prohibited domestic operations.[79c]

Against the massive power of the administration, Fulbright continued in his quest to generate thoughtful public debate. *The Arrogance of Power* received another round of analysis in early 1967, when the *New York Times*, the *Washington Post*, and other national publications featured reviews of the book. Ronald Steel in the *Post* was basically complimentary, saying the work "marks the passage of Senator Fulbright from a relatively orthodox supporter of the liberal line on foreign policy to a spokesman of the post-cold-war generation." Steel acknowledged that there may well be arrogance in the American attitude toward power, and there was deep anguish throughout the nation over the present uses of power. "Senator Fulbright has helped to focus and channel this anguish into constructive criticism," Steel wrote, "that may lead to the changes he desires. Therein lies the courage of his dissent and the importance of this book." The *Post* reviewer also offered a book critic's obligatory criticisms, asserting that Fulbright had failed to explain "the relative benevolence and restraint with which America has exercised our enormous power." Steel would have been well advised to leave well enough alone and not attempt to concoct a criticism in a reviewers' reflexive quest to be "balanced" by adding some criticisms even in a favorable review, for Vietnam was clearly an exception to the "relative benevolence and restraint" with which America had historically exercised its power. Nonetheless, Steel's review was thoughtful and fundamentally fair.[79d]

A more questionable review appeared in the *New York Times Book Review* by Max Frankel, who complained that the book "is not a satisfying prescription for alternatives to the policies it condemns." Frankel was also shocked by the depth of Fulbright's criticism, complaining that "it is one thing to suggest that unnecessary pride and belligerence have compounded error in Vietnam and quite another to describe them as symptoms of messianic zealotry." Fulbright had, of course, taken great pains to state his alternatives in the book, and Frankel was confused by the reality that, at the late date of 1967, any effort to disengage from the now massive involvement in Vietnam would have been exceedingly complex and painful; but the traumatic disengagement, as de Gaulle and others had asserted, should begin forthwith. Frankel's rather indignant reaction to Fulbright's suggestion that America's intervention in Vietnam could be seen as "messianic zealotry" was also rather strained. Many thoughtful observers of American foreign policy have lamented a certain messianic element that has burdened U.S. policy at times, and Fulbright's statement was hardly extreme. Even Frankel conceded, however, that Fulbright's work was "an invaluable antidote to the official rhetoric of government," and that *The Arrogance of Power* "portends, or perhaps already bespeaks, the alienation of a great many thoughtful citizens from our government."[79e]

Fulbright never pretended that *The Arrogance of Power* was a profound work of philosophy; it was a practical effort to promote thought about current American policies and to present alternatives to those policies. It represented the thinking of a realist who was deeply disturbed that American power was massively engaged in a region where no vital U.S. interests were involved, and the concerns of a former academic and advocate of uninhibited free expression who detested what he saw as a stifling conformity of thought in the nation's public discussions. It was rare for an American politician to write a thoughtful book criticizing public policies of his government in the midst of a war. Without attempting to depict the work as a philosophical treatise—which it was not—a fair analysis of *The Arrogance of Power* would acknowledge that on the practical, realistic level upon which it was written, it was an unusual and notable accomplishment in promoting thought and debate about American foreign policy.

The senator should also be given credit for having the candor to admit error. In the book, he conceded that he had seriously erred in supporting the Gulf of Tonkin Resolution in 1964 without a careful examination of the administration's request. In mid-1967, the Foreign Relations Committee began consideration of the National Commitments Resolution, an effort to restrain the executive branch from making foreign commitments that would eventually be passed during the Nixon administration. The original text that Fulbright proposed to the Senate stated the following: "That it is the sense of the Senate that a national commitment by the United States to a foreign power necessarily and exclusively results from affirmative action taken by the executive and legislative branches of the U.S. Government through means of a treaty, convention, or other legislative instrumentality specifically intended to give effect to such a commitment." At hearings on the National Commitments Resolution, Fulbright stressed the lessons he had learned from his mistakes:

> Having now experienced the frenetic mobility of the 1960s, the overheated activism, the ubiquitous involvement and the mounting sense of global mission— often referred to as the 'responsibilities of power'—I now see merit that I used not to see in occasional delay or inaction; I now see how great the Executive's foreign powers are and how limited the Congress' restraining powers are; and I see great merit in the checks and balances of our eighteenth-century Constitution.[79f]

Another disturbing development for the Congressional critics took place in the 1966 elections: many more Republicans were elected to the House of Representatives, so that the new Congress promised to be even more hawkish than the previous one, which had not been notable in opposing the war, except for the Senate Foreign Relations Committee and a few other critics. In October 1966, only 15 percent of the membership favored a greater emphasis on beginning peace talks.[79g]

During the last three years of the Johnson administration Fulbright argued that the Tonkin Resolution did not provide any legal justification for the war in Vietnam. Fulbright emphasized Johnson's almost pacifistic rhetoric during the 1964 presidential campaign and the assurances given by the administration at the time of the resolution's passage that it was intended to prevent a war by demonstrating to the Chinese and North Vietnamese that America was determined to oppose aggression. The Tonkin Resolution, Fulbright continued to maintain, amounted to Congressional acquiescence in the executive's exercise of the war power, which the Constitution vested in Congress and which Congress had no right to renounce.[80]

The significance of the August 1964 resolution lies in its symbolic nature as evidence of Congress' willingness to allow the President to acquire virtually complete control of foreign policy. Senator McGovern later stated that the momentum in favor of escalation in the Johnson administration was already so powerful by August 1964 that the Gulf of Tonkin crisis had no real effect on the administration's thinking concerning Vietnam.[81] McGovern's contention may have been accurate; as early as February 1964, the President authorized the "34A" program of clandestine military operations against North Vietnam.[82] Although Johnson referred to the Gulf of Tonkin Resolution in justifying his Vietnam policy during the early period of his Presidency, he often avoided doing so after 1966. The fact that Fulbright and other dissenting senators were publicizing the doubtful circumstances surrounding the resolution's passage may have contributed to the President's reluctance to rely on the resolution in defending his policies during 1967. In an August 1967 press conference Johnson described the resolution as a courtesy extended to Congress to permit them to "be there on the takeoff as well as on the landing. We did not think the resolution was necessary to do what we did and what we're doing."[83]

President Nixon continued his predecessor's policy of disregarding Congress' views concerning the resolution. When in 1971 Fulbright and other opponents of America's Vietnam policy finally succeeded in repealing the Gulf of Tonkin Resolution—the only legislative instrument that provided (at least in some observers' analysis) some facade of constitutional legitimacy for the Vietnam War—Nixon continued the war as if nothing of consequence had happened.[84]

Fulbright later wrote that the Congress thought it was acting to help prevent a large-scale war in southeast Asia by passing the Tonkin Resolution.[85] Actually, there was considerable confusion in Congress over precisely what the resolution signified. Senator Nelson offered his amendment (declaring it to be the policy of the United States to avoid a military intervention in Vietnam) in order to clarify the meaning of the resolution, for he claimed to be "most disturbed to see that there is no agreement in the Senate on what the joint resolution means."[86] The Pentagon Papers stated that beyond the central belief that "the occasion necessitated demonstrating the nation's unity and collective will in support of the President's action and affirming U.S. determination to oppose further aggression, Congressional opinions varied as to the policy implications and the meaning" of the almost unanimous support for the resolution. According to the Papers, "several spokesmen stressed that the resolution did not constitute a declaration of war, did not abdicate Congressional responsibility for determining national policy commitments and did not give the President carte blanche to involve the nation in a major Asian war."[87]

The Johnson administration claimed that the American commitment to Vietnam centered upon the SEATO treaty. Fulbright argued that the SEATO treaty did not commit the United States to defend member nations against internal revolts. In case of a threat of internal subversion, the only obligation of the SEATO treaty was to consult; in the event of encountering an act of internal aggression, the members were to "meet the common danger" in accordance with their constitutional processes.[88] Even if Johnson had been correct in his view of the conflict as a war of foreign aggression mounted by the North against the South, the war would still have been unconstitutional. Fulbright (as a former constitutional law professor) and many other legal authorities agreed that Congress' power to declare war, as stated in Article I, Section 8 of the U.S. Constitution, cannot be discharged either by a treaty, in which the House of Representatives does not participate, or by provision of appropriations for a war initiated by the President on his own authority.[89]

In addition to his indictment of the war's unconstitutionality, the Arkansas senator increasingly decried the domestic repercussions of America's intervention in southeast Asia. He began describing Johnson's "Great Society" as a "sick society" in 1967. At an American Bar Association meeting of August 1967 Fulbright sadly enumerated the statistics of the American death toll during a single week of July 1967: One hundred sixty-four Americans were killed and 1,442 were wounded in Vietnam, while 65 Americans were killed and 2,100 were wounded in urban riots in the United States.[90] The war not only diverted resources from health, education, and welfare programs, but perhaps even more seriously, it disseminated the idea that violence was an effective means of solving social and political problems.[91]

There was a total dichotomy between the perspectives of Fulbright's August 1967 address, entitled "The Price of Empire," and the Senator's January 1965 speech at Miami. In January 1965, he had believed President Johnson would concentrate on domestic reconstruction and end America's preoccupation with opposing communism abroad. By 1967, he was convinced that Johnson's foreign policy had grievously exacerbated America's domestic maladies. Administration officials produced impressive statistics concerning the gross national product to demonstrate that the United States could afford both the Vietnam War and the Great Society. But the statistics, in Fulbright's view, could not explain "how an anxious and puzzled people, bombarded by press and television with the bad news of American deaths in Vietnam, the 'good news' of enemy deaths—and with vividly horrifying pictures to illustrate them—can be expected to support neighborhood anti-poverty projects and national programs for urban renewal, employment and education. Anxiety about war does not breed compassion for one's neighbors; nor do constant reminders of the cheapness of life abroad strengthen our faith in its sanctity at home. In these ways the war in Vietnam is poisoning and brutalizing our domestic life."[92]

Fulbright responded to the administration's economic statistics with a brief comparison of defense and social spending in recent American history. Since 1946, he observed, 57% of the expenditures in the regular national budget had been devoted to military power, whereas 6% were spent on education, health, labor, housing, and welfare programs. The Johnson administration's budget for fiscal year 1968 was consistent with the postwar trend, calling for $75 billion in military spending and only $15 billion for "social functions."[93] According to Fulbright, Congress had not been reluctant to reduce expenditures on domestic programs, but was much too willing to provide virtually unlimited sums for the military.

The war in southeast Asia severely aggravated the problem of America's overextension of foreign commitments around the globe. Soviet-American relations remained precarious, and in the midst of the Vietnam escalation another international crisis erupted in the Middle East in mid-1967. In May 1967, the administration received CIA reports of an imminent Egyptian invasion of Israel; on June 5, Israel launched a pre-emptive strike and in a six-day war inflicted a devastating defeat upon Egypt, Jordan and Syria. Israel conquered the Sinai Peninsula, the Gaza Strip, the West Bank of the Jordan River, and the Golan Heights, thus seizing control of territory three times the size of Israel itself. Soviet Premier Kosygin used the "hot line" installed after the Cuban missile crisis (the first time it had been used in an actual crisis) to call President Johnson and express his concern over the Israeli military onslaught, at one point intimating that "If you want war, you'll get war." In McNamara's memoirs, the former Secretary of Defense stated that the prospect of military involvement in the Middle East at a time when the United States was massively engaged in Vietnam "was furthest from our thoughts." Johnson replied to Kosygin that the Israelis would accept a cease-fire once the Golan Heights had been secured. The President also moved the Sixth Fleet closer to the Syrian coast to make clear to the Soviet Union that the United States would respond to any Soviet action in the region. Shortly thereafter, Israel and Syria accepted a cease-fire and the Sixth Fleet stopped its eastward maneuver.

The exchange of "hot line" messages had helped prevent a further escalation of the Middle Eastern conflict.[93a] However, the 1967 Arab-Israeli war left numerous festering problems in the region; Arab radicalism increased exponentially in the war's wake, Egypt's policy was still driven by the mercurial Nasser, the burgeoning presence of Palestinian guerrillas in Jordan endangered the moderate, pro-Western King Hussein, and agitation by similar groups in Lebanon left that country without a stable government throughout 1969. The Soviet Union greatly expanded its role in the region by sending huge volumes of military supplies to Egypt, Syria, and Iraq.[93b] President Johnson and Prime Minister Harold Wilson of Great Britain had planned a meeting for June 2 to review all common British-American interests throughout the world, but the Middle East conflict dominated the meeting. McNamara would later admit that the Johnson administration "failed to address systematically and thoroughly questions [regarding Vietnam] whose answers so deeply affected the lives of our citizens and the welfare of our nation."[93c] One of the reasons for this failure, according to McNamara, was the multitude of world problems—including the Middle Eastern crisis—that prevented the administration from devoting full attention to Vietnam. Although McNamara won considerable praise for his belated admission in 1995 that he and the other planners of the war had been "terribly wrong" about Vietnam, by 1967 it could hardly be said that the administration did not devote sufficient attention to southeast Asia; to the contrary, the Vietnam War unfortunately devoured time, attention, energy, and resources that could have been channeled elsewhere. While southeast Asia involved no major national interests of the United States, in contrast, the Middle East was a region of tremendous importance. As Fulbright would observe, the United States had important political and economic interests in the Middle East, and "our major specific interest is a cultural and sentimental attachment to Israel rooted in the strong preference of a great many of the American people and their elected representatives. We also have a crucial stake in the avoidance of conflict with the Soviet Union."[93d]

At the time of the "Six-Day War," Fulbright had been planning to hold more hearings on Vietnam, but he postponed these in order to turn his attention to the Middle East. Fulbright argued that if the Johnson administration took the Middle East crisis to the United Nations and obtained Soviet support for a cease-fire, this precedent could lead to constructive developments elsewhere through the creation of a more appropriate diplomatic environment for a breakthrough regarding southeast Asia. Fulbright again implored the White House to "stop the bombing and to call on Russia and Britain to reconvene the Geneva Conference before the war gets out of hand and involves the Chinese."[93e] Johnson rejected this idea.

In spite of the massive burden placed upon American resources by the war, the Johnson administration persisted in advocating huge foreign aid programs throughout the globe. In the spring of 1967, Johnson asked Congress for a $1.5 billion supplement to the Alliance for Progress, and drafted a "Punta del Este Resolution" that embodied grandiose plans for

Latin American policy, including not only extensive American aid in health, education, telecommunications, highways, and agriculture, but a hemispheric common market. Fulbright criticized the proposed resolution as a usurpation of Congressional prerogatives, and offered a substitute that would provide funds for strengthening the Alliance for Progress "only in keeping with constitutional processes and as specifically authorized and appropriated from time to time by the Congress." The Foreign Relations Committee reported Fulbright's version, and Johnson eventually decided to attend the Punta del Este conference of hemispheric republics without a resolution. The vote was an indication that many of Fulbright's colleagues were beginning to see the merit in the chairman's defense of Congressional prerogatives and his concerns about the damaging effects of "welfare imperialism" in the Third World.[93f]

During the fall of 1967, Fulbright won another victory in his quest to reduce the foreign aid empire. Johnson submitted a $3.2 billion aid package to Congress just after he decided to escalate the air war by bombing targets close to the Vietnamese border, thus angering the doves. Led by Fulbright, Church and others, the Senate cut roughly $850 million from the aid package. Again in 1968, under Fulbright's leadership the Foreign Relations Committee rejected the administration's foreign aid bill and substituted a continuing resolution that extended aid for fiscal 1969 at 80 percent of the previous year's level; thus, foreign aid reached its lowest level yet. Johnson's vindictive response to Fulbright's reductions in foreign aid was an effort to cut the Fulbright Exchange Program by 72 percent. Fulbright prevented some of the reduction in funding, and binational commissions involved in the program in other countries expanded their funding, but it would be more than 20 years before the Exchange Program returned to the funding level it had held before LBJ's vengeful slashing.[93g]

Fulbright was depressed by the President's quest to impose a Pax Americana on the globe. In 1967, even as the war in Vietnam raged, the President sought to undertake a major expansion of aid to Latin America, preserve extensive levels of foreign aid, maintain a "tough" stance against the great communist powers, while simultaneously dealing with regional crises that erupted in the Middle East, Africa, and elsewhere. In June, the administration dispatched cargo planes and 150 soldiers to defend the pro-American, anti-communist regime of President Joseph Mobutu in the Congo. Shortly before the planes departed, Rusk called Senator Russell and Fulbright to tell them that the purpose of the mission to the Congo was to save American lives. A familiar pattern repeated itself when Rusk called back the next day to advise the senators that the planes would be used to help Mobutu deal with insurgents. In this crisis, Russell's reaction mirrored Fulbright's. Russell delivered a Senate speech in which he contended that the conflict in the Congo was a civil war and that no American interests were involved there. He had protested privately to the administration, he said, but to no avail. At a meeting of Congressional leaders shortly thereafter, Fulbright again urged the President to stop the war, and related that Senator Russell had been offended by Rusk's duplicitous, inital justifications for the Congo expedition; he was concerned about American becoming involved in one Vietnam after another. He apprised the President of his profound concerns about the foreign aid program. LBJ lashed out at Fulbright, condemning his position as one that would lead the poor countries of the world to collapse: "Maybe you don't want to help the children of India, but I can't hold back."[93h]

The senator's speeches on foreign policy in the summer of 1967 were not entirely negative. The senator eulogized the burgeoning protest movement against the Vietnam War. He dismissed the notion that young idealists who opposed the war were radical. He predicted that the regenerative influence of the younger generation would eventually prevail over the truly radical super-patriots who were attempting to transform the United States into the self-appointed gendarme of the world. The struggle between these "young idealists" and the advocates of the Vietnam War, Fulbright asserted, was a conflict between "two Americas." The modern ultra-patriots represented an emerging imperial America that contradicted the ideals of the "traditional" America, the America of Jefferson, Lincoln, and Adlai Stevenson. In Fulbright's view, the opponents of the Vietnam War were remaining true to the traditional American values in their desire to abandon the quest for empire and devote the nation's energies to achieving freedom and social justice at home, and the "fulfillment of our flawed democracy."[94]

The Johnson administration persisted in making heated appeals to patriotism. In mid-1967, General William Westmoreland returned to Washington for "consultations," and in public statements vilified critics of the war: "The magnificent men and women I command in Vietnam have earned the unified support of the American people," but a "noisy minority" engaged in "recent unpatriotic acts" that denied the soldier that "unified support." Westmoreland rejected Fulbright's request to appear before the Foreign Relations Committee, although he made numerous other public appearances, including an emotional address to Congress for which he received a lengthy standing ovation. Westmoreland temporarily generated sympathy for his cause, and Fulbright felt compelled to make public statements denying that he had any quarrel with Westmoreland or the troops; he opposed the administration policy that sent the troops to Vietnam. Fulbright and about 15 other Senate critics of the war sent a letter to Ho Chi Minh emphasizing their resistance to a unilateral American withdrawal and urging the North Vietnamese leaders to negotiate.[94a]

Domestic opposition to the Johnson administration's southeast Asian policy increased rapidly during the summer and fall of 1967. By August 1967, draft calls were exceeding 30,000 per month, and more than 13,000 Americans had died in Vietnam. The President announced a 10 percent surtax to cover the spiraling costs of the war. In August, public opinion polls revealed that for the first time a majority of Americans believed the United States had been mistaken in intervening in Vietnam. Public approval of Johnson's handling of the war plummeted to 28 percent by October.[95]

The opposition to the war increasingly focused on the bombing, which many dissenters regarded as futile and immoral. By 1967 the United States had dropped more bombs in southeast Asia than it had dropped in all theaters during World War II. The President expanded the number of sorties in 1967 and authorized air attacks on steel factories, power plants, and other targets around Hanoi and Haiphong, as well as on previously restricted areas along the Chinese border. Civilian casualties mounted as high as 1,000 per week during periods of heavy bombing. The air war inflicted severe damage on North Vietnam's raw materials, vehicles, and military equipment, but these losses were offset by increased Soviet and Chinese aid to North Vietnam. The Soviet Union assisted North Vietnam in the construction of a powerful anti-aircraft system centered around Hanoi and Haiphong. Nine hundred and fifty American aircraft were destroyed over Vietnam from 1965 to 1968.

As George Herring has described the futility of the air strikes, "The limited success of air power as applied on a large scale in Korea raised serious questions" about the military effectiveness of bombing, "and the conditions prevailing in Vietnam, a primitive country with few crucial targets, might have suggested even more." North Vietnamese infiltration into South Vietnam increased from roughly 35,000 men in 1965 to about 90,000 in 1967 despite the intensification of the bombing.[96]

American officials asserted that the United States was "winning" the war, claiming that 220,000 enemy soldiers had been killed in "search and destroy" missions in South Vietnam by late 1967. These figures were based on "body counts" that were notoriously unreliable, since it was not possible to distinguish between Vietcong and noncombatants. Moreover, approximately 200,000 North Vietnamese reached draft age every year, and Hanoi was able to replace its losses and match each American escalation. If the North Vietnamese and Vietcong began to suffer unusually severe casualties in a particular military engagement, they would often simply disappear into the South Vietnamese jungle or retreat into North Vietnam, Laos, or Cambodia. Although there were 450,000 American soldiers in Vietnam by mid-1967, General Westmoreland urged the President to send 200,000 additional troops. The general conceded that even with 650,000 men the war might last two more years; with only a half million troops Westmoreland believed the war could last five more years or longer. [97]

Political, social, and economic conditions in South Vietnam were rapidly deteriorating. American spending had a devastating impact on the fragile economy of South Vietnam, where prices increased 170 percent from 1965 to 1967. The expansion of Vietcong and American military operations had driven four million South Vietnamese (about one-fourth of South Vietnam's population) from their native villages. These refugees drifted into the already overcrowded cities or were herded into refugee camps. The United States furnished $30 million per year to the Saigon government for care of the displaced villagers, but much of the money never reached the refugees. A large portion of South Vietnam's population thus became rootless and embittered, and the refugee camps were often infiltrated by Vietcong fifth columns. In *The Arrogance of Power* Fulbright lamented the "fatal impact" of American economic and military power on South Vietnam and other under-developed countries. "With every good intention," he wrote, "we have intruded on fragile societies, and our intrusion, though successful in uprooting traditional ways of life, has been strikingly unsuccessful in implanting the democracy and advancing the development which are the honest aims of our 'welfare imperialism.'" The senator doubted "the ability of the United States or any other Western nation to go into a small, alien, undeveloped Asian nation and create stability where there is chaos, the will to fight where there is defeatism, democracy where there is no tradition of it, and honest government where corruption is almost a way of life."[98]

Nguyen Cao Ky candidly admitted that "most of the generals are corrupt. Most of the senior officials in the provinces are corrupt." But Ky excused the corruption by claiming that it "exists everywhere, and people can live with some of it. You live with it in Chicago and New York."[99] The September 1967 elections in South Vietnam again revealed the weak and corrupt nature of the Thieu-Ky regime, for even after the Saigon government disqualified many opposition candidates and fraudulently manipulated some of the election returns, the

Thieu-Ky ticket received only a plurality of 35 percent of the vote. The chaos and corruption in America's South Vietnamese ally contributed to the American public's disillusionment with the war.[100]

Despite the depressing news from South Vietnam, many of the establishment Cold Warriors persisted in rallying behind the President. In November 1967, The Citizens Committee for Peace with Freedom in Vietnam was formed, with President Truman, President Eisenhower, former Senator Paul Douglas, the diplomat Arthur Dean, Dean Acheson, and George Meany belonging. The committee's first statement was intended as a warning to the Vietnamese communists that America would not back down: "We want the aggressors to know that there is a solid, stubborn, dedicated, bipartisan majority of private citizens in America who approve our country's policy of patient, responsible, determined resistance."[100a] Johnson would later reflect that "Truman was one of the few comforts I had all during the war... He reminded me of all the hell he'd been through, but somehow he managed to ride it out. Ike was helpful, too. Once I complained to him about the trouble Fulbright and friends were making for me. He told me, 'Why, I'd just go ahead and smack them, just pay no attention to these overeducated senators, that's all there is to it." In another comment Johnson related to Doris Kearns Goodwin, the President stated with considerable embellishment that "Another time when Fulbright was busy talking things over with his Russian friends, I said to Truman, 'Imagine him not wanting the Russians to stop and wanting us to stop.' Truman interrupted me: `But you are the President. You make the policy, not him.'"[100b] Allowance has to be made for Johnson's hyperbole in his interviews, but there is no question that the support for escalation by the Cold War establishment fortified Johnson in his determination to persist in his Vietnam policies.

By late 1967 there was an increasingly vociferous and expanding bloc of senators who agreed with Fulbright's indictment of the war. According to a majority of the members of the Senate Foreign Relations Committee, Dean Rusk should have defended the administration's southeast Asian policies in a public hearing.[101] In December 1967, Rusk rejected the committee's invitation to testify at an open hearing. Fulbright renewed the committee's request in early 1968 shortly after the Vietcong launched the Tet offensive, a massive assault against the major urban areas in South Vietnam.[102] "What is now at stake," the chairman contended in a February 1968 letter to President Johnson, "is no less urgent a question than the Senate's constitutional duty to advise, as well as consent, in the sphere of foreign policy."[103] The members of his committee, Fulbright maintained, were anxious to clarify for the American people the implications of U.S. policy in Vietnam. In the midst of widespread disenchantment with the administration's southeast Asian policies, President Johnson acquiesced to Fulbright's request, and a few weeks later Rusk testified before the committee.

The day before Rusk's testimony in 1968, the New York Times published reports of General William Westmoreland's proposal for 206,000 additional troops in Vietnam. The Pentagon Papers described the publication of the Westmoreland recommendation as a "focus" for political debate that intensified public dissatisfaction with the war.[104] Rusk appeared before the Foreign Relations Committee on March 11, 1968, ostensibly for the purpose of discussing foreign aid. Instead, the televised hearings became a two-day grilling of the Secretary on Vietnam, with Fulbright sharply questioning Rusk over the Tonkin crisis and the administration's interpretation of the Tonkin Resolution, Rusk's views on Lin

Piao's doctrine of world revolution and the reports of Westmoreland's requests for more troops. Rusk refused to discuss possible troop increases, though he confirmed that an "A to Z" policy review was being conducted by the President and his advisers.[105]

During the hearings Fulbright stressed the irrelevance of Indochina to America's vital national interests. The administration described the conflict in Indochina as an "exemplary war" that was discouraging the communists from promoting subversive activities in other Third World nations. Fulbright execrated this notion as a reversion to the crusading anti-communism of the earlier postwar years and averred that far from proving to the communist powers that wars of national liberation could not succeed, the Vietnam War was demonstrating to the world that even with an army of a half million men and expenditures of $30 billion per year America could not win a civil war for a regime that was incapable of inspiring the patriotism of its own people.[106]

Fulbright bluntly dismissed the administration's version of the Gulf of Tonkin incidents as untrue. He stated that if the United States would begin bombing North Vietnam in retaliation against doubtful skirmishes that had not damaged the U.S. armed forces, then the North Vietnamese must have understandably concluded in 1964 that America was determined to attack them regardless of their actions.[107] Two events in early 1968 gave a special poignance to Fulbright's grilling of Rusk regarding the Gulf of Tonkin Resolution: first, the *Pueblo* incident in which the senator had warned that there would be no resolution hurried through Congress in an environment of crisis, and second, the Foreign Relations Committee's recent investigation into the Tonkin incidents. The overextension of the American empire was dramatically illustrated again in early 1968, when the USS *Pueblo*, an intelligence ship, was seized by North Korean vessels about 15 miles offshore. The Johnson administration immediately decided that North Korea's action was a diversionary attack intended to help North Vietnam, and the nuclear carrier *Enterprise* was dispatched to a patrol 12 miles from Korea's shore. At the time, Fulbright was once again investigating the incidents in the Gulf of Tonkin in 1964. Fulbright made it clear that there would be no resolution pushed through Congress in the midst of the North Korean crisis: "An intelligence ship off your coast is very irritating. People for some reason just don't like eavesdropping... I can tell you now that I don't think there will be any 24-hour resolution on this incident." Arthur Schlesinger and some other political analysts contended that the Foreign Relations Committee's pressure may have prevented the administration from launching an attack on North Korea and then presenting a resolution to Congress to ratify its action.

In February 1968, Secretary of Defense McNamara made his last appearance before the Foreign Relations Committee in executive session. The Secretary defended the administration's actions (as discussed previously), although the transcript of the hearings published many years later revealed numerous flaws in McNamara's defense, such as a cable sent by the destroyer task force commander to the Pentagon at the time: "Review of action makes many recorded contacts and torpedoes fire appear doubtful. Freak weather effects and over-eager sonarmen may have accounted for many reports. No actual visual sightings." Although the hearing was closed, parts of the debate continued in public. Fulbright revealed that after a commander in the Pentagon had contacted the senator to express his doubts that the second alleged attack on the American ships had actually occurred, the Pentagon had committed the commander to a psychiatric ward for a month. McNamara asserted that the commander was subsequently cured of his malady and returned to duty. After that exchange, reporters contacted dozens of sailors who were on duty with the destroyers at the time of the incidents in 1964: the great majority of the sailors indicated that the destroyers had been on a secret mission supporting the South Vietnamese and that the famous second attack had never occurred. The administration's credibility was wounded once again.[107a]

By March 1968, of course, the Arkansas senator had criticized the Gulf of Tonkin Resolution on innumerable occasions. The dialogue between Fulbright and Rusk at the 1968 hearings was essentially a repetition of the opposing arguments they had been advancing since 1966. Rusk's sterile, evasive answers did not differ significantly from the testimony he had delivered at Foreign Relations Committee hearings throughout the Johnson Presidency.

If the 1968 Fulbright-Rusk confrontation was not different in substance from earlier debates between the chairman and the Secretary, it was nevertheless true that the political atmosphere in which the debate occurred had changed dramatically. Walter Cronkite had eloquently summarized the prevailing public mood in his widely publicized television broadcast on February 27: "To say that we are closer to victory today is to believe, in the face of evidence, the optimists who have been wrong in the past....We are mired in stalemate."[108] Public opinion polls in March indicated that approximately 75% of the American people believed U.S. policies in Vietnam were failing.[109] The March 11 and 12 Foreign Relations Committee hearings reinforced Secretary of Defense Clark Clifford's nascent conviction that major actions must be taken to reduce America's military involvement in Vietnam.[110]

Immediately after Rusk's testimony Fulbright asked Secretary Clifford, formerly a "hawk" on the Cold War, to testify before the Foreign Relations Committee. The President and Clifford were concerned about the prospect of the Secretary testifying in the hostile Senate forum on national television; therefore, they decided that Clifford's assistant Paul Warnke should testify. In stating that he did not wish to appear before the committee, Clifford informed Fulbright that he needed to devote more time to a review of the Vietnam policy because he was "too new in office," having only recently replaced Robert McNamara (who had earlier become disillusioned with the escalation policy). But Fulbright insisted that either Clifford or Paul Nitze, Deputy Secretary of Defense, must testify, and that the committee would wait until either Clifford or Nitze was prepared to testify. Nitze had previously indicated to Clifford that he would refuse to appear before the Committee because of his private opposition to the administration's Vietnam policy. At this juncture, according to Nitze, Clifford's growing but inchoate doubts about U.S. policy crystallized into a definite conviction that the United States must de-escalate the war and move toward a disengagement from southeast Asia. Clifford was influenced in his burgeoning dissent by the private arguments of his assistants Warnke and Nitze, by the weakness of the Joint Chiefs of Staff's pleas for additional escalation, and by the disaffection of the Congressional critics. In Nitze's analysis, the final deciding factor in Clifford's decision in favor of de-escalation was the Secretary's antipathy toward the idea of having to defend the Johnson policies before a committee of well-informed and assertive Congressional dissenters: "When Clark Clifford had to face up to the possibility that he might have to defend the administration's policy before the Fulbright committee, his views changed," Nitze recalled. William Bundy also later agreed with Nitze's assessment of Clifford's views.[110a]

Nitze's emphasis upon Fulbright's influence on Clifford may or may not have been accurate; but clearly the arguments and pressures from the Congressional critics were among the important considerations leading to Clifford's change of mind. In March Clifford held a private conference with Fulbright and informed the chairman of his profound doubts concerning Johnson's policies. Fulbright agreed that Clifford could testify somewhat later rather than immediately, provided that Clifford (who had known Fulbright well for many years) pressed his views concerning the futility of further escalation during the administration's review of the Vietnam policy. In the next few weeks, Clifford was indeed successful in refuting the military's appeal for continuing the escalation policy. As Clifford later explained his perspective: "I was convinced that the military course we were pursuing was not only endless, but hopeless. A further substantial increase in American forces could only increase the devastation and the Americanization of the war . . . . Henceforth, I was also convinced, our primary goal should be to level off our involvement, and to work toward gradual disengagement."[110b]

Shortly after the conclusion of the second Rusk hearing, the returns from the presidential primary in New Hampshire revealed surprisingly strong support for the President's challenger, Senator Eugene McCarthy.[111] On March 16, Senator Robert Kennedy declared that he would seek the Democratic Presidential nomination on a platform of opposition to the war.[112] Certain reform elements in the ADA had been encouraging Johnson not to run for re-election since early 1967, while promoting a Kennedy-Fulbright ticket for the 1968 nomination. Fulbright publicly repudiated this movement to draft him as RFK's running mate, since he was not interested in the job and correctly felt that erroneous speculation about a Kennedy-Fulbright ticket would only antagonize the President. But Clifford and the Cold War establishment figures were people Johnson could not ignore. Clifford advised Johnson to consult with the Senior Informal Advisory Group—the famous "Wise Men"—for he believed that many of them were beginning to harbor doubts about the war.[112a] A few days later the Senior Informal Advisory Group, consisting of Dean Acheson, George Ball, Matthew Ridgway, Cyrus Vance, McGeorge Bundy, and others advised the President to order a reduction in the bombing.[113] In a shocking, nationally-televised address on March 31, the President announced his withdrawal from the presidential campaign, a token troop increase, and the de-escalation of the air war against North Vietnam in order to obtain Hanoi's entry into negotiations.[114]

The March 10 New York Times, the Foreign Relations Committee hearings, and the apparent political strength of the anti-war candidates, Kennedy and McCarthy, clearly demonstrated that significant and growing elements of the American public believed that the costs of the war had reached unacceptable levels. According to the Pentagon Papers, the President's dramatic change in tactics was based upon two major considerations. One was the opinion of his principal advisers, especially Secretary of Defense Clifford, that the troops General Westmoreland requested would not make a military victory any more likely.[115] The revelation of the Vietnamese communists' power during the Tet offensive was crucial in Johnson's belated acceptance of Clifford's evaluation of the military realities.[116] The Pentagon study described the second major consideration leading to Johnson's March 31 speech as "a deeply felt conviction of the need to restore unity to the American nation."[117]

The March 1968 decisions constituted an end to the Johnson administration's escalation of the Vietnam War. But the administration did not alter its fundamental goals, for Johnson remained determined to secure an independent, non-communist South Vietnam.[118] Fulbright quickly recognized the limited nature of the President's changes. On April 2, he registered his disillusionment with Johnson's address: "Today, within 48 hours, it appears that it [the March 31 de-escalation of the air war] was not a significant change at all."[119] He publicized the disturbing fact that on April 1 U.S. planes bombed North Vietnamese targets 205 miles north of the Demilitarized Zone.[120] On April 1, administration spokesmen revealed that American planes could still strike targets only 45 miles from Hanoi under the terms of Johnson's bombing pause.[121] Fulbright believed a total and unilateral cessation of the bombing would be necessary as a significant inducement toward a cease-fire.[122] The senator refuted the notion that he and Wayne Morse were somehow endangering American lives in Vietnam by their adamant opposition to Johnson's southeast Asian policies, stating: "the idea that what the Senator from Oregon and I and others who seek an end to the war advocate is not protecting the lives of our boys is absurd. What we advocate, is, really, the only effective way to protect their lives; namely, stop the war."[123]

Lyndon Johnson complained in his memoirs that the media devoted considerable attention to Fulbright's views on Vietnam but virtually ignored the pro-administration positions of Frank Lausche and Mike Mansfield.[124] Johnson was correct in arguing that Mansfield approved of the March reductions in the bombing campaign. But the Montana senator had also implied that the bombing halt should have been more extensive, and he described Fulbright's April contributions to the Vietnam debate as "worthwhile."[125] The President claimed in his memoirs that Fulbright's persistent opposition to the war during 1968 interfered with the administration's negotiating efforts at the Paris peace talks, which began on May 13. Johnson lamented that the North Vietnamese could quote the anti-war statements of Charles de Gaulle, Robert Kennedy, and J. William Fulbright in an attempt to "turn the Paris talks into a propaganda sideshow."[126]

Johnson's innuendo concerning the Paris deliberations was obviously an effort to blame the failure of his diplomacy on his domestic critics and Hanoi. Fulbright was deeply interested in the success of the Paris negotiations, as he indicated in a May 7 letter to the President. He vaguely but approvingly referred to "a very cordial and reassuring visit" he had recently enjoyed with his old friend Clark Clifford, one of the primary architects of the de-escalation policy (he did not mention any details of the Clifford conversation.)[127] "I am so pleased," Fulbright informed Johnson, "that Paris was agreed upon, and you certainly have the best wishes of all of us for success. If we could only get a general cease-fire, then the pressure would relax and perhaps a reasonable compromise might be developed."[128]

Unfortunately, the President's inflexible attitude toward the Paris discussions was not conducive to a "reasonable compromise." The interminable quarreling at Paris in 1968 seems to have confirmed Fulbright's April 2 prediction that Johnson's tactical changes would not lead to constructive negotiations. Fulbright's pessimism was further strengthened by a visit with Harry Ashmore, the former editor of the *Arkansas Gazette* who had recently visited Hanoi and attempted to contribute to the peace process; but the White House and the State Department had not been interested in what Ashmore had to report from Hanoi.[128a]

Walt Rostow and other advisers to the President persuaded him that the enemy forces had exhausted their military strength during the Tet offensive and the United States could therefore afford to be demanding at Paris.[129] The North Vietnamese were equally intransigent.[130] By the end of Johnson's Presidency in January 1969, the nominal achievements of the Paris negotiations consisted of an agreement on a speaking arrangement that enabled the United States and Saigon to claim a two-sided conference, and a seating arrangement that permitted Hanoi to claim the presence of four delegations, including the National Liberation Front.[131]

Throughout much of 1968, Fulbright was engrossed in his re-election campaign, which attracted significant national attention. Three Democratic candidates opposed the senator, and all three attacked his foreign policy positions. One opponent, the right-wing political veteran Jim Johnson, repeated the hoary charge that Fulbright was "giving aid and comfort" to America's communist enemies.[132] The senator vigorously maintained his indictment of the Vietnam War during the campaign and defeated his three challengers in the Democratic primary, gaining 53 percent of the vote and thus avoiding a runoff.[133] His right-wing Republican opponent in 1968 was Charles Bernard, a wealthy businessman and landowner. Bernard also utilized the strategy of condemning Fulbright's ideas concerning American foreign policy. Republican presidential nominee Richard Nixon, John Tower, California Governor Ronald Reagan, and the reactionary millionaire H. L. Hunt opposed Fulbright's re-election.[134] Senator Edward Kennedy endorsed Fulbright.[135] The chairman of the Foreign Relations Committee relentlessly advanced his critique of America's crusading anticommunism to the Arkansas electorate (Fulbright also discussed many domestic issues during the 1968 campaign) and eventually defeated the Republican candidate by 100,000 votes.[136]

Fortunately for Fulbright, he decided not to attend the Democratic National Convention, thus sparing him the trauma of the violence between police and anti-war demonstrators that erupted in Chicago. At one point some forces within the Arkansas delegation had tried to draft Fulbright as a favorite son candidate. Fulbright declined to endorse McCarthy or become a candidate himself, and he later stated that he saw nothing to gain from going to Chicago. Despite Johnson's unpopularity, Vice President Humphrey had maintained a strong grip on enough delegates to win the nomination after Robert Kennedy's assassination. Among the dove candidates, Fulbright preferred McGovern over McCarthy. Fulbright was realistic in his assessment that he could not have accomplished anything by attending the Convention; certainly for the purposes of his re-election campaign, it was fortunate that he was not associated with the violence in Chicago in the minds of the voters. Shortly before the Convention, Fulbright appeared before the Platform Committee of the Democratic National Committee and reiterated all of his "arrogance of power" arguments. He offered a peace plank for the platform: the United States should endorse a bombing halt, a cease-fire, and neutralization, and the National Commitments Resolution restraining the executive branch should be approved. Yet he was careful to emphasize that the National Commitments Resolution by itself would not solve the dilemma, informing the Platform Committee that "no legislative enactment can assure the survival of constitutional government. A nation chronically involved in war and crisis abroad must almost inevitably become a nation ruled by centralized executive authority."[136a]

Rusk appeared before the Platform Committee in Washington shortly after Fulbright.

He tirelessly repeated the administration's justifications for the war. Then an event occurred that temporarily revived the fortunes of the Cold Warriors: the Platform Committee apprised Secretary Rusk that a press dispatch reporting the Soviet invasion of Czechoslovakia had just been received. With a wry smile, Rusk excused himself from further testimony: "I think I ought to see what this is all about." Many political observers contended that this startling evidence of Soviet repression made hard-line rhetoric about the Cold War once again respectable.[136b] Even without the Czechoslovakian invasion, the administration controlled enough delegates to secure the nomination for Vice President Humphrey. The anti-war forces failed to control the platform in Chicago, and thousands of anti-war activists confronted the police, leading to an infamous scene along Michigan Boulevard in which officers attacked the demonstrators with night sticks and tear gas, shouting "Kill! Kill! Kill!" As Norman Graebner described the depressing scene, "While millions of distraught viewers witnessed the carnage on television, the Democratic party, since 1936 the majority party of the United States, slowly tore itself to shreds."[136c]

The doves could take some consolation in the electoral victories of several of the leading dissenters in 1968: in addition to Fulbright's victory, McGovern, Frank Church, Harold Hughes of Iowa, and Abraham Ribicoff of Connecticut won re-election to the Senate. There had been a dramatic reversal in Fulbright's political fortunes since 1965. When Fulbright emerged as an adversary of Johnson's foreign policy in late 1965, many political analysts regarded him as a maverick who had wrought his own destruction through his heretical dissent. In February 1966, President Johnson privately boasted that he would destroy the political careers of Fulbright, Robert Kennedy, and other Senate "doves" within six months.[137] By 1968, the public had repudiated Johnson's Vietnam policies so thoroughly that he no longer dared to travel openly around the country.[138] Kennedy was demonstrating impressive political strength at the time of his assassination in June,[139] and Fulbright won a primary race against three opponents and then a triumphant re-election in November after reiterating his opposition to the Vietnam War throughout 1968.

Fulbright was pessimistic at the end of 1968, despite his electoral victory. The anti-war forces lost their two most charismatic and eloquent voices after the assassinations of Kennedy and Martin Luther King, Jr., who became one of the most passionate critics of the war over the last year of his life. A few of the other prominent dissenting senators did not survive politically; Ernest Gruening was defeated in the Alaska primary. Fulbright wrote to his colleague to praise his service and express "great sadness" over the result, adding in a fatalistic comment about his own political future, "I have a rough Republican campaign coming up so I may join you."[139a] Senators Wayne Morse and Joe Clark lost their re-election campaigns. There were still a half-million American soldiers in Vietnam. During the presidential campaign, Richard Nixon proclaimed that "Those who have had a chance for four years and could not produce peace should not be given another chance," but he carefully avoided any explanation of how he planned to end the war.[140] Fulbright believed that if Humphrey had campaigned more resolutely against the war, he would have won, and the war would have ended sooner as a result. Early in the Nixon Presidency, Fulbright would correctly conclude that Nixon was determined to pursue Johnson's fundamental goal of establishing an independent, non-communist South Vietnam.[141] The chairman of the Foreign Relations Committee would oppose Nixon's Vietnam policies at least as adamantly as he had opposed the Johnson escalation policies.

Four years after the Republican presidential candidate had lambasted the Democrats for failing to bring peace to southeast Asia, the deluge of American bombs upon Indochina continued on an ever more destructive scale. By 1972 Nixon had succeeded only in establishing himself as "the greatest bomber of all time," in the words of the *Washington Post*.[142] In Fulbright's scathing indictment of recent U.S. foreign policy, *The Crippled Giant*, the senator lamented President Nixon's failure to deviate from the fundamental objectives of the Johnson administration despite the palpable weakness of Thieu's regime, the military resilience of the Vietnamese communists, and the burgeoning domestic opposition to America's futile crusade in Vietnam: "Employing the insane anti-logic which has characterized this war from its beginning, the Nixon Administration pointed with pride to its troop withdrawals, as if the substitution of a devastating, permanent air war for large-scale American participation in the continuing ground war represented the course of prudence and moderation as between the radical 'extremes' of expanding the war and ending it."[143]

VII. PRESIDENT NIXON AND HENRY KISSINGER

The New Administration

In Richard Nixon's campaign for the Presidency in 1968, he vaguely promised to restore the unity of the American people after the war and divisiveness of the Johnson years.[1] For the first few months of the Nixon administration, Fulbright felt that the new President should be given a fair opportunity to show that he had rejected the Johnson strategy of establishing an anti-communist American client state in South Vietnam, and that he could "bring the American people together" as Nixon had promised.[2] Some writers, such as Seymour Hersh, have contended that Nixon's chief foreign policy adviser, Henry Kissinger, succeeded in manipulating Fulbright and other critics of the war and thus weakened the Foreign Relations Committee chairman's opposition to Vietnam policy.[3] While there is no doubt that Kissinger was a brilliant advocate and Fulbright's enthusiasm for Kissinger's detente policies with the Soviet Union and China in the latter part of the Nixon administration may have occasionally led Fulbright into making some mistakes in his relationship with Kissinger in 1973-74, on balance Fulbright displayed an appropriate adversarial stance toward the administration's Vietnam policy. Fulbright was aggressive throughout most of the Nixon years in opposing the administration's increased military spending for construction of such weapons as the Trident submarine, ABM, and the B-1 bomber.

In fairness to Nixon, the new President deserved a chance to demonstrate a commitment toward ending the war. At a closed-door hearing with Nixon's first Secretary of State, William Rogers, on January 15, 1969, Rogers told the Foreign Relations Committee that he wished to move rapidly in expediting negotiations in Paris, and that amelioration of relations with Moscow ranked high on his agenda. Fulbright stated at a news conference afterward that Rogers was "a broad-gauged man, not doctrinaire, and is capable of adjusting to change." However, even in the early weeks of the Nixon Presidency, Fulbright did not hesitate to oppose the administration when he felt it had erred; the senator opposed the confirmation of Alexis Johnson, an adamant defender of the Vietnam War as Under Secretary of State. (Johnson was easily confirmed despite Fulbright's opposition.) In February, Fulbright created a subcommittee to conduct "a detailed review of the international military commitments of the United States and their relationship to foreign policy." For chairman of the subcommittee, Fulbright selected the former hawk, Stuart Symington, who had been gradually influenced by Fulbright to see that the massive price America was paying for the war was unjustified. Symington would emerge in the Nixon years as one of Fulbright's most formidable allies in the Senate; the Symington Subcommittee would later expose a secret American intervention in Laos. Fulbright opposed the Nixon administration's resistance to the National Commitments Resolution, which stated that a commitment made to a foreign power by the executive branch would not be considered a national commitment unless it received Congress' approval. Another example of Fulbright's determination to exert pressure on the administration to end the war took place in March 1969, when the senator advised Secretary of Defense Melvin Laird "not to delay too long in bringing about this change in the policy which this administration inherited . . . if this administration continues and escalates the war, it will soon be Mr. Nixon's war and there will remain little chance to bring it to a close short of a major catastrophe."[4]

Fulbright met with Nixon and Kissinger for an hour and a half on March 27 in the Oval Office, and both men assured the chairman that they would not repeat Johnson's mistakes and would end the war quickly. In the Oval Office conversation, as well as in a memorandum he presented to the President at the time, Fulbright warned that the continued military activities in Vietnam meant that "the war has regained a momentum which threatens to defeat the political approach to a settlement." The senator recommended American acceptance of a coalition government in South Vietnam, which would evolve in a setting of "natural interplay of indigenous forces within Vietnam." Nixon and Kissinger paid no attention to Fulbright's views, and as the painful similarity between the Johnson and Nixon policies became increasingly apparent by mid-1969, Fulbright urged Secretary Laird that only a much faster rate of withdrawal of American troops could "clear up the horrible and tragic mess in which we are involved." Laird seemed sympathetic to Fulbright's comments, but the senator poignantly wrote in a letter to a friend that Nixon "seems to be too much of an idealogue, committed to last-ditch opposition to communism, than is Laird." The administration's belligerent attitude toward its critics was revealed in Vice President Spiro Agnew's attack on the "self-professed experts" on Vietnam whose opposition was "undermining our negotiations and prolonging the war." Fulbright lambasted Agnew's ad hominem assault on the dissenters, equating his attacks with the previous administration's campaign to discredit its opponents. The senator ridiculed the "offensive" notion that Agnew, who had no experience or knowledge of southeast Asia, would pretend to lecture senators who had by 1969 devoted several years to grappling with the complex, tragic issues in Vietnam.[5]

Agnew's denunciation of the administration's critics was merely one part of a massive propaganda campaign—much of it prompted by the Pentagon—in mid-1969 in support of the President's policies in Vietnam and the "Safeguard" Anti-Ballistic Missile System (ABM). Fulbright and other critics launched a series of criticisms of ABM: ABM would be exorbitantly expensive, but more importantly, it could be perceived by the Soviets as an effort to gain a first-strike capability, since a country with an enormous ABM defense might imagine it could strike first and then use its ABMs to intercept the weakened retaliatory attacks. As Fulbright pointed out during the ABM debate and again in his 1971 book, *The Pentagon Propaganda Machine*, such eminent scientists as Hans Bethe; George Kistiakowsky, who was Eisenhower's science adviser; and Jerome Weisner, Kennedy's science adviser, had contended that ABM was simply unreliable, for it was too technologically complex to operate adequately.[6] Moreover, it could be defeated by various Soviet countermeasures. Kissinger argued that accumulating additional weapons systems would be useful as "bargaining chips" in negotiating limits on current or planned systems, and that in any event ABM was intended to save lives. In building up American "bargaining chips," the United States was developing defensive ABMs as well as offensive multiple-independently-targeted reentry vehicles (MIRVs). The Soviets were deploying a missile defense system around Moscow, accelerating their construction of missile-firing submarines, and deploying gigantic SS-9 intercontinental ballistic missiles. Nixon triumphed by the narrowest of margins on August 6, as the Senate voted 51-50 for the ABM program.[7] The consolation for Fulbright was in having secured 50 votes against the proposal. Opponents succeeded in later years in reducing appropriations until the original 12-site "Safeguard" system had shrunk to three sites by 1972. The 1972 SALT treaty limited ABM to two sites for each country: one for an ICBM field and one for defense of the national command authority. In 1974 the treaty was amended to reduce the number of sites to one for each country, and Congressional opponents scrapped the one remaining American site in 1975. Nonetheless, Kissinger steadfastly maintained that by 1975 "the ABM program had served its minimum purpose of making possible the 1972 SALT agreement, which stopped the numerical buildup of the Soviet offensive strategic forces."[8]

Fulbright commended Kissinger and Nixon for their accomplishments in promoting the 1972 SALT agreement, writing at that time, "giving up the ABM—except for each side retaining the option to two sites—is probably the single most significant commitment the two super powers have made to the principle of coexistence. Insofar as each side abandons the effort to make itself invulnerable to attack or retaliation by the other, it also commits itself to peace and to the survival of the other's power and ideology." Despite the success in SALT in 1972, Kissinger's "bargaining chip" strategy was flawed, for the quest for "bargaining chips" never ends. Shortly after the Moscow SALT agreements of 1972 had been completed, Nixon began campaigning for an expansion of more than $1 billion for offensive strategic weapons, citing the need for "bargaining chips" for the next round of SALT talks. Secretary Laird warned that the 1972 successes with SALT could be undermined if the United States did not immediately pursue development of the Trident submarine, the B-1 bomber, and other offensive weapons not covered by the Moscow SALT agreements.[9] As soon as one arms limitation treaty is signed, the endless search for "bargaining chips" must begin anew.

The confrontational attitude that Nixon and Agnew had assumed in the ABM debate in 1969 intensified as the Nixon Presidency continued. In September 1969, Nixon rejected a suggestion from Fulbright that the President send a representative to Hanoi to attend Ho Chi Minh's funeral. Later in September, Senator Charles Goodell (R-N.Y.) introduced an amendment to the foreign assistance bill requiring a complete suspension of funding for military activity in Vietnam after December 1, 1970. Goodell asserted that this proposal would "help the President and Congress develop a workable plan for ending American participation in the war and the slaughter of American servicemen in the near future." Fulbright commended Goodell's proposal as an original and workable approach to the dilemma of ending the war. In sharp contrast, Nixon denounced the Goodell initiative as a "defeatist" measure that would "inevitably undercut and destroy the negotiating position we have in Paris."[10]

In the summer of 1969, Symington subcommittee staff members Walter Pincus and

Roland Paul traveled to Laos to investigate the Pentagon's covert war in that distant land. American planes based in Thailand were bombarding the Plain of Jars in northeast Laos, a region dominated by the Pathet Lao. U.S. Ambassador George Godley directed the air operations from the American embassy in Vientiane. Utilizing the information uncovered by the committee staff members, Fulbright and his allies challenged a provision for $90 million for military assistance to allegedly neutral Laos. The Senate passed by an overwhelming margin an amendment barring the use of defense funds to finance the deployment of ground combat troops in Laos and Thailand. Capitalizing on the general disenchantment with military aid, the Fulbright forces succeeding in cutting more than $5 billion from the administration's proposed military appropriations bill.[10a]

The war imposed a terrible personal burden upon Fulbright as well as everyone else involved with it. The senator was deluged with abusive mail and occasional personal confrontations by extremists from both sides. He continued to receive threats of violence from the radical right, while radical leftists accused him of being a "racist" who was actually helping the United States kill Vietnamese. Fulbright consistently advised critics of the war to oppose it by legal means and to work for change within the system. He was understanding, however, of those who were so disgusted with the war that they left the country. On one televised appearance, he pointed out that 50,000 young people had emigrated because of the war, and lamented that "the best people, the most sensitive and most intelligent, are the ones who are the most alienated." Of course, this statement rankled for many families of people who were drafted. Some parents of Arkansans serving in Vietnam who had previously backed Fulbright ended their support for him because of the publicity generated by his statement about the intelligent, sensitive people who left the country. Unfortunately for Fulbright, his other comments stressing adherence to law—such as his observation that "I believe that if I were drafted I would serve"—received much less publicity. As Fulbright well knew, many enlightened Americans had served in Vietnam. By 1970, many family members of American POWs and MIAs repeatedly conferred with Fulbright, for most of them favored ending the war to get their loved ones home. Fulbright was an enthusiastic supporter of a young Vietnam veteran named John Kerry, who became prominent in a new organization called Vietnam Veterans Against the War. Fulbright asked Kerry to testify before the Foreign Relations Committee in 1971, when he asked the poignant questions: "How do you ask a man to be the last to die in Vietnam? How do you ask a man to be the last to die for a mistake?"[10b]

When in October 1969 Nixon made the unprecedented request for a 60-day moratorium on criticism of the President, Fulbright responded with a plea for a moratorium on killing.[11] The response came in a Senate speech in which Fulbright emphasized the continuity of the Johnson and Nixon policies. Although Nixon professed to support self-determination for South Vietnam, he had recently praised Thieu as "one of the greatest politicians of the present day."[12] It was contradictory to support Thieu and South Vietnamese self-determination, for Thieu had adamantly refused to permit any communists to participate in a coalition government even through a free election.[13] Fulbright pointed out that it was not exactly a triumph for Nixon's policy that he had been President nine months and withdrawn 60,000 troops, for at that rate there would be an American presence in Vietnam for the next 10 years.[14] He regretted that "the President seems to have lulled the people into the belief that the war is practically over."

The Presidency's tendency to conduct foreign policy with the utmost secrecy and to usurp Congress' war power reached its zenith on April 30, 1970 when Nixon sent American troops plunging into Cambodia without the consent or even the knowledge of Congress.[15] In March, a pro-American group led by Prime Minister Lon Nol had overthrown Cambodia's neutralist Prince Sihanouk, but the weakness of Lon Nol's regime caused Washington to fear that the North Vietnamese might seize control of Cambodia, thus greatly increasing the threat to South Vietnam. In earlier years, Sihanouk had steadfastly championed the cause of Cambodian neutralism, and had worked out a compromise with the North Vietnamese: Sihanouk would not disturb Vietcong sanctuaries in Cambodia, and North Vietnam would not aid the Cambodian communists, the Khmer Rouge, who were a small force at that time. The United States had apparently not been directly involved in Lon Nol's overthrow of Sihanouk, but the new regime quickly began receiving secret U.S. military aid. On April 17, Secretary of State Rogers conferred with the Foreign Relations Committee regarding Cambodia but did not inform the committee that the Nixon administration was planning to invade Cambodia in the next week.[16] Fulbright had publicly warned in mid-April against opening a new front in Cambodia.

On April 23, Senate doves were alarmed by reports that the administration was planning to give extensive military supplies to the Lon Nol regime. That night, Kissinger met informally with Fulbright and other members of the committee at Fulbright's home. Nixon was so agitated about Cambodia that he made three telephone calls to Kissinger at the Fulbright residence during the meeting; Kissinger later described the President as having been in "a monumental rage" over public criticisms of planned assistance to Cambodia.[17] Kissinger did not reveal to committee members that a major decision regarding Cambodia was imminent.

When the invasion began a week later, the President made no effort to justify the invasion on legal grounds other than to refer vaguely to the President's authority as Commander-in-Chief.[18] In a bellicose, nationally televised address on April 30, the President warned that "If when the chips are down the world's most powerful nation acts like a pitiful helpless giant, the forces of totalitarianism and anarchy will threaten free nations and free institutions throughout the world."[19] Nixon claimed that his authority to wage war in Indochina was based upon the need to protect the lives of American personnel.[20] The United States must invade Cambodia to prevent a North Vietnamese attack upon the dwindling numbers of American troops.[21] This pretext was flimsy even by Nixonian standards, for the North Vietnamese had offered to refrain from attacking American troops if the United States would set a withdrawal date.[22]

The American invasion destroyed the Cambodian neutrality that Sihanouk had so carefully sought to preserve when he was in power. In one of his most prescient remarks, Fulbright predicted gloomily to the *Gazette*'s Mike Trimble that "I think the effect is going to be—and already is—a terrible destruction to a rather fine little country that was not bothering anybody."[22a]

The Foreign Relations Committee was so outraged by the Cambodian incursion that it authorized the chairman—for the first time since 1919—to request a private meeting with the President. The committee met with the President at the White House on May 5 and reiterated its opposition to the administration's actions in Cambodia.[23] The public demonstrations against the expansion of the war were so vehement that Nixon withdrew the troops from Cambodia in July 1970.[24] In the aftermath of the Kent State University demonstrations, where four students were killed by the Ohio National Guard, Fulbright lamented the brutalizing impact of the war upon American society. On May 8, Fulbright expressed his grief over the Kent State tragedy and supported the rights of student demonstrators to dissent, praising nonviolent protest as "a reaffirmation of democracy, of youth's commitment to it and of the desire of people of all ages to save American democracy from becoming another casualty of war." In hearings on the moral cost of the war, Fulbright and his colleagues heard testimony from distinguished religious figures such as John C. Bennett of the Union Theological Seminary, Irving Greenberg of Yeshiva University, and Bishop John Dougherty of the United States Catholic Conference; the theologians described the war as a "moral disaster" for the American people.[25] The committee had earlier publicized the operation of the Phoenix program, which had as its goal the "liquidation" of pro-Hanoi people in South Vietnamese villages. Fulbright had characterized Phoenix as a program of assassination, and the committee's interrogation of the CIA's William Colby and other officials who directed the Phoenix campaign elicited admissions that there had been "aberrations" in the campaign at its lower levels.[26] At the May hearings on the moral aspects of the war, Fulbright publicized the reaction of Western European opinion to the Cambodian invasion. He recounted Arnold J. Toynbee's recent statement that the world's phobia concerning CIA subversive activities or direct military interventions by the United States was becoming as "fantastically excessive" as America's phobia about world communism.[27] Toynbee believed that the "roles of America and Russia have been reversed in the world's eyes."[28] He considered the Cambodian incursion to be "a second Vietnam," which had confirmed the prophecy of an anonymous Pentagon representative who said in 1968, "There are going to be many more Vietnams."[29]

At the May 1970 hearings, Fulbright and General James Gavin discussed the reaction of Chancellor Willy Brandt's Social Democratic Party to the Cambodian intervention. Many Social Democrats denounced Nixon's imperialistic policy that had escalated the Vietnam War into the Indochina war.[30] Several speakers at the Social Democratic Party's May 11 national convention spoke of "creeping fascism" in American foreign policy, although Brandt thought the phrase was objectionable.[31] Fulbright described it as a "terrible tragedy of history" that the Germans were accusing the United States of engaging in "what we have accused and reminded them of for 25 years."[32] General Gavin agreed: "As a veteran of over three years in Europe, and one who participated in the liberation of the concentration camps, it is a sad, sad day when such an analogy must be drawn by the Germans."[33]

Fulbright attempted to reach out to the business community and persuade prestigious businessmen to speak out against the war. In the spring of 1970, Louis Lundbourg, chairman of the board of the Bank of America, the nation's largest banking institution, testified before the committee regarding the impact of the war on the economy. "The war in Vietnam," Lundbourg said, "distorts the American economy. It is a major contributor to inflation—our most crucial domestic economic problem. It draws off resources that could be put to work toward solving imperative problems facing this nation at home. And despite the protestations of the New Left to the contrary, the fact is that an end to the war would be good, not bad, for American business." Lundbourg's testimony was distributed to important financial publications, and in the following weeks Fulbright publicized the anti-war views of a group of 1,100 prominent corporate officials.[34] Such comments emanating from conservative business establishment figures gradually strengthened the political weight of the anti-war movement.

The administration counterattacked, with Agnew condemning Fulbright for playing into Hanoi's hands at the Paris peace talks, attempting to "rekindle the debilitating fires of riot and unrest," and advocating the "baldest and most reactionary plea for isolationism heard in the Senate since the heyday of the America firsters." In Arkansas, the Wallace ally Jim Johnson organized a recall campaign against Fulbright, although Johnson eventually failed to obtain the required signatures to challenge Fulbright with a recall in the November elections. Nixon toured 10 states during the Congressional campaign, angrily denouncing critics of the war and urging voters to elect people who would "stand with the President." Although the Republicans scored several notable successes, especially in defeating the prominent doves Albert Gore, Sr. in Tennessee and Charles Goodell in New York, on the whole the confrontational appeal was disappointing for the administration, as the Republicans gained only two seats in the Senate and lost nine in the House.[35]

Despite the growing war weariness, Nixon displayed a persistent ability to persuade or exert pressure upon many members of Congress in support of his southeast Asian policies. In December, the President advocated a $255 million military aid package for Lon Nol. Nixon stressed that American troops would not return to Cambodia and contended that Lon Nol's forces were tying down 40,000 North Vietnamese troops, thus aiding the process of "Vietnamizing" the war. Secretary Laird advised the Foreign Relations Committee that if Hanoi persisted in taking an intransigent attitude in Paris, the United States might resume bombing; he added that "Vietnamization" could not be completed until "there is a resolution of the P.O.W. issue."[36] Such an approach, in Fulbright's view, signified an abandonment of any genuine effort to achieve a negotiated settlement. On December 14, Fulbright, Mansfield, Symington and Gore (in one of his last important votes as a senator) voted against submitting Nixon's funding request to the full Senate, but eight senators supported the administration. In debate in the Senate, Fulbright contended that Nixon's Cambodian policy would only widen the war and open up prospects for untold bloodshed in the future. The senator inserted into the *Congressional Record* a previously classified report by the committee's staff members Richard Moose and James Lowenstein. The staff report conceded that Lon Nol needed help if "Vietnamization" were to become workable, but also concluded that the United States was engaged in training troops in Cambodia and taking part in "close air action" with them, actions which the administration had pledged to avoid.[37] Fulbright, Senator Mike Gravel of Alaska and other dissenting senators were soundly defeated in the Senate's vote.

Yet another expansion of the war erupted in early 1971, as the administration ordered massive B-52 raids against Laos. At the time the raids began, the administration imposed a "blackout" on information about its Laotian policy, so that it was only much later that the public learned that Thieu's forces, backed by American air cover, had advanced into southern Laos to prevent a "dry season" buildup by North Vietnam. Nixon conceived this incursion as an exercise in Vietnamization, imagining that it would strengthen South Vietnam by showing Saigon's will to fight. The Laotian operation was a fiasco; North Vietnamese forces routed the South Vietnamese troops and sent them flying back to South Vietnam, in spite of heavy American air support. Fulbright publicly denounced the Laotian affair as a "massive deception of the American people."[38]

During early 1971, Fulbright was quietly working with former Defense Department official Daniel Ellsberg on a project that would substantially strengthen the forces of dissent. In late 1969, Ellsberg had given Fulbright a copy of the secret Pentagon study of the Vietnam War that McNamara had commissioned in 1967. Fulbright spent some time absorbing the voluminous history, and then attempted to persuade Secretary Laird to declassify the Papers. Unfortunately, Laird rejected Fulbright's repeated requests for declassification. For a time, Fulbright was in a quandary as to what to do with the Papers, at one point in mid-1970 considering making the study public through Foreign Relations Committee hearings. Ellsberg pleaded with Fulbright to publish the Pentagon history through the Foreign Relations Committee, but given Ellsberg's somewhat erratic personality and the fact that he had stolen the papers, Fulbright rejected Ellsberg's arguments. Ultimately Fulbright advised Ellsberg that the best public outlet for the Papers would be the *New York Times*. Ellsberg followed this advice, and after the *Times* meticulously analyzed the study, on June 12 the newspaper began publishing excerpts of it. On June 18 the *Washington Post* published additional excerpts. When reporters asked Fulbright on June 18 for his opinion regarding the publication, he replied, "I think it's very healthy for a democratic country like America to know the facts surrounding their involvement in such a great tragedy as the war in Vietnam. I don't think the documents have any significant effect on our national security; the only effect is embarrassment to a few individuals who were party to the deception of the country."[39]

The administration differed vehemently with Fulbright's view, and its position led to the historic litigation that would culminate in the Supreme Court's decision in *New York Times Co. v. United States; United States v. Washington Post Co*, 403 U.S. 713 (1971). The government filed suit in federal district courts in New York and Washington seeking to enjoin further publication of the Pentagon study, asserting that such publication would interfere with "national security," cause the death of American soldiers, the undermining of our alliances, the inability of U.S. diplomats to negotiate, and the prolongation of the war. The cases worked their way through the federal courts, and on June 26 the Supreme Court heard arguments. Restraining orders were in effect during the Supreme Court's deliberations, and on June 30 the Court issued its decision. In a 6-3 decision, the Court rejected the government's position that the newspapers should be enjoined from publishing the Pentagon study, which was entitled "History of U.S. Decision-Making Process on Vietnam Policy." In a brief per curiam opinion, the Court held that "Any system of prior restraints of expression comes to this Court bearing a heavy presumption against its constitutional validity," and the government had failed to meet its burden of showing a justification for imposing such a restraint. *New York Times*, at 714.

Beyond the Court's per curiam opinion stating the classic principle of the presumption against prior restraints, there were literally as many concurring or dissenting opinions—nine—as there were justices. The opinions that were most similar to Fulbright's view were those of Justices Hugo Black and William O. Douglas. Like Fulbright, Douglas contended that the publication would embarrass some public officials, but that it in no way threatened the nation's security and was essential for the "uninhibited, robust, and wide-open debate" envisaged in the First Amendment. "These disclosures may have a serious impact," Douglas acknowledged, "but that is no basis for sanctioning a previous restraint on the press. The dominant purpose of the First Amendment was to prohibit the widespread practice of governmental suppression of embarrassing information." *New York Times v. United States* (Douglas, J., concurring), at 723-724. Justice Douglas wrote that a debate "of large proportions goes on in the Nation over our posture in Vietnam. That debate antedated the disclosure of the contents of the present documents. The latter are highly relevant to the debate in progress." *Id.* The justice concluded that "secrecy in government is fundamentally antidemocratic, perpetuating bureaucratic errors." *Id.*

Similarly, Justice Black reminded Americans that the First Amendment protected the press "so that it could bare the secrets of government and inform the people." *New York Times v. United States* (Black, J., concurring), at 716. In a resounding opinion, Black praised the newspapers and lectured the government for espousing a view of the First Amendment that contradicted the intentions of the Founding Fathers:

> Only a free and unrestrained press can effectively expose deception in government. And paramount among the responsibilities of a free press is the duty to prevent any part of the government from deceiving the people and sending them off to distant lands to die of foreign fevers and foreign shot and shell. In my view, far from deserving condemnation for their courageous reporting, the *New York Times*, the *Washington Post*, and other newspapers should be commended for serving the purpose that the Founding Fathers saw so clearly. In revealing the workings of government that led to the Vietnam War, the newspapers nobly did precisely that which the Founders hoped and trusted they would do. *Id.* at 718.

Yet in Black's opinion, the government was asking the Court to hold that the executive branch, the Congress, and the federal judiciary "can make laws enjoining publication of current news and abridging freedom of the press in the name of national security. The word 'security' is a broad, vague generality whose contours should not be invoked to abrogate the fundamental law embodied in the First Amendment. The guarding of military and diplomatic secrets at the expense of informed representative government provides no real security for the Republic." *Id.* at 719. The ringing Black-Douglas endorsement of "uninhibited, robust" debate in the setting of Vietnam from the two venerable justices demolished the notion that the government could censor the publication of vital news in the name of "national security."

While other justices did not embrace Black's absolute theory of the First Amendment, Fulbright and other advocates of expansive public debate were pleased by some of the other opinions as well. Justice William Brennan wrote that "The entire thrust of the Government's claim throughout these cases has been that publication of the material sought to be enjoined 'could,' or 'might,' or 'may' prejudice the national interest in various ways. But the First Amendment tolerates absolutely no prior judicial restraints of the press predicated upon surmise or conjecture that untoward consequences may result." *New York Times v. United States*, (Brennan, J., concurring), at 725. Brennan conceded that Supreme Court precedents indicated one exceedingly narrow class of cases in which the First Amendment's ban on prior judicial restraint may be overridden: when the nation "is at war . . . no one would question but that a government might prevent actual obstruction to its recruiting service or the publication of the sailing dates of transports or the number and location of troops." Brennan did not decide whether the world situation as of 1971 could be considered a "time of war," but he stressed that even if that point were conceded, the government had failed to meet its burden, for "only governmental allegation and proof that publication must inevitably, directly and immediately cause the occurrence of an event kindred to imperiling the safety of a transport already at sea can support even the issuance of an interim restraining order." *Id.*

Justice Potter Stewart took a somewhat more restricted view than did Brennan, but eventually concluded that "I cannot say that disclosure of any of them [the papers] will surely result in direct, immediate and irreparable damage to our nation or its people." *New York Times v. United States*, (Stewart, J., concurring), at 730. A different tack was taken by Justice Thurgood Marshall, who emphasized that the Constitution does not provide for government by injunction in which the federal courts and the executive could make law without regard to Congressional action. "It is clear that Congress has specifically rejected passing legislation that would have clearly given the President the power he seeks here and made the current activity of the newspapers unlawful. When Congress specifically declines to make conduct unlawful it is not for this Court to re-decide those issues—to overrule Congress." *New York Times v. United States*, (Marshall, J., concurring), at 745-746.

The three dissenting justices wrote opinions that were strongly supportive of the Nixon administration's viewpoint and diametrically opposed to Fulbright's perspective. Chief Justice Warren Burger lamented the "unseemly haste" in which the cases had been conducted. *New York Times v. United States*, (Burger, C. J., dissenting), at 748. The *Times* had spent three or four months digesting the papers and preparing them for publication; the newspaper, "presumably in its capacity as trustee of the public's 'right to know,' has held up publication for purposes it considered proper and thus public knowledge was delayed." Burger acknowledged that the *Times'* lengthy study of the documents was for a good reason: analyzing 7,000 pages of complex material drawn from a vastly greater volume of material inevitably takes time, as does the composition of thoughtful news articles. "But why should the United States Government, from whom this information was illegally acquired by someone, along with all the counsel, trial judges, and appellate judges be placed under needless pressure?" *Id.* at 750. Burger would have remanded the cases and granted the injunction, with instructions to the lower courts to give the *Times* case priority over all other cases, "but I would not set arbitrary deadlines." *Id.* at 752.

Burger's analysis was flawed in several respects. The public would be deprived of the information while the judges conducted their lengthy scrutiny, and how long would that require? Would the judges have to wade through all 7,000 pages to make certain that a revelation in one section endangered "national security"? The powerful presumption against prior restraints was one of the bedrock principles of American constitutional law; if Burger's opinion had stated the law, this might have set a precedent in which the government could obtain injunctions against publications by asserting that judges would require a substantial amount of time to digest "complex, voluminous" material. Burger failed to address the issue that Brennan had analyzed; the government's arguments were replete with conjectural references that publication "might" prejudice the national interest. Clearly no prior restraint could be based on a mere conjectural argument, and there was simply no need for the courts to devote massive study to whether the government's speculative arguments had carried its heavy burden.

The crusaders for executive authority in the Nixon administration could find solace in Justice Blackmun's dissent, much of which spoke of presidential power as if foreign policy was the exclusive preserve of the executive branch. Blackmun, who at the time embraced a more conservative philosophy than he did during his later years on the Court, stressed that Article II of the Constitution "vests in the Executive Branch primary power over the conduct of foreign affairs and places in that branch the responsibility for the nation's safety." *Id.*, (Blackmun, J., dissenting, 761). Blackmun endorsed the view of Judge Wilkey, a dissenter in the District of Columbia case, that several of the documents, if published, "'could clearly result in great harm to the nation,' and he defined 'harm' to mean 'the death of soldiers, the destruction of alliances, the greatly increased difficulty of negotiation with our enemies, the inability of our diplomats to negotiate,' to which list I might add the factors of prolongation of the war and of further delay in the freeing of United States prisoners . . . . I, for one, have now been able to give at least some cursory study not only to the affidavits, but to the material itself. I regret to say that from this examination I fear that Judge Wilkey's statements have possible foundation." *Id.* Aside from the conjectural nature of these arguments, it was simply far-fetched to argue that publication of the Pentagon study could have had any of the dire consequences about which Blackmun speculated: the papers were a historical account of decision-making in earlier administrations and did not disclose any information about present American actions.

Blackmun's statement that the Constitution placed the conduct of foreign affairs in the executive found an enthusiastic reception in the Nixon administration. Yet, as Fulbright argued, the Constitution entrusted vital foreign policy matters to the legislative branch, such as the treaty power, the war power, and the power of the purse. Justice John Marshall Harlan's dissent also accepted an expansive role of executive powers in foreign policy, but unlike Blackmun, Harlan conceded in one passage of his opinion that the legislative branch had an important role to play in the "political" decisions of foreign policy: Harlan cited Justice Robert Jackson's opinion in *Chicago & Southern Air Lines v. Waterman Steamship Corp*, 333 U.S. 103, 111 (1948): "The very nature of executive decisions as to foreign policy is political, not judicial. Such decisions are wholly confided by our Constitution to the political departments of the government, Executive and Legislative." Harlan contended that the judiciary could review executive determinations that publication would irreparably impair the national security, but such review must be "very narrowly restricted . . . the judiciary must review the initial Executive determination to the point of satisfying itself that the subject matter of the dispute does lie with the proper compass of the President's foreign relations power." *New York Times v. United States*, (Harlan, J., dissenting), at 757. The judiciary could also insist that the head of the department involved—in this case the Secretary of State or Secretary of Defense—should personally review the materials to make certain that irreparable harm would follow from publication. Harlan, like Burger, also complained of the "frenzied train of events" and the "precipitate timetable" through which the Court had decided the case. *Id.* Critics of Harlan's opinion could argue that if foreign policy decisions are political matters entrusted to the executive and legislative branches, then the case involved a "political question" and federal courts had no jurisdiction; if that were so, then the courts should refrain from entering the political thicket by issuing an injunction against the newspapers. Of course, the heart of the case was aptly captured by the Black, Douglas and Brennan opinions, which stressed that the First Amendment protected the press against prior restraints in publishing news concerning vital national issues; vague arguments about "national security" could not override the First Amendment's protection.

Subsequent events vindicated Fulbright's argument that the people had a right to know about Vietnam and publication of the papers would only embarrass the officials who had taken part in deception of the public. Even Nixon administration officials eventually had to concede that the parade of horrors discussed in Blackmun's opinion and in the government's arguments never materialized. Henry Kissinger later wrote that "the sudden release of over 7,000 pages of secret documents came as a profound shock to the Administration." At the time Kissinger was engaged in secret discussions with Peking that would culminate in the President's trip to China in 1972 and the Sino-American detente. "Our nightmare at that moment," Kissinger lamented, "was that Peking might conclude our government was too unsteady, too harassed, and too insecure to be a useful partner. The massive hemorrhage of state secrets was bound to raise doubts about our reliability in the mind of other governments, friend and foe, and indeed about the stability of our political system." The Kissinger-Nixon "nightmares" were unjustified. As Kissinger conceded, "In the event, the release of the Pentagon Papers did not impede our overture to Peking." Kissinger similarly complained that at the time the Papers were published, sensitive negotiations with Hanoi were in progress: "That the villain of the papers was a previous administration did not change our problem. If Hanoi concluded that our domestic support was eroding, for whatever reason, it was bound to hold fast to its position." Yet this possibility, also by Kissinger's admission, did not materialize: "I do not now believe that publication of the Pentagon Papers made the final difference in Hanoi's decision not to conclude a settlement in 1971." The SALT negotiations with the Soviets were also ongoing at that time, but those discussions were not hampered by the publication of the Papers. Finally, by Kissinger's admission, "The documents, of course, were in no way damaging to the Nixon Presidency." Yet in spite of the realities that the Papers' publication inflicted no harm upon American policy and helped inform the American people about the greatest issue of the period, Kissinger's anger at "those who stole the papers" remained unabated in later years, for in his view Ellsberg as well as the government could not have known at the time that the possibilities for problems would never materialize.[40] Nixon administration officials then and later failed to explain how historical material that did not damage the Nixon Presidency and did not harm American policy in China, North Vietnam or the USSR could have posed such a terrible threat to America's security.

The administration's overwrought response to the Pentagon Papers revealed the similarity of Nixon officials to previous administrations in their tendency to view foreign policy in terms of abstractions and conjectural threats. As Fulbright wrote after the Supreme Court's decision, "From the start this war has been rationalized in terms of abstractions, analogies and conjecture, to the neglect of tangible, ascertainable facts. As the Pentagon

Papers showed so strikingly, our policy makers have been preoccupied with ideology and with geopolitical abstractions having to do with our prestige and our power interests, with the possible effects of the war on countries not involved, and hypothetical future conflicts that our inaction now might cause or our action prevent."[41] The preoccupation with secrecy was a formidable weapon in the arsenal of the Cold Warriors as they designed their grandiose geopolitical castles in diplomacy. In essence, the Nixon administration's suit against the *New York Times* and the *Washington Post* was an effort to obtain a British Official Secrets Act—that is, a law making it a crime to disclose classified information to unauthorized Americans as well as to foreign spies—through judicial construction.[42] The administration's lawsuit was one of the most dangerous attacks on freedom of press since the Sedition Act of 1798, and the suit was the first attempt in American history to impose prior restraints on newspapers.[43] Kissinger stated that "I not only supported Nixon in his opposition to this wholesale theft and unauthorized disclosure; I encouraged him" (although Kissinger did not originate the idea of the lawsuit against the newspapers).[44] Kissinger made this statement in spite of his admission that Nixon's vendetta against Ellsberg led him to take actions (of which Kissinger was unaware at the time) "the sordidness, puerility, and ineffectuality of which eventually led to the downfall of the Nixon administration." When Nixon learned of the Supreme Court's decision, he flew into one of his famous rages and approved the creation of a clandestine group of "plumbers" to plug leaks within the government. The President ordered the "plumbers" to use any means necessary to discredit Ellsberg. Nixon unsuccessfully attempted to convict Ellsberg under the Espionage Act. The administration withheld from the court for many months an exculpatory Defense Department study stating that national security had suffered negligible harm from publication of the Pentagon Papers; and for six weeks, Nixon personally suppressed the fact of the burglary at Ellsberg's psychiatrist's office.[45]

In many ways, the publication of the Pentagon Papers marked a turning point in Fulbright's opposition to the Vietnam War. The Papers revealed that Fulbright had been correct in many positions that were bitterly controversial when he first asserted them. The Pentagon history disclosed, among many other subjects, that the Eisenhower administration's attempt to undermine the North Vietnamese regime involved the United States in the breakdown of the 1954 Geneva settlement, that the Johnson administration took actions in waging an overt war against North Vietnam a full year before it disclosed the extent of its involvement to the American people, and that the infiltration of troops and supplies from North to South Vietnam was more important as a means of publicly justifying American involvement than for its military impact. The documents confirmed that the Kennedy and Johnson administrations had misled the public about their intentions in Vietnam. The accuracy of Fulbright's previous criticisms was now demonstrated by a study that was commissioned by McNamara—a man so integrally involved in the early stages of the conflict that it had been christened "McNamara's War." The Papers occasionally suffered from limitations of the Pentagon officials who composed the study—such as a focus on Defense Department planning, at times without sufficient consideration of White House or State Department views—but on balance, the study provided the public with a rare and valuable insight into the decision-making process. The Senate Foreign Relations Committee prepared reports condensing, analyzing and organizing the voluminous study, thus aiding further in the task of informing the public.⁴⁶ Many Americans who had earlier believed that Fulbright's criticisms had been exaggerated or overwrought were now impressed by his stand on the war. Moreover, the Supreme Court's decision strengthened Fulbright's constant pleas for the importance of vigorous public debate in a democratic society. Such pleas coming from a politician were always open to criticisms that they were self-serving; but the thundering defense of First Amendment freedoms, especially in the opinions of Black, Douglas and Brennan, endowed this position with a profound moral and intellectual weight. Of course, the liberal wing of the Supreme Court was anathema for hard-line conservatives, but the stature of a Hugo Black and a William Brennan as giants of constitutional law was undeniable.

It is true that the splintering of the Court into such a diversity of opinions was a disappointment, and the concurrences of Stewart, White and Marshall were somewhat tepid and pedantic, while the three dissenters, of course, reflected a philosophy similar to that of the administration's in many respects. Nonetheless, the publication of the Pentagon Papers increased the inexorable tendency whereby mainstream America came to view the war as a tragic blunder. By the summer of 1971, public dissatisfaction with the war attained an all-time high. Public opinion polls reported that 71 percent of the American people agreed that sending troops to Vietnam had been a mistake, and 58 percent denounced the war as "immoral." Nixon's approval rating on Vietnam policy fell to 31 percent, a near majority felt that troop withdrawals were too slow, and a substantial majority approved removal of all American troops by the end of the year even if this led to a communist takeover of South Vietnam.⁴⁷

The summer of 1971 was replete with depressing news regarding Vietnam. After a heavily publicized trial, a military court found Lt. William Calley guilty of "at least twenty-two murders" in the My Lai massacre of 1968 and sentenced him to life imprisonment, once more bringing home the horrors of the war. Negotiations with the North Vietnamese remained stalemated. For the first time, a house of Congress voted to override the administration's Vietnam policy by legislation. With Fulbright's support, the Senate passed by a vote of 57 to 42 the Mansfield Amendment, which stipulated that the Senate favored the total withdrawal of American troops from Vietnam within nine months after the POWs were returned by Hanoi.⁴⁸ However, the doves were not as strong in the House as they were in the Senate, and the House delayed action on the Mansfield Amendment.

In early 1969, Fulbright wished to give the new administration an opportunity to demonstrate that it would not repeat the Johnson administration's quest for a Pax Americana. Yet, Fulbright would conclude at an early date that the new President suffered from the same tendency as his predecessor in the realm of supporting regimes whose only merit was their staunch anticommunism. In the early months of the Nixon administration, Foreign Relations Committee staff members Walter Pincus and Roland Paul were dispatched to Spain to investigate allegations that the Pentagon was preparing to conclude a major military bases deal with General Francisco Franco. Fulbright doubted that the bases were strategically necessary, and also wondered why the United States should have to pay millions of dollars to build and operate them. The investigation of Pincus and Paul prepared the way for Symington Subcommittee hearings, which revealed that the Pentagon had committed to defend Franco, the autocratic father of the Spanish fascists, from not only external aggression but from a revolt by his own people. This commitment was made without Congressional approval or any public knowledge. In June, the United States and Spain signed an agreement providing the Spanish with $50 million in military assistance, as well as other assistance, but the public pressure from Fulbright and Symington reduced the commitment from the originally proposed 10-year period to a pact of only 15 months. Both governments informed reporters that they held "serious reservations about any long-range extension."[48a]

An even more disturbing example of the administration's support for autocratic regimes was Nixon's support for the military junta in Greece led by Col. George Papadopoulos, who had overthrown the civilian government and declared martial law in 1967. The Johnson administration had withheld military aid to the new Greek regime, which was notorious for its violence against dissidents. The Nixon administration, however, was far less critical of the junta, which (as the later Watergate investigation would demonstrate) had made contributions to Nixon's 1968 campaign through a Greek-American businessman. Nixon envisaged Greece as a crucial strategic base for the Sixth Fleet and American air power, and by 1970 an extensive amount of U.S. aid was funneled to the junta. Fulbright ordered an investigation, and subsequently he co-sponsored a bill with Senator Vance Hartke intended to eliminate all forms of aid to Greece. Spiro Agnew ostentatiously made a trip to Athens and glowingly commended the colonels. Fulbright's campaign to end aid to Greece did not succeed, but he had publicized the plight of the valiant opponents of the junta. Many years later, Fulbright would travel to Greece for a ceremony involving the Fulbright Exchange Program; victims of the colonels' brutal oppression held a huge celebration for the Arkansan. The tribute was gratifying, but in 1970 Fulbright was depressed by American support for the Greek dictatorship.[48b]

If Fulbright could not persuade his colleagues to eliminate aid to the Greek junta in 1970, his overall plea to reduce the overextension of American overseas commitments won an increasingly enthusiastic response as the Nixon Presidency continued. By October, 1971, Fulbright was strong enough to lead the Senate in defeating Nixon's entire foreign aid program by a vote of 41 to 27. Fulbright advocated dispensing aid through multilateral channels in multi-year authorizations. The Senate eventually passed a substitute that provided $1.14 billion in economic aid and $1.5 billion in military aid, a total almost a billion dollars less than the administration's original proposal. Fulbright welcomed his colleagues' burgeoning skepticism toward the foreign aid program, which had often become a device for perpetuating American hegemony in small, underdeveloped nations.[48c]

The Power over War and Peace

In the early 1970s Fulbright supported a series of Congressional measures to prevent the President from expanding the war in southeast Asia. The most significant legislative achievements were the two Cooper-Church amendments, the first prohibiting the use of American ground combat forces in Laos and Thailand, the second prohibiting the use of American ground combat forces or military advisers in Cambodia.[49] In a complex series of votes in the summer of 1970, Senator Robert Dole (R-Kansas), an ardent supporter of

Nixon's Vietnam policy, attempted to add another amendment (sponsored by Senator Robert Byrd of West Virginia) to the Cooper-Church amendment that would have effectively expanded executive power, since it stated that nothing in Cooper-Church would restrict the President's power to protect U.S. forces wherever deployed. Dole combined this amendment with a proposal for repeal of the Gulf of Tonkin Resolution, although the Byrd amendment endowed the executive with such expansive power that repeal would become irrelevant. In the end, the doves succeeded in passing Senator Jacob Javits' amendment, which stated that nothing in the legislation would impugn the "powers of the Congress including the power to declare war and to make rules for the government and regulation of the armed forces of the United States." The Javits amendment precluded any interpretation of Cooper-Church as widening the President's powers. Dole's version of repeal of the Gulf of Tonkin Resolution was attached to a larger bill and hence was vulnerable to a veto, in contrast to Fulbright's version of repeal, which was a concurrent resolution. Fulbright clarified the important differences between the two forms of repeal during the Senate debate, observing that Dole's version "coupled as it is with a legislative enactment which can be read as acquiescence in the Executive's claim to plenary war powers, represents an act of resignation, an attempt by Congress to give away its own constitutional war powers." In contrast, the Foreign Relations Committee's version "would eliminate an illegitimate authorization and, in so doing, reassert the constitutional authority of Congress to 'declare war,' 'raise and support armies,' and 'make rules for the government and regulation of the land and naval forces.'"[49a] The Senate passed Fulbright's version by a huge margin.

Fulbright's amendment to the Defense Appropriation Act for fiscal year 1970 would have prohibited the U.S. government from extending financial aid to foreign forces in Laos and Cambodia, but the Nixon administration continued to finance Thai units in Laos and evaded the law by pretending that the Thai soldiers were "volunteers."[50] The first binding legislative proposal for ending the war was the McGovern-Hatfield amendment, which would have cut off funds for the war after December 31, 1971, subject to recovery of American prisoners of war.[51] Fulbright initially had reservations about McGovern-Hatfield, partly because Kissinger privately urged him to avoid angering the unpredictable Nixon and thus provoking him into another escalation of the war. Yet some of Fulbright's concern stemmed from the fact that McGovern-Hatfield restricted the use of the armed forces, and thus considering the reality that Congress had not authorized the use of such forces, the measure could be interpreted as meaning that the President could do whatever he chose to do unless Congress had explicitly prohibited it. In the end, however, Fulbright supported McGovern-Hatfield. This amendment was defeated twice, in 1970 and 1971. According to a view McGovern later stated, the sentiment in Congress that the President must be supported in his foreign policy was still so strong that the most surprising fact about the amendment was that it received as many as 42 votes.[51a]

The day before the first vote on McGovern's amendment, Fulbright and McGovern appeared together on a televised rebuttal to Nixon's Indochina policy. Fulbright deplored Nixon's attempt to invoke "the specter of a first American defeat," saying that to rectify an error was "not a humiliation but a rational and honorable way of coming to grips with reality."[52] The senator considered "Vietnamization" to be "only the latest in a series of military strategies which would not extricate us completely" but would "keep us involved indefinitely."[53] Fulbright objected to Nixon's contention that "our choice is between Vietnamization and precipitate withdrawal," and offered the alternative of a negotiated settlement based on a "total American military withdrawal from Vietnam to be completed by a specified date."[54]

The Fulbright-McGovern telecast was the first broadcast in compliance with a Federal Communications Commission regulation requiring networks to allow prime-time exposure to critics of the administration's policy, because of five televised presidential speeches on Vietnam in the 10-month period preceding the vote on the "end the war" amendment.[55] Despite the preponderance of Nixon's television exposure in comparison to that of his adversaries, FCC Chairman Dean Burch rejected any interpretation of the FCC ruling as establishing the principle of "equal time" for leaders of the Congressional opposition to match Presidential appearances.[56] The day after the Fulbright-McGovern telecast (September 1, 1970), McGovern's amendment was defeated in the Senate by a vote of 55 to 39.[57]

In late 1971 Congress finally enacted a measure in favor of ending the war, although without specifying a withdrawal date. The Mansfield Amendment declared it to be the "policy of the United States to terminate at the earliest possible date all military operations of the United States in Indochina."[58] Thus the President was at last confronted with a binding provision of law to change his bankrupt policy. Nixon simply defied the Congress, saying the amendment was "without binding force of effects," and the Congress rather obsequiously failed to take any official action regarding the President's intention to violate the law.[59] Fulbright explained Congress' unwillingness to withhold funds for the war by referring to the Nixon administration's success in representing the issue as not being "whether you approve or disapprove of the war, but of whether you wish to support or abandon our boys out there on the firing line and in the prisoner of war camps."[60]

It became apparent during the Nixon administration that Congress lacked the power, and also possibly the will, to stop the presidential war in Vietnam. Nixon's opponents in Congress thus attempted to legislate a generalized reassertion of Congress' authority in foreign affairs in the late 1960s and early 1970s. Fulbright was the floor leader for the National Commitments Resolution of 1969, which expressed the sense of the Senate that no foreign commitment should be made without the prior consent of Congress.[61] This resolution did not deter Nixon in his determination to ignore Congress in the conduct of foreign policy, for the Cambodian invasion occurred a year after its passage. In early 1973, Fulbright testified before Senator Sam Ervin's (D.-N.C.) Subcommittee on the Separation of Powers to discuss the problem of executive claims to what the Arkansan regarded as excessive power, particularly regarding Nixon's arguments in favor of executive privilege, impoundment, and military spending. Fulbright argued that impoundment went to the heart of "Congressional power—the power to appropriate." If Congress permitted the President to impose his policies through impoundment, Fulbright contended that it would be acquiescing in a basic subversion of its constitutional function. The senator stressed that Nixon's repeated reliance on his expansive view of executive privilege had prevented crucial administration officials from testifying to Congress. The President has a great advantage in a contest between the executive and legislative branches, Fulbright told the Ervin subcommittee, because "the power of television is so great and perfectly adaptable to use by an individual already surrounded by a regal atmosphere, the question becomes whether Congress can develop public support."[62] In retrospect, Fulbright was perhaps overly pessimistic; in fact, the two senators who analyzed these constitutional issues at that hearing—Ervin and Fulbright—would play crucial roles within the next 18 months in developing public support for a reassertion of Congress' proper constitutional authority.

The most important legislative enactment directed at preventing "future Vietnams" was probably the War Powers bill that was eventually passed over Nixon's veto. This bill confined unauthorized use of the armed forces by the President to specified conditions of emergency. Even in an emergency the President could not continue hostilities beyond 60 days unless Congress authorized him to do so.[63] Senator Sparkman and Senator Cooper, both of whom supported the bill, privately expressed doubts about its constitutionality during the debate over the bill. The Foreign Relations Committee reported that such legislation would not have been necessary if Congress had defended and exercised its constitutional responsibilities in war and foreign policy.[64]

In the beginning, Fulbright was skeptical about the war powers legislation. With his focus on the crucial importance of public opinion, he was inclined to believe that the real barrier against executive power was in arousing popular political pressures against an administration that had vastly overreached its authority. It was exceedingly difficult for Congress to secure the withdrawal of American troops once they were deployed, and Fulbright believed that Congress must give its approval before troops were sent overseas. Fulbright offered amendments to the bill to strengthen it. One amendment would have simplified the language of the emergency power of the President in order to avoid giving him more latitude for action than he already had. Another Fulbright amendment would have required the President "to report to Congress on peacetime deployments of major units by concurrent resolution." Senator Thomas Eagleton of Missouri and Fulbright supported an amendment that would have placed CIA recruits or civilians under the bill's coverage. All three of these amendments were easily defeated. Senator Jacob Javits successfully blocked substantive changes to the bill on the Senate floor, contending that such alterations could weaken the bill's general appeal. The legislation was then sent to a House-Senate conference committee, led by Fulbright on the Senate side and Rep. Clement Zablocki in the House, to hammer out the final version of the legislation. Fulbright was surprised by his ability to reconcile differences with his House counterparts, and said of the conference committee's accomplishments that "it came out much better than I could have hoped." One of the Resolution's provisions mandated that Presidential authority to use military force shall not be inferred from any law, treaty, or appropriation unless it specifically authorizes such use and "states that it is intended to constitute specific ... authorization within the meaning of this joint resolution." The conference committee summarized the bill's main points:

> The essence of the bill is its imposition of restraints and guidelines on the use of the Armed Forces without congressional authorization. Recognizing the necessity of emergency action under conditions of grave threat to the Nation, the bill restricts unauthorized use of the Armed Forces to a period no longer than 60 days.
>
> By the end of that period, the President would be required to terminate military action unless the Congress explicitly authorized its continuation.

Within the 60-day period, the Congress would have authority to require termination of military action by concurrent resolution, a legislative method which is immune from Presidential veto.

In addition, the bill requires the President to consult in advance with the Congress and to report in detail on any military action he may take.[65]

Nixon condemned the legislation in his veto message on October 24, 1973, complaining that "the restrictions which this resolution would impose upon the authority of the President are both unconstitutional and dangerous to the best interests of our Nation." By the fall of 1973, the combined impetus of the anti-war movement and Watergate had weakened Nixon so seriously that Congress overrode his veto on November 7, a symbolic vote in signaling that the era of the imperial Presidency was drawing to an end.

Fulbright's initial skepticism regarding the Resolution was echoed, in harsher language, by critics who felt it was not strong enough, as well as by Nixonians who thought it encroached upon the executive power. The War Powers Resolution relegated the description of the exclusive circumstances in which the executive can send U.S. forces into a military conflict without a declaration of war to a part of the Resolution entitled "Purpose and Policy." The President could do so only pursuant to a declaration of war, specific statutory authorization, or a national emergency created by an attack upon the United States, its territories or possessions, or its armed forces. Some critics of the War Powers Resolution have contended that it was too weak, insisting that the "Purpose and Policy" section could not have any statutory effect. Critics also argued that rather than restricting the President, the Resolution actually might encourage him to engage in brief military actions, since Congress appeared unlikely, after American troops were militarily involved, to terminate such action before the 60-day period expired. The President could extend the period for not more than an additional 30 days by making written certification to Congress that unavoidable military necessity required this extension in the course of bringing about a removal of the forces. This flexibility could go either way, however; Congress could shorten the 60-day period as well as lengthen it. The Nixonian attack upon the War Powers Resolution was clearly overwrought, for it did not take from the executive any power constitutionally delegated to it, and it did not enlarge upon the powers constitutionally delegated to Congress. Indeed, the Constitution already mandated Congressional supervision of executive military operations, as Article I, Section 8, Clause 12 limits military appropriations to two years. Considering this provision, the war power, the treaty power, and the other constitutional weapons with which the Founding Fathers had armed the legislative branch to enable it to check the power of an overweening executive, the Foreign Relations Committee report was accurate when it concluded that the War Powers Resolution had been made necessary by many years of Congressional laxity in exercising its constitutional prerogatives in the face of a highly aggressive executive branch in previous decades; but the legislation would not have been necessary had Congress "defended and exercised its constitutional responsibility in matters of war and peace."[66]

"The notion that the authority to commit the United States to war is an executive prerogative," Fulbright wrote in 1972, is an argument that emerged in the Cold War epoch.[67] The framers of the Constitution certainly did not entertain any such notion. As Thomas Jefferson wrote to James Madison in 1789: "We have already given in example one effectual check to the dog of war by transferring the power of letting him loose from the executive to the legislative body, from those who are to spend to those who are to pay." The senator cited the position of Alexander Hamilton, famous as an advocate of strong executive power, in *Federalist Number 69*:

> The President is to be Commander-in-Chief of the Army and Navy of the United States. In this respect his authority would be nominally the same with that of the King of Great Britain, but in substance much inferior to it. It would amount to nothing more than the supreme command and direction of the military and naval forces, as first general and admiral of the confederacy, while that of the British King extends to the declaring of war and to the raising and regulating of fleets and armies—all which, by the Constitution, under consideration, would appertain to the legislature.

Fulbright might also have cited the argument in *Federalist Number 23*, in which Hamilton noted that while the Constitution gave each branch constitutional arms for its own defense, the advantage was given to Congress, which has "superior weight and influence of the legislative body in a free government, and the hazard to the executive in a trial of strength with that body."

Fulbright was on stronger ground in quoting Jefferson than Hamilton. In writing *Federalist Number 69* and *Number 23*, Hamilton was concerned as an advocate with promoting the adoption of the Constitution. In a different context, in his debate with certain of his opponents in Congress regarding foreign policy in the 1790s when he was Secretary of the Treasury, Hamilton's *Pacificus* papers sought to define the executive prerogative in foreign policy as broadly as possible, perceiving no limitations to it beyond those expressly stated in the Constitution. The executive branch definitely held the initiative in foreign affairs, Hamilton asserted in *Pacificus*, and while he conceded that Congress was under no explicit constitutional obligation to back the President, he argued that it should necessarily give weight to actions the executive had taken. Both sides in the debate of the 1970s mustered quotations from the great constitutional authorities of the past, and some of the more expansive passages of the *Pacificus* papers were interpreted by the Nixonians as supportive of their view of presidential power. As a matter of constitutional history, however, Fulbright had the stronger argument. Although Hamilton cannot be seen as having exemplified an expansive interpretation of Congress' role in foreign policy throughout his career, Jefferson and Madison, in contrast, did uphold the expansive view of Congress' war power in particular and its major role in foreign policy in general. Madison's *Helvidius* papers answered Pacificus, rejecting Hamilton's "extraordinary doctrine" that the powers of making war and treaties were executive in nature, and asserted that the determination of foreign policy rested with Congress, since that body alone could declare war. John Quincy Adams, one of the great secretaries of state, endorsed Madison's view a generation later, contending that Madison's *Helvidius* "scrutinized the doctrines of *Pacificus* with an acuteness of intellect never perhaps surpassed."[68]

Moreover, Jefferson and Madison did not simply advocate a major Congressional role when it suited their political purposes, yet discard it when they attained power in the executive branch. When Secretary of State James Madison—who had played the single most important intellectual role in the drafting of the Constitution—was grappling with the dilemma of how to navigate between the Scylla and Charybdis of the European powers during the Napoleonic era, he wrote to James Monroe: "As it is a question which belongs to Congress, not to the Executive, that consideration alone forbids any step, on the part of the latter, which would commit the nation, and so far take from the Legislature the free exercise of its power." As the historian Dumas Malone concluded in his magisterial six-volume biography of Jefferson: "Jefferson, Madison, and Gallatin were at one in the desire to infringe in no way on the constitutional prerogatives of Congress, the body in which the authority to declare war was vested." As President in 1812, Madison sent a message to Congress summarizing the aggressions of British naval vessels upon American commerce, but referred the issue to Congress, stating that the question of war or peace was "a solemn question which the Constitution wisely confides to the legislative department of the government." Similarly, in 1824, when the government of Colombia asked the American government what action the United States might take under the Monroe Doctrine to repel possible European intervention in Latin America, Secretary of State John Quincy Adams answered that "by the Constitution of the United States, the ultimate decision of this question belongs to the legislative department." Of course, under the Cold Warrior interpretations of the Monroe Doctrine, this venerable doctrine could serve as a basis for the commitment of military forces by the President acting solely upon his own authority. Another constitutional lawyer who served as Secretary of State, Daniel Webster, argued in 1851 that "I have to say that the warmaking power in this government rests entirely in Congress; and that the President can authorize belligerent operations only in the cases expressly provided for in the Constitution and the laws." The Supreme Court adopted Webster's viewpoint in 1862, ruling that "By the Constitution, Congress alone has the power to declare a national or foreign war." *Prize Cases,* 67 U.S. 635 (1862). The Court confirmed the legitimacy of defensive war waged by the executive in the limited circumstances of repelling an invasion or rebellion; thus the Court upheld President Lincoln's blockade of Southern ports after the attack on Fort Sumter in April, 1861. The President is Commander-in-Chief, the Court held, but "he has no power to initiate or declare a war either against a foreign nation or a domestic state." *Id.*

The constitutional question of war and peace had become more difficult in the World War II and Cold War eras. In the face of isolationist members of Congress—people with whom Fulbright had experienced no little frustration himself in 1940—President Roosevelt had encroached upon Congress' foreign policy powers in the face of the dire threat from the fascist powers. Unfortunately, in Fulbright's view, the reality that Roosevelt was correct in his assessment of the national interest in 1940-41 "in no way diminishes the banefulness of the precedents" set at the time: "FDR's deviousness in a worthy cause made it much easier for LBJ to practice the same kind of deviousness in an unworthy cause." Fulbright made a valid point, although he failed to explain how Roosevelt would have overcome the isolationist resistance had he publicly advocated an interventionist stance at an earlier date. As Dumas Malone aptly stated the conflicts and tensions under which presidents from Jefferson to Roosevelt struggled: "The dilemma created by the necessity for efficacious action on the one hand, and the desirability of popular control on the other, has never been fully resolved under the American system." Yet even in the mid-20th century, when America's gigantic role in international affairs made the war powers issue much more controversial and often revisited, profound constitutional authorities have rejected executive encroachments upon the war power. In his famous concurrence in *Youngstown v. Sawyer*, Justice Robert Jackson rejected the argument of the Solicitor General that American troops in Korea "were sent into the field by an exercise of the President's constitutional powers." Justice Jackson warned that "I cannot foresee all that it might entail if the Court should endorse the argument. Nothing in our Constitution is plainer than that declaration of war is entrusted to Congress." *Id.*

Despite the authority behind the Madisonian view, the federal judiciary was reluctant to become involved in litigation challenging the constitutionality of the war in southeast Asia, with many judges in the first several years of the war denying jurisdiction to such questions under the political question doctrine. In 1967, the Court of Appeals for the District of Columbia, with Judge Warren E. Burger joining in the opinion, held that it was difficult to conceive of "an area less suited for judicial action," and warned future petitioners that resort to the courts would be "futile" and "wasteful of judicial time." The Supreme Court also declined to take war cases on appeal initially. The foundation of the political question doctrine had been established in *Marbury v. Madison*, 5 U.S. 137 (1803), in which Justice John Marshall ruled that "By the constitution of the United States, the president is invested with certain important political powers, in the exercise of which he is to use his own discretion, and is accountable only to his country in his political character, and to his own conscience." The doctrine was extended to Congress in *Foster v. Neilson*, 2 Peters 253 (1829). The scope of this doctrine has been a subject of debate; in 1958, Judge Learned Hand would write that the political question is a term that the Court had "never tried to define—although ... the doctrine has been a stench in the nostrils of strict constructionists." In 1962, Justice Brennan finally offered a series of tests to identify a political question in *Baker v. Carr*, 369 U.S. 186 (1962): there has to be "a textually demonstrable constitutional commitment of the issue to a coordinate political department; or a lack of judicially discoverable and manageable standards for resolving it; or the impossibility of deciding without an initial policy determination of a kind clearly for nonjudicial discretion..." *Baker*, at 188. Other factors included whether it was impossible for a court to undertake independent resolution without expressing disrespect for coordinate branches of government, or the potential of embarrassment from multifarious pronouncements by various departments on the same question. *Id.* Brennan stressed, however, (even though *Baker v. Carr* involved domestic issues) that "it is error to suppose that every case or controversy which touches foreign relations lies beyond judicial cognizance." *Id.*

By 1967, Justices Stewart and Douglas dissented from a Supreme Court denial of certiorari in a war case; they insisted that these cases involved questions of great magnitude and raised a host of problems. *Mora v. McNamara*, 389 U.S. 934 (1967). Many other federal judges were influenced by Douglas and Stewart, as well as by the famous *Youngstown* case in which the Court had invalidated President Truman's seizure of steel mills in order to avert a steel strike during the Korean War. Some judges and constitutional lawyers began to argue that in the case of a conflict between the two other coordinate branches of government, there was necessarily a judicial role. The question as to where the power to decide upon war resides is a constitutional and hence judicial issue, although the question of the wisdom of specific actions was not.[69] Courts began to find jurisdiction to hear such cases, although only in a limited fashion. One court stated that the Constitution envisaged the "joint participation of the Congress and the executive in determining the scale and duration of hostilities... Beyond determining that there has been some mutual participation between Congress and the President, which unquestionably exists here, with action by the Congress sufficient to authorize or ratify the military activity at issue, it is clear that the constitutional propriety of the means by which Congress has chosen to ratify and approve the protracted military operations in southeast Asia is a political question." *Orlando v. Laird*, 443 F.2d 1039 (2d Cir.) *cert. denied*, 404 U.S. 869 (1971). It is crucial to observe that while courts thus continued to avoid challenging the legality of the war, they declined to do so on the grandiose theories of presidential power promoted by Johnson and Nixon.

In cases such as *Orlando v. Laird, supra*, the basis for the Court's ruling rested upon the notion that there had been a collaborative action of the legislative and executive branches from the earliest stages of the military action. The Court cited the continuing appropriations bills for the war, the extension of the Military Service Act, and the Gulf of Tonkin Resolution. The latter resolution had been repealed at the time the Second Circuit ruled in *Orlando*, and the Nixon administration had shifted its reliance to the President's inherent authority as Commander-in-Chief, a simplistic argument that the courts did not accept. Moreover, even if it is assumed that the Resolution in fact delegated Congress' war-making power to the President with respect to southeast Asia—a question that Fulbright and others hotly disputed—there remained the larger question of whether such a delegation of power could comport with the Constitution's allocation of power and responsibility. Fulbright raised a weighty issue on this point, and his position also received the support of some constitutional scholars at the time and later. Harvard law professor Laurence Tribe concluded regarding the resolution that "a generic grant to the President of Congress' war-making power, unaccompanied by any articulated standards, would be unconstitutional as an overbroad delegation of constitutional authority."[70]

As for appropriations, Fulbright had long agonized over that issue. Of course, both branches had participated in providing funds to supply the troops in the field. It was much less clear whether such a vote should constitute "mutual participation" by both branches in the war decisions; as one judge concluded, "The court cannot be unmindful of what every schoolboy knows—that an honorable, decent, compassionate act of aiding those already in peril is no proof of consent to the actions that placed and continued them in that dangerous posture. We should not construe votes cast in pity and piety as though they were votes freely given to express consent." *Mitchell v. Laird*, 476 F.2d 533, 538 (D.C.Cir.1973). Historical examples could be recalled in which honorable leaders had voted money for supplies. At the zenith of his opposition to the Mexican War, Abraham Lincoln had declared, "I have always intended, and still intend, to vote supplies." Another dissenter, John Quincy Adams, also voted money for the troops. Of course, there is no doubt that Congress possessed the constitutional authority to deny the appropriations, and as a last resort the opponents of the Vietnam War eventually exerted that authority. Given the questionable constitutionality of the Gulf of Tonkin Resolution and the questionable significance of appropriations votes as evidence that Congress had "mutually participated" in the war in its earliest stages, a plausible argument could be made that the war in southeast Asia did not pass the "mutual participation" test of both branches utilized in such cases as *Orlando v. Laird*.

Some judges—especially those in the Second Circuit—found the "discoverable and manageable standards" to resolve the controversy under Baker v. Carr in the "mutual participation" test: whether the "reality of the collaborative action of the executive and the legislative required by the Constitution" had been present from the earliest stages. *Orlando v. Laird, supra,; Berk v. Laird*, 429 F.2d 302 (2d Cir. 1970). In *DaCosta v. Laird*, 471 F.2d 1146 (2d Cir. 1973), a plaintiff urged that the President's unilateral decision to mine the harbors of North Vietnam and to bomb targets in that country constituted an escalation of the war, which was illegal in the absence of additional Congressional authorization. Judge Kaufman in *DaCosta* ruled that this was a political question and thus not justiciable, stressing that the Court was deficient in essential military knowledge and institutionally incapable of assessing the facts. "It was the President's view," the Court concluded, "that the mining of North Vietnam's harbors was necessary to preserve the lives of American soldiers in South Vietnam and to bring the war to a close. History will tell whether or not that assessment was correct, but without the benefit of such extended hindsight we are powerless to know." The Second Circuit also rejected the argument that the repeal of the Gulf of Tonkin Resolution removed the earlier judicial finding of Congressional authorization in Orlando: "As the constitutional propriety of the means by which the Executive and Legislative branches engaged in mutual participation in prosecuting the military operations in southeast Asia, is, as we held in Orlando, a political question, so the constitutional propriety of the method and means by which they mutually participate in winding down the conflict and in disengaging the nation from it, is also a political question and outside of the power and competency of the judiciary." *DaCosta v. Laird*, 448 F.2d 1368 (2d Cir. 1971), *cert. denied*, 405 U.S. 979 (1972).

Federal judges began adopting sharply divergent analyses when plaintiffs began challenging the legality of the air war against Cambodia in 1973. In a dissenting opinion on the three-judge panel of the Second Circuit that ruled in *Holtzman v. Schlesinger*, 484 F.2d 1307, 1316 (2d Cir. 1973), Circuit Judge James Oakes rejected the notion that the Cambodian war passed the "mutual participation" test, because "for authorization on the part of Congress by way of an appropriation to be effective, the Congressional action must be based on a knowledge of the facts [Oakes cited a Supreme Court case, *Greene v. McElroy*, 360 U.S. 474 (1959), in support of this legal proposition]." Judges Oakes concluded, therefore, that the Nixon administration's concealment of the reality that the United States engaged in an air war against Cambodia in 1969-1970 invalidated any implied authorization. Oakes stated that he was aware of only one instance in American constitutional history in which a legislator argued that a war was illegal as a result of Congress having been misinformed as to the underlying facts surrounding U.S. involvement in the war. The dissenting judge conceded that the argument had been unique and unsuccessful, but "time has vindicated it." He referred to Congressman Abraham Lincoln's dissent in 1848 against the American "incursion" into Mexico and what later was called the Mexican War. "Here, incredibly enough," Oakes wrote in dissent, "it appears that neither the American public nor the Congress, at the time it was voting appropriations in aid of the war in Vietnam, were given the facts pertaining to our bombing in Cambodia. Recent disclosures have indicated that Air Force B-52 bombers were secretly attacking Cambodia in 1969, 1970 and even later while the United States was publicly proclaiming respect for Cambodian neutrality." *Holtzman*, Oakes, J., dissenting, at 317. Meanwhile, the Congress had declared in the Mansfield Amendment that it was the policy of the United States to terminate at the earliest practicable date all military operations in Indochina. In light of the concealment of the facts and the passage of the Mansfield Amendment, there was no Congressional approval to persist in the Cambodian air war even after withdrawal of troops from Vietnam and return of prisoners of war from North Vietnam, which was the situation by 1973.

The logic of Judge Oakes' argument concerning the concealment of essential truths could also be applied to the Congress in 1964. If, as Fulbright argued at the time and McNamara conceded later, the Congress did not regard its passage of the Gulf of Tonkin Resolution or appropriations for military supplies in Indochina in 1964 as carte blanche for a massive air war and the landing of half a million troops, and if the administration concealed much of the truth about the Tonkin episode from the Congress, then under Oakes' analysis, the entire Vietnam War failed the "mutual participation" test. If the case in favor of the Vietnam escalation in the 1960s was doubtful, Oakes made an even more compelling case against the Cambodian war in the 1970s. The Fulbright proviso had limited military support to Cambodia except to the extent necessary to insure the safe withdrawal of U.S. forces from southeast Asia and the release of American prisoners of war; this proviso was adopted by Congress in the summer of 1970, inserted into the War Forces-Military Procurement Act of 1971, and was signed into law by President Nixon on October 7, 1970. Fulbright's proviso was repeated in every subsequent military appropriation and authorization act, and it stated:

> Nothing [herein] shall be construed as authorizing the use of any such funds to support Vietnamese or other free world forces in actions designed to provide military support and assistance to the Government of Cambodia or Laos: Provided further, that nothing contained in this section shall be construed to prohibit support of actions required to insure the safety and orderly withdrawal or disengagement of U.S. forces from southeast Asia, or to aid in the release of Americans held as prisoners of war.

Despite the language of the Fulbright proviso, Nixon delivered a nationally televised speech on the day of the proviso's passage in which he declared, "The war in Indochina has been proved to be of one piece; it cannot be cured by treating only one of its areas of outbreak."In January 1973, when the Paris Agreement on Ending the War and Restoring Peace in Vietnam was signed, it stated in Article 20(A) that the parties would "refrain from using the territory of Cambodia and the territory of Laos to encroach on the sovereignty and security of one another and of other countries." Despite the Fulbright proviso and Article 20(A) of the Paris Agreement, air operations over Cambodia escalated sharply after January 1973. The last American combat troops were withdrawn from South Vietnam in March 1973 (except for guards at the U.S. Embassy in Saigon) and the last known American prisoners of war were released in April. When Congress passed additional amendments in June 1973 barring the use of "any and all funds" appropriated for the Defense Department for the bombing of Cambodia, Nixon vetoed the bill, and the effort to over-ride failed by a narrow margin, coming within six votes in the House of the two-thirds necessary for an over-ride.[71]

By the summer of 1973, Congress was faced with the dilemma of Nixon's determination to veto any bill containing riders cutting off funds for Cambodian military operations, thus leading to an urgent problem of providing funds for the operation of the federal government. On June 29, Fulbright offered and the Senate passed an amendment to the Continuing Appropriations Resolution prohibiting the use of any funds for military activities in southeast Asia on or after August 15, 1973. The House modified the Fulbright amendment's language to read, "Notwithstanding any other provision of law, on or after August 15, 1973, no funds herein or heretofore appropriated may be obligated or expended to finance directly or indirectly combat activities by United States military forces in or over or from off the shores of North Vietnam, South Vietnam, Laos or Cambodia." In the District Court's opinion in *Holtzman v. Schlesinger,* 361 F.Supp. 553 (E.D., New York, 1973), Judge Orrin Judd—the same judge who had applied the mutual participation test in *Berk v. Laird* in 1970 and found the Vietnam War legal—found that Congress had not participated in the military actions in Cambodia. "Ever since the hostilities in Cambodia were announced by the President in April 1970," Judge Judd contended, "the appropriations bills have all contained the Fulbright proviso forbidding military support to the government of Cambodia, except in support of actions to insure the safe withdrawal of American forces or to aid in the release of prisoners of war." *Holtzman,* 361 F.Supp. at 562-63. As did Judge Oakes in his dissenting opinion, the District Court in *Holtzman* referred to both the Fulbright proviso and the Mansfield Amendment and found no Congressional purpose or authorization to allegedly aid MIAs or POWs by bombing Cambodia. District Judge Judd concluded that Congress had never accepted the President's view that the war in Indochina was "all of one piece." *Id.*

Supporters of the administration tried to torture the August 15 compromise cutoff date for expenditure of any funds over Cambodia as a Congressional endorsement of the Cambodian air war until that date. Judge Judd of the District Court and Judges Oakes' dissenting opinion found that Fulbright had explicitly rejected this view in great detail in debate on the Senate floor:

> The acceptance of an August 15 cutoff date should in no way be interpreted as recognition by the committee of the President's authority to engage U.S. forces in hostilities until that date. The view of most members of the committee has been and continues to be that the President does not have the authority in the absence of specific Congressional approval...As I have said, I do not regard [the President] as having the right to do this... We do not sanction it. It does not mean that we approve of the bombing. This is the best way to stop it. I have never approved of it. And I do not wish my answer to indicate that I approve of the bombing, because I do not.

In a colloquy with Senator Eagleton, even after all of these statements by Fulbright, the Missouri senator was still concerned that the Congress was somehow "permitting" the President to bomb Cambodia for an additional 45 days by passing the legislation with the August 15 cutoff date. Fulbright clearly felt at that point that Senator Eagleton was having inordinate difficulty in getting the point, and stated one more time that the President had the power, but not the constitutional right, to continue the bombing, adding that "The

President has the power to do a lot of things of which I do not approve."[71] Judge Judd was supportive of Fulbright's view of the issue, writing that "Majorities in both Houses had previously made plain that they were opposed to any continuation of bombing in Cambodia, and they included an August 15 cutoff date merely in order to avoid the veto which had met their earlier efforts." *Holtzman*, 361 F.Supp. 564. Judd contended that it cannot be the rule "that the President needs a vote of only one-third plus one of either House in order to conduct a war, but this would be the consequence of holding that Congress must override a Presidential veto in order to terminate hostilities which it has not authorized." The judge observed that the Fulbright compromise had avoided a constitutional crisis that would have resulted in a temporary shutdown of vital federal activities (including issuance of Social Security checks) "due to lack of funds for the new fiscal year, by having Congress to delay the action affirmatively cutting off funds for military purposes until August 15, 1973." *Id.* The District Court agreed with Fulbright that this compromise did not in any way change the reality that Congress—through the Fulbright proviso and numerous other actions—had never authorized the Cambodian war. *Id.* Consequently, Judd held the Presidential war in Cambodia unconstitutional and issued an injunction against further bombing. *Id.* The Second Circuit immediately issued a stay of the District Court's injunction.

Much of Judd's argument was on strong ground. However, he weakened his case by resorting to an unprecedented legal argument in which he applied principles of the law of agency to the issue, stating that "the principal (Congress) may limit the duration of any authorization which it gives to the agent (Executive)." The two Second Circuit judges who formed the majority on the three-judge appellate court panel in *Holtzman* rejected the agency argument, and even the dissenting opinion of Judge Oakes did not rely upon this part of Judd's opinion. Judd's argument on this point ignored the fact that the Second Restatement of Agency promulgated by the American Law Institute had expressly disclaimed the Restatement's applicability to public officers. *Holtzman*, 484 F.2d 1307, 1311n.2. Moreover, the reference to Congress as the principal and the executive as its agent is inconsistent with Judd's view of the collaborative, cooperative sense of the "mutual participation" test. Judd's opinion would have been stronger had he deleted the unusual resort to agency law principles. Nonetheless, Judge Judd and dissenting Circuit Judge Oakes had made compelling legal arguments against the war in Cambodia.

Judd and Oakes were certainly not the only federal judges who had rethought the political question doctrine since the time in 1967 when then-Circuit Judge Burger had warned that any future war cases brought to federal court would simply be a "waste of judicial time." Even in 1967, Justices Douglas and Stewart had dissented from denying certiorari in one of the war cases (*Mora v. McNamara*), and in 1973, Justices Douglas, Stewart and now Brennan were ready to set a similar war case for oral argument. *Atlee v. Richardson*, 411 U.S. 911 (1973). In *Holtzman v. Schlesinger*, a fourth Supreme Court Justice, Thurgood Marshall, stated in analyzing the Second Circuit's decision to stay Judge Judd's injunction against the bombing that he "might well conclude that on the merits that continued American operations in Cambodia are unconstitutional." *Holtzman v. Schlesinger*, 414 U.S. 1321 (1973)(Marshall, Circuit Justice). But Marshall declined to overrule the Second Circuit and reinstate the injunction, because the Supreme Court as a whole had never considered the issue; he felt he should not take upon himself that responsibility. Justice Douglas flatly held that the stay was vacated, relying upon the *Youngstown* decision in Truman's seizure of the steel mills to conclude that "Property is important, but, if Truman could not seize it in violation of the Constitution, I do not see how any President can take 'life' in violation of the Constitution." *Holtzman v. Schlesinger,* 414 U.S. 1316 (1973)(Justice Douglas' order effectively stayed, for one day, the bombing of Cambodia, although his order was shortly replaced by an order of the other justices issuing a new stay). Some legal scholars subsequently questioned the reticence of many federal courts in the war cases and supported the views of such judges as Oakes and Douglas; Laurence Tribe later concluded that it was "by no means clear that federal courts should have refrained from addressing the issue" by reliance upon the political question doctrine.[72]

Justice Marshall promptly polled the other justices by telephone. Chief Justice Burger denied a request that the entire Supreme Court interrupt its recess to hear the case, and the other seven justices immediately supported Marshall in issuing a new stay. The new stay replaced Douglas' order vacating the Second Circuit's stay. The two-judge majority on the Second Circuit was obviously influenced by the Supreme Court to avoid hearing the issue. The Second Circuit found the issue to be a political question, although its logic was not a consistent application of the mutual participation test. The Court found it unnecessary to address the issues regarding the Fulbright proviso that their dissenting colleague, Judge Oakes had analyzed, stating that the proviso predated the Paris Accord, and further concluded that "we have no way of knowing whether the Cambodian bombing furthers or hinders the goals of the Mansfield Amendment." The statement about the Fulbright proviso predating the Paris Accord contradicted the mutual participation test, which was supposed to examine whether the executive and legislative branches had engaged in collaborative action from the earliest stages of the military action (regarding Cambodia). Moreover, the Second Circuit stressed that "since the argument that continuing Congressional approval was necessary was predicated upon a determination that the Cambodian bombing constituted a basic change in the war not within the tactical discretion of the President, and since that is a determination we have found to be a political question, we have not found it necessary to dwell at length upon Congressional participation." *Holtzman,* 484 F.2d 1313. It was ironic that the Second Circuit was holding that the issue was not justiciable as a "political question;" in concluding that whether the Cambodian war was a "basic change" in the situation was a political question, the Court had to use its convoluted argument in essence ignoring the passage of the Fulbright provisos in the early 1970s. Ignoring the Fulbright proviso had been the administration's position for almost three years.

The question remains: why did the remainder of the federal judiciary—primarily the other seven justices of the Supreme Court who were polled by telephone—decline to hear the case? Rather than attempting to answer this question through resort to precise constitutional reasoning in the judicial opinions, the answer can more logically be found in the Court's practical wisdom in recognizing the limits of judicial control over the war-making power. The version of the mutual participation test as formulated by Judge Oakes in his dissent seemed to be a logical test—as Justice Marshall conceded. Yet, as Arthur Schlesinger argued, "what if the Supreme Court were to adopt that test and then confront a President determined to conduct a war without Congressional consent, as Nixon had conducted the bombing of Cambodia after March, 1973?" Such a showdown must be avoided, the Court concluded, as a matter of institutional self-interest, at least until the war was over. Justice Jackson had most succinctly stated the practical realities in time of war in 1944, when he had thought the forced evacuation of the Japanese-Americans unconstitutional but also concluded that the Court could do nothing about it during the war: "I would not lead people to rely on this Court for a review that seems to me wholly delusive... If the people ever let command of the war power fall into irresponsible and unscrupulous hands, the courts wield no power equal to its restraint. The chief restraint upon those who command the physical forces of the country, in the future as in the past, must be their responsibility to the political judgments of their contemporaries and to the moral judgments of history" *Korematsu v. United States*, 323 U.S. 214, 248 (1944)(Jackson, J., dissenting). With his characteristic brutal realism, Justice Jackson elaborated upon this argument in 1948, writing that the war power is usually invoked in haste, when calm legislative consideration of constitutional limitation is difficult, and it is executed in a time of patriotic fervor that makes moderation unpopular. "And, worst of all," Jackson concluded, "it is interpreted by judges under the influence of the same passions and pressures." *Woods v. Cloyd W. Miller*, 333 U.S. 138, 146 (1948)(Jackson, J., concurring).

In a few notable instances, the Supreme Court did question the executive's authority in wartime. In *Ex parte Milligan*, 71 U.S. 2 (1862), the Court held that martial law during the Civil War could not "be applied to citizens in states which have upheld the authority of the government, and where the courts are open and their process unobstructed." In 1946, the Court similarly held that the declaration of martial law in Hawaii after the attack upon Pearl Harbor was unconstitutional. *Duncan v. Kahanamoku*, 327 U.S. 304 (1946). Yet, as Professor Tribe has candidly observed, *Milligan* and *Kahanamoku* regarded executive authority over domestic issues, especially martial law, and "It is noteworthy if sobering that both of these decisions limiting the power of the President to declare and enforce martial law were handed down after hostilities had subsided; one may doubt that the Court would have been so courageous had war still been underway."[73]

Judges who came to differing legal conclusions nonetheless made similarly respectful statements regarding Fulbright's role in the Cambodian debate. A court in Massachusetts decided the Cambodian legality issue was a political question, but used a somewhat different approach from the Second Circuit's in *Holtzman*. In *Drinan v. Nixon*, 364 F.Supp. 854 (D. Massachusetts, 1973), the Court held that the August 15 compromise itself indicated that Congressional and executive branches were not in conflict, and thus there was no need for judicial determination of the issue. The *Drinan* Court rejected the idea that "the courts may never have a proper role to play in the area of foreign relations, particularly with respect to involvement of this country in a war." Judge Tauro in *Drinan* emphasized that "should it be apparent that the political branches themselves are clearly and resolutely in opposition as to the military policy to be followed by the United States, such a conflict could no longer be regarded as a political question, but would rise to the posture of a serious constitutional issue requiring resolution by the judicial branch." *Drinan*, at 858. Of course, Fulbright's objective at the time was to get the war stopped as quickly as possible. His position was a practical political compromise, and the judges recognized it as such. The *Drinan* Court posited that the rule in the First Circuit was that the war in Indochina "is a political question when there is some cooperation by Congress." *Id.* at 859. The Court cited Fulbright's characterization of the legislation as "the result of an accommodation of the views of the committee and the White House following a meeting this morning... It now appears that the executive and legislative branches will, at last, act in a coordinate manner to bring to a close this tragic episode in our Nation's history."[74] The Court discussed Fulbright's role in the debate in a complimentary manner, noting that "the attitude of the branches was cogently characterized by Senator Fulbright: `In reaching agreement upon the terms of this amendment, both the executive branch and the committee receded in part from positions which had been strongly held over a number of years.'"[75] It is highly questionable whether the entire Cambodian legality issue can be boiled down to the two remarks Judge Tauro cited. The *Drinan* view fails to take into consideration the reality that since 1970, the Fulbright proviso had represented a direct rejection by the Congress of any "mutual partic- ipation" in military action in Cambodia, and the Mansfield Amendment reinforced the proviso. Moreover, despite the few conciliatory remarks Fulbright made at the time the final compromise was worked out, the relationship between legislative and executive branches was anything but "collaborative." Tribe more accurately described the episode when he wrote: "To avert a fiscal deadlock, the administration was forced to agree to a compromise under which the President did not veto a provision attached to the Social Security Act" that prohibited use of appropriations for military activities anywhere in Indochina.[76] Neither side gave up its fundamental position. As Fulbright constantly reiterated throughout the lengthy debate, he as well as most other members of the Foreign Relations Committee had always believed and continued to believe that the Cambodian war was unconstitutional, and they did not regard the August 15 compromise as changing their position in any way.

Even legal scholars who have reluctantly concluded that the war in Vietnam was con- stitutional have come to radically different conclusions regarding Cambodia. For example, John Hart Ely disagreed with Laurence Tribe's conclusion regarding the Gulf of Tonkin Resolution that "a generic grant to the President of Congress' war-making power, unac- companied by any articulated standards, would be unconstitutional as an overbroad dele- gation of congressional authority." Ely was sharply critical of Fulbright's role in the 1964 Tonkin Gulf debate, with considerable justification, since Fulbright himself later admitted he made serious mistakes in that controversy. However, Ely wrote of the "troubled consti- tutionality" of the Vietnam War, which "our government told us about—[it] was constitu- tional under currently prevailing notions of congressional authorization." Yet Ely went on to stress the need "to clarify those notions in ways that will more effectively force Congress to face up to its constitutional obligation to decide on war and peace." Ely proposed a change in the law to provide a "bright-line unambiguous authorization rule, so that the nation shouldn't be permitted to "slide into war": "An unambiguous in-or-out vote should be required at the outset (or at least as soon as the President has had time to react to the emergency and bring the matter before Congress)." Where a clear Congressional authoriza- tion has taken place, the military commitment should be supported until both the President and Congress agree in disengaging from it, where Congress overrides a veto, or where the Congressional majority cuts off funding for the war. As with the proposal for any "legal test," problems always arise in that military entanglements can be hypothesized that would becloud the issue. But Ely points out that Congress has unfortunately developed strong incentives to be ambiguous in the war powers area, for its majority has often lacked "the will and/or courage to stop the President from involving us in military ventures, but at the same time has no wish to be held accountable for the wars he gets us into." Ely recalls that the Framers of the Constitution understood that the judgment of one individual should not lead the nation suddenly into war and thus risk the lives of its youth. As Francis Wormuth and Edwin Firmage have written: "The framers did not entrust the war power to Congress for the benefit of congressmen; they did so for the benefit of the citizenry. They believed that a decision for war should be taken by a broadly representative group after debate and deliberation; for that body to shirk its responsibility and transfer the power of decision to a single man was to acquiesce in tyranny." In Ely's view, a bright-line test of authorization would be "a way of forcing our representatives in Congress to take a clear stand, up front, on questions of war and peace."[76a]

In addition to forcing Congressional accountability, Ely contended that a bright-line rule would:

> ...go a long way toward eliminating the tension we must feel when a majority in Congress wishes to terminate a war, but cannot do so without a two-thirds vote [to override a veto] or an act of what has unfortunately come to be regarded as unusual political courage [a vote to cut off funds for the war]... Thus an appropriation to support the troops the President has unilaterally placed `in the field' should not count as authorization—whether or not the feeling is justified, there seems to be too much felt coercion in the appropriations situation. However, once the troops' presence has received the required unambiguous authorization, it should be strongly supported until there has developed a consensus that the war cannot be justified any longer.

Ely further suggested that a bright-line rule would also enable courts to determine whether or not Congress has authorized a given military action: it would render the inquiry amenable to judicial resolution and thus refute the argument that "the question whether a war has been authorized is `political.' Thus, should the President get us involved in an unauthorized war in the future, the courts could help us get out before too many of our young people die—again, not by deciding for themselves whether the war in question is a good idea but rather by insisting that Congress do so." Ely concluded in a scholarly analysis in 1990 that Congress had attempted to devise a "bright-line test" in the War Powers Resolution of 1973, but that instrument was weakened "because the President has not reported military actions to Congress as he is required to, Congress has not had the backbone to call him on it, and the courts have abstained from getting involved even to the extent of `remanding' the case to Congress." In later years, some members of Congress even expressed sentiments in favor of repealing the War Powers Resolution. Ely's more sensible proposal was to repair the flaws in the Resolution rather than repealing it; courts might assist in this project by requiring a "`clear statement doctrine' requiring unusual explicitness in congressional combat authorizations," but the formulation of the specifics of such a doctrine would have to be left to Congress.

Among scholars, Ely and others differed in their analyses but generally conceded, in Ely's words, that "thinking all this through is a tall order" regarding the prevention of future

Presidential actions similar to Vietnam. But if Vietnam itself was of "troubled constitutionality," the argument that the war in Cambodia was unconstitutional should be clearcut for objective analysts. As Ely wrote in addressing the "rest of the war in Indochina—(the part [the government] didn't tell us about)—was (essentially for that reason) unconstitutional." Fulbright at one point during the debate had warned that if Nixon persisted in continuing the bombing after the August 15 deadline, impeachment would become "unavoidable"—a charge that was widely discounted in 1973 as a partisan line. In a scathing conclusion to a scholarly article almost 20 years later, Ely asserted that not only was the war that Nixon had secretly begun in Cambodia during 1969 unconstitutional, but it was clearly grounds for impeaching the President even before the August 15 compromise:

> ...A serious and willful violation of the separation of powers constitutes an impeachable 'high crime or misdemeanor.' Moreover, ... an impeachment inquiry would have been well designed to unravel alleged executive motives and determine which among them constituted only post facto rationalization. Unlike the war in Laos, the secret bombing of Cambodia was an offense consummated by one and only one President [Nixon]. Also unlike Laos, it was a well-kept secret—involving measures as extreme as hoodwinking the Air Force Secretary and Chief of Staff and providing falsified secret documents to the relevant congressional committees for up to four years after the events. The fact that Congress will not be in a moral position to impeach when it has in effect been part of the conspiracy makes it all the more important that it do so in the rare situation where it wasn't.
>
> It is true that other Presidents have masked changes in military strategy in order to avoid criticism from Congress and the public. Lyndon Johnson certainly did some things along these lines at earlier stages of the war in Indochina, McKinley led Congress to believe that our actions in the Philippines during the Spanish-American War were purely defensive... It is, however, the job of Congress in an impeachment proceeding to make just such distinctions of degree. The offense here, viewed even in historical context, was flagrant—the brutal violation of a neutral country (with, we know in retrospect, results of almost unimaginable, and continuing, horror) covered up by a meticulous falsification of records, which falsification was reiterated for years beyond the expiration of the only even remotely colorable (though ultimately incredible) 'innocent' justification for the deception. I'd have impeached him for it...[76b]

What was at stake in this legal debate in 1973? First, the debate would determine whether the bombing of Cambodia would continue for another month, with added civilian casualties at a time when there was no hope of winning the war and the United States was clearly disengaging from southeast Asia. In a war replete with decades of needless violence, that one last rain of death from the skies was utterly senseless. Had the Supreme Court ruled the way Judd, Oakes and Douglas had advocated, the bombing would have been declared unconstitutional and that last paroxysm of violence would not have happened; not even President Nixon, as subsequent events would demonstrate, would defy a direct Court order. Secondly, the manner in which the courts handled the issue would set important precedents for future wars. All realistic observers would have to acknowledge the thoughtfulness and brutal realism of Justice Jackson's argument regarding courts' inability to check executive power in the midst of World War II. Yet, at the least, the situation of World War II—when America's existence was in peril, there had been a declaration of war, and the Congress had unquestionably been wholeheartedly supportive of the war after Pearl Harbor—differed sharply from that of southeast Asia, where there was no declaration of war, Congress' participation in the decision for military action had been questionable (given the lack of candor by the executive branch) in Vietnam, and Congress had clearly opposed the military action in Cambodia. By 1973, from the purely practical standpoint, it would not have been anywhere near as destructive to the judiciary's institutional self-interest as it would have been in World War II for the Court to be seen as opposing the President's conduct of war. The duty to dissent of which Fulbright had so often spoken was a very different duty for a judge than for a member of Congress. Yet, an argument could be made that judges like Douglas and Oakes fulfilled their duties better than those such as Burger who refused to countenance the idea of ruling upon the war issue. Moreover, some commentators have argued that if judges like Jackson had stood up for their views of unconstitutional action regarding the Japanese-Americans—in retrospect it is clear that the Japanese-Americans were not a threat to American security—and decided the case based upon their convictions, this would have saved the Court from one of its most backward and embarrassing decisions. Justice Frank Murphy, in fact, *did* dissent in *Korematsu* on grounds that directly challenged the military's allegation that the Japanese-Americans threatened "sabotage and espionage." *Korematsu*, 323 U.S. 214 (1944)(Murphy, J., dissenting; Jackson and Roberts also dissented, for different reasons).

While in dealing with the prosecution of a war, great respect and consideration must be accorded to the judgments of military authorities, Justice Murphy nonetheless ruled: "It is essential that there be definite limits to military discretion, especially where martial law has not been declared. Individuals must not be left impoverished of their constitutional rights on a plea of military necessity that has neither substance nor support." *Id.* Obviously, there is simply no comparison between World War II and the war in Indochina; during World War II it was vastly more difficult for judges to dissent. On the other hand, the Framers of the Constitution had intended for federal judges to be able to withstand the heat of temporary passions, as did Justice Murphy, hence they were given lifetime tenure with no possibility of a reduction in salary. Of course, judges should make their decisions based upon objective legal standards, and not political judgments. However, Judge Oakes had developed a reasonable legal standard—his interpretation of the mutual participation test, which would not consider Congressional authorization in the face of flagrant deception as "mutual participation" in military activities. Under Oakes' test, the Cambodian issue was an easy one. The Vietnam War would also probably be considered unconstitutional under this test, given the deception of Congress by the Johnson administration in 1964-65, but in the case of Vietnam there could be a valid counter-argument in Congress' approval of appropriations (although there again the question of whether appropriations equal authorization of the war has been a debated judicial issue). The World War II issues would have been a clear-cut issue—at the other end of the spectrum—where courts would be exceedingly reluctant to make any challenge to executive power in the midst of a conflict in which there had been a declaration of war and the Congress and public wholeheartedly approved of it. The difficulty with taking the value of previous judicial decisions as precedents for the future is, of course, that each situation tends to be largely different and not identical to the past one. Neither Oakes' test nor any other test could provide an automatic, mechanical solution that would resolve all constitutional questions regarding the war power. However, if any lessons can be drawn from the debates over the constitutionality of the war, one of the clearest should be that in any future situation analogous to that of the Cambodian debate in 1973, there was simply not any real evidence of Congressional participation in that conflict and abundant evidence of Congressional opposition to that war; the proper legal course was followed by those judges who decided the cases as did Judge Oakes. The air war in Cambodia was an unusual and a clearcut case, for it was clearly unconstitutional. Fulbright and a majority in Congress had consistently opposed the Cambodian war and passed legislation against it from 1970 onwards. In the future, should a situation similar to the Cambodian war arise, courts would be justified in finding the military action unconstitutional.

Although Fulbright and other legislators and scholars were engaging in a valuable enterprise in their efforts to devise additional checks upon the dog of war in the aftermath of the war in Indochina, these efforts were contingent upon Fulbright and his colleagues and successors in Congress as well as the electorate having learned essential lessons: that the people must demand a full public accounting of the war policy from their elected representatives in advance of a military commitment, and that the Congress must not evade its constitutional responsibility confided in the legislative branch by the Framers, who in their wisdom had given an effective "check to the dog of war by transferring the power of letting him loose from the executive to the legislative body, from those who are to spend to those who are to pay."

Ending the War in Indochina

With Fulbright's extensive knowledge of Supreme Court precedents and judges' historic reticence in war cases, he had been realistic enough not to rely upon federal courts to end the war; that struggle would have to be waged in the political arena. In his book *The Crippled Giant,* Fulbright excoriated Nixon's justification for prolonging the war. Nixon had argued that an American withdrawal would precipitate a "blood bath" in South Vietnam and plunge America from the "anguish of war into a nightmare of recrimination" from the radical right.[77] Fulbright charged that it was absurd to sacrifice thousands of American soldiers and the peace of Indochina to the appeasement of the lunatic fringe in the United States. And the administration had failed to explain why it was better for South Vietnamese civilians to be incinerated by American napalm or "blown to bits by American fragmentation bombs" than to confront the hypothetical threat of a future communist blood bath.[78]

Fulbright believed that Nixon's Vietnam policy was the consummation of the ideological anticommunism of the Truman Doctrine. Nixon claimed that he had renounced the international communist conspiracy theory of Dulles and the earlier Cold Warriors, but his contention was belied by many of his statements on Vietnam. By the early 1970s, the Nixon policies were becoming totally contradictory, with the administration's diplomacy toward the great communist powers beginning to display the emphasis upon detente advocated by Henry Kissinger, while the Nixon southeast Asian policies continued in the ideological tradition of the Truman Doctrine. Early in his administration Nixon had spoken of "great powers who have not yet abandoned their goals of world conquest," referring to China and Russia.[79] As late as Nixon's speech of April 1972, the President had repeatedly denounced "communist aggression" in Indochina, not North Vietnamese aggression, in a manner reminiscent of Dean Rusk's view of Ho Chi Minh as a Chinese agent in the grand communist strategy for the conquest of Asia.[80] The thesis of Chinese proxy war should have been discredited long ago, Fulbright held, if not by the evidence of North Vietnamese nationalism then by the fact that no Chinese combat forces ever participated in the war in Vietnam.[81]

Fulbright considered Nixon's "Vietnamization" to be a euphemism for the substitution of an air war of unprecedented dimensions for Johnson's tactics of large-scale American involvement in the ground war. The buildup of the South Vietnamese army and the gradual withdrawal of American forces had reduced American casualties, but Nixon's aerial devastations maintained the total death toll. Thus Fulbright described "Vietnamization" as having succeeded only in "changing the color of the corpses."[82] Nixon had intensified the bombing campaign to the extent that by the middle of 1971 the United States had dropped more bombs on Indochina than it had in both the European and Pacific theaters during World War II.[83] Despite the failures of Vietnamization, Fulbright was further disappointed in the support Nixon still enjoyed from members of Congress. For example, Republican Senator George Aiken, who had been critical of the escalation in the Johnson years, was a steadfast supporter of Vietnamization and an opponent of Congressional efforts to cut off funding for the war. Fulbright later described Aiken as a "cynic."[84]

By mining the North Vietnamese harbors and expanding the air war to unparalleled heights of devastation in 1972 Nixon raised the level of violence in the war beyond any of Johnson's successive acts of escalation. Fulbright listed the sordid record of destruction in Vietnam during the years since Nixon had promised to end the war in 1968: 3.2 million tons of bombs dropped on Indochina, (the figure Fulbright cites here was already greater than the total tonnage dropped during the Johnson administration, with the infamous Christmas bombings of 1972 not included) 20,000 American deaths, 110,000 Americans wounded, 340,000 Asian deaths, and the creation of 4 million new refugees.[85] In the spring of 1972 Fulbright wrote that the Nixon policy "had come back full circle" to that of Johnson four years before; Johnson had partially suspended the bombing of North Vietnam and initiated the Paris peace talks in April 1968, while in April 1972 Nixon suspended the peace talks and resumed massive bombings of North and South Vietnam.[86]

On May 9, 1972, the Foreign Relations Committee hearings on the "Causes, Origins, and Lessons of the Vietnam War" began. Fulbright learned of Nixon's decision to mine the entrances to the ports of North Vietnam against all shipping, including Russian and Chinese shipping, on the afternoon of May 8, a few hours before Nixon's speech that night.[87] It was purely a coincidence that the hearings began the day after Nixon's decision. Fulbright issued an invitation for any member of the administration to appear before the committee, although he did not expect his invitation to be accepted. Kissinger had been asked to testify innumerable times, but he steadfastly refused on the grounds of "executive privilege."[88] Most of the members of the Foreign Relations Committee did not attend the three sessions of the public hearings. The topics that were most frequently discussed were the origins of the American involvement in Vietnam in the 1940s. Thus, while four senators in the half-empty chambers of the Senate Office Building held their dialogue with the past, the President precipitated a crisis that apparently risked a military conflict with Russia or China.

Fulbright had also asked representatives from the Johnson administration to testify about the origins and lessons of Vietnam.[89] Dean Rusk and William Bundy declined. Robert McNamara's refusal to testify was much more disappointing. A quarter of a century later—when it was too late to have any impact in stopping the tragic war—McNamara would belatedly come forward with a detailed, constructive book on Vietnam confessing the Johnson administration's grave errors. McNamara was dutiful to a code followed by many executive branch officials whereby any official who resigned remained silent about his knowledge of the mistakes of his former superior. Such a code would preserve the personal relationships among the officials involved, but it was fundamentally misguided; McNamara was wracked with doubts about the war in the late 1960s, and a higher allegiance to the welfare of the country rather than to the administration that appointed him should have dictated that he come forward with his encyclopedic knowledge of the terrible blunders in southeast Asia, for the benefit of the American public. McNamara's apology in 1995 was beneficial, especially in comparison with Rusk, who never admitted error in Vietnam; but McNamara would have served U.S. foreign policy better had he made the same arguments before Fulbright's committee in 1972, or in the late 1960s shortly after he resigned from the Pentagon.

A few days after the hearings began, the fact that Nixon, Kissinger, Ambassador Dobrynin, and Soviet Minister of Foreign Trade Patolichev were photographed together smiling broadly in the White House seemed to indicate that there had been an understanding between the Soviet Union and the United States, whereby the Russians would accept an ostensible humiliation in return for American wheat and tractors at low prices.[90] Nixon's May 8 speech was, of course, mentioned at the hearings. Fulbright deplored the President's action. Clearly Congress and the public had been notified of decisions already made during the crisis while the President and his men manipulated the entire scenario.

The most important witness at the May 1972 hearings was Frank White, who had been an OSS officer in Hanoi in 1946 and had talked at length with Ho Chi Minh.[91] Fulbright asked White if there was any evidence that Ho had been an ally or representative of "international communism." White replied that Ho believed the Russians had been so devastated by World War II that they would be unable to supply Vietnam with "moral, political, or economic aid."[92] Ho did not mention Mao Tse-tung, and when he did speak of the Chinese he elaborated at "extraordinary length" on the ancient hostility between the Vietnamese and Chinese peoples.[93]

According to White, Ho believed that the United States would be the great power most likely to assist Vietnam because of the American tradition of support for national self-determination. Ho concluded, however, that he did not expect the United States to concern itself with southeast Asia in the postwar era, for Vietnam was "a small country and far away."[94]

Abbot Low Moffat, Chief of the Division of Southeast Asian Affairs at the State Department from 1945 to 1947, discussed the reason for the failure of the Truman administration to reply to eight communications Ho addressed to President Truman between

October 1945 and February 1946 asking America to intervene in favor of Vietnamese independence.[95] Moffat informed the committee that he had written a memorandum arguing
against any reply to Ho, for if the President had officially answered him this would have violated international protocol, (and would have been tantamount to a recognition of Ho as a
head of state) and infuriated the French.[96] Anticommunism was not a factor until late 1946,
according to Moffat, who stated that by February 1947 the Cold War mentality had begun
to permeate the world view of the State Department so thoroughly that speculation about
Ho's "direct communist connection" became common, even though in Moffat's opinion
there never was any evidence that such a connection existed.[97] Moffat was generally accurate in asserting that the Cold Warriors triumphed in the debate within the Truman administration concerning southeast Asian policy; the State Department's debate in the late 1940s
was eventually won by Dean Acheson and those advisers who contended that the Cold War
would be won or lost in Europe, and hence the United States could not risk losing France's
cooperation by opposing French colonialism in southeast Asia. Thus far had American
diplomacy evolved since President Roosevelt's 1944 memorandum to Cordell Hull had
denounced the French for "milking" their colonies and proposed an international trusteeship for Indochina.[98]

At the close of the hearings Moffat mentioned a theory of America's involvement in
Vietnam that stressed economics. He claimed that he had supported the Open Door policy
because he considered "international trade to be one of the big facets of peace."[99] The State
Department was never interested in opening Vietnam to American investors. Insofar as there
was an economic motive, Moffat said that the Department was concerned with southeast
Asia as a source of two raw materials: tin and rubber.[100]

If Moffat intended to refute the economic interpretation of recent American diplomacy,
he had not focused his criticism upon the most plausible economic arguments advanced by
Walter La Feber and other scholars. Some of the radical revisionists alleged that America's
dependence on raw materials in the Third World had forced the United States into the role
of the global defender of the status quo, but the scholars who have most convincingly
stressed the importance of economics in American interventions have not argued that
America became involved in Vietnam in order to protect American investments, which in
fact were quite meager in South Vietnam. Walter La Feber has written that the Eisenhower
and Kennedy administrations emphasized the significance of the domino theory largely
because of its economic implications for Japan—a nation which was crucial to American
strategic policy in the Far East—if southeast Asia fell to communism and hence deprived
the Japanese of important markets and sources of raw materials.[101] The weight of the evidence, however, indicates that these economic considerations exerted only a secondary
influence upon the U.S. officials who determined the early postwar policies in Vietnam.

Fulbright conceded at the hearings that the economic interpretation based upon
America's determination to promote the Open Door policy and the domino theory's economic repercussions for Japan had "a certain consistency," although he was inclined to think
that "it was much more complex than just being economics."[102] In his books that deal with
Vietnam, the senator did not argue that the United States held any significant economic
interests in South Vietnam; and, of course, he constantly reminded the American public that
the war had inflicted massive damage upon the U.S. economy. Moffat's statements about the

State Department's concern with southeast Asian raw materials and the domino theory's hypothetical implications for Japan's economy seem to demonstrate that economic motives were not entirely nonexistent in the American commitment in Vietnam (at least in the 1940s and 1950s) and should not be totally ignored. The domino theory, however, was ultimately based on the ideological assumption that the communist bloc was inherently expansionist and monolithic, an assumption belied by the Chinese-Vietnamese border skirmishes of the mid and late 1970s. Relations among the Far Eastern communist states after the American withdrawal from Indochina were clearly dominated by the traditional national rivalries that Ho Chi Minh had so eloquently lamented in placid conversations with his American friends at the Hanoi Palais du Gouvernement in 1946.

Fulbright convened a brief set of hearings in early 1972 on American policy with respect to China shortly before Nixon's visit to Peking. John Stewart Service appeared before the committee to discuss his recent trip to China. Service had been a Foreign Service officer in the Far East in the 1940s and had predicted a communist victory in the Chinese civil war at least as early as 1944.[103] His accurate prognostications had led to his dismissal in the McCarthy era.[104] The state of the communist world at the time Service testified revealed once again the absurdity in the Cold War mythology of the "monolithic" communist bloc. The Soviet press condemned Nixon's negotiations in Peking as a "dangerous plot."[105] According to Service, the North Vietnamese were extremely suspicious that the Chinese might conspire with the Americans to betray North Vietnam.[106] And in China, Service reported that "the central part of Shanghai is torn up with digging air-raid shelters. In Peking they are digging air-raid shelters. Every school, every factory has air raid shelters." When Service asked people in Shanghai and Peking "the defense is against whom?" The Chinese replied, "the Russians, the Soviets."[107]

The Foreign Relations chairman held the 1972 Vietnam and China hearings in an effort to provoke thought concerning the origins and lessons of the Vietnam War, and he described the sessions as "educational." But the hearings did not attract as much attention or promote as much reflection as Fulbright would have liked. In the early and mid-1970s, unfortunately, most Americans were simply growing weary of thinking about the deeper issues involved in America's tragic experience in Vietnam. The U.S. military involvement in southeast Asia continued for over a year after the 1972 hearings, and the public's attention continued to be focused on the ongoing conflict rather than efforts to analyze and understand the origins and lessons of the war.

Nixon diligently portrayed himself as the moderate, statesmanlike candidate in the 1972 presidential election, while painting the Democrats as irresponsible radicals. He won deserved praise for his visit to China. He cleverly revealed early in the year that Kissinger had secretly been negotiating with Hanoi since 1969, but these efforts had allegedly been frustrated by the North Vietnamese refusal to deal with the Americans, according to the President. He announced that he was now preparing fresh proposals to break the deadlock, and thus scored major public relations victories in early 1972.[108] Fulbright, as a pioneer who had done so much to open up rational discussion of Sino-American relations with the China hearings of 1966, was highly complimentary of the China initiative. He was dismayed, however, by the administration's practice of having the President's lieutenants engage in McCarthyite attacks upon leading Democrats while the President posed as a statesman.

For example, in February, H.R. Haldeman appeared on the "Today" television program to attack the administration's critics as virtually treasonable. The principal target of Haldeman's wrath was Senator Edmund Muskie of Maine, the leading Democratic candidate for President at the time and a vigorous critic of Nixon's Vietnam policy. Shortly afterward, Secretary Rogers condemned Muskie's position on the war as "inappropriate and harmful" to America's best interests. Fulbright responded to Haldeman's attacks by delivering a Senate speech in which he deplored the abusive language of Nixon's political alter ego. But Fulbright's words were lost beneath the din of the public relations extravaganza connected with Nixon's trip to China. Fulbright sadly noted in a letter to Muskie that "with the TV spectaculars of Peking and Moscow pre-empting the airwaves, what you and I or anyone else has to say is going to be difficult to bring to the notice of the public."[109]

Fulbright vigorously supported the eventual Democratic nominee, George McGovern, after the administration's "dirty tricks" campaign and other efforts to discredit Muskie aided in the process of removing the most formidable Democrat from the race. Fulbright argued that McGovern was an honest, decent politician who would end the war quickly, check the power of the military-industrial complex, and respect the liberties "of the ordinary people." At the Democratic Convention in Miami, Fulbright tried to reach McGovern to persuade him to select Congressman Wilbur Mills of Arkansas, the powerful Chairman of the Way and Means Committee, as his running mate. Unfortunately, Fulbright was unable to consult with McGovern before he selected Senator Thomas Eagleton of Missouri.[110] The Eagleton episode ended in a fiasco, as McGovern decided to remove him from the ticket because of Eagleton's previous psychiatric problems. Based on what was generally known about Mills in 1972, he probably would have made an excellent running mate for McGovern, at least from the standpoint of electoral politics; where McGovern's primary political problem was in convincing mainstream America that he was not a wild-eyed radical, Mills epitomized the middle-of-the-road politics of middle-class America. Mills also would have strengthened the Democratic ticket's appeal in the South. Although Mills would later destroy his career by his problem with alcohol, in 1972 that problem was unknown to the public—the Ways and Means chairman was widely respected as a knowledgeable tax expert and legislative powerhouse. While Sargent Shriver, Eagleton's replacement, was an able liberal, he represented precisely the constituency that McGovern had already captivated and hence brought little additional political strength to the ticket. McGovern would still have lost the election to Nixon in the political environment of 1972, but Mills could easily have enabled him to obtain a somewhat larger percentage of the vote and to have helped dispel the administration's propaganda campaign depicting McGovern as a radical. On the other hand, Shriver was an able, progressive man, a former head of the Peace Corps, and a running mate who was ideologically compatible with McGovern and could inspire the young idealists who admired the Democratic ticket in that year.

To Fulbright's credit, he campaigned strenuously for McGovern in 1972. McGovern was unpopular in Arkansas, so that Fulbright's vigorous support for him was politically damaging. Nixon easily carried the state.

The doves in the Senate were disheartened by Nixon's predictable landslide victory in November, yet the pendulum of political momentum began to move in favor of the doves once again after the infamous "Christmas bombings" of North Vietnam in 1972.

The *Arkansas Gazette* called for Nixon's impeachment after this shameless resort to violence from the man who had portrayed himself as the candidate of peace in the election. The vindictiveness of the administration's retaliation against its critics in early 1973 backfired and brought a revulsion against the painful effort to exhume Joe McCarthy. White House Counselor Charles Colson condemned the President's critics for having delayed an end to the war, and impugned the patriotism of what he called the "sellout brigade" of Fulbright, Edward Kennedy, McGovern, Church, and Clark Clifford. The "sellout brigade," Colson ranted in a televised interview, featured the leading advocates of "dishonorable peace," for they would have abandoned Vietnam "without regard to consequences."[111]

In the midst of Fulbright's battle with the Nixon partisans, the senator was saddened by the death of Lyndon Johnson on January 22. Fulbright recalled in a melancholy mood his years of friendship and political collaboration with Johnson before Vietnam and the lasting achievements of Johnson's domestic reform legislation. He issued a statement in which he commended President Johnson as a leader "who had one of the most outstanding careers in American politics of any man in our history. . . . As a senator and as a President he was responsible for some of the most significant legislation of our time. . . . I am saddened by his sudden death and by the fact that he did not live to witness the termination of the war for which we all fervently hope."[112] Ironically, LBJ died the day before Nixon announced that a cease-fire had been worked out in Paris.

The announcement of the cease-fire did not mean the end of American military activities in Indochina. In Foreign Relations Committee hearings in early 1973, Fulbright challenged the legality of the bombing of Cambodia, pointedly regretting that the administration "will not be gotten the better of by anything so trivial as a law . . . (the administration will find) some specious legal justification for doing exactly what it wishes to do."[113]

Even more ominous for the administration was the eruption of the Watergate crisis into a historic scandal. In April Nixon announced the resignations of Haldeman and John Erlichman and the firing of John Dean. The *Gazette's* editor, James Powell, was on Capitol Hill at the time and visited Fulbright's office, witnessing a jubilant celebration that reminded him of a New Year's Eve party. Fulbright proclaimed in a televised interview with Elizabeth Drew in May that "Watergate is the bursting of the boil" on the excessive expansion of executive power in recent American history. Watergate had caused the administration "to re-examine its role and to be more responsive to Congress and public opinion." The senator now believed that Nixon would heed any vote in Congress to end the bombing. Another milestone was reached in May, as the House, which for years had sycophantically stood behind the President, voted to place some restrictions on the bombing.[114]

The power and prestige of the Nixon administration was severely weakened by the Watergate crisis. Watergate had the effect of discrediting in the public mind virtually all of Nixon's policies; the discrediting of Nixon's Vietnam policies was fortunate for the opponents of the war, but Fulbright would later observe that the eventual popular disillusionment with Nixon's detente policies toward the Soviet Union held highly damaging implications for the future of Soviet-American relations.[115] The senator would have preferred that each of Nixon's policies should have been judged on its own merits, rather than allowing Watergate to foster a popular revulsion against all of Nixon's undertakings. While Fulbright always argued that the Nixon administration's crusade in southeast Asia was disastrous, he supported the 1972 Moscow summit and the Kissinger-Nixon detente approach. However, the Foreign Relations chairman was certainly encouraged by the reality that Watergate had weakened Nixon's power to execute his policies in southeast Asia. "In regard to the Watergate affair and related developments," Fulbright informed a constituent in the summer of 1973, "I believe this is indicative of what can happen when too much power is concentrated in the Executive. People in the Executive Branch become so concerned with the preservation and enhancement of their power that they feel above the law. It could, however, be beneficial in the long run by helping to restore some perspective and re-establish the balance between Congress and the Executive."[116]

During the late Nixon administration, Representative Peter Rodino of New Jersey, North Carolina Senator Sam Ervin, and others led the investigations revealing the massive scope of the Watergate scandals. The 1972 burglary of the Democratic National Committee headquarters at the Watergate was only a part of an immense effort to influence the results of the 1972 election through covert and illegal activities; eventually the various investigations of the scandals established that the Nixon administration had been engaged in a systematic attempt to "cover up" its involvement in Watergate.[117] Fulbright was not as vigorously involved in the Watergate inquiries as Ervin, Rodino, Congressman Ray Thornton of Arkansas, and several other members of Congress. When Rodino and others were attempting to gain evidence from the White House as part of the impeachment inquiry in 1974, Fulbright made public statements rejecting Nixon's attempted use of executive privilege to deny Congress the evidence. "I think the Constitution gives the Congress the right," Fulbright argued, "to have all the relevant information of any kind. I think all this parrying and delay by the President is quite unjustified."[118] Fulbright differed from many critics of the Watergate affair in arguing that the proper Congressional response to an "arrogant" administration should have been a censure of the President, as Joe McCarthy had been censured 20 years earlier.[119] Although Fulbright was not one of the principal leaders of the Watergate investigations, during the late 1960s and early 1970s he had played an essential role in beginning the movement to halt the expansion of the executive's power. The Cold Warrior mentality that bred the American intervention in Vietnam also promoted the excessive growth of executive power that culminated in Watergate, for the anti-communist crusaders believed that unethical or even illegal activities were justified in order to ensure that the administration overcame both domestic and foreign foes in its struggle with a supposedly fiendish, global and totalitarian enemy.[120] One of the important motives leading to Watergate was the administration's effort to defend the Vietnam War against its critics during the 1972 presidential campaign.[121] In 1973-74, the Watergate investigations and the anti-Vietnam War movement had combined to check the excesses in the executive branch; the future would show whether other leaders in other generations might attempt to resurrect the "imperial Presidency."

In 1973 the anti-war movement inexorably gained strength, but not until the summer did the Congressional opponents of the war succeed in defeating Nixon's policy of military intervention in southeast Asia. The Paris cease-fire agreements of January 1973 terminated the American phase of the ground warfare by providing for the return of American prisoners in exchange for the withdrawal of U.S. military forces in 60 days. Yet, (as referred to in the previous section discussing the constitutional debate over war powers) massive

American bombing of Cambodia continued in an effort to uphold the fragile pro-American regime of Lon Nol against the Hanoi-supported Khmer Rouge insurgency, and also to maintain what Kissinger called Nixon's "reputation for fierceness."[122] Public opinion polls in May revealed that 60 percent of the public opposed the Cambodian bombing, and 75 percent believed that the President should seek Congressional approval before executing additional hostilities in southeast Asia. During the summer, Congress approved the amendment to end the use of funds for the Cambodian bombing after August 15; the vote in the Senate was 63-19 in favor.[123] Within the administration, Kissinger was disgusted to find many prominent officials—Melvin Laird, for example—urging the President to compromise and accept the August 15 cutoff date. Congressional experts in the White House believed that the administration would face one cutoff bill after another until a veto eventually would be overridden. Kissinger was incensed by the talk of compromise, complaining that "this is one of the most vindictive, cheap actions I've seen the Congress take. And it's not just in Cambodia, it's going to hurt us murderously with the Chinese because if they think that the Congress can do these things to us in Cambodia, what are they going to do to us elsewhere?"[124]

In Fulbright's correspondence in 1973, he explained how the embattled Nixon had used every resource of his dwindling power to prolong the conflict, even though it was obvious that the policy of intervention was politically doomed by that late date. "If I could have had my way," Fulbright explained to a constituent in July, "the U.S. bombing of Cambodia certainly would not have been continued after June 29. Unfortunately, the President had the upper hand and the votes were simply not available to over-ride his veto. That being the case, we did the best we could, which was to write an August 15 cutoff date into a piece of legislation which the President had to sign. Although I regret the prolongation of the bombing, I believe that in finally compelling the President to accept the authority of the Congress in matters pertaining to the use of U.S. military forces we have taken a major step toward the restoration of a proper constitutional balance."[125]

The administration had contended that Hanoi had repeatedly violated Article 20 of the Paris agreement calling for North Vietnam's withdrawal from Cambodia. A Foreign Relations Committee report prepared by Richard Moose and James Lowenstein refuted this argument, asserting that "neither Hanoi's continued presence nor our bombing were violations of Article 20 because it had been clearly understood that Article 20 would not be effective until there was a cease-fire in Cambodia." The report also contended that the State Department had conceded this point when Rogers gave the committee a legal brief outlining its position on Article 20. Fulbright kept up the pressure on the administration in April, supporting the conclusions of Moose and Lowenstein, his two top field investigators, after they visited Phnom Penh. The investigators discovered that American Embassy personnel supervised by Thomas Enders were directly involved in directing the air war in Cambodia. In a report prepared for Senator Symington's subcommittee, the investigators concluded that the bombing "is being employed against the more densely populated areas of Cambodia." Kissinger defended himself against charges that administration policies had led to many civilian deaths in Cambodia; in one of the most resentful passages in his voluminous memoirs, Kissinger essentially blamed Congress for the tragedy of Cambodia, protesting that negotiations regarding Cambodia were "torpedoed by the United States Congress and our domestic turmoil."[126]

In a grudging effort to avoid appearing vindictive, Kissinger acknowledged that no one could have anticipated the hideous campaign of genocide after the Khmer Rouge seized power: "In fairness, the participants on both sides of our domestic debate shared one vast gap of understanding. They could not possibly imagine the evil incarnate represented by the Khmer Rouge." American critics of the southeast Asian war were "incapable of imagining that a government would murder three million of its own people, [and] they thought nothing could be worse than a continuation of the war and they were prepared to ensure its end even at the price of a Communist takeover." Kissinger then stated that American dissenters could not "be blamed" for the Cambodian holocaust, but in the next phrase contradicted himself by complaining that the critics "helped bring about" Pol Pot's bloody rise to power.[127] Kissinger contended that Congress' removal of the bombing deprived him of the pressure needed to force North Vietnam or the Khmer Rouge into accepting a cease-fire, thus setting the stage for the return of Prince Sihanouk as the head of the Cambodian government. According to Kissinger, Chou Enlai had been prepared to provide diplomatic support for the Nixon administration's policies, but Congress' withdrawal had frustrated Chou's plans.

The notion that Kissinger and Chou Enlai had brilliantly masterminded a grand design for peace in Cambodia that was demolished by Fulbright and his allies in Congress was overwrought and inaccurate. Nixon and Kissinger had always regarded Cambodia as a sideshow to the more important issue of who would wield power in South Vietnam, and they had previously realized that if Sihanouk had returned to power in Phnom Penh in the period before 1973, that would have endangered Thieu's regime in Saigon. Had Sihanouk (who had pursued a neutral policy before the coup that removed him in 1970) remained in power, many analysts of Cambodian affairs have concluded that Pol Pot might never have come to power.[128] Both the White House and North Vietnam share responsibility for having militarized the conflict in Cambodia and drawn that small country into the vortex of the war in South Vietnam. In July, the Armed Services Committee revealed that the administration had secretly been bombing Cambodia back in 1969-1970. Fulbright and Mansfield denied administration allegations that they had been informed of the secret bombing. The "Vietnamization" policy paralleled the rise of the Khmer Rouge, which in the post-1975 period would execute a grisly campaign of terrorism, murdering the entire middle class as an obstacle to a "new society," destroying religion and families, and uprooting entire village populations. Nixon and Kissinger had repudiated the position of 75 senators who had voted for the Cooper-Church Amendment in 1970 and thus urged the executive to stay out of Cambodia. The Nixon administration ignored Congress' advice in 1970 and opened up another military front in Cambodia, aggravating that tiny nation's political turmoil and giving life to the Khmer Rouge.[129] In retrospect, it would have been wiser had the United States never intervened militarily in support of the weak pro-American faction of Lon Nol.

In the summer of 1973, Fulbright continued to be wary of the administration, and asked Secretary Rogers to testify about the executive's intentions. Rogers refused to appear before the committee. Fulbright publicly warned that if Nixon disregarded the August 15 deadline regarding halting the bombing, and continued it without congressional approval, such action would "precipitate" impeachment. In the setting of a President severely weakened by Watergate and the anti-war movement, the threat of impeachment was credible. On August 3, Nixon wrote a letter to Congressional leaders indicating that he would reluctantly comply with the law.[130]

Fulbright opposed Nixon's nominations of several ardent defenders of the war to major diplomatic posts in 1973. In July, Fulbright's vote and influence was decisive in the Foreign Relations Committee's rejection by a 9-7 margin of the nomination of George Godley as Assistant Secretary of State for East Asian Affairs. Godley was the Ambassador to Laos, where he had long directed the clandestine war the United States had waged in that remote land. Fulbright argued that an official with Godley's interventionist approach should not be placed in an important State Department position. Godley's defeat was highly unusual, for nominations at that level normally were routinely approved. Fulbright also opposed the nomination of William Sullivan—who, like Godley, had been involved in the covert war in Laos—to be Ambassador to the Philippines, although Fulbright did not succeed in blocking Sullivan's appointment. Nixon also nominated the veteran diplomat Graham Martin as Ambassador to South Vietnam. Fulbright opposed Martin because of his activist background, but Kissinger vigorously backed Martin and eventually won his confirmation. Nixon was incensed at Godley's defeat, complaining that "the consequences of this committee action go far beyond the injustice done to an outstanding Foreign Service officer." The administration's complaints did not deter Fulbright in his conviction that the Senate had a duty to scrutinize all presidential nominations.[131]

Secretary of State Kissinger and the Middle East

In late August 1973, Nixon nominated as Secretary of State the one major administration foreign policy official with whom Fulbright had developed a rapport: Henry Kissinger. Fulbright was basically pleased by the announcement, for Kissinger was clearly a vast improvement over the likes of George Godley and Graham Martin; moreover, Fulbright was painfully aware that if the Senate rejected Kissinger, his probable replacement would be the Texas conservative, John Connally. The senator had ambivalent views of Kissinger. He had clashed repeatedly with Kissinger over southeast Asian policy, of course, and he staunchly opposed Kissinger's support for the B-1 bomber, the Trident submarine, and other increases in military spending. Fulbright was uncertain about whether Kissinger would be forthright with the Foreign Relations Committee, and in fact he would later regret that Kissinger had not revealed the truth about the U.S. role in the overthrow of the Allende regime in Chile in September 1973, a crisis that coincided with his confirmation hearings. The chairman was particularly concerned about allegations that Nixon's foreign policy adviser had been involved in the White House's notorious wiretapping schemes. Fulbright and the other senators subjected Kissinger to extensive questioning at his hearings regarding wiretapping, and the chairman appointed two committee members to make an intensive study of the evidence concerning this issue. Senators Sparkman and Case reported that Kissinger was correct in his denials of wrongdoing.[132]

J. Edgar Hoover (who died in 1972) had proposed the wiretaps to Nixon, and Attorney General John Mitchell authorized them. Kissinger had expressed concern about leaks of sensitive material, and was at least indirectly involved in a few of the wiretaps, although Sparkman and Case concluded that Kissinger's involvement was peripheral and the primary responsibility lay with Hoover, Nixon and Mitchell. Moreover, the wiretaps took place in 1969, well before the Supreme Court's decision in *United States v. U.S. District Court for the Eastern District of Michigan*, 407 U.S. 297 (1972), which held for the first time that wiretaps for national security required a court order. Fulbright was concerned about the wiretapping issue, and was relieved by Kissinger's strong endorsement of the Supreme Court's decision in the wiretapping case, especially in contrast to Nixon's anger at the opinion written by his own nominee, Lewis Powell. As a conservative private citizen in Virginia, Powell had publicly supported the Nixon administration's claim of constitutional authority for wiretapping of "radical" domestic groups without a warrant; yet when the issue reached the high Court, Justice Powell wrote for a unanimous Court that the administration's wiretapping practice was an unconstitutional invasion of Fourth Amendment guarantees as well as being unauthorized under the applicable statute. *Id.* In his testimony, Kissinger stated that after Nixon's wiretapping decision was made, "the Supreme Court has made a new definition of the procedures to be followed in the use of wiretaps, and therefore many of the issues that have been raised with respect to the previous wiretapping by this or by previous administrations have to a very large extent become moot." Kissinger commended Justice Powell's opinion, pledging that in any future national security cases "the weight should be on the side of human liberty, and that if human liberty is to be ever infringed, the demonstration on the national security side must be overwhelming." It might also be noted that former acting FBI Director William Ruckelshaus—later one of the heroes of the "Saturday Night massacre"—stated that "It wasn't his [Kissinger's] idea to tap, he simply complained about the leaks." Of course, Kissinger was telling Fulbright what he wanted to hear in praising the Powell wiretapping opinion. Nonetheless, the committee studied the wiretapping question and eventually concluded—without a dissenting vote—that the wiretapping issue could not bar Kissinger's confirmation by itself.[133]

The wiretapping issue would dog Kissinger for the remainder of the Nixon Presidency. A few days before Nixon resigned in 1974, Kissinger even publicly warned that he would resign if the issue were not "cleared up." At that point Fulbright, Muskie, and Congressman Robert Drinan examined the issue yet again. Drinan, a vociferous administration critic who served on the Judiciary Committee, candidly informed the public that he would be happy to be able to report truthfully that Kissinger was responsible for the wiretap program, but based on the evidence he simply could not do so. Fulbright also gave a public statement of support. Kissinger's threat to resign was overwrought, for given the Nixon administration's horrendous record of violating the constitutional rights of its opponents, the intense media and congressional scrutiny of Bill of Rights issues was a healthy sign. The Foreign Relations Committee conducted another study, and on August 6, 1974, published a report stating that the record "should lay to rest the major questions raised about Secretary Kissinger's role," that there were no significant discrepancies between any information developed after the confirmation hearings and Kissinger's original testimony, and therefore the committee reaffirmed its conclusions that Kissinger's role in the matter did not constitute grounds to bar his service as Secretary of State.[134]

While Fulbright held negative views of Kissinger's record on military spending, southeast Asia, and wiretapping, he was enthusiastic about Kissinger in several other arenas: detente with the Soviet Union and China, expanded educational exchanges, and a more evenhanded policy in the Middle East. Fulbright was enthusiastic about the summit between Brezhnev and the administration in mid-1973 in Washington, and arranged a meeting between the Soviet leader and a group of influential senators. During a lengthy discussion with the senators, Brezhnev told his hosts that "the Cold War is, as far as we are concerned, over." Moreover, Fulbright shared with Kissinger a deep antipathy toward the Jackson Amendment. This amendment was introduced by Democratic Senator Henry Jackson of Washington in October 1972; it barred most-favored-nation trading status to any country that restricted emigration. Jackson's amendment was triggered by the Kremlin's decision in mid-1972 to impose an "exit tax" on emigrants; the Soviets never explained the reason for this decision, although it may have been an attempt to enhance the USSR's standing in the Arab world after the expulsion of Soviet combat troops from Egypt. The Nixon administration had quietly pursued a policy of encouraging the Soviets to permit more Jews to emigrate, so that the number of Jewish emigrants would rise to an annual figure of roughly 35,000 at the time the Jackson Amendment was introduced. The Soviets did discontinue the exit tax, although whether this was a result of Kissinger's detente or the Jackson Amendment is not clear. Fulbright agreed with Kissinger's contention that "What the Jackson Amendment achieved was to make Soviet emigration practices a subject of not just public diplomacy but of legislative action by the American Congress. . . . To Jackson and his supporters, the issue of Jewish emigration was a surrogate for the ideological confrontation with communism."[135] Kissinger had successfully lobbied Anatoly Dobrynin to allow the dissident writer Alexander Solzhenitsyn to leave the USSR. Nixon had originated the concept of encouraging Jewish emigration, and in the context of the detente policy, he and Kissinger had been quite successful; but Fulbright was in agreement with Kissinger that all East-West relations should not be subordinated to the single issue of Jewish emigration. In general, Jackson's efforts to reduce trade, escalate the arms race, and intensify tensions with the USSR were anathema to Fulbright, and he saw Kissinger as a bulwark against the Jackson forces. Kissinger also assured Fulbright that he would assume a cooperative stance toward the committee, and there would be no further American military action in Indochina. The committee voted in Kissinger's favor, 16-1, with McGovern opposed.

Middle Eastern policy was an additional area of compatibility between Kissinger and Fulbright. The senator supported mediation of the continuing conflict, with the objective of having Israel give up land it conquered from Egypt, Syria, and Jordan in the 1967 war in exchange for security guarantees and diplomatic recognition from the Arab states. For many years, Fulbright had believed that American policy was too closely tied up with Israel, and advocated a more balanced and realistic diplomacy in the Middle East. "The critical question for Israel," Fulbright had written in 1972 in a chapter of *The Crippled Giant* analyzing Middle Eastern policy, "is whether it is willing to risk taking the Arabs at their word when they offer to live in peace—as they have done in effect by accepting the Security Council Resolution 242 of November 1967, which calls, among other things, for Israeli withdrawal from occupied territories, the termination of belligerency, the right of Israel and Arab states to "live in peace within secure recognized boundaries,' and a just settlement of the refugee problem." Fulbright argued that both sides in the conflict had committed serious errors.

Since the Six-Day War, the Egyptians had acquired huge arsenals of Soviet weapons, and from 1968 until a cease-fire was accepted in 1970, they waged a war of attrition along the Suez Canal. The senator felt that these Arab actions had only aggravated tensions: the Israelis matched any military buildup by obtaining military hardware from the United States, and Prime Minister Golda Meir refused to make any major concessions. In turn, Israeli policy had been myopic and inflexible, in Fulbright's view; the establishment of Israeli settlements on the occupied West Bank of the Jordan and in the Sinai were seen as efforts to foreclose the return of these territories to their previous Arab owners. Israel's insistence upon the "non-negotiability" of the status of Jerusalem and upon retention of other occupied territories, in Fulbright's analysis, "lends unfortunate credence to the late President Nasser's pessimistic prediction in accepting Secretary Rogers' peace proposal in 1970, that 'While we inform the United States that we have accepted its proposals, we also tell them that our real belief is that whatever is taken by force cannot be returned except by force.'"[136]

Fulbright believed that Israel's diplomatic intransigence was isolating it in the forum of world opinion. For example, the United Nations General Assembly censured Israel's unilateral act in declaring the "non-negotiability" of the Israeli annexation of Arab East Jerusalem by a vote of 99 to 0. In contrast to Foreign Minister Abba Eban's melodramatic proclamation that "a nation must be capable of tenacious solitude," Israel was heavily dependent on the United States for both military aid and economic assistance. U.S. military aid had greatly expanded since the 1967 war, including aircraft, missiles and advanced electronic systems. Fulbright argued that Israel's first Prime Minister and then elder statesman, David Ben-Gurion, had set forth the only realistic path to true security: "Peace, real peace, is now the great necessity for us. It is worth almost any sacrifice. To get it, we must return to the borders before 1967." The senator commended Ben-Gurion's statement that militarily defensible borders would not guarantee Israel's future, for "real peace with our Arab neighbors—mutual trust and friendship—that is the only true security." Fulbright also quoted with approval the ideas of Dr. Nahum Goldmann, President of the World Jewish Congress, that Israel's post-1967 policy had led to a dangerous impasse, because time was on the Arabs' side: "No one can predict how long it will take them to catch up with Israel technologically, especially in the field of weaponry. But sooner or later the balance of power will shift in their favor."[137] The senator was also disenchanted with the Israelis' tendency to portray their nation as the sole bastion of freedom in the Middle East, with Israel supposedly defending American interests by opposing communist imperialism. "I perceive in this," Fulbright argued, "some of the same old Communist-baiting humbuggery that certain other small countries have used to manipulate the United States for their own purpose."[138]

Fulbright also criticized the demonology of the Arabs and their destructive myths: "The Arabs too must face up to certain realities: that Israel has come to stay, that it is demagogic nonsense to talk—as some of the Palestinian guerrillas still do—of driving the Jews into the sea; that in any case the Arab states can have no realistic hope of doing that because they themselves cannot defeat Israel," and that the United States would intervene to save Israel from destruction in the exceedingly unlikely event—given the widespread belief in Israel's overwhelming military superiority at the time—that the Arabs ever did come to endanger Israel militarily. The Arabs must liberate themselves "from futile dreams of revenge, and from the oppressive burden of armaments which slows their development and makes them dependent upon foreign powers." Fulbright saw some encouraging signs that some of the Arab moderates—especially the new Egyptian President Anwar Sadat—were adopting a more realistic policy. Sadat had displayed impressive independence in ordering the expulsion of Soviet military personnel from Egypt, proclaiming as he did so that "Egyptian nationalism and Arab nationalism must stand alone."[139]

For Fulbright, Kissinger's detente policies with the Soviet Union held vital implications for the Middle East, where the senator was concerned that a regional conflict could ignite into a dangerous confrontation between the great powers. However, Fulbright had been concerned about some of Kissinger's statements regarding the Middle East earlier in the Nixon Presidency. In 1970, Nixon and Kissinger had compared the Middle Eastern tinderbox to the explosive situation in the Balkans before World War I; as Kissinger stated, "the situation in the Middle East is roughly analogous, Israel and the Arab states being allied to a super power. . . each of them to some extent not fully under the control of the major country concerned." Kissinger added that World War I came about "as an accident," and similarly the two great powers in the 1970s did not want war over the Middle East. Fulbright acknowledged that Kissinger's bellicose words should not have been taken literally, because it was "designed to scare the Russians." But the senator was not satisfied by that justification, saying that Kissinger's comment reflected a dangerously outmoded way of thinking about international politics, that war was "something fated, controlled by quarrelsome client states if not the iron 'laws' of power policies. Implicit in this outlook is the supposition that the coming of a great war is beyond the control of statesmen—even beyond the control of the Pentagon computers, or of Mr. Kissinger's staff of experts in the White House basement." Fulbright's scholarly analysis was facilitated by the Foreign Relations Committee staff member, Seth Tillman, a scholar who would later teach at Georgetown. Fulbright and Tillman also refuted Kissinger's historical analysis, stating that World War I erupted because "Germany was willing for it to come about and aided and abetted the events which led to the explosion. It was within Germany's power at any time to restrain her Austrian clients, and in so doing, to prevent war." The Germans did not do so because they felt they could win a general European war and it would detract from German pride if they were perceived as shrinking from war. "Left to their own resources," Fulbright and Tillman argued, "the Arabs and Israelis have the power to bring on a local war but not a world war. Only the super powers have that option and—whatever the political usefulness of historical mis-analogies—they had better not forget it."[140]

Fulbright was also critical of the "global policeman" spirit of Kissinger's observations that American interests in the Middle East were based on U.S. allies' dependence on oil from that region: the Japanese obtained 90 percent, and the Western Europeans 75 percent, of their oil from the Middle East. Fulbright asked why the Japanese and Western Europeans could not send their fleets to the region to protect their oil sources themselves.[141] Kissinger's point would gain more validity in future years as the United States itself became more dependent on foreign oil supplies. Yet Kissinger's remark that "American interests" were involved in the question of protecting Japanese and Western European oil routes was an idea symbolic of the Pax Americana: allegedly it was America's burden to preserve the peace throughout the globe.

By 1973, Fulbright's assessment of Kissinger had improved. Kissinger had softened Nixon's refusal—based upon the President's grandiose notions of executive privilege—to let his White House advisers testify before Congress. Kissinger had met "in circumstances we pretended were social but that soon came to resemble a Congressional hearing," first in Fulbright's home, then in a hideaway office in the Senate. Fulbright enjoyed Kissinger's company and found him witty, bright and creative. The senator appreciated the expanded level of communication with Kissinger—although he would have preferred formal hearings—and became aware of Kissinger's understanding of the need for a more balanced American policy in the Middle East.[142]

In the early 1970s, Fulbright made a controversial proposal for peace. First, he argued that a settlement must vindicate the principle stated in Resolution 242 of "the inadmissibility of the acquisition of territory by war." Sadat and King Hussein had both made return of the conquered territories the key to peace. In return for territorial concessions, Israel should be given specific, ironclad guarantees for its security. United Nations forces should be stationed in militarily neutralized zones on both side of the borders at all of the areas critical to Israel's security. Fulbright conceded that Israel had a reasonable security claim to the Golan Heights: "It would be unreasonable to expect the Israelis to withdraw to the Jordan Valley from these highlands from which the Syrians used to fire down on civilian communities—all the more so since the Syrians have refused to accept the Security Council Resolution of 1967." On the other hand, Israel had no justification to a permanent occupation of the entire Syrian territory they held, and he suggested that "a defensible frontier might be drawn along the high ridge line immediately east of the Jordan valley, giving Israel a small, uninhabited but militarily significant strip of previously Syrian territory." As for the West Bank of the Jordan, Fulbright flatly stated that "there is everything to be said for the principle of self-determination."[143]

The senator emphasized the vital importance of remaining sensitive to the real fears of both sides in the conflict: "The Arabs, it must be remembered, are as frightened of the Zionist doctrine of unlimited Jewish immigration leading to a drive for Lebensraum as the Israelis are of an Arab 'holy war' to destroy Israel. Both sides are entitled to explicit guarantees against these deeply rooted fears." Fulbright suggested that this goal could be accomplished by a peace treaty provision that included a more explicit and specific rendition of the section of Resolution 242 that required "termination of all claims or states of belligerency and respect for and acknowledgment of the sovereignty, territorial integrity and political independence of every state in the area." Israel should be entitled to free access through the Suez Canal, the Gulf of Aqaba and the Strait of Tiran.[144]

Fulbright had no specific recommendation for Jerusalem, although he said that some form of international status would seem appropriate for the city. He quoted with approval the American Friends Service Committee's study recommending that Jerusalem "cannot peacefully become the sole possession of one religion or one national state." An even more difficult problem, Fulbright argued, was the refugee problem. He asserted that the Palestinian refugees were entitled to one of two forms of restitution: either repatriation or compensation. Israel ought not to have difficulty meeting the costs of compensating refugees and facilitating their resettlement, "which in any case ought to be accepted as an elementary moral obligation." The Palestinians, in turn, must abandon their futile dreams of destroying the Jewish state, since "Israel has existed as an independent state since 1948, and it would now be as a great an injustice to disrupt that society as it was for the Jews to drive the Arabs from their land in the first place." The Palestinian Arabs would have to accept this bitter reality "if they want an end to futile guerrilla warfare. In any case, the Palestinians are entitled to some form of self-determination on the non-Israeli territory of Palestine." Indispensable to a settlement based on Resolution 242 would be a guarantee of the entire settlement by the United Nations. The Security Council would commit to enforcement of secure and recognized boundaries, neutralized status of border zones, and strict limitations on supply of arms to the Middle East from powers outside the region.[145]

Finally, Fulbright addressed the issue that Israel as well as many other nations had expressed: a lack of confidence in the United Nations. To reassure Israel, the senator advocated a bilateral treaty supplementing the United Nations guarantee, under which the United States would guarantee the territory and independence of Israel within the adjusted borders of 1967. The bilateral treaty between the United States and Israel would not add or detract from the United Nation's multilateral guarantee, which would obligate the United States to defend the boundaries of both Israel and her Arab neighbors. "The supplementary, bilateral arrangement with Israel would obligate the United States to use force if necessary, in accordance with its constitutional processes, to assist Israel against any violation of its 1967 borders, as adjusted, which it could not repel itself, but the agreement would also obligate Israel, firmly and unequivocally, never to violate those borders itself."[146]

Fulbright was roundly condemned by the pro-Israeli forces for allegedly adopting a pro-Arab position. The senator often pointed out the tremendous power wielded by B'nai B'rith, the American-Israel Public Affairs Committee (AIPAC), and other organizations that constituted the "most effective political lobbying group in the United States." Years later, when he was in retirement, Fulbright would recall that the only political contests the Israelis have lost since the 1956 Suez crisis "were over the sale of F-15 fighter planes to Saudi Arabia in 1978 and the sale of AWACs to Saudi Arabia in 1981. The Pentagon was of course involved in the case of the AWACs, and there were also 18 billion dollars of cash involved—which were too persuasive." In a bitter critique of the Israeli lobby that Fulbright wrote in 1989, he complained that "The Israelis and their supporters here—especially the latter—have long taken the position that if you do not do exactly as they wish, you are anti-Israel and anti-Semitic. . . [The Israeli lobby] can elect or defeat nearly any congressman or senator that they wish, with their money and coordinated organizations." (The Israeli lobby was certainly not crucial in Fulbright's defeat in 1974, since he was politically vulnerable for a variety of other reasons). Fulbright's rhetoric may have been overheated, but it was nonetheless true that Israel exerted a powerful political influence upon American politics. In making his proposal for a peace settlement, Fulbright did not pretend that he had worked out all the myriad difficulties of the Middle East labyrinth; to the contrary, he constantly stressed the grave problems afflicting any attempted resolution of the conflict. The Soviets indicated their support of a settlement along the general lines Fulbright had summarized.[147] It was highly unfortunate for American policy in the Middle East that instead of having the merits or flaws of his proposal debated as an attempt to arrive at an evenhanded approach to the Arab-Israeli conflict, the pro-Israeli lobby and its many supporters frequently succeeded in depicting his ideas as suffering from a pro-Arab bias that did not devote sufficient attention to Israel's security needs.

Given his own frustrating experiences regarding the Middle East, Fulbright was sympathetic to the pressures Kissinger faced in dealing with that chaotic, byzantine region. Kissinger later admitted that he knew little of the Middle East when he entered office in 1969. By 1973, however, Kissinger had dealt with a number of Middle East crises and had greatly increased his knowledge of the Arab-Israeli conflict. The dangers in the region, of course, were not confined to Egypt and Israel. In 1970, the Palestinian Liberation Organization (PLO), which Kissinger would describe as having established "almost a state within a state in Jordan," hijacked several aircraft and flew them to Jordan. King Hussein ordered his army to attack the PLO, and the organization's leaders were expelled from Jordan. At that point, Syria invaded Jordan, Israel mobilized, and the entire region appeared on the verge of another war. The United States reinforced its naval armada in the Mediterranean and warned that no outside intervention would be tolerated; the Soviets made clear that they were unwilling to risk a confrontation, and Syria withdrew. The crisis ended, leaving Kissinger with the conviction that the Arab moderates had been strengthened and that the United States should continue to attract realistic, moderate leaders among the Arabs.[148]

A vastly more serious conflict erupted on Yom Kippur, 1973, a few weeks after Kissinger's confirmation as Secretary of State. Egypt attacked Israeli forces on the east bank of the Suez Canal, while the Syrian army simultaneously attacked Israel on the north. The United States and Israel were stunned by the Arab offensive, for their assessments of the situation were so dominated by the belief in overwhelming Israeli superiority that they had discounted all Arab warnings as bluffs. Even more shocking was the military reality that in the early fighting, the Egyptian army succeeded in crossing the canal and establishing a bridgehead on the other side, while the Syrians advanced into part of the Golan area. Soviet weaponry enabled the Arabs to neutralize the Israeli air force, which had devastated Arab forces in the 1967 war. Sadat's objectives in the attack did not become known until much later. The Egyptian leader sought not territorial gain, but to show enough flexibility and strength to alter the positions into which Arabs and Israelis had become frozen; he wished to obliterate the myth of Arab weakness, disunity and ineptitude, as well as the myth of Israeli invincibility. He was seeking psychological and diplomatic objectives, to restore Arab self-respect and increase its diplomatic flexibility in order to open the way for subsequent negotiations. Syria, in contrast, was apparently fighting only in the hopes of gaining territory and inflicting casualties in Israel.[149]

On October 8, 1973, two days after the war began, Fulbright and Kissinger appeared together at the Pacem in Terris conference held in Washington. Kissinger's heightened rapport and communications with the Soviet Union were exceedingly valuable during the Middle East crisis; he was in constant communication with Soviet diplomats throughout the conflict. Fulbright facilitated this communication, as he acted as an intermediary between Kissinger and Anatoly Dobrynin during the latter part of October. The senator defended Kissinger in his informal talks with Dobrynin, assuring the Soviet diplomat that the United States genuinely sought a cease-fire and that Kissinger had not been conspiring with the Israelis to deceive the Soviets and Arabs. In their speeches in Washington on October 8, Fulbright and Kissinger reiterated their support for detente and their repudiation of the hard-line philosophy represented by the Jackson Amendment. Fulbright delivered his familiar, limited approval of Kissinger's balance of power diplomacy, commending it as a tremendous improvement over the rigid ideological anticommunism of his predecessors. Yet, while conceding that Kissinger had demonstrated an impressive ability to conduct effective responses to crises in the Middle East and to maintain the complex balance of power approach, he wondered whether Kissinger's successors would be as brilliant; if not, the traditional power politics could break down into war. The solution must be an advance over traditional Realpolitik and a transition into policies aimed at strengthening the United Nations as a forum for settling international crises. The senator again criticized Kissinger's "bargaining chip" mentality and called for a reduction in America's global involvements and a concentration on reviving the deteriorating U.S. domestic economy. The major thrust of his speech, however, was a vigorous endorsement of detente with the Soviet Union. In Kissinger's speech on October 8, he affirmed that the United States was deeply committed to detente, but warned the Soviets not to take advantage of that commitment to pursue a policy of adventurism during the Middle East crisis: "Our policy with respect to detente is clear: We shall resist aggressive foreign policies. Detente cannot survive irresponsibility in any area, including the Middle East."[150]

While Fulbright's friendship with Dobrynin was useful in easing tensions with the Soviets during the crisis, his high standing in the Arab world enabled him to communicate with President Sadat and King Faisal of Saudi Arabia. King Faisal and Sadat implored Fulbright to travel to the Middle East and help mediate the dispute. Later in October, the Organization of Petroleum Exporting Countries (OPEC) had sharply raised prices, and Saudi Arabia embargoed oil exports to the United States. In November Fulbright urged Faisal to use his influence with the Arab oil powers to relax their use of the oil weapon against the West. Fulbright ultimately responded to the request from Sadat and Faisal to come to the Middle East by sending Seth Tillman, who met with government officials in Riyadh, Cairo, Tel Aviv, and other major cities in the region. Meanwhile, Fulbright met with Arab oil ministers in Washington. The senator publicly advocated a peace plan that would include a rejection of the Nixon administration's request for $2.2 billion in emergency military aid for Israel and the "land-for-peace" arrangement he had been promoting in the early 1970s. Kissinger was in Peking at the time, but he endorsed Fulbright's proposal. Sentiment in the public and in Congress was strongly in favor of the Israelis, however, and the Senate passed the additional aid to Israel by a wide margin.[150a]

The Soviets were pressing Sadat for a cease-fire from almost the beginning of the war. An American airlift to Israel far outstripped Soviet efforts to resupply the Arabs. In a few days, the Israelis counterattacked and drove the Egyptians back across the canal and advanced into Syrian territory toward Damascus. Nonetheless, at war's end, the Arab military forces had fought much more effectively than in any previous war. In many ways, the 1973 war was not a defeat for Egypt: the military campaigns had been carefully planned and executed; Egypt had gained financial and military support from other Arab countries; and the conflict ended in a cease-fire worked out by the superpowers, demonstrating that the United States would not allow Israel to be defeated, but also that both superpowers would not allow Egypt to be overrun. The two great powers held the omnipresent concern of avoiding being drawn into the war after the client states had escalated it. The United States adroitly avoided humiliating Sadat, and facilitated the development of future negotiations and a balance of forces conducive to a settlement.[151]

An additional force leading to the intervention of the great powers was the Arabs' use of what was apparently their strongest weapon—an oil embargo. The Arab oil producers decided to reduce their production as long as Israel remained in Arab lands, and Saudi Arabia imposed a total embargo on exports to the United States. Demand for Middle Eastern oil had been expanding, as the industrial countries' requirements grew faster than their production. By the end of 1973, another critical decision regarding oil was made: OPEC decided to increase oil prices by 300 percent, with Iran and the Arab oil-exporting countries being the prime movers in the decision.[152] In retrospect, Kissinger's concerns about Western dependence on Middle Eastern oil stated years earlier had been correct. This political and economic setting tremendously enhanced the need to reach out to the Arab world moderates, of whom the most prominent was Sadat.

Of the two great powers, Sadat recognized that only the United States possessed the military and political power as well as the flexibility to make progress toward peace. Consequently, in the aftermath of the Yom Kippur War he turned from Moscow to Washington for help in a gradual process toward peace. Sadat had engaged in secret diplomatic contacts with Kissinger and Nixon since the 1972 expulsion of Soviet military personnel, and he had come to regard them as flexible enough to cooperate with the moderate forces in the Arab world. At one point during Kissinger's direct negotiations with Sadat in Egypt during the crisis, Sadat dramatically asked Kissinger to take a personal message to Golda Meir. The message stated: "You must take my word seriously. When I made my initiative in 1971, I meant it. When I threatened war, I meant it. When I talk of peace now, I mean it. We never have had contact before. We now have the services of Dr. Kissinger. Let us use him and talk."

Fulbright, of course, had been advocating a strategy of working with the Arab moderates for many years. Sadat's historic overtures to the West would inaugurate a constructive, if painfully slow process through which limited progress was achieved over the years in ameliorating at least some phases of the Middle Eastern conflict. Some of the components of the Fulbright plan for the Middle East were evident in these negotiations. In 1974, there were interim agreements with Egypt and Syria that initiated a process of Israeli withdrawal in return for Arab security guarantees; in 1975, Israel and Egypt signed a second disengagement agreement. Under the aegis of President Carter in 1979, Egypt and Israel signed a formal peace agreement. Finally, Fulbright would live to see more moderate forces—the philosophical heirs of Ben-Gurion—gain power in Israel just as his protégé, Bill Clinton, attained the Presidency: the result would be the Israeli-Palestinian agreement concluded in September 1993.[153]

The End of the Imperial Presidency

When Kissinger returned from his "shuttle diplomacy" trip to the Middle East to facilitate negotiations in January 1974, he found the President extraordinarily proud that in the midst of domestic scandals that were ravaging his administration, he had presided over the diplomacy orchestrated by Kissinger that prevented the conflict from escalating. In late 1973 Agnew resigned amid charges of accepting kickbacks from contractors and businessmen while he was governor of Maryland. The firing of Watergate investigator Archibald Cox and the resignation of Attorney General Elliot Richardson and his deputy, William Ruckelshaus, took place in a conflict over access to tapes of Nixon's White House conversations; the new Solicitor General, Robert Bork, ultimately removed Cox in the infamous "Saturday Night Massacre." And in early 1974, a grand jury indicted Haldeman, Ehrlichman, Mitchell, Colson, and three others on charges of covering up the 1972 burglary of the Democratic National Committee headquarters by destroying evidence, lying to investigators, buying silence, and offering clemency. Nixon was named an unindicted co-conspirator in the cover-up. Most of the Congressional leaders were so immersed in Watergate and so incensed at Nixon's apparent transgressions that they could not bring themselves to give the administration the praise it deserved for its foreign policy achievements. Yet Kissinger pointedly noted that only one senator gave the President the accolades he had long sought for what he considered his forte—foreign policy—and that senator was, in Kissinger's words, "ironically enough, J. William Fulbright." Administration officials found this surprising; in William Safire's description, Fulbright was a man Nixon had always "cordially despised and distrusted."[154] Fulbright believed that the trauma of Watergate should not be allowed to discredit all the administration's achievements, especially in foreign policy.

Kissinger returned the favor by coming to Little Rock in February 1974 to appear at a press conference that was intended to strengthen Fulbright's chances for reelection. The *Arkansas Gazette* editorial editor, James Powell, was at the conference and recalls Fulbright and Kissinger—both of them at the zenith of their international fame and prestige—demonstrating the cordial, mutually respectful relationship they had come to enjoy. In the end, the conference held little value in Arkansas politics, but it showed Kissinger's appreciation for Fulbright's role in American foreign policy.[155]

Fulbright was ambivalent about Watergate. He regretted the scandal's impact on Nixon's ability to pursue his foreign policy initiatives in detente. Yet, Watergate led to a restoration of a proper constitutional balance between the branches of government after the Cold War era of aggrandized executive power. In July 1974, the legislative and judicial branches issued decisions that sealed the President's fate. The House of Representatives Judiciary Committee voted articles of impeachment against Nixon for obstruction of justice with respect to the Watergate break-in and other activities, willful disobedience of subpoenas issued by the Judiciary Committee, and abuse of power by misusing executive agencies and violating constitutional rights of the citizenry. On July 25, the Supreme Court handed down its decision in *United States v. Nixon*, 418 U.S. 683 (1974), rejecting President Nixon's argument that the Court should quash a *subpoena duces* tecum directing the President to produce certain tapes and documents relating to White House conversations with his advisers. Nixon's counsel made three arguments: first, that while in office the President was immune to judicial process and could be subject only to the explicit constitutional sanction of impeachment; second, that the President had absolute discretion to determine the scope of executive privilege; and third, that even if the President's determination was subject to judicial review, Nixon was correct in this case. In an 8-0 decision (with Nixon's appointee William Rehnquist having recused because of his former association with John Mitchell), the Court upheld U.S. District Judge John J. Sirica's ruling denying the motion to quash the subpoena. *Nixon*, 418 U.S. 683.

Chief Justice Burger's opinion for the Court rejected Nixon's absolute interpretation of executive privilege. Although the Court in *Nixon* acknowledged the existence of executive privilege for the first time (this doctrine is not explicitly mentioned in the Constitution, but the Court found it was constitutionally based to the extent the interest in confidentiality of presidential communications "relates to the effective discharge of a President's powers"), it repudiated the absolute version of the privilege that Fulbright felt had so often been used by the executive in the Cold War to conceal unpleasant realities that might have caused political difficulties for administrations had they become public knowledge. Burger wrote that in the performance of assigned constitutional duties, each branch of the government must initially interpret the Constitution, and that interpretation is due great respect from the other branches. The chief justice rejected the President's counsel's reading of the Constitution "as providing an absolute privilege of confidentiality for all communications. Many decisions of this Court, however, have unequivocally reaffirmed the holding of *Marbury v. Madison* (1803) that it is emphatically the province and duty of the judicial department to say what the law is." *Nixon*, at 685. The Supreme Court ruled that neither the doctrine of separation of powers, nor the need for confidentiality of high-level communications by themselves could "sustain an absolute, unqualified Presidential privilege of immunity from judicial process under all circumstances." The Court could not accept the argument that in the absence of any need to protect military, diplomatic or national security secrets, the interest in confidentiality could be significantly diminished by production of materials for "in camera inspection with all the protection that a district court will be obliged to provide. The impediment that an absolute, unqualified privilege would place in the way of the primary constitutional duty of the Judicial Branch to do justice in criminal prosecutions would plainly conflict with the function of the Courts under Article III." The Court stressed that Nixon was basing his argument on "no more than a generalized claim of the public interest in confidentiality of nonmilitary and nondiplomatic discussions." *Id.* In concluding that the needs of the judicial process may outweigh presidential privilege, the Court stressed that "The very integrity of the judicial system and public confidence in the system depend on full disclosure of all the facts, within the framework of the rules of evidence. To ensure that justice is done, it is imperative to the function of courts that compulsory process be available for the production of evidence needed either by the prosecution or by the defense." *Id.* at 709.

The opinion in *Nixon* was confined to the factual and procedural setting of the case, and Burger acknowledged that the interest in preserving confidentiality "is weighty indeed and entitled to great respect," but that interest would not be vitiated by disclosure of a limited number of conversations "preliminarily shown to have some bearing on the pending criminal cases." The Court's conclusion followed: "When the ground for asserting privilege as to subpoenaed materials sought for use in a criminal trial is based only on the generalized interest of confidentiality, it cannot prevail over the fundamental demands of due process of law in the fair administration of criminal justice." *Id.* at 713..

After the justices analyzed the case in *United States v. Nixon*, the issue in their deliberations became not whether the President would lose—the justices had no doubt of that question—but upon what terms he would lose it. A question that was shared by many thoughtful leaders in both the judicial and legislative branches in Washington focused on whether the pendulum could swing too far in a direction against the executive branch in an understandable reaction against the excesses of the Cold War, Vietnam and Watergate era Presidency. In the Supreme Court, Justice Lewis Powell had shocked many conservatives by writing the famous wiretapping opinion in *United States v. United States District Court*, rejecting the Nixon administration's position on that question; and now Powell was stunned by the revelation that White House officials were involved in felonies. Yet Powell was careful to admonish his colleagues on the Court in a pre-conference memorandum that "We decide and write not just as to Nixon and Watergate, but for the long term."[156] Although Powell was much more conservative than Fulbright on many issues, the two men shared a general concern by 1973 that the revulsion against the excesses of Watergate must not go too far in creating problems for future Presidents who might be hounded by future McCarthyites in Congress. Powell conceded the possibility that any President could be involved personally in criminal conduct or the deliberate concealment of such conduct by administration officials, and in that case it would be unthinkable to "allow the President himself to be the sole judge of what, if anything, to disclose to an investigating grand jury." Yet the President should not be vulnerable to any prosecutor or Congressional committee with the subpoena power. The experience of Joe McCarthy's demagogy in the 1950s was more than enough to remind experienced leaders in Washington that the Court should not set a precedent that would play into the hands of a latter-day McCarthy. The Court ruled that the President had to cooperate with grand jury investigations when a court ordered it, but as Professor John Calvin Jeffries of the University of Virginia Law School contended, the Court's recognition of executive privilege actually gave a firm position to future Presidents, who have argued that they have no legal obligation to comply with every Congressional subpoena. Some critics of the Nixon decision have argued it went too far in strengthening the Presidency in this respect. Jeffries has argued, to the contrary, that the frequent conflicts between the President and Congress—aside from the specifics involved in the Nixon tapes case, an incredible set of facts unlikely to be repeated often (at least, everyone hopes so)—were left by the Court to the incessant, kaleidoscopic "political tug of war between the President and Congress—a conflict in which each side has both the means to defend its interests and the need to compromise. This political give-and-take, though untidy and frustrating, is in the long run far more tolerable than a rule that routinely allows Congress to go to court to gain the upper hand in its perpetual battles with executive authority."[157]

However one regards the Court's opinion as a precedent for the future, it was clear the decision—combined with the vote from the House Judiciary Committee regarding impeachment—signified a historic victory for the rule of law. As Jeffries aptly wrote, Powell was justifiably proud of the Nixon decision: "in drawing attention to the real and legitimate pride that every American can feel in a nation whose head of state and commander-in-chief resigns his office rather than defy a court order. That, in Powell's view, was the real triumph of the Nixon tapes case." *Id.*, 397. In a hospital bed at Georgetown University, the former chief justice of the Supreme Court was overjoyed when Justice Brennan came to visit him and told him that the justices had held their conference on the case earlier that day and unanimously decided against the President's claim that he could refuse to turn over crucial tapes to the District Court. Just a few hours before his death, Earl Warren exclaimed to

Justice Brennan, "Thank God! Thank God! Thank God! If you don't do it this way, Bill, it's the end of the country as we know it."[158]

Over the decades, Fulbright had witnessed abuses of power from both branches of government. By the late Nixon administration, the Arkansan was becoming increasingly concerned that the momentum against the executive might become excessive. As the Foreign Relations Committee concluded shortly after the end of the Cambodian bombing and during the controversial hearings over Kissinger's appointment as Secretary of State:

> It would be naive to assume that the Executive and Legislative branches will always agree. But, if the issues are debated openly and clearly, it should be possible to avoid the public confusion, mistrust and alienation which have developed during the last decade.
>
> Each of the branches has its respective powers and responsibilities. Some conflict between the two is inevitable and may, on occasion, serve the national interest. From time to time in recent years each of the branches may have become overly assertive of its own powers but it is clear that the American constitutional system works best when each branch has a clear sense of the limits of its authority and of the rights of the other. We hope that this balance can be restored, for neither branch is all-wise or all-powerful. [159]

The Nixon decision and the House Judiciary Committee's vote for articles of impeachment were the final actions ending an era of executive dominance. While Fulbright commended the restoration in the constitutional balance that he had done so much to promote over the years, he also continued his struggle to support detente even in the midst of Nixon's downfall. Shortly after Fulbright's defeat in the May primary election (which will be discussed in later chapters), the senator planned hearings featuring Kissinger and an impressive gallery of the nation's leading diplomatic experts—James Schlesinger, Henry Jackson, George Kennan, Averell Harriman—in an effort to promote a thoughtful public debate concerning detente. Kissinger was fully prepared to assist the Foreign Relations Committee, and he was scheduled to testify on August 9, 1974—which ironically, turned out to be the day Nixon resigned. On August 5, Nixon released transcripts of conversations with Haldeman in 1972 revealing that he had used the CIA to stall an FBI investigation of Watergate.[160] Understandably, Kissinger became so immersed in the end of the Watergate debacle that he was unable to testify on August 9, and although later hearings were held, the ambitious design to foster a public debate that would shed fierce light upon the arguments of the Jackson forces as well as the champions of detente never materialized.

On August 9, President Nixon delivered his resignation to Secretary of State Kissinger. On the day Nixon resigned, Fulbright took the floor of the Senate to deliver a compassionate appeal to America to end the trauma and bitterness of Vietnam and Watergate. Each side in the debates, he said, should adopt a spirit of forgiveness for the human failings of the other. Therefore, he proposed a simultaneous pardon for President Nixon and an amnesty for the draft resisters. Fulbright had experienced personal suffering—as had most Americans—through the divisive years of the 1960s and early 1970s. He had witnessed the great promise of the Johnson Presidency collapse into the abyss of Vietnam, and he had seen

Watergate explode into the greatest domestic political scandal in American history. Lee Williams would recall how Fulbright became depressed and the lines deepened in his face as he fought against the war day after day, year after year. In his August 9 speech, Fulbright praised his old adversary for Nixon's improvement of relations with Russia and China, as well as his diplomacy in the Middle East. Nixon had grasped and acted upon "the preeminent necessity of the postwar era," which the President had eloquently described: "In the nuclear age our first responsibility must be the prevention of the war that could destroy all societies. We must never lose sight of this fundamental truth of modern international life." In Fulbright's view, Nixon's detente policies had implemented that fundamental truth, and "Mr. Nixon has earned our gratitude and approbation." Shortly thereafter, President Gerald Ford pardoned Nixon—in an action that was bitterly controversial—and outlined plans for a limited amnesty program for those who had resisted the Vietnam draft.[161]

In one sense, Fulbright's August 9 Senate address embodied an admirable spirit of magnanimity toward his former opponent, and surely the recriminations that flowed from that period would hound the nation for decades to come. Yet, in some of Fulbright's statements, he perhaps displayed a tendency to be too lenient on a President who had defied the law. In a speech in December to the National Press Club in which he complained of the media's tendency to sensationalize scandals and play up conflicts of personalities to the exclusion of thoughtful reporting on the substance of vital issues, Fulbright stated that "I am not convinced, for example, that Watergate was as significant for the national interest as Mr. Nixon's extraordinary innovations in foreign policy."[162] This statement, considered together with the recommendation of a pardon for Nixon and his earlier suggestion that perhaps a censure of Nixon would be sufficient (as it had been for Joe McCarthy), indicate that to some extent, Fulbright had allowed his appreciation for the Kissinger-Nixon detente to soften his criticism of Nixon on Watergate. While a trial of the former President would have been controversial, Nixon's flagrant violations of the principle of the rule of law and not of men were so severe that he deserved to stand trial. Nonetheless, Fulbright's melancholy over the state of the nation's affairs in 1974 and his plea for a spirit of forgiveness were serious arguments, and serious observers of American public affairs would develop opposing views in future years on both sides of the debate as to whether Nixon should have been pardoned.

In assessing Fulbright's overall performance regarding southeast Asian policy during the Nixon years, it is clear that on the whole he continued his courageous and historic dissent that began in the Johnson administration. Again, however, some critics have argued that Fulbright occasionally allowed his support for Kissinger to weaken his opposition to the war.[163] These critics cite Fulbright's lackluster support for the Church-Case Amendment at one juncture late in the Nixon administration; at the time, Brezhnev was holding a summit meeting with Nixon in Washington. Fulbright should have been more supportive of his anti-war colleagues on this occasion, and perhaps one or two other occasions when he could have been more active in supporting the McGovern-Hatfield Amendment. However, it should also be recognized that Fulbright was aware of the need to allow other senators to adopt a prominent role among the anti-war forces so as to avoid the impression that the dissenters were only a faction led by the Foreign Relations Committee; as Fulbright phrased it, he did not wish to "play the same records over and over again." Moreover, after having suffered so many defeats for so many years concerning Vietnam, he sought to take actions and

pursue strategies that would be effective in ending the war. He had appeared on many televised news programs and delivered countless speeches against the war by the late Nixon
years, so that his concern about "playing the same records over and over again" is understandable. Yet, the most important conclusion to draw from Fulbright's record in the Nixon
years should focus on the central reality that Fulbright *did* valiantly oppose the Vietnam War
in the vast majority of issues and votes that took place. He did have a few temporary lapses—such as with the Church-Case Amendment—but those should not obscure his fundamental record of forceful dissent.

Fulbright's political career was at an end. President Ford and Secretary Kissinger offered
him the post of U.S. Ambassador to Great Britain, but he turned it down. His main consideration was Betty Fulbright's fragile health. In any event, he certainly had reason to be weary
of public life.

In his valedictory address to the Senate on December 19, Fulbright recalled that his early
career was devoted to support for expanded international education and an international
peacekeeping organization, although the results of the latter had been disappointing. His later
career had been directed to dissent against the excesses of Vietnam and the Cold War. His
positions were not based upon pacifism, he said, but upon the convictions of a rationalist who
deplored "the vanity and emotionalism which leads a nation to fight unnecessarily, or to arm
to the teeth far beyond the necessities of defense or deterrence, at a colossal and debilitating
cost, with the overkill serving no purpose but prestige." His views were seldom solicited, "but
I crashed the party and offered them anyway—for better or worse. . . . If I am remembered, I
suppose it will be as a dissenter. That was not what I had in mind, but when things go contrary to your highest hopes and strongest convictions, there is nothing you can do except dissent or drop out."[164]

While Fulbright had worked out a constructive relationship with Kissinger during the
late Nixon period, he continued to battle administration officials who defended continuing
aid requests for South Vietnam in terms that did not differ significantly from justifications
that Johnson administration officials had given a decade earlier. With the withdrawal of the
American military intervention, southeast Asia had at last been relegated to a position of
lesser importance in the administration's policies. Yet, in June 1974, Secretary of Defense
James Schlesinger advocated continuing aid, citing America's "moral commitment" and the
goal of preserving a "free choice" for the people of South Vietnam and Cambodia. Fulbright
was perplexed by Schlesinger's reference to America's alleged "moral commitment": was the
United States committed because it "made a great mistake in intervening and brought
destruction on a country?" He contended that "there may be a moral commitment when it
is settled to help some of the restoration of the basic infrastructure that we destroyed, but I
do not see by any stretch of the imagination that we have a commitment just to maintain
Mr. Thieu and this particular type of government. It is obviously not a government of free
choice."[165]

Again, in July, Graham Martin, Ambassador to South Vietnam, supported a large funding request for Thieu. Kissinger himself advocated a figure of $1.5 billion. Fulbright told
Ambassador Martin that if the Congress accepted the administration's position, American
involvement in South Vietnam would be endless. In the end, Congress approved in
September a drastically reduced aid program of $700 million. Fulbright's consternation at

the frozen Cold Warrior mentality of Martin—a man whose nomination he had opposed—was understandable. To the bitter end, Martin remained stubborn in his backing for Thieu, long after it was clear that Thieu had no real support in South Vietnam. Martin blocked several coup attempts and encouraged Thieu's refusal to resign. Moreover, out of a misguided fear of spreading panic, Martin postponed implementation of evacuation plans until the last minute. When the final, inevitable North Vietnamese offensive crushed the last South Vietnamese resistance in 1975, the United States managed to evacuate its own people and 150,000 Vietnamese, but the operation was chaotic. Martin himself escaped from the U.S. Embassy roof, but tens of thousands of Vietnamese on the U.S. payroll could not be saved, along with billions of dollars in American equipment and secret files abandoned in the last rush for the helicopters. Many South Vietnamese who wished to leave could not do so because of the inadequacy of transport.[166] In the sad spectacle in the spring of 1975, American Marines used rifle butts to prevent desperate Vietnamese from blocking escape routes, and some South Vietnamese fired on the departing Americans; the final debacle symbolized the disastrous lost crusade that America had begun and maintained with such grand hubris for a quarter of a century.

By 1973, Fulbright was in the unfamiliar position of enjoying the support of the majority in Congress and in public opinion. After many years of suffering overwhelming defeats in his efforts to end the U.S. military involvement in southeast Asia, Fulbright and his allies had achieved a momentous victory of their own in the 63-19 Senate vote to cut off funds for the Cambodian bombing. Although the senator would have greatly preferred that the air war had ended much earlier, he was nevertheless encouraged that the military crusade in Indochina was at last coming to an end. After a seemingly endless era of public allegiance to presidential domination of foreign policy, opinion polls and other measures of the public's views revealed widespread support throughout the nation for Fulbright and the Congressional critics of Nixon's southeast Asian policies. Thus, in 1973, in the senator's eighth year of public opposition to the war, the mainstream of America had finally rejoined Fulbright.

Book Five:

FULBRIGHT, CIVIL RIGHTS, AND THE SUPREME COURT, 1960S-1974

FULBRIGHT, CIVIL RIGHTS AND THE SUPREME COURT, 1960s-1974

I. Introduction

In the latter part of his 30-year career in the United States Senate, Fulbright faced the challenge of responding to a series of Supreme Court nominations that posed explosive political problems for him, especially in the realm of civil rights. Throughout his career until the late 1960s, Fulbright had pursued a policy of protecting his flank against an attack from the right wing by voting in favor of the segregationist position on civil rights issues. The senator made occasional statements stressing that the *Brown* decision, the Civil Rights Act of 1964 and the Voting Rights Act of 1965 were the "law of the land" and would have to be obeyed, but he avoided opposition to Governor Orval Faubus' racist demagogy and failed, as we have noted, to exert any leadership in calling for moderation in race relations. He was vulnerable politically to charges that he was too "liberal" and excessively concerned with national and international affairs to the alleged detriment of his constituents' local concerns. In the Arkansas of the 1950s and early 1960s, he believed it would have been political suicide to assume the additional burden of adopting a controversial leadership position on civil rights. As he said, he had "no desire for martyrdom."[1]

Given Fulbright's policy of avoiding civil rights controversies, the nominations of Thurgood Marshall, G. Harrold Carswell and William Rehnquist created severe political problems for him. Most of the debate on these nominations in Arkansas focused on civil rights, despite the presence of other important issues such as judicial ability or, in Rehnquist's case, the nominee's role as an apologist for the Vietnam War. Lee Williams recalled that the nominations of the later era ignited a remarkable controversy among the constituents who had displayed indifference to Court appointments over the first 25 years of Fulbright's career.[2]

Many Arkansans were disturbed by the social and political turbulence of the late 1960s, and blamed this unrest on what they regarded as the excessively liberal civil rights and criminal law decisions of the Warren Court and the Johnson administration's domestic reforms. Fulbright's surprising votes on the Marshall, Carswell and Rehnquist nominations and the 1970 extension of the Voting Rights Act antagonized many conservatives who had previously provided vital political support. Fulbright had never been an admirer of the Warren Court, at the time or even in his 1989 book, *The Price of Empire*. Writing in 1989 with no political pressures to consider, Fulbright's arguments did not differ from what he had said during the Nixon era. The senator commended equal access to public accommodations and voting rights and acknowledged that "the South has profited from the successes of the civil rights movement." Yet he persisted in arguing that a more "gradualist" approach toward integration that would have fomented less segregationist resistance, combined with much greater public investments in federal aid to education and anti-poverty programs, might have been an effective solution to the dilemma of racial injustice.[3] Critics argued that Fulbright's gradualist approach was so glacially slow as to prevent any meaningful progress toward integration. In contrast, his argument was on much more viable ground where he advocated a re-assessment of national priorities toward greater emphasis on education and social spending to correct the economic inequalities between the races.[4] The issue in Fulbright's responses to the nominations was not whether he would embrace a liberal position, since his "gradualist" approach on integration obviously differed from those of the Arkansas civil rights leader Wiley Branton, the *Arkansas Gazette* editors and other racial progressives in the state; the relevant issue would focus on whether Fulbright would oppose extremism despite a deluge of political pressure in favor of a segregationist position. When faced with this choice earlier in his career, the extremist pressure prevailed.

Faubus' political domination of the state persisted from his landslide re-election in 1958 until the mid-1960s, when he faced a substantial challenge from the progressive Republican, Winthrop Rockefeller. The 1964 presidential election in Arkansas was the harbinger of a more moderate era in the state's politics, as Fulbright campaigned aggressively for President Johnson and helped win the state for the national Democratic ticket. Fulbright's vote against the Civil Rights Act of 1964 strengthened his political credentials as he campaigned for Johnson that year, telling his constituents that the Civil Rights Act controversy had been settled, "so let's move on to other things." With Faubus' decision not to run in 1966 and Rockefeller's subsequent election that year, followed by Thurgood Marshall's nomination to the Supreme Court in 1967, Fulbright would face his first major civil rights-related vote in the post-Faubus era of Arkansas politics. As a Justice Department attorney in the New Deal, a former law professor and veteran lawmaker, he knew that Supreme Court nominations exert a powerful influence upon the course of events decades into the future.[5]

II. FULBRIGHT, THE SUPREME COURT AND THE POLITICS OF REACTION, 1967-69

In the summer of 1967, the Marshall nomination generated substantial opposition from the right wing. Arkansas conservatives looked to the leadership of the state's senior senator, John McClellan, a Judiciary Committee member who had opposed Marshall's nomination as Solicitor General in 1965 and criticized him in 1967 as a "constitutional iconoclast" who would worsen the "lopsided division of the Court in favor of ultraliberal activists."[6] In the opinions of many Arkansas conservatives, Marshall was associated with a "permissiveness" that had led to what they regarded as radical school desegregation decisions and lenient treatment of criminal defendants. As one constituent from southern Arkansas wrote to Fulbright, "Since he is a former chief counsel of the NAACP, I consider him one of the originators and activists of the crime wave that now plagues America. His utter contempt and hatred of white Southerners should disqualify him from sitting on any suit involving white Southerners."[7] Another constituent complained that "I cannot believe that after spending his life fighting for the cause of the Negro he could possibly be fair and impartial in any related cases."[8]

Fulbright initially responded to Marshall's critics in a bland form letter thanking them for their views and indicating he planned to study the nomination. Most of the criticisms consisted of vague, rambling attacks on Marshall and the Court that did not reveal any particular knowledge of Marshall's record. While most of the constituent responses concerning the nomination were negative, the senator also heard from Marshall's supporters. The *Arkansas Gazette* editorialized that Marshall was a highly qualified nominee who would eventually be confirmed despite the resistance of Chairman James Eastland of the Judiciary Committee (Fulbright was not a member of Judiciary.) In the *Gazette's* view, "The nation will have its first Negro member of the Supreme Court. All, really, that we need to say is, 'It's about time.'"[9] The *Pine Bluff Commercial* similarly commended the President's statement that "race no longer serves as a bar to the exercise of experience and skill."[10]

Fulbright attached substantial importance to the analysis of Marshall's record given to him by Wiley Branton, who had worked with Marshall on Arkansas desegregation cases in the 1950s.[11] The senator had avoided voting on President Kennedy's appointment of Marshall to the Second Circuit Court of Appeals, at a time when Eastland, McClellan and other Southerners had engaged in race-baiting attacks on the nominee and held up the confirmation for a year. Marshall, who graduated first in his class from Howard Law School, won the approval of the American Bar Association, which rated him "highly acceptable from the viewpoint of professional qualifications."[12] Branton lauded Marshall's 23 years of service for the NAACP, in which he won 29 of 32 cases he argued before the Supreme Court, including *Brown*. As a federal circuit judge from 1962 to 1965, Marshall had written more than 100 opinions, with none of his majority opinions being reversed and some of his dissenting opinions becoming law. Fulbright replied in late June that he appreciated receiving the views of someone who had been associated with the nominee, and he was inclined to support Marshall.[13]

After waiting to discover if further scrutiny of Marshall's record led to any revelations of unfitness to serve on the Court, Fulbright voted for Marshall, who was confirmed by 69-11 on August 30.[14] Staunchly conservative constituents criticized his vote for "further packing" of the Court with liberals.[15] The senator responded that "I regret that my vote to confirm Mr. Justice Marshall was not in line with your thinking, but to paraphrase a familiar statement of Abraham Lincoln, I have learned that I can never please all of the people all of the time."[16] Fulbright informed his critics that the Judiciary Committee had approved the nominee by a vote of 11 to 4, the great majority of the Senate approved, and he had found no flaws in Marshall's record. "I do not believe it would be beneficial to the people of Arkansas," he concluded, "for me to disapprove the appointment because of the nominee's race."[17]

Fulbright's matter-of-fact justifications proved effective in helping to reduce the political damage from his vote in Arkansas. The growing sentiment for abandoning the racist excesses of the Faubus era contributed to making his vote more palatable in the state. The Marshall vote did not provoke the torrent of controversy that President Nixon's "Southern strategy" appointments would incite in 1969-70. Fulbright succeeded in handling the criticism through a series of succinct statements and never had to delve in detail into the substance of Marshall's positions on desegregation. One of the basic reasons for the relatively lower profile of the Marshall debate centered on the "imperial Presidency" notion that the President virtually wielded a royal prerogative in making Court appointments. The Senate must not tamper with that prerogative, according to the prevailing orthodoxy, unless the nominee was either flagrantly unethical or incompetent. At the time, the President was so vindictive over their break concerning southeast Asian policy that there was no consideration of substantially improving relations with the White House through a vote for Marshall.[18]

Fulbright never based his vote on any theory of an alleged need to stand behind the President in order to promote national harmony, but in this case he inadvertently benefited from his constituents' deeply ingrained conviction that it was patriotic and proper to support the President. Ironically, Fulbright led the opposition to the mystique of the imperial Presidency and by 1967 was beginning to erode the myth that the Congress must blindly follow the leadership of the White House, particularly in foreign policy. This expansive notion of executive prerogative would bring considerable grief to Fulbright in the Carswell and Rehnquist nominations, but in the Marshall case it helped blunt the effect of the right wing attack on his vote.[19]

Fulbright responded to the Marshall nomination on relatively simple grounds: a strong record and the need to reject racial bias in appointments. Yet the Marshall nomination was one in a series of historic episodes that raised deeper issues forcing Fulbright to reflect seriously about the dilemma of racial inequality in America, and to give those reflections public expression for the first time in his career. The senator was deeply troubled by riots in Detroit and other cities in mid-1967, poverty in the inner cities, and the administration's declining commitment to invest in the Great Society reforms while continuing to pour billions of dollars into the war. Constituent attacks on Marshall exemplified a burgeoning attitude among many Arkansans blaming the Court's alleged "ultraliberal permissiveness" for racial unrest and violence.[20] This reaction would culminate in the electoral strength in 1968 of George Wallace and Nixon, who may have differed in style and rhetoric but both stressed opposition to the Court's desegregation decisions, the need for a "law and order" crackdown on dissenters, and a pledge to appoint conservatives to the Court. Wallace carried Arkansas with a plurality of 39 percent, and Nixon edged Vice President Humphrey in the previously solid Democratic state, 31 to 30 percent.[21]

Fulbright differed from the majority of his constituents in his view of the riots and dissent. The senator saw the basic cause of the unrest in the failure to persist in making investments of time, funds and energy for the domestic reforms that were inaugurated with so much promise in 1964-65, combined with what he believed was the reactionary impact of the war on the people's attitudes and hopes toward reform. Fulbright's speeches in mid-1967 were unprecedented in his career in showing pronounced concern for racial inequality.[22]

In Fulbright's widely publicized address to the ABA in August entitled "The Price of Empire," he lamented that proportionally twice as many blacks as whites were engaged in combat in Vietnam by early 1967 and twice as many blacks died in action (20.6 percent) in proportion to their numbers in the population.[23] "We are truly fighting a two-front war and doing badly in both . . . Congress has been all too willing to provide unlimited sums for the military and not very reluctant at all to offset these costs to a small degree by cutting away funds for the poverty program and urban renewal, for rent supplements for the poor and even for a program to help protect slum children from being bitten by rats." Twenty million dollars a year—about one percent of the war's monthly cost—to eliminate rats in the ghettoes exemplified the kinds of investments Fulbright advocated, not as a panacea that would eliminate racial unrest, but "it would suggest that somebody cared. The discrepancy of attitudes tells at least as much about our national values as the discrepancy of dollars."[24]

The dilemma of racial inequality, Fulbright argued, was primarily caused by a lack of educational and economic opportunities, and thus substantial funds needed to be devoted to federal aid to education, anti-poverty programs, and other public investments that would be required to attack the economic plight of blacks; but these were not investments the prosperous classes were prepared to undertake, at least not for the long-term commitment that would be required to eradicate problems created by centuries of discrimination. One of the greatest tragedies of the Vietnam War, in "The Price of Empire" analysis, was that the political and financial resources that might have been channeled into the promising beginnings of the Great Society program of domestic reforms were being devoured by the war. Although the war had magnified what Fulbright regarded as the discrepancy in national priorities, the imbalance in favor of military spending during the Cold War had afflicted America for a quarter of a century: "At home—largely because of the neglect resulting from 25 years of preoccupation with foreign involvements—our cities are exploding in violent protest against generations of social injustice." Since 1946 total expenditures in the U.S.

budget were $1,578 billion, and $904 billion was devoted to the military. In contrast, less than $96 billion was spent on education, health, and community development programs.[25]

The senator stressed that the damage to domestic policy was not strictly financial; not only did the war divert human and material resources and "foster the conviction on the part of slum Negroes that their country is indifferent to their plight: in addition the war feeds the idea of violence as a way of solving problems." Why should not "riots and snipers' bullets bring the white man to an awareness of the Negro's plight" when peaceful programs for jobs and education had become more rhetoric than reality?[26] In the bleak atmosphere of interventionism abroad and violence and reaction at home, Fulbright did not find the emergence of radicalism among youth surprising. His tolerant attitude toward even those dissenters who held radical views with which he disagreed provided a stark contrast to Nixon's attacks on student dissenters, as symbolized by his famous diatribe in 1970 that "you see these bums, you know, blowing up the campuses."[27]

"The Price of Empire" sounded dissonant for many Americans, who were accustomed to hearing politicians regale them with all-encompassing solutions to military conflicts. In C. Vann Woodward's view of the anti-war dissent, "Senator J. William Fulbright, who harbors a keen awareness of the incongruity between national myth and national policies, has observed that 'a nation whose modern history has been an almost uninterrupted chronicle of success. . . should be so sure of its own power as to be capable of magnanimity.'" Anyone entertaining a solution for a war other than a military triumph, Woodward argued,

> is clearly out of tune with the chorus of the American Way . . . . In the American past, and in the predominant mind of the present as well, all wars end in victory and all problems have solutions. Both victory and solution might require some patience—but not very much. The idea of admitting defeat and the prospect of living patiently with an unsolved social problem, are, to borrow Senator Fulbright's expression, 'unthinkable thoughts' for most Americans.[28]

Woodward (who was addressing Fulbright's antiwar stance, of course, not his votes against civil rights bills) was accurate to stress the dissonance of Fulbright's anti-war views with the attitudes of many Americans; in the 1968 election, constituents tolerated his dissent on the war, but became increasingly impatient and restive during the Nixon years as Fulbright incessantly drove home his depressing message on the war's devastation of the nation's domestic life and the illusory search for "total victory."[29]

With the Johnson administration's characteristic tendency to make two diametrically opposed arguments during the same period without acknowledging any inconsistency, Johnson usually assured the public that the country could indeed afford both "guns and butter." But on one occasion, the President candidly acknowledged that "Because of Vietnam, we cannot do all that we might have done, or all that we should."[30] Although Fulbright differed substantially in political strategy, philosophy and other respects from Martin Luther King, Jr., his emphasis upon the inseparability of domestic and foreign policy and the war's onslaught on reform were similar to King's lament that "The Great Society has been shot down on the battlefields of Vietnam."[31] King had earlier praised the Arkansan's antiwar stance: "Yours is one voice crying in the wilderness that may ultimately awaken our people to the international facts of life."[32]

Fulbright's constant emphasis on his anti-war themes led many political observers in Arkansas to think that he would be vulnerable in the 1968 election. His anti-war positions had been controversial since late 1965, and the controversy escalated when he connected the antiwar stance to the issues of budgetary priorities and racial unrest. However, by communicating in a forthright, aggressive manner, he was able to gain support from some of the Arkansas electorate and blunt the criticism of the right in 1968. The antiwar movement was gaining strength in late 1967 and early 1968. Faubus had publicly speculated about running against either Governor Rockefeller or Fulbright, and his decision not to run was critical in the outcome of the election. In early 1967, Faubus stated that it was "mostly likely"that he would run against Fulbright, adding ominously that "I agree with Governor George Romney of Michigan when he said that Fulbright is aiding the enemy by his comments." Yet, as in 1961, Fulbright toured the state in the fall of 1967, and impressed many constituents with his courage and determination in standing up to the President on issues in which he deeply believed. Even some constituents who disagreed with his positions admired his integrity and courage. As Governor Rockefeller explained it, "The folks here in Arkansas are proud of our boy [Fulbright] who stands up and takes a position." Once again, Fulbright lined up support from Witt Stephens, Jack Pickens and other major sources of campaign funding. In explaining the benefits of Fulbright's seniority and clout in Congress for Arkansas, he could cite the massive $1.2 billion Arkansas River Navigation Project that he and the other members of the powerful Arkansas Congressional delegation had secured. Benefactors all along the Arkansas River Valley promised to hold a series of events in 1968 to express appreciation for Fulbright's work on the river project. Moreover, former Governor McMath, a hawk on Vietnam and a racial progressive, also considered running against Fulbright, but decided against it after President Johnson announced he would not run in the aftermath of the Tet offensive and McCarthy's unexpectedly strong showing in the New Hampshire primary. McMath said his candidacy for the Senate would no longer be viable with Johnson out of the race "and the Democratic front-runner a peace candidate like Senator Kennedy."[33]

Faubus and the extreme segregationist, Jim Johnson, failed to weaken Fulbright politically on the civil rights front, as he cited his votes against the earlier civil rights legislation and the 1968 Fair Housing Act. The latter act prohibited racial discrimination in the sale or rental of housing, but also included a provision to placate conservatives by making incitement to riot a serious federal offense.[33] In Fulbright's correspondence, he assured constituents in vague terms that he shared "your concern about the Supreme Court." Fulbright cultivated a network of moderately conservative supporters, the most important of whom was Little Rock banking tycoon Witt Stephens, one of the most influential king-makers in Arkansas' political history. Stephens was a long-time supporter of both Faubus and Fulbright. The multi-millionaire investment banker disliked the image of racial strife the Faubus era had inflicted on the state, and he felt it damaged the business climate and the quality of the schools. The idea of Faubus representing the state in Washington hardly furthered those goals, and Stephens took pride in Fulbright's prestige and candor as Foreign Relations Committee chairman, even if he often disagreed with him. As long as Fulbright did not adopt a liberal attitude toward the Warren Court's "activism," Stephens was willing to tolerate his controversial statements on the war. Stephens' support for Fulbright was highly significant because his views typified those of many businessmen in 1968, and Stephens was the single most influential member of the Arkansas business community. Stephens would always remain a Fulbright supporter because of personal loyalty and faithfulness, but when Fulbright's controversial positions on the Court nominations were added to his persistent anti-war stance, most of the moderately conservative bankers, lawyers and businessmen in the state left the senator, and the Fulbright coalition began to disintegrate.[34]

Fulbright was helped in the campaign by the large number of enemies Jim Johnson had made over the years. The relationship between Faubus and his former opponent for the gubernatorial race in 1956 was strained, and Faubus refused to support Johnson. The head of the state's AFL-CIO, J. Bill Becker, was so disgusted with "Justice Jim" that he engineered his labor organization's endorsement of Fulbright, despite the fact that Fulbright had usually voted against the wishes of the AFL-CIO. Blacks had traditionally been disillusioned by Fulbright's weak civil rights record, but Johnson was anathema for Arkansas blacks. Fulbright hired a black civil rights activist, Ben Grinage, to coordinate his campaign among blacks. Moreover, by 1968, Fulbright's staunch support of the Great Society antipoverty programs and his vote for Thurgood Marshall's elevation to the Supreme Court made it easier for blacks to support Fulbright, especially when the alternative was the notorious racist, Johnson. As always, Fulbright cultivated his network of connections with the east Arkansas oligarchy.[34a]

"Justice Jim" Johnson and two obscure businessmen opposed Fulbright in the 1968 primary, and Johnson condemned the senator as the "pinup boy from Hanoi."[35] Johnson represented the extreme right of Arkansas politics and had accused Faubus of being too weak in defending segregation in an unsuccessful campaign against the governor in 1956. A former Arkansas Supreme Court justice, Johnson was a talented orator who had won the Democratic nomination for governor in 1966 and was narrowly defeated by Rockefeller in the general election, with the black vote making the difference. "Justice Jim," who in 1968 became Wallace's chief lieutenant in the state, launched an endless succession of tirades against the senator, ranting that "Fulbright and the liberal, left-wing political elements and groups such as the ADA are . . . eroding constitutional guarantees, destroying Americans' rights to law and order, to control schools and local institutions, to reasonably restrict premiums paid to mothers of illegitimate children, and even to say a simple prayer in school." Johnson gained only limited political mileage out of these charges or the Marshall nomination vote. Fulbright's only answer was to remark, "I don't respond to trash and hogwash." Most Arkansans had become weary of Johnson's brand of strident rhetoric by 1968, and this proved crucial. Fulbright won, although with only 53 percent.[36]

In weaving his way through the labyrinth of Arkansas politics in the late 1960s, Fulbright had to make judgments about several unpredictable political factions. The factions, based on election returns, could be roughly estimated: white progressives and blacks made up roughly 25 percent, the right wing roughly 35 percent, and the crucial middle ground was held by the most unpredictable group of roughly 40 percent. The middle-of-the-road faction tended to be moderately conservative, but could be swayed either way by an effective message and candidate. The peculiarity of the state's voters was the subject of considerable bewilderment among political analysts, especially after the 1968 election results, when Fulbright won the Senate, the progressive Republican Rockefeller survived in the governor's race, and Wallace, the hero of the radical right, won the presidential vote; the combined Wallace and Nixon vote reached 70 percent, as Humphrey was perceived as too liberal by the middle faction. A moderate candidate such as Rockefeller or Fulbright could survive only by attracting votes from the moderately conservative faction, which Fulbright basically accomplished by stressing the advantages to Arkansas of his seniority in Congress, and his civil rights record. He easily held the blacks and progressives based on his social and economic policy positions and the extremism of "Justice Jim." The influence of black voters was growing in the late 1960s: Rockefeller promoted registration drives; poll taxes and other formal barriers had been outlawed, and manipulation by planters who "voted" local blacks in the delta was being reduced by the increased political activity of black leaders and Rockefeller. Progressive Democrats realized by 1968 the need to compete with Rockefeller for black votes.[37]

It should be emphasized that even candidates who were popularly described as "moderate" in the 1960s tended to avoid controversial civil rights positions. Rockefeller, the symbol of the state's repudiation of the Faubus era's racial excesses, had commended Barry Goldwater's opposition to the Civil Rights Act of 1964 during his gubernatorial campaign of that year, and in the late 1960s and 1970 he opposed busing. Fulbright usually avoided any commentary on specific Supreme Court decisions such as the 1971 *Swann v. Charlotte-Mecklenburg* case and generally did not discuss the issue beyond terse statements that he opposed busing.[38]

Fulbright succeeded in gaining the middle faction in the general election, because of the Republican Party's weakness. The opponent was a wealthy, engaging businessman, Charles Bernard, but Republican strength was entirely dependent on Rockefeller's vast financial power and personal talents, and Bernard won only 41 percent. Despite the difference in parties, the governor's organization helped Fulbright, much to Bernard's chagrin. Many Rockefeller supporters were also Fulbright supporters, and the governor's campaign funds promoted a Rockefeller-Humphrey-Fulbright ticket, especially among blacks.[39] The Fulbright-Rockefeller relationship was always tenuous, however, as Rockefeller attempted to avoid offending Bernard while staying on good terms with Fulbright. The senator was a loyal Democrat and preferred to have a progressive Democrat in the governor's mansion.[40] By late 1969, he was encouraging a talented northwest Arkansas lawyer, Dale Bumpers, to fill the void.[41]

In 1969, Fulbright demonstrated some independence from the Southern bloc on some important votes. Rather than supporting Russell Long of Louisiana as majority whip, Fulbright supported Edward Kennedy, the liberal who was so detested by Southern segregationists. In late 1969, conservatives supported legislation that would have denied tax-exempt status to the Southern Regional Council Voter Registration Project and thus destroyed it. The Southern Regional Council, a famous Southern progressive institution, had played a particularly constructive role in the civil rights movement, and Fulbright supported the Council, to the consternation of reactionaries in Arkansas and elsewhere.[41a]

Having survived the 1968 election, Fulbright soon learned that Nixon's criticisms of the Warren Court were increasingly popular in Arkansas. Nixon fulfilled one of his campaign pledges in 1969 by nominating Judge Clement Haynsworth of the Fourth Circuit to fill the vacancy created by Justice Abe Fortas' resignation because of unethical conduct. The debate over the Haynsworth nomination was less difficult for Fulbright than the Carswell nomination in 1970, since much of the Haynsworth debate focused on conflict of interest charges that were not related to civil rights. Haynsworth had held stock in corporations with subsidiaries that came before his court, but his financial interest ranged from small to infinitesimal.[42] Fulbright was troubled by Haynsworth's failure to avoid the appearance of impropriety, but he eventually concluded that under prevailing judicial ethical standards the conflict of interest charges against him were insubstantial. The Arkansan suspected that the liberal criticism of Haynsworth was a vindictive effort to counterattack against the conservatives who had, in many liberals' estimation, hounded Fortas from the Court for ideological reasons.[43] Not all of the criticism of Fortas came from conservatives; some of Fortas' critics were concerned about his continuing service to Johnson as an adviser even after his elevation to the Supreme Court, a practice that compromised the separation of powers. On Vietnam policy, Fortas was a hawk, who frequently discussed the war with the President. Johnson initially nominated Fortas to be Chief Justice when Warren announced plans to retire, but the Senate blocked the nomination based on initial evidence of ethical problems, and more serious revelations later forced Fortas to resign. In retrospect, legal scholars including Laurence Tribe later concluded that the Haynsworth allegations were not comparable to the seriously unethical conduct of Fortas, and critics of his nomination probably erred in concentrating their fire on the dubious ethical question.[44]

The *Gazette* asserted that the Court's stature would be seriously damaged by the appointment of Haynsworth, "an obscure judge in the federal appeals court in South Carolina whose principal recommendation lay in the favor he had with Strom Thurmond, the South Carolina king-maker who was an influential figure in Nixon's 'Southern strategy' of wooing southern whites away from the Democrats."[45] In the *Gazette's* analysis, Haynsworth "has almost never gone beyond the minimum, literal requirements of the Supreme Court in implementing desegregation. His opinions show reluctance, even timidity, in applying the doctrine that was the crowning achievement of the Warren Court." The *Gazette* acknowledged that "the record does not show that Haynsworth is one of those scattered federal judges who actually reject the interpretations of the Supreme Court itself."[46] The newspaper concluded that the nominee's civil rights record by itself would be justifiable grounds for voting against Haynsworth. Fulbright believed that if Haynsworth had not actually rejected Supreme Court precedents but had merely been "timid" in applying them, as the *Gazette* argued, such decisions were distasteful but did not rise to the level of prejudiced adjudication that would disqualify him from service on the highest court. In Fulbright's view at that time, philosophy should disqualify a nominee only if it were so extreme as to prevent impartial adjudication.[47]

A case could be made, however, that the description of Haynsworth's record as merely a "timid" effort to apply *Brown* was incorrect. For example, in *School Board of the City of Charlottesville v. Dillard*, 374 U.S. 827 (1963), Haynsworth dissented from a majority opinion prohibiting transfers of children in schools where desegregation was taking place. Haynsworth contended that the "sense of inferiority" that the Court associated with segregation in *Brown* would be intensified if integration were to be achieved. Subsequently, the Supreme Court in *Goss v. Board of Education*, 373 U.S. 683 (1963) ruled that transfer systems of the type Haynsworth approved in *Dillard* were inconsistent with *Brown*. Haynsworth's opinion in *Dillard* was diametrically opposed to the reasoning in *Brown*; the decision raised the issue whether Haynsworth had simply attempted a good-faith, erroneous effort to apply *Brown*, or was engaging in a reactionary effort to obstruct integration. Fulbright concluded that the former was the correct analysis of Haynsworth, but it should be stressed that there was so much discussion of the conflict of interest allegations that the senator never had to discuss the nominee's civil rights record in detail.[48]

Similar questions could have been raised about other Haynsworth decisions. For example, in *Griffin v. Prince Edward School Board*, 377 U.S. 218 (1964), the Supreme Court held that the county could not shut down its public school system to evade its duty to desegregate. Haynsworth had previously decided that black children denied public education through such practices could not assert an equal protection clause violation. Again, in *Bowman v. County School Board of Charles City, Virginia*, 382 F.2d 326 (1967), Haynsworth supported the "freedom of choice" approach to desegregation. In *Green v. School Board of New Kent County*, 391 U.S. 430 (1969), the Supreme Court rejected a "freedom of choice" plan that the district had adopted to avoid loss of federal funds; the Court emphasized its impatience with the slow pace of desegregation: "10 years after *Brown II* directed the making of a 'prompt and reasonable start.' . . . The burden on a school board today is to come forward with a plan that promises realistically to work, and promises realistically to work *now*." Judges Sobeloff and Winter of the Fourth Circuit were in accord with the Supreme Court's view, having dissented from Haynsworth's opinion in writing, "It is time for this Circuit to speak plainly to its district courts to tell them to require the school boards to get on with their tasks—no longer avoidable or deferrable—to integrate their facilities."[49] Haynsworth defended his earlier rulings by contending that they reflected the prevailing view of most judges in the Fourth Circuit at the time. He and his supporters contended that he would consider himself bound by the Court's reversals of his earlier decisions after being elevated to the high court.[50]

In analyzing the nomination, Fulbright gave great weight to the advice of his former colleague, Robert A. Leflar of the University of Arkansas School of Law, and Bill Penix, a progressive Jonesboro lawyer. Leflar, a nationally renowned legal scholar and probably the single most prestigious academic figure in Arkansas' history, contended that Haynsworth was a conservative, but was reasonably fair and impartial.[51] Leflar had taught Haynsworth in a seminar for judges, and he believed that Haynsworth would honor the Supreme Court reversals of his earlier opinions. Penix's analysis was similar.[52]

The *Gazette's* editorial taking issue with Fulbright for his vote envisaged the issue in terms of a political compromise the senator allegedly made to placate his segregationist supporters. Fulbright's vote was sharply criticized by the *Gazette*, (which in criticizing Haynsworth also stressed the ethical issues that later proved exaggerated), labor leaders who argued that Haynsworth was biased against unions, and the NAACP. The Gazette over-simplified the issue in describing Fulbright's vote as solely an effort to appease the right on civil rights, but it was certainly true that Fulbright's vote reflected majority sentiment in the state. In contrast to the *Gazette*, McClellan condemned Nixon's opponents for criticizing Haynsworth solely because, "One, he is from the South; and two, he is not completely subservient to modern liberalism."[53] Powerful constituents such as the influential east Arkansas planter, R.E.L. Wilson, weighed in for Haynsworth. Wilson wrote the senator, "you would be happy with the reaction throughout the state among those that really were so terribly concerned."[54] A wealthy Little Rock businessman told Fulbright his vote was wise and added, "I have never seen the people so rabid."[55] In a memo before the vote, Lee Williams advised the senator that constituents were arguing that "it is good you are not running in Arkansas this year because you are hurting yourself badly by your continued adamant stand on the war," and a vote against Haynsworth would further complicate his political situation.[56]

Williams' memo also noted opposition calls from the *Gazette* and others. However, even the *Gazette* editorial on the issue softened the blow by conceding, "Fulbright is still the man who has done as much for the cause of peace as any man of his time."[57] The attitude of Fulbright and his allies was summarized by a late 1969 letter from Dale Bumpers to the senator, in which he said the *Gazette* publisher, Hugh Patterson, "had been much exercised over the Haynsworth nomination, but he'll get over it in a few weeks. After all, Haynsworth wasn't confirmed and that was his primary concern."[58] Fulbright remained undecided until an announcement that several other senators would oppose Haynsworth, thus removing any doubt as to the outcome.[59] Bumpers advised the senator that his vote had been politically wise. While Fulbright was troubled by the criticisms of friends like Patterson, he did not think he would lose their votes by supporting Haynsworth; on the other hand, many conservatives from the east Arkansas delta very well might have changed their votes over the Haynsworth affair. Fulbright made few statements to the press, except to warn that if Haynsworth were defeated Nixon would nominate someone "worse."[60]

The political pressures were certainly important in the Haynsworth vote, but the *Gazette* was severe in analyzing the decision as being based solely on a desire to placate the right. Fulbright had the esteemed advice of Leflar that Haynsworth was a reasonable, ethical nominee. If Fulbright agreed with Bumpers' political analysis, he was more deeply troubled by the liberal criticism than his young ally was. The senator continued to agonize over the debate in an extended exchange of letters in December with an old friend, Guy Berry of Fayetteville. After Haynsworth's defeat, 55 to 45, Fulbright noted that he was the first nominee to be rejected since President Hoover's nomination of Judge John Parker, and then cited the tradition that a President's choice should be supported; but these arguments were so fragile, especially for the leading advocate of a revitalized role for the Congress in the nation's policy formulation, that he jettisoned the traditional argument in his next paragraph: "All of this, of course, is no proper or adequate answer for my vote." He said the vote was wise considering his political relations in the state and other goals he hoped to achieve by remaining in power; and he emphasized that "If the President now nominates Strom Thurmond or John Mitchell and he is confirmed, I wonder if you will think that you were right in objecting to a rather bland and innocuous small-town lawyer."[61] Berry replied that while he would find a "responsible conservative" acceptable, each nomination ought to be judged on its own merits, and it was no answer to support a mediocre nominee on the grounds that Nixon might later appoint "someone worse."[62] The *Gazette* also rejected Fulbright's reasoning.

Both Fulbright and Berry had plausible points to make. The defeat of Haynsworth led Nixon to accept John Mitchell's advice to nominate G. Harrold Carswell. After the protracted Haynsworth debate, the Senate first responded with the attitude that it did not want to appear to the nation as an obstructionist body that would vindictively oppose every appointment Nixon offered. Weariness with battling the executive had also set in, and at first it seemed that Carswell would be confirmed. Even at the end of the debate, Carswell was opposed by four fewer senators than Haynsworth, even though Carswell was vastly inferior to Haynsworth as a judge. Given the reality that Carswell came so close to confirmation, Fulbright was understandably concerned that the Senate's reluctance to defeat two successive nominees would lead to a disastrous confirmation of an extremist. Of course, Fulbright himself was in a position to help defeat the future nomination of an extremist, but at the time of the Haynsworth debate he understandably looked with anxiety on the prospect of another such furor. In retrospect, the view that each nomination must be considered on its own merits regardless of political problems was probably the stronger. In this instance, the Senate's defeats of Haynsworth and Carswell finally led to the appointment of Harry Blackmun, who would become a highly respected justice. In Haynsworth, the Court lost a judge who had been subjected to unfair criticism and probably would have made a respectable justice, but even many of his supporters such as Leflar and Fulbright regarded him as a passable but undistinguished choice.[63] If Fulbright's argument were accepted, then the President could bludgeon the Senate into accepting weak nominees by holding over it the threat of nominating far worse candidates.

III. CARSWELL AND REHNQUIST

T he nomination of G. Harrold Carswell in 1970 posed the civil rights issue in stark, unavoidable terms for Fulbright. There was no conflict of interest issue and the debate focused squarely on the nominee's civil rights record. Carswell, then a resident of Tallahassee, Florida, and a judge on the Fifth Circuit, had made statements while campaigning for the Georgia Legislature in 1948 that "I yield to no man as a fellow-candidate, as a fellow-citizen, in the firm, vigorous belief in the principles of white supremacy, and I shall always be so governed."[64] The nominee had not repudiated this statement until he testified at the Judiciary Committee hearings on his confirmation. In 1956 he had taken part in the transfer of a golf course in Tallahassee from municipal control to private hands in order to evade desegregation of the municipal recreation facilities. At the Judiciary Committee hearings, Carswell had at one juncture denied his involvement in the golf course episode, but later acknowledged it. As a district judge and later a circuit judge, Carswell was reversed on appeal 40 percent of the time—a rate of reversal much higher than average for Fifth Circuit judges. The great majority of the reversals involved either race-related cases or criminal law cases. Carswell had been abusive to civil rights lawyers in his court and often dismissed their suits without a hearing. Privately, even Mitchell rated Carswell far below Haynsworth, so that the choice represented vengeance for rejection of the first nominee and a heavy-handed effort to impose the "Southern strategy."[65]

Senator Birch Bayh (D.-Ind.), a Judiciary Committee member, led the Northern liberal opposition to Carswell. In March, Fulbright privately informed Bayh that he was inclined to vote with the opposition. Bayh was encouraged by Fulbright's position, and advised him that "since the prospective votes in opposition to Carswell are not as firm as they were against Haynsworth," the best strategy would be to intensify the investigation into Carswell's record and to recommit the nomination to the Judiciary Committee (which reported the nomination to the full Senate). Bayh believed that Fulbright would be the best choice of a senator for a prominent opposing role, because his prestige in Washington might persuade moderates who were intimidated by administration pressures, and his conservative record on civil rights issues strengthened his credibility, "particularly since you voted for Haynsworth." The senator's record, ironically, strengthened his credentials as an opponent of Carswell, for his vote could not be discounted as a "knee-jerk liberal" response.[66]

The administration succeeded in dictating much of the phraseology of the debate, such as describing Carswell as mediocre. Actually, Carswell was so biased as to be simply unqualified to serve on the Court, so that "mediocrity" was a misnomer in describing him. Carswell's tendency to prejudge issues based on his reactionary philosophy distinguished him from Warren Burger, who was inept as a legal craftsman but eventually became a respectable justice because of his decency, desire to be fair, and willingness to listen to colleagues' advice. As revealed by a high reversal vote on civil rights issues and unfair treatment of civil rights plaintiffs, Fulbright argued that Carswell was simply devoid of the qualities of impartiality and fairness that made Haynsworth and Burger competent judges. Even the nominee's defenders found it rather difficult to praise him; the best Senator Roman Hruska (R-Neb.) could do was to laud Carswell's "mediocrity" by saying that many Americans were mediocre and Carswell could thus be their voice on the Court.[67]

Most legal scholars strongly opposed Carswell. William Van Alstyne of Duke advised Fulbright that Carswell suffered from "a conscious or unconscious hostility to Negro plaintiffs, volunteer attorneys in race cases, and Northern lawyers." Van Alstyne, a witness at the confirmation hearings, decried the nominee's "pattern of reversals by the court of appeals in the many cases where civil rights complaints were dismissed out of hand without a hearing." Similarly, Dean Louis Pollak of Yale argued that "the nominee presents more slender credentials than any nominee for the Supreme Court in this century." Leflar informed Fulbright and McClellan that "One reason why I favored Haynsworth was that I feared the alternative would be someone much less qualified than he. That is what has happened."[68] Wiley Branton advised Fulbright that "I can tell you quite honestly that the confirmation of Judge Carswell would greatly undermine the confidence which many black Americans hold in the use of the legal system for the enforcement of rights." Branton, then with the Alliance for Labor Action in Washington, had a lengthy conference with Fulbright on Carswell. Leflar and Branton were Fulbright's crucial advisers on the nomination.[69]

Fulbright and Bayh placed great emphasis upon the need for an extensive public debate on the nomination. The Arkansan stressed in a March 26 Senate speech that Judge John Minor Wisdom of the Fifth Circuit opposed the nomination, and Chief Judge Elbert Tuttle had declined to testify for Carswell. Fulbright acknowledged that there were other judges who supported Carswell, and the ABA had approved him. But the ABA endorsement was complicated by numerous state and local bar associations, such as those of New York, Vermont, San Francisco, Philadelphia and others who rejected the nominee. Fulbright referred to numerous allegations of Carswell's prejudice from civil rights attorneys who sent telegrams and letters to the Senate opposition. A Florida attorney who had practiced before Carswell stated, "Judge Carswell is the most prejudiced judge before whom I have had the honor to practice." Former Justice Department attorney Norman Knopf said "Judge Carswell made clear . . . that he did not approve of any of this voter registration going on." Leroy Clark, a law professor active in civil rights litigation, described Carswell as "the most hostile federal district court judge I have ever appeared before with respect to civil rights matters." Fulbright concluded his March 26 statement by stipulating that he was still undecided, but would support recommittal. A front-page New York Times story on his statement interpreted it as a surprise and a major blow to Carswell's prospects. The Boston Globe similarly commended Fulbright's support for recommittal and his plea that the "sundry allegations of racial bias" must be resolved.[70]

Questions of "competence" in the Carswell debate were closely related to the question of racial bias, because the basis for the charge of incompetence was his prejudiced treatment of civil rights issues. The vote to recommit was eventually blocked by Chairman Eastland and McClellan on April 6, but the overall strategy succeeded in prolonging the debate and giving undecided senators time to reflect about the weaknesses of the nomination. The extension of the debate effectively doomed the nomination, for it meant that the Senate would subject Carswell's record to a searching analysis it could not withstand. The lengthy debate also magnified the issue in Arkansas, and gave Fulbright's critics more time to attack his position. The final 51-45 vote was delayed until April 8.

Fulbright's correspondence with his constituents makes painfully clear that the Nixon administration and McClellan won the public relations and mass communications battles in Arkansas, for they succeeded in portraying the issue as a vendetta by Northern liberals to block the appointment of a "Southern strict constructionist, conservative constitutional judge" who opposed the Warren Court's activism on civil rights. Fulbright protested in his responses to constituents that Carswell was not a strict constructionist conservative, but was a reactionary activist; in light of all the other highly qualified nominees from the South, the senator felt that Carswell's selection was an insult to the region. The former law professor reminded his constituents that Southerners already sat on the Court: Hugo Black of Alabama, Marshall of Maryland, and Warren Burger, who had lived in Virginia for a number of years. "I consider myself a strict constitutional constructionist," Fulbright told his constituents, "and in turning down an incompetent nominee, I believe I was following the duty imposed upon the Senate by the Constitution to approve or disapprove nominees of the President in accordance with their qualifications."[71]

The volume and virulence of the reaction against his vote came as a shock to Fulbright's aides. J.E. Bunch, a banker from northwest Arkansas and a long-time supporter of Fulbright, ended his political support for the senator over the nomination. Although the conservative banker had been concerned about many of Fulbright's other positions and the Carswell vote was probably the culmination of his restlessness, Bunch's response typified a widespread feeling of alienation from Fulbright's stance among many lawyers, bankers and businessmen throughout the state. Fulbright reiterated his arguments about strict constructionism in replying to Bunch, and added plaintively, "I do not quarrel with you about your views, but only regret that you feel my vote on a single nomination is sufficient to offset 25 years of what you formerly led me to believe you thought was a reasonably satisfactory performance." Similarly, Gazzola Vaccaro, a prominent businessman in the delta, erroneously complained that Fulbright had voted against Haynsworth, Burger and Carswell, and concluded "This indicates to me that you are not interested in anyone who is considered conservative and a strict constructionist. . . You and the other ultra-liberals will not live to see the harm which you are bestowing on our country." This letter revealed a common misconception that developed in the aftermath of the Carswell vote, as many constituents became confused and thought the senator had opposed all the Nixon nominees. Although Fulbright never advocated anything resembling a "liberal" civil rights position throughout the debate, constituents perceived his vote as such a position. Actually, Fulbright had voted for Haynsworth and Burger, and would vote for the later nominations of Harry Blackmun of Minnesota and Lewis Powell of Virginia. The senator explained this to Vaccaro and expressed his enthusiasm for Blackmun. But the misconception that Carswell was a fair-minded conservative who was smeared by vindictive liberals recurred in complaints from planters, local bar associations, in a letter signed by the sheriffs of seven east Arkansas counties, and other responses.[72]

Penix, the progressive east Arkansas Democrat, aptly summarized the public's perception of the Carswell debate. "Sitting up there in Washington," he wrote to Lee Williams in April, "it is easy to forget how very unsophisticated the rest of our country really is. Right now many good people believe that Carswell was turned down solely because he was a Southerner."[73] After consulting with Penix and Branton, Fulbright compiled a list of well-qualified Southern jurists. They included Judge J. Smith Henley, a life-long Republican appointed by Eisenhower; Ed Wright, an attorney from Little Rock and president-elect of the ABA; District Judge Frank Johnson of Alabama; John R. Brown, John Minor Wisdom, Griffin Bell, and Irving Goldberg of the Fifth Circuit; John Butzner of the Fourth Circuit; and Robert Leflar.[74] Fulbright publicized this list in a counterattack against Nixon, in showing that there were numerous qualified Southerners who could have been chosen.[75]

Nixon lashed out at the Senate for rejecting Carswell, charging that "Judges Haynsworth and Carswell have endured with admirable dignity vicious assaults on their intelligence, their honesty, and their character. . . . They have been falsely charged with being racist, but when all the hypocrisy is stripped away, the real issue was their philosophy of strict construction of the Constitution—a philosophy that I share—and the fact that they had the misfortune of being born in the South." Nixon condemned the Senate's rejection of Carswell as a sheer act of "regional discrimination."[76] The affair exemplified Nixon's decision to accept the counsel of Mitchell and White House adviser Patrick Buchanan, who advocated in internal administration memos a politically divisive strategy in which the administration would "cut the Democratic Party and country in half; my view is that we would have the larger half." Nixon had campaigned in 1968 on a theme that he would "bring the country together," but in the White House he was one of the most divisive presidents in the nation's history.[77]

Fulbright led the opposition's counterattack on Nixon. A national wire service report on April 10 stated that "Senator J. William Fulbright, whose break with the majority of his fellow Southerners was a key factor in Carswell's defeat, said of Mr. Nixon's statement: `I think it is an affront to the many eminent Southern jurists that the President has ruled them out of consideration.'"[78] The senator reiterated his pledge to support a genuine strict constructionist and regretted Nixon's complaint that he would not now nominate a Southerner to the Court because of the alleged regional bias.[79] In a farcical episode after the vote that attracted national notoriety, Martha Mitchell, wife of the Attorney General, called the *Gazette* at 2 a.m. looking for the *Gazette* editorial editor in an effort to get the state's largest newspaper to condemn Fulbright. Mrs. Mitchell had made the cardinal error of thinking that editorial writers actually stay up late plying their trade. In reality, unlike people who have to work for a living, editorial writers have to go home early each day to preserve their creative powers. In any event, Powell was deeply impressed with Fulbright's vote against Carswell and would have declined Mrs. Mitchell's suggestion. Not being able to find the editorial editor—who happened to be in the Netherlands that night, making certain that the *Gazette's* positions on Dutch-American relations were correct—Mrs. Mitchell told a reporter, "I want you to crucify Fulbright" for his vote, which she said did not reflect the views of his constituents and was a "disgrace" to the state. Mrs. Mitchell, who was from a prominent Pine Bluff family, charged that Fulbright "could have swung" the vote for Carswell.[80] Vice President Spiro T. Agnew seconded Mrs. Mitchell's comments in a speech at Little Rock a few weeks later, saying that she had told him to "tell it like it is about Bill Fulbright," and then delivered a sarcastic tirade against "Fulbright and his radic-lib friends."[81] Fulbright responded to the call for his crucifixion by saying "Mrs. Mitchell is a little unrestrained in the way in which she expresses herself." The senator gallantly thanked Mrs. Mitchell for giving him the credit for Carswell's defeat.[82]

In the aftermath of his defeat, Carswell resigned to run for the Senate. In his fund-raising letters, Carswell attributed the Senate vote to the opposition of "the ultra-liberals (Kennedy, Fulbright, McGovern) who united to defeat my appointment by President Nixon, thus giving fresh proof of the liberals' domination over American politics." When Carswell lost his race and Nixon nominated Blackmun, Fulbright felt encouraged by the result of his efforts.[83]

In contrast to the administration's vituperation, Fulbright received accolades from the *Gazette* and other allies. The *New York Times* lauded the vote as a triumph of conscience and constitutional responsibility over partisanship. Bayh praised Fulbright's vote as "one of a handful which helped write a new chapter in Profiles in Courage." Ben Grinage, Fulbright's black aide in Little Rock, reported that "The reaction here among blacks and so-called liberals has been a combination of awe, wonder, surprise and pride." Grinage, a civil rights activist who had joined Fulbright's congressional staff after having worked in the 1968 campaign, told Fulbright that "I personally am prouder than ever to be a part of your team." Grinage also dutifully reported that some outraged white constituents had called to say that they would never again vote for Fulbright.[84]

The Carswell debate occurred during one of the most frenetic, if exciting, periods in Fulbright's career, when the senator was under political pressure on several fronts. At home, the long-awaited emergence of a progressive Democrat who could win the governor's race was nearing a reality, as Bumpers was running a strong campaign and would eventually defeat Faubus in the primary and Rockefeller in the general election. Fulbright helped raise funds and gave speeches for Bumpers, who at first was a dark horse candidate. The senator also had to take a position on the Voting Rights Act extension and five-year suspension of literacy tests; he voted in favor while McClellan and most other Southern senators opposed it. As early as the Voting Rights Act's initial passage in 1965, Fulbright had stated publicly when asked by a reporter about the Act:

> I am for it. I think the decision last year about this long-standing quarrel about the role of the federal government in this area was made. I mean that with all that went on last year—from here on, it is the law of the land, and I think they should be allowed to vote. They do vote in my state. They should be allowed to in the other states. These are the last gasps, I would say, of the opposition that we are seeing now.

Those were obviously not "the last gasps of opposition" in 1965, but the Voting Rights Act was much less controversial in 1970 than it had been in 1965. The moderates were strengthened in Arkansas by the emergence of a progressive young congressman, David Pryor, who supported extension. Branton conferred with Fulbright at length about the Voting Rights Act extension. The Attorney General had testified on Capitol Hill against renewal of the Act, so that Fulbright was faced with two major civil rights controversies in 1970. The vote was a departure from Fulbright's earlier policy, especially in the context of opposition to renewal of the Act by the Attorney General and McClellan. McClellan remained the state's most powerful politician and would defeat the moderate Pryor in a runoff in the 1972 Senate race. While some conservatives criticized Fulbright's support for the Voting Rights Act extension, it was overshadowed by the deluge of criticism on the Carswell debate.[85]

Those who felt Nixon was chastened by the Carswell affair did not reckon with the President's affinity for the politics of confrontation. If the Blackmun appointment was widely applauded, his release of a list of six highly questionable candidates in 1971 (to replace John Harlan and Hugo Black) replayed the earlier debates. The six included Senator Robert Byrd, a former member of the Ku Klux Klan who was not a member of the bar and had never practiced law; and Herschel Friday, a Little Rock lawyer who was rejected by the ABA. Friday was a successful lawyer, but he was out of his depth in being considered for elevation to the Supreme Court. Friday had not made even Fulbright's expansive list, which had included conservative Arkansas Republicans, and his credentials seemed to be his work in attempting to prevent integration in Little Rock and his friendship with Mitchell. After the release of the six possible nominees provoked a number of fratricidal quarrels among Democrats, Nixon withdrew "the list of six" and nominated Lewis Powell and Assistant Attorney General William Rehnquist.[86]

The basic issues in the Rehnquist nomination were his role as an apologist for the Vietnam War, including the suppression of dissent and the justification for executive domination of foreign policy, and his extreme stands on civil rights. Not surprisingly, Fulbright reiterated and emphasized all his arguments against the war in the Rehnquist debate. The issue for Fulbright focused on whether he would allow the political problems posed by right-wing sentiment in favor of Rehnquist to override other considerations, as had happened in the Central High crisis and the initial passage of the Voting Rights Act. After the previous debates over nominations, it was abundantly clear to Fulbright that the controversy in Arkansas would focus on civil rights, regardless of how much he highlighted the war and the other issues in his speeches.[87]

There was no question of ethics or intellect in Rehnquist's case. An honors graduate of Stanford Law School, Rehnquist was one of the chosen few among young law graduates who clerk for the Supreme Court. Fulbright believed that Rehnquist's intellectual ability was hardly comforting if that ability was to be employed to justify a radical, reactionary view of constitutional law. The Rehnquist nomination would stand or fall strictly on whether the Senate judged the nominee's philosophy too extreme for him to render impartial adjudication on the Court. There was no mechanistic set of guidelines that could distinguish an extremist from someone who merely held controversial views, Fulbright recognized; the Senate would simply have to use its discretion. As Justice Robert Jackson's law clerk before *Brown* was decided, Rehnquist had written a memorandum contending that Thurgood Marshall was wrong to argue for the NAACP that a majority may not deprive a minority of its constitutional rights, for "the answer must be made that while this is sound in theory, in the long run it is the majority who will determine what the constitutional rights of the minority are." Rehnquist advised Justice Jackson that over-ruling *Plessy* would amount to liberal activism that would be as improper constitutionally as the conservative activism of Justice James Reynolds' faction on the Court, and thus "I think *Plessy v. Ferguson* was right and should be re-affirmed." At the time of the debate on his confirmation in 1971, Rehnquist asserted that his memorandum only reflected Jackson's views at the time. But that assertion was contradicted by a draft concurrence (prepared but not delivered) in the Jackson Papers in which the Justice wrote, "I am convinced that present-day conditions require us to strike from our books the doctrine of separate-but-equal facilities."[88] The documents in the Jackson Papers tending to refute Rehnquist's view were not publicized until years later, however, and Rehnquist's explanation for his memo was widely accepted in the Senate in 1971.

Perhaps even more serious than his memorandum as a law clerk were Rehnquist's continued pro-segregationist actions in the 1960s. In 1964, several months after the passage of the Civil Rights Act, Rehnquist opposed a Phoenix municipal ordinance and an Arizona state law requiring non-discriminatory policies in public accommodations, laws that by late 1964 had won the support of even Rehnquist's conservative mentor, Barry Goldwater. As late as 1967, Rehnquist wrote a letter to the *Arizona Republic* criticizing the desegregation of the Phoenix schools: "We are no more dedicated to an integrated society than we are to a segregated society." As Nixon's Assistant Attorney General during the Carswell nomination, Rehnquist had defended Carswell's civil rights record as evidence merely of "an overall constitutional conservatism, rather than to any animus directed only at civil rights cases or civil rights litigants."[89]

During the Carswell debate, Rehnquist drafted Nixon's letter to Senator William Saxbe (R-Ohio) contending that the President possessed exclusive authority to appoint Supreme Court justices, for the President is "the one person entrusted by the Constitution with the power of appointment."[90] Rehnquist had ventured out of his depth on the constitutional law issue. Fulbright correctly pointed out in a December, 1971 Senate speech that the Constitution explicitly grants the Senate the role of advising and consenting to nominations. The former constitutional law professor observed that during the Constitutional Convention of 1787 the Framers originally anticipated that Congress or the Senate alone would have the power to appoint Supreme Court justices, and "only near the end of the Convention was the existing system adopted under which the President has the power to appoint judges but only with the advice and consent of the Senate."[91] Fulbright argued that far from being a strict constructionist, as Nixon had portrayed him, Rehnquist was a judicial activist who advocated an unprecedented expansive role of the executive at the expense of Supreme Court precedents, the role of Congress and the rights of individuals. During the May Day demonstrations against the war, Rehnquist justified mass arrests under a doctrine that the executive had the power to declare "qualified martial law," a position subsequently rejected by the U.S. Court of Appeals in invalidating the arrests. Rehnquist had argued that Nixon had not approached "anything like the outer limits of his power" in ordering the invasion of Cambodia, a view Fulbright decried as a usurpation of Congress' constitutional war powers. Similarly, Fulbright opposed Rehnquist's views on executive use of surveillance; Rehnquist had testified to Senator Sam Ervin's Subcommittee on Constitutional Rights that the executive would not violate the First Amendment if it ordered surveillance of a U.S. senator, "if the executive thought it necessary." Fulbright concluded that "Mr. Rehnquist is committed to the supremacy of the Executive power to such an extent that his influence on the Court would undermine that essential virtue of our Constitution."[92]

Fulbright's status as an advocate of judicial conservatism strengthened his credibility with many conservatives, in the Rehnquist and especially in the Carswell debate. From the 1930s to the 1980s, the Rhodes Scholar was consistently critical of Supreme Court decisions he regarded as based on the personal values of the justices. As a Justice Department attorney in the 1930s he had been critical of the "outstandingly reactionary bunch of old fogey activists" who blocked the New Deal reforms.[93] He was uneasy with *Brown* and more comfortable with *Brown II*'s "all deliberate speed" (although the Court disagreed with his glacial interpretation of "deliberate" in *Cooper v. Aaron*) and greater leeway for local district judges, and in later years he criticized what he regarded as the reactionary activism of Rehnquist. There were serious problems with both activist and conservative approaches; Fulbright would prefer that the political process should resolve profound policy questions, yet he would concede that the Court must play a limited role in intervening as an objective referee in such cases as *Reynolds v. Sims* or other situations where the political process is not functioning properly because of geographical or racial discrimination. But neither Fulbright nor anyone else ever definitively resolved the dilemma of how far the "referee" role should extend, when the Court should decide sensitive issues and when it should not. Whatever the merits or lack of merit of judicial conservatism, Rehnquist would not qualify as a conservative in the sense of respecting precedent and judicial restraint. In a 1959 *Harvard Law Record* article, Rehnquist had written, "In the same sense that an inferior court may bemoan precedents, there are those who bemoan the absence of *stare decisis* in constitutional law, but of its absence there can be no doubt."[94] Fulbright may or may not have been correct in holding his convictions in favor of greater judicial restraint, but arguments couched in such language were comforting to the Arkansan's colleagues, who frequently complimented the former law professor's erudition.[95]

Bayh and other opponents of Rehnquist regarded Fulbright's focus on the anti-war arguments and the constitutional role of the Senate as highly beneficial, given his prestige as chairman of Foreign Relations and leading advocate for a revitalized Congress. Fulbright briefly acknowledged the criticisms of Rehnquist's civil rights record in the debate, but his detailed arguments focused on the other flaws in the nominee's record. The critics managed to generate considerable concern over the nomination by publicizing their arguments concerning civil liberties, war powers, and civil rights; but at the time, Nixon was at the height of his power and Rehnquist was an able advocate who defended his previous positions as taken in a political context that would differ sharply from his role on the Court. After Haynsworth and Carswell, most senators were exceedingly reluctant to undergo a third ordeal. Fulbright and Bayh attempted to extend the investigation, as had been done in the Carswell case. Cloture was supported by many Southerners who had been valiant defenders of the right to unlimited debate in the Senate when they were filibustering against civil rights legislation.[96] In the end, Rehnquist was confirmed, 68-26, with Fulbright the only Southerner in opposition. Of the three Southerners who joined him in opposing Carswell,

Gore of Tennessee and Ralph Yarborough of Texas were defeated in 1970 and William Spong of Virginia voted for Rehnquist.[97]

The responses to Fulbright's vote were predictable. Branton had advised the senator to support Powell but oppose Rehnquist and was naturally delighted that his counsel was followed. Right-wingers in Arkansas and elsewhere were again antagonized. Since a Deep South nominee was not involved, and the Virginian Powell was confirmed at about the same time, the regional animosities of the Carswell debate were not inflamed in the Rehnquist vote; and the reality that Rehnquist was not rejected reduced the controversy over the appointment. Fulbright and Bayh consoled themselves with their conviction that their position was correct, and possibly that the debate over his record would serve as a restraint on Rehnquist's decisions while on the Court. After Rehnquist consistently voted to reverse Warren Court precedents on racial issues and criminal cases in later years, Fulbright would concede that his hopes concerning the confirmation debate as a restraining influence on the nominee were forlorn.

Fulbright had implored his colleagues in the Rehnquist debate to fulfill the Senate's proper investigative role. In retrospect, it is unfortunate that a thorough examination of the nominee's record did not take place. Some of the controversies continued to hang over Rehnquist's head years later, such as an issue concerning his alleged intimidation of blacks in an effort to keep them from voting in Arizona in 1964. The Judiciary Committee refused to conduct a thorough investigation into the voting allegations in 1971, but they surfaced again in 1986 at the hearings on Rehnquist's confirmation to be Chief Justice. By 1986 Arizona party officials no longer had the relevant voting records on the incident, and some participants in those elections were no longer living. This situation damaged the Court and all parties concerned, for if the charges were unfounded, then Rehnquist was unfairly deprived of an opportunity in 1971 to refute them when the evidence still existed to do so. If the charges were true, then his nomination would have been in jeopardy.[98] Those who called for a searching debate were perceptive.

In 1972, in the context of yet another historic debate in the arena of civil rights, Fulbright again demonstrated that he was much more amenable to change than were many of his Southern colleagues. President Nixon doggedly pursued his Southern strategy in 1972, and one of his favorite weapons in that campaign was antibusing legislation. The President had proposed a moratorium on all court desegregation orders involving busing until mid-1973, and sought permanent legislation that would have prohibited federal courts and agencies from requiring that any student be assigned to a school other than the one "closest or next closest" to his home that provided the proper grade level. The House passed an antibusing bill containing that provision, as well as another provision enabling desegregation suits already settled by the courts to be re-opened to insure that they conformed to the new antibusing bill. The bill had the administration's support, as well as that of a majority not only in the House but in the Senate. The Northern progressive senators of both parties found themselves in the ironic position of engaging in a filibuster against the bill, since this was the identical tactic that Southerners had relied upon in earlier years to block civil rights legislation. If the measure had been enacted, it would have been challenged in the courts, but there was little doubt that for the long term, the bill would have established Congressional limits on who could and could not be bused, and it would have wielded an impact on desegregation plans throughout the nation. Nixon's supporters in the South and elsewhere contended that there was nationwide opposition to busing and the antibusing bill would stop federal courts from expanding the use of busing. Opponents of the bill argued that it would have obstructed progress toward desegregation made so painstakingly during the previous two decades. Moreover, critics contended that Congress did not have the constitutional authority to pass legislation restricting the remedies courts could order in correcting violations of the equal protection clause.[99a]

Two thirds of the members would have to vote for cloture of the filibuster in the Senate; hence the moderate Republicans and moderate Southerners—above all, Fulbright—became the crucial bloc of votes. The Senate voted three times regarding cloture of the filibuster, which kept the Senate in deadlock for as long as it continued. Fulbright and McClellan faced intense pressure to stand with the Southerners. On the same week of the antibusing debate, Nixon campaigned in the South and received warm, tumultuous receptions; the President's enthusiastic reception in Atlanta on the day of the final vote on the antibusing bill prompted the *New York Times* to proclaim that the Georgia crowds "gave President Nixon visual evidence of what the pollsters have been saying for months: Wallace country is now Nixon country."[99b] McClellan had always regarded the right to filibuster as a hallowed principle of the Senate: the right of extended debate in the great deliberative body. Before the antibusing debate, he was the only man in the Senate with a perfect record in having always opposed closure. In the early voting, both Fulbright and McClellan stood by their principles in the teeth of the clamor against busing, as both senators voted against ending the debate on October 10, 1972. These votes placed the *Arkansas Gazette* in the unique position of complimenting Fulbright and McClellan for their votes on a civil-rights-related issue. In the end, however, the clamor was too virulent; McClellan abandoned his 30-year devotion to the extended debate principle and voted for cloture.[99c] In contrast, Fulbright was one of nine senators who were the crucial swing votes in the failure to invoke cloture. As the *New York Times* pointedly observed in a lengthy front-page news article, "Today, every Southern senator except J.W. Fulbright, the Arkansas Democrat, voted for closure."[99d] Not only did Fulbright vote against cloture; he also voted with a majority of the Senate that voted after the unsuccessful cloture effort to set the antibusing bill aside and move on to other legislation. The *Gazette* lamented McClellan's failure to adhere to the Senate's principle of unlimited debate: "Great conservatives make a big thing of their devotion to principle and it is disillusioning when they can't stand up under pressure." The *Gazette* commended Fulbright, "who is made of stouter stuff" than McClellan and other defenders of the status quo.[99e]

Fulbright's important role in helping to kill the antibusing bill—just as his vote against Carswell had—demonstrated that in the later period of his Senate career, he would not allow right wing sentiment on desegregation issues to force him into taking stands that violated his principles. Of course, Fulbright always had doubts about busing and had opposed it on several other occasions, but the antibusing bill was a challenge to the courts and a clear effort by Congress to meddle in judicial matters. Earlier in his career, if the conservative position on race had threatened fundamental principles—such as in the Central High crisis—he had nonetheless acquiesced to the greater political power of the right. Although the segregationists were not as powerful in the South in 1972 as they had been in 1957, it is still true that Nixon and his conservative supporters in the South and elsewhere were attempting to impede progress toward desegregation—albeit in less spectacular and demagogical ways than had Faubus and the massive resisters of the 1950s. It is clearly a tribute to Fulbright's statesmanship that he weathered the Nixon storm in 1972 and stood fast for the principles of extended debate, moderation in desegregation matters, and respect for the proper role of the federal courts in fashioning remedies in desegregation lawsuits. His behavior in the debate was truly that of a "great conservative."

IV. CONCLUSION:
"SHOUTING IN A HIGH WIND"

The Carswell and Rehnquist nominations damaged Fulbright politically in Arkansas. They were not sufficient in themselves, however, to cause his defeat in 1974, but were symptomatic of a series of controversial positions Fulbright assumed that weakened his position and created a sense of alienation from the senator among many constituents, who felt he took stands foreign to their opinions. Many Arkansans were uneasy with such brave innovations as Fulbright constantly advocated throughout the late 1960s and early 1970s, and even though many of them may have had the uncomfortable feeling that Fulbright was right in calling for a searching public debate before nominees were elevated to the nation's highest court, this feeling did not enhance his popularity. Bumpers was philosophically similar to Fulbright, although that was not revealed fully until his later career in the Senate. The governor felt that he had no choice but to run against Fulbright if his political career were to continue, for there was a tradition in Arkansas that governors do not run for a third term. Bumpers believed that Fulbright was so vulnerable that anyone would have beaten him, and it was vastly preferable to have someone with similar views replace him rather than a right-wing candidate. Bumpers demolished Fulbright among the staunchly conservative voters, for whom Fulbright was the arch-villain, as well as among the middle-of-the-road voters, who were weary of the succession of Fulbright's controversial positions on Court appointments, national priorities, and foreign policy.

Over the long term, it was fortunate for the moderates that Bumpers survived the era of reaction ignited by the war and the Nixon administration in the early 1970s. The pendulum of public opinion experienced several major swings during the last 10 years of Fulbright's career; the moderates gained strength from late 1964 until roughly 1967, when a period of reaction set in that would culminate in McClellan's defeat of the moderate Congressman Pryor and Nixon's landslide victory in the state's presidential race in 1972. With the end of the war and Watergate, the moderates' political fortunes again began to revive in roughly 1973-74 and afterwards. By the era of Watergate, however, Fulbright's support had deteriorated beyond restoration because of his long succession of controversial stands. As a noncontroversial figure, Bumpers survived the Nixon years and then became a dominant politician in a more moderate era beginning in the mid-1970s and continuing into the 1980s, when Bumpers, Congressman Bill Alexander, Pryor (who came back from the 1972 loss to McClellan to win the 1974 governor's race), Governor Bill Clinton and other progressives dominated the state's politics as they had never done before; all these younger men shared an admiration for Fulbright. For supporters of Fulbright's sober, thoughtful approach to the role of senator, Bumpers was one of the best replacements he could have found. Bumpers acquired a reputation in the Senate for courage and intellect reminiscent of Fulbright; Bumper's opposition to President Reagan's nomination of Robert Bork, in fact, bore similarities to Fulbright's role in the Carswell and Rehnquist debates, although the strength of the black and moderate vote by 1987 rendered Bumpers' opposition to Bork somewhat less controversial than the Carswell affair had been.[99]

Fulbright's votes on the Court nominations appear perceptive, in retrospect. His votes on all of the nominations except the controversial cases of Haynsworth and Rehnquist would be almost universally recognized among legal scholars as correct.[100] Fulbright's justification for his Haynsworth vote—to prevent "someone worse" from being appointed—was inept, since each case needs to be judged on its own merits. But it is nevertheless true that Haynsworth was a decent judge who was subjected to a barrage of overheated criticism; if the appointment process is to be a cooperative venture between President and Congress, such choices probably have to be honored. The only possible caveat to that argument might be the South Carolinian's civil rights record, but even in that realm disagreement with a judge's decisions is insufficient to preclude him from appointment, as long as extreme ideological prejudice is not involved. As the Rehnquist nomination demonstrated, distinguishing sharp disagreement with a judge's opinions from ideological extremism can be a difficult, intricate matter. In Rehnquist's case, some legal scholars would argue that Rehnquist merely provided faithful conservative adjudication after his elevation to the Court, while others would be sharply critical of him as a reactionary. Whatever the merits of the Rehnquist case, Fulbright was certainly correct to lead the revitalized role of the Congress in fostering exhaustive investigations into the nominations. In the Nixon years, the process involving both an aggressive legislative as well as executive involvement in the process was one of the pressures leading Nixon to make the widely acclaimed appointments of Blackmun and Powell, and the Nixon-era Court controversies furnished precedents on which opponents of the Bork nomination could rely.[101]

With all of the political burdens Fulbright was already laboring under, the question arises as to why he would take controversial positions on Supreme Court nominations, vote for the Voting Rights Act extension, and embrace the highly dissonant arguments lamenting the Vietnam War's impact on America's domestic life. Previously he had focused his anti-war dissent on the argument that the United State should not intervene in a civil war between two authoritarian regimes in a country where no American vital interests were threatened. One of the important explanations for the departures from Fulbright's earlier strategy was the gradual strengthening of the moderates in Arkansas politics. The Voting Rights Act extension episode could be explained by the political changes. But it would be an over-simplification to attribute all of Fulbright's votes to gradual political change, for the Carswell nomination presented an issue that was basically similar to what he had faced in the 1950s: in both cases there was a progressive faction, a reactionary faction and a large group in the middle that was unpredictable, although McClellan believed, with some justification, that it was much more likely to move to the right. Certainly in the Rehnquist case, the Vietnam War issue was more important in Fulbright's scale of values than the civil rights issues; but he had still taken a controversial position on a vote that was primarily perceived in Arkansas as a civil rights issue. The Carswell nomination unleashed a reaction as virulent as any single civil-rights related issue he faced in his career with the exception of the Central High crisis. Fulbright's votes cannot be explained strictly by the gradual movement of the state's politics away from the racist demagogy of the 1950s.

In addition to this growth of a stronger moderate faction, in his later career Fulbright was simply less inclined to believe that his seat in Congress was worth making concessions on meaningful issues. He would recall that "When I was first elected, I was concerned about getting re-elected, but after I'd been up here a good while and was getting older, the prospect of losing an election just didn't hold that much anxiety any more."[102] Lee Williams would recall that when he implored Fulbright to make the rounds of the Rotary Clubs to revive his political fortunes after the Carswell battle, the senator at first halfheartedly agreed; but whenever a substantive committee assignment produced a scheduling conflict with the Little Rock Rotary Club, alas, the Rotary Club would be the loser.[103] In 1961 and 1967 the senator had engaged in intensive pre-election year tours of the state and had greatly solidified his political situation in the process. But when Williams emphasized that he would have to spend a great deal of time again making the local rounds in Arkansas in 1973, Fulbright either grudgingly acknowledged the point or simply replied that he had too many vital duties in American foreign policy in Washington. The senator was offended by the new political techniques that focused on television, political consultants, extensive political research and public opinion polls, and fund-raising through the use of computers. When Williams, his press aide Hoyt Purvis, and his campaign consultant Mark Shields tried to impress upon Fulbright the importance of utilizing the new mass communications techniques, the senator was never enthusiastic and at times irritated. The idea of selling J. William Fulbright on a television commercial was repugnant to him, although he reluctantly agreed to it, after considerable delay. Fulbright had always been willing to risk political defeat for his stands on education and foreign policy; in the later years, his votes were carried wherever his intellectual analysis led him, causing his range of adversarial positions to embrace virtually all of the controversial issues of the time. By the early 1970s his political position appeared so bleak he considered not running. The senator's private polls showed in early 1973 that if Bumpers opposed him the race would be utterly hopeless, but Fulbright clung to the hope that Bumpers would not oppose his former mentor, and there might be no opposition. There was also some speculation that if Bumpers decided to run, he might privately relay his decision through intermediaries to Fulbright, thus giving the senator the choice of either running for re-election or retiring without a defeat. It seemed that the hope of no opposition might become a reality until just hours before the filing deadline, when Bumpers suddenly announced his candidacy in March.

Lee Williams had previously met with members of Bumpers' staff in Little Rock to urge the governor not to run, and he had been assured at that time that Bumpers would not enter the Senate race. Fulbright and Bumpers had worked together in Arkansas politics until 1974, and the thought of philosophical blood brothers opposing each other was painful for many people in both camps. Back in 1970, James Powell encouraged Fulbright to support the able but unknown young lawyer from Charleston in his first run for the governor's mansion. Williams had also urged Fulbright to support Bumpers against Faubus. Fulbright agreed to back the newcomer, and the work of the *Gazette* and Fulbright were significant forces contributing to Bumpers' victory in 1970.[103a]

No issues about civil rights or any other issue were hotly debated in the campaign; although Fulbright unsuccessfully tried to provoke some discussion of substance to at least give the final chapter of his career some meaning, he would later concede "it was like shouting in a high wind." The voters had become weary of the man who forever urged them to "think unthinkable thoughts" about war or poverty or the Supreme Court. If he was often right too far in advance of the voters, it seemed more important to them in 1974 that he gave the impression of always knowing that he was right. With Bumpers' amiable genius for evading issues, in 1974 the governor did not trouble the people with complex, challenging ideas about the Supreme Court or any other issue, but vaguely preached about the "mess in Washington" in the heyday of Watergate and inflation, and his own local status as strictly an Arkansas politician. Bumpers and everyone else knew that Fulbright had nothing to do with Watergate or the "mess in Washington," of course, but Bumpers' 2-to-1 landslide was foretold from the moment of his announcement.[104]

Many blacks had appreciated Fulbright's leadership on socio-economic policies and the Court appointments; but Bumpers, on the other hand, had appointed numerous blacks to state government posts. Fulbright's strength among blacks deteriorated in the 1974 campaign when Ben Grinage, the black aide who had written so effusively of Fulbright's courage in the Carswell vote, publicly voiced criticism during the campaign that a white lawyer was placed in charge of paying and supervising 12 black campaign workers. Grinage complained that "I was hurt and I was agonized not because the money [$15,000] was spent, but because they felt this machinery [placing the white lawyer in charge] was necessary."[105] It was a fleeting episode in a campaign that was already lost at the time, despite overall campaign expenditures of more than half a million dollars as opposed to Bumpers' spending of $250,000. It was partly the result of a disgruntled staff member, although it also may have represented an offensive, paternalistic attitude on the part of the Fulbright campaign. If the problem was Grinage's disgruntlement, the campaign erred in not correcting it earlier. Although it would be impossible to prove whether any of the payments the Fulbright campaign made were improper, (Grinage did not criticize the payments themselves and had advocated similar expenditures in the 1968 campaign) in the larger sense the massive expenditures of the senator's campaign contradicted one of his arguments for reform, for he had previously decried the corrosive impact of huge expenditures on the electoral process.[106] Even if Grinage's complaint was motivated by some personal grudge against the campaign, it nonetheless further weakened Fulbright's appeal among a group of voters who had previously supported him. It was one of the more dismal events of a campaign in disarray. Fulbright would naturally recall 1974 with distaste, later saying simply, "I'm sorry I ran."[107] Previously, Fulbright's lowest total black vote had been 70 percent against Bernard; the black vote was roughly even against Bumpers.[108]

The Bumpers challenge was unique in Fulbright's career, for the Rhodes Scholar's opposition in the past had always come from the right. By 1974, the moderates and blacks had become potent voting forces in the state. Fulbright's voting record had become substantially more liberal, with the Americans for Democratic Action giving him the highest rating (55) of any member of the Arkansas delegation. On issues regarding medical care and Social Security, the National Council of Senior Citizens gave Fulbright a 78 percent score, again the highest in the state's delegation. On labor issues, the senator's record again reflected a liberal trend, as he voted in 1973 for significant increases in the minimum wage and cosponsored a bill providing an additional $44.5 million in funding for the Neighborhood Youth Corps Project. The latter vote was well received among blacks, since the Youth Corps provided jobs for unemployed and underemployed people, and blacks in the delta and in other areas of the state still suffered from discrimination and a severe lack of employment opportunities. Despite a record that was now quite progressive on the great majority of issues, Fulbright still had great difficulty in competing with Bumpers for many moderate voters. Bumpers also had a progressive record; more importantly, on such issues as civil rights and labor, Fulbright's recent changes could not erase the memory of his earlier record on those issues. Moreover, Fulbright had so thoroughly antagonized the hard-line right wing through his stance on Vietnam, the Carswell nomination, the Middle East, and other controversial positions that they would have voted for virtually anyone rather than the "Great Dissenter."[108a]

Fulbright was also damaged by his position on the Middle East. Although he had advocated an evenhanded approach, he was perceived as anti-Israeli and pro-Arab. Paul Greenberg of the *Pine Bluff Commercial* incessantly condemned the senator as an appeaser. Dr. Elijah Palnick, a Rabbi in Little Rock, excoriated Fulbright for allegedly promoting "anti-Semitic canards and propaganda of Joseph Goebbels or the Klan at its worst." Protestants shared in the sympathy for Israel. The Baptist Missionary Association passed a resolution commending American support for Israel in the 1973 Middle East war.[108b] Pro-Israeli elements made substantial contributions to Bumpers' campaign, although this was not a major factor in the outcome since campaign funding was one of the few major areas where Fulbright had an advantage over Bumpers.

The senator did not campaign as effectively in 1974 as he had in previous years. In his earlier campaigns, he had had been careful to cite his positions on such Arkansas issues as agricultural exports, river navigation projects, and local economic questions. But rather than conveying the image of concern for local issues, the 1974 campaign projected the opposite view by bringing in such national figures as Henry Kissinger and constantly harping upon Fulbright's great stature as a national and international figure. The fact that Fulbright received substantial out-of-state campaign contributions was also a negative, for Arkansans traditionally disliked the idea of interests outside of the state becoming involved in its elections. Bumpers also skillfully played up the contrast between Fulbright's deep pockets supporters—Stephens, Murphy, Pickens and others—and his own decision to restrict contributions to less than $1,000. Bumpers had powerful backers as well, but since his position was so strong he had no compelling need for a massive campaign war chest.

To compound all of Fulbright's problems, throughout 1973-74 the senator just did not have the fire in his heart for that last campaign. His answers to questions on the stump at times became undisciplined and rambling. Once, when he was asked about how to increase funding to impoverished areas of east Arkansas, he replied that there had been a good harvest that year and he thought the delta was potentially one of the most prosperous areas of the state. Of course, this answer simply reflected the fact that Fulbright had been talking too much in east Arkansas to the narrow class of planters and businessmen who had traditionally controlled the politics in that region earlier in his career. Agribusiness was booming in some areas, but many people who lived in east Arkansas were still afflicted by inadequate health care and abject poverty.[108c]

The Grinage episode touched a chord with NAACP leader Daisy Bates and many other blacks who had long sensed a certain paternalism in Fulbright's attitude toward them. It might have been more accurate to say that Fulbright, the patrician intellectual from one of Arkansas' most prominent families, was equally condescending to many people of all races. The Rhodes Scholar whose life had been an unbroken chronicle of personal successes, from the nation's youngest university president to senator to chairman of Foreign Relations, displayed an insensitivity to personal failures of others, and particularly the individual trauma inflicted by racial injustice. Reporters and scholars who discussed the issue with him in later years would notice the sharp divergence between his willingness to admit error and the acuity of his observations on other issues, as opposed to the defensive denial of error and the rigidity of his reflections on civil rights. It was paradoxical that a man with such vision on so many issues seemingly failed to see the full tragedy of race relations in the South, and no candid observer could ever plausibly say that he or she had fully resolved the enigma of Fulbright's relative insensitivity on racial issues. Certainly there was nothing in his youthful experiences that would have exposed him to racial injustice, for there were almost no blacks in the hill country of Arkansas when he was growing up; he would always recall that "there was no interest in integration in Fayetteville," and the town's schools made comparatively early progress toward desegregation in the 1950s. His first exposure to racial politics in the delta during the 1940s and 1950s indelibly imprinted on him the virulence of racial passions and fears of miscegenation; he was shocked at first, but eventually settled into his comfortable rationalization that there was nothing he could do in dealing with such irrational behavior. An insensitivity, but a studied insensitivity, hardened in him over the years, as if he wanted to make sure he never reflected too long or too hard about the issue, for such reflection might have led him to views contradicting his facile rationalizations that "nothing could be done."[109]

The senator's substantive record on race issues did not differ markedly in the later period from those of Rockefeller or Bumpers, who also opposed busing and were careful to avoid controversy on civil rights as much as possible. But Rockefeller and Bumpers shared a talent of showing their personal warmth and compassion, of some feeling for the human dimensions of the racial problem. A shaken Rockefeller, for example, took part in a memorial for Martin Luther King on the capitol steps in Little Rock after King's assassination, and was fond of symbolic gestures and glowing speeches in support of racial justice. Fulbright would regard such gestures as rhetorical flourishes, which in part they were; but the effect over the years of having those in power set such examples gradually ameliorated Arkansans' feelings about race relations.[110] Even when Fulbright was engaged in activities that were substantively quite effective, such as his dissent on the Carswell nomination, he was ever the detached, profound intellectual viewing the panorama of life from the Capitol committee chambers. If he opposed a segregationist who was nominated to the Court, he would cite high reversal rates and the opposition of Judge John Minor Wisdom or legal scholars who were unknown to the vast majority of the people. Most Arkansans, of whatever race or political philosophy, needed to see some sense of a personal sympathy for a profound social problem, and without that there would remain a distance between them and the senator.

Even at the moment of triumph—the elevation of Blackmun to the Court instead of Carswell—civil rights leaders remained somewhat cold and reluctant to praise Fulbright, and some of them used the occasion to criticize him for his earlier positions, or even to condemn him for what some of them regarded as hypocrisy. The *Gazette* enthusiastically supported Fulbright in the 1974 election, but its editorial complimenting his Carswell vote could not refrain from reminding its readers of his earlier civil rights record; this deepened Fulbright's frustration.[111]

What so many of the black leaders could not fathom in Fulbright was the lack of any sense that racial injustice was one of the greatest tragedies of the era, and perhaps fundamentally, his refusal to ever admit that he had made any errors in his civil rights policies. "Why does he have to sell his people and his soul like that?" Bates had asked in harsh tones when Faubus was still in power, " . . . I'll listen to Faubus more than I'll listen to Fulbright." Fulbright only aggravated the stress by his patronizing explanations that the annoying liberals did not understand his dilemma in the Senate, about the strain he was under and the concessions he had to make "to help them in the long run."[112] What the liberals and black political leaders resented most, perhaps, was his failure to reflect upon their dilemma in being in a political minority or a racially oppressed minority. In their endless debate, neither Fulbright nor his critics seemed particularly sensitive toward developing empathy for the other's point of view.

The liberal criticism resonated with poignancy in 1957, but may have been at times harsh in 1970. If some of the black civil rights leaders in Arkansas or Hugh Patterson thought their criticisms of Fulbright never touched his conscience, perhaps they were mistaken. While he would often become somewhat irascible with his liberal critics, it is also impressive that he never cut off the lines of communication with them, never questioned their responsibility to criticize a senator. And any reporter or civil rights leader would find open access to the senator to debate civil rights questions. Behind the defensiveness, one sensed that conscience influenced the departures in the later years. Perhaps the lofty intellect that offended so many people over the years was not so much arrogance, as simply the professorial demeanor of an academic figure who was thrust into politics accidentally by his family's involvement in politics, rather than a conscious choice of his own.[113] In a career rich with ironies, the final irony came in the Carswell nomination. In previous decades, his historic role had essentially been that of a courageous dissenter in international affairs or in opposition to anti-communist extremism. In 1954, for example, he cast the only dissenting vote in the entire Senate opposing the appropriations for Senator Joe McCarthy's demagogical investigations. Again in 1961 he was the only adviser at the final review session before the Bay of Pigs to advise Kennedy not to go through with the invasion of Cuba. He had publicly opposed the Vietnam War in late 1965 when Johnson still commanded an imposing majority of support. Finally, Fulbright had advocated detente years before it was popular. Throughout all those years he fashioned a record that many lauded for serving as the nation's conscience, but he was almost always in lonely dissent in McCarthyism, the Bay of Pigs, and Vietnam. All the while he often seemed to regard civil rights as a frustrating sideshow that was his "admission ticket" to the Senate. Then in the twilight of his career, it was in a Supreme Court nomination that focused on civil rights issues that at last offered the opportunity to not merely establish a courageous record of dissent but to exert a profound influence in deciding a vote. Fulbright's influence by itself may or may not have defeated Carswell, but he was one among several senators whose opposition was indispensable. And it was his judicial conservatism and his conservative civil rights record—for so long his greatest flaw—that gave his vote such a powerful political impact among his colleagues when he finally decided to take risks on such a volatile issue. Thus, in one of the few votes on a historic political controversy in his entire career where his personal influence was critical to success, Fulbright played a crucial role in helping to prevent a judge with a record of racial extremism from being elevated to the nation's highest Court.

Book Six:

FULBRIGHT AND HIS LEGACY

I. PERSPECTIVE AFTER DEFEAT

Senator Fulbright's record in the Nixon nominations to the Supreme Court was, in a word, exemplary, because in each case he followed his judgment and his conscience. His opposition to the nomination of G. Harrold Carswell was critical and prescient. In the same period his stand against the Vietnam War finally came to coincide with the opinion of the popular majority. So it was that in the early 1970s he had reached the pinnacle of his career—even as his time was running out with his own constituency. After 30 years Arkansas was growing weary of its most celebrated son and was captivated, at the same time, by a popular and talented governor. In early 1974, Fulbright's defeat was ordained from the time Bumpers announced his candidacy for the Senate.

In January 1975, when his career ended, he could look at U.S. foreign policy and see that it had matured and sobered in the 15 years since he had assumed the chair of Foreign Relations.

Fulbright's opposition to the obsessive anti-communism of recent American diplomacy was not a failure, despite the interminable and disastrous intervention in Vietnam. The Arkansas senator had contributed to the creation of a general American consensus against military expeditions into regions of the globe where vital American interests were not involved: by the late 1970s public opinion polls revealed that the vast majority of the American people opposed U.S. military involvement in the Third World and believed that the Vietnam War was "more than a mistake, it was fundamentally wrong and immoral." Whether a large majority of Americans agreed with Fulbright's dissent against the anti-communist ideology by the 1970s was not clear. However, his constant appeals for the amelioration of American relations with the great communist powers throughout the 1960s foreshadowed and facilitated the detente policies that National Security Adviser Henry Kissinger pursued in the early 1970s.

Fulbright maintained in *The Crippled Giant* that by the time of the President's journey to China in February 1972, Nixon's foreign policy was no longer dominated by the rigid anti-communism of the Truman Doctrine. Henry Kissinger had persuaded Nixon by the early 1970s that China's policies in Indochina were no more than conventional great-power maneuverings in a region the Chinese had always considered to be their "sphere of influence." Fulbright was not optimistic about the prospects for establishing a permanent foundation of international peace and security on the basis of Kissinger's "geopolitical or balance of power approach," for he believed the 19th century European "balance of power policies" had culminated in the first world war. Yet Fulbright supported the Kissinger foreign policy (except in Indochina), which was based upon a scholarly, dispassionate analysis of specific advantages and threats to America's vital national interests. The Foreign Relations Committee chairman described the geopolitical diplomacy of Dr. Kissinger as an "enormous improvement" upon the policies of the Cold War crusaders, whose ideological prejudices led them to imagine that all communist states were aggressive and united in their determination to destroy the free world.

During Nixon's visit to China he declared it to be the objective of the United States to withdraw its soldiers from Vietnam (the 1973 cease-fire agreements would provide for the withdrawal of the last 27,000 American troops from South Vietnam), and at some unspecified date in the future to remove its military installations from Taiwan. Both the Chinese and American governments agreed to seek a "normalization of relations." Nixon did not attempt to explain why it was necessary for thousands of Americans to continue risking their lives in Vietnam to "contain" the alleged Chinese imperialism when the President could drink toasts of friendship with the Chinese leaders in Peking. Fulbright continued to denounce the administration's "unreconstructed" policies in Vietnam.

Fulbright's defeat in his 1974 re-election campaign cannot be interpreted as a repudiation of his opposition to the Vietnam War. The senator's opponent, Governor Dale Bumpers, agreed with his dissent against the war. No differences concerning Vietnam emerged during the nationally televised debate between Fulbright and Bumpers just before the May 1974 Democratic primary. During the debate, Bumpers agreed with Fulbright that the United States should not have intervened in Vietnam, asserting that "I didn't think that it was a moral war for us to be involved in." Bumpers' only sharp disagreement with Fulbright during the May debate focused on the senator's defense of the seniority system, which the governor claimed had prevented Congress from responding to "the grass-roots problems in this country." Fulbright countered by observing (and his observation was accurate) that he and the other senior members of Arkansas' Congressional delegation had used their seniority to obtain federal government funds to assist the economic development of Arkansas, which had enjoyed substantial economic progress over the previous 30 years. Bumpers' overwhelming margin of victory (approximately two to one) in the election was difficult to explain. A few political observers argued that some Arkansans regarded Fulbright as a foreign affairs specialist who did not devote sufficient attention to the domestic concerns of his constituents: this argument was speculative, however, and Fulbright actually devoted great amounts of time and energy to Arkansas affairs. One reason for the primary's denouement was simply the talent of Bumpers, who in some ways was as gifted as Fulbright. Bumpers had fashioned a successful and constructive record in his two terms as governor. The year 1974—a year of inflationary troubles and the height of the Watergate crisis—was an unfortunate time for any national incumbent to seek re-election, even though Fulbright had absolutely nothing to do with the Nixon administration's domestic wrongdoing. The senator attempted to disassociate himself from the administration, and one of his campaign slogans proclaimed that "Nothing would make Richard Nixon happier than a Fulbright defeat." In the televised debate Bumpers acknowledged that "Senator Fulbright is a man of integrity who has disagreed very vigorously with the President." However, the voters displayed a somewhat illogical mood of resentment against all national incumbents in that year.

Daniel Yergin described Fulbright as the major political casualty of "the Incumbent Syndrome of 1974."

In one sense, the senator was identified with the administration, since he continued to encourage Kissinger's detente with China and the USSR. During the election year, Kissinger rather ostentatiously visited Arkansas to confer with Fulbright about U.S. diplomacy. At a Little Rock press conference with the Foreign Relations Committee chairman, Secretary of State Kissinger first evaded reporters' suggestions that his conference with Fulbright had political implications by joking that "I am not in my job for my competence in domestic politics." But he added that he had always respected Fulbright's advice, and claimed that during his years at Harvard "When I was a professor, I used to assign his books in my courses." The senator's identification with the Kissinger policy was not necessarily a political disadvantage, since there was little strong evidence that detente was highly unpopular in Arkansas: and Bumpers was also a moderate in foreign policy. Whatever the explanation for the Fulbright defeat, it is clear that his dissent on Vietnam and his support for detente were not the crucial factors in his loss to Bumpers.

During his career as a senator, Bumpers adopted a moderate, realistic approach to international issues that was reasonably similar to Fulbright's, although for obvious reasons the two men rarely acknowledged the similarities in their foreign policy positions. The 1974 election provoked bitter animosities among admirers of the two candidates, for Fulbright had assisted Bumpers' 1970 gubernatorial campaign and Bumpers had previously supported Fulbright. Admirers of Fulbright argued that Bumpers should have waited for future opportunities to run for the Senate. The Bumpers camp would respond that there was a traditional resistance in Arkansas to third gubernatorial campaigns, so that if the governor's political career was to continue then he had no choice but to declare his candidacy in the Senate election of 1974: the Bumpers partisans also contended that Fulbright, who was 69 in 1974, should have retired. The Fulbright admirers would answer that the senator was perfectly alert and capable of serving brilliantly for one last term at the prestigious post of Foreign Relations Committee chairman. Indeed, Fulbright was still remarkably perspicacious as late as 10 years after 1974. The debate between the Fulbright and Bumpers advocates was endless; an objective observer could only regret the unfortunate situation in which two of the most eloquent and enlightened statesmen in recent American history had campaigned against each other.

In later years, Senator Bumpers opposed President Ronald Reagan's military interventionism abroad, although by 1984 he was not yet as prominent a critic of the Cold Warriors as Fulbright had been. Bumpers criticized the expanding U.S. involvement in Central America in 1983, stating that many Americans feared that Reagan "may be heading us into a war in Central America that they don't want." The senator was even more outspoken in his dissent from the President's decision to deploy Marines in Lebanon in a quest to uphold the tottering government of Amin Gemayel. In September 1983, Bumpers was among the minority of the members of Congress voting against a measure to allow the President to keep the Marines in Lebanon for another 18 months. During the Senate's emotional debate over Lebanon, Bumpers announced: "The people in this country do not want another 55,000 dead sons for something they do not understand . . . The parallel is not perfect, but there are enough lessons to be learned from Vietnam that we ought not to do what we are about to do." The senator maintained that most Americans did not believe U.S. national security was endangered by the civil war in tiny

Lebanon. He also opposed the measure in part because Reagan had not fulfilled his obligation under the War Powers Resolution "to tell Congress and the American people the conditions under which we will leave Lebanon." Bumpers warned his colleagues not to be influenced by a recent announcement of a cease-fire, for "This is the 172nd cease-fire in Lebanon since 1975." Arkansas' junior Senator David Pryor joined Bumpers in attempting to prevent the United States from becoming entangled in a Vietnam-like quagmire in the Middle East.

In addition to the two U.S. senators, U.S. Representative Bill Alexander of Arkansas continued in the Fulbright tradition in opposing the Reagan administration's interventionism. Alexander's criticisms of Reagan's policies in Lebanon and Central America were surprising, for in his early career he had not challenged the Cold Warrior approach to foreign policy. But during the Reagan Presidency he charged that the President was speaking publicly about negotiation while quietly continuing to escalate hostilities in Nicaragua. When a reporter asked Alexander if he sought to emulate Fulbright's former role as an advocate of the amelioration of U.S.-Latin American relations, Alexander first avoided the question by remarking, "This is a different day and generation," but then added, "It's already done, don't you think?" The representative supported Congressional efforts to prohibit the administration from supplying covert aid to the Nicaraguan rebels. Alexander observed that most Latin Americans envisaged the 1980 Nicaraguan revolution in which the leftists came to power as the beginning of a historic rebellion against the oligarchy, oppression, and right-wing dictatorships that had previously dominated most Latin American governments. In the Arkansas congressman's view, Latins were being united against U.S. policy by the administration's actions in Nicaragua and El Salvador, which they regarded as "Yankee imperialism." Alexander proposed a plan for peace in Central America, beginning with a hemispheric peace conference including Cuba and four countries—Colombia, Mexico, Panama, and Venezuela—that had offered to help negotiate a settlement. According to Alexander, the United States should concentrate on food and economic aid rather than military aid in Latin America.

Alexander developed themes reminiscent of Fulbright's career when he professed that even if his constituents displayed no concern about Central America, he would feel obligated to educate them: "I think I can convince my people it's in their best interest to pursue a rational policy in Latin America. It's a [political] risk but I see it as a challenge." In making this statement, Alexander appeared to be pursuing the fundamental attitude advocated by Fulbright in *The Arrogance of Power*, where the senator explained the educational motivations behind the decision to hold the Vietnam hearings. "The hearings were criticized," Fulbright observed, "on the ground that they conveyed an 'image' of the United States as divided over the war." But the country clearly was divided, so that the hearings conveyed a fact rather than an image. The Vietnam hearings were undertaken, Fulbright declared, "in the belief that the best way to assure the prevalence of truth over falsehood is by exposing all tendencies of opinion to free competition in the marketplace of ideas. They were undertaken in something of the spirit of Thomas Jefferson's words:

'I know no safe depository of the ultimate powers of the society but the people themselves: and if we think them not enlightened enough to exercise their control with a wholesome discretion, the remedy is not to take it from them, but to inform their discretion.' "

Alexander joined Fulbright (then of counsel to the Hogan and Hartson law firm in Washington) in opposing President Reagan's policies in Lebanon. Fulbright was more sharply critical of the President's intervention and placed great emphasis upon the danger that crises might erupt from the war in Lebanon that could precipitate a clash between the superpowers. In February 1984, Alexander asserted that "the American Marines have been viewed by the majority Moslem population as the enemy because of the American support of a minority Christian government that has not shared power with a majority Moslem population." Alexander approved of the President's February decision to move the Marines from Beirut to U.S. naval vessels near the Lebanon coast, but he predicted that the ground forces' redeployment was a "prelude to a major escalation" of U.S. air and naval assaults against the enemies of the Gemayel government.

Fulbright's influence upon Alexander was direct. As a young lawyer in east Arkansas, the congressman had admired Fulbright's statesmanship, and as he began to gather seniority and influence in Congress, he consciously moved in the direction of Fulbright's realistic, thoughtful approach to foreign policy. The congressman would have occasional luncheons with Fulbright in Washington in the 1980s in which the two Arkansans would discuss a wide array of national and international issues. In particular, Fulbright and Alexander would discuss the congressman's ideas regarding U.S. policy toward Cuba, particularly Alexander's proposed legislation for ending the embargo. Fulbright and Alexander also shared the view that when confronted by a right-wing extremist, such as a Joe McCarthy, Democrats should not maintain a craven silence, but should develop forthright, public answers to the demagogues. On one occasion, Fulbright, Alexander, and an Alexander staff member working on political issues discussed an idea for an op-ed article that eventually was published in a lengthy column in the *New York Times* in late April, 1989 under the headline, "Democrats: Answer Gingrich or Lose." The basic idea of Alexander's column was that latter day demagogues of the right were using mudslinging tactics that were not fundamentally different from those McCarthy had employed; just as Fulbright had been proven right in the light of history for his stalwart opposition to McCarthy, the Democrats should have answered the Republican "Willie Horton" ads accusing Mike Dukakis of allowing a rapist to go free, and the diatribes of Congressman Newt Gingrich of Georgia (in the earlier stages of his career, before he became Speaker of the House) against the Democratic Party. Alexander's *New York Times* article was symbolic of a determination upon the part of the Democrats to avoid repeating the errors of Dukakis in 1988, when the Democratic nominee had avoided making any rejoinders to the Republican charges until it was too late. In 1992, Bill Clinton had clearly taken this lesson to heart, and aggressively answered Republican charges in the Presidential campaign of that year. As for Alexander, he was destined never to attain the national and international prominence enjoyed by Fulbright; although he rose to become the fourth ranking Democrat in the House of Representatives national leadership in the 1980s, he encountered a series of political setbacks, antagonized many of his conservative constituents through his constant feuding with Presidents Reagan and Bush, and eventually was defeated for re-election in 1992.

In 1984, as the removal of the Marines began, American naval vessels bombarded Moslem positions east of Beirut in the most massive U.S. naval barrage since the Vietnam War. The bombardment provoked warnings by pro-Syrian factions that they would retaliate if the shelling continued. Thus, by early 1984 it was not yet clear whether the movement of the Marines would be followed by naval and aerial warfare that could heighten international tensions and risk a conflict between the superpowers. It was clear, however, that public opinion opposed the American military involvement in Lebanon: in September 1983, a public opinion poll indicated that 58 percent of the Americans surveyed thought the Marines should be withdrawn in six months or less, and public opposition to intervention in Lebanon increased after terrorist attacks and other hostilities led to the deaths of more than 260 soldiers in the last months of 1983.

A minority of Arkansas politicians, including the Republican U.S. Representative Ed Bethune, supported Reagan's crusading approach to international controversies. However, most of the major Arkansas politicians dissented from Reagan's policies. (Governor Bill Clinton had worked for the Foreign Relations Committee during the latter part of Fulbright's chairmanship, and most Arkansans generally regarded him as a Fulbright protege: of course, as a governor, Clinton's attention was primarily focused on Arkansas rather than diplomatic issues.) Thus, in the years after Fulbright's defeat, the former senator's plea for moderation and realism was sometimes echoed in the statements of Alexander, Bumpers, Pryor, and other Arkansas figures, although by 1984 these younger men had not attained the international stature of Fulbright.

Fulbright was unquestionably one of the historical giants of his time. One measure of his stature was the praise he received from intellectuals and politicians of widely divergent philosophies. For example, John F. Kennedy lauded the Fulbright exchange program as "the classic modern example of beating swords into plow shares." Edward Kennedy once said of the Arkansan: "Only a small handful of senators in our history have even begun to rival his stature in foreign affairs and his impact on the conduct of U.S. foreign relations . . . From the Fulbright scholarship program to his unflagging courage and insight during the national trial of Vietnam, to divining a new course for America in the post-Vietnam era, Senator Fulbright has set the highest standards for wisdom, statesmanship, and leadership. One cannot travel anywhere without hearing him spoken of as the personification of what is best in America and best in our foreign policy." Walter Lippmann praised Fulbright as "the bravest and wisest of advisers," and John Kenneth Galbraith described him as "perhaps the most diversely intelligent legislator" of the post-World War II era. In an endorsement for Fulbright's last book, *The Price of Empire*, Galbraith wrote: "Of all persons who, for their foreign policy, I've wished might be president, Bill Fulbright stands first." It was not surprising that Lippmann and Galbraith honored Fulbright, since they agreed with his basic perspective on American diplomacy; but perhaps the most impressive tributes to the senator were delivered by men who had usually disagreed with him during most of his career. For example, Fulbright and Henry Kissinger, though basically in agreement concerning detente, had assumed totally antagonistic positions regarding the Vietnam War and U.S. interventionism in the Third World. Yet in the second volume of Kissinger's memoirs, the former Secretary of State wrote, "I greatly respected Senator Fulbright across the chasm of our policy differences for his erudition, fairness, and patriotism." At the opposite end of the philosophical spectrum from Fulbright, was John McClellan, a "hawk" and a hard-line anti-communist. Yet near the end of his career, McClellan once conceded that Fulbright had "gained the recognition of being regarded as a prophet in his own time. Often in defiance of conventional wisdom he has taken a sometimes lonely and unpopular stand on some of the great issues of our day. Often, it has turned out that his position was correct."

Perhaps the man who was the most unlikely admirer of Fulbright was Dr. Martin Luther King, Jr., who wrote an encomium to Fulbright in 1965 when the senator had just begun his historic opposition to Johnson's foreign adventures in southeast Asia and the Caribbean. The famous civil rights leader and the Southern senator obviously held divergent views and different constituencies in the realm of civil rights: nevertheless, King had encouraged the Arkansan to continue publicizing his dissenting ideas about foreign policy:

> In many respects the destiny of our nation may rest largely in your hands. I know the tremendous price you pay for your outspoken critique of administration policy, and I write to you these few words simply as personal encouragement and to let you know that there are many of us who admire and respect your role in our nation's international affairs . . . Yours is one voice crying in the wilderness that may ultimately awaken our people to the international facts of life. I trust that you will not let any pressure silence you.

The senator had responded to King's epistle by confessing that "my influence is not sufficiently strong in the highest echelons of our Nation's Government to do much about the policy which is now being followed" in 1965. It was not unusual for famous senators to receive panegyrics: but only a unique statesman could have been praised by such heterogeneous leaders as Kennedy, John McClellan, Walter Lippmann, Henry Kissinger, and Martin Luther King.

There were other leaders, of course, who denounced the Arkansas senator during the course of his career. Joe McCarthy lambasted him as "Halfbright." President Nixon's private denunciations of the Arkansan were reportedly too profane to be printed by most writers, while in the early 1970s General Alexander Haig privately told his associates that Fulbright was a "traitor" because of his opposition to the Vietnam War. President Johnson delivered some of the most abrasive criticisms of his former colleague, charging that Fulbright had opposed his Vietnam policies merely to attract publicity: or, in Johnsonian language, "even a blind hog can find an acorn once in a while." The President attempted to discredit Fulbright's motives, explaining to Doris Kearns that the anti-war movement was

> Nothing but a lot of sound and poppycock stimulated by the personal needs of William Fulbright . . . Fulbright's problem is that he's never found any President who would appoint him Secretary of State. He is frustrated up there on the Hill. And he takes out his frustration by making all those noises about Vietnam. He wants the nation to stand up and take notice of Bill Fulbright, and he knows the best way to get that attention is to put himself in the role of critic. He would have taken that role whichever way I moved on Vietnam.

The charge that Fulbright was frustrated because he had not been appointed Secretary of State was incorrect, for Johnson himself had complained in December 1960 that Fulbright had made no effort to persuade President-Elect Kennedy to select him for the State

Department post. Ironically, in 1960 Johnson had been one of the most vigorous advocates of the idea of appointing Fulbright to be Secretary of State. The truth seems to have been that the senator would have accepted the Cabinet post if Kennedy had offered it to him, but that he was also quite happy to remain as Foreign Relations chairman. In any event, Johnson was obviously vindictive and emotional in accusing Fulbright of opposing the war because of alleged frustrations over his career, for Fulbright never displayed any great zeal to become Secretary of State.

In the late 1970s and 1980s, Fulbright enjoyed the relatively quiet role of an elder statesman. He became a registered lobbyist with the United Arab Emirates and an informal counselor to the Saudi Arabian government. President Sadat awarded Fulbright the Order of the Republic, a high honor in Egypt. The former senator occasionally consulted with Kissinger and President Ford on Middle Eastern policy; in an impressive tribute to Fulbright at a ceremony given by the Board of Foreign Scholarships in the mid-1970s, Secretary of State Kissinger gave a speech in which he commended Fulbright for championing an "even-handed approach to settlement in the Middle East." Some commentators, including Bernard Kalb, later argued that Kissinger did not agree with Fulbright's Middle East positions as much as he led the Arkansan to believe. Yet, Fulbright was hardly duped by Kissinger. As he wrote to James Powell in March, 1975 after the Senate had once again indicated support for military aid that would assure Israeli military domination in the Middle East, Kissinger was cornered between "the Israelis in the Middle East and the Senate... between a rock and a hard place," and the Secretary "is going to have a very hard time bringing anything off."

Throughout most of the Carter administration, Fulbright was sharply critical of the Georgian. Carter's emphasis on being a born-again Christian left Fulbright unimpressed, because the Arkansan felt that a public figure's religious beliefs should remain a private matter. Fulbright was also less than enamored of the President's vague promise to make defense of human rights the basis of his foreign policy. Of course, everyone supports human rights, but how were "human rights" defined, how could the nation's foreign policy be based upon a moralistic crusade to protect human rights throughout the globe, and how would the United States enforce such a crusade? It smacked of the moralistic approach to diplomacy that had failed in the past. Fulbright was especially disdainful of the Cold Warrior, Zbigniew Brzezinski, Carter's National Security Adviser, for reviving the Cold War after the hopeful support for detente under Kissinger. The Arkansan was much more favorable toward the more restrained and cerebral Secretary of State, Cyrus Vance, and Fulbright was a staunch supporter of President Carter's attempts to successfully complete a SALT II agreement. Fulbright was congenial with the Carter administration regarding Middle Eastern policy. He admired UN Ambassador Andrew Young, who was sympathetic to the plight of the Palestinians. Fulbright developed a cordial relationship with Young, who served as a means of communication to the administration. In the middle of the Camp David negotiations attended in 1978 by Sadat, Israeli Prime Minister Menachem Begin and Carter, Fulbright commended the conference and wrote an article in *Newsweek* reiterating his land-for-peace proposal and a great power guarantee of Israel's boundaries.

Fulbright continued to encourage the growth of the Fulbright Scholarship program; he also agreed to the establishment of a Fulbright Institute of International Relations at the University of Arkansas and the naming of the College of Arts and Sciences at the university as the J. William Fulbright College of Arts and Sciences. The former senator usually did not actively involve himself in controversies over U.S. diplomacy during this period. However, Fulbright once again began to receive national attention in 1982-83 when journalists frequently sought his opinions concerning President Reagan's attempt to revive Lyndon Johnson's approach to foreign policy. One of the most memorable episodes in his post-1975 career occurred in the autumn of 1983, when the Illinois Republican Charles Percy, chairman of the Senate Foreign Relations Committee, invited Fulbright to testify on the future of Soviet-American relations. Fulbright's testimony promised to be dramatic: at a time of escalating tensions between the superpowers, he was returning to the chamber where the Vietnam hearings had been held and appeared before the committee he had led from 1959 until the end of his Senate career—the longest chairmanship over the Foreign Relations Committee of any senator in American history.

"Perhaps I should preface my remarks with the personal observation that I am an old man of 78 years," Fulbright announced in his opening statement, "40 of which have been intimately connected with public affairs. I have witnessed many hopeful events which, with only a few exceptions, have been frustrated, so that I well may be more pessimistic than one should be." According to Fulbright, one of the greatest disappointments was the abandonment of the Nixon-Kissinger detente approach before it gained a fair trial. The former senator emphasized that Nixon's 1972 policy eventually lost the support of Congress "for causes quite irrelevant to the validity of the process initiated and the agreements [SALT I and the "confidence-building" joint ventures for cooperative research in medicine, pollution control, space, and cultural exchange] made at that time. The failure of the President's policy was influenced by the circumstances of Watergate and the disastrous Vietnam War, which undermined the power and prestige of that administration. Fulbright observed that "some of the most disturbing aspects of our present condition are that the rhetoric of our government is so ideological and so hostile toward the Soviet Union that an objective and reasoned discussion of our relations seldom takes place." In his view, the arms race had developed a dangerous momentum propelled by vast economic power and heated ideological rivalry. Although he believed that the horror of a nuclear war acted as a restraining force upon both Russia and America, the former senator warned that "Crises are likely to arise out of the ongoing war in the Middle East, which could lead to a clash between the super powers."

Fulbright contended that Reagan's interventionism in Lebanon, Grenada, and Central America was escalating the super-powers' "dangerous game of 'Tit for Tat.'" in which "a move by one calls for a response from the other." The Reagan administration frequently attempted to justify its interventions by claiming that agents of what the President had called the "evil empire" of the Soviet Union were the real enemies the United States was fighting in Central America and the Middle East. Reagan's justifications were obviously similar to the preachments of John Foster Dulles in the 1950s, when Dulles portrayed Ho Chi Minh and other anti-Western Third World leaders as puppets of the Soviet bloc. Fulbright warned Reagan, just as he had warned Dulles a quarter of a century before, that military crusades in the Third World would wreak havoc upon the prospects for a peaceful international order. The former senator noted several volatile regions where great power confrontations might occur: "For example, in case of a conflict between Israel and Syria and the occupation of Damascus, the Soviets may come to the aid of Syria, and the U.S. is not likely to stand aside;" or, he observed, in response to the administration's decision to invade Grenada the USSR might accelerate its military aid to Nicaragua and Cuba. He also reminded the committee that the Soviets might "increase the number of submarines off our coast ready to send missiles to Washington as quickly as our Pershings can reach Moscow from Germany. Such a game is likely to end in a conflict." The former senator advocated a reduction in Soviet-American tensions by negotiating and ratifying strategic arms limitation treaties (such as SALT II, which the Senate never approved) and other cooperative agreements, and by ending the reckless game of intervening against leftists or alleged Soviet agents anywhere in the world. Such moderate and realistic policies, Fulbright contended, would affect the climate of hostility that contributed to the outbreak of violence by both superpowers in crises such as "the Korean plane tragedy, the Grenada affair, and the ongoing conflict in the Middle East."

Fulbright quoted several famous statements by historical figures in an effort to support his plea for an end to the rigid and chronic American animosity toward the Soviet Union. He asked the committee to remember that in Washington's Farewell Address, the first President had counseled his countrymen to avoid indulging in ideological or emotional biases toward other nations: "A nation which indulges toward another an habitual hatred, or an habitual fondness, is in some degree a slave. It is a slave to its animosity or to its affection, either of which is sufficient to lead it astray from its duty and its interest." Fulbright compared the Soviet-American arms race to the militaristic rivalries that had afflicted Europe before World War I. He recalled that after the first World War, Lord Edward Grey (British Foreign Minister before and during World War I) had analyzed the origins of that war in these words: "Every country had been piling up armaments and perfecting preparations for war. The object in each case had been security. The effect had been precisely the contrary." The perfecting and stockpiling of armaments, Fulbright asserted, "is exactly what we are doing today." The former chairman argued that a more enlightened approach to international relations was suggested in Sigmund Freud's celebrated 1932 letter to Albert Einstein: "Anything that creates emotional ties between human beings must inevitably counteract war . . . Everything that leads to important shared action creates such common feelings, such identifications. On them the structure of human society in good measure rests." In Fulbright's view, these sentiments in the Freud-Einstein correspondence were consistent with the policies advocated by the supporters of detente in 1972.

During the November 1983 testimony, the former chairman implored the committee members to acquire a sense of empathy for the Soviets' world view. The United States had never been invaded and enjoyed borders with two friendly and comparatively weak nations, while the great Russian plains, Fulbright reminded the senators, "have throughout history been tempting to foreign invaders, and since the 13th century, they have succumbed to that temptation on numerous occasions. We should recognize that these experiences have affected and do affect the Soviets point of view." He suggested that the members of the committee might reflect upon the thought that if they were members of the Politburo, they would probably be "deeply disturbed by the installation of Pershing missiles in Germany and Western Europe, and by the congressional appropriations of $250 billion for armaments." He believed the Politburo would probably be even more disturbed by the prospect that in a future war, the Soviets might be opposed not only by their traditional enemies to the west and south, but also by Britain, France, and the United States—nations that had been Soviet allies in the previous World War—and by some of the disaffected Soviet satellites. According to Fulbright, any nation would be anxious about its national security when confronted by the possibility of facing such an unprecedented combination of power.

Fulbright proposed that Reagan should reverse the direction of his Soviet policies, just as Presidents Kennedy and Nixon had during the course of their administrations. Nixon had been a zealous Cold Warrior throughout most of his career, Fulbright recalled, until he displayed the flexibility to change his policies toward the great communist powers in the early 1970s. The former chairman did not state the obvious point, which all the senators were aware of, that he had always been an ardent critic of Nixon's dogged adherence to military intervention in southeast Asia in the early 1970s: Nixon's southeast Asian policies remained the central blot on the former President's diplomatic record.

Fulbright regarded President Kennedy's emergence as an advocate of stable and normal Soviet-American relations in 1963 as an even more impressive example of intellectual growth and flexibility than Nixon's reversal of his Soviet policies in 1971-1972. He observed that Kennedy had pursued "a very hard line indeed with the Russians" during the years 1960-1962, pledging to end the "so-called missile gap," authorizing the Bay of Pigs debacle, and threatening war over the Berlin crisis and over Russian missiles in Cuba. "However," Fulbright concluded, "after looking `down the abyss,' as it is said, at the time of the missile crisis in October 1962, Kennedy abruptly changed course and negotiated the Test Ban Treaty in August of 1963, after making the most enlightened and conciliatory speech about the Soviet Union of any President in June 1963, at American University. It was the hope for the establishment of more normal relations with the Soviet Union aroused by that speech and the treaty that, in my opinion, accounts for much of the faith in and respect for what is often called the Kennedy `Legend' or Camelot."

Fulbright did not argue that in 1963 Kennedy had attempted to alter the Cold War policies of interventionism in Vietnam. Several months before his assassination, Kennedy asked Canadian Prime Minister Lester Pearson for his advice concerning U.S. policy in southeast Asia, and Pearson answered, "Get out." The President bluntly replied, "That's a stupid answer. Everybody knows that. The question is: How do we get out?" Mike Mansfield and White House official Kenneth O'Donnell later contended that the President had privately informed them in 1963 that he planned to withdraw the U.S. military presence from South Vietnam, but he would have to wait until 1965 to do so in order to avoid right-wing charges of "appeasement" in his 1964 re-election campaign. At a high-level administration policy meeting in the autumn of 1963, Robert Kennedy noted the chaotic nature of the Saigon regime and the devastating impact of the war upon the Vietnamese people: he then proposed that the United States should consider withdrawing from Vietnam. Robert Kennedy was the first powerful presidential adviser to privately suggest the possibility of a withdrawal as a solution to the American dilemma in southeast Asia. There was no public reversal of U.S. southeast Asian policy in 1963, of course, and it will never be known whether President Kennedy would have changed America's course in Vietnam if he had lived to serve a second term.

Senator Percy or one of the other senators who attended the November 1983 hearing might have asked Fulbright if he felt that the changes in the Kennedy foreign policy in 1963 were confined to the arena of the direct relationship between America and Russia, or if he believed that Kennedy had also considered changing the policy of interventionism in the Third World. No senator asked Fulbright this fairly obvious question, even though the Arkansan had stressed in his statement that military interventionism by the superpowers in favor of their respective Third World clients had frequently damaged Soviet-American relations. In fact, Percy and his colleagues generated very little debate at the hearing with the former chairman. Percy had been a member of the Foreign Relations Committee during the last few years of Fulbright's Senate career, but as chairman he did not follow in Fulbright's tradition of utilizing hearings to promote a candid national discussion of American diplomacy. In the early 1980s the Foreign Relations Committee was a shadow of what it had been at the height of Fulbright's chairmanship. For example, a clear majority of the committee members had attended each of the Vietnam hearings; and at most of the important hearings during the late 1960s and early 1970s several senators, notably Fulbright, Morse (until his defeat in 1968), Gore, McCarthy, Church, and (after 1967) John Sherman Cooper had consistently promoted an extensive and perceptive dialogue with the witnesses. In contrast, only four senators attended the November 1983 hearing, and only Percy and ranking Democrat Claiborne Pell of Rhode Island asked a few perfunctory questions.

No one asked Fulbright for his thoughts concerning the recent Soviet shooting of a Korean airliner (although he had briefly mentioned it in his statement), and other important questions were not raised by the senators. The exchange between Fulbright and Percy was amicable: Fulbright commended the committee for holding the hearing and Percy praised Fulbright's record as chairman, stating, "The longer I serve in this chair, the more I realize the burden and load that you carried and the greatness and the dignity with which you carried this gavel." But Percy was a supporter of the administration, and he clearly did not wish to encourage and prolong a dialogue in which the former chairman was trenchantly pointing out the dangerous flaws in Reagan's foreign adventures. During the early 1980s, the Republican Mark Hatfield of Oregon, Edward Kennedy, the Arkansas senators, and others promoted educational discussion of and debate over U.S. foreign policy, but the Senate Foreign Relations Committee under Percy did not provide vigorous leadership in this discussion.

Percy was pleased by the former chairman's observation that "if President Reagan would change course, revive the spirit of detente, negotiate a significant agreement with the Russians, stop and reverse the arms race in a credible manner, that confidence in peace would be restored, the budget could be balanced, interest rates would come down, and the economy of the world, certainly including that of the United States, would revive, and he would be elected next year by a landslide. If he did such things, I surely would be tempted to vote for him." The Illinois senator chuckled at the notion that Fulbright might vote for Reagan, whereupon Fulbright asserted that Reagan was not serious about arms control and a reversal in his policies was unlikely. According to the Arkansan, the President was interested not in arms control but in achieving military superiority for the United States. He maintained that from the beginning of the Reagan administration the President had demanded a $1.5 trillion arms program and that after "he gets that $1.5 trillion and he has what he considers superiority over the Russians," then he might attempt to freeze the strategic arms ratio at a level of U.S. superiority. An obvious difficulty with the Reagan approach was that the Soviets had always attempted to match the Reagan arms escalation, and they could not be expected to acquiesce in their own strategic inferiority.

One might also argue that the entire concept of strategic superiority was chimerical in an age when both superpowers could destroy each other many times over. Fulbright observed that Dean Rusk had proclaimed after the Cuban missile crisis that the Americans and Russians were "eyeball to eyeball, and the Russians blinked first." "But it was rumored," the former chairman informed the Senators, "that Mr. Khrushchev said after that, `Yes, but the next time we won't be the one to blink first.' I think that next time may well have arrived. In other words, they have enough weapons now that they won't be bluffed as easily as then [1962] because they obviously were inferior." Fulbright regarded the relative military power of America and Russia in the 1980s as "a condition of parity, or as near parity as you are likely to get." In a condition of inferiority on the part of one of the powers, the superior side usually attempted to preserve its advantage, while the inferior side tended to engage in feverish efforts to expand its strategic arsenal; hence Fulbright envisaged the contemporary situation of relative strategic parity as providing a historic opportunity for progress in arms control.

Most of Fulbright's conclusions were generally supported by retired Admiral Noel Gayler, one of the other witnesses at the November 1983 hearing; while two bitterly anti-Soviet witnesses, especially Reagan's former National Security Adviser Richard Allen, sharply disagreed with the former chairman. In contrast to Fulbright's perspective, Richard Allen used phrases redolent of John Foster Dulles' pronouncements in condemning the Soviet Union as an allegedly fiendish threat to the peace and civilization of the world. According to Allen, Reagan was not a "gun-slinging Western cowboy," but rather a thoughtful man who believed that the Soviets respected only military strength in their rivals. The President's former adviser alleged that ultimate Soviet objectives encompassed the control of the Panama Canal and the Marxist "liberation" of Mexico, and that the Soviets were constantly engaged in revolutionary warfare and "the unbridled use of terrorism as a destabilizing force throughout the world." Allen did not adduce any evidence to prove that the Soviets intended to control Mexico and the Panama Canal, he merely asserted it; he also implied that the Russians were basically responsible for all revolution or terrorism throughout the globe, ignoring the reality that much of this subversion and violence emanated from indigenous sources in the Third World.

The hearing was not long enough for Fulbright to answer all of Allen's allegations, but he did respond to the complaint that Reagan sincerely desired arms control but had been frustrated by Soviet unwillingness to end the arms race. The former senator recalled that the Soviets had offered to reduce their SS-20s to 140, if the Reagan administration would not deploy Pershing missiles in Europe, but the administration dismissed the Soviet proposal "as of no consequence." In Fulbright's opinion, the President had agreed to the INF (intermediate nuclear force) talks in Geneva only after the nuclear freeze movement had acquired an imposing momentum within the United States, when there were "stories in the paper, bills in the Congress, and people like Kennedy and Hatfield, the chairman of the Appropriations Committee, and others, very prominent senior members, who were beginning to show an interest and get a following." Fulbright argued that the Geneva talks were charades, which Reagan had undertaken to "pull the teeth" of the domestic nuclear freeze movement, so that the President "said we will go to Geneva. It did have that effect. People thought, well after all, he has made a gesture." But Fulbright could not detect any evidence of a genuine negotiating effort by the President, and he pointedly noted that Reagan had appointed as leader of the Geneva talks a general, Edward Rowny, who had not demonstrated a serious concern for arms control.

The Arkansan generally avoided attempts to predict specific future events, but he did maintain that the Russians would leave INF if the administration deployed the Pershing missiles in western Europe. Allen had prophesied that the Soviets would be impressed by Reagan's "toughness" and begin to negotiate after the deployment occurred. When the Pershings were deployed shortly after the November 1983 hearing, Allen was proven to be somewhat lacking as a prophet, as the Soviets at least temporarily withdrew from INF and warned that they would escalate their buildup and deployment of nuclear weapons in response to the President's action.

Senator Pell's questioning fostered the most acid exchange of the hearing between Allen and Fulbright. Pell complimented Fulbright's achievement in influencing many Americans to question the "hawkish" consensus that had dominated U.S. foreign policy before the mid-1960s. "Looking back at the Vietnam War," the Rhode Island senator said, "I think it was thanks to Senator Fulbright and the committee that public opinion got turned around." Pell hoped that the advocates of a moderate American foreign policy in the 1980s would continue to attempt to encourage an enlightened public dialogue, just as the opponents of the Vietnam War had done. He asked Allen to respond to a report Pell and several other senators (including Bumpers) had written after they had conferred with Soviet leader Andropov in August. The report concluded that both the Reagan administration and the Soviet leadership had failed to advance constructive proposals for nuclear arms control, and that many Soviet leaders "believe that the U.S. Government has no interest in better relations with the Soviet Union." As Allen conceded, Reagan had been one of the vociferous critics of SALT II and contributed to the eventual demise of that treaty, and by early 1984 he had not fulfilled his 1980 campaign pledge to negotiate arms reduction agreements with the USSR. Nevertheless, Allen simply argued that Reagan's opponents were irresponsible and the American people should trust their President. Allen assured the committee that he had known the President for years and understood Reagan's intentions: "I am going to continue to believe him as long as he gives his word that he does want such an agreement." Fulbright disagreed with the notion that Americans should dutifully trust Reagan's intentions; in his view, presidents and their policies should be judged by their effects and actions, not by their promises. "With regard to what Mr. Allen just said," Fulbright countered, "in my position I do not have to believe the President, and in my experience with former Presidents, I know they don't always tell the truth. There is no reason why anybody has to believe any President. You have to judge him by circumstances, by what he actually does and the effect of it. I used to believe President Johnson until I learned better."

Allen condemned as "an abysmal failure" the detente policy Fulbright had supported. Instead of exerting a moderating effect on Soviet behavior, Allen asserted that detente had led to a massive Soviet military buildup and the brutal communist conquest of Cambodia, South Vietnam, and Laos in the years after America withdrew from southeast Asia. He neglected to mention the American failure to give detente a fair trial. And he did not explain how the detente policies of the early 1970s had supposedly caused the results of the Indochina wars.

Allen ignored the reality that southeast Asia has always been outside the range of vital American interests. If the United States constantly followed Allen's suggestion that America must halt all repression, then the United States should intervene to stop the brutal actions of regimes in South Africa, El Salvador, Iran, Vietnam, Chile, and dozens of other repressive nations in every corner of the globe; but such a policy was clearly beyond the power of America or any other nation to enforce. Allen's argument was disconnected and vague on this point; but he seemed to be arguing that detente had caused the fall of South Vietnam and Cambodia to the communists and that the United States should have prevented the violence that occurred in southeast Asia after the fall of Saigon in 1975. The obvious question arises as to how the United States could have done this, unless Allen meant that another massive U.S. military expedition should have been dispatched to Vietnam and Cambodia in the late 1970s. One wonders how many more billions of dollars, and how many more tens of thousands of American lives Allen might have wished that the United States had hurled into the maelstrom of southeast Asia. The violence and repression in southeast Asia after 1975 were brutal, but the entire history of the U.S. involvement had demonstrated the virtually insurmountable difficulties America experienced in its futile quest to control events in far-away Indochina. Neither the United States nor any other nation possessed the power to eradicate all brutality from the world. If the republic continued to dissipate its resources on adventures such as the Vietnam War, then America might find itself too over-extended and exhausted to confront a genuine threat to its vital interests at some time in the future.

American public attitudes toward interventionism had changed in the years from the height of the Cold War until the post Vietnam era. However, many of the Richard Allens, Ronald Reagans, and other rigid anti-communists had not changed their views. Reagan had been a supporter of the Vietnam War, and in 1980 he called the war a noble cause that failed. Although the Cold Warriors had not altered their basic assumptions even in the aftermath of Vietnam, it was nevertheless true that in the 1980s Reagan's attempts to escalate U.S. involvement in Lebanon and Central America encountered greater resistance from the public and Congress than earlier presidents had faced in executing interventions in the 1950s and 1960s. Johnson had received strong Congressional and public support for his Vietnam policy in 1964 and 1965. In contrast, in the 1980s opinion polls and other indications of public attitudes registered extensive opposition to escalation in Lebanon and Central America. By early 1984, the administration had ordered a military withdrawal, at least for the time being, from Lebanon. Richard Allen claimed that Reagan had been elected because of his "tough" anti-Soviet stance in foreign policy, but the assertion was inaccurate. Reagan was elected primarily because of some of his domestic positions, his promises in 1980 to reduce the federal deficits (a promise much further than ever from fulfillment by 1984), the Iranian hostage crisis, popular dissatisfaction with the incumbent administration, and a variety of other reasons; but one of his greatest political disadvantages was the widespread misgiving that he was reckless in foreign policy. By early 1984, this misgiving remained one of the most serious of Reagan's political liabilities.

Concerns about Reagan's recklessness and lack of control over foreign policy were confirmed in his second term by the Iran-Contra scandals, one of the worst debacles in

American diplomatic history. On November 3, 1986, *Al Shiraa*, a Lebanese publication, reported that the United States had secretly sold arms to the government of the Ayatollah Khomeini of Iran. Later reports indicated that the sales were made in an effort to gain the release of American hostages held in Lebanon. These reports were shocking, for U.S. officials had repeatedly stated that they refused to traffic with terrorists or sell arms to Khomeini's Iran. The administration at first denied the reports, but within a few weeks it became clear that they were true. Although the Iranians received the arms, just as many Americans were held hostage as before: three were freed, but three more hostages were taken during the period of the arms sales to Iran.

Yet another revelation came in late November, when Attorney General Edwin Meese announced that profits from the Iranian arms sales were secretly diverted to the Nicaraguan rebels at a time when U.S. military aid to the Contras was prohibited by Congress. The issue of Contra aid had been exhaustively debated during the Reagan years, and Congress had barred U.S. support of Contra military operations for two years. Senior administration officials repeatedly assured congressional committees that the executive branch would abide by the law.

Although Fulbright made no active effort to join in the public debate over the Iran-Contra affair, he often privately discussed these issues with his friends in Washington and in interviews with writers. The former senator believed that Reagan's efforts to intervene in Central America met with greater resistance in Congress and in the general public than earlier presidents had experienced in ordering military interventions in the 1950s and 1960s. He reflected that one of the major reasons for this change was the legacy of Vietnam. Despite CIA assistance, the Nicaraguan Contras failed to win widespread support within Nicaragua in their effort to overthrow the Sandinista regime. The President persisted in his determination to support the Contras, many of whom had formerly supported the dictatorship of Anastasio Somoza, who was overthrown in 1979. Yet opinion polls indicated that a majority of the public did not support him on that issue. This was typical, Fulbright observed, for many Americans disagreed with the President on a wide range of specific important issues, but because of Reagan's magnetic personality and his ability to speak his lines so convincingly on television, those same people who disagreed with his policy positions continued to say they supported the President.

The consensus against "future Vietnams" that Fulbright had been instrumental in building was crucial in ultimately determining the outcome of the debates over Contra aid in the 1980s. Congress prohibited aid for the purpose of overthrowing the Sandinista government in fiscal year 1983 and restricted all aid to the Contras in fiscal year 1984 to $24 million. After revelations in the spring of 1984 that the CIA had been engaged in the mining of Nicaraguan harbors without notifying Congress, public criticism grew and congressional support for the policy waned. Congress exercised its constitutional power over appropriations and ended all funds for Contra operations by the Boland Amendment, which was included in a fiscal year 1985 omnibus appropriations bill. The President signed the legislation including the Boland Amendment into law on October 12, 1984. As the Senate and House committees chaired by Senator Daniel Inouye of Hawaii and Representative Lee Hamilton of Indiana concluded in their massive 1987 volume, *Report of the Congressional Committees Investigating the Iran-Contra Affair*, supporters of the policy feared that "the

Soviets would gain a dangerous toehold." But critics of the Reagan policy in Congress and in the public ultimately prevailed: "Opponents of the administration's policy feared that U.S. involvement with the Contras would embroil the United States in another Vietnam." The Contra aid debate again posed the dilemma Fulbright had analyzed during the debate on funding the Vietnam War: "In our system, withholding funds is a legitimate, appropriate—and all too often the only effective—means of restraining the executive from initiating, continuing, or extending an unauthorized war, or from taking steps which might lead to war."

Despite the law, the President privately ordered his staff to find ways to keep the Contras' "body and soul together." The National Security Council, which is supposed to be a White House advisory body, became an operational body that ran the clandestine Contra aid campaign—and subsequently, the Iranian arms sales—under the supervision of Lt. Col. Oliver North. The administration turned to funding from private sources and from third countries, raising $34 million from the latter and $2.7 million from private contributors between 1984 and early 1986. The NSC concealed many of its activities not only from Congress and the people, but also even from other administration officials. For example, Assistant Secretary of State Langhorne Motley, who was not informed of the secret fund-raising, assured Congress that the administration was not "soliciting and/or encouraging third countries" to provide aid to the Contras, because the Boland Amendment prohibited that solicitation.

President Reagan had issued an Executive Order and a National Security Decision Directive ordering that all covert operations must be approved by the President personally and in writing. By law, Congress must be notified of each covert act, and the funds must be strictly accounted for. Yet the NSC's covert program received no written approval from the President. Congress was not notified, and there was no accounting of the funds. The Iran-Contra affair thus represented a clear violation of one of the Constitution's fundamental checks on executive power, which is Congress' authority to grant or deny funding for government actions. In 1985, National Security Adviser Robert C. McFarlane testified to Congress that the NSC staff was obeying both the spirit and the letter of the law and was not soliciting funds or organizing military aid for the Contras. Again in 1986, McFarlane's successor, Vice Admiral John Poindexter, and North himself repeated those pledges to Congress. The pattern of deception persisted in October 1986, when one of the planes involved in the Contra aid enterprise run by North's associate, retired Air Force Major General Richard V. Secord, was shot down over Nicaragua. The President and his spokesmen denied to the American people that the U.S. government had any involvement with the flight or the captured American, Eugene Hasenfus. Elliott Abrams, Motley's successor as Assistant Secretary of State for Inter-American Affairs, continued the deception of Congress, repeating the assurance that the plane was not engaged in a U.S. covert operation.

In Fulbright's view, the Iran-Contra fiasco was in some respects worse than Watergate, since it damaged the reputation of the United States in the conduct of its international policies, whereas Watergate was basically a domestic scandal. Fulbright argued that while the Reagan administration loved to portray itself as "conservative," the Iran-Contra affair showed a profound disrespect for the true conservative principle of the rule of law. The former senator rejected the contentions of North, Poindexter and others who argued at the Iran-Contra hearings that the Boland Amendment did not apply to the President or the

NSC. Poindexter's reasoning was clearly fallacious, in Fulbright's opinion, for officials could not select which laws they would obey and which laws they would not obey. As he had observed in *The Arrogance of Power*, the genuine conservative must always uphold the rule of law, which by its nature is a buttress of the status quo: "It is not rational for conservatives to play fast and loose with the law in a seizure of anti-revolutionary zeal. When they do, it is rather like the defenders of a besieged fort firing their artillery *through* the protecting walls instead of over them; they may blow up some of the attackers on the other side but in the process they are making a nice opening through which the enemy can pour into the fort in their next attack." Fulbright's views on the rule of law became a focus for some of the debate during the summer of the hearings; for example, Senator John Kerry (D.-Mass), a Vietnam veteran, wrote an op-ed article for the *Washington Post* on the day the hearings began, recalling Fulbright's views in The *Arrogance of Power* on the rule of law as the embodiment of "true conservatism."

The administration's assertions in 1987 that the Boland law did not apply to the President or the NSC were contradicted not only by congressional critics, but by administration statements that were made from 1982-1986. Reagan's supporters in Congress ardently fought the Boland Amendments. Among them was Republican Congressman Gene Taylor of Missouri, who said during debate in 1983 that "it severely restricts the President's ability to conduct an effective foreign policy in Central America." No less an authority than McFarlane himself testified at the Iran-Contra hearings that "it was very evident that the intent of the Congress was that this amendment applied to the NSC staff. . . . Otherwise, why would we have worked so hard to get rid of it after it was passed?" Not once during the voluminous debate from 1982 through 1986 did the President or his supporters in Congress assert that the President or the NSC was not to be bound by the Boland Amendment. North admitted at the Iran-Contra hearings that he made statements to Congress that were "false," "misleading," and "wrong." The President did not make the argument of immunity when he signed the bill. Shortly after he signed it into law, Langhorne Motley testified that the restriction was written in "pretty plain English": no money would be spent "directly or indirectly" promoting the Contra war. After losing the battle in Congress, the administration was not restrained and embarked upon its clandestine effort to circumvent the law. In late 1986, NSC staff members shredded many of the relevant documents in the affair. If the majority of the American people had modified their views in the post-Vietnam era, the Elliot Abramses and the John Poindexters would never change; in their zeal, they neglected the counsel of Thomas Jefferson, who once wrote, "The whole art of government consists in the art of being honest."

Many years before the Iran-Contra scandal erupted, Reagan made powerful statements in support of the principle of obedience to the law. One of the most memorable was uttered on September 3, 1981, when Reagan had faced a very different crisis—the firing of the air traffic controllers after they went out on strike. Reagan said: "They were in violation of the law and of sworn oaths . . . We have the means to change the laws if they become unjust or erroneous. We cannot, as citizens, pick and choose the laws we will or will not obey." If only the President had heeded his own eloquent words uttered during that crisis early in his administration, the nation would have been spared the travail of the Iran-Contra debacle.

During the period when the administration was denying that it was involved in supporting the Contras' war effort, it engaged in a massive campaign to alter public opinion and change the congressional vote on Contra aid. This effort included "white propaganda," in which pro-Contra news articles were written by paid consultants who did not disclose their connection to the administration. North, Carl R. "Spitz" Channell, and Richard Miller helped raise $10 million in private donations, most of which went to Channell's National Endowment for the Preservation of Liberty. They organized White House briefings on Central America for potential contributors, after which Channell would re-assemble them at the Hay-Adams Hotel and solicit tax-deductible contributions to NEPL's Central America "public education" program, or for weapons for the Contras. North and President Reagan also took part in some of the briefings. Channell used part of the funds to unleash a media blitz against Congressional opponents of Contra aid. For example, one series of the pro-Contra NEPL radio and TV ads in early 1986 was broadcast in the Memphis media market serving the most populous east Arkansas counties in the district of Fulbright's former colleague, Congressman Bill Alexander, during his primary election campaign against a right-wing supporter of the Contras. Channell was especially concerned about defeating the Senate campaign of Congressman Mike Barnes of Maryland and later boasted to North that Barnes' electoral defeat "signals an end to much of the disinformation and unwise effort directed at crippling your foreign policy goals." Channell said he was proud that he participated in a campaign "to ensure Congressman Barnes' defeat." Unfortunately for Mr. Channell, Alexander and most of the principal opponents of Contra aid survived the 1986 elections. Moreover, NEPL's charter did not contemplate raising funds for a covert war in Nicaragua, and the IRS never approved such actions when NEPL gained tax-exempt status. Channell and Miller eventually pleaded guilty to criminal charges of conspiring to defraud the U.S. Treasury of revenues by "corrupting the lawful purposes of NEPL."

North was charged with lying to Congress, accepting an illegal gratuity, shredding documents, and conspiring to defraud the government by setting up an unauthorized covert operation to support the Contras and engage in other illegal covert activities. His trial had been delayed on several occasions. North was convicted on several charges at trial, but the conviction was overturned on appeal on several grounds. The government compelled his testimony at the Iran-Contra hearings by a grant of use immunity, but the District of Columbia Circuit Court ruled that the District Court erred in not having held a full hearing to insure that the Independent Counsel made no use of North's immunized congressional testimony. *United States v. North*, 910 F.2d 843, 851-852 (U.S.App.D.C. 1990). After the case was remanded to the trial court to hold the proper hearings, Judge Gerhard Gesell ordered the convictions dropped in September, 1991, after the hearings examined the question of whether the jury was biased by North's nationally televised testimony. North gave the testimony on condition that he would be immune from prosecution for any statements he made, and the prosecutors were unable to prove that his convictions had not been tainted by the hearing testimony. *North*, at 353-355; (see Reuters, "Verdict in CIA Case Adds to Iran-Contra Scandal Record," December 9, 1992). Ultimately, North was narrowly defeated by Lyndon Johnson's son-in-law, Charles Robb, in a campaign for the U.S. Senate in Virginia in 1994.

While Fulbright was disturbed by the Iran-Contra fiasco, he did not believe that it would necessarily arm the Democratic presidential nominee, Governor Michael Dukakis, with an invincible issue in his campaign against Vice President George Bush. Although Fulbright, of course, was for Dukakis, he said that by 1988, the Iran-Contra affair had become stale in many people's memory; moreover, while the affair was appalling to serious analysts of foreign policy, it was too complex and distant to be seen as tragic in the views of many Americans who were preoccupied with local issues. He also remarked that the U.S. naval presence in the Persian Gulf in the midst of the Iran-Iraq war was also unlikely to be damaging to the administration, since most Americans supported U.S. policy in the gulf. Support for the U.S. presence there was an exception to the generally more cautious attitude taken by Americans in the post-Vietnam era. Despite an Iraqi warplane's apparently inadvertent attack on the *USS Stark* in 1987 in which 37 sailors were killed, and the *USS Vincennes'* tragic accidental shooting of an Iranian airliner with 290 people aboard in 1988, Americans tended to rally behind the U.S. presence there. Talks concerning a U.N.-sponsored cease-fire between Iran and Iraq were proceeding as the campaign began, although the chronic violence and volatility in the Persian Gulf made it precarious to venture any optimistic assessments of the long-term prospects for peace in the region. Fulbright believed that a more likely prospect for an issue that would help propel the Democrats to victory in 1988 would be the scandals regarding massive fraud in defense procurement. The defense scandals broke in mid-1988, and Fulbright said that unlike the Iran-Contra affair, the defense procurement scandal would be alarming and easily comprehensible to all Americans, "since everybody understands corruption."

Nevertheless, Fulbright believed that Iran-Contra would inflict a certain amount of damage on Bush's political fortunes, for the Vice President faced the dilemma of explaining why he failed to join Secretary of Defense Caspar Weinberger and Secretary of State George Shultz in privately advising the President of their opposition to arms sales to Khomeini. Bush attended several high-level meetings where the arms sales were discussed, but he did not join Shultz and Weinberger in their objections. Moreover, while Bush as well as Reagan apparently did not know of the diversion of funds to the Contras, they had a responsibility to know. The President clearly has a responsibility to inform his aides that they must advise him of all important actions, and his constitutional duty to "take care that the laws be faithfully executed" mandates the rule, in the words of the congressional Iran-Contra report, "to leave the members of his administration in no doubt that the rule of law governs." Bush's National Security Adviser, Donald Gregg, knew that North was running the Contra resupply operation in August 1986, but he testified that he did not inform Bush, even after the Hasenfus plane was shot down and the administration had denied any involvement with it. Bush's record in the scandal was one of failure of leadership regarding the NSC's secret war, and silence on the profound moral question of selling arms to terrorists.

The future of Latin America loomed as volatile and unpredictable as any region on the globe by 1988. In addition to the conflict in Nicaragua, Panama's General Manuel Noriega presented a major embarrassment for the administration. For many years, Noriega provided political intelligence to the U.S. government, but in February 1988 two federal grand juries in Florida indicted him on drug trafficking charges. The indictments embarrassed U.S. anti-drug efforts and revealed that at times one agency of the government was unaware of what another was doing. For example, John Lawn, head of the Drug Enforcement

Administration, testified to a congressional committee that he had written letters before 1988 praising Noriega for supposedly fighting the international traffic in narcotics; Lawn said he had been "left out of the loop" by intelligence agencies and did not know that Noriega had been under investigation for drug trafficking. Economic sanctions against Panama failed to topple the Noriega regime, and the Reagan administration offered to drop the charges if the general would resign and leave Panama, but he refused. The White House blocked a Congressional investigation into the ways that information about drug trafficking by foreign officials influenced U.S. foreign policy decision. Administration officials said the investigation by the General Accounting Office raised "statutory and constitutional issues" involving access to sensitive data, while critics countered that the NSC was allegedly "stonewalling" an investigation that could delve into the politically controversial question of when Vice President Bush learned that Noriega might be engaged in drug trafficking. Bush had been in charge of the administration's overall anti-drug effort, but he denied having any knowledge of Noriega's ties to the drug world.

Not all developments were depressing for those who had agreed with Fulbright's moderate, realistic approach to foreign policy in the 1980s. In contrast to the debacle in Panama, the Arias peace plan signed by the Central American presidents offered a positive sign. But then the continuing intransigence of the Contras, compounded by the serious blunders of Sandinista President Daniel Ortega in repressing dissent and freedom of the press in Nicaragua, held out the potential for a revival of pro-Contra sentiment. Yet, by 1988, there was no massive, Vietnam-like intervention in Central America; the consensus against future Vietnams had been sorely tested in the 1980s, but ultimately the consensus held throughout the Reagan years.

Despite Fulbright's decades of disagreement with Ronald Reagan over most of the great issues of recent American history, he displayed a sense of objectivity and fairness in complimenting the President late in his administration for negotiating the INF Treaty. Fulbright believed that after all Reagan's scandals and failures, and the domestic controversy over the soaring trade and budget deficits, Nancy Reagan and other advisers convinced him that a treaty with the Soviets was his only recourse to gain a positive historic place in the pantheon of American Presidents. He also felt that the emergence of the new, more conciliatory leadership of Soviet General Secretary Mikhail Gorbachev was a major factor leading to the successful negotiation of the treaty. Whatever the reasons, Fulbright was generous in commending Reagan for the Washington and Moscow summit meetings with Gorbachev and the signing of the INF Treaty, which eliminated medium-range and short-range missiles. Fulbright said that while the provisions of the treaty itself involved only a small part of the nuclear arsenals of the superpowers, it was nevertheless a positive, initial step that was a welcome reversal from the "evil empire" rhetoric of the early Reagan administration. The treaty tended to produce an environment that could lead to further arms control treaties in the future, if the next administration continued to pursue the more cooperative line of the late Reagan years. In his 1983 testimony to the Foreign Relations Committee, Fulbright had predicted that the President would win acclaim if he began to pursue a more conciliatory policy toward the Soviet Union. This proved to be an accurate statement, as the President won accolades even from many of his former critics, although ironically, some of his former champions on the extreme right denounced him for supposedly betraying the Reagan revolution's earlier anti-Soviet crusade.

Fulbright noted with pride that one of Gorbachev's most influential advisers, Alexander Yakovlev, was a Fulbright Scholar. He said that the presence in the highest councils of the Soviet regime of a Yakovlev, who understood the United States, was vastly more valuable for the defense of the country than another expensive aircraft carrier. This was true, he said, not because Yakovlev was necessarily an admirer of the United States, for he might or might not be; but a man who had studied and lived in the United States would have a more accurate perception of the American people, of how their leaders might react under duress, and thus the Soviets would be less likely to act upon the basis of rash miscalculations. The continuing success of the exchange program and rise to prominence of Fulbright Scholars such as Yakovlev was a source of immense gratification for the program's founder.

The relaxation in Soviet-American tensions also held out prospects for reductions in regional conflicts. If the Soviet Union was no longer perceived as the "evil empire" fomenting communist revolutions throughout the globe, it was vastly more difficult for the administration to justify military interventions abroad to block movements that had previously been identified as Soviet clients. In the case of Cuba, there were tentative signs of a relaxation in tensions. A public opinion poll in 1988 showed that a majority of people supported negotiating with Cuba. Although the administration was reluctant to modify its rigid hostility toward Castro, it made a significant move in having a dialogue with Cuba concerning a political settlement in Angola, where Cuban troops backed the Marxist government while the United States backed the anti-communist forces of Jonas Savimbi. The process of discussion itself was a departure from the early Reagan years, when little or no constructive discussion of issues took place between the two countries.

There were even more significant signs of change in Congress, where Congressman Alexander's bill to prohibit agricultural embargoes (except in times of war or when the President certified that a country is engaged in hostilities against the United States) was gaining a large number of Congressional supporters in 1988. One of the important effects of the bill would be to end the Cuban trade embargo on agricultural goods, thus opening up a potential market estimated at roughly $489 million annually for American rice, poultry and other farm products. With the advantages of excellent quality and lower transportation costs, American producers would likely win a competition against China for the Cuban rice market, as well as against other trading competitors for many other agricultural commodities. The benefits to America in reducing the trade deficits and helping to revive the depressed farm economy were obvious. The authors of this book, along with two professors from Arkansas State University, made a trip to Cuba in the summer of 1988 and discussed prospects for future Cuban-American trade at length with several Cuban officials, including Ricardo Alarcon, an important adviser to Castro. The Cubans were eager to resume trade and initiated a number of steps designed to increase their hard currency reserves (including a major expansion of their tourist industry and other measures) in the event that the embargo were lifted, in order to be able to purchase the U.S. products.

Trade with Cuba was an intriguing issue for Fulbright, for Cuban policy was an arena of special interest for him. The Bay of Pigs, the Cuban missile crisis, and the intervention in the Dominican Republic in 1965 to "prevent another Cuba" had been among the most important events in his career in the 1960s. He had been one of the first politicians to oppose the Cuban trade embargo as a failure. In his "Old Myths and New Realities" speech in 1964, he had argued that the embargo had not and would not succeed in overthrowing Castro, and he urged that the United States should accept the reality that the Castro regime was a "distasteful nuisance but not an intolerable danger" and should cease flattering "a noisy but minor demagogue by treating him as if he were a Napoleonic menace."

Regarding the Alexander bill (which applied to agricultural embargoes in general and was not restricted to Cuba, and was primarily motivated by a desire to develop the U.S. domestic economy), Fulbright recalled that the 1980 Soviet grain embargo as well as other food embargoes in the past had failed. Such policies failed to punish the embargoed nations, which simply bought the farm products elsewhere, and America's trading competitors were enriched by filling the vacuum created by the American decision to abandon those markets. Soviet policies in 1980, as well as Cuban policies in the decades after the revolution, were not altered by the pressure of the embargo, and the true victim was the American producer and the U.S. domestic economy.

Fulbright remarked in a Capitol Hill conversation in June 1988 that the only way trade policies could wield any influence over Cuban behavior would be to resume trade, for then the United States would have leverage to bestow or withhold trading incentives for Cuba. The former senator was aware that the bill faced opposition from many Cuban-Americans, especially from the Florida congressional delegation, the executive branch, and the extreme right wing. Nevertheless, he was pleased that the bill was attracting so many co-sponsors (about 100 by mid-1988). He was amused by Alexander's accomplishment of making the bill a political boon in agricultural east Arkansas; the Arkansas legislature and a series of farm, academic and church organizations had endorsed it. In commenting on Alexander's 2-to-1 electoral victory in 1988 after a right-wing opponent had accused the congressman of being "an apologist for communism" because of his stance on farm trade to Cuba and his Central America positions, Fulbright said of the opponent's neo-McCarthyite tactics, "that old song won't play any more." While recognizing that Alexander's positions were controversial, Fulbright was gratified by his former colleagues's labors. Alexander defeated another virulent right-wing challenge in his 1990 campaign from the arch-conservative Democrat, Mike Gibson. Although Alexander was ultimately defeated for re-election in 1992, his opposition came not from the right, but from a former member of his own staff—Blanche Lambert—who had no clearly defined philosophy but was not a right-wing Democrat. Alexander's defeat came as a result of the anti-incumbent sentiment in 1992, (of which the so-called "House bank" controversy was foremost) rather than any repudiation of his positions on Iran-Contra or trade with Cuba. In the late 1980s and early 1990s Fulbright commended the efforts of Alexander and other members of Congress to prevent American producers from being sacrificed on the altar of foreign policy. One of the principal themes of his career had been his plea that rather than expending the nation's political, economic and moral resources in the crusade to annihilate the communist demons throughout the globe, America should focus its energies on building its productive base, on economic development and trade as a source of domestic strength. As he wrote in *The Arrogance of Power*, "An excessive preoccupation with foreign relations over a long period of time is more than a manifestation of arrogance; it is a drain on the power that gave rise to it, because it diverts a nation from the sources of its strength, which are in its domestic life."

After the collapse of communism in the Soviet Union and Eastern Europe, the administration of Fulbright's old friend and former protege, President Bill Clinton, would enjoy historic opportunities for focusing on economic development in foreign policy rather than Cold War militarism. Of course, conflicts still confronted America in Bosnia, Africa, the Middle East, and elsewhere, but the fixation on countering the "communist monolith" did not dominate the American mind as it often had during the Cold War and Vietnam.

It was always possible that the crusading militarism of the 1950s and 1960s might revive at some point in the future, of course. But in the late 1970s and 1980s the political environment had changed (not necessarily permanently) since the earlier Cold War epoch, when presidents could wield a virtually unrestricted anti-communist consensus in support of their decisions for intervention. To a certain extent, this change emanated from the military labyrinth that had frustrated America in Vietnam; but in addition to the obvious military difficulties of the southeast Asian conflict, an enlightened group of intellectual and political leaders had educated most thoughtful Americans regarding the fallacies and prejudices that led to the disastrous Vietnam War. In that endeavor, no one exercised more vigorous, historic leadership than J. William Fulbright.

Conclusion

During the Nixon Presidency Fulbright had been active in the Congressional movement to terminate funds for the war. His reluctance to sponsor legislation ending appropriations for the war had probably been the only significant flaw in his opposition to the Vietnam War in the later years of the Johnson administration. Fulbright believed that the senators who would have voted for an amendment cutting off the war funds would have been a small minority, and President Johnson would have characterized such an amendment's resounding defeat as an another triumphant Congressional endorsement of his Vietnam policy. The anti-war forces, in Fulbright's view during the Johnson years, would have to change public opinion concerning the war and gather strength in the Senate before introducing amendments to terminate the funds. Yet it might also be argued that if Fulbright had voted against the appropriations in the early years of the escalation, he might have established the precedent that no member of Congress should ever feel obligated to support funds for a war he detested. A dissenting vote by Fulbright might have encouraged other senators to become more resolute in opposing the Vietnam War. These arguments are conjectural, however, and one could easily sympathize with Fulbright's perspective, since the dissident bloc of senators constituted a small minority throughout most of the Johnson Presidency.

It is clear that Fulbright was dilatory in publicly challenging the escalation policy in Vietnam during 1964 and 1965. The crucial reasons for his indecisive public responses to Johnson's Vietnam policies in late 1964 and early 1965 were his conviction that Johnson was moderate and reluctant to use force, his fear of the Goldwater presidential candidacy, his inaccurate view of China as an aggressive power, and his belief until the summer of 1965 that he could influence Johnson through private communications. Fulbright envisaged his emerging adversary role with distaste, for in the years before 1965 he had usually preferred to exert influence quietly within the policy-making process. The senator's scholarly approach to foreign policy controversies also tended to delay the presentation of his public positions, for he would deliver important statements on U.S. policies only after extended periods of laborious research. His careful strategy, however, had the salutary effect of convincing many Americans that Fulbright was not an irresponsible radical, but a moderate who had arrived at his adversary role only after a painful and judicious re-evaluation of American diplomacy.

Frequently during the senator's career, one could sense the tension within Fulbright created by pressures to remain in the mainstream and cultivate his ties to the Establishment, and the conflicting pressures to speak for the dissenters and those who believed that the republic was abandoning the profound, realistic diplomatic tradition established by the Founding Fathers. Fulbright's greatest accomplishments would come when he assumed the duties of the dissenter and eschewed the dream of influencing the panorama of events by private remonstrances through the elite, as he had devoted much time and energy in doing in the period from roughly 1961 until mid-1965. Under Fulbright's leadership in 1966, the Senate Foreign Relations Committee had indeed embarked upon the historic task of educating the nation about the realities of Asia and American foreign policy; but the program of enlightening and changing public opinion through speeches, books, and hearings was an arduous, time-consuming struggle that would require years to complete its full effects. For years after the vast American armies began to enter the rice paddies and elephant grass of Vietnam in 1965, critics of America's lost crusade would be haunted by somber reflections about the delay in the Senate's challenge to the intervention. If there was any possibility that the dissenters might have prevented the escalation, that possibility may have existed in inaugurating the campaign of enlightenment concerning the Far East in the early 1960s, before hundreds of thousands of Amerian soldiers had arrived in Vietnam, before many Americans imagined that the national honor and prestige were in peril, and before the Vietnam policy had become enshrouded in the flag. Whether these disturbing doubts embraced the truth can never be determined.

Fulbright's record after 1965 is much more difficult to criticize (with the possible exception of the controversy over termination of the war appropriations). The journalist I. F. Stone, an early critic of America's involvement in the southeast Asian conflict who had disparaged Fulbright's views on Vietnam in 1964-1965, argued that Fulbright's opposition to the Vietnam War after 1965 was so courageous and eloquent "that it makes much that went before forgivable." According to Robert Beisner, Fulbright and other dissenters directed an attack on the Vietnam War that was among "the most comprehensive, meticulously detailed, merciless and unremitting ever to be directed at a government of the United States in its conduct of foreign affairs." David Halberstam described the Senate Foreign Relations Committee and its chairman as "the center of opposition" to the war. The historian Daniel Yergin delivered an unusually perceptive assessment of Fulbright's opposition to the Vietnam War: "What is most important to say about Fulbright and Vietnam is that, though he was not the first senator to oppose the United States' involvement in war there, he, more than any other politician except perhaps Eugene McCarthy, made opposition respectable, even possible. His example seemed to say that you could still be a loyal American and not subscribe to the militant anti-Communist creed."

During the later 1960s, Fulbright used his position as chairman of the Foreign Relations Committee to disseminate the knowledge that China was not a relentlessly expansionist power and North Vietnam was not a Chinese satellite. Fulbright further argued that the Vietnam War was not simply a unique aberration arising from the dynamics of an incredibly complicated situation, but a manifestation of a historical phenomenon that had afflicted all the great nations of the past. The United States was exhibiting in Vietnam "the arrogance of power," the tendency of nations at the apogee of their power to see their economic and political ascendancy as proof of their national virtue and to confuse their immense responsibilities with an obligation to eradicate evil from the universe. If the United States hoped to avoid allowing "the arrogance of power" to dominate its foreign policy, the people of America must recognize that communism might be a harsh system for organizing society, but it is not a nefarious conspiracy to exterminate the Western way of life throughout the world. Communism, in historical fact, has been destined to collapse under the weight of its internal weaknesses and contradictions in the vast majority—if not all—of the nations that have embraced it.

It should be acknowledged that some Americans remained hostile to Fulbright's ideas concerning U.S. foreign policy. The Congressional movement to terminate funds for the war did not succeed until late in the Nixon administration. Many of the more zealous anti-communists remained unrepentant, lamenting that America had failed to unleash sufficient violence against the Vietnamese communists. In the late 1970s the scholar Guenter Lewy, the columnist George Will, and others began an intellectual counter-offensive against the "no more Vietnams" consensus. Will vaguely asserted that a failure to intervene in future foreign crises could lead to the "loss" of the Middle East and the collapse of N.A.T.O. In contrast with Fulbright's "arrogance of power" thesis, McGeorge Bundy contended that Vietnam was unique, and therefore no lessons could be learned from America's tragic experience in southeast Asia.

It is likely that from the perspective of the small group of elitists who essentially directed American diplomacy during the 1960s, the American withdrawal from Vietnam did not symbolize the repudiation of the policy of enhancing America's credibility in the role of the global anti-communist gendarme. McGeorge Bundy, one of the principal architects of America's strategy in Vietnam, had written in 1965 that the plan of "sustained reprisal against North Vietnam may fail. . . . What we can say is that even if it fails, the policy will be worth it." Bundy's implication was that even a disastrous war effort would strengthen American credibility by demonstrating that the United States was not only a powerful nation but was utterly determined to exercise its power. America evacuated Vietnam only after the terror bombings of North Vietnam completed the most massive campaign of aerial devastation in the history of warfare. This senseless paroxysm of violence in 1972 could only be explained as one last, defiant affirmation by the United States that even after the expenditure of more than $200 billion, after the "roles of America and Russia have been reversed in the world's eyes" in Arnold Toynbee's words, and after decades of war in which as many as two million people may have been killed in Indochina, America remained undaunted in its will to use its matchless power, in its resolve to confront what Kissinger had called "the risks of Armageddon." Six years after the Foreign Relations Committee hearings on Vietnam had revitalized the essential process of serious, sustained dialogue between the public and the policy-making elite, the United States was not only still fighting in Vietnam, but the quest for upholding America's "credibility" had attained its frenzied zenith.

Nixon's tactics of escalating the air war, expanding the South Vietnamese ground forces, and withdrawing American troops were clearly effective in delaying the success of the Congressional movement to end the war. Yet when Richard Nixon, the infamous anti-communist of the 1950s, could visit Peking and drink toasts to Mao Tse-tung in February 1972, then travel to Moscow in May and simultaneously address the Russian and American peoples on international television, Fulbright was not naive when he approved of the welcome reversal in American diplomacy with respect to the great communist powers. The improvement of American relations with the Soviet Union and China rendered the U.S. involvement in Vietnam completely irrational, for the United States had originally intervened in southeast Asia to block the expansionism of an allegedly Soviet-controlled communist monolith across Asia, and America had enlarged its commitment to South Vietnam to halt the presumed aggression of China. Nixon evaded charges of pursuing contradictory foreign policies by increasingly referring to Vietnam as a test of American determination to maintain world order, but Fulbright dismissed this nebulous concept as no more convincing than the earlier rationalizations for the Vietnam War. Nevertheless, Fulbright continued to support the Kissinger-Nixon detente policies until the end of his Senate career.

President Johnson's diplomacy had not deviated from the post-war anti-communist dogmas, either in Vietnam or in his policies toward the great communist powers. E. W. Kenworthy had obviously been correct when he predicted in 1965 that the Johnson administration would repeatedly reject the Arkansas senator's advice regarding the southeast Asian conflict. Fulbright's influence upon American thought constituted the basic significance of his opposition to the Vietnam War. The chairman of the Foreign Relations Committee had gradually changed the ideas of many Americans concerning U.S. foreign policy; if the public opinion polls and foreign affairs analysts such as Daniel Yergin and David Halberstam were correct, then by the mid-1970s the vast majority of the American people belatedly endorsed Fulbright's dissent. Whether Fulbright and the other major critics of the war had fostered a permanent re-evaluation of public attitudes toward American foreign policy was uncertain, however, and it was clear that even in the 1970s the senator's plea for an amelioration of American relations with the Soviet Union frequently encountered hostility.

Yet it is true that many Americans eventually recognized the validity in Fulbright's indictment of anti-communist military expeditions abroad, especially when he appealed for a return to the "traditional America" of Jefferson, John Quincy Adams, Lincoln, and Adlai Stevenson, the America that abhorred the dream of a militaristic destiny for the United States. Any claim of a partial and belated victory for the Vietnam War's adversaries must be juxtaposed, of course, with the Johnson and Nixon administration's long succession of political "triumphs" in escalating and prolonging the tragic American military commitment to South Vietnam. Nevertheless, Fulbright and the other antagonists of the rigid anti-communist world view had helped to create a general consensus against "future Vietnams" by the mid-1970s, so that the opponents of the Vietnam War may have achieved a certain limited (and not necessarily permanent) victory in the political struggle that began in 1965-1966 and continued through the 1970s. Perhaps this limited victory of the dissenters had been assured, in a symbolic sense, from the day at the 1966 Vietnam hearings when George Kennan and J. William Fulbright endorsed the proposition that John Quincy Adams' famous pronouncement of July 4, 1821 had directly addressed the America of the latter

20th century: "Wherever the standard of freedom and independence has been or shall be unfurled, there will be America's heart, her benedictions, and her prayers. But she goes not abroad in search of monsters to destroy."

II. ELDER STATESMAN

On the night of May 28, 1974, the returns from the Democratic primary in Arkansas started rolling in soon after the polls closed and it was immediately clear that Senator Fulbright had been badly beaten by his opponent, Governor Dale Bumpers. Fulbright and his wife, Betty, watched the returns from their suite in the Sam Peck Hotel, a popular hostelry owned by his old friend, Henrietta Peck. He had gained only about 34 percent of the vote, one in three, in his re-election bid after 30 years of service in the Senate that had won him worldwide recognition and acclaim.

The huge margin of defeat was a shock to the senator because he and some of his backers had been under an illusion that the race had tightened up and become close in the last two weeks before the voting. Jim Blair reported that Fulbright's poll had indicated a dramatic improvement. The veteran political reporter, Ernest Dumas, said later that pollster Jim Ranchino had not showed any dramatic improvement for Fulbright in his latest polls during the campaign. Another private poll, done by postcard, had been taken for several weeks by Ike Murry, a former attorney general, and it showed the same kind of turnaround that Blair alleged. The Murry poll was admittedly amateur although it had gained in the past a reputation for accuracy, but the senator's own poll was supposed to be professional. There were strong indications that Fulbright's managers, or some of them, had given him a doctored report to keep him from giving up while the campaign was still on.[1]

Fulbright was bitter and hurt, as his friends knew, but took his defeat in the best tradition of American politics. The authors of this book were present in the Fulbright suite on that melancholy night, and both were impressed with the senator's composure and philosophical attitude. At one point Dale Bumpers appeared on the television screen stating some of the generalities that had marked his campaign, and Fulbright remarked, wryly, about the governor's tendency to express himself in platitudes. The senator joked, with considerable irony, that the Fulbright forces could have saved themselves the trouble of traversing the state campaigning in the hot Arkansas sun, because all their efforts "never moved a vote against Bumpers." In an amiable manner, he mused about the way Bumpers would campaign on the vague basis that "if you'll vote for me, 'we'll turn this country around,' but he never said which way we'd turn it;" Bumpers' message usually did not get much more specific than that on the campaign trail. That was about all Fulbright said in reference to his opponent. He was able to look defeat, and the end of his Senate career, in the face without losing his dignity.

He went down to the campaign headquarters at 11:30 p.m. and read a prepared state-ment congratulating the governor for a "vigorous and effective campaign." There was no trace of bitterness, although he acknowledged, in answer to a reporter's question, that he was astonished by such "an overwhelming majority for the governor." Fulbright had carried only a few counties out of 75; he had lost his own home town and county, the scene of his successes and triumphs as a young man.[2]

In the early stages of the senatorial campaign it would have been hard to foresee such a landslide for Dale Bumpers, even though Bumpers' own polls always showed an unbalanced contest. Fulbright had been in the Senate 30 years, and in the Congress 32 years; he had won international renown that brought to the state "a good measure of reflected glory," in the words of Bill Lewis, a reporter writing in the Arkansas Gazette.[3] His campaign was well financed by a number of rich friends including Charles Murphy, a multimillionaire oil man from El Dorado; Bill Darby, the developer of a major insurance company: and Witt Stephens, the famous utility executive and bond dealer who had become one of Fortune's 400. Fulbright had the enthusiastic editorial support of the state's largest newspaper, the Arkansas Gazette, even though the Gazette had been instrumental in Dale Bumpers' own election as governor in 1970. The Gazette had hailed Bumpers as governor and was sad about his entering the primary against Fulbright. In a singularly unprophetic editorial, the editor proclaimed that Bumpers' "days of wine and roses" had come to an end.

In actuality, Fulbright's bid for re-election was doomed from the start. He was opposed by the most popular man in Arkansas politics, who had already earned a reputation as a giant killer when he defeated the legendary Orval Faubus (who was trying for a comeback) in the 1970 primary and Governor Winthrop Rockefeller in the November 1970 general election. Bumpers' powers in politics would be affirmed again in three re-election cam-paigns—in 1980, 1986 and 1992—and he would earn prestige in the Senate where, among other things, he would be regarded as perhaps the most eloquent orator in the chamber.

The Senate campaign of 1974 was a civil war of sorts because so many of the people active for Fulbright in the past had also been backers of Dale Bumpers. Indeed, Fulbright helped Bumpers get elected governor, not foreseeing that after Bumpers was elected to the statehouse he would have to decide four years later where he was going next and whether he had any place to go except to the Senate. In one sense the campaign of 1974 was mean, because old friendships were broken up in the state's liberal and moderate communities. At the same time, the campaign was one of the cleaner races in contemporary Arkansas poli-tics. The differences between the candidates were not very important, as in Fulbright's emphasis on seniority and Bumpers' denial that seniority should govern. Fulbright wanted to debate on television but Bumpers declined, with one small exception, because he knew he was ahead. Neither of the candidates was capable of waging a really dirty campaign. Possibly the "low" level was reached at a rally in Levy, near Little Rock, on the weekend before the election. On this occasion Bumpers was considering a Fulbright claim, which was correct, that he, Fulbright, had "stood up to Nixon," and the governor asserted that it was more important "what you stood up for" than "who you stood up to."[4]

The governor's remark sounded like an implied defense of Nixon, who had a large fol-lowing in Arkansas even though he was under threat of impeachment. But Fulbright rose to the occasion by noting that Bumpers had "doubled the state income tax" and raised the gasoline tax. In fact, Bumpers' achievement in raising the income tax did more to redress a regressive tax system than anything done in the state's recent history.

The race was less than epic, certainly, but it never got really nasty. If it had, the result wouldn't have changed, for Bumpers was the winner from the start, on the record of his private polls and his two-to-one margin in the end. Senator Fulbright, for his part, was a model of elegance in his concession, although the senator's partisans felt no compulsion to be similarly sportsmanlike. The *Gazette* said, "the loser is not Fulbright, the loser is the Republic," adding: "In marking the end of the historic career of J. W. Fulbright, it is good to remember that the peacemakers are blessed and rewarded in the kingdom of heaven, for, God knows, their reward is not given below."

What was most notable in the campaign was the absence of any argument over the war in Vietnam, which had made Fulbright the storm center of a raging national controversy. Bumpers agreed with Fulbright on the Vietnam War.

If the *Gazette* had claimed, poignantly, that the peacemakers are unrewarded on this earth, the next 20 years—the years of Fulbright's retirement from public life—suggested that he was one peacemaker who won rewards everywhere. For nearly 20 years he was the recipient of accolades, rewards and awards. At the very start he was employed by a leading Washington law firm to lend it his prestige and influence. He became "of counsel" to the firm of Hogan and Hartson immediately after leaving the Senate in 1975. It was easy work with a nice office and the compensation had to be substantial. The preceding May he had told reporters the day after the primary election that he would come back to Arkansas to live. Actually, he was never going back to Fayetteville, any more than the legendary legislator who never went back to Pocatello, but he didn't have any trouble explaining to critics why he remained in Washington. He always remarked in good humor, irrefutably, that nobody in Arkansas offered him a job.

A year later he registered in Washington as an agent for a group of Arab sheikdoms, as required by law. He had always believed and argued that the Arabs were not treated fairly in the Middle East, and he was a natural lobbyist for their point of view in the capital. Then, in August 1977, he was appointed to the board of Stephens, Inc., in Little Rock, which was one of the largest bond houses off Wall Street in America. He would fly to Little Rock every quarter for the Stephens board meetings and visit his old friend Witt Stephens, and the younger brother, Jack Stephens. On these occasions Fulbright would often go on to Fayetteville, where he was forming a new connection with the College of Arts and Sciences, and, alternatively, to Hot Springs, where he had always enjoyed and claimed beneficial effects from the mineral baths. It was not clear how much business advice he gave to the Stephens, but he could tell them about what was going on in Washington, and had entertaining arguments with Witt, whose favorite sport was arguing with prominent guests at luncheon round tables or provoking them into heated exchanges with each other.[5]

The honors poured in continuously over two decades, even though one day in 1976 he told Hugh B. Patterson Jr., publisher of the *Arkansas Gazette*, along with the editorial page editor, in Patterson's office, that he, Fulbright, was "ready for the boneyard." In 1977 he was awarded a medal in London by the Royal Society of the Arts. In 1978 a new public school was opened in Little Rock and named the Fulbright Elementary School. In 1981 the College of Arts and Sciences at the University in Fayetteville was renamed the J. William Fulbright

College of Arts and Sciences, and the Fulbright Institute of International Relations was established simultaneously, with a million-dollar gift by Jack Stephens. James Powell, who was a member of the original advisory board to the Fulbright College, recalls that considerable work behind the scenes was required in establishing it. At one point, Fulbright had doubts about the idea when he had gotten the impression that he might have to do some promoting and lobbying for the College; Powell impressed upon him that he would not have to do any such thing. Powell, Fayetteville lawyer Jim Blair and others continued to work in putting the program for the Fulbright College together; in the end, the Fulbright College became, along with the highly regarded Hendrix College in Conway, one of the two best undergraduate institutions in Arkansas. In 1982 John Kenneth Galbraith dedicated the renamed college, and when he called for a standing show of former Fulbright staff members, Bill Clinton was among those to rise. At the dedication in Fayetteville, Dean John C. Guilds, who was a driving force behind the creation of the Fulbright College, said that Fulbright was "the state's greatest man." In 1985 Fulbright received an honorary doctorate from Georgetown University. In 1986 and 1987 he traveled across the country and to London on the occasion of the 40th anniversary of the Fulbright exchange program.[6]

In 1989 Fulbright traveled to Athens to receive the Aristotle Onassis Award—and a prize of $100,000—from the Onassis Foundation. Premier Andreas Papandreou made the presentation in April. Fulbright was honored for "his major contribution to education by establishing this century's largest international study fellowship program of academic and cultural exchanges," the Foundation declared.

In October the former senator received the Roosevelt Freedom Medal, not long after his home town, Fayetteville, rolled out the carpet again in a native-son celebration. Then, in 1990 a bronze bust of Fulbright was unveiled in the Kennedy Center in Washington. In Moscow, he was awarded an honorary degree by Moscow State University in tribute to the Fulbright exchange program. Since 1974, the Fulbright Foundation had provided professors from American universities to teach American history in Moscow State University. "For many of us," said Anatoly Lognov, director of the University, "Fulbright is the living history of America."[7] Back home, the Arkansas Historical Association honored him as a charter member on its 50th anniversary, and an honorary doctorate was conferred upon him at Arkansas College, a small but well-regarded private school in Batesville.

In 1993, President Clinton pinned upon Fulbright the Presidential Medal of Freedom. It was the climactic accolade, bestowed, fortuitously, a few weeks before Fulbright suffered a stroke that left him partially paralyzed. Clearly, J. William Fulbright had not anticipated what was in store for him that day in the office of Hugh Patterson. In the two decades after his defeat, moreover, the furious denunciations by his critics during the Vietnam War, and in other confrontations, abated for the most part. He could still provoke majority opinion, as in doubts expressed about the U.S. action against Panama's Manuel Noriega. But only a few of his old adversaries never let up, as in the notable instance of Paul Greenberg, an Arkansas columnist and editor who at last account was still fighting the Vietnam War 20 years after its end and never forgave Fulbright for his views on Israel.

Fulbright was anathema to the forces of the right wing. Unlike the zeal of the Pat Robertsons and Jerry Falwells in enlisting the cause of religion for the sake of political objectives, Fulbright did not mix politics and religion. He admired Jefferson for having declined to publicize his religious views or make his religious opinions known—even in the teeth of scurrilous accusations that Jefferson was an atheist—and agreed with the sage of Monticello that a political leader's religious beliefs were his own private affair and were not a public concern.[7a]

Fulbright again antagonized the right with his vote in 1972 in favor of the Equal Rights Amendment, which stated that "Equality of rights under the law shall not be denied or abridged... on account of sex." Although the legal effect of this language was debatable, it would have outlawed virtually all legal distinctions based on sex.[7b] When the ERA came to a vote in the Senate on March 22, 1972, Fulbright voted for it, while such conservative stalwarts as Goldwater, Eastland, Stennis, Ervin, and Buckley opposed it, with McClellan not voting.[7c] The Congress approved ERA and sent it to the states for ratification, but time ultimately ran out on the amendment.

In the field of environmentalism, Fulbright's stand in favor of preserving the Buffalo River earned him the disapproval of those who argued that business development was more important than saving the Buffalo. Over the years, the Army Corps of Engineers built dams that created numerous large lakes in Arkansas that supplied electricity and flood control, and led to the growth of large real estate investment projects. Some of the lakes were beginning to have problems with boat traffic jams and excessive sewage caused in part by the presence of too many septic tanks. Undeterred by these problems, Arkansas promoters in the 1960s and 1970s encouraged the Corps to dam more and more free-flowing streams. The influx of retirees from the North encouraged the promoters in their business ventures. The Buffalo River was one of the major free-flowing streams in Arkansas, and it provided spectacular scenery as it passed through the heart of the Ozark Mountains. The river's preservation was championed not only by Fulbright and other Arkansans, but by environmentalists from around the country. Justice William O. Douglas floated down the Buffalo River and afterward exclaimed that "it is worth fighting to the death to preserve." Secretary of the Interior Stewart Udall called it a "national treasure." The painter Thomas Hart Benton, who frequently painted Arkansas scenes, endorsed the movement to save the scenic river. Nonetheless, the business promoters maintained a powerful coalition, and the entire House of Representatives delegation from Arkansas endorsed the proposal for yet another dam. Fulbright fortunately found unlikely allies in McClellan and Governor Faubus, who surprisingly supported the environmentalists. Fulbright endorsed National Park Service status for the river, and in 1972, Congress made the Buffalo a national river.[7d] Fulbright's positions were especially galling to the hard-line conservatives, for his moderate, restrained positions simply could not be assailed as the reflexive positions of a knee-jerk liberal.

Above all, the end of the Cold War and Russian-American relations were the fields in which his views were most clearly vindicated. In the 20 years following his involuntary retirement from the Senate, the pages of history unfolded in patterns that Fulbright could hardly have predicted even with his considerable powers of prescience. The collapse of the Soviet Union was the most dramatic event. It was symbolic of the changes in Soviet-American relations that when Fulbright married again in the 1980s, he and his new bride traveled to Moscow shortly after their marriage for the senator to receive an honorary degree from Moscow State University.

Fulbright's personal life had surprises as well, even though the death of his wife, Betty, had been foreshadowed for many years. Betty Fulbright had been ill and frail during the 1970s and became an invalid during the 1980s. She died in October 1985. It had been a time of sorrow for the senator, but in February 1989 he announced his impending marriage to Harriet Mayor, the executive director of the Fulbright Alumni Association. She had been married to a Foreign Service officer, but they were divorced in 1976. She was 56, Fulbright was 84; she had three daughters, Fulbright had two. They were married March 10, in a private ceremony. Clearly they had much in common, and they got along very well. Fulbright had begun to experience a series of slight strokes, but he was active and alert and staying busy traveling often, both abroad and in Arkansas. It was in late June that the newlyweds journeyed to Moscow for Fulbright to receive his degree from Moscow State University.[8]

They visited Arkansas in 1990 where Fulbright took the mineral baths and visited old friends. He loved to tell friends, acting as if they had been married a long time, that Harriet set their agenda. There was a memorable luncheon at Witt Stephens' in honor of the Fulbrights; Stephens and his wife, Bess, brought in Hillary Clinton, then the First Lady of Arkansas, along with the former editorial page editor of the *Gazette*. The senator took the opportunity to suggest that Witt Stephens give a million dollars to the university, as his brother, Jack, had done in 1982. Stephens, whose philanthropies emphasized the personal, declined. Fulbright was always looking for opportunities to help the university, the arts and sciences in particular.

Meantime, there was a gradual change in Fulbright's relations with Senator Bumpers. The two men had so much in common in their views—their skepticism about the indiscriminate use of power, their loathing of McCarthyism, their belief in education—that Fulbright might have personally chosen Bumpers as his successor if he had been leaving the Senate voluntarily. Aside from such conjecture, supportable as it may be, Fulbright and Bumpers had been moving toward an understanding.

In the relationship between Fulbright and Dale Bumpers, they were finally to affirm an old truth of politics and warfare: Old adversaries have so many memories in common that they eventually can become friends, unless their differences are rooted in irreconcilable principle. Over the years Bumpers and Fulbright gradually reached an accommodation, helped along by Lee Williams, Fulbright's old administrative assistant and alter ego. Their reconciliation was dramatized one bright September afternoon in 1991, at Fayetteville. The occasion was the formal reopening of Old Main, the lovely, towered, historic centerpiece of the university campus which had been renovated at a cost of $10 million over the objections of a few Arkansans who had no sense of history. Bumpers and Fulbright were on the platform together, exchanging pleasantries and enjoying the afternoon. Bumpers set the tone with droll remarks in which he said, mournfully, that in spite of all the millions in federal appropriations he had rolled for the university, it was Fulbright who got all the recognition. Bumpers said he hoped one day that a great old tree nearby might be named the "Bumpers Oak." Fulbright enjoyed the day and remarked at an earlier meeting in the Old Main auditorium that "this may be the last time I go to a meeting in this room."[9] It was. (Fulbright had even gone to kindergarten in the basement of Old Main.)

In the end the friendship was established, or perhaps, to be more accurate, re-established, considering Fulbright's support for the young lawyer Bumpers in the 1970 gubernatorial campaign. In the summer of 1992 the Fulbrights and the Bumpers would have lunch together now and then and showed real warmth in their relationship. The authors remember well the pleasure shown by both couples when they encountered each other at lunch in the 116 Club near the Capitol the July when Bill Clinton was running for the Presidency. Invigorated by the news that Clinton was waging a strong campaign, Fulbright enjoyed himself immensely that day, speaking and looking much younger than his 86 years.

Fulbright was 69 when he lost his seat to Dale Bumpers. It was an early retirement from the Senate, whose members have commonly held places of great responsibility when they were in their 70s and even their 80s. He knew that he would never be at the center of power as he was in his 15 years as chairman of the Foreign Relations Committee. He was prone to remark, as the years went by, that he would have been *the* senior member of the Senate had he stayed a few years longer. But the worldwide respect accorded him as an elder statesman and the honors paid him in such profusion were more than an ordinary consolation. At the same time, in at least two areas of international relations, history turned around in a way that had to be a source of great satisfaction to Fulbright, even if he never would have asserted that anything he had said or done was prophetic.

He had always been skeptical of the Cold War and found Ronald Reagan's inflammatory rhetoric—the "evil empire"—distasteful and damaging to the cause of peace, but when the Cold War came to an end, almost abruptly, and the President of the new Russian republic emerged as a friend of the United States, such a reversal of history might have been foreshadowed in Fulbright's enduring themes on relations between the Americans and the Russians. He was fond of saying that the two nationalities had much in common in their personalities, and he had been an ardent supporter of the detente built by President Nixon and Henry Kissinger. Cold Warriors might argue that the Soviet Union was driven into collapse, but Fulbright felt all along that both sides had contributed unnecessarily to the Cold War. In actuality the Soviet system was in the end unviable.

In the same way that Fulbright tried to diminish the terrible tensions between the American and the Soviet colossi, he had tried in the Senate to work out accommodations between the Israelis and the Arabs, the bitterest enemies in the Middle East. In a way the conflict between Israel and the Palestinians seemed more intractable than the Cold War, for their hatred was rooted in thousands of years of history and virulent religious animosity. Nevertheless, in September 1993, Israel and the Palestinians signed a peace agreement at the White House that was much like what Fulbright had proposed 23 years earlier when he was chairman of Foreign Relations.

Yitzhak Rabin, the prime minister of Israel, and Yassir Arafat, chairman of the Palestinian Liberation Organization (PLO), signed the peace agreement on the White House lawn with President Clinton towering over them. They agreed formally that the West Bank of the Jordan and the Gaza Strip should have a phased-in autonomy, which is to say self-government. Israel had finally broken the shackles of the Likud Party and abandoned the fiction that it owned the West Bank of the Jordan and the Gaza Strip because the Lord had decreed it thousands of years earlier.

The presence of President Clinton as mediator made the United States effectively the guarantor of the agreement and of the peace, which was a role that Fulbright had proposed beginning in the 1970s in the Senate. In 1970 Israel and the Arabs were halfway between two wars, the Six-Day War of 1967 and the much more perilous (for Israel) war of 1973.

Israel was comfortable in its role as victor, and the timing seemed ideal for a movement toward autonomy for the Palestinians, who had an overwhelming majority of the population in the occupied territories. The Labor Party was still in power in Israel, and whatever hopes there were for peace rested in the Labor Party, heir to the tradition of Ben Gurion. Peace talks were opening in the U.N. headquarters in New York; U.N. mediators prepared to hold separate conversations with representatives from Israel, Jordan and Egypt. Israel had a deep distrust of a peace fashioned in the United Nations.

Three days before the U.N. talks began in 1970, Fulbright had released a plan to make the United States the guarantor of a settlement in the Middle East that would be imposed by the United Nations if necessary. The borders that preceded the Six-Day War would be re-established, the Arabs would agree to honor them, and so would Israel; the United States would sign a bilateral agreement with Israel committing American power to defend the Israeli borders. In this fashion the territories occupied by Israel after the war would be restored. Fulbright saw that no peace was possible while Israel occupied and governed the Arab lands on the West Bank and in Gaza.

Fulbright's proposal was somewhat more direct than what Rabin and Arafat would agree to in 1993, but the essentials were the same. He called upon Israel, the victor, to take the lead, committing itself to the return of the occupied territories and to a fair settlement of the Palestinian refugee problem. He declared that the prospects for peace would be better than at any time since the 1967 war, adding: "... in due course the Palestinian Arabs will find it necessary to accept the existence of the state of Israel and to recognize that further, futile efforts to destroy the Jewish state will only compound their suffering." Further, he suggested that an international police force be set up under the United Nations to enforce the terms of the peace.[10]

The auguries for Fulbright's daring proposal were unfavorable from the start. On the very day the New York Times carried the story, the venerable James Reston reacted skeptically in his column on the editorial page. He even went so far as to compare the idea to Spiro T. Agnew offering to take over the editorial page of the New York Times. He wrote that Fulbright, "to put it as gently as possible, is no Zionist." He made a gesture by describing the Fulbright proposal as "worth considering" and he did recall that Arthur T. Vandenberg, another famous chairman of Foreign Relations, had switched from isolationist to internationalist in a celebrated speech made in January of 1945.

On August 25, 1970, the Times reported that the Israelis at the United Nations declined comment on the Fulbright speech. By Tuesday the Times was able to report that Abba Eban, the Israeli foreign minister, and Menachem Begin, head of the opposition Likud Party, were joined in expressing suspicion of what Fulbright offered. The same day the Times reacted editorially, grandly conceding "an effort to be constructive" but dismissing the idea of a peace "imposed" by the United Nations. The editorial even claimed that the Fulbright ploy might be damaging because Israel would react so strongly against losing "any hope for more defensible borders." In actuality, the argument for Israel's having "more defensible borders" required, then and now, keeping territory that belonged to the Palestinians.

The Arabs liked what Fulbright had to say. Al Ahram, the authoritative newspaper in Cairo, described Fulbright as "one of the few American statesmen who are genuinely working for peace."

Fulbright's plan never got off the ground. Israel's champions in the American Jewish community didn't trust Fulbright (and some of them worked against him in the 1974 Arkansas election). He had always worried about injustice in Palestine and he was popular in the Arab countries. His effort to settle the Palestinian question attracted little support in the United States even though he was at the peak of his influence and prestige as chairman of Foreign Relations.

Fulbright might have left one item for later—international status of Jerusalem, which is terribly complicated and of doubtful practicality—but he had advanced a design for peace and a scheme for establishing it. In any case no progress was made at all for 20 years. In 1973 another bloody war was fought, and Israel very nearly lost it. Then the chauvinistic Likud Party came to power in Israel under Menachem Begin. The Israelis marched into Lebanon all the way to Beirut and brought more bloody conflict into that troubled country. Meanwhile, back on the West Bank, Israel started resettling Arab land with Israeli squatters, in a policy that was totally indefensible in the world's view and invited barbaric acts of Arab terrorism.

In the end, Fulbright lived to see the beginning of the redress he had proposed. Arafat and Rabin agreed to it, with Clinton's blessing, and the next year, after all manner of atrocities committed by extremists on both sides, Jericho and Gaza were turned over to the Palestinian police, with Arafat in charge of the new local government. The Middle East was still plagued by myriad problems, but the agreements during the Clinton administration represented real, if limited, progress; and these agreements embodied the more evenhanded approach to Middle Eastern policy that the President's mentor had advocated 20 years earlier.

III. THE FULBRIGHT PROGRAM AND ITS CRITICS

As has repeatedly been discussed throughout this book, one of Fulbright's great joys was his work for the Fulbright Program. From the program's founding, to the senator's defense of international scholar exchanges against the depredations of Joe McCarthy, to Yugoslavia's joining the program as its first communist member, to the pride Fulbright displayed when such Fulbright Scholars as Alexander Yakovlev rose to the heights of international prominence, the exchange program was the one unshakable consolation the senator enjoyed throughout the many strains and disappointments of his lengthy, controversial career. Few figures in the United States Congress have had such instant name recognition as Fulbright in the elite circles of the world, and the Fulbright exchange program was a key factor in his international fame. The Fulbright Scholars are scattered throughout the world and for nearly a half century they have felt a sense of personal identification with the program and the man. By 1995, approximately 140 countries had participated in the program, with more than 200,000 scholarships having been awarded since it began. About 72,000 Americans and 140,000 foreigners have received the scholarships. The Fulbright alumni feel that their own lives, their own accomplishments, have been influenced positively by the opportunity that the program afforded them. Fulbright has been honored abroad at least as much as he has at home, as he found in his travels in the 1980s. Two great industrial countries, Germany and Japan, now contribute more to support the Fulbright Program than does the U.S. government; the German contribution was twice the U.S. contribution in 1988, as reflected in the Fulbright exchange's 25th annual report. In Japan, during the celebration of the program's 40th anniversary, a major newspaper, *Nikkei* published a long series of short, first-person articles by Fulbright relating his life. The list of Fulbright alumni features celebrated names in the United States and abroad. These alumni are in many fields of endeavor—education, government, journalism, science, the arts. In education there is a roster of presidents of great American universities, alongside such distinguished professors as Henry Steel Commager and Paul Samuelson; in arts and letters, the actor Stacy Keach and the writer Roger Rosenblatt; in government, Daniel Patrick Moynihan and Walt Rostow are among the alumni; in journalism Fox Butterfield of the *New York Times* and Garrick Utley of NBC News; in music, the composer Aaron Copeland and the soprano Anna Moffo; in science there are no less than six Nobel laureates. Foreign Fulbright alumni have their own great roster of distinction: U.N. Secretary General Boutros Boutros-Ghali,

Alexander Yakovlev, the adviser to Mikhail Gorbachev, and countless academic figures throughout the world, including Martin Noel, professor of Spanish-American Literature at the University of Buenos Aires, Solly Cohen, dean of the faculty of science at Hebrew University, and many others.[10a]

The role of the Fulbright exchange has changed in a number of ways. In its early years it was the predominant program in the world for the exchange of scholars between countries: now there are many such programs in many countries and Fulbrighters are a fairly small percentage of the total each year. Another change was administrative: during the Carter administration the Fulbright program began receiving its money through the U.S. Information Agency. Fulbright was highly displeased by the move. The USIA is in a sense a propaganda agency. Fulbright felt that the program should have been kept strictly under its own independent agency. Over the decades the U.S. government has appropriated well over a billion dollars for the Fulbright scholarships. If the principle of exchanging scholars is now implemented on a much larger, broader scale, with many programs (including the Hubert H. Humphrey scholarships that were inaugurated in this country in 1978), it was the Fulbright Program that was the pioneer.

Despite the program's imposing achievements, some have always criticized the program. Joe McCarthy charged that Fulbright Scholars had been soft on communism, and some anti-intellectual forces had always been suspicious of the international scholar exchange program. If the Carter administration was mistaken in making the administrative change that led the program to receive its funds through USIA, that decision was minor compared with the full-scale assault on the program launched by Republicans in the mid-1990s. In an alleged quest to balance the federal budget, Congressional Republicans targeted the Fulbright Program for drastic cutbacks or even elimination. Daniel Pipes, a former Republican appointee to the program's supervisory board and one of the conservative critics of the Fulbright Program, complained: "At a time of severe retrenchment, it's a luxury we can't afford...A lot of these programs are essentially middle-class pork." On its face, the Republican attack was a preposterous political ploy. Even if the USIA's budget for educational and cultural exchange programs were destroyed, it only amounted to $265 million in fiscal 1995. Such a tiny amount was irrelevant to the gargantuan task of reducing the federal deficits that had become mammoth during the Reagan and Bush administrations, and that the Clinton administration was able to reduce only with great difficulty. Only a few months after Fulbright's death in 1995, the assault on the program was front-page news, as headlines warned that the budgetary "Ax Dangles over Legacy of Fulbright." Senator Moynihan and many other enthusiasts of the program rushed to its defense. Perhaps most helpful of all were the efforts of moderate Republicans, notably Senator Richard Lugar (R.-Ind.) in championing the program.[10b]

Of all the controversies in which Fulbright became involved in his career, his defense of the Fulbright Program was undeniably the one in which he pursued the correct, statesmanship position in supporting a program that was a triumph. With the exception of Joe McCarthy and the neo-McCarthyites who attacked the program in the late 20th century, the program generally enjoyed overwhelming support among most members of Congress throughout its history. Newspapers were generally warmly supportive. As the *New York Times* observed in 1950, "What is important is that Americans should understand that the program is proving a success and that it holds real possibilities of becoming the greatest medium for the exchange of students and teachers that has yet been seen." The apogee of public support for the program was probably attained with the passage of the Fulbright-Hays Act of 1961 (co-sponsored by Congressman Wayne Hays of Ohio), which endorsed the cooperative approach of the Fulbright Program, enlarged its scope, and identified its activities as a significant phase of American foreign policy. As President Kennedy pronounced in commemorating its 15th anniversary in 1961: "This program has been most important in bettering the relations of the United States with other parts of the world. It has been a major constructive step on the road toward peace."[10c]

Kennedy's accolades were echoed across the world. In August 1964, the Sydney, Australia, *Daily Mirror* announced that the program would be shifted to a cost-sharing basis: "Most welcome news of the day is that the Fulbright brain exchange between America and Australia will continue by means of a joint education Foundation, even though the original fund is exhausted. The Fulbright Program was one good thing to emerge from the evil of war... The two governments will share the cost of the new Foundation, and we can't think of a better way of spending the money." As the British Foreign Office phrased it, the program represented one of the great experiments of the post-World War II world, for the scholarships "are based on the feeling that if the mass of the people in all countries can be brought to know each other, and can be allowed to communicate as free men, a solution can be found for their common problems." Similarly, in 1949, the *Evening Post* of Wellington, New Zealand, commented: "The fact that American dollars, changed into pounds by American sacrifice sales in New Zealand, are to be spent, as pounds, to the full extent that New Zealand policy will permit, and in support of a wider education and atmosphere for New Zealanders, is another piece of evidence that the Americans desire to use dollar power to help the outside world."[10d]

The multitude of contributions of the program was as diverse as the countries around the world in which the scholars were exchanged. In Greece, the program allowed more Americans to gain direct knowledge of Athens, the fabled city that was the birthplace of many Western democratic ideals. Many of the Fulbright research scholars worked on restoring the magnificent Agora, beneath the heights of the Acropolis. Not only did the program make a contribution to the study and preservation of the ancient glory of Athens, but teachers also went out into the smaller Greek cities and worked on a less grandiose, but highly constructive process of sending American secondary school teachers of English into the provinces. As George Stewart, a Fulbright lecturer in Greece in 1952-53, phrased it, the work of the teachers in the smaller Greek towns assured "that some contact with the United States has been made, not only by the Athenian (who is a good deal of an international anyway) but also by the grass-roots Greek of the provinces."[10e]

During the height of the Cold War, some of the most interesting developments took place in Third World countries that had considerable tension in their relations with the United States. In Egypt, for example, there was substantial anti-American sentiment flowing from American recognition of Israel and U.S. private and governmental support of Israel. Yet, despite the strains in Egyptian-American relations, American grantees were well-received and developed constructive relationships with Egyptian colleagues in the early years of the program. At the time of the Suez crisis, the program suffered a serious, but temporary setback. In June 1957, after the Egyptian nationalization of the Suez Canal Company and the Israeli-British-French attack on Egypt, the Fulbright Program was terminated and the office closed because of lack of funds; but within two years, Egypt and the United States signed a new agreement, as funds were now made available from the sale of surplus agricultural products. In particular, the Egyptians requested extensive aid in strengthening its science departments and constructing laboratories. The Fulbright Program responded to this request for scientific assistance in 1959, and many other fields of learning were included as well. One of the most poignant achievements of how the Fulbright Program made contributions to the world of the human mind and civilization that would otherwise not have occurred was summarized in the comments of John A. Wilson, former director of the Oriental Institute of the University of Chicago in 1964:

> The study of ancient Egypt in the United States had been limited by the high cost of field work several thousand miles away. The Fulbright Program met this difficulty. Research scholars were given a year of study in Egypt, in some mutually advantageous relation to their Egyptian colleagues. Students ... had the chance to use the field as a laboratory, enrolling at the Egyptian national university, joining an excavation, or working on a thesis based upon the materials in the museum of antiquities. The field enjoyed an enormous stimulus from the good relations between Egyptian and American scholars.[10f]

Fulbright Scholars contributed to a heightened appreciation of preserving the Egyptian heritage at Luxor and elsewhere, and President Kennedy recommended funding in 1963 to preserve the great Egyptian monuments that were endangered by the rising waters behind the Aswan Dam. For a culture as ethnocentric as that of America, it was indeed an educational experience for American scholars to not only be reminded of, but to participate in the preservation of the ancient wonders of a Third World country in the Middle East.

A similar accomplishment in the appreciation of foreign cultures took place in India. In 1961, the Fulbright Program initiated an annual Institute on Indian Civilization, which was intended not for research specialists but for professors of small American colleges and high school teachers. The idea was to help the generalists teach American students in world history classes. In addition, American students and research scholars won grants to study India's language, history, literature, music and art. The Indian-American binational foundation wrote to the Board of Foreign Scholarships in 1952 that the program was motivated by the concept that "mutual understanding and sympathy between peoples is promoted not only by the exchange of purely utilitarian knowledge and skills but also, and perhaps more effectively, by the dissemination of knowledge about each other's cultural and artistic achievements." The reciprocity of the program was vital to its success in India, as elsewhere: Indian specialists lectured at American universities, while American professors and graduate students traveled to India to increase their knowledge of south Asia. One of the cardinal features of the Fulbright Program was its provision for two-way traffic in exchanges. In this respect, it provided a sharp contrast with most other U.S. government programs and with programs of other countries. The older countries had traditionally focused on the education of foreign visitors in their universities and sending their teachers and professors abroad. The newer, developing countries had emphasized the education of some of their best students overseas and the importation of foreign scholars. In contrast, the Fulbright Program emphasized reciprocal contacts among all grantees. For one observer—Robert Trumbull, who wrote from New Delhi in the *New York Times* in 1952—the Fulbright Program, the Point Four Technical Cooperation Administration, and the Rockefeller and Ford foundations had all contributed to "a remarkable improvement" in Indian-American relations. Trumbull commended the contributions of those who traveled to India as Fulbright Scholars or with other cultural and educational exchange endeavors, writing, "The presence of the Americans here, meeting Indians from Cabinet Ministers down to the poorest peasants, has had its effects."[10g]

The success of the program in India contributed to its expansion elsewhere in southern Asia. Agreements were signed with Burma, the Philippines, Pakistan, Thailand, Korea, Japan and other Asian countries. In the Philippines, the program was instrumental in rehabilitating an educational system that had been ravaged during World War II, when vast numbers of laboratories, museums, libraries, and books, particularly books in English, had been destroyed. Many Filipino teachers were killed by the Japanese or died of disease during the war. In the early postwar years, the Philippines had just won its independence from the United States and was plagued by the communist-led Huk guerrilla war. American teachers came to the Philippines to make contributions in the fields of vocational training, education, agriculture, natural sciences and other fields. A major contribution of the program in the Philippines was the teaching of English, which was the only common language of all the people in the archipelago and the linguistic highway to much of the rest of the world. The reciprocity of the program was again evident: Fulbright grantees' attempts to improve the teaching of English led to the creation of the Center for Language Study in Manila, and by 1963, Filipinos who had been granted Fulbright Scholarships in the United States numbered more than 100 of the faculty of the University of the Philippines. The educational needs of the Philippines still required much greater efforts, and the social, political and economic problems of that sprawling country were of course, beyond the capacity of one educational program to solve; but the many students and teachers who participated in the Fulbright Program contributed to the improvement of Filipino education. As the Foreign Service officer Jack Bryan would observe: "the magic name Fulbright has become in the Philippines synonymous with quality in the field of education."[10h]

In Japan, a Fulbright agreement was signed in 1951, as the military occupation was coming to a close. The program emphasized work in the social sciences, since scholarship in that field had been partly suppressed during World War II. Historians, geographers, and cultural anthropologists came to Japan and attempted to separate historical reality from myth and to end the militaristic, ultra-nationalistic tradition in Japan that had previously disseminated the false views that Japan was self-sufficient and destined to be the predominant power throughout Asia and the Pacific. American economists who were knowledgeable about Keynesian theory came to provide an alternative to the outmoded Marxian economics that had frequently been taught in Japan in earlier periods. The Fulbright Commission brought American lecturers to Japan to promote better knowledge of the United States. The program, along with the efforts of the American Embassy, were the main catalysts in leading influential Japanese to see the need to expand their country's understanding of America, and in 1962, a group of Japanese businessmen and educators established the American Studies Foundation. Fulbright believed that relations with Japan were unusually important for the United States. Shortly after John F. Kennedy's election, Fulbright had urged the President to appoint Edwin O. Reischauer, a scholar of Japanese culture and a former president of Harvard, as Ambassador to Japan. The ambassadorship to that nation, Fulbright told Kennedy, was possibly "the most difficult, the most sensitive, and one where an inadequate representative would result in the greatest harm to our prestige and influence." With Reischauer's deep background in Japanese studies, he indeed made an effective American representative. As he would observe in 1963: "We Americans and Japanese in particular have much to learn from each other. The Fulbright Program between our two countries, which has succeeded in being both binational in its direction and mutually beneficial, has contributed greatly to the achievement of this task."[10i]

One of the great successes of the Fulbright Program was that it worked with widely divergent societies and cultures, from Europe, Japan, and the Philippines to Africa and Latin America. At first, the program grew slowly in Latin America; not until foreign currencies from the sale of surplus agricultural products became available was a Fulbright agreement signed with a Latin American country. (Originally, of course, the Fulbright Act of 1946 had permitted the sale of American surplus war material abroad after World War II to be devoted to the exchange of students; see Book Two.) In 1955, an agreement was signed with Chile, and in the following years Brazil, Colombia, Peru, Argentina, and Ecuador joined, and the program continued to expand in later years to include Mexico and other Latin countries. The program in Latin America expanded contacts among educators across the Americas and added significantly to investments in human capital. As Theodore Schultz wrote in analyzing economic growth in certain parts of Latin America, investment in human capital is the wisest investment a nation can make, and the crucial investment in human capital is education: "One simply could not explain a very substantial amount of the economic growth in particular parts of Latin America—Mexico, for example—by just measuring and quantifying the additional labor and capital going into the economic system." Rather than attributing these advances to technology, Schultz concluded that "Clearly, the improvement in the quality of people's skills really mattered." In Latin America the Fulbright Program was one program among many, such as State Department and major foundation activities, that contributed to advances in education. The American effort to make a bona-fide attempt to help in a *reciprocal* program was appreciated even in countries that admittedly had vast problems in their educational systems.

In Africa, the Fulbright Program also sought to address the dire problems of inadequate food sources and conservation. As Prime Minister J. K. Nyerere of Tanganyika once stated, the survival of African wildlife was vital not only as a source of inspiration, but was a crucial part of Africa's natural resources "and of our future livelihood and well-being." The Fulbright Wildlife Project in East Africa promoted intensive study of the problem of conservation. In one example of the type of exhaustive studies of the problem that the program produced, Fulbright grantees Raymond Dasmann and Archie Mossman concluded that in rational planning for land use in Africa, the place of wild game as a producer of meat and income should be seriously considered. With the newly independent nations of Africa faced with the crisis of how to feed rapidly expanding populations, game ranching projects could be helpful, although the grantees did not pretend to have solved the problem of food sources. Dasmann also stressed the esthetic and cultural values in maintaining African parks and preserves for "the sheer pleasure that people gain from seeing them, in the scientific value to be obtained from studying them, but mostly in the ethical obligation which all people have to preserve for the people of tomorrow a part of the world that was here in the Past."

Dasmann and others engaged in the wildlife project, however, were worried about the future; Dasmann felt that many African government officials had not clearly recognized the value of wildlife as a natural resource, and that there had been far too few efforts to establish its place in a permanent land-use plan. Another Fulbright Scholar, Harold Heady of the University of California, concluded after studying problems in Kenya, Tanganyika and Uganda, that the most important step should be to gain control of the number of livestock, for excessive grazing had resulted in a severe deterioration of the soil. Heady concluded that the East African nations must require grazing control, and in order for the land to recover from erosion, "there was a need for reseeding, water development, fencing, control of the bush, and grazing management schemes." A milestone in the work of such grantees as Dasmann and other Fulbright Scholars came in 1961, when the International Union for the Conservation of Nature and Natural Resources met in Arusha, Tanganyika, with representatives from all over the world, and analyzed the results of recent research, much of it facilitated by the Fulbright Program. A United Nations Educational, Scientific, and Cultural Organization study confirmed the conclusions of Fulbright grantees that African wildlife yielded significant tourist revenue, sources of protein, international prestige, and scientific knowledge. The Fulbright Wildlife Project in East Africa stimulated programs adopted by many of the newly independent governments, as well as by the UN Food and Agricultural Organization. Although the problem of food sources and conservation in Africa and elsewhere in the Third World will challenge the world community for many years to come, the Fulbright Program was a constructive effort to put America's finest minds to work in trying to solve the problem. As a contribution to true international understanding between the United States and the countries involved, such a program was immensely more valuable than arms sales, Cold War politics, or an ideological crusade.

The Fulbright Program achievements in Africa, Greece, Egypt, India and other countries discussed above are only a few examples, of course, of the work of tens of thousands of scholars involved in the program over the decades. Although the particular triumphs of Fulbright Scholars and the program in eastern Africa, Japan, India, and around the world are impressive, probably the greatest impact of the program was in terms of its effect on the predispositions and attitudes of peoples toward each other. As Fulbright wrote in "Old Myths and New Realities": "In our quest for world peace, the alteration of attitudes is no less important, perhaps more important, than the resolution of issues. It is in the minds of men, after all, that wars are spawned; to act upon the human mind, regardless of the issue or occasion for doing so, is to act upon the course of conflict and a potential source of redemption and reconciliation."[10] The Fulbright-Hays Act required the U.S. Advisory Commission on International Educational and Cultural Affairs to provide a critical analysis of the effectiveness of all exchange programs. The commission was nonpartisan in character and advised the President, the State Department, and relevant agencies of the executive branch regarding cultural and educational policies. In 1963 the commission reported that "There is no other international activity of our government that enjoys so much spontaneous public approval, elicits such extensive citizen participation, and yields such impressive evidences of success." In an epoch when international relations had become oppressively complex and obscure in results, the commission concluded that "the success of educational exchange is a beacon of hope." The principal features of the Fulbright Program have been abundantly vindicated: its search for academic excellence and prevention of political influences from tainting the program, its partnership with non-governmental organizations, its stress on the individual as the primary catalyst of international educational exchange, and its reciprocity.

Despite its great merit, the exchange program always had its critics. Even soon after its creation, Senator Kenneth McKellar of Tennessee complained that if he had been aware of the bill, he would have opposed the dangerous idea of subjecting fine young Americans to foreign "isms" of socialism, communism, or other ideas foreign to those in America. Fulbright's strategy of quietly guiding the bill through the Senate without fanfare had clearly succeeded in avoiding opposition from such anti-intellectuals as McKellar. Even after it cleared the Senate, Congressman Will Whittington of Mississippi attempted for a time to bottle up the bill in a House subcommittee. Fulbright made no impact upon Whittington in talking to him directly, even after explaining that the program would not require appropriations. Fulbright's proposal, of course, had focused on the vast stores of American military supplies-trucks, food, blankets, drugs, other equipment—left by U.S. forces all over the world after the war. Another bill had been pending at the time Fulbright was conceiving the idea for his program regarding the disposal of war properties, in which the Secretary of State was to be given authority to dispose of assets outside of the United States, and to take credits for them, since the countries involved did not have dollars to pay for these assets. As Fulbright would recall years later: "Our principal allies owed us more money than they could possibly pay, and they had no dollars and no access to dollars. So it was a question of taking IOUs or noncontrovertible credits in payment."[10k] Fulbright thought he had devised a way to get the bill through Congress by the selling point that it would not require appropriations from the Treasury. Yet, had it not been for the fortuitous help of Undersecretary of State Will Clayton, the wealthy founder of the Anderson-Clayton Cotton Company, Fulbright's bill might never have cleared the House. Whittington had regarded Fulbright as a young upstart with a program that the Mississippi congressman did not appreciate. However, Clayton was a friend of Fulbright's who had also done business in Whittington's district and knew the congressman. The cotton tycoon persuaded Whittington that the credits in the program could not be used in Mississippi or anywhere else in this country, and that no appropriations would be involved. Whittington relented and the bill barely got through before the recess in August 1946. Fulbright recalled many years later that if the legislation creating the program had not passed then, given the Congressional reluctance to pass legislation supporting cultural and educational activities "I doubt it would have gotten through later."[10l]

The bill also had to clear a legal hurdle: whether funds could be allocated without an appropriation. The Attorney General researched the issue and decided that it was constitutional because the credits involved were not Treasury funds under the Constitution.

After its creation, support in Congress greatly increased over the years as the successes of the program continued. By 1961, the program had become so large that new sources of funding were required, for the foreign credits from the war had been exhausted in all but a few countries. Appropriations were needed if the program were to survive and flourish. Fulbright gained the support of the Kennedy administration and of Congressman Hays, who was influential with other members because of his chairmanship of the "housekeeping" committee in the House that handled office allowances and perquisites. When President Kennedy sent a message to the U.S. Educational Commission in West Germany on its 10th anniversary, he encouraged the continuing growth of international educational exchange: "It is now my hope that we will tarry at this milestone only long enough to consolidate our successes. For the times are urgent and the road ahead is long."[10m]

One flaw of the program was the problem of "brain drain." Pakistan's Ambassador to the United States discussed this problem with Fulbright, saying that some of the brightest people from Pakistan would come to the United States, obtain excellent educations in the fields of medicine and the sciences, and then remain in America because the opportunities were much greater than in Pakistan. "We can't go on like that," the Pakistani said, "it's taking some of our best brains." Fulbright had failed to anticipate this problem in the original program, but having been apprised of it, he agreed that the rules should be changed. Thereafter, both American students studying abroad and foreign students studying in America would have to leave the country where they studied for at least two years. This change became part of the law in an effort to deal with the problem of "brain drain."[10n]

The program had fundamental characteristics that assured its success. One was the Board of Foreign Scholarships, which was the basic policy-making body and was insulated from threats of political interference in the selection procedures. Moreover, it was not a program dominated by the United States, but stressed reciprocity. In each country, binational commissions developed programs meeting that country's needs for students, teachers and professors and types of research. The Board of Foreign Scholarships had the final authority, but it usually followed the recommendations of the binational commissions. Indira Gandhi once charged that the program was a form of cultural imperialism, because allegedly the United States was imposing its ideas upon other nations. Fulbright responded that the charge was unjustified, and his response was accurate: given the reciprocal nature of the binational commissions, the program was cosmopolitan and resisted political and cultural biases.[10o]

One of Fulbright's greatest hopes for the program was to expand it greatly with the Russians. The senator once wrote that he had long admired the writings of George Kennan, "perhaps because he was the equivalent of a Fulbright scholar, having lived for so long in Moscow." When he considered other major American diplomatic figures, he contrasted the more accurate views of those such as Kennan and Charles Bohlen who had lived in the U.S.S.R. with "others who did not, Acheson, Rusk, and Lovett, for example... Acheson was a brilliant man, but he didn't have any feeling for what the Russians were like; he simply mistrusted them." In the early 1970s, Fulbright discussed prospects for expanding the scope of the Fulbright Program in the Soviet Union. He talked to Madame Kruglova, who represented the Soviet ministry of cultural affairs, and she was supportive and agreed to discuss expansion of the program with her government. Unfortunately, the anti-detente forces led by Senator Jackson and the Jackson amendment obstructed progress in the amelioration of Soviet-American relations at that time, and the project came to naught.[10p]

In the Carter years, another frustration for Fulbright took place, as the program was placed under USIA. During the Reagan administration, some of the Republicans and conservative Democrats who posed as valiant budget-cutters advocated reducing funding for the program; while the Fulbright Program continued to succeed, it deserved greater financial resources. As Lee Williams observed, "The cost of one B-2 bomber is equal to the amount invested in this program over a nearly 50-year period."[10q]

The attacks on the Fulbright Program in the mid-1990s, after the Republicans regained control of Congress for the first time since the 1950s, were not unique; Kenneth McKellar, Joe McCarthy and others had criticized the program in the past, and President Johnson had slashed funding for the program in 1968, in retaliation for Fulbright's successful efforts to cut the foreign aid program. Fulbright had fought for the international educational program since 1946, and the fight continued after his death. "It would be a tragedy for the country," Lee Williams was quoted in the media as saying in May, 1995, if the critics succeeded in eliminating or severely reducing the Fulbright Program, for "this is one of the strongest arms of U.S. foreign policy... It provides a tremendous return for the investment. I just can't believe they would be that Draconian, even in their talk." Harriet Mayor Fulbright; who served on the program's supervisory board, said that the program was just as important for new countries emerging in the post-Cold War environment as it had been in the wake of World War II.[10r] Fulbright had eloquently stated the essential merit in looking back on the first 40 years of the program in 1989, without exaggerating the program's import: "The vital mortar to seal the bricks of world order is education across international boundaries, not with the expectation that knowledge would make us love each other, but in the hope that it would encourage empathy between nations, and foster the emergence of leaders whose sense of other nations and cultures would enable them to shape specific policies based on tolerance and rational restraint."[10s] No objective observer could challenge Fulbright's belief that the relatively tiny funds devoted to the exchange program were among the wisest investments ever made by America in its relations with the international community.

Fulbright and McDougal: A Losing Excursion

Fulbright's adventures in retirement included a losing excursion into Arkansas real estate development with a former staffer, James McDougal, who was to become famous in the celebrated Whitewater affair. The former senator was one of several prominent investors in projects that McDougal initiated after leaving the Senate's employ.

In 1975 McDougal went home to Arkansas and turned into an accomplished promoter. He taught political science briefly at Ouachita Baptist University, his alma mater, and then obtained charters for two small banks, one of which, Madison Guaranty, got into trouble and failed in 1989 after lending money for McDougal's land developments. He enlisted well-known investors for his real estate enterprises including Fulbright, Bill Clinton and Hillary Clinton, and Jim Guy Tucker—who would become governor after Clinton was elected president in 1992. He married a handsome and ambitious young woman who helped him launch developments including Whitewater, which is in the scenic mountain country of Northern Arkansas. The Clintons' investment in Whitewater finally became the focus of a federal investigation on whether there were improprieties and violations of law in Whitewater financing.

In the early 1980s McDougal was riding high. He ran for Congress in 1982 in Northwest Arkansas, in the Third District, and won the Democratic nomination. In 1974 Bill Clinton had gotten 48 percent in the general election against the incumbent, John Paul Hammerschmidt, a Republican icon, and McDougal hoped to equal or improve on Clinton's performance. Hammerschmidt beat McDougal 2 to 1, but McDougal, who loved campaigning, had a wonderful time stumping the district on a New Deal platform, making rousing speeches and invoking the shades of his idol, Franklin Roosevelt.

The McDougals had charm and ambition and they looked like winners, especially in an era of bold, risky investment. Fulbright, for his part, wanted to help his old staffer get started, and the investment prospects seemed attractive. McDougal was looking in several directions. One morning in the late 1970s he had breakfast with Fulbright and James Powell at the Sam Peck Hotel and outlined an idea for a land development north of Little Rock, near the town of Mayflower. The third party at the breakfast, as an underfunded inky wretch, was surprised by the proposal, did not pursue the matter and heard no more of it.

Fulbright was persuaded to put $700,000 into a proposed industrial park called Castle Grande, a few miles south of Little Rock. He borrowed the money from Madison Guaranty and learned later than McDougal was being forced out of the bank. The year was 1986. Fulbright had to pay off the loan and borrowed $270,000 from his old friend, Witt Stephens; he paid off the latter loan, with interest, writing Stephens: "It is a sad tale of misplaced trust but I expect you have encountered it before."[11]

McDougal was indicted for fraud in 1989 but was acquitted at trial in 1990. Meantime, he and Susan McDougal had been divorced and his health had failed. He went into seclusion in the scandal, for a time, but then came out fighting, interviewing every journalist he could talk to—and even ran for Congress again in the spring of 1994, this time in the Fourth (South Arkansas) District. He lost the Democratic nomination but he got enough votes to force the leading candidates into a runoff.

By the time the Castle Grande reached the headlines, Fulbright had suffered his stroke and was unable to discuss it with the federal investigators, who were looking into everything McDougal had done. Inquiries to Fulbright were handled by his old friend and aide, Lee Williams, and David Capes, another former aide. Williams said in an interview that Fulbright was simply helping his old staffer, McDougal, and that he, Fulbright, was accustomed to taking the word of people he was in business with, as his family had done earlier in the family enterprises in Fayetteville.[12] The *Washington Post's* Susan Schmidt, covering the Castle Grande story, wrote that "Fulbright's integrity has been above reproach throughout his career." Robert Fiske, Jr., the first special counsel conducting the Whitewater investigation, said that Fulbright was not under investigation.

Fulbright was perhaps fortunate that his name was not brought up in the context of Whitewater after Kenneth Starr took over the investigation. While Fiske had been statesmanlike and reasonably careful to avoid destroying reputations in the course of his prosecutorial duties, Starr's activities were more doubtful. Of course, no competent person ever alleged any improper conduct on Fulbright's part, but Fiske had at least officially stated that the senator was not under investigation after misleading media reports gave the impression that Fulbright might have done something wrong. The major Clinton administration casualty was the high-ranking Justice Department official Webster Hubbell, who pled guilty to stealing money from the Rose law firm and some of his clients back when he had practiced law in Little Rock; Hubbell's crimes were gross violations of a lawyer's profession, but they had nothing to do with the Whitewater real estate project. The charges brought in the first indictment against Gov. Jim Guy Tucker—which tucker vehemently denied—also had nothing to do with Whitewater; that indictment was dismissed by Judge Henry Woods. A second indictment was still pending against Tucker as of this writing in the early fall of 1995. After years of scrutiny of the real estate deals, the special prosecutor had uncovered no evidence that the Clintons had been involved in an illegal scheme regarding Whitewater. Fiske had incurred the wrath of many Republicans because he had not made any revelations damaging to the administration. An appellate federal court panel appointed Starr rather than Fiske to continue the investigation. *In the Matter of a Charge of Judicial Misconduct or Disability*, 39 F.3d 374 (1994); (*see also Washington Post*, August 12, 1994, "Judge Met Sen. Faircloth before Fiske was Ousted"). Rather than envisioning Fiske's conduct as lenient, it may be that he had simply been objective in not having found any evidence of illegal activity. As of this writing in mid-1995, it was too early to tell whether the investigation under Kenneth Starr might develop evidence that could lead to indictments regarding Whitewater itself, although none had been forthcoming after years of inquiry. In June, 1995, a report prepared by a Republican critic of President Clinton indicated that the President and the First Lady had only minimal knowledge of or involvement in the financial transactions conducted by their Whitewater partner, McDougal. The report was prepared by Jay Stephens, a former Republican U.S. attorney in Washington, and submitted to the Resolution Trust Corporation. In any event, there was no doubt that Fulbright had been guilty of nothing in his dealings with McDougal, except for weak business judgment and sentimentality toward a former aide.

IV. ROLE MODEL FOR CLINTON

One of Fulbright's most important legacies was his direct influence upon political leaders of the younger generation, including Bumpers, Pryor, Alexander, and above all, Bill Clinton. Fulbright met Clinton when the young student from Hot Springs came to Washington as one of the Boys Nation leaders in July, 1963. Clinton and Larry Taunton, another Arkansas student, enjoyed a luncheon appointment with Fulbright and John McClellan. Taunton later reflected that Clinton and Fulbright talked at length and developed an instant affinity for each other; Clinton even as a teenager displayed great ease in the presence of powerful politicians, and the young Arkansan had studied Fulbright's career before he visited Washington. Clinton considered Fulbright his first political role model. In 1992, Clinton would recall thinking that the senator was "the cat's meow. Fulbright I admired no end.... He had a real impact on my wanting to be a citizen of the world." After the lunch with Fulbright, Clinton proceeded to the highlight of his visit to Washington: a visit to the Rose Garden to hear President Kennedy speak. Clinton was the first to shake JFK's hand, a moment captured by a photographer as the President greeted the future President.[12a]

In 1966 Senator Fulbright had opened a great national debate that was to change the course of the public debate regarding the Vietnam War. The Senate hearings on Vietnam were coming to center stage and stirring widespread doubt about the war's conduct. It was in this setting that Fulbright hired Clinton to come to work as an intern on the staff of the Foreign Relations Committee. Clinton needed the job to help pay for his undergraduate education at Georgetown University, but it was a fortuitous event for both parties. Fulbright, in his turn, was to become a role model for a young man who would be elected President of the United States a quarter century later.

The convergence of the lives of Fulbright and Clinton came about rather by accident. Young Clinton had returned home briefly to work in the Arkansas gubernatorial primary, as a driver and campaign worker for one of the leading Democratic candidates, Frank Holt, a state Supreme Court justice. In this campaign Clinton caught the attention of the candidate's brother, Jack Holt, an influential Little Rock lawyer who was later to become chief justice of the state Supreme Court. As it happened, Jack Holt had been a classmate in law school of Lee Williams, later the administrative assistant and leading aide to Senator Fulbright; Holt was taken with Clinton and he asked Williams if there might be a job in the Senate for the young Arkansan.

Lee Williams telephoned Clinton to talk to him about a job on the Foreign Relations Committee, and was instantly impressed in the same way that Jack Holt had been. "Indeed," Williams recalled in a 1993 interview, "the more he talked the more impressed I was." He found Clinton bright and resourceful and ambitious. Williams asked Clinton if he would like a full-time job or a part-time job, and Clinton replied, "How about two part-time jobs?" Williams hired him on the spot and Clinton spent valuable time in association with Fulbright on the committee, at a time when the chairman was engaged in his momentous dissent on Vietnam.[13] Clinton, Phil Dozier, and another college student filled the hundreds of requests for committee reports that came in each week, carefully read several major newspapers for articles related to foreign affairs, sorted the mail, and ran errands. Clinton was able to occasionally have lunch with or talk to Fulbright, and he had frequent and lengthy conversations with Williams and Norvill Jones, who worked on Vietnam policy for the committee. Clinton developed an immense pride in his state for having sent to Washington such a deep intellect as Fulbright, in contrast to the stereotype of Arkansans as anti-intellectual rednecks.

The young Arkansan's staff work was a tremendous educational experience. When he first began working for the committee, Clinton held a student deferment and was two years away from being drafted. At first he recalled being "for the war—or at least not against it," but his views changed after his intense exposure to Fulbright and his staff. For a class at Georgetown on American relations in the Far East, Clinton wrote a 28-page paper on the Gulf of Tonkin Resolution—with the resource materials at hand in the back room of the committee where he worked. Clinton's paper followed Fulbright's conclusions regarding the Resolution. Fulbright's influence upon Clinton was also extensive in the manner in which the young Arkansan's dissent was expressed: Clinton was not at that time an antiwar activist and he did not take part in the early mass demonstrations against the war. Clinton had absorbed Fulbright's philosophy that the most effective dissenters remained within the system and worked for change through traditional forms of opposition.[13a]

Clinton's relatively placid world as a student leader at Georgetown and intern with Senator Fulbright was devastated in early 1968 on "Black Friday," when President Johnson abolished draft deferments for graduate students except those in various fields of medicine. This was a stark day for Clinton and roughly 226,000 other young men who were then college seniors or in their first year of graduate school. The Johnson administration was responding to criticisms that the graduate school deferments were one of the inequities of the draft, for they allowed the educated elite to avoid the war that working class people were fighting. A year earlier, only 14,000 college graduates had been drafted; with the deferments eliminated, that number would skyrocket to 150,000, with another 75,000 expected to enlist voluntarily.[13b]

With the threat of the draft now looming in the near future, Clinton returned to Arkansas to work in the re-election campaign for Fulbright, whose principal opponent, of course, was "Justice Jim" Johnson, the same extremist candidate who had defeated Frank Holt in the gubernatorial Democratic primary that Clinton had worked in two years earlier. Clinton's deep respect for Fulbright was not blind adulation; at the time he confided to his friends that he regarded Fulbright's unwillingness to speak out on civil rights issues as a relic of the South's melancholy past, and he would break from the Fulbright pattern on that issue. On international issues, he would emulate the senator in his future plans for a political career. He sought to avoid developing Fulbright's political image of schizophrenia, in which many people unfortunately perceived the senator as playing two contradictory roles with two radically different personas: the patrician, cosmopolitan Rhodes Scholar in Washington, who became "just plain Bill" in flannel shirts when he went home to campaign.

Clinton asked Lee Williams (who left Washington temporarily to run the campaign) for an assignment close to the senator. Williams was known for his political sagacity, but his decision to let Clinton be Fulbright's driver was not one of his master strokes. Fulbright generally preferred to do quite a bit of talking, although he was careful to periodically throw questions back at the other person. But when he was campaigning and had dozens of issues on his mind, he preferred to talk more and not to be troubled by difficult questions. Unfortunately, Clinton was intellectually Fulbright's equal, and was young, vigorous and full of difficult questions. The Fulbright-Clinton-mobile had two brilliant minds who, in retrospect, were two of the most famous statesmen the South ever produced. But their brilliance was fully matched by their absent-mindedness. One day, Fulbright called the headquarters to report that the car's floorboard was drenched, and it was left to Jim McDougal, then director of the senator's Little Rock office, to deduce that Clinton had precipitated this flood by running the air conditioning with the vents closed. McDougal joked to Williams: "Two goddamn Rhodes Scholars in one car and they can't figure out why they're making rain!" In another misadventure, Clinton drove for over an hour and a half in the wrong direction, until Fulbright, relying upon his greater knowledge of Arkansas geography, realized that they were nowhere near where they were supposed to be and told him to turn around. Fulbright irritated Clinton because he could never win an argument with the senator, while Clinton exasperated Fulbright because he was constantly talking and asking difficult questions. On the next day, Fulbright decided to drive himself around alone. Clinton was assigned to other tasks, including occasionally talking to small groups, and the young student leader still remained upbeat: as he wrote to a friend that summer, "Lately I have returned to my speechmaking."[13c] Clinton had taken a minor part and gained more political experience in Fulbright's victory in the 1968 primary.

Despite the comical irritations between Fulbright and Clinton in the midst of a hectic political campaign, Fulbright always took a strong interest in Clinton and encouraged him to apply for a Rhodes Scholarship. Fulbright arranged for Clinton to meet other influential, talented people. For example, he helped him meet the writer, Willie Morris, the Rhodes Scholar who wrote *North Toward Home*, the autobiographical account of a Mississippi-born writer; later, Fulbright would get Clinton in touch with Rudy Moore, a Fayetteville lawyer with connections to Fulbright who ultimately served in Clinton's gubernatorial administration and was one among many young, influential lawyers who supported Clinton's rise to power in Arkansas. In November, 1968, after Clinton won his Rhodes and was watching the election returns at Oxford, one of the few consolations after Nixon's triumph was the news that Fulbright had defeated his Republican opponent in the general election. Clinton sent a telegram to Fulbright the next day: "Got results at Rhodes House election party. You received a great cheer. Everything fine here. Happy for you and Mrs. Fulbright. Congratulations!"[13d] Fulbright replied, "Dear Bill: I appreciate so much your warm telegram. It was thoughtful of you to wire me at such a busy time. I am looking forward to seeing you on your return."[13e]

Clinton obtained help from numerous sources in his desire to avoid fighting in a war he detested in Vietnam. Fulbright was certainly willing to help Clinton or any other young man who opposed the war in Vietnam, but the senator was not the first one to help. Raymond Clinton, Bill's uncle, had important connections to the Hot Springs power structure, including the Garland County Draft Board. Raymond Clinton contacted an influential Hot Springs lawyer, Henry Britt, who asked the chairman of the board to put Bill Clinton's draft notice in a drawer to give him a chance to go to Oxford. Bill Clinton himself may not have known about this action—or inaction—on his behalf. It was common at the time for Rhodes Scholars to receive preferential treatment—at least five other Rhodes Scholars that year received treatment that was at least as or more explicit than that given to Bill Clinton. The mother of Rhodes Scholar Paul Parish, for example, received a letter from the governor of Mississippi telling her to allow Paul to go to England because they were trying to get an exemption for Rhodes Scholars. The board in Alameda County, California, granted Tom Williamson of Harvard a graduate school deferment even though such deferments were supposed to have been abolished.[13f] Such preferential treatment obviously increased the inequities of the war, and heightened the guilt that some of the best and brightest felt about not being drafted when the less educated were. However, it is clear that this preference for Rhodes Scholars emanated from those in positions of power: obviously the Mississippi governor, the Alameda County Draft Board and other power structures were determined to give the Rhodes Scholars their chance at Oxford.

Clinton, like countless others of his generation, became preoccupied by the specter of the draft. At Oxford, he wrote a meticulously researched paper on the conscientious objector statute, citing Supreme Court opinions. He finally received his dreaded Order to Report for Induction, but he had started another term by the time he received it, and under draft regulations he could complete the term in which he was already enrolled. Clinton consulted Lee Williams and Fulbright about his dilemma. He could either submit to the draft and enter the Army that summer, resist the draft like his stalwart fellow Rhodes Scholar Frank Aller, or find a way to void the induction notice in exchange for a military alternative such as a Reserve Officer Training Corps (ROTC) program. Williams, a veteran of World War II, was routinely advising hundreds of young men at the time. Fulbright and Williams helped the young in any legal way that they could.[13g] "We would call and find out where they were looking for people in the National Guard, where there might be an ROTC slot," Williams recalled. Clinton made an effort to obtain an ROTC deferment at the University of Arkansas Law School. This program had become known as a safe haven for those wishing to avoid the draft. Lee Williams, himself a graduate of the law school, made several phone calls in support of Clinton's deferment, including one to the director of the program, Colonel Eugene Holmes. At the same time, Clinton had also arranged for contacts in Governor Rockefeller's office to make similar calls in support of his deferment, which was to figure dramatically in the 1992 presidential campaign. Clinton paid a visit to Col. Holmes, who decided to enroll Clinton in the program, and as a result the July 28 induction notice was nullified.

As David Maraniss pointed out in his book on Clinton, *First in His Class*, millions of either privileged or just lucky young men could tell similar stories of escaping the draft.

Gimpy knees, bad backs or migraines kept some men out who were in fact rather robust and excelled in sports. During the entire Vietnam era, there were 26.8 million men of draft age, of whom 8.7 million enlisted and 2.2 million were drafted. Many who served were poor and undereducated. Most of them—about 16 million—avoided service entirely through deferments, disqualification, exemptions, or—the smallest category—resistance. Only 209,000 were accused of resisting or dodging the draft, and only 8,8750 were convicted. Another Rhodes Scholar from Mississippi, Tom Ward, found a job in a National Guard unit through the influence of his father, an influential Republican lawyer who supported Nixon. Maraniss' book—which in some respects was favorable to Clinton, in other respects was critical and dwelled upon his alleged flaws—was candid in noting the genuine distress that Clinton and Ward felt about escaping the draft that those without connections were unable to do. Yet, Ward also believed that even the limited vulnerability to the war that the golden boys of the influential classes faced in 1969 hastened an end to the war. As Maraniss quoted Ward, who later became an Episcopalian minister in Nashville: "I just think historically the war broke down when we started drafting the Bill Clintons and Tom Wards. People like my father were not going to have their sons dying in that war and were politically influential enough to stop it. That is the moral ambiguity of the situation." In similar terms, Clinton would speak of his ambivalence, of his detestation of the war and yet his guilt that he held the ROTC deferment.[13h]

For Bill Clinton, the Fulbright connection would prove important to him in surviving one of the crucial tests he encountered in the 1992 presidential race. In both the primaries and the general election campaign a troublesome issue arose in the fact that Clinton had avoided the draft. Clinton's responses in the 1992 campaign to questions about his draft record seemed confused and even contradictory at times. In September of the election year, Lee Williams was able to give Clinton support that helped substantially in maintaining the credibility of the candidate's recollections of the Vietnam period. As the fall campaign got under way a fresh attack on Clinton was made in early September by Colonel Holmes, who claimed that Clinton had "defrauded the military" and "purposely deceived me" in 1969. The contacts between Clinton and the colonel took place in the summer of 1969. Clinton was then only a few weeks away from the draft unless he was accepted for ROTC training. In Holmes' version of the contacts, Clinton led Holmes to believe he would enter the ROTC right away, but Clinton, for his part, said that the colonel had agreed to let him return to Oxford University, as a Rhodes Scholar, and then enter the Law School at the University of Arkansas in the following year, 1970.[14]

Enter Lee Williams. Newspaper reporters had taken a fascinated interest in a memorandum by Williams in the Fulbright Archives at the University. It showed that Williams had made contacts, in July 1969, with the University of Arkansas ROTC on behalf of a deferment for Bill Clinton, whom Williams had gotten to know well when Clinton worked earlier for Fulbright while a student at Georgetown and in the 1968 campaign. Williams was interviewed by the *New York Times*. He acknowledged that the memorandum had to be his, and that "obviously" he had been in contact with the ROTC, although he did not remember the memorandum.

The memorandum was written in cryptic, unconnected phrases but it made reference to the university "law school," and another abbreviated note suggested that Clinton would not undertake the required basic training for the ROTC program until the following summer, suggesting the very terms that Clinton said he had proposed to arrange with the ROTC for deferment.[15]

Interestingly, the Fulbright archives showed that the Fulbright office was routinely giving help to a number of Arkansans at the time in requests for draft deferment. The reporter for the *New York Times* concluded, in the article of September 13, that Williams' explanation of the memorandum supported Clinton's interpretation of it.

Williams' account of the draft episode lent support to Clinton on this issue at a time when he needed all the support he could find. Fulbright had been for Clinton from the start in the Presidential race. In June 1991 he told the author in an interview that he was for Clinton although he doubted that a candidate from Arkansas, such a small and poor state, could be nominated. In 1992, he pitched in his own comment backing Clinton on the draft. He told the Associated Press in Washington that he did not remember being approached to help Clinton avoid the draft but that if he, Fulbright, had been asked for advice he would have told Clinton to avoid it. Fulbright went on to accuse George Bush of using the draft issue against Clinton in the same way he had used the Willie Horton issue against Michael Dukakis, the Democratic nominee in the 1988 campaign. The Republicans had employed a bitterly controversial television advertisement, in 1988, suggesting that Dukakis was soft on crime because a black felon named Willie Horton had raped a woman while on a furlough in Massachusetts, where Dukakis was governor.

"I think the whole thing is disgraceful that national politics has fallen into this sort of thing," Fulbright said at his office in Washington, adding: "I can see where the President [Bush] has nothing else to talk about. That's his main issue."

In analyzing the draft controversy, Col. Holmes cannot be regarded as an accurate, objective source. Holmes' recollections of the episode have fluctuated radically over the years, ranging from innocuous comments in the 1970s to the bitterly hostile comments he made at the height of the 1992 campaign. When he was asked about it in 1978, he said that he could not remember any specifics. In 1991, he said that he treated Clinton "just like any other kid." In September, 1992, despite his earlier statement that he could not remember any details, his memory suddenly became acute. He wrote a statement questioning Clinton's "patriotism and his integrity" and accusing him of deception; this statement was written with the assistance of his daughter, Linda Burnett, a Republican activist, and released with assistance from the office of former Republican Congressman John Paul Hammerschmidt. Even Bush campaign officials were disappointed by the letter, because it was "full of rhetoric and precious few facts," according to David Tell of Bush's opposition research staff. On some points, Holmes' statement was simply erroneous. "At no time," Holmes complained, "during this long conversation about his desire to join the program did he inform me of his involvement, participation and actually organizing protests against the United States involvement in Southeast Asia." Holmes said that if he had known of Clinton's alleged "anti-war activism," he would not have been accepted into the ROTC program as a potential officer of the U.S. Army. The fallacy in Holmes' argument rested on a factual error: Clinton did not take part in organizing protests against the war until after their meeting. In fact, Clinton had been influenced by Fulbright's mainstream philosophy of promoting change within the system, and during most of his student days his dissent went no further than oral criticisms and an occasional research paper. Clinton did help organize a demonstration against the war in October, 1969, in England. Even at the London demonstrations, which were in sympathy with the Vietnam Moratorium in the United States at the same time, Clinton's activities were perfectly consistent with mainstream opposition tactics: Clinton merely led a teach-in against the war, endorsed an antiwar petition signed by nearly all the American Rhodes Scholars of the time, and took part in a peaceful march to the American Embassy by about 500 American and British protesters. With his ties to Fulbright and his stature as a Rhodes Scholar, he was somewhat prestigious in the student antiwar movement, but he did not become directly involved in protests until the fall of 1969. Moreover, regarding his views on the war, although Clinton did not discuss them with Holmes in their conversation, Holmes knew that he had worked for and admired Fulbright, the famous opponent of the war. The ROTC drill instructor, Ed Howard, acknowledged that Holmes' ROTC unit had enrolled law students who were seeking to escape Vietnam, and his unit had expanded in 1969 for that reason.[15a] Whatever opinions anyone might hold regarding Clinton and Fulbright in this episode, it is clear that Holmes' attacks were shrill and incorrect.

David Maraniss' book was marred in some passages by his reliance upon source material (the book was based upon interviews far more than documents) that was essentially gossip, but in most passages he was reasonably objective, if occasionally rather critical of Clinton. Even Maraniss, however, acknowledged the weaknesses in Holmes' recollections of events. "A letter that Clinton wrote Holmes from Oxford in December 1969 in which he apologized for not writing more often—'I know I promised to let you hear from me at least once a month'—is the strongest evidence that Holmes was aware of and approved Clinton's plan to go back to Oxford." Holmes later argued that he had wanted to enroll in the Arkansas law school after a couple of months at Oxford. Even if Holmes' account was not objective, there is no doubt that other members of the ROTC staff had thought Clinton would enroll that fall and were irritated when he did not. In any event, it is often forgotten that the final event that led to Clinton's avoidance of the draft was determined not by the influence of Fulbright or anyone else, but largely by the Nixon administration changes in the draft system and pure luck. Later in 1969, Clinton decided to give up his deferment, reject the University of Arkansas law school and ROTC proposal altogether, and resubmit himself to the draft. On October 1, Nixon sought to reduce antiwar dissent by ordering the Selective Service System to change its policy for graduate students, who would now be allowed to finish the entire school year rather than just the term they were in when they received draft notices. The President announced a withdrawal of 35,000 troops and a temporary suspension of the draft. Under a draft lottery system, young men would be vulnerable to the draft for only one year, with their vulnerability determined by selection of numbers corresponding to their birthdays. Clinton was safe from the draft that year because of the change in policy, and he was obviously aware that in the climate of reduced draft calls and the pressures of dissent from Congress and the public, his chances of getting drafted were reduced. By resubmitting his name, however, he exposed himself to a still real chance of getting drafted. Part of the motivation may have been guilt over having obtained the ROTC deferment earlier, although the ultimate answer to that question lies only in Clinton's mind. Like many young opponents of the war of his generation, Clinton was understandably appreciative of the role Fulbright and other titans of the antiwar movement had played in hastening America's disengagement from Vietnam. In the end, a combination of the reduced American military commitment in Vietnam and luck removed the possibility that Clinton might be drafted: his draft number was 311.[15b]

In fairness to Holmes and all those involved in both sides of the draft controversy, the Vietnam War evoked feelings of bitterness more than any other issue of its time (with the exception of the civil rights movement), and it was hardly surprising that emotions might becloud descriptions of those events, both at the time and in later years. Clinton had added a few inaccuracies to his activities during those years in a lengthy letter he wrote to Holmes on December 3, 1969, explaining why he had decided not to enroll in the ROTC. Clinton referred to his two years of work for the Senate Foreign Relations Committee, saying that "I did it for the experience and the salary but also for the opportunity, however small, of working every day against a war I opposed and despised with a depth of feeling I had reserved solely for racism in America before Vietnam. I did not take the matter lightly but studied it carefully, and there was a time when not many people had more information about Vietnam at hand than I did." Clinton's vehement opposition to the war as of late 1969 colored his view of what his position had been in the fall of 1966 when he began work for Fulbright's staff. At that time, he had no strong feelings on the war and may have even leaned toward supporting Johnson, and his experience in the environment of Fulbright's committee—as well as his independent thinking on the issue—was a major catalyst in changing his views. Clinton also recalled that he had "written and spoken and marched against the war," and after he left Arkansas in the summer he had worked in the national headquarters of the Vietnam Moratorium in Washington. Actually, Clinton was cleancut and quite tame while at Georgetown; Father McSorley, Georgetown's leading antiwar activist in those years, did not meet Clinton until he became more of an activist at the London demonstrations in 1969. On the other hand, Clinton was correct to stress his activism after he left Arkansas that summer. At Oxford, he became more critical of American policy, although he was hardly unusual in that respect during the Nixon years. His hair became fairly long and he grew a beard—in fact, when Fulbright saw him in those years he would frequently tell him to get a haircut. Other than his outward appearance, however, Clinton never departed from Fulbright's fundamental philosophy of remaining within the system to bring about change. On a tour of Europe to Oslo, Moscow and elsewhere, he attended meetings with peace groups, and in the summer of 1970, he worked in Washington for Project Pursestrings, an organization that lobbied Congress to cut off funds for the war. During this period, Clinton was more critical of leading politicians, including Fulbright, than he had been before. At a time when Cliff Jackson, a young Republican from Arkansan who would later become a bitter critic of Clinton, was seeking a job in the Nixon White House, Clinton wrote to him in a reference to Fulbright's civil rights record that "His [Fulbright's] politics are probably closer to yours than to mine."[15c] In the next couple of years, Clinton would work for the antiwar candidate Joe Duffey's Senate campaign in Connecticut and then for the McGovern campaign in Texas in 1972; none of these activities support later notions disseminated by right-wing critics that Fulbright had encouraged Clinton to persist in a radical, counterculture rebellion.

The Fulbright-Clinton relationship remained amicable through the years. In 1974, when Clinton made a valiant, if ultimately unsuccessful race for Congress against the entrenched Republican Congressman John Paul Hammerschmidt, he had planned to assist Fulbright's campaign as well, according to James Blair, Fulbright's campaign manager that year. Given the imposing strength of the Bumpers campaign in that year, it would not have made any difference, and Clinton understandably became so involved in his own race—in which he gave the incumbent a surprisingly strong fight—that he was not able to help his former boss.[15d]

In 1993, after Clinton was inaugurated President, Senator Fulbright would have occasion to influence Clinton again, on a familiar theme of Fulbright's, the dangers of foreign adventuring. In February, Fulbright conferred with the president in the White House, along with Lee Williams and certain presidential aides. "We kicked the gong around with Clinton" in a foreign policy discussion featuring what to do about Bosnia, Williams said. Fulbright had not yet suffered the heavy stroke that would partially paralyze him a few months later.

In retrospect, Williams recalled, "we may have overdone it," in warning the President against military entanglement in the Balkans, citing the awful Vietnam example. Many influential supporters of the President shared the desire to prevent another promising era of American reform from disappearing into the jaws of a foreign military quagmire. But if only Bill Clinton can say how much influence Fulbright had upon him in the White House meeting, the record shows restraint on the part of the President in action if not in rhetoric, as the civil war in Bosnia raged on through Clinton's first two years in the Oval Office.

At the same time that Fulbright was criticizing Bush's overwrought attacks on the Vietnam draft question, the former senator was interviewed at length by a Vermont columnist writing for the *Valley News*. The interview didn't receive a lot of attention but it was vintage Fulbright. He was in Vermont with his wife visiting her parents. He was lively and loquacious, ranging across many subjects, from Ronald Reagan's film career to taxes to selection of a Clinton cabinet.

Whether facetiously or not, Fulbright warned against the selection of too many Rhodes Scholars in the next government. He said he was surprised that an Arkansan was so close to the White House, noting that Arkansas is a poor state with few electoral votes. He expressed confidence that Clinton would make a fine president, but said he should not try to move too fast.

"But if Bill does move too fast, I'm confident Hillary will slow him down . . . I don't think he will absorb arrogance the way most men do in the White House," Fulbright asserted. In a truly expansive mood, he declared Ross Perot to be right about Americans having to tighten their belts and he unloaded a remark about Ronald Reagan that revealed the true contempt he had for the ex-president: "The Republicans squawk about taxes because that silly movie actor Reagan made people believe we can live on air like they do in Hollywood. I've often thought Ronald Reagan really believed he was in the war. That's not any more ridiculous than his being in the White House. Only trouble was, he really was in the White House."[16] Unquestionably, Fulbright was having a grand vacation in Vermont, partly because he could sense that Bill Clinton was going to be elected president.

Fulbright's association with Bill Clinton brought the senator one of his most gratifying experiences as his health declined and the shadows of his life lengthened. On May 5, 1993, the Fulbright Association, which is made up of Fulbright Scholars, held a great dinner in his honor attended by 400 guests. President Clinton appeared and conferred upon

Fulbright the Presidential Medal of Freedom, which is the highest honor that may be conferred upon a civilian. It was, to Fulbright, a complete surprise.

The timing was fortuitous. Fulbright, at 88, was infirm, having continued to suffer a series of small strokes, but he was still able to go to the microphone with the help of his wife, Harriet, and respond to the tribute paid him by the President. He thanked Clinton and the audience and said it was "just wonderful to have my old students here." The President, in his turn, regaled the audience with stories of Fulbright's political career and told the crowd that Fulbright "doubled the IQ of any room he entered." The Fulbright Association announced the inauguration of a $50,000 prize, the J. William Fulbright Award for International Understanding, funded by the Coca-Cola Company.[17]

Fulbright was never lacking in confidence but he was always skeptical about his own impact on events. He would remark to friends in his best mood that "perhaps I did make a difference." The bestowal of the Presidential Medal might have convinced Fulbright of his own accomplishment. In any case, the climactic award of his life was made a few weeks before he sustained the stroke that left him in a wheelchair, his speech impaired.

In July, 1995, a few months after Fulbright died, Bill Clinton would become the President who established full diplomatic relations with Vietnam. Clinton gained some bipartisan support, especially from Senator John McCain (R.-Arizona), who had been a prisoner of war for more than five years. The President appealed for an end to the decades of divisiveness over Vietnam: "This moment offers us the opportunity to bind up our own wounds. They have resisted time for too long." In contrast to McCain's support for the President in having shown "courage and honor" in the decision to normalize relations, Senator Jesse Helms, the Chairman of the Senate Foreign Relations Committee, denounced the President's action as a "mistake of the highest order," and vowed to use his chairmanship to hinder implementation of recognition. Senator Robert Dole also condemned the President's "tragic"" mistake. Yet, in 1995, it was Fulbright's protege who held power in the White House. "I wish Fulbright" the President reminisced that summer, "had been alive to see our nation normalize relations with Vietnam."

V. A MAN OF STOUT IDEAS

In his 90th year Fulbright was felled by an ancient disease once called apoplexy, which has been in history the cruelest affliction for a man of brilliant mind and unusual gifts of expression. Even then, he was not disposed to self-pity, for, as the authors of this book found, he could still make jokes about the harsh limitations suddenly imposed upon him. Fulbright had always been a realist in considering what life had done for him and how he had been favored. In the years of his retirement from the center of power on Capitol Hill, he was ever prone to say that whatever else happened to him he had no complaints about the hand that fortune had dealt him.

He could look back and know that he had been blessed with talent and advantages that he had employed resourcefully to become one of the leading American legislators of his century. Fulbright himself, especially in his late years, often spoke of the accidents that fashioned his life. What was fascinating was the absence of an early driving personal ambition to become a great figure, a president or other historic personage, wielding power and gaining glory. In this respect, he was unlike his protégé, Bill Clinton, who was thinking of a great career in politics at least as early as when he met John F. Kennedy when he was a teenager visiting the White House as a member of Boys State. Fulbright was a natural patrician, by inheritance and inclination, and he did not set out early to be a politician. Fate shaped his course at critical points, dramatically in Governor Homer Adkins' decision in 1941 to fire Fulbright as president of the University of Arkansas. If Fulbright had been allowed to remain as head of the university, he might have spent his life in academe, as he was disposed to do when he left the Justice Department in Washington, first to teach law at George Washington University and then to return to the Fayetteville law school. Moreover, ambition came to Fulbright late. As a young man he was in no great hurry. Even though he did well as a Rhodes Scholar, it wasn't until he reached George Washington Law School that he settled down to hard studying and finished second in his class.

When he finally wandered into politics, his timing was right, not only in his ability to get elected but also in the condition of the Congress when he rose in its ranks. In the 1950s and 1960s, committee chairmen wielded more power than they did in the late 1970s and the 1980s. Seniority governed the road to power but the individual member of the House and Senate was then much less disposed to challenge the authority of the elders. At one time Arkansas exercised extraordinary, perhaps unique, power in having three enormously powerful committee chairmen at work. Fulbright presided over the Senate's role in foreign policy; Senator John McClellan was chairman of Appropriations; and, in the House, Wilbur

Mills exercised legendary power as chairman of the Ways and Means of the government. Seniority had its dark side, and the members in both houses finally managed to reduce the powers of the chairmen; it was supposed to be reform and it looked like reform, but Congress lost some of its ability to function directly and effectively. In the 1980s and since, Congress has sometimes resembled a self-shorn Samson. Certainly, no chairman of Foreign Relations has made much of an impact since Fulbright left the Senate. Fulbright was splendidly equipped for the chairmanship and, in the decades since, it is doubtful that most Americans have even known who holds the position. When Fulbright was in power, the whole country knew it, unloading veneration and vilification upon him, both in full measure.

Fulbright's rise in the Senate was also due in part to his willingness to play by the rules of the game. Luckily, in the late 1950s, he and Lyndon Johnson were great friends in a period when Johnson was majority leader and the single greatest power in the Senate. It was seven years later before Fulbright broke with President Johnson. Factors that made Fulbright such a powerful senator worked against his successor, Dale Bumpers, a man of talent and principle with views rather like those of the man he displaced. Early on, Bumpers came into conflict with Majority Leader Robert Byrd of West Virginia, and Bumpers' committee assignments have not been at the places of greatest power. Bumpers commands wide respect in Washington and his personality and eloquence twice made him a realistic prospect for the Democratic presidential nomination. On both occasions, he decided not to run, perhaps unwilling to make the formidable sacrifice that is required and clearly not driven to become president, as his fellow Arkansan, Bill Clinton, was driven. The record on Bumpers is not nearly completed after 20 years in the Senate. Fulbright is now taking his place in history and is likely to loom large in its pages.

In his career Fulbright was a man of stout opinions and a set of principles that he developed as a young man under the influence of his mother and leading scholars in the universities where he was educated. He did not modify his views dramatically as the decades passed. His themes recurred again and again in his speeches and conversation, rather like a symphony. As his interests matured and his sphere of influence focused, his central concern became the proper exercise of American power in the international community.

There is little evidence that he changed his mind often, or that he went through the dreary experience, fairly common, of spending his early years as a liberal and then reacting into conservatism in his advancing years. Fulbright was Fulbright. He could be stubborn in defending his actions and his record, notably in the case of civil rights, which is surely the main liability on his record. He voted against civil rights bills in the 1950s and he signed the notorious Southern Manifesto, although with clear distaste. A fellow Southern senator, George Smathers of Florida, told his new administrative assistant in 1956: "if you think the Southern Manifesto was bad, hell, you should have seen it before Fulbright and I toned it down."[18]

Fulbright's votes on issues related to civil rights were significantly separated from the Southern norm in the late 1960s and early 1970s, particularly in nominations to the Supreme Court that became highly controversial due to the civil rights positions of the nominees. He had voted to extend the Voting Rights Act in 1970. His position on the earlier racial controversies was, as he had said, motivated by the desire to avoid a political martyr's fate, like that of Congressman Brooks Hays. Even in the 1980s he would sometimes get into rambling, illogical remarks suggesting that the South might have straightened itself out if given time. He never recanted on his accommodation with Southern segregation in the crucial massive resistance era. The subject irritated him, but if he ever changed his mind regarding his early civil rights record, nobody could tell it. Yet, in his last years in the Senate, he was able to change, at least to some degree; as his young liberal aide, David Capes, recalls the senator's statements on the few occasions they discussed civil rights in the early 1970s: "He always made the point that nobody's too old or too smart to grow."[18a]

The late Senator Paul Douglas of Illinois, a man of keen intellect himself, regarded Fulbright as an intellectual whose roots were in the eighteenth century and its emphasis upon reason. It was reason, not patriotism or religious fervor, that Fulbright sought to bring to bear on American policy. The only crusade he ever joined was the one against Naziism, which he recognized as nationalism gone berserk.

Fulbright served in the Congress for a third of his century. His legacy is substantial—he did "make a difference"—both in his own country and abroad. He helped create an international agency which, in spite of its failures and aberrations, has given the world a central forum. At times, the United Nations has responded effectively to crises, although its lapses—such as in Bosnia and elsewhere—demonstrate how far the world community has yet to rise in order to make the UN a genuine collective security organization. As Fulbright had lamented at its creation, the nations must begin to delegate their national sovereignty in the field of armaments to the international body, and given the still vast power of nationalism, such a reform will be an exceedingly difficult goal for the long term. Yet, the difficulty of the objective, as the Arkansas senator had urged in 1945 and for 40 years thereafter, could not diminish the imperative need to restrain the growth of armaments that threatened human civilization with extinction. Near the end of his career, Fulbright was still realistic about the UN, but also still convinced that the world community must strengthen the international organization over the long term. "I still believe in the United Nations," he wrote in 1989, but "not the debilitated, often irresponsible body that sits in New York, but the concept underlying the United Nations, which cannot be said to have failed because it has never been seriously tried."[19] After his death in 1995, Fulbright's voice would be sorely missed as an advocate for the establishment for a meaningful, powerful United Nations. The resurgent Republicans in Congress waged a renewed assault on American commitment to the United Nations. At his death, a melancholy irony emerged concerning Fulbright's role as champion of the United Nations: while his protege and supporter of a stronger UN, Bill Clinton, held power in the White House, the devotees of the "Contract With America" in Congress sought to restrict the American role in the UN so drastically as to render the world organization impotent. At the 50th anniversary of the UN Charter's adoption, Clinton conceded that many UN agencies had grown too bloated and that reforms to streamline the organization and make it more effective would be essential. Yet he emphatically rejected the "siren song of the new isolationists": "So I say, especially to the opponents of the United Nations here in the United States, turning our back on the UN and going it alone will lead to far more economic, political and military burdens on our people in the future and would ignore the lessons of our own history. Let us say no to isolation, yes to reform." While Clinton's mentor was famous for a tenacity that could compel him to clash with the likes of

Joe McCarthy or Lyndon Johnson, the Arkansas President has always been known as more of a conciliator and consensus builder. The champions of internationalism could now hope that the President would show some of Fulbright's pertinacity in defending the remnants of support for the UN against the neo-isolationists in Congress.

More than any other senator of his time, Fulbright made dissent respectable in the national debates on foreign policy. He dared to think "unthinkable thoughts" and express them against the will of a furious majority opinion and a bitter enemy in the White House. If dissent is sometimes even fashionable, now, it is Fulbright who set the pattern. Recurrently, Fulbright's was a profile in courage—the lone dissenter voting against giving more money to the Joe McCarthy investigation, or the lone counselor ádvising President Kennedy against the foolish U.S. adventure in Cuba's Bay of Pigs in 1961. Future generations will long remember his long and powerful dissent against the Vietnam War.

What Fulbright warned against most was the "arrogance of power," a phrase that lingers in the national discourse long after Fulbright flourished his rhetoric in the Senate. He was wary of the indiscriminate exercise of power, especially when the United States wields more power than any nation on earth. He did not believe in a Pax Americana; he was among the first to see what a terrible price in blood and treasure that we would pay for the lost crusade in Vietnam.

His counsel to the nation, during his time of greatest influence, may echo into the next century. In 1972, the Vietnam War was still dragging on toward its humiliating conclusion, and Fulbright penned this counsel to the country in *The Crippled Giant*: "All things considered I would place my bet on the regenerative powers of the idealism of our younger generation—this generation who reject the inhumanity of war in a poor and distant land, who reject the poverty and sham in their own country, this generation who are telling their elders what their elders ought to have known, that the price of empire is America's soul and that price is too high."

VII. THE DEATH OF FULBRIGHT

In mid-January of 1995, Fulbright suffered another major stroke and was taken to George Washington University Hospital. The attack left him completely paralyzed and his doctors sent him back home to await the end, which came three weeks later at 1:15 on the morning of February 9. As of that moment, he belonged to history. The *New York Times* reported his death the next day under the headline, "J. William Fulbright, Senate Giant, Dead at 89."[1]

Fulbright's funeral service was held on February 17 at the great Washington Cathedral. Two days later a memorial service was held in Fayetteville at the University of Arkansas's historic Old Main building, now the home of the Fulbright College of Arts and Sciences, and his ashes were interred in a private service at his family's burial plot not far from the University.

The death of the former senator shared the front pages around the country with the announcement of Dan Quayle, the former vice president, that he would not run for the Republican nomination for president in 1996. All of the Fulbright obituaries centered upon the furious confrontations of his career, his record in opposing the Vietnam War and his sponsorship of the Fulbright scholarship program. The service at the Washington Cathedral was tantamount to a state funeral, for the central eulogy was delivered by the President, Bill Clinton, who said that Fulbright was the heir of Thomas Jefferson and "stood against the 20th century's most destructive forces and fought to advance its brightest hopes." Other tributes were given by family members and by the Very Rev. Nathan D. Baxter, dean of the cathedral; Baxter recalled that he had been an army private serving in Vietnam in the war that Fulbright had helped bring to an end.[2]

In Arkansas most of the newspapers hailed Fulbright as a statesman, although the largest, the *Arkansas Democrat-Gazette*, took the occasion of his death to assail the senator's record yet another time, not only for his admittedly weak civil rights record, but also for his dissent during the Vietnam War and the Cold War. The *Jonesboro Sun* said that Fulbright served his country "with extraordinary dedication and strength of benign purpose," adding that his "conduct in office over a period spanning three decades can serve as a lofty model for senators now and in years to come." The *Sun* and a few other newspapers remained as voices of moderation and thoughtfulness, in the tradition of Roberta Fulbright and the old *Arkansas Gazette*, the demise of which Fulbright had often lamented in his final years; yet the *Democrat-Gazette* now held by far the largest circulation in the state.

Both news and commentary in major newspapers underlined the different evaluations of his career and the common question of which counted most—his work against the Vietnam War or his work in the international student exchange. The *New York Times'* veteran reporter, R. W. Apple, Jr., led with a description of Fulbright as the "Arkansas Democrat whose powerful mind and eloquent voice helped to rally opposition to the Vietnam War." The *Dallas Morning News*, in its news account, described him as "a foreign affairs specialist whose legislation led to the forming of the United Nations and a renowned scholarship program bearing his name."

Sharp differences in the appraisal of Fulbright's service emerged in the royal pronouncements on the editorial pages of the two leading national newspapers, the *New York Times* and the *Washington Post*. The *Times* did not spare Fulbright for his opposition to civil rights legislation but added that "most congressional careers featured the same sellouts without rising to the heights in a transcendental issue." The *Times* went on to say that Fulbright "challenged powerful enemies and bad ideas at the flood tide of their power... His courage saved lives. Few politicians can lay claim to that epitaph."

The *Washington Post*, in its turn, was harsh in its editorial treatment of Fulbright, denouncing the "rotten argument" made in defense of his civil rights compromises and giving him scant credit for his opposition to the war. It was clear that the *Post* could not forgive Fulbright for his differences with the newspaper at the time when the *Post* was advocating the war and supporting President Johnson's conduct of it. The *Post* gave Fulbright credit, of course, for standing against Senator Joseph McCarthy and claimed his leading achievement was in the scholarship program, which was the least controversial of his services, no matter how worthy.

The attendance at the Fulbright funeral, 20 years after he ended his career in the Senate, held a poignant reminder how the great figures of Congress can neglect their respects to a once famous and powerful colleague. Henry Allen, the *Washington Post* staff writer covering the funeral, reported under the headline, "Elegy for a Statesman," that only about 900 people turned out in a cathedral that would accommodate 3,000 or more. A few of the senator's colleagues were there—notably George McGovern, the one-time presidential nominee, along with Gene McCarthy of Minnesota and George Smathers of Florida. Gene McCarthy remarked to the *Post* that Fulbright had been a great defender of the Senate, while Senator Robert Byrd of West Virginia was now the only one left to defend the body. "Where," the writer asked, "was Byrd yesterday . . . where was Strom Thurmond, Pat Moynihan, Bob Dole, the elders who had known Fulbright?" The *Post* reporter went on to observe that "almost everyone there was a friend or admirer, a rare thing in Washington, even at memorial services."

The warmest tribute to Fulbright in the Washington newspaper was in a feature story on February 10 by Walter Pincus, once a Fulbright staff member: "On television in the '50s, '60s and '70s he was always asking the right questions, raising reasonable doubts. He never got accolades for being right, not for his exposure of the 'deepfreezes' in the Truman administration, not for the early opposition to the red-baiting Senator Joseph McCarthy (R., Wis.) not for rallying public opposition to the Vietnam War or laying the groundwork for Nixon's recognition of China." Pincus visited Fulbright after the last stroke and was saddened to see the senator lying there in a hospital bed, unable to speak. In his *Washington Post* article, he wrote of learning that Fulbright "was gone, and with him the civilized world of politics and dissent that he personified."[3]

The services at the cathedral in Washington and the memorial service in Arkansas were elegant and beautifully conceived. At Fayetteville the ceremony was held on a bright, beautiful February day, in the Giffel Auditorium in Old Main. The eulogies were led by Mack McLarty, the influential White House aide and confidant of the President; Governor Jim Guy Tucker; Senator David Pryor; and there was a round of tributes from old, old friends and from one former adversary, Senator Dale Bumpers, who had beaten Fulbright 21 years earlier in one of the more civil campaigns in Arkansas history. Bumpers said that Fulbright had "turned me against the Vietnam War long before he ever heard my name." The accolades were long and sentimental, on the last homecoming of one of Arkansas' most celebrated sons. The ceremony ended with a short film of Fulbright speaking outside several years earlier at the rededication of Old Main: The senator's remarks on that earlier occasion had been interrupted by the chimes in the watchtower, striking the hour. Fulbright had paused in his oration, grinning happily, waving his hands and shoulders in time to the bells. Then he looked at his watch, gazed with a warm smile up at Old Main and praised the faithful old clock: "Right on time." It was a charming scene in a light-hearted moment at home, perfectly suited for saying goodbye.

AFTERWORD ON THE COLD WAR AND VIETNAM

Written by J. William Fulbright in 1988

This intensive study of the role of a senator in the events preceding and during the Vietnam war will be useful to present or future senators who, of necessity, must vote upon matters of importance affecting our relations with foreign nations. It is also useful to anyone considering the adequacy of our form of government in the conduct of our foreign relations. Many serious students of government are presently concerned about the obvious disarray in our foreign relations, especially the alienation of our NATO allies and the escalation of the arms race with the Soviet Union. They are concerned that the absence of continuity and experience in the higher echelons of our leaders is inherent in our system and is a serious disadvantage in the conduct of our foreign relations.

It is clear from this study that a typical senator assumes that office with a very limited understanding of foreign relations. Due to our geographical location and our history prior to World War II, we have had very little involvement in foreign affairs. For the first 200 years of our national existence we generally followed George Washington's advice not to become entangled in the affairs of Europe or other foreign nations. We are the only major nation that has never been occupied by a hostile army, a very educational experience. Under this policy of isolation, we prospered materially, but our understanding of our proper role in the world and how to play it successfully has not developed in a manner commensurate with our economic and military power. As some observers have said, we are like a loose cannon, unpredictable, emotional and often arrogant. Above all, perhaps we are self-righteous and hypocritical, and superior in our attitude toward less powerful nations, evidence I believe of our "immaturity as a nation."

This study by Mr. Powell reveals in many instances all of these characteristics of problems in American foreign policy. Personally it reveals my own lack of knowledge of China and Vietnam especially and consequently my vulnerability to misinformation supplied by an administration concerned only with its own purposes and not with candid consultation.

The structure of our government, with its separation of powers between the Executive and Legislative results in an adversary relationship which inhibits candid consultation and which puts the Congress at a disadvantage with regard to knowledge of foreign affairs. Senators and congressmen are experts on the conditions in their own constituencies and do not need to rely upon the executive for information, but very few speak a foreign language or have any significant experience in or knowledge about any foreign lands. These circumstances in addition to many others too extensive to deal with in this brief piece—such as the proliferation of primaries and the cost of elections, the low esteem of Congress as revealed by the polls, and the effect of television on rational discussion of issues—all indicate that it is time to review and re-evaluate the relevance and the validity of our present constitutional system to present world conditions. It suggests to me that it may be time to consider changing our adversarial division of power to a system combining these powers in the legislative body in which a more cooperative spirit would prevail between those who enact the laws and treaties and those who execute them.

The years of the Vietnam war and my differences with President Johnson were not only tragic for the country and the people suffering personal mutilation and death, but were personally painful and unhappy years for me. It is obvious that in the early period of the war I was quite unaware of the relevant history of the area and the issues involved, that I was unduly influenced by my former close association with the President as Majority Leader and by the power of "groupthink" as Professor Janis described it. It was only at the end of that experience that I developed sufficient knowledge and skepticism about the executive to have the confidence in my judgment that I should have had at the beginning. However, I think that could be said of most of the other senators.

The most consistent theme in my conduct, although with some lapses, was my conviction that a war with the Soviet Union would be a catastrophe and therefore I supported a policy of detente rather than confrontation. I still do. I believe the agreements made in 1972 between Nixon and Brezhnev, if implemented in good faith as I believe they could and would have been by more experienced leaders, would serve the interests of our country and the world.

Mr. Powell has given us the material from which we can learn much about our government if we are willing to recognize that conditions have changed and our Constitution is not a divine instrument for eternity, but is a human document well suited for its time and now in need of review. The 200th anniversary of its adoption was in 1987, an appropriate time for all thoughtful citizens to consider how we can make this great country live up to its traditions and aspirations—which we have been unable to do in recent years.

J. William Fulbright, Washington, D.C., 1988.

BIBLIOGRAPHY AND ENDNOTES

Bibliographical Notes

In writing this book the author relied upon a wide variety of sources too numerous to discuss in their entirety. However, I might note the most important sources, especially the J. William Fulbright Papers at the University of Arkansas. This book makes extensive use of the correspondence, memoranda, and the large collection of various other types of documents in the Fulbright Papers. For the massive resistance era, I also used some documents from the Brooks Hays Papers and the Orval E. Faubus Papers at the University of Arkansas. Almost all of the correspondence I have discussed refers to documents in the Fulbright Papers.

Transcripts of Senate Foreign Relations Committee hearings were important sources. Fulbright was involved in an extraordinarily large number of important hearings. I have listed some of the most important hearings in the bibliography.

A useful collection of Fulbright's speeches and memoranda from 1940 to 1962 can be found in *Fulbright of Arkansas: The Public Positions of a Private Thinker* (Washington: Robert B. Luce, Inc., 1963) edited with an introduction by Karl E. Meyer, and with a forward by Walter Lippmann. The *Congressional Record* is another source for some of Fulbright's comments. For Fulbright's most detailed expositions of his dissent from postwar American foreign policy, see the books written by the senator, especially *The Arrogance of Power* (New York: Random House-Vintage Books, 1967), *The Pentagon Propaganda Machine* (New York: Random House-Vintage Books, 1971), *The Crippled Giant: American Foreign Policy and Its Domestic Consequences* (New York: Random House-Vintage Books, 1972), and *The Price of Empire* (with Seth Tillman) (New York: Pantheon, 1989). I have discussed *The Arrogance of Power* and *The Crippled Giant* in detail, of course. *The Pentagon Propaganda Machine* is an expansion of a series of Senate speeches Fulbright delivered in 1969 in an effort to make the Senate and the public aware of the quietly pervasive nature of the Defense Department's public relations activities. For the Senator's foreign policy positions in 1964, *Old Myths and New Realities* (New York: Random House-Vintage Books, 1964), is a useful source. The earliest and probably the least important of Fulbright's books was *Prospects for the West* (Cambridge, Massachusetts: Harvard University Press, 1963). *The Role of Congress in Foreign Policy* (Washington: American Enterprise Institute for Public Policy Research, 1971) is a transcript of a debate between Fulbright and Senator John C. Stennis of Mississippi concerning the proper roles of Congress and the President in the formulation of foreign policy. Fulbright stressed his familiar theme of opposition to the excessive expansion of the executive's power, while Stennis, an opponent of both the Cooper-Church and McGovern-Hatfield amendments, did not express any particular concern over the Presidency's leadership in foreign policy decision-making in recent American history.

I consulted various State Department publications and the *Public Papers of the Presidents of the United States* for the administrations from Truman through Nixon. The memoirs of the Presidents and their principal aides are also interesting, such as Dean Acheson's *Present at the Creation: My Years in the State Department* (New York: Norton, 1969); Dwight D. Eisenhower's *Mandate for Change, 1953-*

1956 and *Waging Peace, 1956-1961* (Garden City, New York: Doubleday, 1963-1965); Lyndon Baines Johnson's *The Vantage Point: Perspectives of the Presidency, 1963-1969* (New York: Holt, Rinehart, Winston, 1971); Henry A. Kissinger's *White House Years* and *Years of Upheaval* (Boston: Little, Brown and Company, 1979 and 1982); George Ball, *The Past Has Another Pattern: Memoirs* (New York: Norton, 1982); Robert S. McNamara's *In Retrospect: The Tragedy and Lessons of Vietnam* (New York: Random House, 1995); and many other memoirs. For a collection of Adlai Stevenson's correspondence and other documents relating to his career, I used *The Papers of Adlai E. Stevenson*, edited by Walter Johnson, especially Volume VIII, Ambassador to the United Nations, 1961-1965 (Boston: 1969).

For contemporary journalistic accounts and analyses of postwar American diplomacy, I studied past editions of the *New York Times, Washington Post, Arkansas Gazette, St. Louis Post-Dispatch, Time, Newsweek*, and *U.S. News and World Report*, and other journals. We read these newspapers and magazines basically to capture the mood of some of the public responses to events as they happened.

In a few passages I relied upon three letters (each consisting of three or four single-spaced pages) Senator Fulbright had written me in which he commented upon rough drafts of some of the book's chapters. We also had interviews with Fulbright, John Sparkman, Claude Pepper, George McGovern, Bob Snider (a former aide to John McClellan), Lee Williams and others.

In January, 1966, Clyde Edwin Pettit wrote what was probably the most brilliant letter Fulbright ever received. Pettit was a journalist, an aide to Fulbright and at other times to Senator Carl Hayden, then the President of the U.S. Senate. Mr. Pettit sent a copy of this letter, along with an extensive collection of related materials, to James Powell (Clyde Edwin Pettit to Lee Williams and J. William Fulbright, January 13, 1966, copy in authors' possession, also in the Fulbright Papers and the Congressional Record of April 6, 1966). Pettit was a graduate of Yale and the University of Arkansas Law School, and he was a friend of Lee Williams and Fulbright. In addition to the passages of the lengthy letter quoted on page 270, Pettit made several other insightful observations in his famous letter, which had a substantial impact on Fulbright and deserves thorough discussion. Fulbright praised Pettit's letter as "remarkable" and "prophetic" and published it in the Congressional Record on April 6, 1966.

In 1992, Fulbright would write that Pettit made many distinguished radio broadcasts from Vietnam in 1965 and 1966, and was "one of the very first Americans to predict that the United States could not prevail in that tragic undertaking. He wrote a long and prescient letter to me from Saigon that was a substantial influence upon my long opposition to America's adventure in Indochina." (Letter of introduction for Clyde Pettit from J. William Fulbright, given to the authors from Clyde Pettit; a similar letter of introduction was written in December, 1992, by President-Elect Bill Clinton at a time when Pettit was working to normalize relations between the United States and Vietnam; Bill Clinton's letter of introduction for Clyde Pettit, December 9, 1992, given to the authors by Clyde Pettit). Pettit's January, 1966 letter summarized the intellectual analysis that was the foundation of his book, *The Experts* (Secaucus, N.J.: Lyle Stuart, 1975), which Fulbright would later describe as "the definitive chronicle of the Vietnam War." Pettit's *The Experts* was a massive compilation of commentary about Vietnam that proved the folly of the "experts" over the centuries.

To quote a few of the most memorable statements from Pettit's book:

> The enemy must fight his battles far from home for a long time... We must weaken him by drawing him into protracted campaigns. Once his initial dash is broken, it will be easier to destroy him... When the enemy is away from home for a long time and produces no victories and families learn of their dead, then the enemy population at home becomes dissatisfied and considers it a Mandate from Heaven that the armies be recalled.

> Time is always in our favor. Our climate, mountains and jungles discourage the enemy; but for us they offer both sanctuary and a place from which to attack.

> —Marshal Tran Hung Dao, Vietnamese general who defeated the Mongols, 1280 A.D.

Why should we take Chinese troops, horses, money and supplies and waste them in such a hot, desolate and useless place? It is definitely in the class of not being worth it... Even if we chase away the [Vietnamese rebels], how can we guarantee that there will not be more [rebels]... again coming out to cause trouble? The environment of that place is inhospitable. It is not worth any great involvement.

—Chinese Emperor Ch'ien-lung, 1789

Your country belongs to the Western seas, ours to the Eastern. As the horse and the buffalo differ, so do we--in language, literature, customs. If you persist in putting the torch to us, disorder will be long. But we shall act according to the laws of heaven, and our cause will triumph in the end.

—Vietnamese proclamation to the first group of French sailors
venturing up the Saigon River in the 19th century;
Pettit quoting Buttinger's *Vietnam: A Dragon Embattled*
and Pierre Dabezies, *Forces Politiques au Vietnam*

The Vietnamese are ripe for servitude.

—Paul Doumer, French Minister of Finance, 1867

[America's] Pacific era,... destined to be the greatest of all, is just at its dawn.

—President Theodore Roosevelt, San Francisco, 1903

Indochina of course is not in the Far East. You have to define what you are talking about really. Indochina is in the Middle East. It's not in the Far East.

—Secretary of the Treasury George M. Humphrey,
speaking on *Meet the Press*, NBC, January 23, 1955

By every quantitative measure we are winning the war in Vietnam... There is a new feeling of confidence.

—Secretary of Defense Robert S. McNamara, February 5, 1963

They are swinging wildly. They are suffering substantial losses in their sneak attacks.

—President Lyndon Baines Johnson, July 9, 1964

We are very pleased that the casualties are no higher than they are. We lost 100 American lives last week.

—President Lyndon Baines Johnson, October 24, 1968

Peace is within reach... I am confident we will succeed in achieving our objective.

—President Richard Milhous Nixon, October 26, 1972

SAIGON--American B-52s and F-111 swing-wing fighter bombers pounded insurgent forces Tuesday in some of the heaviest air attacks of the Cambodian war.... Approximately 60 B-52s participated in the massive bombings.

—Associated Press, April 3, 1973

Quotations from *The Experts*, pp. 435-440 (quotes from early Vietnamese history); pp. 2-3 (quotes from Paul Doumer and Theodore Roosevelt); p. 181 and p. 365, (President Johnson quotes); p. 426, (President Nixon); pp. 432-433, (AP report from Saigon).

In the January, 1966 letter to Fulbright, Pettit warned that Americans had little understanding of the effectiveness of Vietcong "tax collection methods" throughout South Vietnam. The Vietcong needed money badly, and they got it through "'rent' or what in the Capone era we called 'protection money.'" A prominent French-owned hotel paid this protection money to the Vietcong, and "this whole problem of blackmail to buy off terrorists leads us to the point of terrorism itself as a modus vivendi of modern insurgency. It is effective; it is cheap in cost; and it is demoralizing. It has convinced hundreds of thousands of South Vietnamese who would otherwise (for selfish, not ideological reasons) be for us of the prudence of 'playing both sides.'"

Pettit lambasted the notion that the Vietnamese war was analogous to the war in Korea. "There we had a battle line most of the time; here we have none; there we had a relatively defensible terrain, here we have none; there we had a people who had some faith, however misplaced, in the prospects for an eventual American victory, here we lack even that."

As for the fantasy that the United States was building up the South Vietnamese army's ability to some day stand and fight by itself, Pettit was pessimistic: "The sad fact is that the ARVNs (Army of the Republic of Vietnam) are pretty generally ineffective." Corruption and inefficiency weakened ARVN, but an even more serious problems "is the fact that most lieutenants and captains of experience have been killed off." The Ky regime tended to seek new officers from the ranks of the educated class and were loathe "to promote a country boy of demonstrated leadership ability under combat conditions... and it is getting increasingly difficult to find South Vietnamese officers who have been schooled in Switzerland."

Pettit advised Fulbright and Williams that the United States was losing the battle for the hearts and minds of the Vietnamese people. While Ho Chi Minh "traveled very far on a road paved with words like 'freedom' and liberty,'" the Americans had failed in the realm of psychological and philosophical warfare. Pettit found this to be a symptom of the American preoccupation with the use of force: "I question both our original involvement and the deepening of our commitment. But so long as we are there it would seem vitally incumbent that we speak and speak with sincerity to these people; and not in terms of defending them from communism, either, which, rightly or wrongly, strikes most of them as a bit silly."

Pettit regretted the sad story of America's newfound marriage to the status quo: "...when many nations cried out for sudden emergence, we chose to issue pallid policy statements from State on stability. It is fundamental in the affairs of men that when you see the imminent and inevitable death of an ancient regime, that you go to the funeral, but you are amiable to the heirs and do not sit forever holding hands with the corpse in necrophilial devotion."

Pettit proceeded to make the obvious comment in 1966 that of course he opposed communist expansion, but he gloomily pointed out that "Ho, the former cook at the Carlton in London is so strong with the peasant that even were he to be killed, his posthumous influence as a legend would sharply imperil our interests." Pettit stated the following syllogism: 1) the war cannot be won without support of the Vietnamese people; 2) in view of the magnitude of Ho's appeal and the diffuse nature of the American appeal as "liberators, it is highly questionable whether we can ever get more than token support, and that largely the result of our money;" 3) thus, "it is highly questionable whether we can ever have victory."

Fulbright's confidant did not pretend to have an easy solution to the war, but he emphasized that just having returned from Vietnam,

I am very frightened. I could talk about bright spots; there are many. I do not think they override the stark, terrifying realities of a stalemate, at best, purchased at inconceivable cost and coupled with humiliating setbacks and losses. Then always, and I do not say this lightly, there is the unlikely but ever-present possibility of catastrophe. The road from Valley

Forge to Vietnam has been a long one, and the analogy is more than alliterative: there are some similarities, only this time we are the British and they are barefoot. Too long have we taken our invincibility for granted.

Pettit suggested that direct negotiations with the Vietcong and major concessions to Hanoi should be pursued: "In short, I would rather America err on the side of being overly generous than on the side of military miscalculation of inconceivable cost." Although Fulbright had been profoundly wary of the deepening commitment in Vietnam before he received Pettit's letter, the communication from a confidant strengthened his skepticism about the escalation policy. The letter was indeed prophetic.

******

For the background of the Supreme Court decisions in which Fulbright was directly or indirectly involved, see Roger K. Newman, *Hugo Black: A Biography* (New York: Pantheon, 1994); John C. Jeffries, Jr., *Justice Lewis F. Powell, Jr.* (New York: Charles Scribner's Sons, 1994); Bernard Schwartz, *Super Chief: Earl Warren and His Supreme Court—A Judicial Biography* (Unabridged edition; New York: New York University Press, 1983); Bernard Schwartz, *The Ascent of Pragmatism: The Burger Court in Action* (New York: Addison-Wesley, 1990). The most comprehensive liberal activist view is found in Laurence H. Tribe, *American Constitutional Law* (New York: The Foundation Press, 1988). For a staunchly conservative view, see Robert H. Bork, *The Tempting of America: The Political Seduction of the Law* (New York: Touchstone, 1990).

The literature on Southern politics and civil rights is voluminous. A few of the notable works that were important for the broad context of Fulbright's time include C. Vann Woodward's books: *The Burden of Southern History*, Revised edition, (LSU Press, 1968); *The Strange Career of Jim Crow*, Third revised edition (New York: Oxford University Press, 1974); *Origins of the New South*, 1877-1913 (LSU, 1951); Paul Gaston, *The New South Creed: A Study in Southern Mythmaking* (LSU, 1970); Harvard Sitkoff, *The Struggle for Black Equality, 1954-1981* (New York: Hill and Wang, 1981); and Carl Brauer, *John F. Kennedy and the Second Reconstruction* (New York: Columbia University Press, 1977). Harry Ashmore recalled the Little Rock crisis of 1957 as well as his other involvement in civil rights issues over the decades in *Civil Rights and Wrongs: A Memoir of Race and Politics, 1944-1994* (Pantheon, 1994), and *An Epitaph for Dixie* (Norton, 1958). Brooks Hays chronicled his role in the civil rights controversies in *A Southern Moderate Speaks* (Chapel Hill: University of North Carolina Press, 1959), and *Politics Is My Parish*, (LSU Press, 1981). For the background of the civil rights movement, see David J. Garrow, *Bearing the Cross: Martin Luther King, Jr., and the Southern Christian Leadership Conference* (Vintage, 1986). Judge Henry Woods and Beth Deere wrote a poignant analysis of the Central crisis in "Reflections on the Little Rock School Case," 44 Arkansas Law Review 971 (1991).

The most notable secondary work which has been previously published concerning Fulbright's career is the biography by Haynes Johnson and Bernard Gwertzman, *Fulbright the Dissenter* (Garden City, New York: Doubleday, 1968). I have cited chapters from Johnson and Gwertzman in the treatment of Fulbright and U.S. foreign policy in the 1940s, the Bay of Pigs, and the Dominican controversy of 1965. Generally, *Fulbright the Dissenter* is a perceptive biography; as the title indicates, in most chapters it emphasizes Fulbright's activities as a critic of crusading anti-communism during much of his career. Johnson and Gwertzman's book was limited by the fact that it was published in early 1968, when many important events were still in the future, including the last five years of Fulbright's opposition to the Vietnam war. Their biography's treatment of the period from mid-1966 until early 1968 is very brief. However, *Fulbright the Dissenter* is an interesting account of the Senator's career up to early 1966.

There is at least one significant inaccuracy in the Johnson and Gwertzman volume. They stated that Fulbright "always refused to try and repeal" (Page 222, Johnson and Gwertzman) the Gulf of Tonkin Resolution. In fact, Fulbright *did* vote to repeal the Tonkin Resolution on March 1, 1966. Only four other senators voted with Fulbright in favor of repealing the Resolution, and thus the March 1, 1966 vote was one of the memorable acts of political courage in the Arkansas Senator's career. It was true that after the debacle of the ninety-two to five vote defeating repeal, Fulbright did not advocate attempts to obtain repeal until the dissenters could expect to attract considerably more than five votes; in 1966 such attempts had no chance of gaining a majority, and the administration publicized such results as the March 1, 1966 vote as triumphant endorsements of the escalation policy. Johnson and Gwertzman mentioned the reasons for Fulbright's reluctance to support repeal in 1967-68, but they neglected to discuss the senator's vote for repeal in 1966; apparently they did not know about it. The important fact was that Fulbright had been courageous enough to publicly repudiate the Tonkin Resolution at a relatively early date, in comparison to the vast majority of senators. Many political analysts were surprised in 1966 that Fulbright would go so far in opposing the President as to vote for repeal. There were so many momentous events happening in 1966 that many foreign policy analysts and historians seem to have later forgotten the effort to repeal the Resolution.

In addition to Haynes Johnson's book, William Berman has written *William Fulbright and the Vietnam War: The Dissent of a Political Realist* (Kent, Ohio: Kent State University Press, 1988). Berman refers to Lee Riley Powell, *J. William Fulbright and America's Lost Crusade: Fulbright, the Cold War and the Vietnam War* (Little Rock, Rose, 1984; expanded edition, 1988) in a number of his footnotes, thus proving Mr. Berman's superb taste in sources. Berman's book does not cover the early years of the Cold War. Regarding the Kennedy and Johnson administrations, Berman's book is solid, but it basically covers ground that had been covered before; however, Berman's treatment of the Nixon years did cover new ground in a diligent, careful fashion. Therefore, Berman's book does make a significant contribution to our knowledge of Fulbright and of U.S. foreign policy in the 1960s and 1970s, particularly the Nixon era.

Kurt Tweraser's *Changing Patterns of Political Beliefs: The Foreign Policy Operational Codes of J. William Fulbright, 1943-1967* (Beverly Hills, California: Sage Publications, 1974) is written in the jargon of political science, and hence, unfortunately, is relevant only for political scientists. A more useful source is Tweraser's 1971 Ph.D. dissertation at American University, "The Advice and Dissent of Senator Fulbright" (which has not been published, to our knowledge). This dissertation is based on extensive research and focuses on Fulbright's responses to the Cold War. Tweraser acknowledges that the senator was a dissenter after 1965, but we would not agree with his depiction of Fulbright as a standard "Cold Warrior" during the period from 1946 to 1964. Fulbright made anti-communist statements during those years, especially the late 1940s and early 1950s, but what deserves the greatest emphasis was Fulbright's opposition to the most destructive and extreme manifestations of anti-communism, such as McCarthyism, some of Dulles' more erratic actions in the late 1950s, the U-2 fiasco, the Bay of Pigs, and the senator's frequent criticism of the radical right. Our view is closer to that in Daniel Yergin's article, "Fulbright's Last Frustration," in *The New York Times Magazine*, November 24, 1974. Yergin argues that the Arkansan was quietly and carefully beginning to question the Cold War consensus at an early date: "While Henry Kissinger was just turning his Ph.D. thesis into a book and describing scenarios for limited nuclear warfare, Fulbright was pointing the direction toward what a decade and a half later became known as detente."

Tristram Coffin's *Senator Fulbright: Portrait of a Public Philosopher* (New York: E.P. Dutton, 1966) is an exercise in hero-worship and has little intellectual value.

Thirty years ago Walter Johnson and Francis Colligan wrote *The Fulbright Program: A History* (Chicago: The University of Chicago Press, 1965), a detailed, careful account of the exchange program up to 1965, with a foreword by J. William Fulbright.

In 1973, Naomi Lynn and Arthur McClure wrote *The Fulbright Premise: Senator J. William Fulbright's Views on Presidential Power* (Lewisburg: Bucknell University Press, 1973). This work is a 168-page sketch of Fulbright's views on Presidential power. Eugene Brown's *J. William Fulbright: Advice and Dissent* (Iowa City: University of Iowa Press, 1985) is a sketchy, 124-page account that seeks to cover ground that has already been covered in much greater detail and depth by many other books.

Students of Senator Fulbright's career have long awaited publication of Seth Tillman's biography of Fulbright. Tillman was one of Fulbright's most important aides, and he is now a professor at Georgetown University. Tillman has been working on the book for many years, and it will undoubtedly be a major achievement when it is published.

The most recent and longest book (700 pages of small print) on Fulbright was written by Randall Woods of the University of Arkansas. Woods' *Fulbright: A Biography*, is a revisionist work that was published in 1995. Given its length and the revisionist nature of many of its comments, *Fulbright: A Biography* requires several comments. Woods alleges that it was "indisputable" that Fulbright was a "racist." The authors of *J. William Fulbright and His Time* have extensive backgrounds in the fields of constitutional law and in Southern politics, and while we are sharply critical of Fulbright's civil rights record, it is shrill and superficial to not only dismiss Fulbright as a racist, but to claim that his alleged "racism" was "indisputable." This view of Fulbright as a racist is contradicted by numerous facts. If Fulbright had been a racist, why was he one of the few Southern senators who voted for Thurgood Marshall's elevation to the Supreme Court, and why did he oppose the nomination of the extreme segregationist Carswell to the Supreme Court? He voted for the extension of the Voting Rights Act at a time when the Attorney General of the United States opposed it. He was the only Southern senator to assist the Northern bloc in killing the antibusing bill in 1972. Even in his earlier career, he eschewed the kind of race-baiting rhetoric that enhanced the popularity of so many Southern politicians in the 1950s; had he been a racist it would have been natural for him to have engaged in such rhetoric. We are sharply critical of the senator for having signed the Southern Manifesto, failing to stand against Faubus' assault on the rule of law in 1957, and making his other compromises to the right wing on this issue; but to call him a "racist" simply takes a simplistic view. Our own treatment of Fulbright's civil rights record, of course, is stated in great detail in Books Three and Five of *J. William Fulbright and His Time*.

In another revisionist argument, Woods asserts that Fulbright "invoked the neo-isolationist theories he had once attacked" in opposing the Pax Americana that Johnson and Nixon attempted to impose. He also adds that Fulbright, "like Gerald P. Nye, the famous isolationist of the Roosevelt era with whom he [Fulbright] struck up a brief correspondence in 1969, he preferred the term 'noninterventionist.'" Readers will arrive at their own conclusions as to whether Fulbright was a "neo-isolationist," but I find it incorrect to compare Fulbright's opposition to Johnsonian and Nixonian globalism to the old isolationists. Of course, Fulbright had opposed the isolationists in the period just before World War II because of the grave threat the Nazis posed to America. It is difficult to imagine how Fulbright's enthusiastic support of detente with the Soviet Union and mainland China, as well as his interests in constructive engagement with Europe, Latin America and Japan could be interpreted as isolationism. Readers will no doubt form their opinions after reading Book Four of *J. William Fulbright and His Time* concerning Fulbright and the Pax Americana.

Woods also adds numerous passages in the book that consist of psychological evaluations of Fulbright and members of his family. "Periodically during his career, J. William Fulbright demonstrated the most striking ignorance of human nature and lack of insight into the simple rules of psychology. Nowhere was this more apparent than in his relations with Lyndon Johnson," Woods writes. Rather than engaging in such psychological speculation, I would emphasize that the crucial point to be made about Fulbright's relationship with Lyndon Johnson is the Arkansan's courage and integrity

in opposing a man who was not only a former friend and colleague, but one of the most powerful political leaders in American history. In addition, Woods engages in frequent speculation about the psychological condition of Fulbright, Roberta Fulbright, Fulbright's brother Jack, and others. There is much
truth in the comments in a review by Paul Spillenger, a former literature professor at Columbia, when
he said that while Woods' book is provocative and engrossing, such psychological evaluations belong
in a Gothic romance but not in a historical account. Spillenger refers to Woods' "utterly gratuitous,
unprepared, and subsequently undeveloped remark that `Fulbright's fits of garrulousness ... were as
much as anything diversions to keep from discussing his emotional and psychological experiences.' We
wait in vain for some serious exploration of this theme.'" (Paul Spillenger, Review in *Arkansas Democrat-
Gazette*, July 9, 1995).

Another questionable argument in Woods' book is his treatment of the Vietnam draft controversy
regarding Bill Clinton. Woods charges that "In 1969 Bill Clinton was politically inconsequential. What
was significant was that an aide to J. William Fulbright had attempted to use the prestige of the senator's office to help the young man avoid going to Vietnam. Had that fact become known in 1969,
Richard Nixon, Spiro Agnew, Henry Jackson, and Strom Thurmond would have used it to devastating
effect." This argument is riddled with flaws. First of all, it is a fact that Fulbright and his administrative
assistant, Lee Williams, were routinely helping large numbers of constituents who sought National
Guard or ROTC slots to escape the draft. The senator advised young men who had already been drafted that he would go to Vietnam if drafted and ordered to go there, but Fulbright had stated repeatedly
that he would assist opponents of the war in legal efforts to avoid fighting in Vietnam. Secondly, as for
Woods' charge that the Nixonians could have used knowledge of his help for Clinton to "devastating
effect" against Fulbright, that attack strains credulity; Fulbright could scarcely have provoked any more
vituperation from Nixon's cohorts than he was already enduring merely by helping one more young
man—then unknown, of course—from Hot Springs, Arkansas. Moreover, the foundation of Woods'
argument is based upon a highly questionable use of sources. In a footnote referring to Williams' recommendation to Col. Eugene Holmes that Clinton be accepted in the ROTC, Woods states: "Interview
with Lee Williams, June 20, 1989, Washington, D.C. According to Robert Corrado, the only surviving
member of the Hot Springs draft board, Williams had earlier called him and other members of the
board asking that Clinton be given time to finish his course of study at Oxford." Woods cites as his
source for Corrado's alleged comments an article by William C. Rempel, "Draft Inquiry Hints Lobbying
Helped Clinton," *Los Angeles Times*, (and *Arkansas Democrat-Gazette*), September 2, 1992. (Footnote
41, page 544, Woods, *Fulbright*). In Rempel's article, Corrado was quoted as saying that "an aide" to
Fulbright had called him to lobby for Clinton; Rempel had been careful to identify Corrado as a
Republican who was speaking at the height of the 1992 Presidential campaign in which the Bush campaign was attacking Clinton on the draft question. Corrado's comments may or may not have been true,
but at a minimum, the nature of his comments as emanating from a Republican source should have
been stated, yet Woods failed to do so (unlike Rempel). Woods' contention that Corrado stated that
"Williams had earlier called him [Corrado] and other members of the board asking that Clinton be
given time to finish his course of study at Oxford" is flatly erroneous in the charge that Lee Williams
had made these alleged calls; in fact, the article by Rempel states that "Corrado also complained that he
was called by an aide to then Sen. J. William Fulbright" regarding Bill Clinton and the draft. Even if
Woods might contend that it did not matter which aide to Fulbright made the call, it still remains true
that we do not know that any such calls were ever made; we only know that Corrado alleged that some
unidentified aide in Fulbright's office made such calls. Yet, Woods stated, as if it were a fact, that
Williams had called Corrado.

Woods makes the further gratuitous criticism that "Apparently unbeknownst to Fulbright, his legislative aide, Lee Williams, was putting that reputation [Fulbright's reputation for advocating only lawful opposition to the war and working for change within the legal system] at grave risk at the same time

Fulbright was advising" others to serve. In an interview in the summer of 1995, Lee Williams flatly denied ever having called any draft board on Clinton's behalf. (Telephone interview with the author, June, 1995). Williams also emphatically stated that any actions he took in advising young critics of the war were taken with the full knowledge and approval of the senator. Congressional aides learn very quickly on Capitol Hill that if they take action without the senator or congressman's knowledge, they will probably be fired. It is highly doubtful that Williams—a veteran Congressional aide—would have taken any important actions without the senator's knowledge. As a matter of historical fact, it is highly doubtful that Fulbright or Williams did anything improper at all, yet Woods described the episode as if Williams had, as a matter of fact, taken actions that would have gravely damaged Fulbright's reputation had it become public in Washington at the time. In light of the reality that Fulbright and Williams were vigorously helping other young opponents of the war—just as they helped Clinton—and the other facts discussed above, this argument is simply erroneous.

Woods' only significant interviews with Fulbright were conducted in the fall of 1988, when Fulbright was 84 years old and had already suffered two mild strokes. Woods stated that Fulbright occasionally dozed, repeated himself, and that many of his recollections were taken "straight out of books and articles written about him"; yet Woods also contended that for an hour each day Fulbright was lucid and provided "remarkable and insightful" comments. There was still certainly a limited value to Fulbright's recollections in the late 1980s, although interviews conducted much earlier were more valuable. It is questionable to place significant reliance upon an interview conducted at a time when the senator was elderly, had suffered two minor strokes, and was attempting to recall events that had happened many years or decades before. Nonetheless, Woods' description of this interview figures prominently in his preface and he does not hesitate to use this interview in 1988 as a source in footnotes. In contrast, the authors of *J. William Fulbright and His Time* interviewed Fulbright more than 100 times from the 1950s until the early 1990s. Some of these interviews were conducted at the time events were unfolding; many of them were conducted in the 1970s—when Fulbright was still quite intellectually vigorous—and some took place in the early 1980s. We continued to converse with Fulbright in the late 1980s and early 1990s, but the later interviews, naturally, were less important than those conducted when Fulbright was still at the height of his intellectual powers.

In fairness to Woods, most of his book is based on substantial research into the Fulbright Papers and other sources. However, despite the tremendous length of his work and the massive detail devoted to many issues, he curiously failed to deal with a number of important areas: there is very little coverage of Fulbright's positions on Vietnam during the Kennedy era (although his treatment of the Nixon and Johnson Vietnam policies is lengthy). Woods covers the Vietnam hearings in several pages, but glosses over the highly important China hearings in only a page or so. In general, Woods has only a small number of footnotes to Senate Foreign Relations Committee hearings. There are only a couple of passing references to Fulbright's encouragement of the career of a young man named Bill Clinton who later became President. Regardless of what one thinks about President Clinton, Fulbright's support for his career in the early years is clearly an important topic. Similarly, there is virtually no coverage of Fulbright and Brooks Hays, a friend of Fulbright's who was perhaps the most important moderate in Arkansas during the Central crisis. Woods' book lacks a bibliography or a bibliographical essay. The coverage is, in short, voluminous on some issues but sketchy on others. The central flaws in Woods' book are his frequent editorializing, constant value judgments, and lack of objectivity in resorting to such epithets as "racist" and "neo-isolationist."

For a perceptive analysis of the Truman Doctrine, see Norman Graebner's *Cold War Diplomacy*, where Mr. Graebner aptly wrote that far from being "realistic," the Doctrine "seemed to promise salvation to the world":

some thoughtful Americans criticized the new doctrine for confusing the issue between the United States and the Soviet Union and for defining the American commitment in vague generalities at a time of trial. Western security demanded the prevention of further Russian expansion. But the President's message identified American interest in Greece and Turkey, not with the maintenance of the European balance of power, but with the defense of freedom even where it scarcely existed. The Truman Doctrine seemed to promise salvation to the world. It perpetuated the nation's habit of refusing to separate what was essential from what was desired. Kennan objected to the President's reference to an ideological struggle between two ways of life and to the open-end commitment to aid free peoples everywhere. To Walter Lippmann the new policy was so general that it had no visible limits. He reminded the national leadership that a crusade was not a policy. (Norman A. Graebner, *Cold War Diplomacy: American Foreign Policy, 1945-1975* (New York: Van Nostrand, 1977), pp. 39-40.

There are vast numbers of articles on Senator Fulbright. The following is a short list of some of the most important articles: Charles B. Seib and Alan L. Otten, "Fulbright: Arkansas Paradox," in *Harper's*, June, 1956; Sidney Hyman, "Fulbright—The Wedding of Arkansas and the World," *The New Republic*, May 14, 1962; Brock Brower, "The Roots of the Arkansas Questioner," *Life*, May 13, 1966; Russell Warren Howe and Sarah Trott, "J. William Fulbright: Reflections on a Troubled World," *Saturday Review*, January 11, 1975; Gary Herlick, "J.W. Fulbright: Democratic Senator from Arkansas," in *Ralph Nader Congress Project: Citizens Look at Congress,* (Washington: Grossman, 1972), edited by Ralph Nader. Lloyd E. Ambrosius, "The Goldwater-Fulbright Controversy," *The Arkansas Historical Quarterly*, Autumn, 1970, deal with Fulbright's debate with Goldwater concerning Soviet-American relations in the early 1960s. In a series of articles written in 1967, I. F. Stone delivered a sympathetic yet searching criticism of Fulbright's evolution from pro-administration figure to dissenter: "Fulbright of Arkansas, Part 1," December 29, 1966; "Fulbright: From Hawk to Dove, Part 2," January 12, 1967; "Fulbright: The Timid Opposition, Part 3," January 26, 1967, in *The New York Review of Books*. One should also consult the many articles on recent U.S. foreign policy in *Foreign Affairs*.

The scholarly literature on the Cold War and the Vietnam war is voluminous. We might note a few of the works that were useful in research. For McCarthyism, see Richard M. Fried, *Men Against McCarthy* (New York: Columbia University Press, 1976); Robert Griffith, *The Politics of Fear: Joseph R. McCarthy and the Senate* (Lexington, Kentucky: The University Press of Kentucky, 1970); and Richard Rovere, *Senator Joe McCarthy* (New York: Harper and Row, 1959). A few of the best volumes on Vietnam are Frances Fitzgerald, *Fire in the Lake: The Vietnamese and the Americans in Vietnam* (New York: Random House-Vintage Books, 1972); George C. Herring, *America's Longest War: The United States and Vietnam, 1950-1975* (New York: John Wiley and Sons, 1979); David Halberstam, *The Best and the Brightest* (Greenwich, Connecticut: Fawcett Crest, 1972); Halberstam, *The Powers That Be* (New York: Dell, 1979) Stanley Karnow, *Vietnam: A History*, Second edition (New York: Viking, 1991); and Bernard B. Fall, *Last Reflections on a War* (New York: Schocken Books, 1967). The best book on Sino-American relations is John King Fairbank's *The United States and China*, Fourth edition (Cambridge, Massachusetts: 1979). We also profited from Fairbank's lecture, "The Chinese Revolution," at Newcomb Hall, the University of Virginia, April, 1983. For a journalist's observations on the China of 1973, see the collection of articles, *A Visit To the People's Republic of China* (Little Rock: 1973, Arkansas Gazette) (In the James O. Powell Collection, in the Arkansas Collection at the University of Arkansas Library) written by James Powell, when he led a group of journalists on a month-long visit through the mainland; this was one of the first groups to enter China after President Nixon's journey to Peking in 1972.

The following is a short list of works on the Kennedy, Johnson and Nixon years. Two of Arthur M. Schlesinger's books were particularly valuable *A Thousand Days: John F. Kennedy in the White House* (Boston: Houghton Mifflin, 1965); and *Robert Kennedy and His Times* (New York: Ballantine, 1978).

Also see John Kenneth Galbraith, *A Life in Our Times* (New York: Ballantine, 1981). Schlesinger's *The Imperial Presidency* (New York: Popular Library, 1974) includes several discussions of Fulbright's responses to the expanding power of the postwar Presidency. Doris Kearns' *Lyndon Johnson and the American Dream* (New York: Signet, 1976) is an interesting biography, although it does not provide a thorough analysis of the Fulbright-Johnson conflict over Vietnam. For Clark Clifford, Fulbright, and Johnson in 1968, we relied upon Herbert Y. Schandler, *Lyndon Johnson and Vietnam: The Unmaking of a President* (Princeton, New Jersey: Princeton University Press, 1977). Also see Harry S. Ashmore and William C. Baggs, *Mission to Hanoi: A Chronicle of Double-Dealing in High Places* (New York: G.P. Putnam's Sons, 1968); and Neal Sheehan, et al., editors, *The Pentagon Papers* (Based on investigative reporting by Neil Sheehan, written by Neil Sheehan, Hedrick Smith, E. W. Kenworthy, and Fox Butterfield. New York: Bantam 1971); and McNamara's memoirs published in 1995, as previously cited. Three of the most engrossing volumes on the Nixon years are Jonathan Schell, *The Time of Illusion* (New York: Vintage, 1975); William Shawcross, *Sideshow: Kissinger, Nixon, and the Destruction of Cambodia* (New York: Washington Square Press, 1979); and William Safire, *Before the Fall* (New York: Ballantine, 1975).

Ronald Steel's biography, *Walter Lippman and the American Century* (Boston: Little, Brown and Company, 1980) was a significant source because of Fulbright's long and rewarding friendship with the famous columnist. Especially interesting are the chapters which describe Lippmann's initial euphoria for Johnson's leadership, followed by his gradual disillusionment with the President, and finally his outrage at the colossal blunders of the U.S. intervention in Vietnam.

For the background of American diplomatic history, we have relied upon several of the works of George F. Kennan and Norman A. Graebner. Kennan's realistic analysis of U.S. foreign policy and of Soviet-American relations is presented in many of his writings, among them *Russia and the West Under Lenin and Stalin* (New York: Mentor, 1961); and *Memoirs, II: 1950-1963* (Boston: 1972). Norman A. Graebner's *The Age of Global Power: The United States Since 1939* (New York: John Wiley and Sons, 1979), is a general history of America from the late 1930s to the late 1970s. Graebner's *The New Isolationism* (New York: The Ronald Press Company, 1956) was one of the earliest critical evaluations of the Eisenhower-Dulles foreign policies; the historian stressed the administration's attempt to create the impression of more determined foreign policies than those of Truman, basically by employing Dulles' dramatic rhetoric. The Republican administration's rhetoric promised greater success at less risk and cost than the Truman administration accomplished; in reality, Dulles' dramatic phrases left American policy exactly where it had been in the later Truman era. For the Cold War see Graebner's *Cold War Diplomacy, 1945-1975* (New York: D. Van Nostrand, 1977, Second edition).

Graebner's *Ideas and Diplomacy* (New York: Oxford University Press, 1964) is a massive collection of readings in the intellectual tradition of American foreign policy, edited with extended commentary by the author. This book analyzes the conflict between the realistic and ideological approaches to diplomacy from the 18th century to the post-World War II epoch. As Graebner demonstrates, during the early history of the republic, George Washington, Thomas Jefferson, John Quincy Adams, and other realists controlled the basic U.S. foreign policy decisions. These decisions (along with other historical factors) facilitated the effective and often brilliant U.S. diplomacy of early American history. In the 20th century (for a variety of involved reasons) those who advocated the ideological approach came to dominate the formulation of U.S. foreign policy. Interestingly, *Ideas and Diplomacy* ends with a chapter including two of Fulbright's speeches: "Old Myths and New Realities" of 1964 and one of the addresses Fulbright delivered in his debate with Goldwater in the early 1960s. Graebner describes Fulbright's positions as following the realistic tradition; the senator pleaded that the nation's commitments abroad should be limited by the interests, power, and capabilities of the United States. Fulbright's conservative approach to the use of power seems reminiscent of one of Jefferson's realistic statements, quoted near the beginning of *Ideas and Diplomacy*: "I hope our wisdom will grow with our power, and teach us, that the less we use our power, the greater it will be."

General Bibliography on Senator Fulbright

I. Primary Sources

Correspondence, Articles, Speeches, and Books by J. William Fulbright

James William Fulbright Papers, Special Collections, University of Arkansas Library, Fayetteville, Arkansas.

. *Fulbright of Arkansas: The Public Positions of a Private Thinker*, ed. Karl E. Meyer, with a Foreward by Walter Lippmann. [A collection of Fulbright's speeches and memoranda.] Washington: Robert B. Luce, Inc., 1963

. *Prospects for the West*. Cambridge: Harvard University Press, 1963.

. *Old Myths and New Realities*. New York: Random House-Vintage Books, 1964.

. *The Arrogance of Power.* New York: Random House-Vintage Books, 1967.

. *The Crippled Giant: American Foreign Policy and Its Domestic Consequences*. New York: Random House-Vintage Books, 1972.

. *The Pentagon Propaganda Machine*. New York: Random House-Vintage Books, 1971.

. *The Price of Empire*. (with Seth Tillman)(New York: Pantheon, 1989)

. Letter to the author, November 2, 1978.

. Letter to the author, January 29, 1979.

. Letter to the author, October 1, 1981.

, and John Stennis. *The Role of Congress in Foreign Policy*. [Transcript of the Fulbright-Stennis debate, Rational Debate Seminars]. Washington: American Enterprise Institute for Public Policy Research, 1971.

Government Publications

a. *Congressional Record*, 1940-1975

b. Short List of Major Congressional Hearings

U.S. Congress. Senate. Committee on Foreign Relations. Extension of European Recovery. February, 1949. Washington: Government Printing Office, 1949. (The hearings listed here were published by the Government Printing Office.)

———. *North Atlantic Treaty*. Parts 1 and 2, April-May, 1949.

———. (Joint hearings of the Foreign Relations Committee and the Armed Services Committee) *Assignment of Ground Forces of the United States to Duty in the European Area*. February, 1951.

———. *Military Situation in the Far East*. May 3-August 17, 1951.

———. Subcommittee. *Nomination of Philip C. Jessup to be United States Representative to the Sixth General Assembly of the United Nations*. September-October, 1951.

———. *Mutual Security Act of 1952*. March 13-April 4, 1952.

———. *Mutual Security Act of 1953*. May, 1953.

———. *Mutual Security Act of 1954*. June, 1954.

———. *The Southeast Asia Collective Defense Treaty*. November, 1954.

———. (Joint hearings of the Foreign Relations Committee and the Armed Services Committee) *The President's Proposal on the Middle East*. January-February, 1957.

———. *United States Foreign Policy*. January, 1959.

———. *United States Foreign Policy*. January-March, 1960.

————. *Proposed Nomination of Chester Bowles as Under Secretary of State*. January 19, 1961.

————. *Mutual Education and Cultural Exchange Act*. March-April, 1961.

————. *Problems and Trends in Atlantic Partnership*, 1962.

————. *Nuclear Test Ban Treaty*. August, 1963.

————. Committee on Armed Services and Committee on Foreign Relations, Joint Hearing. *The Southeast Asia Resolution*. August, 1964.

————. *Foreign Assistance, 1965*. March and April, 1965.

————. *Executive Sessions of the Senate Foreign Relations Committee, Vol. 17, 1965* [The Dominican hearings](Washington: 1995)

————. *Supplemental Foreign Assistance, Fiscal Year 1966—Vietnam*. [Known as the Vietnam hearings.] January and February, 1966.

————. *U.S. Policy with Respect to Mainland China*. March, 1966.

————. *Foreign Assistance, 1966*. April and May, 1966.

————. *Harrison Salisbury's Trip to North Vietnam*. February, 1967.

————. *United States Commitments to Foreign Powers*. August-September, 1967.

————. *The Gulf of Tonkin, 1964 Incidents*. February, 1968.

————. *Foreign Assistance Act of 1968*. March, 1968.

————. *Briefing by Secretary of State William P. Rogers*. March, 1969.

————. *Strategic and Foreign Policy Implications of ABM Systems*. March, 1969.

————. *The Impact of the War in Southeast Asia on the United States Economy*. April, 1970.

————. *The Moral and Military Aspects of the War in Southeast Asia*. May, 1970.

————. *Cambodia: May, 1970*. (Staff Report). June, 1970.

————. *The Military Budget and National Priorities*. June, 1970.

————. *Supplemental Foreign Assistance Authorization: 1970*. December, 1970.

————. *War Powers Legislation*. March-October, 1971.

————. *Laos: April, 1971*. (Staff Report). August, 1971.

————. *China and the United States: Today and Yesterday*. February, 1972.

————. *The Causes, Origins, and Lessons of the Vietnam War*. May, 1972.

————. *Thailand, Laos and Cambodia*, January 1972. May, 1972.

————. *U.S. Involvement in the Overthrow of Diem*. July, 1972.

————. *U.S. and Vietnam, 1944-1947*. (Staff Study No. 2, 1972).

————. *Vietnam Commitments, 1961*. (Staff Study, 1972).

————. *Bombing as a Policy Tool in Vietnam Effectiveness*. October, 1972.

————. *Briefing on Major Foreign Policy Questions by Secretary of State William P. Rogers*. February, 1973.

————. *U.S. Air Operations in Cambodia, April, 1973*. April, 1973.

————. *Nomination of Henry A. Kissinger*. September, 1973.

————. *Legislative History of the Committee on Foreign Relations, 1963-64*. 1972-75.

————. *U.S. POWs and MIAs in Southeast Asia*. January, 1974.

————. *The Future of United States-Soviet Relations*. November, 1983.

————. *The United States Government and the Vietnam War: Executive and Legislative Roles and Relationships, Part I, 1945-1961*. April, 1984.

————. *The United States Government and the Vietnam War: Executive and Legislative Roles and Relationships, Part II, 1961-1964*. December, 1984.

Hearings before the Committee on the Judiciary, U.S. Senate:

Nomination of Thurgood Marshall to be an Associate Justice of the Supreme Court of the United States. 90th Congress, First Session, July, 1967. U.S. Government Printing Office, Washington: 1967.

Nomination of Clement F. Haynsworth to be an Associate Justice of the Supreme Court of the United States. 91st Congress, First Session. September, 1969. Washington: U.S. Government Printing Office, 1969.

Nomination of George Harrold Carswell to be an Associate Justice of the Supreme Court of the United States. 91st Congress, Second Session. January and February, 1970. Washington: U.S. Government Printing Office, 1970.

Nominations of William H. Rehnquist and Lewis F. Powell, Jr. to be Associate Justices of the Supreme Court of the United States. 92nd Congress, First Session, November, 1971. U.S. Government Printing Office: Washington: 1971

Short List of Major Cases

Schechter Poultry Corp. v. the United States, 295 U.S. 495 (1935)

Brown v. Board of Education of Topeka, 347 U.S. 483 (1954)

Brown v. Board of Education of Topeka, Brown II, 349 U.S. 294 (1955)

Cooper v. Aaron, 358 U.S. 1 (1958)

School Board of the City of Charlottesville v. Dillard, 374 U.S. 827 (1963)

Goss v. Board of Education, 373 U.S. 683 (1963)

Griffin v. Prince Edward School Board, 377 U.S. 218 (1964)

Bowman v. County School Board of Charles City, Virginia, 382 F.2d 326 (1967)

Green v. School Board of New Kent County, 391 U.S. 430 (1969)

New York Times Co. v. United States; United States v. Washington Post Co., 403 U.S. 713 (1971)

United States v. United States District Court for the Eastern District of Michigan, 407 U.S. 297 (1972)

Holtzman v. Schlesinger, 361 F.Supp. 553 (Eastern District, New York, 1973); 484 F.2d 1307 (2d Cir. 1973)(Oakes, J., dissenting); 414 U.S. 1316 (opinion of William O. Douglas)) 414 U.S. 1321 (opinion of Thurgood Marshall).

United States v. Nixon, 418 U.S. 683 (1974)

c. Presidential Papers

Truman, Harry S. *Public Papers of the Presidents of the United States: Harry S. Truman, April 12, 1945 to January 20, 1953.* Volumes I-VIII. Washington: Government Printing Office, 1961-1966.

Eisenhower, Dwight D. *Public Papers of the Presidents of the United States: Dwight D. Eisenhower, January 20, 1953 to December 31, 1955.* Volumes I-III. Washington: Government Printing Office, 1960.

Kennedy, John F. *Public Papers of the Presidents of the United States: John F. Kennedy, 1963.* Washington: Government Printing Office, 1964.

Johnson, Lyndon B. *Public Papers of the Presidents of the United States: Lyndon B. Johnson, 1963-1966.* Washington: Government Printing Office, 1965-1967.

Nixon, Richard M. *Public Papers of the Presidents of the United States: Richard M. Nixon, 1969-1974.* Washington: Government Printing Office.

d. State Department Publications: *Foreign Relations of the United States, 1945-1974.* Washington: Government Printing Office.

Foreign Relations of the United States, 1945, Volume General: The United Nations. Washington: Government Printing Office, 1967.

Foreign Relations of the United States, 1948, Volume II, Germany and Austria. Washington: Government Printing Office, 1973.

Foreign Relations of the United States, 1948, Volume III, The Far East: China. Washington: Government Printing Office, 1973.

Foreign Relations of the United States, 1950, Volume VI, East Asia and the Pacific. Washington: Government Printing Office, 1976.

Foreign Relations of the United States, 1950, Volume VII, Korea. Washington: Government Printing Office, 1976.

Foreign Relations of the United States, 1952-1954. United Nations Affairs. Washington: Government Printing Office, 1979.

Foreign Relations of the United States, 1952-1954, Volume XVI, The Geneva Conference. Washington: Government Printing Office, 1981.

Foreign Relations of the United States, 1961-1963, Vol. I, Vietnam, 1961. Washington: U.S. Government Printing Office, 1988.

Foreign Relations of the United States, 1961-1963, Vol. II, Vietnam, 1962. Washington: U.S. Government Printing Office, 1990.

Foreign Relations of the United States, 1961-1963, Vol. III, Vietnam, January-August, 1963. Washington: U.S. Government Printing Office, 1991.

Foreign Relations of the United States, 1961-1963, Vol. IV, Vietnam, August-December, 1963. Washington: U.S. Government Printing Office, 1991.

Foreign Relations of the United States, 1964-1968, Vol. I, Vietnam. Washington, U.S. Government Printing Office, 1992.

Newspapers

Arkansas Gazette.
Baltimore Sun.
Boston Globe.
New York Times.
St. Louis Post-Dispatch.
Washington Post.
Fort Smith Southwest Times Record.
Arkansas Democrat.
Jonesboro Sun.
Northwest Arkansas Times.

Magazines

Life
Newsweek.
Time.
U.S. News and World Report.

Interviews

Senator J. William Fulbright	A total of roughly 100 interviews from 1958-1993.
Senator George McGovern	August 6, 1978
Senator Claude Pepper	May 19, 1981
Senator John Sparkman	July 28, 1978
Carl Marcy (former chief of Staff of the Senate Foreign Relations Committee	July 14, 1978
Norville Jones (former member of Senator Fulbright's staff)	July 14, 1978
Bob Snider (former member of Senator John McClellan's staff)	July 11, 1978.
U.S. District Judge Henry Woods	May 4, 1995
Lee Williams	May 24, 1991; October, 1993; June, 1995.
Witt Stephens	May, 1990.
David Capes	June, 1995.
Memorandum from U.S. District Judge William R. Wilson, Jr., to the author	March, 1995.

II. Secondary Sources

Acheson, Dean. *Present at the Creation: My Years in the State Department.* New York: Norton, 1969.

Adler, Renata. *Reckless Disregard:Westmoreland v. CBS et al; Sharon v. Time.* New York: Knopf, 1986.

Alexander, Charles C. *Holding the Line: The Eisenhower Era, 1952-1961.* Bloomington: Indiana University Press, 1975.

Ambrose, Stephen E. *Rise to Globalism: American Foreign Policy, 1938-1976.* New York: Penguin Books, 1976.

Ambrosius, Lloyd E. "The Goldwater-Fulbright Controversy," *The Arkansas Historical Quarterly,* Autumn, 1970.

Ashmore, Harry S. *An Epitaph for Dixie.* New York: Norton, 1958.

————. *Arkansas: A History.* New York: Norton, 1978.

————. and William C. Baggs. *Mission to Hanoi: A Chronicle of Double-Dealing in High Places.* New York: G.P. Putnam's Sons, 1968.

————. *Civil Rights and Wrongs: A Memoir of Race and Politics, 1944-1994* New York: Pantheon, 1994.

Bailey, Thomas A. *A Diplomatic History of the American People.* Englewood Cliffs, New Jersey: Prentice-Hall, 1974.

Ball, George. *The Past Has Another Pattern: Memoirs.* New York: Norton, 1982.

Barnet, Richard J. *Roots of War.* New York: Penguin Books, 1972.

Barnes, Steve. "Fulbright Remembered," *Active Years,* September, 1995.

Berman, William. *William Fulbright and the Vietnam War: The Dissent of a Political Realist* Kent, Ohio: Kent State University Press, 1988.

Bernstein, Barton, ed. *Towards a New Past: Dissenting Essays in American History.* New York: Random House-Vintage Books, 1968.

Blum, John Morton. *V Was for Victory.* New York: Harcourt, Brace, Jovanovich, 1970.

Bork, Robert. *The Tempting of America: The Political Seduction of the Law.* New York: Touchstone, 1990.

Brauer, Carl M. *John F. Kennedy and the Second Reconstruction.* New York: Columbia University Press, 1977.

Brower, Brock. "The Roots of the Arkansas Questioner," *Life,* May 13, 1966.

Burns, James MacGregor. *Roosevelt: The Soldier of Freedom.* New York: Harcourt, Brace, Jovanovich, 1970.

Clifford, Clark, with Richard Holbrooke. *Counsel to the President: A Memoir.* New York: Random House, 1991.

Coffin, Tristram. *Senator Fulbright: Portrait of a Public Philosopher.* New York: E.P. Dutton, 1966.

Donovan, Robert J. *Conflict and Crisis: The Presidency of Harry S. Truman, 1945-1948.* New York: Norton, 1977.

————. *Tumultuous Years: The Presidency of Harry S. Truman, 1949-1953.* New York: Norton, 1982.

Donovan, Timothy, and Willard Gatewood, eds. *The Governors of Arkansas: Essays in Political Biography.* Fayetteville, Arkansas: University of Arkansas Press, 1981.

Dougan, Michael B. *Arkansas Odyssey: The Saga of Arkansas from Prehistoric Times to the Present.* Little Rock, Rose, 1994.

Eisenhower, Dwight D. *Mandate for Change, 1953-1956.* Garden City, New York: Doubleday, 1963.

————. *Waging Peace, 1956-1961.* Garden City, New York: Doubleday, 1965.

Ely, John Hart, "The American War in Indochina: The (Troubled) Constitutionality of the War They Told Us About," 42 *Stanford Law Review* 877 (April, 1990) (PART I).

————. "The American War in Indochina: The Unconstitutionality of the War They Didn't Tell Us About," 42 *Stanford Law Review* 1093 (May, 1990) (PART II).

————. *Democracy and Distrust: A Theory of Judicial Review.* Cambridge: Harvard University Press, 1980.

————. *War and Responsibility: Constitutional Lessons of Vietnam and its Aftermath.* Princeton: Princeton University Press, 1993.

Fairbank, John King. *The United States and China.* Fourth Edition. Cambridge, Massachusetts: Harvard University Press, 1979.

Fall, Bernard B. *Last Reflections on a War.* New York: Schocken Books, 1967.

Fitzgerald, Frances. *Fire in the Lake: The Vietnamese and the Americans in Vietnam.* New York: Random House-Vintage Books, 1972.

Freund, Paul, "Appointment of Justices: Some Historical Perspectives," in *Essays on the Supreme Court Appointment Process,* 101 Harv.L.Rev. 1,155 (1988)

Freyer, Tony. *The Little Rock Crisis: A Constitutional Interpretation* (1984)

Fried, Richard M. *Men Against McCarthy*. New York: Columbia University Press, 1976.

Feis, Herbert. *The Atomic Bomb and the End of World War II*. Princeton, New Jersey: Princeton University Press, 1966.

Gaddis, John Lewis. *The United States and the Origins of the Cold War, 1941-1947*. New York: Columbia University Press, 1972.

Galbraith, John Kenneth. *Annals of an Abiding Liberal*. New York: The New American Library, 1979.

————. *A Life in our Times*. New York: Ballantine, 1981.

Gallagher, Hugh Gregory. *Advise and Obstruct: The Role of the United States Senate in Foreign Policy Decisions*. New York: 1969.

Garrow, David J. *Bearing the Cross: Martin Luther King, Jr. and the Southern Christian Leadership Conference*. New York: Vintage, 1986

Gaston, Paul M., *The New South Creed: A Study in Southern Mythmaking*. Baton Rouge: Louisiana State University Press, 1970.

Gilbert, Felix. *The End of the European Era, 1890 to the Present*. New York: Norton, 1970.

Glennon, Michael. *Constitutional Diplomacy* (1990).

Graebner, Norman A. *The New Isolationism: A Study in Politics and Foreign Policy Since 1950*. New York: The Ronald Press Company, 1956.

————. *Ideas and Diplomacy: Readings in the Intellectual Tradition of American Foreign Policy*. (Edited with commentary by Norman Graebner). New York: Oxford University Press, 1964.

————. "The Extension of the Cold War to Asia," in *The Origins of the Cold War*, ed. Thomas G. Paterson. Lexington, Massachusetts: D.C. Heath, 1974.

————, ed. *The Cold War: A Conflict of Ideology and Power*. Second edition. Lexington, Massachusetts: D.C. Heath, 1976.

————. *Cold War Diplomacy: American Foreign Policy, 1945-1975*. Second edition. New York: D. Van Nostrand, 1977.

————. *The Age of Global Power: The United States Since 1939*. New York: John Wiley and Sons, 1979.

Graff, Henry. *The Tuesday Cabinet: Deliberation and Decision on Peace and War under Lyndon B. Johnson*. Englewood Cliffs, Prentice Hall, 1970.

Griffith, Robert. *The Politics of Fear: Joseph R. McCarthy and the Senate*. Lexington, Kentucky: The University Press of Kentucky, 1970.

————, and Athan Theoharis, eds. *The Specter: Original Essays on the Cold War and the Origins of McCarthyism*. New York: Franklin Watts, 1974.

Halberstam, David. *The Best and the Brightest*. Greenwich, Connecticut: Fawcett, Crest, 1972.

————. *The Powers That Be*. New York: Dell, 1979.

Hamby, Alonzo L. *Beyond the New Deal: Harry S. Truman and American Liberalism*. New York: Columbia University Press, 1973.

Herlick, Gary. "J. W. Fulbright: Democratic Senator from Arkansas," in *Ralph Nader Congress Project: Citizens Look at Congress*, ed. Ralph Nader. Washington: Grossman, 1972.

Hays, Brooks. *A Southern Moderate Speaks*. Chapel Hill: University of North Carolina Press, 1959.

————. *Politics Is My Parish*. Foreward by Arthur M. Schlesinger, Jr. Baton Rouge: Louisiana State University Press, 1981.

Herring, George C. *America's Longest War: The United States and Vietnam, 1950-1975*. New York: John Wiley and Sons, 1979.

Horowitz, David. *The Free World Colossus: A Critique of American Foreign Policy in the Cold War*. New York: Hill and Wang, 1965.

Howe, Russell Warren, and Sarah Trott. "J. William Fulbright: Reflections on a Troubled World," *Saturday Review*, January 11, 1975.

Hull, Cordell. *The Memoirs of Cordell Hull: Volume II*. New York: The MacMillan Company, 1948.

Hyman, Sidney. "Fulbright—The Wedding of Arkansas and the World," *The New Republic*, May 14, 1962.

Isaacson, Walter. *Kissinger: A Biography*. New York: Simon & Schuster, 1992.

Jeffries, John C. *Justice Lewis F. Powell, Jr.: A Biography* New York: Charles Scribner's Sons, 1994.

Johnson, Haynes, and Bernard M. Gwertzman. *Fulbright the Dissenter*. Garden City, New York: Doubleday, 1968.

Johnson, Lyndon B. *The Vantage Point: Perspectives on the Presidency, 1963-1969*. New York: Holt, Rinehart, Winston, 1971.

Johnson, Walter, ed. *The Papers of Adlai E. Stevenson, Volume VIII: Ambassador to the United Nations, 1961-1965*. Boston: 1969.

Johnson, Walter, and Francis J. Colligan. *The Fulbright Program: A History*. Foreword by J. William Fulbright. Chicago: The University of Chicago Press, 1965.

Karnow, Stanley. *Vietnam: A History*. 2d ed. New York: Viking, 1991.

Kearns, Doris. *Lyndon Johnson and the American Dream*. New York: Signet, 1976.

Kennan, George F. *American Diplomacy, 1900-1950*. New York: Mentor, 1951.

————. *Russia and the West Under Lenin and Stalin*. New York: Mentor, 1961.

————. "A Fresh Look at Our China Policy," *The New York Times Magazine*, November 22, 1964.

Kennedy, Paul. *The Rise and Fall of the Great Powers: Economic Change and Military Conflict from 1500 to 2000*. New York: Random House, 1987.

Kissinger, Henry A. *White House Years*. Boston: Little, Brown and Company, 1982.

————. *Years of Upheaval*. Boston: Little, Brown and Company, 1982.

————. *Diplomacy*. New York: 1994.

Klarman, Michael.. *Brown, Racial Change, and the Civil Rights Movement*. 80 Virginia Law Review 7 (February, 1994)

Kolko, Gabriel. *The Roots of American Foreign Policy: An Analysis of Power and Purpose*. Boston: Beacon Press, 1969.

Lake, Anthony, ed. *The Legacy of Vietnam*. New York: New York University Press, 1976.

Lamis, Alexander P., *The Two-Party South*. Second Expanded Edition (New York: Oxford University Press, 1990)

LaFeber, Walter. *America, Russia, and the Cold War, 1945-1971*. Second edition. New York: John Wiley and Sons, 1972.

Leflar, Robert A. *One Life in the Law: A Sixty-Year Review*. Fayetteville: University of Arkansas Press, 1985.

Lester, Jim. *A Man for Arkansas: Sid McMath and the Southern Reform Tradition* Little Rock: Rose, 1976.

Lippmann, Walter. *The Public Philosophy*. New York: Mentor, 1955.

Malone, Dumas. *Jefferson and His Time*. Six volumes. (Boston: Little, Brown, 1948-1981). *Jefferson the Virginian*, Volume I; *Jefferson and the Rights of Man*, Volume II; *Jefferson and the Ordeal of Liberty*, Volume III; *Jefferson the President: First Term, 1801-1805*, Volume IV; *Jefferson the President: 1805-1809*, Volume V; *The Sage of Monticello*, Volume VI. [Mr. Malone did most of his writing and research for this 40-year project at the University of Virginia. This biography received a glowing endorsement from Senator Fulbright when the first volume was published in 1948, and it was awarded the Pulitzer Prize for History in 1975.]

Maraniss, David. *First in His Class: A Biography of Bill Clinton*. New York: 1995.

McCallum, R.B. *Public Opinion and the Last Peace*. London: Oxford University Press, 1944.

McCullough, David. *Truman*. New York: Simon & Schuster, 1992.

Martin, John Bartlow. *Adlai Stevenson and the World: The Life of Adlai E. Stevenson*. Garden City, New York: Doubleday, 1978.

Newman, Roger. *Hugo Black: A Biography*. New York: Pantheon, 1994.

Paterson, Thomas G. *On Every Front: The Making of the Cold War.* New York: Norton, 1979.

————, ed. *The Origins of the Cold War*. Second edition. Lexington, Massachusetts: D.C. Heath, 1974.

Pettit, Clyde Edwin. *The Experts*. Secaucus, NJ: Lyle Stuart, 1975.

Powell, Lee Riley. *J. William Fulbright and America's Lost Crusade: Fulbright, the Cold War and the Vietnam War* Little Rock: Rose, 1984; Expanded edition, 1988. (Foreword by J. William Fulbright).

Rehnquist, William, *The Supreme Court: The Way It Was, The Way It Is* (New York: William Morrow and Company, 1987)

Reedy, George E. *The Twilight of the Presidency*. New York: Mentor, 1970.

Richardson, Elmo. *The Presidency of Dwight D. Eisenhower.* Lawrence: The Regents Press of Kansas, 1979.

Rovere, Richard. *Senator Joe McCarthy*. New York: Harper and Row, 1959.

Rusk, Dean, as told to Richard Rusk. *As I Saw It*. New York: Norton, 1990.

Safire, William, *Before the Fall: An Inside View of the Pre-Watergate White House* (New York: Ballantine, 1977)

Schell, Jonathan, *The Time of Illusion* (New York: Vintage, 1975)

Schlesinger, Arthur M., Jr. *The Age of Roosevelt: Volume II, The Coming of the New Deal; Volume III, the Politics of Upheaval*. Boston: Houghton, Mifflin, 1958-1960.

————. *A Thousand Days: John F. Kennedy in the White House*. Boston: Houghton, Mifflin, 1965.

————. *The Imperial Presidency*. New York: Popular Library, 1974.

————. *Robert Kennedy and His Times*. New York: Ballantine, 1978.

Schwartz, Bernard. *Super Chief: Earl Warren and The Supreme Court—A Judicial Biography* (New York: New York University Press, 1983)

————. *The Ascent of Pragmatism: The Burger Court in Action* (New York: Addison-Wesley, 1990)

Seib, Charles, and Alan Otten. "Fulbright: Arkansas Paradox," *Harper's*, June, 1956.

Sharp, U.S. Grant, and Westmoreland, W.C. *Report on the War in Vietnam, 1964-68.* Washington: U.S. Government Printing Office, 1968.

Sheehan, Neil. *A Bright Shining Lie: John Paul Vann and America in Vietnam.* New York: Random House, 1988.

Sheehan, Neil, et al., eds. *The Pentagon Papers.* (Based on investigative reporting by Neil Sheehan, written by Neil Sheehan, Hedrick Smith, E.W. Kenworthy, and Fox Butterfield.) New York: Bantam, 1971.

Sitkoff, Harvard. *The Struggle for Black Equality, 1954-1981* (New York: Hill and Wang, 1981)

Smith, Beverly. "Egghead From the Ozarks," *Saturday Evening Post*, May 2, 1959.

Smith, Gaddis. *American Diplomacy During the Second World War, 1941-1945.* New York: John Wiley and Sons, 1965.

Snow, Edgar. *Red China Today.* New York: Random House-Vintage Books, 1970.

Spanier, John W. *The Truman-MacArthur Controversy and the Korean War.* Cambridge, Massachusetts: Belknap Press of Harvard University Press, 1959.

Steel, Ronald. *Pax Americana.* New York: The Viking Press, 1970.

————. *Walter Lippman and the American Century.* Boston: Little, Brown, and Company, 1980.

Stone, I. F. "Fulbright of Arkansas: Part 1," December 29, 1966, *The New York Review of Books*, Volume VII, Number 11.

————. "Fulbright: From Hawk to Dove, Part 2," January 12, 1967, *The New York Review of Books*, Volume VII, Number 12

————. "Fulbright: The Timid Opposition, Part 3," January 26, 1967, *The New York Review of Books*, Volume VIII, Number 1.

Totenberg, Nina, "The Confirmation Process and the Public: To Know or Not to Know," in *Essays on the Supreme Court Appointment Process*, 101 Harv.L.Rev. 1,212 (1988)

Tribe, Laurence, *American Constitutional Law* New York: The Foundation Press, 1988.

————. *God Save this Honorable Court* (New York: Random House, 1968)

Tweraser, Kurt. "The Advice and Dissent of Senator Fulbright: A Longitudinal Analysis of His Images of International Politics and His Political Role Conceptions," Ph.D. dissertation, American University, Washington, D.C., 1971.

———. *Changing Patterns of Political Beliefs: The Foreign Policy Operational Codes of J. William Fulbright, 1943-1967.* Beverly Hills, California: Sage Publications, 1974.

Ward, John, *The Arkansas Rockefeller* (Baton Rouge: Louisiana State University Press, 1978)

Williams, William Appleman. *The Tragedy of American Diplomacy.* Second revised edition. New York: Delta, 1971.

Woods, Henry (United States District Judge, Eastern District of Arkansas) and Deere, Beth, "Reflections on the Little Rock School Case," 44 *Arkansas Law Review* 971 (1991)

Woods, Randall. *Fulbright: A Biography* (1995).

Woodward, Bob, and Scott Armstrong. *The Brethren.* New York: Simon and Schuster, 1979.

———. and Carl Bernstein. *All the President's Men.* New York: Simon and Schuster, 1974.

———. and Carl Bernstein. *The Final Days.* New York: Simon and Schuster, 1976.

———. *The Secret Wars of the CIA,* 1981-1987. New York: Simon and Schuster, 1988.

Woodward, C. Vann. *The Burden of Southern History.* Revised edition. Baton Rouge: Louisiana State University Press, 1968.

———. *The Strange Career of Jim Crow.* Third revised edition. New York: Oxford University Press, 1974.

Yergin, Daniel. "Fulbright's Last Frustration," *The New York Times Magazine,* November 24, 1974.

Notes

(NOTE: In most paragraphs in this book, there is one endnote at the end of the paragraph that contains the notes for that paragraph. In some cases, however, where I chose to pinpoint a particular page number for a quotation or source, I placed several endnotes after particular sentences in the paragraph.)

Book One
Prologue and The Early Years

1. Brock Brower, *Roots of the Arkansas Traveler,* in *Life* magazine, New York, May 13, 1966; page 98.

2. Walter Lippmann, syndicated column, *The Toledo Blade,* October 10, 1961; in the Fulbright Papers at the University of Arkansas library, Fayetteville.

3. Tweraser, Kurt K., *The Advice and Dissent of Senator Fulbright*; unpublished dissertation in the Arkansas Collection at the University of Arkansas, Fayetteville.

3a. Mark Twain, *Life on the Mississippi* (New York: 1907), at 32.

3b. Haynes Johnson and Bernard Gwertzman, *Fulbright the Dissenter,* (Garden City, N.Y., Doubleday, 1968); pg. 12.

4. William S. Campbell, *One Hundred Years of Fayetteville,* published by the author, 1920; in the Arkansas Collection at the University of Arkansas, Fayetteville; pg. 105. Jay Fulbright had often thought of moving to Memphis, where he had bought some land along the Mississippi. He thought Memphis was destined to become the great city of the New South. However, he became successful in Arkansas and never left.

5. In May of 1991, *Nikkei,* one of the largest newspapers in Tokyo, published 30 consecutive daily articles by J. W. Fulbright, entitled *My Personal History.* Fulbright's story was told to Michio Katsumata, journalist. Each article covered a stage in Fulbright's life. The 30 articles, in Japanese and in English, are in the Fulbright Papers, where each has a page number in the English translation. This reference is from pp. 22-24, inc.

6. Ibid, pg. 23.

7. Roberta Fulbright, *As I See It,* column in the *Daily Democrat* at Fayetteville, AR, February 22, 1938; columns collected in the Fulbright Papers at the University of Arkansas, Fayetteville.

8. Ibid, column of March 4, 1936; in the Fulbright Papers.

9. Ibid, column of May 8, 1935; in the Fulbright Papers.

10. Ibid, column of July 18, 1940; in the Fulbright Papers. Roberta Fulbright also crusaded for reform in local government, supporting the Good Government League in Fayetteville, an organization that fought corruption in Washington County.

11. Ibid, column of February 19, 1938; in the Fulbright Papers.

12. Ibid, column of September 12, 1934; in the Fulbright Papers.

13. Ibid, column of March 2, 1939; in the Fulbright Papers.

14. Ibid, column of November 26, 1934; in the Fulbright Papers.

15. J. W. Fulbright in *Nikkei,* Tokyo; pg. 22 in the collection of the series in the Fulbright Papers.

16. J. W. Fulbright and Harriet Fulbright, interview with the authors, September 15, 1993.

17. J. W. Fulbright in *Nikkei,* Tokyo; pp. 19-20 in the collection of the series in the Fulbright Papers.

18. Haynes Johnson and Bernard Gwertzman, *Fulbright the Dissenter,* (Garden City, N.Y., Doubleday, 1968); pg. 17.

19. J. W. Fulbright in *Nikkei,* Tokyo; pp. 20-21 in the collection of the series in the Fulbright Papers.

20. Ibid, pg. 16 in the collection in the Fulbright papers.

21. Ibid, pg. 18 in the collection in the Fulbright Papers.

22. Johnson & Gwertzman, pg. 14.

23. J. W. Fulbright in *Nikkei,* Tokyo; pg. 21 in the collection in the Fulbright Papers.

24. James O. Powell, covering session of the Florida legislature for the *Tampa Tribune*; April, 1949.

25. J. W. Fulbright in *Nikkei,* Tokyo; pg. 21 in the collection in the Fulbright Papers.

26. Leflar, Robert A., *Legal Education in Arkansas,* Arkansas Historical Quarterly XXI; 1961; pg. 1.

27. J W. Fulbright in *Nikkei,* pp. 20-21 in the collection in the Fulbright Paper.

28. Ibid, pg. 27 in the collection in the Fulbright Papers. Despite Fulbright's highly beneficial experience at Oxford, there were also some problems. Although Fulbright would develop an excellent relationship with R.B. McCallum, to his surprise he also encountered anti-Americanism among

some of the people at Oxford. Some Oxonians engaged in the popular sport of portraying Americans as rich and foolish. Oxford intellectuals generally held little respect for the quality of American colleges. In addition, when Fulbright made a tour of America as a member of the Oxford-Cambridge lacrosse team, he suffered serious injuries to both knees in a match against Yale. The injuries left him with gimpy knees for the rest of his life. Fulbright was an athletic 5 feet 11 inches, 165 pounds. Johnson and Gwertzman, pp. 26-29.

29. *Arkansas Gazette*, magazine section, Rhodes Scholars from Arkansas; Little Rock, October 29, 1939; pg. 1.

30. Ibid, pg. 2.

32. Herb Gunn, *The Continuing Friendship of James William Fulbright and Ronald Buchanan McCallum*; South Atlantic Quarterly; Autumn, 1984, pg. 416.

33. Tweraser, pp. 33-34.

34. James O. Powell, interview with Walker Stone at Washington, February, 1950.

35. Johnson and Gwertzman, pp. 38-39. Fulbright was particularly impressed by the St. Sulpice church in Paris, writing to Roberta Fulbright: "It had the most beautiful music I have ever heard... Religion, seems to me, appeals to the senses and emotions more than to the intellect, and rightly so." (J.W. Fulbright to Roberta Fulbright, December 24, 1926, Fulbright Papers; quoted in Randall Woods, *Fulbright: A Biography* (1995), p. 33. The Fulbright family had attended the First Christian Church in Fayetteville. Bill Fulbright rarely talked about religion, although he believed in a Supreme Being.

36. J. W. Fulbright in *Nikkei*, Tokyo, pp. 32-33 in the Fulbright Papers.

37. Interview with J. W. Fulbright, by James O. Powell at Miami Beach, August 15, 1972.

38a. Geoffrey Stone, Louis Seidman, Cass Sunstein, and Mark Tushnet, *Constitutional Law* (2d ed., 1991), at 416.

38b. Ibid.

38c. Interview with J. W. Fulbright by Lee Powell in Washington, June 4, 1991.

38d. Roger Newman, *Hugo Black: A Biography* (1994) at 159-161.

38e. Arthur M. Schlesinger, Jr., *The Age of Roosevelt: The Politics of Upheaval* (Boston: 1960) at 277-285.

38f. Felix Frankfurter and Henry Hart, Jr., "The Business of the Supreme Court at October Term, 1934, *Harvard Law Review*, November, 1935.

39. J. W. Fulbright in *Nikkei*, Tokyo; pg. 34 in the collection in the Fulbright Papers.

39a. June 4, 1991 interview with J.W. Fulbright, supra, note 38c.

39b. Robert A. Leflar, *One Life in the Law: A Sixty-Year Review* (Fayetteville, 1985), at 14-15.

39c. Interview with United States District Judge Henry Woods with the authors, May 4, 1995, Little Rock.

39d. *Leflar, One Life in the Law*, at 6-9.

39e. Interview with Henry Woods, *supra*, note 39c.

40. Johnson and Gwertzman, pg. 46.

40a. "The Social Function of the University," speech by J. William Fulbright, Fort Smith, Arkansas Civic Club, December 10, 1939; Johnson and Gwertzman, at 42. Regarding Fulbright's elevation to the university presidency, there are different interpretations about Julian Waterman's views. Eloise Baerg, who knew both the Fulbrights and Watermans, stated that Mrs. Waterman had been deeply disappointed when Mr. Waterman did not become president. Woods, supra, at 55. Hal Douglas, Fulbright's brother-in-law, contended that Fulbright was initially astounded that he was the choice to succeed Futrall, and insisted that Waterman should be president. According to Haynes Johnson, Waterman, "then the university vice president as well as law dean, was contacted, but declined for a singular reason: he was a Jew, he pointed out, and, because he would have to be dealing with the Arkansas Legislature, he probably would be leading the university into controversy." Johnson and Gwertzman, pp. 40-41.

In fairness to Fulbright, it should be noted that his credentials as a Rhodes Scholar, honors graduate of George Washington University Law School, Justice Department attorney, and law professor indicated a brilliant promise. It could be seen as perfectly justifiable that the university would choose a brilliant—if young—scholar rather than an older, more experienced, but also more pedestrian candidate. When Fulbright was fired by Governor Adkins' supporters for political reasons, the Rhodes Scholar's replacement was the competent, but rather forgettable Dean of the College of Agriculture, A. M. Harding.

40b. "Economic Problems of Arkansas," speech by J. William Fulbright, Little Rock Chamber of Commerce, October 18, 1940; Johnson and Gwertzman, at 44.

40c. Congressional Record, March 6, 1940.

41. The *Arkansas Gazette*, May 15, 1941, editorial page.

42. Alan Gilbert, *A Fulbright Chronicle*, the Fulbright Foundation, Fayetteville, 1980; pg. 142.

43. Ibid, pg. 142. The Democratic State Committee had tried to persuade Fulbright to run for public office in 1942. Fulbright had turned down overtures to run for the gubernatorial nomination, saying that he had decided to enlist in the armed forces in the autumn. Democratic leaders countered that his age (37), his bad knees and his dependents would keep him out of military duty, and he could better serve the country by entering politics. Carl Bailey's forces sought an opponent for Governor Homer Adkins, who had defeated Bailey in the 1940 gubernatorial nomination. Adkins used the fact that Bailey was seeking a third term, a move that contradicted Arkansas' two-term tradition. Adkins had been a protege of the late Senator Joseph T. Robinson, the U.S. Senator who created a powerful political organization. Governor Adkins was a former member of the Ku Klux Klan.

43a. Johnson and Gwertzman, at 42.

44. J. W. Fulbright in *Nikkei*, Tokyo; pg. 48 in the collection in the Fulbright Papers. In 1942, John McClellan defeated Clyde Ellis in the Senate race. McClellan had powerful support from the Arkansas Power & Light Company. Ellis became a prominent supporter of public power as head of the Rural Electrification Administration.

45. Alan Gilbert, *A Fulbright Chronicle*, the Fulbright Foundation, Fayetteville, 1980; pg. 246. Ms. Luce had stressed that the nation that dominated air power could gain global hegemony. She had denounced the Atlantic Charter and the views of Vice President Henry Wallace. Fulbright countered that her attacks on Wallace were clearly intended to "ridicule the Vice President of the United States," and that the Atlantic Charter was, contrary to Ms. Luce's views, "no more of a monumental generality or virtuous platitude than is the preamble of our own Constitution or our own sacred Declaration of Independence." He warned against a strategy of grasping all commercial advantages and endorsed a policy of "freedom of the skies." Congressional Record, February 16, 1943, 1011-12.

46. Johnson and Gwertzman, pp. 83-87. Fulbright maintained a conservative voting record on labor issues. In Arkansas, anti-union sentiment was strong. He voted against minimum-wage bills and supported measures designed to allow government to restrict labor unions. Fulbright acknowledged that the labor union movement in America had been beneficial on the whole, as it had ended the most flagrant abuses of workers. Yet, it was much easier for large Northern states to support a minimum wage, because they already had attracted industry; but Arkansas needed to be able to attract new industry by offering lower labor costs.

Regarding agricultural issues, Fulbright voted for acreage allotments and endorsed legislation that was helpful to agricultural interests. At times he had to make a difficult political choice, however, between the large and small farm interests. The large landowners' interests were represented by the conservative American Farm Bureau Federation. The Farm Bureau was allied with the Agricultural Extension Service of the University of Arkansas' College of Agriculture. The Farm Bureau forces were bitterly opposed to the Farm Securities Administration (FSA), which gave long-term, low-interest loans and free technical advice to tenants. R.E. Short, president of the Arkansas Farm Bureau, advised Fulbright in 1943 that the FSA was "building a gigantic bureaucracy under the guise of aiding low income farmers to be used as a pressure group in prosecuting the philosophy of state land socialism." Fulbright antagonized the agribusiness interests by opposing efforts to abolish the FSA. Fulbright had grown up in the area of Arkansas where there were no plantations as there were in the delta, and his family's lumber company did business with small farmers. Douglas Bradley of the Arkansas Farmers' Union wrote Congressman Fulbright in 1943: "Our Washington office informs us that you did a splendid job in support of the FSA." R.E. Short to Fulbright, April 19, 1943, Fulbright Papers; Douglas Bradley to Fulbright, Fulbright Papers, April 26, 1943; quoted in Woods, 85-87. Interview with Jack Stephens, February, 1995; Interview with Witt Stephens, May, 1990. James Powell and Lee Powell discussed the 1944 Senate campaign on several occasions at the Stephens luncheons in the late 1970s and 1980s.

46a. Johnson and Gwertzman, pp. 82-84; Woods, 94-96; Witt Stephens interview, May, 1990; Jack Stephens interview, February, 1995.

47. Johnson and Gwertzman, p. 83; Interview with Fulbright, October, 1981; Woods, 96; Interview with Witt Stephens, May, 1990; Jack Stephens interview, February, 1995.

Book Two
Fulbright and the Cold War

Chapter 1
Introduction.
1. Haynes Johnson and Bernard Gwertzman, *Fulbright the Dissenter* (Garden City, New York: Doubleday, 1968), pg. 92.
   1a.*Chicago Tribune*, September 22, 1943.
2. Karl E. Meyer, ed., *Fulbright of Arkansas: The Public Positions of a Private Thinker* (Washington: Robert B. Luce, Inc., 1963), pg. 21.
3. Tristram Coffin, *Senator Fulbright: Portrait of a Public Philosopher* (New York: E.P. Dutton, 1966), pg. 64.
4. Meyer, ed. *Fulbright of Arkansas,* pg. 24. At the United Nations San Francisco Conference, Fulbright had also been disturbed by American support for the admission of Argentina, which not only had an autocratic government, but had maintained diplomatic relations with the Axis powers for two years after America entered the war. Fulbright attributed this support for Argentina to the inexperience and lack of knowledge of Secretary of State Edward Stettinius (who was soon to be replaced, as it happened). Woods, 106. Soviet diplomat Molotov justifiably objected to the admission of Argentina, because of its pro-Fascist sympathies for much of the war; he also pointed out that at Yalta, it had been agreed that Argentina would be excluded from the UN. American diplomats supported Argentina in an effort to improve relations with South American countries, and 20 countries in the Americas voted for Argentina, winning the vote over Soviet opposition. Robert J. Donovan, *Conflict and Crisis: The Presidency of Harry S. Truman, 1945-1948* (New York: Norton, 1977), pp. 54-55.
5. Johnson and Gwertzman, pg. 99.
6. Ibid.
7. Ibid.
8. Meyer, ed., *Fulbright of Arkansas*, pg. 35.
9. Johnson and Gwertzman, pg. 92.
10. Coffin, *Senator Fulbright*, pg. 82.
11. J. William Fulbright, *The Crippled Giant: American Foreign Policy and Its Domestic Consequences* (New York: Vintage, 1972), pg. 4.
12. J. William Fulbright, *The Arrogance of Power* (New York: Vintage, 1966), pg. 219.
13. Ibid., pg. 220.
14. Ibid.
15. Fulbright, *The Crippled Giant*, pg. 6.
16. Ibid., pg. 154.
17. Ibid., pp. 5-6.
18. Ibid.
19. Ibid., pg. 23.
20. Ibid., pg. 63.
21. Ibid., pg. 19.
22. Johnson and Gwertzman, pg. 47.
23. Meyer, ed., pp. 1-2; Johnson and Gwertzman, pp. 46-47.
24. Johnson and Gwertzman, pg. 47. Also, see Fulbright's letter to President Roosevelt, June 19, 1940, (quoted in Woods, p. 60) urging him to take stronger actions supporting Great Britain: "We cannot expect Congress to be decisive. I am convinced that the people of this country, especially the youth, will follow you enthusiastically if you are daring and bold in this crisis."
25. Doris Kearns, *Lyndon Johnson and the American Dream* (New York: New American Library), pg. 336.

1943 - 1946
1. James MacGregor Burns, *Roosevelt: The Soldier of Freedom* (New York: Harcourt, Brace, Jovanovich, 1970), pg. 427; Cordell Hull, *The Memoirs of Cordell Hull* (New York: The MacMillan Company, 1948), pg. 1,262; Kurt Tweraser, "The Advice and Dissent of Senator Fulbright: A Longitudinal Analysis of His Images of International Politics and His Political Role Conceptions," (Ph.D. dissertation, American University, Washington, D.C., 1971), pg. 94.
2. Ibid.
3. Personal interview with J. William Fulbright, February 6, 1981; Johnson and Gwertzman, pp. 79-81.
4. Johnson and Gwertzman, pp. 80-90.
5. J. William Fulbright to R. B. McCallum, January 24, 1945, James William Fulbright Papers, University of Arkansas Library, Fayetteville, Arkansas; R. B. McCallum to J. William Fulbright, February 19, 1945, James William Fulbright Papers; R. B. McCallum, *Public Opinion and the Last Peace* (London: Oxford University Press, 1944), pp. 192-194
6. *Congressional Record*, March 28, 1945, pp. 2,896-2,900.
6a. *New York Times*, April 13, 1945; Johnson and Gwertzman, p. 94.
6b. Johnson and Gwertzman, 94.
7. President Harry S. Truman to J. William Fulbright, April 13, 1945, Fulbright Papers: Johnson and Gwertzman, pg. 96.

7a. *Arkansas Gazette*, May 29, 1945.

7b. Johnson and Gwertzman, 96.

8. John Morton Blum, *V Was for Victory: Politics and American Culture During World War II* (New York: Harcourt, Brace, Jovanovich, 1976), pp. 316-317; J. William Fulbright, "This Malady of Mankind Is Not a Recent Affliction," in Karl E. Meyer, ed., *Fulbright of Arkansas: The Public Positions of a Private Thinker* (Washington: Robert B. Luce, Inc., 1963), pp. 22-33; *Congressional Record*, October 29, 1945, pg. A4,653.

9. *Congressional Record*, October 29, 1945, pp. A4,652-4,65. Fulbright visited the White House in the autumn, 1945, to persuade the President to give stronger support for the United Nations, but Fulbright later stated that the meeting was fruitless: "I didn't make a bit of an impression on the President. He didn't know what I was talking about." Alfred Steinberg, *The Man from Missouri: The Life and Times of Harry S. Truman* (New York, 1962), p. 263.

10. *Congressional Record*, November 26, 1945, pp. 10,962-10,964; Harry S. Truman, *Public Papers of the Presidents of the United States: Harry S. Truman, 1945* (Washington: Government Printing Office, 1961-1966), pg. 513.

11. Claude Pepper to J. William Fulbright, August 14, 1944, James William Fulbright Papers; Claude Pepper to J. William Fulbright, March 29, 1945, James William Fulbright Papers; James William Fulbright to Claude Pepper, March 30, 1945; Tweraser, "Advice and Dissent," pg. 213.

12. J. William Fulbright, "Our Foreign Policy," in *Academy Papers: Addresses on the Evangeline Wilbour Blashfield Foundation of the American Academy of Arts and Letters, Volume Two*, pp. 204-214, in James William Fulbright Papers.

After the end of Lend-Lease aid to Great Britain, Fulbright worked closely with the administration in steering the Anglo-American Financial Agreement through the Banking and Currency Committee and then through the Senate. Woods, 121. This agreement extended to Great Britain a total credit of $4.4 billion to be repaid at 2 percent interest. The United States, led by Under Secretary of State for Economic Affairs Will Clayton, drove a hard bargain and extracted a number of trade concessions from the British; once again, Fulbright's interest in international policy was relevant for Arkansas economic interests, for economic aid to develop foreign markets would expand exports of cotton, rice, poultry and soybean farmers. The *Chicago Tribune* and other midwestern isolationists condemned Fulbright and the agreement as an Anglo-American alliance in disguise. Congress eventually passed it over isolationist opposition. Donovan, Conflict and Crisis, pp. 185-186.

13. John Lewis Gaddis, *The United States and the Origins of the Cold War, 1941-1947* (New York: Columbia University Pres, 1972), pp. 333-334; William Appleman Williams, *The Tragedy of American Diplomacy* (New York: Delta, second revised edition, 1972), pg. 264; Walter LaFeber, *America, Russia, and the Cold War, 1945-1971* (New York: John Wiley and Sons, 1972), pg. 35; Tweraser, "Advice and Dissent," pg. 134.

14. Johnson and Gwertzman, pp. 107-115; interview with J. William Fulbright, August 4, 1978.

14a. Johnson and Gwertzman, pg. 108.

14b. *Congressional Record*, Senate, September 27, 1945.

14c. *Id.*

14d. Speech by J. William Fulbright, "Education in International Relations," University of Colorado, August 1, 1966.

14e. Hearings before a subcommittee of the Committee on Military Affairs, United States Senate, 79th Congress, 2nd Session, February 25, 1946, U.S. Government Printing Office, pp. 5-6.

14f. Johnson and Gwertzman, pg. 112.

14g. Department of State press release No. 532, August 1, 1946.

14h. Johnson and Gwertzman, pg. 111.

14i. *Id.*

14j. *International Educational Exchange: The Opening Decades, 1945-1966.* A report of the Board of Foreign Scholarships, 1966. U.S. Government Printing Office.

14k. *The New Yorker.* May 10, 1958; undated statement from Fulbright files, Fulbright Papers, cited in Johnson and Gwertzman, pg. 113.

14m. *Congressional Record*, Senate, April 11, 1951.

15. "It's the Thinking of Fulbright We're Fighting:" Political Advertisement of Homer Adkins, August 4, 1944, *Arkansas Gazette*, pg. 11; Johnson and Gwertzman, pp. 91-100.

16. Norman A. Graebner, *Cold War Diplomacy: American Foreign Policy, 1945-1975* (New York: Van Nostrand, Second edition, 1977), Pg. 19; LaFeber, pg. 36.

17. Johnson and Gwertzman, pg. 102.

18. Meyer, ed., pp. 52-55; Johnson and Gwertzman, pp. 103-105. After Fulbright's suggestion,

Truman supported the Presidential Succession Act of 1947, which placed the Speaker of the House and the President Pro Tempore of the Senate ahead of the Secretary of State and other cabinet members in the line of presidential succession after the Vice President. In the event of the death or incapacity of the President and Vice President, Truman wanted elected rather than appointed officials to become President.

18a. Harry S. Truman to Fulbright, March 14, 1960.

19. Ronald Steel, *Walter Lippman and the American Century* (Boston: Little, Brown and Company, 1980), pg. 454; Alonzo L. Hamby, *Beyond the New Deal: Harry S. Truman and American Liberalism* (New York: Columbia University Press, 1973), pg. 138; Meyer, ed., pp. 52-55; personal interview with J. William Fulbright, February 6, 1981; Johnson and Gwertzman, pg. 121.

20. Ernest K. Lindley, "Kefauver and Fulbright," *Newsweek*, April 2, 1951, pg. 25; Johnson and Gwertzman, pg. 121.

21. J. William Fulbright to President Harry S. Truman, March 10, 1947, James William Fulbright Papers.

22. Norman A. Graebner, *The Age of Global Power: The United States Since 1939* (New York: John Wiley and Sons, 1979), pg. 77. Fulbright won support for his ideas regarding a United States of Europe among diverse political leaders: former President Hoover, former isolationists Robert LaFollette and Burton Wheeler, and Clare Booth Luce were among the members of the American Committee for a Free and United Europe; Fulbright was elected chairman of this committee. Fulbright stated that a federation of Europe would eventually become strong enough to counter the power of the Soviet Union. Woods, 141. J. William Fulbright, "A United States of Europe: It Is Not an Idealistic Dream" April 7, 1947, Meyer, ed., pp. 155-159.

22a. Robert J. Donovan, *Conflict and Crisis: The Presidency of Harry S. Truman, 1945-1948* (New York: 1977), at 292.

22b. Harry S. Truman to George Earle, former governor of Pennsylvania, February 28, 1947, Official File, Truman Papers, Harry S. Truman Library, Independence, Missouri.

22c. Donovan, *Conflict and Crisis*, at 294.

22d. Harry S. Truman, *Years of Trial and Hope,* (Garden City: 1956), 3-4.

22e. Clark Clifford, memorandum to President Truman, May 23, 1947, Papers of George Elsey, Harry S. Truman Library.

22f. Fulbright, *The Crippled Giant*, at 208.

23. J. William Fulbright, "Your Role in America's Future," speech at Southwestern at Memphis, June, 1948 (Memphis: Committee on Publication of Southwestern at Memphis, 1948), pp. 1-10, in James William Fulbright Papers; Tweraser, "Advice and Dissent," p. 222.

24. George C. Marshall to J. William Fulbright, July 1, 1947, Fulbright Papers; Graebner, *The Age of Global Power*, 77; Tweraser, "Advice and Dissent," p. 224.

25. Tweraser, "Advice and Dissent," pg 226; Graebner, *The Age of Global Power*, pp. 91-92; J. William Fulbright, Carlos P. Romulo, Charles F. Brannan, Eric A. Johnston, speakers, George V. Denny, Jr., moderator, "How Can the Free Peoples of the World Best Share Peace and Well-Being?" in *Bulletin of America's Town Meeting of the Air* (New York: The Town Hall, Inc. 1949), pp. 1-13.

26. Harold F. Gosnell, *Truman's Crises: A Political Biography of Harry S. Truman* (London: Greenwood Press, 1980), pg. 435; Graebner, *The Age of Global Power*, pg. 99.

27. Personal interview with Claude Pepper, March 19, 1981; Richard M. Fried, *Men Against McCarthy* (New York: Columbia University Press, 1976), pp. 95-117.

28. Walter Davenport, "Just a Boy from the Ozarks," Collier's, February 10, 1945, pg. 52; Johnson and Gwertzman, pp. 79-83;" It's the Thinking of Fulbright We're Fighting," Political Advertisement of Homer Adkins, *Arkansas Gazette*, pg. 11; Gary Herlick, "J. W. Fulbright: Democratic Senator from Arkansas," in *Ralph Nader Congress Project*, ed. Ralph Nader (Washington: Grossman, 1972), pg. 6.

29. J. William Fulbright to Dean Acheson, November 25, 1950, James William Fulbright Papers; William S. White, "Senate Shelves GOP Attack on Truman's Foreign Policy," December 19, 1950, *New York Times*, pg. 1, pg. 12.

30. Johnson and Gwertzman, pg. 119; David Horowitz, *The Free World Colossus: A Critique of American Foreign Policy in the Cold War* (New York: Hill and Want, 1965), pg. 112.

30a. Norman A. Graebner, *The New Isolationism: A Study in Politics and Foreign Policy Since 1950* (New York: The Ronald Press Company, 1956); *Congressional Record*, January 22, 1951, 520-523.

31. Douglas MacArthur, Address to Congress, April 19, 1951, in Norman A. Graebner, ed., *Ideas and Diplomacy: Readings in the Intellectual Tradition of American Foreign Policy* (New York: Oxford

University Press, 1964), pg. 778; Thomas A. Bailey, *A Diplomatic History of the American People* (Englewood Cliffs, New Jersey: Prentice Hall, 1974), pg. 823.

32. J. William Fulbright, "General MacArthur's Dismissal: The Ricks of Recklessness," in Meyer, ed., pp. 61-67.
33. Ibid.
34. U. S. Congress. Senate. Committee on Foreign Relations. *Military Situation in the Far East,* Hearings, 82nd Congress, May-August, 1951, (Washington: Government Printing Office, 1951), pp. 138-142, pg. 298.
35. Ibid.
36. Norman A. Graebner, *The New Isolationism: A Study in Politics and Foreign Policy Since 1950* (New York: The Ronald Press Company, 1956), pp. 57-59.
37. Fried, pp. 185-191.
38. Robert Griffith, *The Politics of Fear: Joseph R. McCarthy and the Senate* (Lexington, Kentucky: The University Press of Kentucky, 1970), pp. 148-150. The nomination was held over until after adjournment of the Senate, and thus Truman could give Jessup a recess appointment. Woods, 179. Members of McCarthy's staff also cooperated with the notorious anti-Semite, Gerald L.K. Smith, to smear the reputation of Anna Rosenberg, Truman's nominee for assistant secretary of defense. Griffith, p. 136. In remarks in the Senate in December 1950, Fulbright condemned the "false charges" against Rosenberg. *Congressional Record*, Senate, December 18, 1950, 16692. Fried, pg. 185.
39. George H. Hall, "Stevenson Backers Charge GOP Blitz Plan Is Based on Deception," October 6, 1952, *St. Louis Post-Dispatch*, pg. 1, pg. 10; Fried, pp. 239-249.
40. R. B. McCallum to J. William Fulbright, November 13, 1952, James William Fulbright Papers; J. William Fulbright to R. B. McCallum, February 2, 1953, James William Fulbright Papers.
41. J. William Fulbright to William Benton, March 4, 1953, James William Fulbright Papers; William Benton to J. William Fulbright, February 25, 1953, James William Fulbright Papers; Fried, pp. 239-249.
42. Johnson and Gwertzman, pg. 131; Fried, pp. 261-262.
43. Walter Johnson and Francis J. Colligan, *The Fulbright Program* (Chicago: The University of Chicago Press, 1965), pp. 86-104.
44. *Congressional Record*, February 2, 1954, pg.

1,103; Johnson and Gwertzman, pg. 137; W. H. Lawrence, "Senate, 85-1, Votes McCarthy's $214,000; Fulbright Only One Opposed," *New York Times*, February 3, 1954, pg. 1.
44a. "Fulbright Boycotts FBI, Charges Files Opened to McCarthy: Confidential Information Used for Smears, Arkansan Complains," Associated Press report, *Arkansas Gazette*, March 14, 1954, p.1. Hoover had met the Fulbrights previously in a friendly setting: Hoover delivered the commencement address at the University of Arkansas in 1943 and was a guest in Roberta Fulbright's home. Fulbright spoke to the Academy's graduating class in 1949. Fulbright interview, August 4, 1978. Hoover was indignant at Fulbright, and defended McCarthy as the victim of "vicious criticism." "FBI Chief Calls McCarthy Man Who Won't Be Pushed Around," *Washington Star,* August 26, 1953.
45. Meyer, ed., pp. 71-72.
46. Ronald Steel, *Walter Lippmann,* pg. 504; John Kenneth Galbraith, *Annals of an Abiding Liberal* (New York: Meridian, 1979), pg. 256; J. William Fulbright to Walter Lippmann, December 29, 1955, James William Fulbright Papers; Walter Lippman to J. William Fulbright, December 31, 1955, James William Fulbright Papers.
47. J. William Fulbright, *The Arrogance of Power* (New York: Random House-Vintage Books, 1967), pp. 106-120.
47a. *Arkansas Gazette*, April 18, 1954, p. 1.
47b. *Arkansas Gazette*, March 2, 1955, p. 1.
48. "Mr. Dulles Explains—What America Is Up Against in Europe and Asia," *U. S. News and World Report*, July 23, 1954, pp. 73-78.
49. U. S. Congress. Senate. Committee on Foreign Relations. *Mutual Security Act of 1954.* Hearings, 83rd Congress, June, 1954, pp. 21-25, pg. 137.
50. "Fulbright Lays Rift with Allies to McCarthy: Arkansan is Opposed to U. S. Quitting U. N. If Red China Gets In," *Arkansas Gazette*, July 5, 1954, pg. 1; Tweraser," Advice and Dissent," pg. 247. In the fall of 1954, Fulbright served in New York as U.S. delegate to the United Nations.
51. Tweraser, "Advice and Dissent," pg. 437; "Fulbright Lays Rift with Allies to McCarthy," *Arkansas Gazette*, July 5, 1954, pg. 1. On February 2, 1954, Fulbright attacked the supporters of the Bricker Amendment for attempting to "throttle the President of the United States in his conduct of foreign relations." The Arkansan regarded the amendment as an isolationist effort to evade the world's unpleasant realities. Fulbright expressed his faith in "the traditions

and history of the institutions of the Presidency, the Senate, and the Supreme Court, and in the ability of our people, present and future, to regulate those institutions through the processes of government, as they have in the past. *Congressional Record*, Senate, February 2, 1954, 1106.

52. David Halberstam, *The Powers That Be* (New York: Dell, 1979), pg. 285; Johnson and Gwertzman, pp. 137-138.

53. J. William Fulbright, "Six Counts of Censure: 'Thou Shalt not Raise a False Report,'" July 31, 1954, in Meyer, ed., pp. 73-81; Griffith, pg. 282; Fried, pp. 295-315.

54. Johnson and Gwertzman, pp. 139-141.

55. "Sickness," *Time*, December 13, 1954, pg. 14; Johnson and Gwertzman, pg. 140.

56. Arthur M. Schlesinger, Jr., *A Thousand Days: John F. Kennedy in the White House* (Boston: Houghton Mifflin, 1965), Pg. 12; Graebner, The Age of Global Power, pg. 117; Johnson and Gwertzman, pg. 138; William Benton to J. William Fulbright, September 16, 1954, James William Fulbright Papers.

57. Fulbright, Frances Fitzgerald, *Fire in the Lake: The Vietnamese and the Americans in Vietnam* (New York: Vintage, 1972).

59. Graebner, *Cold War Diplomacy*, pg. 131; Graebner, *The Age of Global Power*, pg. 237; Lyndon Baines Johnson, *The Vantage Point: Perspectives of the Presidency, 1963-1969* (New York: Holt, Rinehart, and Winston, 1971), pg. 152.

60. Fulbright, *The Crippled Giant*, pg. 160.

61. Daniel Yergin, "Fulbright's Last Frustration," The *New York Times* Magazine, November 24, 1974, pg. 77.

Chapter II

1. J. William Fulbright and John Stennis, *The Role of Congress in Foreign Policy* (Washington: American Enterprise Institute for Public Policy Research, 1971), pg. 43.

2. Fulbright, *The Crippled Giant*, pg. 209.

3. Tristram Coffin, *Senator Fulbright: Portrait of a Public Philosopher* (New York: E. P. Dutton), pg. 124.

4. Meyer, ed., pg. 97.

5. Coffin, pg. 126.

6. Johnson and Gwertzman, pg. 161.

7. Coffin, pg. 127.

8. Meyer, ed., pg. 103.

9. Coffin, pg. 123.

10. Meyer, ed., pg. 98.

11. Ibid., pg. 102.

12. Ibid., pg. 101.

13. Johnson and Gwertzman, pg. 159.

14. Coffin, pg. 123.

15. Meyer, ed., pg. 101.

16. Ibid.

17. Johnson and Gwertzman, pg. 160.

18. Coffin, pg. 124.

19. Meyer, ed., pg. 102.

20. Ibid., pg. 101.

21. Ibid., pg. 102.

22. Johnson and Gwertzman, pg. 161.

23. Coffin, pg. 120.

24. Meyer, ed., pg. 109.

25. Ibid., pg. 115.

26. Ibid., pg. 114.

26a. Robert S. McNamara, *In Retrospect: The Tragedy and Lessons of Vietnam* (Random House, 1995), Appendix at 343.

27. Coffin, pg. 127.

28. *Congressional Record*, August 6, 1958, pg. 16,317.

29. Ibid., pg. 16,319. Fulbright, of course, was also concerned about expanding America's investment in domestic education, and he cosponsored a bill that was the forerunner to the National Defense Education Act in 1958. Woods, 243. The 1958 bill was intended to assure the intellectual preeminence of the United States, strengthen defense, and promote peace by developing programs to "stimulate the development and to increase the number of students in science, engineering, mathematics, modern foreign languages, and other disciplines." *Congressional Record*, Senate, January 23, 1958, 871-77.

30. Coffin, pg. 126.

31. Ibid.

32. *Congressional Record*, August 6, 1958, pg. 16,319.

33. Ibid.

34. William Appleman Williams, *The Tragedy of American Diplomacy* (New York: Second revised edition, Delta, 1972), pg. 12.

35. *Congressional Record*, August 6, 1958, pg. 16,317.

36. Ibid., pg. 16,318.

37. Johnson and Gwertzman, pg. 161.

38. Coffin, pg. 128.

39. *Congressional Record*, August 6, 1958, pg. 16,319.

40. Ibid.

41. Ibid.

42. Ibid.

42a. James Reston, "Dulles and Fulbright—Feud or Truce, *New York Times*, February 1, 1959, p. 10E; William Harlan Hale, "The Man from Arkansas Goes After Mr. Dulles," *Reporter*, April 18, 1957, p. 31; Brown, *Advice and Dissent*, p. 38.

43. Coffin, pg. 144.
44. Meyer, ed., pg. 142.
45. Coffin, pg. 144.
46. Meyer, ed., pg. 141.
47. Ibid., pg. 143.
48. Coffin, pg. 144; Dewey W. Grantham, *The United States Since 1945: The Ordeal of Power* (New York: McGraw Hill, 1976), pg. 105.
49. Meyer, ed., pg. 145.
50. Bailey, pg. 857.
51. Johnson and Gwertzman, pg. 165.
52. Fulbright, *The Crippled Giant*, pg. 26.
53. Ibid., pg. 32.
54. Coffin, pg. 143.
55. Meyer, ed., pg. 147.
55a. Fulbright to W.W. Jackson, July 30, 1959, Fulbright Papers, quoted in Woods, 264.
56. Sidney Hyman, "Fulbright—The Wedding of Arkansas and the World," *The New Republic*, May 14, 1962, pg. 24.
57. J. William Fulbright, Memorandum to President John F. Kennedy, March 29, 1961, warning him against the Bay of Pigs invasion, in Meyer, ed., pg. 194-205; also in Fulbright Papers.
58. Ibid.
59. Ibid.
60. Ibid.
61. Ibid.
62. Ibid.
63. Ibid.
64. Johnson and Gwertzman, pg. 175.
65. McNamara, *In Retrospect*, pp. 25-26.
66. Williams, pg. 11.
67. J. William Fulbright, Memorandum to President John F. Kennedy, March 29, 1961, warning him against the Bay of Pigs invasion, in Meyer, ed., pp. 194-205.
68. Ibid.
69. Ibid.
70. Schlesinger, *A Thousand Days*, p. 252; McNamara, *In Retrospect,* pp. 25-26.
71. Johnson and Gwertzman, 177.
72. Ibid.
73. Coffin, pg. 148.
74. Arthur M. Schlesinger, Jr., *Robert Kennedy and His Times* (New York: Ballantine, 1978), pg. 481.
75. Ibid., pg. 477.
76. Johnson and Gwertzman, pg. 158.
77. Ibid.
78. Schlesinger, *Robert Kennedy and His Times*, pg. 487; Johnson and Gwertzman, pg. 176.
79. Coffin, pg. 149.
80. Schlesinger, *Robert Kennedy and His Times*, pg. 482.
81. Johnson and Gwertzman, p. 178.
81a. McNamara, *In Retrospect*, pp. 25-27.
81b. Ibid.
81c. Theodore Sorensen, *Kennedy*, (New York: Harper and Row, 1965), p. 307.
81d. Schlesinger, *A Thousand Days*, p. 252.
81e. Walter Lippmann, *Washington Post*, May 2, 1961; Woods, 269; Leslie Carpenter, "Fulbright Rates High in Councils at White House," *Arkansas Gazette*, May 2, 1961.
82. Johnson and Gwertzman, p. 178.
83. Ibid., pg. 228; Interview with Fulbright, August 4, 1978.
84. Fulbright, *The Arrogance of Power*, pp. 48-49.
85. McNamara, In Retrospect, p. 340; Schlesinger, Robert Kennedy and His Times, pg. 573.
86. Fulbright, *The Arrogance of Power*, pg. 48.
87. Coffin, pg. 150.
88. Schlesinger, *Robert Kennedy and His Times*, pg. 565.
89. Johnson and Gwertzman, pg. 183.
90. Arthur M. Schlesinger, Jr., *The Imperial Presidency* (New York: Popular Library, 1973), pp. 174-175.
91. Williams, pg. 302.
92. Fulbright, *The Crippled Giant*, pp. 31-32.
93. Ibid., pg. 28.
94. Personal interview with J. William Fulbright, August 4, 1978.
95. Fulbright, *The Crippled Giant*, pg. 33.
96. Ibid., pg. 28.
97. Ibid., pg. 29.
98. Ibid.
99. Ibid.

Book Three
Fulbright and Civil Rights

Chapter I

1. Charles Alexander, *Holding the Line: The Eisenhower Era, 1952-1961*, (1975) at 199.
2. Robert Bork, *The Tempting of America: The Political Seduction of the Law* (1990), at 77.
3. "Hays Concedes, States Rights Victory Seen by Alford," *Arkansas Gazette*, November 6, 1958, at 1.
4. Tony Freyer, *The Little Rock Crisis: A Constitutional Interpretation*, (1984) at 158.
5. Numan V. Bartley, "Looking Back at Little Rock," XXV *Arkansas Historical Quarterly*, pg. 101 and 107 (Summer, 1966); Freyer, supra note 4, at 147.
6. "Election Officials Distribute Stickers for Alford, But Nobody Seems to Care.," *Arkansas Gazette*, November 5, 1958, at B1.
7. Brooks Hays, *Politics Is My Parish*, (1981) at 190-191.
8. Harvard Sitkoff, *The Struggle for Black Equality*, 1954-1980 (1981) at 37.
9. *Id.*
10. Freyer, supra note 4, at 22.
11. *Id.* at 88.
12. Brooks Hays, *A Southern Moderate Speaks* (1959), at 184.
13. C. Vann Woodward, *Origins of the New South, 1877-1913* (1971) at 321.
13a. *Id.* At 326.
14. *Arkansas Democrat*, June 26, 1934, at 6.
15. James E. Lester, "Sidney Sanders McMath," in *The Governors of Arkansas*, Willard Gatewood and Timothy Donovan, editors, (1981) at 206.
16. Gubernatorial primary election results, July 29, 1958, records in office of the Secretary of State of Arkansas.
17. Id.
18. Id., "How to Tell a Voter," *Arkansas Gazette*, July 31, 1958, at B12.
18a. Freyer, supra note 4, at 88; Robert Sherrill, *Gothic Politics in the Deep South: Stars of the New Confederacy* (1968), at 109.
19. Bill Penix to Brooks Hays, November 6, 1958, Brooks Hays Papers, University of Arkansas, Fayetteville, Arkansas.
20. David Wallace, "Orval Eugene Faubus," in *The Governors of Arkansas,* supra note 15, at 217.
21. Sikoff, supra note 8, at 30.
22. Wallace, supra note 20, at 225.
23. Freyer, supra note 4, at 124.
24. Numan V. Bartley, *The Rise of Massive Resistance: Race and Politics in the South During the 1950s* 1969), at 269.
25. Harry Ashmore, *An Epitaph for Dixie*, (1958), at 44.
26. Sitkoff, supra note 4, at 30.
27. Harry Ashmore, *An Epitaph for Dixie,* (1958), at 44.

Chapter II

1. Johnson and Gwertzman, 103-104.
2. Robert J. Donovan, *Tumultuous Years: The Presidency of Harry S. Truman, 1949-1953* (New York, 1982), at 332.
3. Ibid.
4. J. William Fulbright, "The Legislator," in *The Works of the Mind,* (University of Chicago Press, 1947).
5. Johnson and Gwertzman, 131-132.
6. Donovan, *Tumultous Years*, 333. In David McCullough's biography, Truman (1992), McCullough reports Douglas as having said to Truman, "You have been loyal to friends who have not been loyal to you," whereupon Truman replied, "I guess you are right." McCullough then immediately skips over to Truman's later appointment of Stuart Symington as head of the RFC and Symington's expeditious work "to straighten things out." This description of the meeting with Fulbright and Douglas makes it appear that Truman responded positively to the observations privately made at the White House by the two senators. In reality, of course, Truman renominated Dunham and Willett at the expiration of their terms as RFC directors, in direct contradiction of the advice given by Fulbright and Douglas. Fulbright then made public the subcommittee's preliminary conclusions, held public hearings, and Truman belatedly instituted the reforms—including reorganization of the RFC under one administrator, with Symington receiving the appointment to the post—that Fulbright and Douglas had originally suggested.
   Moreover, McCullough provides the following description of the subcommittee's *Study of the Reconstruction Finance Corporation: Favoritism and Influence*: "Truman denounced the report, called it 'asinine,' because while its insinuations were in effect serious charges, it also piously stressed that no charges were being made." *Truman*, p. 864. The full Senate, such commentators as Walter Lippmann, and the majority of thoughtful

observers of this episode regarded the Fulbright subcommittee's preliminary report as having been careful and restrained; as the full Senate Banking and Currency Committee officially stated after the public hearings on the RFC, the hearings had substantiated Fulbright's preliminary report. McCullough's biography is generally good, but his passage on Fulbright, Douglas and the RFC controversy inaccurately portrays Fulbright and the senators as having made "pious" arguments and "insinuations." Such pejorative language was entirely inaccurate; the fact is that Fulbright had been concerned about being careful and restrained in the controversy. The authors of this book have no doubt that Truman was in many ways one of the great Presidents of the twentieth century, but the RFC controversy was simply one of his weak moments. Robert J. Donovan's chapter in *Tumultuous Years*, 332-339, is more objective and accurate than McCullough's treatment, which is too apologetic for the President.

7. U.S. Congress. Senate. Committee on Banking and Currency. *Study of Reconstruction Finance Corporation: Favoritism and Influence*, S. Report 76, Eighty-Second Congress. First Session, 1951.

8. *Public Papers of the Presidents, Harry S. Truman*, 1951, at 144-146.

9. Johnson and Gwertzman, 122.

10. Donovan, *Tumultuous Years*, 337.

11. Text of Richard M. Nixon's "Checkers" speech in *New York Times*, September 24, 1952, at 1.

12. Donovan, *Tumultuous Years*, 334.

13. President Harry S. Truman to Clark M. Clifford, April 27, 1951, President's Secretary's File, Clifford folder, Harry S. Truman Library.

14. See Dumas Malone, *Jefferson the President* (two volumes on Jefferson's Presidency in Mr. Malone's six-volume magisterial biography of Jefferson, published 1947-1981).

15. Oral History Transcript, John Steelman, Harry S. Truman Library.

16. U.S. Congress. Senate. Committee on Banking and Currency. Subcommittee on Reconstruction Finance Corporation. *Study of Reconstruction Finance Corporation: Lending Policy, Parts II and III*, Hearings before the Subcommittee pursuant to S. Res. 219, Eighty-Second Congress, First Session, 1951, at 1710-16, 1759-76.

17. Paul H. Douglas, *The Memoirs of Paul H. Douglas*, (New York: 1971), 224.

18. RFC hearings, at 1811-27.

19. Ibid.

20. *New York Times*, August 21, 1951, at 1.

21. Donovan, *Tumultuous Years*, 338.

22. Walter Lippmann, *Washington Post*, March 29, 1951.

23. *Buffalo Evening News*, March 8, 1951.

24. Ibid.

25. Seib and Otten, "Fulbright: The Arkansas Paradox," *Harper's*, June, 1956.

26. *Congressional Record*, Senate, March 27, 1951.

27. Ibid.

28. *Arkansas Gazette*, May 20, 1952.

29. *Congressional Record*, April 8, 1948.

30. As C. Vann Woodward explained in *The Strange Career of Jim Crow* (Oxford, third revised edition, 1974): The phase of Reconstruction "that began in 1877 was inaugurated by the witdrawal of federal troops from the South, the abandonment of the Negro as a ward of the nation, the giving up of the attempt to guarantee the freedman his civil and political equality, and the acquiescence of the rest of the country in the South's demand that the whole problem be left to the disposition of the dominant Southern white people... In the early years of the twentieth century, it was becoming clear that the Negro would be effectively disfranchised throughout the South, that he would be firmly relegated to the lower rungs of the economic ladder, and that neither equality nor aspirations for equality in any department of life were for him." pp. 6-7.

31. Karl Meyer, Introduction to *Fulbright of Arkansas*, at xxvi; John Kenneth Galbraith, The Great Crash (1955); Woods, 199.

32. Johnson and Gwertzman, at 149-150.

33. Ibid., at 119.

Chapter III

28. Haynes Johnson and Bernard M. Gwertzman, *Fulbright the Dissenter* (1968), at 151.

29. "Your Role in America's Future," Southwestern Bulletin, Speech by Senator J. William Fulbright at Southwestern at Memphis, July 1948, J. William Fulbright Papers, University of Arkansas, Fayetteville, Arkansas.

29a. McCullough, Truman, 586-589.

29b. Johnson and Gwertzman, 91; Woods, 117-118, 149-151, McCullough, Truman, at 702. In addition, in 1950 Fulbright had supported an amendment to a military appropriations bill aimed at allowing individual soldiers to decide whether they would serve in an integrated unit.

30. Lester, supra note 15, at 206.

31. Id.

32. Richard Yates, "Arkansas: Independent and Unpredictable," in *The Changing Politics of the South*, William Havard, ed., (1972), at 260.

33. Hays, *Southern Moderate*, supra note 12, at 82.
34. *Id.* At 86.
35. "Congressmen Express Temperance," *Arkansas Gazette*, May 18, 1954, 6A.
36. *Id.*
37. "Cherry Says Arkansas to Meet Requirements," *Arkansas Gazette*, at 1.
38. J. William Fulbright to Mrs. R. A. Cameron, April 6, 1955, Fulbright Papers.
39. *Id.*
40. Johnson and Gwertzman, supra note 28, at 151.
41. Jack Bass and Walter Devries, *The Transformation of Southern Politics: Social Change and Political Consequences Since 1945* (1977) at 91.
42. J. William Fulbright to W. C. Rodgers, June 27, 1955, Fulbright Papers.
43. *Brown v. Board of Education (Brown II)* 349 U.S. 294 (195).
44. J. William Fulbright to W. C. Rodgers, June 27, 1955, Fulbright Papers.
45. *Id.*
46. C. Vann Woodward, *The Strange Career of Jim Crow*, (Third Revised Edition, 1974), at 154.
47. *Id.*
48. George Yarbrough, William Duerson, and Joe Foster to J. William Fulbright, June 22, 1955, Fulbright Papers.
49. J. William Fulbright to William Duerson, George Yarbrough, and Joe Foster, June 22, 1955, Fulbright Papers.
50. *Id.*
51. Wallace, supra note 20, at 218.
52. *Id.*
52a. Interview with J. William Fulbright, Columbia University, 1956, Fulbright Papers (Fulbright stipulated that this interview would only become public five years after his death; permission was obtained from Mrs. Harriet Mayor Fulbright to refer to it.)
53. Timothy Donovan, "Francis Adams Cherry," in *The Governors of Arkansas*, supra note 15, at 214.
54. Wallace, supra note 20, at 218.
55. *Id.* At 216.
56. *Congressional Record*, February 2, 1954, at 1,103.
57. Charles McCarry "Mourning Becomes Senator Fulbright," *Esquire,* June 1970, at 116-123; Richard Rovere, *Senator Joe McCarthy* (1959) at 38-39.
58. Bass and Devries, supra note 41, at 91.
59. Freyer, supra note 4, at 80.
59a. Woodward, *The Strange Career of Jim Crow*, at 166.
60. Johnson and Gwertzman, supra note 28, at 143-145.
61. Wallace, supra note 20, at 218.
62. Johnson and Gwertzman, supra note 28, at 146.
63. *Id.* at 143.
64. J. William Fulbright, Statement on the "Declaration of Constitutional Principles," Southern Manifesto File, February, 1956, Fulbright Papers.
65. *Id.*
66. Woodward, Jim Crow, at 156.
67. Fulbright statement, supra note 64, Fulbright Papers.
68. *Id.*
69. *Id.*
70. Johnson and Gwertzman, supra note 28, at 145-147.
71. Brock Brower, "Roots of the Arkansas Questioner," *Life*, May 13, 1966 at 106.
72. Theo Epperson to J. William Fulbright, February 6, 1956, Fulbright Papers.
73. J. William Fulbright to Theo Epperson, February 11, 1956, Fulbright Papers.
74. Theo Epperson to J. William Fulbright, February 6, 1956, Fulbright Papers.
75. Brower, supra note 71, at 107.
76. Brower, at 107. Randall Woods states that Fulbright explained to Isaac McClinton, a black businessman from Little Rock, that had he not intervened against the early drafts of the Southern Manifesto, that segregationist statement "would have been much more extreme than it actually was. For the most part, Arkansas' black leadership generally accepted that gloss." Of course, Woods' comment neglects the reality that the Southern Manifesto in final form was an extremist statement. While some blacks may have been more willing to listen to Fulbright's political justifications than others, most of them were quite disappointed. Daisy Bates was more outspoken than many, but most of them agreed with Theo Epperson and the NAACP leaders that Fulbright's signature on the Manifesto was highly disillusioning, and Woods' contention that black leaders "for the most part" generally accepted his "gloss" is dubious.
76a. Author's interview with J. William Fulbright, June 4, 1991.
77. Sherrill, supra note 18a, at 66.
78. Charles Seib and Alan Otten, "J. William Fulbright: Arkansas Paradox," *Harper's*, June 1956.
79. *Id.*
80. *Congressional Record*, March 12, 1956, at 4,460.
81. Sitkoff, supra note 8, at 26.
82. Woodward, *Jim Crow*, supra note 46, at 161.

83. Ashmore, *Epitaph*, supra note 27, at 34-35.
84. Woodward, *Jim Crow*, supra note 46, at 161.
85. *Id.*
86. Johnson and Gwertzman, supra note 28, at 148.
87. Mrs. J. O. Powell to J. William Fulbright, March 15, 1956, Fulbright Papers.
88. Hays, *Southern Moderate*, supra note 12, at 89.
89. *Id.*
90. Woodward, *Jim Crow*, supra note 46, at 162.
91. Freyer, supra note 4, at 92.
92. Bartley, "Looking Back," supra note 5, at 101.
93. Freyer, supra note 4, at 92-98.
94. Bartley, "Looking Back," supra note 5, at 103.
95. *Id.*
96. Bartley, *Massive Resistance,* supra note 24, at 254.
97. *Id.*
98. *Id.* at 255.
99. *Id.*
100. Freyer, supra note 4, at 42.
101. *Id.* at 43.
102. *Id.* at 56.
103. *Id.* at 56-57.
104. *Id.* at 58; *Arkansas Gazette*, August 29, 1956, at 4.
105. Bartley, "Looking Back," at 105-106.
106. *Id.* at 110.
107. Wallace, supra note 20, at 221.
107a. U.S. District Judge William R. Wilson, memorandum to the authors, March 13, 1995.
108. *Id.* at 219.
109. Bartley, "Looking Back," at 108.
110. *Id.* at 109.
111. Carl Brauer, *John F. Kennedy and the Second Reconstruction* (1977) at 3-4.
112. *Id.* at 9.
113. Woodward, *Jim Crow,* supra note 46, at 163.
114. *Id.*
115. Brauer, supra note 111, at 2-3.
116. Freyer, supra note 4, at 95.
117. Alexander, supra note 1, at 199.
118. Sitkoff, supra note 8, at 31.
119. Freyer, supra note 4, at 93.
120. Wallace, supra note 20, at 220.
121. Freyer, supra note 4, at 101.
122. Bartley, *Massive Resistance,* supra note 24, at 262.
123. Freyer, supra note 4, at 92.
124. Bartley, *Massive Resistance,* supra note 24, at 265.
125. Sitkoff, supra note 8, at 31.
126. Bartley, *Massive Resistance,* supra note 24, at 266.

126a. Fulbright, *The Price of Empire*, at 91.
127. Bartley, "Looking Back," supra note 5, at 115.
128. Freyer, supra note 4, at 116.
129. Sitkoff, supra note 8, at 30; Brauer, supra note 111, at 4; Wallace, supra note 20, at 221.
130. Wallace, supra note 20, at 221.
131. Bartley, "Looking Back," supra note 5, at 116.
132. Sherrill, supra note 18a, at 89.
133. *Id.*
133a. Fulbright, *The Price of Empire*, at 91.
134. Freyer, supra note 4, at 19.
135. *Congressional Record*, July 23, 1957; Russell Warren Howe and Sarah Troutt, "J. William Fulbright: Reflections on a Troubled World," *Saturday Review*, January 11, 1975, at 19.
136. Brauer, supra note 111, at 10.
137. *Congressional Record*, July 23, 1957, at 12,448.
137a. Woods, 229-233.
137a. Harry S. Ashmore, *Civil Rights and Wrongs: A Memoir of Race and Politics, 1944-1994* (New York: 1994), at 130.
137b. Id.
137c. Id.
138. Alexander, supra note 1, at 197.
139. Freyer, supra note 4, at 119.
140. *Id.* at 106.
141. Hays, *Southern Moderate,* supra note 12, at 151.
142. Freyer, supra note 4, at 144.
143. Sitkoff, supra note 8, at 31.
144. Hays, *Southern Moderate,* supra note 12, at 174.
145. Freyer, supra note 4.
146. Brower, supra note 71, at 106.
147. Johnson and Gwertzman, supra note 28, at 153.
148. Ashmore, *Arkansas*, at 152.
149. Johnson and Gwertzman, supra note 28, at 152.
150. "Arkansas: Just Plain Bill," *Time*, November 3, 1961, at 18.
151. Johnson and Gwertzman, supra note 28, at 152.
152. *Id.* at 152.
153. Charles Johnston to J. William Fulbright, October 25, 1957, Fulbright Papers.
154. J. William Fulbright to Charles Johnson, October 28, 1957, Fulbright Papers.
155. *Id.*
156. J. William Fulbright to Fred Pickens, October 28, 1957, Fulbright Papers.
157. *Id.*
157a. Fulbright, *The Price of Empire*, at 91.
157a. Wallace, supra note 20, at 221.
158. Les Gibbs to J. William Fulbright, September 20, 1957, Fulbright Papers.

159. *Id.*
160. J. William Fulbright to Les Gibbs, September 18, 1959, Fulbright Papers.
161. Johnson and Gwertzman, supra note 28.
162. Ben F. Jordan to Orval E. Faubus, September 24, 1957, Orval E. Faubus Paper, University of Arkansas, Fayetteville, Arkansas.
163. *Id.*
164. *Id.*
165. Roy White to Orval E. Faubus, September 5, 1957, Faubus Papers.
166. *Id.*
167. Harold Caplin to Winthrop Rockefeller, September 17, 1957, Faubus Papers.
168. *Id.*
169. *Id.*
170. Freyer, supra note 4, at 89.
171. *Id.*
172. Bernard Schwartz, *Super Chief: Earl Warren and His Supreme Court—A Judicial Biography* (1983), at 290.
173. Freyer, supra note 4, at 145.
174. *Aaron v. Cooper*, 163 F.Supp. 13 (E.D. Ark., 1958); Schwartz, supra note 172, at 290.
175. Schwartz, supra note 172, at 290.
176. *Id.*
177. *Id.* at 291.
177a. Schwartz, supra note 172, at 275-279.
177b. Woods, 233.
178. Schwartz, supra note 172, 291.
179. J. William Fulbright, *amicus curiae* brief, *Cooper v. Aaron*, August 1958, Fulbright Papers.
180. *Aaron v. Cooper,* 163 F.Supp. 14 (1958).
181. *Aaron v. Cooper*, 257 F2d 33 (85h Cir. 1958) (Gardner, C.J., dissenting).
182. *Id.*
183. Fulbright, supra note 179, *Cooper* brief, Fulbright Papers.
184. Author's interview with Lee Williams, May 30, 1991, Fayetteville, Arkansas.
185. Ashmore, *Arkansas*, supra note 25, at 152-153.
186. Elizabeth Huckaby, *Crisis at Central High, Little Rock, 1957-58* (1980), at 156.
187. Griffin, *Politics and the Supreme Court: The Case of the Bork Nomination*, Virginia Journal of Law and Politics 551, 598 (1989).
188. Schwartz, supra note 172, at 291.
189. *Id.* at 292.
190. *Id.* at 291.
191. *Id.* At 302.
192. Freyer, supra note 4, at 150-151.
193 Schwartz, supra note 172, at 302.
194. *Cooper v. Aaron,* 358 U.S. 1, (1958) (Frankfurter, J., concurring).
195. *Id.* at 20.
195a. Roger K. Newman, *Hugo Black: A Biography* (New York, 1994) at 475-476.
196. *Id.* at 303.
196a. Leflar, *One Life in the Law*, 6-8.
197. Freyer, supra note 4, at 157.
198. Schwartz, supra note 172, at 299.
199. *Id.* at 297.
200. *Cooper,* supra note 194, at 1-2.
201. *Id.* at 3.
202. *Id.* at 19.
203. Schwartz, supra note 172, at 297.
204. Freyer, supra note 4, at 157.
205. *Cooper,* supra note 194, at 19.
206. Schwartz, supra note 172, at 293.
207. *Id.*
208. Sitkoff, supra note 8, at 37.
208a. Newman, *Black,* at 474.
209. Freyer, supra note 4, at 158-159.
209a. Michael B. Dougan, *Arkansas Odyssey: The Saga of Arkansas from Prehistoric Times to Present*, (Little Rock, Rose, 1995), 502-505.
210. *Id.*
211. *Id.* at 131.
212. Hays, *Politics*, supra note 7, at 196.
213. Freyer, supra note 4, at 162.
213a. Charles Johnston to J. William Fulbright, October 25, 1957, Fulbright Papers.
214. *Congressional Record*, May 6, 1958, at 8,108.
215. *Id.*
216. "Fulbright Says Faubus Erred in School Crisis," *Arkansas Gazette*, August 24, 1959, agt 1.
217. *Id.*
218. Sherrill, supra note 18a, at 112.
219. Interview with J. William Fulbright, October 16, 1981, Washington, D.C.
220. "Hays Takes Race 3 to 2," *Arkansas Gazette*, at 1.
221. *Id.*
222. Lloyd M .Conyers to Brooks Hays, October 23, 1958, Hays Papers.
223. "Hays Concedes; State Rights Victory Seen by Alford," *Arkansas Gazette*, November 6, 1958, at 1.
224. Sherrill, supra note 18a, at 109.
225. "Election Officials Distribute Stickers for Alford, But Nobody Seems to Care," *Arkansas Gazette*, November 5, 1958.
226. Hays, *Politics*, supra note 7, at 196.
227. J. W. Fulbright, *The Price of Empire*, at 92 (1989).
228. *Id.*
229. Arthur M. Schlesinger, Foreword to Hays, *Politics Is My Parish*, supra note 7 at ix.
230. J. William Fulbright to Brooks Hays, November

22, 1958, Hays Papers.

231. Bill Penix to Brooks Hays, November 6, 1958, Hays Papers.

232. Dwight D. Eisenhower to Brooks Hays, January 11, 1961, Hays Papers.

233. Richard Milhous Nixon to Brooks Hays, November 18, 1958, Hays Papers.

234. *Id.*

235. Freyer, supra note 4, at 147.

236. July, 1958, gubernatorial election return records, Pulaski County Clerk's Office

237. Gubernatorial primary election results, July 29, 1958, records in office of Secretary of State of Arkansas.

238. Freyer, supra note 4, at 147.

239. "How to Tell a Voter," *Arkansas Gazette*, July 31, 1958.

240. John Ward, *The Arkansas Rockefeller*, (1978) at 115.

240a. Interview with U.S. District Judge Henry Woods, Little Rock, 1995; Jim Lester, *A Man for Arkansas: Sid McMath and the Southern Reform Tradition* (Rose: Little Rock, 1976), 238.

240b. Editor Troutt's comments on Melton and the 1962 campaign came from a telephone interview, Jonesboro, Arkansas, May 23, 1995; Lee Riley Powell, *J. William Fulbright and America's Lost Crusade: Fulbright, the Cold War and the Vietnam War* (Rose: Little Rock, 1988), at 79; Interview with Witt Stephens, Little Rock, May 22, 1991.

240c. Brauer, at 270-271.

240d. *President John F. Kennedy, Public Papers of the Presidents, 1963*, 760-765, 877.

240e. *Arkansas Gazette*, October 6, 1963; to make sure the President read it, Brooks Hays, then a Kennedy administration official, sent a copy to JFK.

240f. Brauer, at 302.

240g. Id., at 302; Lee White to Lawrence O'Brien, October 30, 1963, Lee White Files, John F. Kennedy Library, Massachusetts; Theodore Sorensen and Lawrence O'Brien to President Kennedy, September 10, 17, October 22, 1963, Kennedy Library; Woods, 329.

241. Sitkoff, supra note 8, at 186.

242. "An Analysis of Negro Voting in the General Election of 1966—Governor's Race," Internal Memorandum from Ben Grinage to Lee Williams, September 4, 1968, Fulbright Papers, at 5.

The analysis of black voting in Arkansas was prepared by Ben Grinage, a civil rights activist who joined Fulbright's campaign staff in the 1968 election and later became a full-time staff member in the Senator's Little Rock office.

243. Ben Grinage Memorandum to Lee Williams, Fulbright Papers, at 3.

244. *Id.* at 3-7.

245. *Id.* at 3.

245. Bork, supra note 2, at 77.

246. Sitkoff, supra note 8, at 37.

247. Stone, Seidman, Sunstein, Tushnet, *Constitutional Law*, 2d ed. (1991) at 511, 517.

248. Freyer, supra note 4, at 175.

249. Sitkoff, supra note 8, at 186.

250. Lloyd M. Conyers to Brooks Hays, October 23, 1958, Hays Papers.

251. Stone, et al., supra note 247, at 508.

252. Dworkin, *The Bork Nomination*, 9 Cardozo L.Rev. 101, 104 (1987).

253. Posner, *Bork and Beethoven*, 42 Stan.L.Rev. 1,363, 1,373-1,374, (1990)

254. Freyer, supra note 4, at 20.

255. Bartley, *Massive Resistance*, at 251.

256. Bass and Devries, supra note 41, at 92.

257. Wallace, supra note 20, at 225.

258. Frank Smith, *Congressman from Mississippi*, (1964) at 273.

259. J. William Fulbright, "The Legislator," in *The Works of the Mind*, University of Chicago Press, 1947.

259a. Fulbright's comments on the recent history of the Little Rock school case, interview with J. William Fulbright, Washington, D.C., June 4, 1991; James O. Powell, "Judge Woods Has Left Mark on State," *Jonesboro Sun*, March 10, 1995, at C1.

260. Daniel Yergin, "Fulbright's Last Frustration," *New York Times Magazine*, November 24, 1974, at 14.

261. David Halberstam, *The Best and the Brightest*, (1972) at 41.

262. Martin Luther King, Jr., to J. William Fulbright, November 8, 1965.

263. Arthur M. Schlesinger, Jr., *Robert Kennedy and His Times*, (1978) at 239; "Fulbright Still is Front-Runner for Secretary of State Post," December 8, 1960, at 1; "Rights Unit Opposes Fulbright in Cabinet," December 10, 1960, *New York Times*, at 1; Ronald Steel, *Walter Lippmann and The American Century* (1980), at 523.

Book Four
Fulbright and the Pax Americana

Chapter I
1. Coffin, pg. 141.
2. Ibid., pg. 140.
3. David Halberstam, *The Best and the Brightest* (Greenwich, Connecticut: Fawcett Crest, 1972), pg. 296.
4. Ibid., pg. 505.
5. Ibid.
6. Johnson and Gwertzman, pg. 165.
7. Halberstam, *The Best and the Brightest*, pg. 28.
8. Coffin, pg. 118.
9. Halberstam, *The Best and the Brightest*, pg. 188.
10. Ibid., pg. 717.
10a. "No Colossus of Rhodes," Editorial, March 3, 1960, *Washington Post*, p. A16.
10b. Ibid.
10c. "The Negro Question," December 8, 1960, *Washington Post*, p. A31; "Rights Units Oppose Fulbright in Cabinet," December 10, 1960, *New York Times*, p. 1, p. 14; Schlesinger, *Robert Kennedy and His Times*, p. 239. Schlesinger also wrote, "In later years Robert Kennedy repented his fight against Fulbright." p. 240.
10d. "Fulbright Still Is Front-runner for Secretary of State Post," December 8, 1960, *Washington Post*, p. 1; "Johnson Reported Seeking Stronger Vice-Presidency," November 10, 1960, *New York Times*, p. 1; "Johnson Will Go to Paris Session," November 12, 1960, *New York Times*, p. 10; Ronald Steel, *Walter Lippmann and the American Century* (Boston: Little, Brown, 1980), p. 523.
11b. James O. Powell, interview with J. William Fulbright, December, 1960, Sam Peck Hotel, Little Rock.
11c. Halberstam, *The Best and the Brightest*, p. 41.
11d. David Halberstam, *The Powers That Be* (new York: Dell, 1979), pg. 493.
11d. Regarding Acheson's criticism of Fulbright in 1960, see" The Dilettante," *Nation*, September 7, 1970.
11e. "Arkansas' Interest in Cabinet Selection," November 28, 1960, *Arkansas Gazette*, p. 5A; Schlesinger, *Robert Kennedy and His Times*, pg. 239.
11f. Brauer, p. 77.
12. Schlesinger, *A Thousand Days*, pp. 148-149.
13. Transcript of Voice of America program, "Press Conference USA," broadcast for overseas audience, November 30, 1963; Johnson and Gwertzman, pp. 171-172.

14. Johnson and Gwertzman, p. 172.
15. Fulbright to R.B. McCallum, January 7, 1961, Fulbright Papers.
16. J. William Fulbright, Doherty Lecture, University of Virginia, April 21, 1961, in Meyer, ed., 263-273; Fulbright, *The Arrogance of Power*, p. 46.
17. J. William Fulbright, Memorandum on Propaganda Activities of Military Personnel Directed at the Public, *Congressional Record*, August 2, 1961. Meyer, ed., pg. 221. In 1959, Fulbright had criticized *The Ugly American* (the novel by Eugene Burdick and William Lederer that was made into a movie starring Marlon Brando) as a libel on the Foreign Service and an attack on American foreign aid. The novel depicted incompetent, lazy American officials who were isolated from the common people of Sarkhan, an imaginary southeast Asian country that was threatened by communism in spite of huge U.S. aid. Woods, 277; *Congressional Record*, Senate May 19, 1959.
18. Johnson and Gwertzman, pg. 180.
19. Fulbright, Memorandum on Military Propaganda, in Meyer, ed., p. 228.
20. Coffin, pg. 162.
21. Fulbright, Memorandum on Military Propaganda, in Meyer, ed., p. 225.
22. Ibid., pg. 226.
22a. Johnson and Gwertzman, pp. 18-181; Fulbright, Memorandum Submitted to the Department of Defense on Propaganda Activities of Military Activities, *Congressional Record*, August 2, 1961; Woods, 288.
22b. *Congressional Record*, Senate, June 27, 1962, 11879. In 1960, the United States had suspended the Dominican Republic's sugar quota in order to weaken Trujillo. The Kennedy administration continued this policy, but Pincus' investigation uncovered evidence that the administration was considering changing its policy. Pincus found a contract between the late Trujillo and Igor Cassini, brother of the famous designer, Oleg Cassini. Igor Cassini tried to use his brother's connections with Mrs. Jacqueline Kennedy to get the Dominican sugar quota restored. Upon Pincus' return, Fulbright told him to apprise Robert Kennedy of the evidence he had found in the Dominican Republic, and give the administration six months to indict Igor Cassini. If it did not, the Foreign Relations Committee would

hold public hearings. Robert Kennedy came to Fulbright's office at the time the six-month deadline had almost expired, and advised the senator that Igor Cassini had been indicted. Woods, 307-308.

22c. Schlesinger, *A Thousand Days*, 596; Woods, 312.

22d. Kissinger, *Diplomacy* (Touchstone, New York: 1994), p. 650. Kissinger read into Fulbright's concern about the extent of Vietnamese and Thai internal support for American assistance an excessive concern about "America's legal and moral position." Kissinger's criticism is clearly misplaced; Fulbright was notable, in comparison to most American politicians, for his realistic concern about serving America's vital interests, and he did not suffer from a John Foster Dulles-like "legalistic-moralistic" complex, as Kissinger implies.

22e. Ibid.

23. *Congressional Record*, June 29, 1961, pg. 11,703.

24. Ibid.

25. Ibid.

26. Ibid.

27. Ibid.

28. Fulbright, *The Crippled Giant*, pg. 93.

29. *Congressional Record*, June 29, 1961, pg. 11,703.

30. Ibid., pg. 11,704.

31. Ibid.

32. Ibid.

33. Ibid.

34. Ibid.

35. Ibid., pg. 11,703.

36. Ibid., pg. 11,702.

37. Meyer, ed., pg. 213.

38. Norman A. Graebner, *Ideas and Diplomacy: Readings in the Intellectual Tradition of American Foreign Policy* (New York: Oxford University Press, 1964), pg. 844.

39. Frances Fitzgerald, *Fire in the Lake: The Vietnamese and the Americans in Vietnam* (New York: Random House-Vintage Books, 1972), pg. 162.

40. *Congressional Record*, June 29, 1961, pg. 11,704.

41. Ibid.

42. Ibid.

43. Fitzgerald, pg. 123.

44. Ibid., pg. 139.

45. Ibid., pg. 123.

46. U. S. Congress. Senate. Committee on Foreign Relations. *Supplemental Foreign Assistance: Fiscal Year 1966—Vietnam* Hearings, 89th Congress, 2d Session, January-February 1966. (Washington: Government Printing Office, 1966), pg. 537.

47. *Congressional Record*, June 29, 1961, pg. 11,702.

48. Ibid., pg. 11,703.

49. Ibid., pg. 11,704.

50. Fitzgerald, pg. 141.

51. Ibid., pg. 168.

52. Ibid., pg. 121.

53. Ibid., pg. 114.

54. U. S. Congress. Senate. Committee on Foreign Relations. *Foreign Assistance, 1966* Hearings, 89th Congress, 2d Session, April-May 1966. (Washington: Government Printing Office, 1966), pg. 698.

55. Ibid.

56. Coffin, pg. 165.

57. Powell, 79; "Back in Arkansas," *Newsweek*, November 13, 1961, 24-5; Woods, 296; "Fulbright Says Chaffee Slated for Reopening," *Arkansas Gazette*, September 27, 1961; Interview with Witt Stephens, May, 1990.

58. Johnson and Gwertzman, pg. 182.

59. Halberstam, *The Best and the Brightest*, pg. 209.

60. Johnson and Gwertzman, pg. 229.

61. Halberstam, *The Best and the Brightest*, pg. 217.

62. LaFeber, pg. 229.

63. Coffin, pg. 171.

63a. Television transcript of CBS "Face the Nation," September 15, 1963, Fulbright Papers; William Berman, *William Fulbright and the Vietnam War: The Dissent of a Political Realist* (Kent State University Press: Kent, Ohio, 1988), pp. 12-13.

64. Johnson and Gwertzman, pg. 183.

65. Ibid., pg. 193.

66. Fitzgerald, pg. 164.

67. Memorandum of Conference with the President, November 2, 1963, National Security File, John F. Kennedy Library; Williams, pg. 303; Grantham, *The United States Since 1945*, pg. 187.

68. Fitzgerald, pg 364.

69. Ibid., pg. 364.

70. Johnson and Gwertzman, pg. 205.

71. Fitzgerald, pg. 138.

72. U. S. Congress. Senate. Committee on Foreign Relations. *The Impact of the War in Southeast Asia on the Economy*, Hearings, 91st Congress, April-August 1970. (Washington: Government Printing Office, 1970), pg. 3.

73. Ibid., pg. 316.

74. Ibid.

74a. Memorandum, Secretary of Defense Robert McNamara and the Chairman of the Joint Chiefs of Staff, to the President, October 2, 1963; Summary Record of the 519th meeting of the National Security Council, October 2, 1963, 350-352; National Security File, John F. Kennedy Library.

74b. McNamara, *In Retrospect*, p. 96.
74c. *Public Papers of the Presidents, John F. Kennedy, 1963*, pp. 652, 659, 846, 848.
75. Personal interview with J. William Fulbright, August 4, 1978.
75a. "Fulbright Calls on U.S. to Take Lead in Dispute over Berlin," *Arkansas Gazette*, July 30, 1961; Woods, 315-316; Michael Beschloss, *The Crisis Years: Kennedy and Khrushchev, 1960-1963* (New York, 1991), 278.
76. Ibid.
77. Arthur M. Schlesinger, Jr., *A Thousand Days: John F. Kennedy in the White House* (Boston: Houghton Mifflin, 1965), pg. 902.
78. Ibid., pg. 910.
79. Ibid.
80. Fulbright, *The Arrogance of Power*, pg. 57.
81. Schlesinger, *A Thousand Days*, pg. 913.
81a. Memorandum by J. William Fulbright, July 16, 1958, Fulbright Papers.
81b. Nan Robertson, "Glittering Audience Attends Kennedy Center Opening," *New York Times*, September 10, 1971.
81c. Fulbright to Mrs. John F. Kennedy, January 24, 1964, Fulbright Papers.
82. Johnson and Gwertzman, pg. 184.
83. Ibid.
84. Ibid., pg. 185.
85. Ibid., pg. 186.
86. Ibid.

Chapter II
1. Brock Brower, "The Roots of the Arkansas Questioner," *Life*, May 13, 1966, pg. 107.
2. Kurt Tweraser, "The Advice and Dissent of Senator Fulbright: A Longitudinal Analysis of His Images of International Politics and His Political Role Conceptions," Diss. American University, 1971, pg. 560.
3. *Congressional Record*, March 25, 1964, pg. 6,232.
4. Ibid., pg. 6,232.
5. Ibid., pg. 6,232.
6. Haynes Johnson and Bernard M. Gwertzman, *Fulbright the Dissenter* (Garden City, New York: Doubleday, 1968), pg. 188.
7. Norman A. Graebner, *Cold War Diplomacy: American Foreign Policy, 1945-1975* (New York: D. Van Nostrand, 1977), pg. 214.
8. J. William Fulbright, *Old Myths and New Realities* (New York: Vintage, 1964), pg. 44.
9. Tweraser, "The Advice and Dissent of Senator Fulbright," pg. 567.
9a. McNamara, *In Retrospect*, pp. 115-116, 102-103.
10. Fulbright, *Old Myths and New Realities*, pg. 8.

11. Ibid., pg. 8.
12. Ibid., pg. 9.
13. Ibid., pg. 10.
14. Ibid., pg. 10.
15. *Congressional Record*, March 25, 1964, pg. 6,230:
16. Ibid., pg. 6,230.
17. Johnson and Gwertzman, pg. 187.
18. Walter Lippman, "A Senator Speaks Out," *Newsweek*, April 13, 1964, pg. 19.
19. Johnson and Gwertzman, pg. 187.
20. Ibid., pg. 187.
21. J. William Fulbright, *The Crippled Giant: American Foreign Policy and Its Domestic Consequences* (New York: Vintage, 1972), pg. 24.
22. Ibid., pg. 24.
23. Ibid., pg. 24.
24. Fulbright, *Old Myths and New Realities*, pg. 44.
25. *Congressional Record*, March 25, 1964, pg. 6,231.
26. Ibid., pg. 6,232.
27. Ibid., pg. 6,232.
28. Ibid., pg. 6,232.
29. J. William Fulbright, "Old Myths and New Realities", in *Ideas and Diplomacy: Readings in the Intellectual Tradition of American Foreign Policy*, edited with commentary by Norman A. Graebner (New York: Oxford University Press, 1964), pg. 868.
30. U.S. Congress. Senate. Committee on Foreign Relations. *Supplemental Foreign Assistance: Fiscal Year 1966—Vietnam.* Hearings, 89th Congress, 2d Session, on S. 2793, To Amend Further the Foreign Assistance Act of 1961, As Amended, January 28, February 4, 8, 10, and 18, 1966. (Washington: Government Printing Office, 1966), pg. 56.
31. J. William Fulbright, *The Arrogance of Power* (New York: Vintage, 1966), pg. 52.
32. Johnson and Gwertzman, pg. 195.
33. Coffin, pg. 216.
34. U. S. Congress. Senate. Committee on Foreign Relations and Committee on Armed Serviced. *Southeast Asia Resolution.* Joint Hearing on a Joint Resolution to Promote the Maintenance of International Peace and Security in Southeast Asia. 88th Congress, 2d. Session August 6, 1964. (Washington: Government Printing Office, 1966), pg. 1.
35. Coffin, pg. 216.
36. U. S. Congress. Senate. *Southeast Asia Resolution,* pg. 3.
37. Johnson and Gwertzman, pg. 227.
38. U. S. Congress. Senate. *Southeast Asia Resolution,* pg. 5.
39. Ibid., pg. 1.

40. Johnson and Gwertzman, pg. 194.
41. U. S. Congress. Senate. *Southeast Asia Resolution*, pg. 7.
42. Ibid., pg. 18.
43. Ibid., pg. 10.
44. Ibid., pg. 13.
45. Ibid., pg. 16.
46. Walter LaFeber, *America, Russia, and the Cold War, 19455-1971* (New York: John Wiley and Sons, 1972), pg 250.
47. U. S. Congress. Senate. *Southeast Asia Resolution*, pg. 16.
48. *Congressional Record*, August 6, 1964, pg. 18,402.
49. Neil Sheehan, et al., *The Pentagon Papers* (New York: Bantam, 1971), pg. 265.
50. LaFeber, pg. 250.
51. U. S. Congress. Senate. *Supplemental Foreign Assistance: Fiscal Year 1966—Vietnam*, pg. 54.
52. Fulbright, *The Crippled Giant*, pg. 190.
53. Doris Kearns, *Lyndon Johnson and the American Dream* (New York: Signet, 1976), pg. 205.
54. LaFeber, pg. 251.
55. Fulbright, *The Crippled Giant*, pg. 188.
56. Ibid., pg. 189.
56a. *Congressional Record*, Senate, July 23, 1964, 16764; *Congressional Record*, June 1, 1965, 12152.
56b. Lyndon Johnson to Fulbright, July 23, 1964, Lyndon Baines Johnson Papers, Lyndon Baines Johnson Library; Woods, 332; Graebner, *The Age of Global Power*, 215; Interview with Fulbright, October 6, 1981.
57. *Congressional Record*, August 6, 1964, pg. 18,406.
58. Fulbright, *The Arrogance of Power*, pg. 52.
59. Johnson and Gwertzman, pg. 190.
60. Ibid., pg. 191.
61. Fulbright, *The Crippled Giant*, pg. 191.
62. Hugh Gregory Gallagher, *Advise and Obstruct: The Role of the United States in Foreign Policy Decisions* (New York: Delacorte Press, 1969), pg. 317.
63. Ibid., pg. 318.
64. Fulbright, *The Crippled Giant*, pg. 182.
65. Ibid., pg. 182.
66. Daniel Yergin, "Fulbright's Last Frustration," The *New York Times Magazine*, November 24, 1974, pg. 78.
67. Fulbright, *The Arrogance of Power*, pg. 52.
68. George C. Herring, *America's Longest War: The United States and Vietnam, 1950-1975*, (New York: John Wiley and Sons, 1979), pg. 123.
69. Ibid., pg. 123.
70. Ibid., pg. 123.
71. David Halberstam, *The Best and the Brightest* (New York: Fawcett Crest, 1972), pg. 506.

72. Fulbright, *The Arrogance of Power*, pg. 51.
73. Halberstam, *The Best and the Brightest*, pg. 506.
74. Yergin, pg. 78.
75. Ibid., pg. 78.
76. Johnson and Gwertzman, pp. 193-199.
77. Ibid., pg. 194.
78. Coffin, pg. 218.
79. Johnson and Gwertzman, pg. 199.
80. Herring, pp. 120-121.
81. Johnson and Gwertzman, pg. 198.
82. Personal interview with J. William Fulbright, August 4, 1978.
83. Walter Lippmann, "In the Gulf of Tonkin," *Washington Post*, August 6, 1964, Sec. A., pg. 21.
84. Tweraser, "The Advice and Dissent of Senator Fulbright," pg. 52.
85. Halberstam, *The Best and the Brightest*, pp. 507-509; Kearns, pg 211.
86. Johnson and Gwertzman, pg. 205.
87. Tweraser, "The Advice and Dissent of Senator Fulbright," pg. 522.
88. Ibid., pg. 566.
89. J. William Fulbright, "The Senate and Foreign Affairs," Doherty Lecture, University of Virginia, April 21, 1961, in Meyer, ed., pg. 266.
90. Ibid., pg. 266.
91. Halberstam, *The Best and the Brightest*, pg. 522.
92. Fulbright, *The Arrogance of Power*, pg. 44.
93. Fulbright, *The Crippled Giant*, pg. 229.
94. Johnson and Gwertzman, pg. 190; Halberstam, *The Best and the Brightest*, pg. 489.
95. Halberstam, *The Best and the Brightest*, pg. 489.
96. Herring, pg. 108.
97. Halberstam, *The Best and the Brightest*, pg. 489.
98. Yergin, pg. 77.
99. Ibid., pg. 77.
100. Kearns, pg. 205.
101. Tweraser, "The Advice and Dissent of Senator Fulbright," pg. 578.
102. Johnson and Gwertzman, pg. 205; Personal interview with J. William Fulbright, August 4, 1978.
103. Personal interview with J. William Fulbright, May 21, 1981.
104. Johnson and Gwertzman, pg. 232.
105. Fulbright, *The Crippled Giant*, pg. 197.
106. Herring, pg. 122, pp. 143-144.
107. Fulbright, *The Crippled Giant*, pg. 189
108. Halberstam, *The Best and the Brightest*, pg. 512.
109. Walter Lippman, "In the Gulf of Tonkin," *Washington Post*, August 6, 1964, Sec. A, pg. 21.
110. *Congressional Record*, August 6, 1964, pg. 18,403.
110a. McNamara, *In Retrospect*, p. 128.

110b. Ibid., p. 141.

110c. Ibid., pp. 129-134.

110d. Ibid., 128-129.

110e. Ibid., pp. 142-143.

111. Lloyd E. Ambrosius, "The Goldwater-Fulbright Controversy," *The Arkansas Historical Quarterly*, Volume XXIX, Number 3, Autumn, 1970, pg. 268.

112. Ibid., pg. 268.

113. Ibid., pg. 268.

114. Ibid., pg. 267.

115. Ibid., pg. 269.

Chapter III.

1. Tweraser, "The Advice and Dissent of Senator Fulbright," pg. 526.

2. Johnson and Gwertzman, pg. 191.

3. Ronald Steel, *Walter Lippmann and the American Century* (Boston: Little, Brown, and Company, 1980), pg. 50; Halberstam, *The Powers That Be*, pg. 696; Personal interview with J. William Fulbright, May 21, 1981.

4. Johnson and Gwertzman, pg. 191.

5. J. William Fulbright, letter to the author, October 1, 1981.

6. Halberstam, *The Powers That Be*, pg. 687.

7. Personal interview with J. William Fulbright, August 4, 1978.

8. Fulbright, *The Arrogance of Power*, pg. 49.

9. Sheehan, et al., pg. xiii.

10. Ibid., pg. 363.

11. Ibid., pg. 363.

12. Ibid., pg. 363.

13. Johnson and Gwertzman, pg. 192.

14. Ibid., pg. 192.

15. *Congressional Record*, January 6, 1965, pg. 315.

16. J. William Fulbright, Letter to President Lyndon Johnson, March 3, 1965, J. William Fulbright Papers, University of Arkansas Library, Fayetteville, Arkansas.

17. Tweraser, "The Advice and Dissent of Senator Fulbright," pg. 582.

18. Coffin, pg. 243.

19. *Congressional Record*, January 6, 1965, pg. 315.

20. Ibid., pg. 317.

21. Ibid., pg. 317.

22. Ibid., pg. 318.

23. Ibid., pg. 318.

24. Ibid., pg. 318.

25. Ibid., pg. 318.

26. Ibid., pg. 318.

27. Yergin, pg. 78.

28. Tweraser, "The Advice and Dissent of Senator Fulbright," pg. 608.

29. Yergin, pg. 78.

30. *Congressional Record*, January 6, 1965, pg. 315.

31. Ibid., pg. 315.

32. *Congressional Record*, January 12, 1965, pg. 538.

33. Tweraser, "The Advice and Dissent of Senator Fulbright," pg. 579.

34. *Congressional Record*, January 12, 1965, pg. 539.

35. Ibid., pg. 539.

36. Ibid., pg. 539.

37. Coffin, pg. 226.

38. *Congressional Record*, January 12, 1965, pg. 539.

39. Ibid., pg. 541.

40. Johnson and Gwertzman, pg. 201.

41. Ibid., pg. 202.

42. Ibid., pg. 202.

43. Tweraser, "The Advice and Dissent of Senator Fulbright," pg. 578.

44. Johnson and Gwertzman, pg. 202.

45. "Foreign Relations: The Ultimate Self-Interest," *Time*, January 22, 1965, pp. 14-18.

46. Ibid., pg. 15.

47. Tweraser, "The Advice and Dissent of Senator Fulbright," pg. 579.

48. Johnson and Gwertzman, pg. 201.

49. Kearns, pg. 272.

50. Halberstam, *The Best and the Brightest*, pg. 628.

51. Johnson and Gwertzman, pg. 203.

52. Personal interview with J. William Fulbright, February 6, 1981.

53. "Fulbright Urges U.S. to Drop Cold War Stress," Washington Post, January 17, 1965, Sec. A, pg. 4.

54. Ibid., pg. 4.

55. Ibid., pg. 4.

56. Ibid., pg. 4.

57. David Halberstam, *The Powers That Be* (new York: Dell, 1979), pg. 696.

58. Walter Lippmann, "The Johnson Beginning," *Washington Post*, February 2,1965, Sec A, pg. 11.

59. Ibid., pg. 11.

60. Ibid., pg. 11.

61. Ibid., pg. 11.

62. Walter Lippmann, "The Principle of the Great Society," *Washington Post*, January 12, Sec A, pg. 13.

63. Kearns, pg. 222.

64. Halberstam, *The Powers That Be*, pg. 763.

65. Herring, pg. 129.

66. Ibid., pg. 130.

67. Ibid., pg. 130.

68. Ibid., pg. 127.

69. Ibid., pg. 128.

70. Sheehan, et al, pg. 363.

71. Halberstam, *The Best and the Brightest*, pg. 646.

72. Ibid., pg. 632.

73. Ibid., pg. 632.
74. Personal interview with J. William Fulbright, February 6, 1981.
75. Halberstam, *The Best and the Brightest*, pg. 632.
76. Ibid., pg. 633.
77. Tweraser, "The Advice and Dissent of Senator Fulbright," pg. 580.
78. Ibid., pg. 580.
79. Halberstam, *The Best and the Brightest*, pg. 728.
80. Ibid., pg. 729.
81. Ibid., pg. 279.
82. Yergin, pg. 80.
83. Personal interview with J. William Fulbright, February 6, 1981.
84. Johnson and Gwertzman, pg 233.
85. Letter received from J. William Fulbright, November 2, 1978.
86. Personal interview with Carl Marcy, August 4, 1978.
87. Carroll Kilpatrick, "Peace Talks Urged by Thant," *Washington Post*, February 13, 1965, Sec. A., pg. 1.
88. Ibid., pg. 1.
89. Ibid., pg. 11.
90. Ibid., pg. 11.
91. Ibid., pg. 1.
92. Ibid., pg. 1.
93. Drew Pearson, "Side-Door to Viet-Nam," *Washington Post*, February 21, 1965, Sec. E, pg. 7.
94. John Chamberlain, "Churchillian Voice of Tom Dodd," *Washington Post*, February 23, 1965, Sec. A, pg. 18.
95. "Fulbright Red Policy Ridiculed by Dirksen," *Arkansas Gazette*, March 7, 1965, Sec. A, pg. 3.
96. Yergin, pg. 78.
97. J. William Fulbright, Letter to President Lyndon Baines Johnson, March 3, 1965, J. William Fulbright Papers, University of Arkansas Library, Fayetteville, Arkansas.
98. Ibid.
99. Ibid.
100. Johnson and Gwertzman, pg. 204.
101. Coffin, pg. 242.
102. Johnson and Gwertzman, pg. 204.
103. Tweraser, "The Advice and Dissent of Senator Fulbright," pg. 579.
104. Johnson and Gwertzman, pg. 204.
105. *Meet the Press*, produced by Lawrence E. Spivak, guest: Senator J. W. Fulbright, National Broadcasting Company, March 14, 1965, pg. 2.
106. Ibid., pg. 9.
107. "Fulbright Red Policy Ridiculed by Dirksen," *Arkansas Gazette*, March 7, 1965, Sec. A., pg. 5.

108. *Meet the Press,* March 14, 1965, pg. 3.
109. Ibid., pg. 4.
110. Ibid., pg. 6.
111. Ibid., pg. 5.
112. Ibid., pg. 3.
113. Tweraser, "The Advice and Dissent of Senator Fulbright," pg. 579.
114. *Meet the Press*, March 14, 1965, pg. 1.
115. Ibid., pg. 1.
116. Ibid., pg. 2.
117. Ibid., pg. 3.
118. Ibid., pg. 3.
119. Halberstam, *The Best and the Brightest*, pg. 507.
120. Tweraser, "The Advice and Dissent of Senator Fulbright," pg. 580.
121. Herring, pg. 132.
122. Halberstam, *The Powers That Be*, pg. 699.
123. Johnson and Gwertzman, Pg. 219.
124. Halberstam, *The Powers That Be*, pg. 697.

Chapter IV

1. Warren Unna, "Aid Bill Task Is Given up by Fulbright," *Washington Post*, December 24, Sec. A, pg. 1.
2. William S. White, "Schoolboy Antics," *Washington Post*, February 1, 1965, Sec. A, pg. 16.
3. Walter Lippman, "Money and Foreign Policy," *Washington Post*, March 9, 1965, Sec. A, pg. 17.
4. Ibid., pg. 17.
5. Warren Unna, "Aid Bill Task Is Given up by Fulbright," *Washington Post*, December 24, 1965, Sec. A, pg. 10.
6. Rowland Evans and Robert Novak, "Foreign Aid by Consensus," *Washington Post*, February 8, 1965, Sec. A, pg. 17.
7. U. S. Congress. Senate. Committee on Foreign Relations. *Foreign Assistance, 1965*. Hearing, 89th Congress, 1st Sess., on the Foreign Assistance Program, March 9, 10, 12, 15, 17, 19, 22, 23, 24, 25, 29, and April 7, 1965. (Washington: Government Printing Office, 1965), pg. 168.
8. Ibid., pg. 169.
9. Ibid., pg. 169.
10. Ibid., pg. 169.
11. Ibid., pg. 164.
12. Ibid., pg. 168.
13. Ibid., pg. 169.
14. Ibid., pg. 645.
15. Ibid., pg. 646.
16. Ibid., pg. 647.
17. Ibid., pg. 645.
18. Ibid., pg. 645.

19. Ibid., pg. 646.
20. Ibid., pg. 646.
21. Ibid., pg. 648.
22. Herring, pg. 135.
23. U. S. Congress. Senate. *Foreign Assistance*, 1965, pg. 649.
24. Schlesinger, *Robert Kennedy*, pg. 799.
25. U. S. Congress. Senate. *Foreign Assistance*, 1965, pg. 649.
26. Ibid., pg. 649.
27. Ibid., pg. 481.
28. Sheehan, et al, pg. 607.
29. Johnson and Gwertzman, pg. 240.
30. Fulbright, *The Arrogance of Power*, pg. 234.
31. Halberstam, *The Powers That Be*, pg. 706.
32. U. S. Congress. Senate. *Foreign Assistance*, 1965, pg. 319.
33. Ibid., pg. ii.
34. Ibid., pg. 491.
34a. Woods, 367.
35. Johnson and Gwertzman, pg. 205.
36. John W. Finney, "U. S. Plans Step-Up in Troops and Aid for Vietnam War," *New York Times*, April 3, 1965, Sec. 1, pg. 1.
37. "LBJ to Increase Pressure on Hanoi with Troops, Aid," *Arkansas Gazette*, April 3, 1965, Sec A, pg. 1.
38. John W. Finney, "U.S. Plans Step-Up in Troops and Aid for Vietnam War," *New York Times*, April 3, 1965, Sec. 1, pg. 3.
38a. Berman, p. 44.
39. John W. Finney, "U.S. Plans Step-Up in Troops and Aid for Vietnam War," *New York Times*, April 3, 1965, Sec. 1, pg. 3..
40. "'Most Unhappy,' Fulbright Says," *Arkansas Gazette*, April 3, 1965, Sec. A, pg. 1.
41. John W. Finney, "U. S. Plans Step-Up in Troops and Aid for Vietnam War," *New York Times*, April 3, 1965, Sec 1, pg. 3.
42. Tweraser, "The Advice and Dissent of Senator Fulbright," pg. 581.
43. Coffin, pg. 243.
44. Johnson and Gwertzman, pg. 205.
45. Yergin, pg. 78.
46. Ibid., pg. 78.
47. Coffin, pg. 243.
48. Yergin, pg. 78.
49. Fulbright, *The Arrogance of Power*, pg. 150.
50. Ibid., pg. 152.
51. Tweraser, "The Advice and Dissent of Senator Fulbright," pg. 582.
52. Ibid., pg. 582.
53. Coffin, pg. 243.
54. Johnson and Gwertzman, pg. 206.
55. Coffin, pg. 244.
56. Tweraser, "The Advice and Dissent of Senator Fulbright," pg. 582.
57. Johnson and Gwertzman, pg. 206.
58. Ibid., pg. 206.
59. E. W. Kenworthy, "Fulbright: Dissenter," *New York Times*, October 31, 1965, Sec. E, pg. 4
60. "Stopping Raids Might Pay Off, Fulbright Says," *Arkansas Gazette*, April 19, 1965, Sec. A, pg. 1.
61. Personal interview with J. William Fulbright, February 6, 1981.
62. Graebner, *Cold War Diplomacy*, pg. 135.
63. Herring, pg. 136.
64. Rowland Evans and Robert Novak, "Quieting the Peace Bloc," *Washington Post*, April 14, 1965, Sec. A, pg. 21.
65. "Stopping Raids Might Pay Off, Fulbright Says," *Arkansas Gazette*, April 19, 1965, Sec. A, pg. 1.
66. Fulbright Urges Halt in Bombings," *New York Times*, April 19, 1965, Sec. 1, pg. 1.
67. Jack Bell, "Viet Pause Is Urged by Fulbright," *Washington Post*, April 19, 1965, Sec. A, pg 1.
68. Ibid., pg. 2.
69. "Stopping Raids Might Pay Off, Fulbright Says," *Arkansas Gazette*, April 19, 1965, Sec. A, pg. 1.
70. "Fulbright Urges Halt in Bombings," *New York Times*, April, 19, 1965, Sec. 1, pg. 3.
71. "Stopping Raids Might Pay Off, Fulbright Says," *Arkansas Gazette*, April 19, 1965, Sec. A, pg. 1.
72. Ibid., pg. 1.
73. "Fulbright Urges Halt in Bombings," *New York Times*, April 19, 1965, Sec. 1, pg. 3..
74. "Stopping Raids Might Pay Off, Fulbright Says," *Arkansas Gazette*, April 19, 1965, Sec. A, pg. 2.
75. Ibid., pg. 1.
76. *Congressional Record*, April 28, 1965, pg. 8800.
77. Ibid., pg. 8800.
78. Ibid., pg. 8801.
79. Ibid., pg. 8800.
80. Ibid., pg. 8801.
81. Ibid., pg. 8802.
82. Ibid., pg. 8802.
83. Ibid., pg. 8802.
84. *Congressional Record*, April 28, 1965, pg. 8785.
85. Ibid., pg. 8784.
86. Ibid., pg. 8784.
87. William S. White, "Congressmen Support President," *Washington Post*, April 30, 1965, Sec. A, pg. 27.
88. Ibid., pg. 27.
89. Ibid., pg. 27.
90. Fulbright, *The Arrogance of Power*, pg. 86..
91. Tweraser, "The Advice and Dissent of Senator Fulbright," pg. 591.

92. Fulbright, *The Arrogance of Power*, pp. 89-90.
93. Johnson and Gwertzman, pg. 208.
94. Ibid., pg. 209.
95. Fulbright, *The Arrogance of Power*, pg. 49.
96. Johnson and Gwertzman, pg. 209.
97. Fulbright, *The Arrogance of Power*, pg. 49.
98. Lyndon Baines Johnson, *The Vantage Point: Perspectives of the Presidency, 1963-1969* (New York: Holt, Rinehart, and Winston, 1971), pg. 196.
99. Ibid., pg. 196.
100. Johnson and Gwertzman, pg. 209.
101. Ibid., pg. 210.
102. Ibid., pp. 212-215.
103. Ibid., pg. 210.
104. *Congressional Record*, September 17, 1965, pg. 24,222; Johnson and Gwertzman, pg. 215.
105. Johnson and Gwertzman, pg. 205.
105a. Berman, 38-39.
105b. Fulbright to Harry Sions, June 2, 1965, Fulbright Papers.
106. Schlesinger, *Robert Kennedy and His Times*, pg. 786.
107. Ibid., pg. 786.
108. "Fulbright Urges Vietnam Solution," *New York Times*, May 6, 1965, Sec. 1, pg. 4.
109. Ibid., pg. 4.
110. Ibid., pg. 4.
111. Tweraser, "The Advice and Dissent of Senator Fulbright," pg. 586.
112. "Fulbright Urges Vietnam Solution," *New York Times*, May 6, 1965, Sec. 1, pg. 4.
113. Arthur Krock, "In the Nation: The Stone the Builders Refused," *New York Times*, May 18, 1965, Sec. 1, pg. 38.
114. Ibid., pg. 38.
115. Tom Wicker, "U. S. Raids North Vietnam After 6-Day Lull Brings No Overture from Hanoi," May 19, 1965, Sec 1, pg. 1.
116. *Meet the Press*, produced by Lawrence E. Spivak, guest: Senator J. W. Fulbright, National Broadcasting Company, October 24, 1965, pg. 7.
117. Herring, pg. 136.
118. Tweraser, "The Advice and Dissent of Senator Fulbright," pg. 586.
119. *Congressional Record*, June 7, 1965, pg. 12,733.
120. Ibid., pg. 12,733.
121. Ibid., pg. 12,733.
122. Ibid., pg. 12,732.
123. *Congressional Record*, March 4, 1965, pg. 4,191.
124. U. S. Congress. Senate. Foreign Assistance, 1965, pg. 168.
125. *Congressional Record*, June 7, 1965, pg. 12,734.
126. Ibid., pg. 12,737.

127. I. F. Stone, "Fulbright: From Hawk to Dove," *The New York Review of Books*, January 12, 1967, pg. 8.
128. *Congressional Record*, June 7, 1965, pg. 12,740.
129. Ibid., pg. 12,738.
130. Ibid., pg. 12,738.
131. Ibid., pg. 12,731.
132. Ibid., pg. 12,739.
133. Frances Fitzgerald, *Fire in the Lake: The Vietnamese and the Americans in Vietnam* (New York: Vintage, 1972), pg. 168; Coffin, pg. 236.
134. Bernard Fall, *Last Reflections on a War* (New York: Schocken, 1972), pg. 190.
135. Johnson and Gwertzman, pg. 214.
136. Ibid., pg. 214.
137. *Congressional Record*, June 15, 1965, pg. 13,656.
138. Ibid., pg. 13,656.
139. Ibid., pg. 13,656.
140. Ibid., pg. 13,656.
141. Ibid., pg. 13,657.
142. Ibid., pg. 13,657.
143. E. W. Kenworthy, "Fulbright Urges a Holding Action in Vietnam War," *New York Times*, June 16, 1965, Sec. 1, pg. 1.
144. *Congressional Record*, June 15, 1965, pg. 13,656.
145. *Congressional Record*, January 12, 1965, pg. 539.
146. Johnson and Gwertzman, pg. 214.
147. Yergin, pg. 80.
148. "Foreign Relations: The Ultimate Self-Interest," *Time*, January 22, 1965, pg. 16.
149. Halberstam, *The Powers That Be*, pg. 692; Johnson and Gwertzman, pg. 233.
150. "Foreign Relations: The Ultimate Self-Interest," *Time*, January 22, 1965, pg. 16.
151. Walter Lippmann, "Whom We Support," *Washington Post*, June 17, 1965, Sec. A, pg. 21.
152. Ronald Steel, *Walter Lippmann and the American Century* (Boston: Little, Brown, and Company, 1980), pg. 575.
153. Walter Lippmann, "Whom We Support," *Washington Post*, June 17, 1965, Sec. A, pg. 21.
154. Ibid., pg. 21.
155. *Congressional Record*, June 15, 1965, pg. 13,658; Tweraser," The Advice and Dissent of Senator Fulbright," pg. 588.
156. *Congressional Record*, June 15, 1965, pg. 13,658.
157. Ibid., pg. 13,658.
158. Ibid., pg. 13,658.
159. Ibid., pg. 13,658.
160. "Fulbright Proposal Attacked by G. O. P.," *New York Times*, June 19, 1965, Sec. 1, pg. 12.
161. Ibid., pg. 12.
162. E. W. Kenworthy, "G. O. P. House Leader Urges Bombing Hanoi's Missile Sites," *New York Times*,

July 8, 1965, Sec. 1, pg. 6.

163. Ibid., pg. 6.
164. Neil Sheehan, "Nixon Bids U. S. Press for Victory," *New York Times*, September 6, 1965, Sec. 1, pg. 2.
165. Ibid., pg. 2.
166. Ibid., pg. 2.
167. Ibid., pg. 2.
168. Ibid., pg. 2.
169. Coffin, pg. 257.
170. Ibid., pg. 257.
171. William S. White, "Power Counts: Viet Nam Peacemakers Irrelevant," *Washington Post*, June 23, 1965, Sec. A, pg. 27.
172. Ibid., pg. 27.
173. Howard Margolis, "Fulbright Would Ease Viet Stand," *Washington Post*, June 16, 1965, Sec. A, pg. 1, pg. 20; E. W. Kenworthy, "Fulbright Urges a Holding Action in Vietnam War," *New York Times*, June 16, 1965, Sec. 1, pg. 1, pg. 4.
174. E. W. Kenworthy, "Fulbright Urges a Holding Action in Vietnam War," *New York Times*, June 16, 1965, Sec. 1, pg. 4.
175. Howard Margolis, "Fulbright Would East Viet Stand," *Washington Post*, June 28, 1965, Sec. A, pg. 15.
176. Rowland Evans and Robert Novak, "LBJ and the Peace Bloc," *Washington Post*, June 28, 1965, Sec. A, pg.15.
177. Halberstam, *The Best and the Brightest*, pg. 729; Rowland Evans and Robert Novak, "LBJ and the Peace Bloc," *Washington Post*, June 28, 1965, Sec. A, pg. 15.
178. *Congressional Record*, June 17, 1965, pg. 14,016.
179. Ibid., pg. 14,016.
180. "A Limited Objective in Vietnam," Editorial, *New York Times*, June 17, 1965, Sec. 1, pg. 32.
181. Ibid., pg. 32.
182. Johnson and Gwertzman, pg. 207.
183. *Congressional Record*, July 1, 1965, pg. 15,460.
184. Ibid., pg. 15,460.
185. Ibid., pg. 15,460.
186. Ibid., pg. 15,460.
187. Personal interview with J. William Fulbright, August 4, 1978; Johnson and Gwertzman, pg. 214.
188. *Congressional Record*, July 1, 1965, pg. 15,460.
189. Ibid., pg. 15,460.
190. *Meet the Press*, October 24, 1965, pg. 2; Halberstam, *The Powers That Be*, pg. 699.

Chapter V.
1.   Personal interview with J. William Fulbright, February 6, 1981.

2.   Murrey Marder, "Fulbright Scores Pressure Groups," *Washington Post*, July 26, 1965, Sec. A, pg. 1.
3.   Fulbright, *The Arrogance of Power*, pg. 124.
4.   Murrey Marder, "Fulbright Scores Pressure Groups," *Washington Post*, July 26, 1965, Sec. A, pg. 1.
5.   *Congressional Record*, August 10, 1965, pg. 19,754.
6.   Joseph Kraft, "The United States and Europe," *Washington Post*, September 1, 1965, Sec. A, pg. 25; *Congressional Record*, July 26, 1965, pg. 18,233.
7.   *Congressional Record*, August 10, 1965, pg. 19,755.
8.   Fulbright, *The Arrogance of Power*, pg. 125.
9.   J. William Fulbright, Letter to President Lyndon Baines Johnson, October 12, 1965, J. William Fulbright Papers, University of Arkansas Library, Fayetteville, Arkansas.
10. *Congressional Record*, July 26, 1965, pg. 18,233.
11. Ibid., pg. 18,233.
12. Fulbright, *The Arrogance of Power,*, pg. 63.
13. Ibid., pg. 63; Halberstam, *The Best and the Brightest*, pg. 729.
14. Ibid., pg. 729.
15. Walter Johnson, ed., *The Papers of Adlai E. Stevenson, Volume VIII: Ambassador to the United Nations, 1961-1965* (Boston: Little, Brown, and Company, 1979), P. 833.
16. John Bartlow Martin, *Adlai Stevenson and the World: The Life of Adlai E. Stevenson* (Garden City, New York: Anchor, 1978), pg. 798.
17. Walter Johnson, ed., pg. 723.
18. Ibid., pg. 724.
19. Ibid., pg. 747.
20. Ibid., pg. 747.
21. Ibid., pg. 748.
22. Ibid., pg. 813.
23. Halberstam, *The Best and the Brightest*, pg. 128.
24. Walter Johnson, ed., pg. 830.
25. Martin, pg. 861.
26. Walter Johnson, ed., pg. 765.
27. Martin, pg. 844.
28. Walter Johnson, ed., pg. 836.
39. Martin, pg. 848.
30. Johnson and Gwertzman, pg. 216.
31. Ibid., pg. 216.
32. Lyndon Baines Johnson, pg. 150.
33. Halberstam, *The Best and the Brightest*, pg. 729.
34. Ibid., pg. 729.
35. Herring, pg. 142.
36. Lyndon Baines Johnson, pg. 150.
37. Halberstam, *The Best and the Brightest*, pg. 729.

38. Ibid., pg. 729.
39. Herring, pg. 142; Graebner, *Cold War Diplomacy*, pg. 133; Lyndon Baines Johnson, pg. 153; Halberstam, *The Best and the Brightest*, pg. 729.
40. Herring, pg. 140.
41. Graebner, *Cold War Diplomacy*, pg. 133.
42. Tweraser, "The Advice and Dissent of Senator Fulbright," pg. 593.
43. Johnson and Gwertzman, pg. 210.
44. Tweraser, "The Advice and Dissent of Senator Fulbright," pg. 593.
45. Ibid., pg. 594.
46. Ibid., pg. 495.
47. Johnson and Gwertzman, pg. 211.
48. Ibid., pg. 212.
49. Ibid., pg. 216.
50. Ibid., pg. 266.
51. U.S. Senate, Committee on Foreign Relations, *Executive Sessions of the Senate Foreign Relations Committee, Vol. 17, 1965* [The Dominican hearings](Washington: 1995), 491-514, 805.
52. Ibid.
53. Ibid.
54. Ibid.
55. Ibid.
56. Ibid.
57. Ibid.
58. Ibid.
59. Tweraser, "The Advice and Dissent of Senator Fulbright," pg. 595.
60. Ibid., pg. 595.
61. Ibid., pg. 595.
62. *Congressional Record*, August 25, 1965, pg. 21,663.
63. Coffin, pg. 203.
64. Johnson and Gwertzman, pg. 217.
65. Coffin, pg. 206.
66. Personal interview with J. William Fulbright, February 6, 1981.
67. Personal interview with Carl Marcy, February 6, 1981.
68. *Congressional Record*, September 15, 1965, pg. 23,859.
69. Ibid., pg. 23,856.
70. Ibid., pg. 23,859.
71. Ibid., pg. 23,857.
72. Ibid., pg. 23,857.
73. Ibid., pg. 23,858.
74. Ibid., pg. 23,858.
75. Ibid., pg. 23, 858.
76. Ibid., pg. 23,858.
77. Ibid., pg. 23,859.
78. Ibid., pg. 23,855.
79. Ibid., pg. 23,861.
80. Ibid., pg. 23,860.
81. Ibid., pg. 23,858.
82. Ibid., pg. 23,858.
83. Ibid., pg. 23,859.
84. Johnson and Gwertzman, pg. 218.
85. Yergin, pg. 78.
86. *Congressional Record*, September 15, 1965, pg. 23,859.
87. Fulbright, *The Arrogance of Power*, pg. 63.
88. Richard J. Barnet, *Intervention and Revolution* (New York: New American Library, 1968, 1972), pg. 208.
89. Ibid., pg. 84.
90. *Congressional Record*, September 15, 1965, pg. 23,856; Fulbright, *The Arrogance of Power*, pg. 92.
91. *Congressional Record*, October 22, 1965, pg. 28,402.
92. Ibid., pg. 28,402.
93. Ibid., pg. 28,404.
94. Ibid., pg. 28,402.
95. *Congressional Record*, September 15, 1965, pg. 23,862.
96. Ibid., pg. 23,863.
97. *Congressional Record*, October 22, 1965, pg. 23,402.
98. William S. White, "Fulbright's Folly: An Irresponsible Speech," *Washington Post*, September 17, 1965, Sec. A, pg. 22.
99. *Congressional Record*, October 6, 1965, pg. 26,107.
100. *Congressional Record*, October 22, 1965, pg. 28,389.
101. Ibid., pg. 28,389.
102. *Congressional Record*, September 17, 1965, pg. 24,223.
103. I. F. Stone, "Fulbright: The Timid Opposition," *The New York Review of Books*, January 26, 1967, pg. 10; *Congressional Record*, September 17, 1965, pg. 24,223.
104. I. F. Stone, "Fulbright: The Timid Question," *The New York Review of Books*, January 26, 1967, pg. 10.
105. Johnson and Gwertzman, pg. 218.
106. *Congressional Record*, September 17, 1965, pg. 24,224; Johnson and Gwertzman, pg. 218; Lyndon Baines Johnson, pg. 494; I. F. Stone, "Fulbright: The Timid Opposition," *The New York Review of Books*, January 26, 1967, pg. 10.
107. *Congressional Record*, October 22, 1965, pg. 28,386.
108. Ibid., pg. 28,387.
109. Ibid., pg. 28,387.

110. Ibid., pg. 28,387.
111. Ibid., pg. 28,387.
112. Ibid., pg. 28,387.
113. Ibid., pg. 28,387.
114. Walter Lippmann, "Soviet-American Relations," *Washington Post*, September 28, 1965, Sec. A, pg. 15.
115. Ibid., pg. 15.
116. Ibid., pg. 15.
117. Yergin, pg. 78.
118. Johnson and Gwertzman, pg. 218.
119. Yergin, pg. 78.
120. Ibid., pg. 78.
121. J. William Fulbright, letter to President Lyndon Baines Johnson, October 12, 1965, J. William Fulbright Papers, University of Arkansas Library, Fayetteville, Arkansas.
122. Ibid., pg. 1.
123. Johnson and Gwertzman, pg. 220; Fulbright also contacted Jack Valenti, a White House aide, in an effort to restore communication with the President, but LBJ rejected this overture. Jack Valenti to President Johnson, October 19, 1965, White House Central File, Lyndon Baines Johnson Papers, Lyndon Baines Johnson Library, Austin, Texas.
123a. Ibid.
124. Yergin, pg. 78; Personal interview with J. William Fulbright, August 4, 1978.
125. *Meet the Press*, October 24, 1965, pg. 7.
126. Ibid., pg. 3.
127. "Johnson's Stand on Vietnam Raids is Affirmed Again," *New York Times*, October 26, 1965, Sec. 1, pg. 1.
128. Ibid., pg. 1.
129. E. W. Kenworthy, "Fulbright: Dissenter," *New York Times*, October 31, 1965, Sec. 3, pg. 4.
130. Ibid., pg. 4.
131. Ibid., pg. 4.
132. Ibid., pg. 4.
132a. McNamara, *In Retrospect*, 215-216.
133. *Congressional Record*, October 22, 1965, pg. 28,405.
134. Graebner, Ideas and Diplomacy, pg. 864; Tweraser, "The Advice and Dissent of Senator Fulbright," pg. 512.
135. Schlesinger, *Robert Kennedy and His Times*, pg. 781; Tweraser, "The Advice and Dissent of Senator Fulbright," pg. 538.
136. Johnson and Gwertzman, pg. 187.
137. Ibid., pg. 188.
138. Ibid., pg. 187.
139. Walter Lippmann, Preface to *Fulbright of Arkansas: The Public Positions of a Private Thinker*,
ed. Karl Meyer, pg. ix.
140. Johnson and Gwertzman, pg. 189.
141. Walter Lippmann, "Money and Foreign Policy," *Washington Post*, March 9, 1965, Sec. A, pg. 17.
142. Steel, pg. 550.
143. Steel, pg. 557; Yergin, pg. 78.
144. Steel, pg. 566.
145. Ibid., pg. 567.
146. Walter Lippmann, "Soviet-American Relations," *Washington Post*, September 28, 1965, Sec. A, pg. 15.
147. Yergin, pg. 78.
148. Ibid., pg. 78.
149. Ibid., pg. 80.
150. Ibid., pg. 82.
151. Ibid., pg. 82.
152. Fulbright, *The Crippled Giant*, pg. 194.
153. Yergin, pg. 82.
154. Graebner, Cold War Diplomacy, pg. 163.
155. Fulbright, *The Crippled Giant*, pg. 197.
156. Ibid., pg. 194.
157. Yergin, pg. 82.
158. Fulbright, *The Crippled Giant*, 193-197.
159. Ibid., 194.

Chapter VI.
1. Johnson and Gwertzman, pg. 224.
2. Halberstam, *The Powers That Be*, pg. 700.
3. Coffin, pg. 271.
4. J. William Fulbright, Letter to Jack L. Bodie, January 13, 1966, J. William Fulbright Papers, University of Arkansas Library, Fayetteville, Arkansas.
5. Ibid., pg. 1.
6. William A. Williams, *The Tragedy of American Diplomacy* (New York: Delta, 1972), pg. 12.
7. Tweraser, "The Advice and Dissent of Senator Fulbright," pg. 572.
8. Johnson and Gwertzman, pg. 233; Fulbright, *The Arrogance of Power*, pg. 147.
9. Fulbright, *The Arrogance of Power*, pp. 140-150.
10. Johnson and Gwertzman, pg. 232.
11. U.S. Congress. Senate. *Supplemental Foreign Assistance: Fiscal Year 1966—Vietnam*, p. 2.
12. Johnson and Gwertzman, pg. 232.
13. Ibid., pg. 233.
14. U. S. Congress. Senate. *Supplemental Foreign Assistance: Fiscal Year 1966—Vietnam*, pg. 2.
15. Ibid., pg. 53.
16. Ibid., pg. 53.
17. Ibid., pg. 54.
18. Halberstam, *The Powers That Be*, pg. 706.
19. Fulbright, *The Arrogance of Power*, pg. 116.
20. Ibid., pg. 48.

22. Williams, pg. 300.
23. U. S. Congress. Senate. *Supplemental Foreign Assistance: Fiscal Year 1966—Vietnam*, pg. 49.
24. Ibid., pg. 668.
25. Ibid., pg. 545.
26. Johnson and Gwertzman, pg. 235.
27. U. S. Congress. Senate. *Supplemental Foreign Assistance: Fiscal Year 1966—Vietnam*, pg. 400.
28. Ibid., pg. 401.
29. Fulbright, *The Arrogance of Power*, pg. 53.
30. Coffin, pg. 276.
31. U. S. Congress. Senate. *Supplemental Foreign Assistance: Fiscal Year 1966—Vietnam*, pg. 391.
32. Ibid., pg. 577.
33. Ibid., pg. 2.
34. U. S. Congress. Senate. Committee on Foreign Relations. *Foreign Assistance Act of 1968, Part 1—Vietnam. Hearings*, 90th Congress, 2d. Session, on S. 3091, A Bill to Amend Further the Foreign Assistance Act of 1961, as Amended, and for Other Purposes, March 11, 12, 1968. (Washington: Government Printing Office, 1968), pg. 97.
35. U. S. Congress. Senate. *Supplemental Foreign Assistance: Fiscal Year 1966—Vietnam*, pg. 73.
36. Johnson and Gwertzman, pg. 236.
37. Thomas A. Bailey, *A Diplomatic History of the American People* (Englewood Cliffs, New Jersey: Prentice-Hall, 1974), pg. 919.
38. U. S. Congress. Senate. *Supplemental Foreign Assistance: Fiscal Year 1966—Vietnam*, pg. 337.
39. Ibid., pg. 367.
40. Ibid., pg. 393.
41. Ibid., pg. 535.
42. Ibid., pg. 392.
43. Ibid., pg. 367.
44. Ibid., pg. 676.
45. Ibid, pg. 367.
46. Ibid., pg. 235.
47. Coffin, pg. 283.
48. U. S. Congress. Senate. *Supplemental Foreign Assistance: Fiscal Year 1966—Vietnam*, pg. 244.
49. Ibid., pg. 230.
50. Ibid., pg. 299.
51. Ibid., pg. 233.
52. Ibid., pg. 240.
53. Ibid., pg. 617.
54. Ibid., pg. 596.
55. Ibid., pg. 82.
56. Fulbright, *The Arrogance of Power*, pg. 151.
57. Ibid., pg. 152.
58. U. S. Congress. Senate. *Supplemental Foreign Assistance: Fiscal Year 1966—Vietnam*, pg. 367.
59. Fulbright, *The Arrogance of Power*, pg. 155.
60. Ibid., pg. 108.
61. Ibid., pg. 118.
62. U. S. Congress. Senate. *Supplemental Foreign Assistance: Fiscal Year 1966—Vietnam*, p. 663.
63. Ibid., pg. 662.
64. Halberstam, *The Powers That Be*, pg. 706.
65. I. F. Stone, "Fulbright: The Timid Opposition," *The New York Review of Books*, January 26, 1967, pg. 13.
66. Halberstam, *The Powers That Be*, pg. 704.
67. Ibid., pg. 706.
68. Ibid., pg. 706.
68a. "Talk of Killing Fulbright Laid to Minutemen," *Arkansas Gazette*, April 8, 1966; Woods, 416.

Subchapter on China Hearings

4. Louis Harris, "See-It-Through Viet Policy Favored 2 to 1 But Support for Johnson Wanes," Washington Post, February 28, 1966, pg. 1;" Slackening of War Costs LBJ Support, White House Says," *Arkansas Gazette*, March 10, 1966, pg. 1
5. Arthur M. Schlesinger, Jr., *Robert Kennedy and His Times* (New York: Ballantine, 1978), pg. 827.
6. "Slackening of War Costs LBJ Support, White House Says," *Arkansas Gazette*, March 10, 1966, pg. 1.
7. *Congressional Record*, March 1, 1966, pg. 4380.
8. U.S. Congress. Senate. Committee on Foreign Relations. *U. S. Policy With Respect to Mainland China*, March 1966. (Washington: Government Printing Office, 1966), pg. 1.
9. Iriye, ed., "Introduction," *U.S. Policy Toward China*, pg. xiv.
10. Committee on Foreign Relations, *U.S. Policy With Respect to Mainland China*, pg. 99.
11. Ibid., pp. 100-101.
12. Ibid., pp. 101-103
13. "China Expert Suggests U.S. May Be Worrying Too Much," *Arkansas Gazette*, March 11, 1966, pg. 16.
14. Committee on Foreign Relations. *U.S. Policy With Respect to Mainland China*, pp. 98-101; John King Fairbank, *The United States and China*, Fourth edition (Cambridge, Massachusetts: Harvard University Press, 1979), pp. 425-426.
15. Committee on Foreign Relations. *U.S. Policy With Respect to Mainland China*, pg. 98.
16. Ibid., pg. 107.
17. Ibid., pg. 133.
18. Ibid., pp. 107-141.
19. "Fulbright Proposes U.S. Withdrawal for Peace in Asia," *Arkansas Gazette*, March 23, 1966, pg. 1; Committee on Foreign Relations, *U.S. Policy*

With Respect to Mainland China, pg. 139.

20. Committee on Foreign Relations, *U.S. Policy With Respect to Mainland China*, pg. 142.

21. John King Fairbank, *Chinabound: A Fifty-Year Memoir* (New York: Harper and Row, 1982), pp. 396-400; Fairbank, *The United States and China*, pg. 454; Committee on Foreign Relations, *U.S. Policy With Respect to Mainland China*, pg. 142.

22. Committee on Foreign Relations, *U.S. Policy With Respect to Mainland China*, pg. 178.

23. J. William Fulbright, *The Arrogance of Power* (New York: Random House-Vintage Books, 1967), pg. 150; "U.S. Urged to Seek a Moderate China," E.W. Kenworthy, *New York Times*, March 31, 1966, pg. 1, pg. 10; Committee on Foreign Relations, *U.S. Policy With Respect to Mainland China*, pp. 561-614.

24. Committee on Foreign Relations, *U.S. Policy With Respect to Mainland China*; "U.S. Urged to Seek a Moderate China," E. W. Kenworthy, *New York Times*, March 31, 1966, pg. 1, pg. 10.

25. Committee on Foreign Relations, *U.S. Policy With Respect to Mainland China*, pp. 94-96.

26. Ibid.

27. Fulbright, *The Arrogance of Power*, pp. 106-119; Committee on Foreign Relations, *U.S. Policy With Respect to Mainland China*, pp. 94-96.

28. Committee on Foreign Relations, *U.S. Policy With Respect to Mainland China*, pp. 269-290.

29. Stephen E. Ambrose, *Rise to Globalism: American Foreign Policy 1938-1980* (New York: Penguin, 1980), pg. 205; Committee on Foreign Relations, *U.S. Policy With Respect to Mainland China*, pp. 325-328.

30. I. F. Stone, "Fulbright: The Timid Opposition," *The New York Review of Books*, January 26, 1967, pg. 10.

31. Chalmers Roberts, "Any Shift Opposed in China Policy," *Washington Post*, March 29, 1966, pg. 1.

32. J. William Fulbright to Gene Farmer, March 22, 1966, James William Fulbright Papers, University of Arkansas Library, Fayetteville, Arkansas; Robert J. Donovan, *Tumultuous Years: The Presidency of Harry S. Truman, 1949-1953* (New York: North, 1982), pp. 75-76.

33. Committee on Foreign Relations, *U.S. Policy With Respect to Mainland China*, pp. 435-548.

34. Ibid., pp. 505-541.

35. Chalmers Roberts, "Any Shift Opposed in China Policy," *Washington Post*, March 29, 1966, pg. 1.

36. Committee on Foreign Relations, *U.S. Policy With Respect to Mainland China*, pp. 179-268.

37. Ibid., pp. 181-186.

38. Ibid., pg. 182.

39. Fulbright, *The Arrogance of Power*, pg. 149.

40. Haynes Johnson and Bernard M. Gwertzman, *Fulbright the Dissenter*, (Garden City, New York: Doubleday, 1968), pp. 128-141, pg. 239.

41. Committee on Foreign Relations, *U.S. Policy With Respect to Mainland China*, pp. 597-598.

42. Ibid., pp. 551-553.

43. Committee on Foreign Relations, *Supplemental Foreign Assistance, Vietnam*, pp. 392-393; Committee on Foreign Relations, *U.S. Policy With Respect to Mainland China*, pg. 227, pg. 552.

44. Committee on Foreign Relations, *U.S. Policy With Respect to Mainland Chain*, pp. 551-562.

45. Ibid., pp. 551-562.

46. Ibid., pg. 594.

47. Norman A. Graebner, *Cold War Diplomacy: American Foreign Policy, 1945-1975* (New York: D Van Nostrand, 1977), pg. 152.

48. John Kenneth Galbraith, *A Life in Our Times* (New York: Ballantine, 1981), pg. 490; J. William Fulbright, *The Crippled Giant: American Foreign Policy and Its Domestic Consequences* (New York: Random House-Vintage Books, 1972), pg. 24.

49. Committee on Foreign Relations, *U.S. Policy With Respect to Mainland China*, pg. 612.

50. Ibid., pg. 611.

51. Stephen E. Ambrose, *Rise to Globalism: American Foreign Policy, 1938-1980* (New York: Penguin, 1980), pg. 202.

52. Committee on Foreign Relations, *U.S. Policy With Respect to Mainland China*, pp. 609-610.

53. David Halberstam, *The Powers That Be* (New York: Dell, 1979), pp. 688-706.

54. James Reston, "Some Hopeful Stirrings in Official Washington," *Arkansas Gazette*, March 29, 1966, pg. 6; Reinhold Niebuhr, Letter to the editors of the *New York Times*, March 20, 1966.

55. Ibid.

56. Walter Lippmann, "The Dead Hand in Foreign Policy," *Washington Post*, March 24, 1966, pg. 25.

57. Ibid.

58. Fulbright, *The Arrogance of Power*, pg. 57.

59. *Congressional Record*, April 5, 1966, pg. 7,629; Eric Sevareid, "Why Our Foreign Policy Is Failing," Interview with J. William Fulbright, *Look*, May 3, 1966; Kurt Tweraser, "The Advice and Dissent of Senator Fulbright," Ph.D. dissertation, American University, Washington, D.C., 1971, pg. 609.

60. "Rusk Rules Out Policy Change Toward Peking," *Arkansas Gazette*, March 26, 1966, pg. 1.

61. Committee on Foreign Relations, *U.S. Policy With Respect to Mainland China*, pp. 336-337.

62. David Halberstam, *The Best and the Brightest* (New

York: Fawcett Crest, 1972), pg. 719. Fulbright sent another letter to the President in March, 1966 advocating the neutralization proposal for Vietnam. Johnson replied that "until Hanoi and Peking are prepared to permit solutions other than force against South Vietnam and Laos, I see no prospect of achieving the result you have in mind. They won't even talk about what you have in mind." President Johnson to Fulbright, March 22, 1966, National Security File, Country File, Vietnam, Lyndon Baines Johnson Library.

63. Fulbright, *The Crippled Giant*, pg. 63.

64. Henry F. Graff, *The Tuesday Cabinet: Deliberation and Decision on Peace and War under Lyndon B. Johnson* (Englewood Cliffs, New Jersey: Prentice Hall, 1970), pg. 106; George C. Herring, *America's Longest War: The United States and Vietnam, 1950-1975* (New York: John Wiley and Sons, 1979), pg. 181.

65. Lyndon Baines Johnson, *The Vantage Point: Perspectives of the Presidency, 1963-1969* (New York: Holt, Rinehart, Winston, 1971), pg. 152.

66. Schlesinger, *Robert Kennedy*, pp. 838-829.

67. Fairbank, *Chinabound*, pg. 408.

68. Henry Kissinger, *Years of Upheaval* (Boston: Little, Brown and Company, 1982), pg. 426.

69. Doris Kearns, *Lyndon Johnson and the American Dream* (New York: New American Library, 1976), pg. 341.

70. Iriye, ed., "Introduction," U.S. Policy Toward China, pg. xiii.

71. Fulbright, *The Arrogance of Power*, pg. 152; Committee on Foreign Relations, Supplemental Foreign Assistance, Vietnam, pg. 535.

72. Committee on Foreign Relations, *U.S. Policy With Respect to Mainland China*, pp. 328.346.

73. Fairbank, *The United States and China*, pp. 436-439.

74. Kearns, *Lyndon Johnson*, pg. 341.

75. *Congresional Record,* March 1, 1966, pg. 4,404.

76. J. William Fulbright to Arthur M. Schlesinger, Jr., March 15, 1966, Fulbright Papers

77. Fairbank, *Chinabound*, pp. 396-397.

77a. David W. Levy, *The Debate Over Vietnam* (Baltimore and London: Johns Hopkins University Press, 1991), pp. 104-105; there is a discussion of censorship at the University of Arkansas and the Ellis and Loudermilk controversies in Michael B. Dougan, *Arkansas Odyssey: The Saga of Arkansas from Prehistoric Times to Present* (Little Rock: Rose, 1995), p. 516.

77b. Fulbright, *The Arrogance of Power*, pp. 40-43.

77c. Levy, pp. 105-108.

77d. Fulbright, *The Arrogance of Power*, p. 36.

77e. Levy, pp. 103-106.

77f. *Washington Post*, June 14, 1966; Berman, p. 61, pp. 77-78; Ronald Steel, review of *The Arrogance of Power* in *Washington Post Book Week*, February 19, 1967.

The Arrogance of Power

69. Fulbright, *The Arrogance of Power*, pg. 189.

70. Ibid., pg. 192.

71. Ibid., pg. 193.

72. Ibid., pp. 188-197.

73. Ibid., pg. 200.

74. Ibid., pg. 22.

75. Tweraser, "The Advice and Dissent of Senator Fulbright," pg. 575; Fulbright, *The Arrogance of Power*, pg. 9.

75a. S.F.R.C. hearings, *U. S. Policy to Mainland China*, pp. 94-96.

76. J. William Fulbright, Letter to President Lyndon Baines Johnson, May 9, 1966, J. William Fulbright Papers.

77. J. William Fulbright, Letter to President Lyndon Baines Johnson, March 19, 1966, J. William Fulbright Papers.

78. Ibid.

79. Johnson and Gwertzman, pg. 242.

79a. Kearns, *Lyndon Johnson,* pg. 341; *Congressional Record*, March 1, 1966, pg. 4,404; Fulbright to Arthur M. Schlesinger, March 15, 1966, Fulbright Papers.

79b. President Johnson to Fulbright, May 27, 1966, White House Confidential File, Lyndon Baines Johnson Papers, Lyndon Baines Johnson Library.

79c. William Sullivan, *The Bureau: My Thirty Years in Hoover's FBI* (New York: Norton, 1979), pp. 64-65, 235; Berman, p. 68.

79c. Gilbert C. Fite, *Richard B. Russell, Jr., Senator from Georgia* (Chapel Hill, 1991), p. 391; Woods, 464.

79d. Ronald Steel, review of *The Arrogance of Power* in *Washington Post Book Review*, February 19, 1967.

79e. Max Frankel, review of *The Arrogance of Power* in *New York Times Book Review*, February 19, 1967.

79f. Statement of Senator Fulbright at August 16, 1967 hearing on the National Commitments Resolution, Series 72, Box 29, Folder 3, Fulbright Papers.

79g. Berman, p. 74.

80. Fulbright, *The Crippled Giant*, pg. 186.

81. Personal interview with George McGovern.

82. Sheehan, et al, pg. 235.

83. Fulbright, *The Crippled Giant*, pg. 186.

84. Ibid., pg. 182.

85. Ibid., pg. 188.

86. U. S. Congress. Senate. *Supplemental Foreign*

Assistance: Fiscal Year 1966—Vietnam, pg. 58.

87. Sheehan, et al., pg. 268.

88. J. William Fulbright and John Stennis, *The Role of Congress in Foreign Policy*, (Washington: American Enterprise Institute for Public Policy Research, 1971), transcript of Fulbright-Stennis debate, Rational Debate Seminars Series, July 1971, pg. 5.

89. Ibid., pg. 54.

90. Johnson and Gwertzman, pg. 308.

91. Ibid., pg. 308.

92. Ibid., pg. 304.

93. Ibid., pg. 309.

93a. McNamara, *In Retrospect*, pp. 277-280.

93b. Henry Kissinger, *White House Years*, (Boston: 1979), p. 344.

93c. McNamara, *In Retrospect*, p. 277.

93d. Fulbright, *The Crippled Giant*, p. 139.

93e. Fulbright to Irma Jennings, May 22, 1967, Fulbright Papers; Fulbright to R.B. McCallum, June 7, 1967, Fulbright Papers.

93f. *Congressional Record*, Senate, March 16, 1967, 7057; Woods, 447.

93g. "Budget Cuts Imperil Fulbright's Program on Scholar Exchange," *Arkansas Gazette*, September 27, 1968; Woods, 490.

93h. W.W. Rostow to President Johnson, August 3, 1967, National Security File, Lyndon Baines Johnson Library;

94. Ibid., pg. 304

95. The analysis of the war on pages 314 to 315 relies upon statistics found in George Herring's chapter on the war in 1967, "On the Tiger's Back: The United States at War, 1965-1967," in *America's Longest War*, pages 145 to 183.

96. Herring, pp. 145-183.

97. Ibid., pp.145-183.

98. Fulbright, *The Arrogance of Power*, pp. 15-19.

99. Herring, pg. 163.

100. Ibid., pp. 145-183.

100a. Levy, p. 141.

100b. Kearns, p. 366.

101. J. William Fulbright, Letter to President Lyndon Baines Johnson, February 7, 1968, J. William Fulbright Papers, University of Arkansas Library, Fayetteville, Arkansas.

102. Herring, pg. 183.

103. J. William Fulbright, Letter to President Lyndon Baines Johnson, February 7, 1968, J. William Fulbright Papers, University of Arkansas Library, Fayetteville, Arkansas.

104. Sheehan, et al, pg. 607.

105. U. S. Congress. Senate. *Foreign Assistance Act of 1968, Part 1, Vietnam*, pg. 9.

106. Ibid., pg. 13.

107. Ibid.

107a. *The Gulf of Tonkin, 1964 Incidents*. February, 1968; Woods, 476..

108 Herring, pg. 198.

109. Ibid., pg. 199.

110. Ibid.

110a. Herbert Y. Schandler, *Lyndon Johnson and Vietnam: The Unmaking of a President* (Princeton, New Jersey: Princeton University Press, 1977), pp. 213-215.

110b. Ibid., pp. 215-217.

111. Halberstam, *The Best and the Brightest*, pg. 790.

112. Schlesinger, *Robert Kennedy and His Times*, pg. 920. A few days earlier, Johnson met with Fulbright and several other Foreign Relations Committee members in an attempt to soften their criticism of the war, but, of course, the President did not succeed and Fulbright continued blasting the Vietnam policy. Harry McPherson to President Johnson, February 26, 1968, McPherson File, Lyndon Baines Johnson Library; President's Appointment File, Lyndon Baines Johnson Library.

112a. Schandler, *Lyndon Johnson and Vietnam*, pg. 255; Lyndon Johnson, *The Vantage Point*, pg. 409.

113. Sheehan, et al., pg. 610.

114. LaFeber, pg. 272.

115. Sheehan, et al., pg. 612.

116. Ibid., pg. 611.

117. Ibid., pg. 612.

118. Herring, pg. 205.

119. *Congressional Record*, April 2, 1968, pg. 8,569.

120. Ibid., pg. 8,670.

121. Ibid., pg. 8,571.

122. Ibid., pg. 8,569.

123. Ibid., pg. 8,576.

124. Lyndon Johnson, pp. 493-495.

125. *Congressional Record*, April 2, 1968, pg. 8,577.

126. Lyndon Baines Johnson, pg. 508.

127. J. William Fulbright, Letter to President Lyndon Baines Johnson, May 7, 1968, J. William Fulbright Papers, University of Arkansas Library, Fayetteville, Arkansas.

128. Ibid.

128a. Berman, p. 100.

129. Herring, pg. 205; Graebner, *Cold War Diplomacy*, pg. 139; Halberstam, *The Best and the Brightest*, pg. 787.

130. Graebner, *Cold War Diplomacy*, pg. 139.

131. Ibid., pg. 141.

132. Gary Herlick, "J. W. Fulbright, Senator from Arkansas," in *Ralph Nader Congress Project: Citizens Look at Congress* (Washington:

Grossman, 1972), pg. 9.

133. Ibid., pg. 9.

134. Ibid., pg. 9.

135. Ibid., pg. 10.

136. Ibid., pg. 10.

136a. J. William Fulbright, proposal for a peace plank in the Democratic National Platform, August, 1968, Fulbright Papers.

136b. Lewis Chester, Godfrey Hodgson, Bruce Page, *An American Melodrama: The Presidential Campaign of 1968* (New York: Viking Press, 1969), p. 532.

136c. Graebner, *The Age of Global Power*, p. 250.

137. Schlesinger, *Robert Kennedy and His Times*, pg. 827.

138. Graebner, *Cold War Diplomacy*, pg. 139.

139. Schlesinger, *Robert Kennedy and His Times*, pg. 981.

139a. Fulbright to Ernest Gruening, September 2, 1968, Fulbright Papers.

140. Jonathan Schell, *The Time of Illusion* (New York: Vintage, 1975), pg. 18.

141. J. William Fulbright, Letter to General W. Peyton Campbell and Reverend Mouzon Mann, September 8, 1969, J. William Fulbright Papers, University of Arkansas Library, Fayetteville, Arkansas; J. William Fulbright, Letter to Ted Crabtree, June 10, 1969, J. William Fulbright Papers, University of Arkansas Library, Fayetteville, Arkansas; Herring, pg. 217.

142. Fulbright, *The Crippled Giant*, pg. 74.

143. Ibid., pg. 74.

Chapter VII

1. Jonathan Schell. *The Time of Illusion*, (New York: Vintage, 1975), pg. 19.

2. Ibid., pg. 74.

3. Seymour Hersh, *The Price of Power: Kissinger in the Nixon White House* (New York: 1983), at 122-123.

4. Senate Committee on Foreign Relations. *Strategic and Foreign Policy Implications of ABM Systems*, Hearings, 91st Congress, 1st Session, March 1969, at 184-185; William Berman, *William Fulbright and the Vietnam War: The Dissent of a Political Realist* (Kent State University Press, Kent, Ohio, 1988), at 104-107.

5. J. William Fulbright to Fagan Dickson, September 6, 1969, J. William Fulbright Papers; Berman, 107-114.

6. Fulbright, *The Pentagon Propaganda Machine*, (New York, 1971), at 5.

7. Kissinger, *The White House Years*, at 206-210.

8. Id. at 210.

9. Fulbright, *The Crippled Giant*, at 46-47.

10. *Public Papers of the Presidents, Richard Nixon, 1969*, 748-749.

10a. Woods, 525-528.

10b. Interview with United States District Judge William R. Wilson, Jr., March, 1995; Woods, 599.

11. *Congressional Record*, October 1, 1969, pg. 27,864.

12. Ibid.

13. Ibid., pg. 27,865.

14. Ibid., pg. 27,862.

15. Fulbright, *The Role of Congress in Foreign Policy*, pg. 47.

16. Ibid., pg. 47.

17. Kissinger, *White House Years*, at 495.

18. Fulbright, *The Crippled Giant*, p. 183.

19. *Public Papers of the Presidents, Richard M. Nixon*, (Washington: 1971) at 405-410.

20. Fulbright, *The Crippled Giant*, pg. 183.

21. Fitzgerald, pg. 552.

22. Ibid.

22a. Mike Trimble, "Allied Troops' Invasion to Destroy Cambodia, Fulbright Forecasts," *Arkansas Gazette*, June 17, 1970.

23. Berman, at 126.

24. Bailey, pg. 924.

25. U.S. Congress. Senate. Committee on Foreign Relations. *The Moral and Military Aspect of the War in Southeast Asia*. 91st Congress, May, 1970, (Washington: Government Printing Office, 1970).

26. Berman, at 121.

27. U. S. Congress. Senate. Committee on Foreign Relations. *The Moral and Military Aspects of the War in Southeast Asia*. 91st Congress, May 1970, (Washington: Government Printing Office, 1970), pg. 92.

28. Ibid.

29. Ibid., pg. 93.

30. Ibid., pg. 64.

31. Ibid.

32. Ibid., pg. 65.

33. Ibid.

34. Senate. Committee on Foreign Relations. *Impact of the War in Southeast Asia on the U.S. Economy*. Hearings. 91st Cong. 2d Sess., April 15-16, 1970.

35. Herring, at 234.

36. *Public Papers, Richard M. Nixon, 1970*, at 1106-1109; *Washington Post*, December 12, 1970.

37. Berman, at 138; *Washington Post*, December 16, 1970.

38. *Congressional Record*, March 30, 1971, at 8608-

8611.

39. UPI report, June 18, 1971; Berman, at 144-145.

40. Kissinger, *White House Years*, at 729-730, 1021.

41. Fulbright, *The Crippled Giant*, at 83.

42. Schlesinger, *The Imperial Presidency*, at 331.

43. Id.

44. Kissinger, *White House Years*, at 730.

45. Schlesinger, *The Imperial Presidency*, at 332; Herring, at 237; Kissinger, *White House Years*, at 730.

46. Senate Foreign Relations Committee staff study, *Vietnam Commitments, 1961*, (1972); SFRC staff study, *U.S. & Vietnam, 1944-1947* (1972); SFRC staff study, *U.S. Involvement in the Overthrow of Diem, 1963*, (1972).

47. Herring, at 237.

48. *Congressional Record*, 117 (June 16, 1971) at 20216, 21308.

48a. Fulbright, *The Crippled Giant*, 218-220; "Fulbright Panel Opens Probe on Spanish Bases," *Arkansas Gazette*, April 3, 1969.

48b. "Hill Report Cites Greek Repression," *Washington Post*, March 5, 1971; Woods, 590-592.

48c. Woods, 610; Spencer Rich, "Military Aid Voted in Senate; $1.5 Billion Provided for Revived Bill," *Washington Post*, November 12, 1971.

49. Fulbright, *The Crippled Giant*, pg. 194.

50. Ibid.

51. Fulbright, *The Role of Congress in Foreign Policy* , pg. 75.

51a. Interview with George McGovern, August 6, 1978; *Congressional Record*, Senate, February 3, 1971, 1868-9.

52. *New York Times*, September 1, 1970, pg. 4.

53. Ibid.

54. Ibid.

55. Ibid.

56. *Facts on File Yearbook*, (New York: 1970).

57. Fulbright, *The Crippled Giant*, pg. 194.

58. Ibid., pg. 194.

59. Ibid.

60. Ibid, pg. 197.

61. *Congressional Record*, June 25, 1969, pg. 17,232.

62. *Congressional Record*, 119 (February 15, 1973) 4210-12; *Arkansas Gazette*, February 4 and February 16, 1973.

63. Fulbright, *The Crippled Giant*, pg. 216.

64. Ibid.

65. U.S. Congress. House of Representatives, Foreign Affairs Committee, *War Powers Resolution: A Special Report* (Washington, 1973).

66. War Powers Resolution of 1973, 87 Stat. 555, Public Law 93-148, 93d Congress. (H.J. Res. 542, adopted over Presidential veto on November 7, 1973); Laurence Tribe, *American Constitutional Law,* (2d edition, 1988) at 233-237; "War Powers," *Report by the Committee on Foreign Relations*, 92nd Congress, 2nd Sess., No. 92-606, p. 21.

67. Fulbright, *The Crippled Giant*, p. 216.

68. Hamilton, *Federalist Number 69*; Hamilton, *Federalist Number 23*; Dumas Malone, *Jefferson and the Ordeal of Liberty* (Little Brown, 1962), 110-112.

69. *Youngstown Sheet and Tube Company v. Bowers*, 343 U.S. 579 (1952); for the views of Jefferson, Madison and Gallatin during the Jefferson Presidency on the war powers issue, see Dumas Malone, *Jefferson the President, Second Term, 1805-1809* (Little Brown, 1974), 55-56; Schlesinger, *The Imperial Presidency*, pp. 280-282.

70. *Orlando v. Laird*, 443 F.2d 1039 (2d Cir.) *cert. denied*, 404 U.S. 869 (1971); *Mora v. McNamara*, 389 U.S. 934 (1967); *Commonwealth of Massachusetts v. Laird*, 400 U.S. 886 (1970); *Holtzman v. Schlesinger*, 414 U.S. 1304 (1973)(Marshall, Circuit Justice); *Holtzman v. Schlesinger*, 414 U.S. 1321 (1973)(Marshall, Circuit Justice); *Holtzman v. Schlesinger*, 414 U.S. 1316 (1973)(Douglas, Circuit Justice)(effectively staying, for less than one day, the bombing of Cambodia); Tribe, supra note 66, at 234.

While Fulbright was immersed in the controversy over Indochina in 1973, another crisis erupted concerning oppression of American Indians. Sioux members of the American Indian Movement (AIM) seized a Roman Catholic Church and a trading post near Wounded Knee, South Dakota, the place where U.S. troops massacred a large number of Sioux men, women and children in 1890. Russell Means, the leader of AIM, held 10 hostages and became surrounded by a large numbers of law enforcement officers. Means demanded a conference with Senator Fulbright and Senator Kennedy, requesting hearings on the many treaties with American Indians that they alleged had been violated by the United States. Fulbright said he would do anything to help solve the crisis, and stressed that the Nixon administration ought to be devoting more of its attention to such domestic problems as the plight of the American Indians. The Arkansan, however, acknowledged that he was not familiar with Indian issues, and after conferring with the two senators from South Dakota, George McGovern and James Abourezk, decided that the two South Dakota senators and Carl Marcy should go to Wounded Knee. McGovern,

Abourezk and Marcy met with the Indian dissidents, who eventually surrendered to the authorities. For the historical background, see Dee Brown, *Bury My Heart at Wounded Knee, An Indian History of the American West* (New York: Henry Holt and Company, 1970).

The Interior Department often leased reservation lands to corporations for logging, mining and ranching. Militants organized AIM in order to preserve Indian culture, recover ancestral lands, and improve economic conditions among the Indians. The Wounded Knee incident served to focus attention on the plight of the Indians. Half of the nation's Indian population lived on $3,000 a year or less, and unemployment on some reservations exceeded 50 percent. The Interior Department's Bureau of Indian Affairs employed many bureaucrats who contributed little to the improvement of the Indians' condition. Graebner, *The Age of Global Power*, 186-187; "400 Indians Seize 10 Hostages, Ask to See Fulbright, Kennedy," *Arkansas Gazette*, March 1, 1973.

71. *Congressional Record*, June 29, 1973, 12,562.
72. *Holtzman v. Schlesinger*, 414 U.S. 1316 (1973)(Douglas, Circuit Justice)(effectively staying, for less than one day, the bombing of Cambodia); Tribe, at 231.
73. *Korematsu v. United States*, 323 U.S. 214, 248 (1944)(Jackson, J., dissenting); Woods v. Cloyd W. Miller, 333 U.S. 138, 146 (1948)(Jackson, J., concurring); Tribe, at 238.
74. *Congressional Record*, June 29, 1973, 12,560.
75. Id.
76. *Drinan v. Nixon*, 364 F.Supp. 854 (D.Mass.1973); *Congressional Record*, June 29, 1973, 12,560-62; Tribe, at 237.
76a. Tribe, supra note 66, at 234; John Hart Ely, *War and Responsibility: Constitutional Lessons of Vietnam and Its Aftermath* (Princeton: Princeton University Press, 1993); Michael Glennon, *Constitutional Diplomacy* (1990); John Hart Ely, "The American War in Indochina, Part I: The (Troubled) Constitutionality of the War They Told Us About," 42 *Stanford Law Review* 877 (April, 1990), 895-923. We agree with Ely regarding Cambodia and parts of his analysis concerning Vietnam, but we do not agree with all his conclusions.

Ely stated that the "Fulbright Proviso has conventionally been read to have meant that American forces could not bomb Cambodia except to protect our troops or prisoners of war." He also contended that the language, nothing herein shall be construed as authorizing the use of any such funds to support Vietnamese or other free world forces" in military actions in Cambodia or Laos should not be read to include American forces of any sort:

"It seems mildly breathtaking in light of the literature, but some further attention to context demonstrates that the Fulbright Proviso wasn't intended to control the use of American forces in the first place... The common assumption has been that 'other free world forces' included American troops, and certainly in some contexts such language might mean that. However, other sections of the appropriations acts to which the Fulbright Proviso was attached quite pointedly differentiated between 'free world forces' and 'Armed Forces of the United States,' and at one point during the debates Senator Fulbright characterized the Proviso as operative in respect to 'South Vietnamese or other foreign military operations in support of the Cambodian or Laotian governments.'" Ely, at 919.

76b. Ely, "The American War in Indochina, Part I," supra note 76a, at 921-926; Francis Wormuth and Edwin Firmage, To Chain the Dog of War: The War Power of Congress in History and Law (1986) at 214; John Hart Ely, "The American War in Indochina, Part II: The Unconstitutionality of the War They Didn't Tell Us About," 42 Stanford Law Review 1093 (May, 1990), 1146-1148. For Fulbright's comment that if Nixon persisted in the bombing, his action would precipitate impeachment, see *Arkansas Gazette*, July 29, 1973.
77. Fulbright, *The Crippled Giant*, p. 87.
78. *Id.*
79. *Public Papers of the Presidents: Richard Nixon, 1969*, pp. 901-10.
80. *Public Papers of the Presidents: Richard Nixon, 1972*, pp. 550-54.
81. Fulbright, *The Crippled Giant*, pp. 86-95.
82. Id., at 81.
83. Statistics compiled, among others, by Indochina Resource Center, Washington, D.C. in the early 1970s; Fulbright, *The Crippled Giant*, 73-74; Herring, 185, 209.
84. Berman, 153.
85. Fulbright, *The Crippled Giant*, p. 74.
86. *Id.*, 74-106.
87. U. S. Congress. Senate. Committee on Foreign Relations. *The Causes, Origins, and Lessons of the Vietnam War, Hearings*, 92d Congress, May 1972. (Washington: Government Printing Office, 1972), pg. 4.

88. Ibid., pg. 90.
89. Ibid., p. 2.
90. Schell, p. 244, 341.
91. Fulbright, *The Crippled Giant*, pg. 61.
92. Ibid.
93. U.S. Congress. Senate. *The Causes, Origins, and Lessons of the Vietnam War*, pg 159.
94. Ibid.
95. Ibid., pg 159.
96. Ibid., pg. 190.
97. Ibid., pg. 157.
98. Fulbright, *The Crippled Giant*, pp. 48-71.
99. U. S. Congress. Senate. *The Causes, Origins, and Lessons of the Vietnam War*, pg. 187.
100. Ibid., pg. 170.
101. LaFeber, p. 241; for an economic interpretation, see Gabriel Kolko, *The Roots of American Foreign Policy* (Boston: Beacon Press, 1969), p. 89.
102. U. S. Congress. Senate. The Causes, Origins, and Lessons of the Vietnam War, pg. 204-105.
103. U. S. Congress. Senate. Committee on Foreign Relations. *China and the United States: Today and Yesterday*. February 1972 (Washington: Government Printing Office, 1972), pg. 13-19.
104. Ibid.
105. Ibid.
106. Ibid.
107. Ibid.
108. *Public Papers of the Presidents: Richard M. Nixon, 1972* , at 100-106.
109. J. William Fulbright to Edmund Muskie, February 10, 1972, Fulbright Papers.
110. Berman, at 158-159.
111. *Public Papers of the Presidents: Richard M. Nixon, 1973*, at 55.
112. Berman, at 167.
113. *Arkansas Gazette*, April 12, 1973.
114. *Public Papers of the Presidents: Richard M. Nixon, 1973*, at 328-333.
115. Herring, *America's Longest War*, pp. 254-255.
116. J. William Fulbright to Mary Jean Antrim, July 31, 1973, J. William Fulbright Papers, University of Arkansas Library, Fayetteville, Arkansas.
117. Graebner, *The Age of Global Power*, pp. 274-278.
118. Bill Lewis, "Both Expect a Victory in Election: Little New from Bumpers, Fulbright Elicited During ABC-TV Program," *Arkansas Gazette*, May 27, 1974, p. 3.
119. Yergin, p. 88.
120. Grantham, *The United States Since 1945*, p. 292.
121. Herring, p. 251.
122. Senate Foreign Relations Committee Staff Report, *U.S. Air Operations in Cambodia*, April 1973, 93d Congress, 1st Session., at 2-10; Berman, at 171-173; Henry Kissinger, *Years of Upheaval* (Boston: 1982) at 369.
123. Kissinger, *Years of Upheaval*, at 347-369.
124. *Id.*, at 359.
125. J. William Fulbright to Mary Jean Antrim, Fulbright Papers, July 31, 1973.
126. Kissinger, *Years of Upheaval*, at 369; Berman, at 173.
127. *Id;* Kissinger's estimate of three million deaths at the hands of the Khmer Rouge may have been high; other estimates are in the vicinity of 1.2 million. In any event, the Khmer Rouge rank with Hitler and the Nazis among the most vicious murderers in human history.
128. Berman, p. 178.
129. Id., at 179.
130. *Public Papers of the Presidents: Richard M. Nixon, 1973*, at 686; *Arkansas Gazette*, July 29, 1973.
131. *New York Times*, July 12, 1973; Berman, at 179.
132. Kissinger, *Years of Upheaval*, at 427-430; Berman, at 182-183.
133. Senate. Committee on Foreign Relations. *Hearings on the Role of Dr. Henry Kissinger in the Wiretapping of Certain Goverment Officials and Newsmen*, 93d Cong., 2d sess., 1974 (includes Kissinger's testimony in both 1973 and 1974); *Justices and Presidents*, Henry Abraham (Oxford, 1985) 2d ed., at 307; Kissinger, *Years of Upheaval,* at 1246.
134. Kissinger, *Years of Upheaval*, at 116-1123; Richard Nixon to Fulbright, July 12, 1974.
135. Henry Kissinger, *Diplomacy*, (New York: 1994), at 753-755.
136. Fulbright, *The Crippled Giant*, 113-121.
137. Id., 107-133.
138. Id., 123, 132.
139. Id., 136-138.
140. Id.
141. Id.
142. Kissinger, *Years of Upheaval*, at 426.
143. Fulbright, *The Crippled Giant*, 141-143.
144. Id., at 144.
145. Id., at 144-146.
146. Id., 146-149.
147. Fulbright, *The Price of Empire*, at 186.
148. Kissinger, *White House Years*, at 341, 631; Albert Hourani, *A History of the Arab Peoples* (New York: 1991), 416-417; Kissinger, *Diplomacy*, at 739.
149. Hourani, 418; Kissinger, *Years of Upheaval*, at 460.
150. *Congressional Record*, October 9, 1973, 33,262-66; Kissinger, Years of Upheaval, at 490-491.

150a."Report: Fulbright Cooled Off Soviets," *Fort Smith Southwest Times Record*, October 28, 1973; Woods, 650.

151. Hourani, 418-420.

152. Id.

153. Kissinger, *Years of Upheaval*, at 836; Kissinger, *Diplomacy*, at 739-740.

154. Graebner, *The Age of Global Power*, at 275-276; Kissinger, *Years of Upheaval*, at 853; William Safire, *Before the Fall: An Inside View of the Pre-Watergate White House* (New York, 1975) at 486.

155. Interview with J. William Fulbright by James Powell, Little Rock, February 15, 1974.

156. John C. Jeffries, *Justice Lewis F. Powell, Jr.: A Biography* (New York: Scribner's, 1994), p. 385.

157. Id., at 396.

158. Bernard Schwartz, *Super Chief: Earl Warren and His Supreme Court-A Judicial Biography* (New York University Press, 1983), p. 772.

159. Kissinger, *Years of Upheaval*, p. 430.

160. Graebner, *The Age of Global Power*, at 278; Berman, at 194.

161. *Congressional Record*, August 9, 1974, 27,624-25; Berman, at 194.

162. J. William Fulbright, address to the National Press Club, December 18, 1974, Fulbright Papers; Berman, at 195.

163. Berman, at 199; Hersh, *The Price of Power,* 122-123.

164. *Congressional Record*, December 19, 1974, 41,075-76.

165. Senate. Committee on Foreign Relations. *Foreign Assistance Authorization*, Hearings on S. 3394, 93d Congress, 2d Session, June 7-July 25, 1974.

166. Herring, 261-262; Graebner, *The Age of Global Power*, at 283.

Book Five
Fulbright, Civil Rights and the Supreme Court

1. Johnson and Gwertzman, pp. 146-149; Interview with J. William Fulbright, Washington, D.C., October 16, 1981.

2. Interview with Lee Williams, Fayetteville, Arkansas, May 24, 1991.

3. J. William Fulbright, *The Price of Empire* (New York: Pantheon, 1989), pg. 94.

4. J. William Fulbright, "The Price of Empire," address to the American Bar Association, August 1967, in Honolulu, reprinted in Johnson and Gwertzman, *Fulbright*, pp. 303-311. Fulbright's speeches always received substantial coverage in Arkansas through wire services or Washington correspondents of the state's papers, so that the location of his speeches was not important. Politics was a popular subject in the state, and politician's speeches received prominent coverage in the *Arkansas Gazette*, the conservative *Arkansas Democrat* (the state's second largest paper), the *Jonesboro Sun* and *Pine Bluff Commercial* in east Arkansas, Fayetteville's *Northwest Arkansas Times*, (which the Fulbright family owned during his earlier career), and other papers.

5. Johnson and Gwertzman, *Fulbright*, pg. 191; Interview with J. William Fulbright, November 17, 1981.

6. "Senate Confirms Marshall," August 31, 1967, *Arkansas Democrat*, pg. 1.

7. Mrs. Claude E. Haswell to J. William Fulbright, June 1967, Fulbright Papers.

8. George Kelley to J. William Fulbright, June 1967, Fulbright Papers.

9. "Thurgood Marshall to the High Court," Editorial, June 15, 1967, *Arkansas Gazette*, pg. 6A.

10. "Mr. Justice Marshall," Editorial, June 14, 1967, *Pine Bluff Commercial*, pg. 4.

11. J. William Fulbright to Wiley Branton, June 28, 1967, Fulbright Papers.

12. Carl M. Brauer, *John F. Kennedy and the Second Reconstruction* (New York: Columbia University Press, 1977), pg. 121; Wiley Branton to J. William Fulbright, June 21, 1967, Fulbright Papers.

13. J. William Fulbright to Wiley Branton, June 28, 1967, Fulbright Papers.

14. *Congressional Record*, August 30, 1967, pg. 24,656.

15. E. L. Hutchison to J. William Fulbright, August 30, 1967.

16. J. William Fulbright to E. L. Hutchison, September 15, 1967.

17. Ibid.

18. Jonathan Schell, *The Time of Illusion*, (New York: Vintage, 1975), pp. 80-84; Johnson and Gwertzman, Fulbright.

19. J. William Fulbright, *The Arrogance of Power*

(New York: Vintage, 1967); Fines Batchelor to J. William Fulbright, March 28, 1970, Fulbright Papers.

20. J. William Fulbright to Robert A. Leflar, October 21, 1969, Fulbright Papers; Bernard Schwartz, *Super Chief: Earl Warren and His Court: A Judicial Biography* (New York: New York University Press, 1983), pg. 760.

21. Schwartz, Super Chief, pp. 761-762; Dougan, *Arkansas Odyssey*, at 513-514.

22. Fulbright, "The Price of Empire," reprinted in Johnson and Gwertzman, *Fulbright*, pp. 304-311. Fulbright stressed the themes of "The Price of Empire" in his Arkansas campaign statements as well. "Senator Fulbright Says Poverty Is No. 1 U. S. Problem, War Delaying Solution," Fulbright 1968 campaign advertisement, June 1968, J. William Fulbright Papers, Special Collections, University of Arkansas Library, Fayetteville, Arkansas. A. C. Duke to J. William Fulbright, July 1967, Fulbright Papers. Gary Herlick, "J. W. Fulbright: Democratic Senator from Arkansas," in *Ralph Nader Congress Project: Citizens Look at Congress*, Edited by Ralph Nader (Washington, D.C.: Grossman, 1972), pg. 3.

23. Fulbright, "The Price of Empire" pp. 303-310.

24. Ibid., pg. 304.

25. Ibid., pg. 310.

26. Ibid., pp. 306-310.

27. Schell, *The Time of Illusion*, pg. 97.

28. C. Vann Woodward, *The Burden of Southern History* Enlarged edition (Baton Rouge: Louisiana State University Press, 1968), pp. 216-218.

29. Memorandum, Lee Williams to J. William Fulbright, November 17, 1969, Fulbright Papers.

30. Harvard Sitkoff, *The Struggle for Black Equality, 1954-1980* (New York: Hill and Wang, 1981), pg. 200.

31. Martin Luther King, Jr., *The Trumpet of Conscience* (New York: Harper and Row, 1967) pp. 22-23.

32. Martin Luther King, Jr. to J. William Fulbright, November 8, 1965, Fulbright Papers.

33. "McMath Decides Not to Run," April 1, 1968, *Arkansas Gazette*, pg. 1. Woods, 465; "Faubus Says Fulbright Vulnerable," Arkansas Democrat, April 27, 1967.

34. Sitkoff, *The Struggle for Black Equality*, pg. 223.

34a. Bill Lewis, "COPE Endorses Boswell, Fulbright After Hot Debate," *Arkansas Gazette*, June 16, 1968.

35. "Faubus, McMath Weighing Race Against Fulbright," May 15, 1967, *Arkansas Gazette*, pg. 1; Interview with Witt Stephens, Little Rock, Arkansas, May 22, 1991.

36. "Fulbright Builds Safe Lead," July 31, 1968, *Arkansas Gazette*, pg. 1.

37. Memorandum, Ben Grinage to Lee Williams, September 4, 1968, Fulbright Papers; Herlick, "J. William Fulbright," pg. 9; "Fulbright Voting Record Comforts Communists, Johnson Charges on TV," July 3, 1968, *Arkansas Gazette*, pg. 1.

38. Irene Samuel to Edwin Dunaway, "An Analysis of Negro Voting in the General Election, 1966—Governor's Race," November 17, 1966, Fulbright Papers; Ben Grinage to Lee Williams, "Analysis of the Black Vote for Senator Fulbright," July 30, 1968. Fulbright won a bloc vote from blacks against Jim Johnson and the two minor Democratic opponents. Bernard tried to gain support from black voters, but Fulbright still won 70 percent of the black vote in the general election.

39. John Ward, *The Arkansas Rockefeller* (Baton Rouge: Louisiana State University Press, 1978), pg. 162, 176.

40. Ward, *The Arkansas Rockefeller*, pp. 114-117.

41. Ibid.

41a. David Garrow, *Bearing the Cross: Martin Luther King, Jr., and the Southern Christian Leadership Conference*, (New York: 1986), 162-163; Woods, 541; Woodward, *The Strange Career of Jim Crow*, 127. In early 1970, Fulbright voted for an amendment to the HEW appropriations bill requiring that the country desegregate its schools at the same speed. This measure reflected the concerns of Southerners that they were having to desegregate faster than some Northern areas.

42. J. William Fulbright to Dale Bumpers, December 16, 1969, Fulbright Papers.

43. Laurence Tribe, *God Save This Honorable Court* (New York: Random House, 1985); Roman Hruska and Marlow Cook to J. William Fulbright, October 15, 1969, Fulbright Papers; Robert A. Leflar to J. William Fulbright, October 9, 1969.

In fact, it would have been unethical if Haynsworth had recused himself from the cases, because judges were required by judicial canons of ethics as well as by federal law to hear all cases in which they did not have a "substantial interest." Some judges had avoided hearing controversial civil rights or labor cases by citing infinitesimal financial interests. Such evasiveness tended to discredit the bench, led to further delays in assigning the cases after judges recused themselves, and any disqualification disrupted the random pattern of assigning appellate cases.

Critics unleashed a wide assortment of

ethics charges against Haynsworth. Many of the charges focused on the nominee's interest in Carolina Vend-a-Matic, which did business with a parent company, Deering—Milliken, that came before Haynsworth's court in *Darlington v. NLRB*, 325 F.2d 682 (1963) Haynsworth had resigned as a corporate officer in 1957, although record-keeping errors continued to list him as a vice president until 1964. He did no work and was not paid as an officer, and he sold his shares in the company in 1964. In addition to the ethics question, Haynsworth's opinion in Darlington was also criticized for an alleged anti-labor philosophical bias.

When the Haynsworth nomination was first announced, Fulbright was leaning toward opposing it, writing to constituents that "having voted against Mr. Fortas' elevation to the Chief Justiceship because of his fees and indiscretions, I find it difficult to accept Judge Haynsworth." Upon further study of the issue, and after receiving Leflar's endorsement of Haynsworth, he changed his view. The standard that the critics set would also have disqualified Justice William O. Douglas and numerous district and circuit judges. Fulbright agreed with Earl Warren and others who contended for a higher ethical standard in such matters, but until the standards were actually changed, Haynsworth's activities were common among judges.

44. Paul A. Freund, "Appointment of Justice: Some Historical Perspectives," 101 Harvard Law Review 1,15 (1988); Tribe, *God Save This Honorable Court*, pg. 82, 89.
45. J. William Fulbright to Griffin Smith, October 24, 1969, Fulbright Papers; J. William Fulbright to Mr. and Mrs. Thomas Lamb, December 9, 1969; Richard Arnold to J. William Fulbright, November 24, 1969.
46. "The Compelling Case Against Haynsworth," Editorial, November 16, 1969, *Arkansas Gazette*, pg. 2E.
47. Ibid.
48. Edward L. Wright to J. William Fulbright, November 12, 1969, Fulbright Papers; J. William Fulbright to Robert Parker, December 11, 1969, Fulbright Papers; J. William Fulbright to Guy Berry, November 28, 1969.
49. *School Board of the City of Charlottesville v. Dillard*, 374 U.S. 827 (1963); Goss v. Board of Education, 373 U.S. 683 (1963); Members of the U. S. House of Representatives Adam Clayton Powell, Augustus Hawkins, John Conyers, Shirley Chisholm, William Clay, and Louis Stokes to J.

William Fulbright, October 2, 1969, Fulbright Papers.
50. *Griffin v. Prince Edward School Board*, 377 U.S. 218 (1964); *Bowman v. County School Board of Charles City, Virginia*, 382 F.2d 326 (1967); *Green v. School Board of New Kent County* 391 U.A. 430 (1969); Adam Clayton Powell, et al to J. William Fulbright, October 2, 1969, Fulbright Papers.
51. Robert A. Leflar to J. William Fulbright, October 9, 1969, Fulbright Papers.
52. Ibid.
53. Bill Penix to Lee Williams, April 10, 1970, Fulbright Papers.
54. "Fulbright Vote Likely Judge's," November 21, 1969, *Arkansas Gazette*, pg. 1.
55. R. E. L. Wilson, 3rd to J. William Fulbright, December 2, 1969, Fulbright Papers.
56. Jack Pickens to J. William Fulbright, November 26, 1969, Fulbright Papers.
57. Memorandum, Lee Williams to J. William Fulbright, November 17, 1969, Fulbright Papers.
58. "Victory for the Court in Haynsworth Affair . . . And Fulbright's Vote," Editorial, November 23, 1969, *Arkansas Gazette*, pg. 2E.
59. Dale Bumpers to J. William Fulbright, December 2, 1969, Fulbright Papers.
60. "Fulbright Vote Likely Judge's," November 21, 1969, *Arkansas Gazette*, pg. 1.
61. Dale Bumpers to J. William Fulbright, December 2, 1969, Fulbright Papers; Interview with Lee Williams, May 24, 1991, Fayetteville, Arkansas; "Fulbright Vote Likely Judge's," November 21, 1969, *Arkansas Gazette*, pg. 1.
62. J. William Fulbright to Guy Berry, on November 28, 1969 and December 18, 1969, Fulbright Papers.
63. Guy Berry to J. William Fulbright on November 25, 1969 and December 11, 1969, Fulbright Papers.
64. Schell, *The Time of Illusion*, pg. 81. As Schell summarized the initial period of the debate: "The Senate, having just turned down a Supreme Court nominee for the first time in forty years, was at first strongly inclined to accept almost anyone the President chose." J. William Fulbright to Guy Berry, November 28, 1969, Fulbright Papers.
65. *Congressional Record*, April 8, 1970, pg. 10,763.
66. William Safire, *Before the Fall: An Inside View of the Pre-Watergate White House* (New York: Ballantine, 1977), pp. 342-344; Schell, The Time of Illusion, pg. 82.
67. Birch Bayh to J. William Fulbright, March 24, 1970, Fulbright Papers; Memorandum, David

Lambert (Fulbright aide) to J. William Fulbright, March 24, 1970, Fulbright Papers.

68. *Congressional Record*, April 3, 1970, pg. 10,319. James J. Kilpatrick also tried his hand at defending Carswell, dismissing Judge John Minor Wisdom's opposition to the Floridian as the biased outlook of a "kneejerk liberal." Kilpatrick gave Carswell's opponents further ammunition in a column that basically defended the nominee, but blasted his "evasive account" to the Judiciary Committee of his role in transferring the Tallahassee municipal golf course to a private country club. "Forgive my incredulity," Kilpatrick wrote, "but if Carswell didn't understand the racial purpose of this legal legerdemain, he was the only one in north Florida who didn't understand it." *Congressional Record*, April 2, 1970, pg. 10,177.

69. William Van Alstyne to J. William Fulbright, February 23, 1970, Fulbright Papers; Robert Leflar to John McClellan and J. William Fulbright, March 11, 1970; J. William Fulbright to Leflar, March 16, 1970.

70. Wiley Branton to J. William Fulbright, March 6, 1970, Fulbright Papers; J. William Fulbright to Wiley Branton, March 16, 1970.

71. *Congressional Record*, March 26, 1970, pp. 9,610-9,614; *Congressional Record*, April 2, 1970, pg. 10,104; "Carswell Foes Gain Senate Support," March 27, 1970, *New York Times*, pg. 1; *Congressional Record*, April 3, 1970, pg. 10,322. The following is a brief analysis of the Carswell vote in the Senate:

Chairman Eastland, McClellan, the second-ranking Democrat on the Committee, and Hruska, the ranking minority member, correctly saw the motion to recommit as a criticism of the Committee's work. In a Senate that required specialization and respected committees' prerogatives, these were formidable political arguments. A letter asking Fulbright to reconsider his position and oppose the motion to recommit was sent to him by ten members of the committee: including Eastland, McClellan, Hruska (R-Neb.), Sam Ervin (D-N.C.), Strom Thurmond (R-S.C.), Robert Byrd (D-W.Va.), Robert Griffin (R-Mich.), Hugh Scott (R-Pa.), Hiram Fong (R-Hawaii), and Marlow Cook (R-Ky) to J. William Fulbright, April 3, 1970, Fulbright Papers. Committee members supporting recommittal were Bayh, Edward Kennedy (D-Mass.), Charles McMathias (R-Md.) Philip Hart (D-Mich.), and Joseph Tydings (D-Md.)

Eastland's letter simply referred to the committee majority's opposition to further hearings and did not discuss the merits of the issue. Fulbright, of course, rejected the committee majority's argument and continued to support recommittal.

The vote to recommit failed, 52-44, on April 6. *Congressional Record*, April 6, 1970. As a parliamentary maneuver and political strategy, however, it succeeded, since the Senate engaged in lengthy and spectacularly obtuse debates over whether to recommit. *Congressional Record*, April 6, 1970, pg. 10,393.

Only four Southerners in the entire Senate supported recommittal: Fulbright, Albert Gore of Tennessee, Ralph Yarborough of Texas, and William Spong of Virginia. All of them were defeated the next time they ran for re-election, although the Carswell vote was not necessarily the crucial reason for the losses. Several other Senators from border states, such as Fred Harris of Oklahoma, supported recommittal.

The biggest disappointment for the dissenters was John Sherman Cooper (R-Ky.), who had opposed Haynsworth but balked at the idea of rejecting a second consecutive nominee and voted for Carswell. Marlow Cook (R-Ky.) and Margaret Chase Smith (R-Maine) were Republicans whose votes against Carswell were important.

Fulbright was in touch with the other three Southerners and the moderate Republicans on the nomination although it is not possible to prove how influential he was. Thomas Eagleton of Missouri and John Pastore of Rhode Island, in particular, emphasized at the time that they were influenced by Fulbright's example. Fulbright's seniority, prestige, conservatism on civil rights, and reputation for erudition also may have influenced moderate Republicans and Democrats who were subjected to administration pressures to support the nomination. There were about 15 statements commending Fulbright's role in the debate.

72. J. William Fulbright to Randall Mathis, May 12, 1970, Fulbright Papers; J. William Fulbright to Bruce Switzer, April 3, 1970, Fulbright Papers. Fulbright was trying to defend his argument and was undoubtedly aware that his description of Maryland as a Southern state would have an odd ring in the ear of an Arkansan, who would consider Maryland a border state. Burger lived in Virginia after his appointment as a federal judge but he was from Minnesota, forming half of the "Minnesota Twins" on the Court along with

Blackmun. Arkansans considered Black of Alabama the only legitimate Southerner. Fulbright's effort to emphasize the "Southernness" of the Court was strained and unpersuasive to constituents.

73. J. E. Bunch to J. William Fulbright, April 8, 1970, Fulbright Papers; J. William Fulbright to J. E. Bunch, April 13, 1970; Gazzola Vaccaro, Jr. to J. William Fulbright, April 27, 1970; J. William Fulbright to Gazzola Vaccaro, Jr., May 21, 1970.

Other critics recalled their resentment over the Marshall vote; West Memphis lawyer Jim Hale ranted that "Carswell's background is no more biased or prejudiced than Thurgood Marshall, yet the Senate approved Marshall without a fight even though his entire life had been grooved with racism and prejudice." James Hale to Fulbright, March 28, 1970.

74. Bill Penix to Lee Williams, April 10, 1970.

75. Wiley Branton to J. William Fulbright, April 16, 1970.

76. "Nixon Says Senate Biased Against South: 'Incredible' Statement, Critics Reply," April 10, 1970, Arkansas Gazette, pg. 1; "Names of Two On the Mind of Fulbright," April 11, 1970, Arkansas Gazette, pg. 2A.

77. "Nixon Says Senate Biased Against South," April 10, 1970, Arkansas Gazette, pg. 1.

78. Schell, The Time of Illusion, pg. 185.

79. "President Angers Foes of Carswell," April 10, 1970, New York Times; "Nixon Says Senate Biased Against South," April 10, 1970, Arkansas Gazette, pg. 1.

80. Ibid.

81. "Mrs. Mitchell Bids Newspaper 'Crucify' Fulbright," April 10, 1970, New York Times, pg. 14;" Fulbright Shrugs Off Call to 'Crucify' Him by Mitchell's Wife," April 10, 1970, Arkansas Gazette, pg. 1.

82. Ward, The Arkansas Rockefeller, pg. 176.

83. "Fulbright Shrugs Off Call to 'Crucify' Him by Mitchell's Wife," April 10, 1970, Arkansas Gazette, pg. 1.

84. G. Harrold Carswell to Mr. and Mrs. Thomas Owens, August 5, 1970, Fulbright Papers; "Blackmun Gets Confirmation," May 13, 1970, Arkansas Gazette, pg. 1. Blackmun was confirmed 94-0 on May 12.

85. "The Carswell Decision," Editorial, April 9, 1970, New York Times; "Fulbright's Vote," April 10, 1970, Arkansas Gazette, pg. 6A; Birch Bayh to J. William Fulbright, April 10, 1970, Fulbright Papers; Ben Grinage to J. William Fulbright, March 27, 1970, Grinage wrote, "I personally am

prouder than ever to be a part of your team."

86. Interview with Lee Williams, May 24, 1991; J. William Fulbright to Dale Bumpers, December 16, 1970; Meet the Press, March 14, 1965, Produced by Lawrence Spivak (Washington, D.C.: Merkle Press, 1965); Congressional Record, March 13, 1970, pg. 7,336.

87. Schell, The Time of Illusion, pp. 186-187.

88. "Wrote Memo, Nominee Says, Views Not His, Rehnquist Asserts," December 9, 1971, Arkansas Gazette, pg. 1; Congressional Record, December 10, 1971, pp. 46,110-46,114.

89. Bernard Schwartz, The Ascent of Pragmatism: The Burger Court in Action (New York: Addison-Wesley, 1990), pp. 29-30; Congressional Record, December 10, 1971, pg. 46,170.

90. Memorandum on the Rehnquist Nomination, David Capes (a Fulbright aide) to J. William Fulbright, December 7, 1971, Fulbright Papers; "Summary of the Judiciary Committee Minority Memorandum in Opposition to the Nomination of William Rehnquist," Birch Bayh to J. William Fulbright, December 7, 1971, Fulbright Papers.

92. Congressional Record, December 9, 1971, pp. 45,791-45,793.

93. Tribe, God Save This Honorable Court, pg. 137; Congressional Record, December 9, 1971, pp. 45,791-45,793.

94. Interview with J. William Fulbright, Washington, D.C., June 4, 1991.

95. Nomination of William H. Rehnquist and Lewis F. Powell, Jr. to be Associate Justices of the Supreme Court of the United States, Hearings before the committee on the Judiciary, United States Senate, 92nd Congress, First Session, November 1971. (Washington: U.S. Government Printing Office, 1971), pg. 303.

96. Congressional Record, March 26, 1970, pp. 9,610-9,614; Congressional Record, pp. 45,791-45,794.

97. Congressional Record, December 10, 1971, pg. 46,121.

98. Congressional Record, December 10, 1971, pg. 46,197.

99. J. William Fulbright to Birch Bayh, December 13, 1971, Fulbright Papers; Nina Totenberg, "The Confirmation Process and the Public: To Know or Not to Know," in Essays on the Supreme Court Appointment Process, 101 Harvard Law Review 1,214-1,215 (1988).

100. Interview with J. William Fulbright, Washington, D.C., June 4, 1991.

101. Freund, "Appointment of Justices: Some Historical Perspectives," in Essays, 101 Harvard Law Review, 1,155-1,156 (1988); Nina

Totenberg, "The Confirmation Process and the Public: To Know or Not to Know," in *Essays,* 101 Harvard Law Review 1,214-1,217 (1988).

102. Interview with Lee Williams, May 24, 1991. Williams continued to be an adviser to Democratic Party officials in Washington until returning to Arkansas in 1990; he returned to Washington again about a year later.

103. Interview with J. William Fulbright, Washington, D.C., June 4, 1991.

103a. Interview with Lee Williams, May 24, 1991.

104. Interview with Lee Williams, May 24, 1991.

105. Daniel Yergin, "Fulbright's Last Frustration," *New York Times Magazine,* November 24, 1974, pg. 14.

106. "Black Aide Criticizes Use of White in Fulbright Effort," May 23, 1974, *Arkansas Gazette,* pg. 1.

107. Interview with J. William Fulbright, Washington, D.C., June 4, 1991. Secretary of State Henry Kissinger came to Arkansas to campaign for Fulbright, who was then cooperating with Kissinger in building the nascent detente policy with the Soviet Union. Kissinger's visit, however, only deepened the impression that Fulbright regarded himself as indispensable and devoted most of his time and energy to international issues. Fulbright was magnanimous in praising Kissinger and Nixon, formerly his adversaries, for their detente policies.

108. "No Vote Trend, Bumpers Says," May 30, 1974, *Arkansas Gazette*, pg. 1. Randall Woods states that "blacks voted by a 4-to-1 margin for Bumpers." Woods, at 670. Wood's statement is inaccurate. In the 1974 primary, black voters were narrowly divided between Governor Bumpers and Senator Fulbright. The returns from the large delta counties, where the black population is heavy, showed that the delta was the only section of the state where the race for the Senate was close. Mississippi, Phillips, Crittenden and Lee counties gave Bumpers a margin of 194 votes—total—17,377 to 17,183 for Fulbright. Fulbright carried Phillips County, 4854 to 4265. It was one of only three counties in the state that Fulbright won. One of the other two was Conway County, then ruled by a famous sheriff named Marlin Hawkins, in Central Arkansas. The returns are recorded in the office of the Arkansas Secretary of State.

The pattern was underscored in the returns from key black precincts in Little rock, long used by political analysts for interpretation. There were five bellwether black precincts— Granite Mountain, College Station, the Arkansas Arts Center, the Dunbar Community Center and Wrightsville. Fulbright got about 45 percent of the vote in these five (Bumpers got 1331 votes to Fulbright's 1068.) The incumbent senator polled 12 points higher in the black precincts of Little Rock than he did in statewide totals.

Outside of the black precincts, Fulbright ran well in the fashionable country club section of Little Rock, where he outpolled Bumpers, but he was beaten badly in the lower-income white sections of Southwest Little Rock and North Little Rock and the outlying rural precincts.

The division in the black vote in Little Rock was indicative substantially of the division in sentiment among the white liberal-moderate community, which was split between the senator and the governor. For example, Fulbright had the ardent support of Mrs. Calvin (Brownie) Ledbetter while Bumpers was ardently backed by Mrs. Irene Samuel. The two women had fought side by side in the Central High crisis. Fulbright's standing in the black community was also influenced by the *Arkansas Gazette* editorial page, which volleyed and thundered for the incumbent senator.

108a. Interview with Fulbright, October, 1981; Woods, 665.

108b. Woods, 665.

109. Alexander P. Lamis, *The Two-Party South* Second Expanded Edition (New York: Oxford University Press, 1990), pg. 122.

110. Fulbright, *The Price of Empire,* pg. 82; Interview with J. William Fulbright, Washington, D.C., October 16, 1981; Interview with J. William Fulbright, June 4, 1991.

111. Ward, *The Arkansas Rockefeller,* pp. 165-166.

112. "Fulbright's Vote," April 10, 1970, *Arkansas Gazette,* pg. 6A.

113. Johnson and Gwertzman, *Fulbright,* pg. 153; Interview with J. William Fulbright, October 16, 1981.

114. Johnson and Gwertzman, *Fulbright,* pp. 40-50.

Book Six
Fulbright and His Legacy

I. Perspective After Defeat

For a contemporary report on the 1974 campaign and the Kissinger-Fulbright press conference in Little Rock, see Bill Lewis, "Kissinger Makes Stop at LR, Meets Fulbright at the Airport," *Arkansas Gazette*, February 16, 1974. For some contemporary reports on Arkansas politicians' responses to President Reagan's policies, see "Bumpers Says Trip Might Further Open Road to Better U.S.-Soviet Relations," *Arkansas Gazette*, August 14, 1983;" Congress Votes for Compromise on War Powers," *Arkansas Gazette*, September 30, 1983; Carol Matlack, "Reagan Policy Draws Wrath of Alexander: Congressman a Leader in Criticism of Handling of Latin America Crisis," *Arkansas Gazette*, July 24, 1983; "Marines Ordered to Ships," *Arkansas Gazette*, February 8, 1984.

For the reflections of Senator McClellan and Senator Kennedy on Fulbright, see *Congressional Record*, pp. 22,182-22,183, p. 22,193; John Kenneth Galbraith on Fulbright is in Galbraith's *A Life in Our Times: Memoirs* (1981), pp. 309-310; Kissinger's compliments for Fulbright, Henry Kissinger, *Years of Upheaval*, (1982), p. 426; for Martin Luther King's praise for Fulbright, Martin Luther King, Jr. to J. W. Fulbright, November 8, 1965; Fulbright to Martin Luther King, Jr., December 13, 1965; for President Johnson's criticisms of Fulbright, see Kearns, pp. 326-341. For Fulbright's remarks on Kissinger and the Middle East, Fulbright letter to James O. Powell, March 20, 1975. For Carter and the Middle East, "J. William Fulbright," *Newsweek*, September 11, 1978; Interview with Fulbright, August 4, 1978.

For Fulbright's testimony to the Senate Foreign Relations Committee in 1983, see *The Future of United States-Soviet Relations*, November 16, 1983. For President Kennedy's private observations about Vietnam to Senator Mansfield and Kenneth O'Donnell, see Schlesinger, *Robert Kennedy and His Times*, pp. 767-768; for Robert Kennedy's private comments on Vietnam in 1963, see Halberstam, *The Best and the Brightest*, pp. 336-337.

A starting point for the Iran-Contra affair is *Report of the Congressional Committees Investigating the Iran-Contra Affair, With Supplemental, Minority, and Additional Views*, November, 1987. 100th Congress. 1st Session. U.S. House of Representatives Select Committee to Investigate Covert Arms Transactions with Iran, U.S. Senate Select Committee on Secret Military Assistance to Iran and the Nicaraguan Opposition (Washington: Government Printing Office, 1987). For differing examples of views on the scandal, see Jack Kemp,I"ran-Contra Boomerang Hits Democrats," *Charlottesville Daily Progress*, August 9, 1987, and Senator John Kerry," When We Disregard the Rule of Law," *Washington Post*, May 5, 1987.

For the Boland Amendments, the Congressional Research Service's complete legislative history of the Amendments was written and compiled at the request of Congressman Bill Alexander, and published in Volume 133, Number 97, *Congressional Record*, June 15, 1987, pp. 4,577-4,990.

II. Elder Statesman

1. *Arkansas Gazette*, Little Rock, AR, May 25, 1974, pg. 5A.
2. *Arkansas Gazette*, May 30, 1974, pg. 6A.
3. Ibid., May 26, 1974, pg. 3A.
4. Ibid., May 27,1974, pg 3A.
5. James O. Powell, a frequent visitor at the Witt Stephens luncheons over fifteen years. Fulbright lived in a lovely, spacious home in Washington. On one occasion in 1987, Lee Powell called the senator to ask him a quick question about Cuban policy, whereupon the senator asked him out to the house to elaborate for another 40 minutes or so. Fulbright was preparing to go to a dinner at the British Ambassador's home and was wearing a tuxedo, while Powell, alas, was not expecting to be invited out to the Fulbright home and was dressed casually in tennis shoes. Fulbright was amused by the contrast in dress, and gallantly remarked that the "tennis shoes must be very comfortable, I'm sure."
6. The chronology of Fulbright's honors and rewards is excerpted rom the *Arkansas Gazette Index*, Arkansas Tech University library; by Shannon J. Henderson.
7. *Arkansas Gazette*, July 1, 1990, pg. 10A.
7a. Interview with David Capes, June 15, 1995; Dumas Malone, Jefferson the President: Second Term, 1805-1809 (Boston: Little Brown, 1974), pp. 7-8; Malone, *Jefferson and the Ordeal of Liberty* (Boston: 1962), pp. 480-483.
7b. *Congressional Record*, March 22, 1972, p. 9,598; John C. Jeffries, Justice Lewis F. Powell, Jr., supra, p. 509.
7c. *Congressional Record*, March 22, 1972, p. 9,598.
7d. Dougan, *Arkansas Odyssey*, supra, pp. 594-597; see also Neil Compton, The Battle for the Buffalo River (Fayetteville, 1992).
8. *Arkansas Gazette*, March 10, 1990; pg. 1A.

9. Ibid., September 1991.

10. *New York Times*, August 24, 1970, pg. 1.

III. The Fulbright Program and Its Critics

10a. Johnson and Gwertzman, p. 114; Jane Fullerton, "Ax Dangles over Legacy of Fulbright," *Arkansas Democrat-Gazette*, May 11, 1995, p. 1A, 11A.

10b. Fullerton, "Ax Dangles over Legacy of Fulbright," supra note 10a.

10c. Walter Johnson and Francis Colligan, *The Fulbright Program: A History* (Chicago: University of Chicago Press, 1965), Foreword by J. William Fulbright; p. 5.

10d. Sydney, Australia, *Daily Mirror,* August 11, 1964; Wellington, New Zealand, *Evening Post*, January 15, 1949; Johnson and Colligan, 107-131.

10e. "Fulbrighting in Greece," *Harper's* Magazine, October, 1953, pp. 75-80; Johnson and Colligan, 136-141.

10f. John A. Wilson to Walter Johnson, April 13, 1964, quoted in Johnson and Colligan, p. 144.

10g. See Norman Dawes, *A Two-Way Street: The Indo-American Fulbright Program, 1950-1960* (Bombay: Asia Publishing House, 1962); *New York Times*, March 9, 1952.

10h. "Fulbright Is a Magic Name in the Philippines," *The Record*, VII, March-April, 1951, 18; Johnson and Colligan, 152-165.

10i. Johnson and Gwertzman, 172; The Fulbright Exchange Program In Japan, 1962-1963 (Tokyo: U.S. Educational Commission in Japan, 1963), p. 1.

10j. Fulbright, *Old Myths and New Realities*, p. 59; Johnson and Colligan, pp. 172-191.

10k. Fulbright, *The Price of Empire,* 210-211.

10l. Id., 214.

10m.U.S. Educational Commission in the Federal Republic of Germany, *The Funnel: Tenth Anniversary Edition* (Bad Godesberg: The Commission, 1962), p. 41.

10n. Fulbright, *The Price of Empire*, 216.

10o. Id., 215.

10p. Id., 217.

10q. Jane Fullerton, "Ax Dangles over Legacy of Fulbright," *Arkansas Democrat-Gazette*, May 11, 1995, p. 1A, 11A.

10r. Id.

10s. Fulbright, *The Price of Empire*, 199.

11. *Arkansas Democrat-Gazette*, July 7, 1994; pg. 5A.

12. Interview with Lee Williams, July 21, 1994.

IV. Role Model for Clinton

12a. David Maraniss, *First in His Class: A Biography of Bill Clinton* (New York: Simon & Schuster, 1995), p. 17.

13. Interview with Lee Williams, October 12, 1993.

13a. Maraniss, p. 94.

13b. Id., p. 106.

13c. Id., 114-115.

13d. Bill Clinton telegram to J. William Fulbright, November 6, 1968, Fulbright Papers.

13e. J. William Fulbright to Bill Clinton, December 3, 1968, Fulbright Papers.

13f. Maraniss, p. 120.

13g. Interview with Lee Williams, June 5, 1995.

13h. Maraniss, pp. 176-178.

14. *New York Times*, September 12, 1992, pg. 1.

15. Lee Williams, memorandum in the Fulbright Archives at the University of Arkansas, Fayetteville.

15a. *Arkansas Gazette*, October 28, 1978; *Arkansas Democrat*, October 29, 1991; statement of Col. Holmes, September 16, 1992; Maraniss, 204-205.

15b. Maraniss, 197-203.

15c. Id., 261.

15d. Id., 322-323.

16. Interview of Fulbright in the *Valley News* reported in the *Arkansas Democrat-Gazette*, November 6, 1992, pg 1B.

17. *Arkansas Democrat-Gazette*, May 6, 1993, pg. 1. Skip Rutherford, one of President Clinton's most prominent advisors in Arkansas, was one of the influential people who urged the President to confer the Presidential Medal of freedom upon Fulbright.

18. James O. Powell, then administrative assistant to Senator George Smathers, Spring 1956.

18a. Interview with David Capes, June 18, 1995.

VII. The Death of Fulbright

1. "J. William Fulbright, Senate Giant, Dead at 89," February 10, 1995, *New York Times*.

2. Memorial Services for J. William Fulbright, Washington Cathedral, February 17, 1995. Many of those in attendance at the services for the senator were much impressed by the senator's attractive and eloquent sons-in-law, wife, children and grandchildren. His daughter Bosey had married Thaddeus Foote, a cousin of Adlai Stevenson, and his daughter Betsy married John Winnacker. Both Winnacker and Foote had successful professional careers; Foote as president of the University of Miami, and Winnacker as a distinguished teacher at the University of Missouri School of Medicine.

3. Walter Pincus, February 10, 1995, *Washington Post*.

INDEX